EGYPT AND NUBIA

GIFTS OF THE DESERT

EGYPT AND NUBIA

GIFTS OF THE DESERT

edited by Renée Friedman

THE BRITISH MUSEUM PRESS

Dedicated to Thomas and Linda Heagy
with gratitude

© 2002 The Trustees of the British Museum

Published by The British Museum Press
A division of The British Museum Company Ltd
46 Bloomsbury Street, London WC1B 3QQ

A catalogue record for this book is available from the British Library

ISBN 0 7141 1954 7

Text designed and typeset by Nigel Strudwick
Cover, pp. 1–4 and plate section designed and typeset by John Hawkins
Printed in Hong Kong by C&C Offset

Contents

Plates

List of contributors

Sydney H Aufrère
UPRES-A 5052 du CNRS
Université Paul Valéry
Montpellier
France

Janine Bourriau
The MacDonald Institute for Archaeological Research
Downing Street
Cambridge CB2 3ER
UK

John Coleman Darnell
Department of Near Eastern Languages
Yale University
102 HGS Drawer 1504 A
Yale Station
New Haven, CT 06520-7425
USA

Deborah Darnell
Department of Near Eastern Languages
Yale University
102 HGS Drawer 1504 A
Yale Station
New Haven, CT 06520-7425
USA

Mark A J Eccleston
Centre for Archaeology & Ancient History
Monash University
Clayton, Victoria 3800
Australia

Renée Friedman
Department of Ancient Egypt and Sudan
The British Museum
London WC1B 3DG
UK.

James A Harrell
Professor of Geology
The University of Toledo
Toledo, OH 43606-3390
USA

Joseph J Hobbs
Department of Geography
3 Stewart Hall
University of Missouri - Columbia
Columbia MO 65211
USA

Colin A Hope
Centre for Archaeology & Ancient History
Monash University
Clayton, Victoria 3800
Australia

Dirk Huyge
Royal Museums of Art and History
Jubelpark 10
1000 Brussels
Belgium

Olaf E Kaper
Centre for Archaeology & Ancient History
Monash University
Clayton, Victoria 3800
Australia

Dietrich D Klemm
Department of Geosciences
Ludwig-Maximilians Universität München
Luisenstrasse 37
80333 München
Germany

Rosemarie Klemm
Institut für Ägyptologie
Ludwig Maximilians Universität München
Meiserstrasse 10
80333 München
Germany

Rudolph Kuper
Heinrich-Barth-Institut
Jennerstrasse 8
50823 Köln
Germany

Mary M A MacDonald
Department of Archaeology
University of Calgary
Calgary, Alberta 2N 1N4.
Canada

Mark G Macklin
Institute of Geography and Earth Sciences
University of Wales
Aberystwyth
Ceredigion SY23 3DB
Wales
UK

Anthony J Mills
Dakhleh Oasis Project
The Barn Above Town
Egloshayle, Wadesbridge
Cornwall PL27 6HW
UK

Andreas Murr
Department of Geosciences
Ludwig-Maximilians Universität München
Luisenstrasse 37
80333 München
Germany

Pamela Rose
The Egypt Exploration Society
3 Doughty Mews
London WC1N 2PG
UK

Romauld Schild
Institute of Archaeology and Ethnology
Polish Academy of Sciences
Al. Solidarnosci 105
00-140 Warsaw
Poland

Ian Shaw
School of Archaeology
Classics and Oriental Studies
The University of Liverpool
14 Abercromby Square
Liverpool L69 3BX
UK

Derek A Welsby
Department of Ancient Egypt and Sudan
The British Museum
London WC1B 3DG
UK

Fred Wendorf
Department of Anthropology
Southern Methodist University
Dallas TX 75275
USA

Harco Willems
Department of Near Eastern and Slavic Studies
Katholieke Universiteit Leuven
Blijde-Inkomststraat 21
3000 Leuven
Belgium

Jamie C Woodward
School of Geography
University of Leeds
Leeds LS2 9JT
UK

Foreword

Renée Friedman

Egypt has often been called the gift of the Nile, paraphrasing Herodotus' famous words; its life-giving flood provided the water, soil, and the regular rhythms of life from which ancient Egyptian civilization was created and on which it flourished. Surrounding it, and isolating it, were two of the driest deserts on earth, the antithesis of life. Beyond the flood plain, the desert was chaotic, an area inhabited by the forces of disorder that surrounded the created world, a place to be avoided. One of the purposes of this volume and the international colloquium held in the British Museum in 1998, on which it is based, was to reveal the imbalance in this assessment, which has been influenced to a great extent by religious conceptions. In reality the Egyptians did not view the world in such black and 'red' terms. Recent and on-going investigation of a wide variety of archaeological remains in the Western (eastern Sahara or Libyan) and Eastern (Arabian) Deserts is showing that in fact these forbidding yet fascinating realms played a significant role in the making, maintaining and sometimes the breaking of Egyptian and Nubian civilization.

A major aim of the colloquium was to bring together Prehistorians, Egyptologists, Geologists, Geomorphologists and Geographers, the desert researchers in different disciplines, for a mutually beneficial dialogue with a view toward making more widely accessible the current issues and new lines of thought about the desert milieu across time. We are grateful to all of those who participated in the original colloquium for making it such a stimulating event.

Contributions in this volume show that the gifts of the deserts are surprisingly varied and manifold, if difficult to obtain. As Rudolph Kuper describes in his paper, their acquisition requires masterful logistics, detailed information, stamina and determination. These gifts go far beyond the abundant and well-known mineral resources of the deserts to include less tangible but no less important benefits in the form of conduits for commerce and travel, strategic military routes and strongholds, reliable communications, areas for colonization and loci for personal religious expression. Perhaps the most remarkable of the recent revelations about the deserts are that they may also have served as the spring-board for Egyptian civilization itself. One of the greatest gifts the deserts still have to bestow is that of preservation. Unlike the Nile Valley where an active river has washed away or later occupation has deeply buried the earliest evidence of the Neolithic past, the desert has saved it, and more – from the artefacts of early nomads to the modern Bedouin who still make the desert their home (Hobbs).

By its very nature desert exploration is wide-ranging, and as many of the contributions to this volume straddle a variety of topics and time periods, they have been arranged in rough geographical order from south and west to north and east. The papers focus mainly on the time period from the beginning of the Holocene, approximately 11,000 years ago, when the onset of more clement climatic conditions following the end of the last ice age allowed the desert to be reoccupied, to the end of the Egyptian dynastic period. This focus is not to diminish the important wealth of information to be derived from the extensive Roman presence in the desert, but this topic has been well served by the 1996 colloquium *Life on the Fringe*, the proceedings of which were published by Kaper (1998).

Making up over 95% of the landmass of Egypt and 30% of the Sudan, the deserts are a final frontier in many ways. But, when exploring their numerous gifts, it is important to understand from the outset that the deserts were not always the barren and hostile lands they are now. The Western Desert today is one of driest places on earth (only the Atacama Desert of Chile is drier) and it makes up a substantial part of the only 4% of the world that is classified as hyper-arid, receiving statistically less than 5 mm of rain per year. Yet, the work of desert researchers has shown that in the early and mid-Holocene (c. 9500–5500 bp, or roughly 8500–4300 BC) the climate was wetter, with as much as 100–200 mm of seasonal rain falling per year. This was enough to create grassy savannas and playa lakes for at least part of the year, which supported a variety of desert-adapted life and cultures. Investigations around seasonal lakes, natural cisterns and wells and within wadis and oases have yielded evidence, so far lacking in the Nile Valley itself, for the development of an indigenous Neolithic (food producing rather than only food gathering) way of life and the independent invention of ceramics (Kuper; Wendorf and Schild; Hope; Eccleston). Such work has also revealed the desert as a great meeting-point of north and south, preserving evidence that will help us date and understand both the African and Near Eastern contributions to early Nilotic society. Finally, the discovery at Nabta Playa in the last phase, before the onset of arid conditions made continued occupation untenable, of 'public architecture', including calendar circles, megalithic alignments, sculptures and other constructed features, indicates a political or religious authority with control over human resources, in other words, a higher level of social complexity than was ever supposed for a desert region (Wendorf and Schild). This and other newly collected data leave us much food for thought regarding the impact such social developments may have had on the emergence of Predynastic societies along the Nile Valley. These early desert dwellers were far from isolated and their contributions to and interactions with the Nile Valley are becoming clearer with the recent finds in the Eastern Desert (Friedman and Hobbs) and along routes to the western oases in and around the Qena Bend of the Nile and beyond (D Darnell).

The impact of climatic change is of importance not only for understanding developments deep within what is now arid desert, but also for comprehending events along the banks of the Nile. Recent archaeological and geomorphological investigations in the Northern Dongola Reach, just upstream of the Third Cataract, have highlighted the close relationship between environmental change and human activity in the Nubian Nile Valley with specific relevance to the rise and fall of the Kerma state (Welsby, Macklin and Woodward).

Protected from the worst of the deteriorating climate, the oasis of Dakhleh, the largest in the Western Desert, is of especial interest. The work of the Dakhleh Oasis Project provides a unique view of a distinct desert culture able to persist after other areas had been abandoned (Hope), and to remain relatively unaffected by events in the Nile Valley until the oasis was apparently forcefully colonised by Egyptians in the Old Kingdom (Mills; Kaper and Willems). This Egyptian occupation of the oasis, which at least in its early stages involved major outlay for its protection and supply, was not designed simply to acquire agricultural wealth, although the quality of its wine was well-appreciated in New Kingdom times as the dispersal of oasis amphorae attests (Hope *et al.*). The number of addenda to the papers in this volume indicate that new gifts of the desert are being found every year, obliging us to reassess earlier interpretations. Most recently, the discovery of inscriptions relating to a major mining expedition undertaken during the reign of Khufu deep into the Western Desert (Bergmann and Kuhlmann 2001), and the investigation of nearly 30 watering stations, deposits of water jars, stretching from Dakhleh to the cliffs of the Gilf Kebir (Kuper), suggest that the original value of Dakhleh was as a supply-point for the transdesert caravans and mining expeditions, which went further and occurred earlier than previously imagined. These remarkable finds also serve to answer some of the chronological questions about Egyptian state activity in the desert and oases posed here in the papers of Kuper and Kaper and Willems.

That the oases and the routes leading to and through them had strategic value was fully appreciated by the ancient Egyptians, as the evidence for a robust military presence documented by The Theban Desert Road Survey at a variety of desert sites makes abundantly clear (J Darnell; D Darnell). In addition, this material demonstrates how geography and the strategic importance of the Western Desert contributed to the rise of Thebes as the political head of Upper Egypt during the Eleventh Dynasty, and to its resurgence in the Seventeenth Dynasty.

Thus even when arid and hyper-arid conditions prevailed within the deserts, contrary to popular belief, the ancient inhabitants of the Nile Valley were not afraid to venture within them. The sheer extent of gold mining (Klemm,

Klemm and Murr) and the effort put into the extraction of hard stone (Harrell) and gemstones (Shaw) leave little doubt that the mineral resources to be found not only in the Eastern Desert but, as new research (Harrell) shows, also in the West, were of vast importance to the economy at state and local levels. Careers were made in the desert by the successful handling of these difficult enterprises (Aufrère). Further, the study of the logistics, methods and timing of these mining expeditions is providing new insights into the working of the Egyptian state as well as additional evidence for interpreting the internal and external political situation from perhaps the very dawn of Egyptian history known sometimes only obliquely from other sources (J Darnell; Shaw; Klemm, Klemm and Murr).

The great trade caravans and state mining expeditions have made their way into popular romantic imagination, but long overlooked has been the more humble traffic that made use of the desert routes. The Nile is considered the great artery of communication that knit a long narrow Egypt together politically, economically and socially. While it did serve as a major corridor of communication, it was by no means a super-highway. With a current flowing from south to north at an average speed of four knots (7.4 kph) during the time of inundation, a voyage from Thebes to Memphis took about two weeks. However, when the Nile was low, the same journey could take up to two months. The great bends in the Nile like that around the Qena Bend not only added miles to the journey, but the east-west flow made river travel problematic especially on a southward journey. That the Egyptians took to the desert to cut the distance and save the trouble is not remarkable; more surprising is the extent and type of traffic found upon these routes. Literally paved with potsherds and lined with inscriptions, the exploration of these desert routes is leading to a new understanding of state and private travel for business and pilgrimage, internal communications, ancient geography and, in the early periods, the spread of culture and ideas (J Darnell; D Darnell).

In addition to its economic value, the desert retained its religious resonance as a locus for practices that went beyond the burial of the dead. The desert was a land of spirits, and as such a place where one might get closer to the spiritual world and interact with it. Huyge presents a thought provoking explanation for rock art in these terms, and J Darnell provides an overview of the numerous religious documents within the desert realm. Of particular interest are the inscriptions which relate how people came to the desert to 'spend the day' on holiday as part of the worship of Hathor, the goddess of fertility and love.

As the papers in this volume demonstrate, the desert was never an invariably frightening and impenetrable barrier, but often served as a conduit through which flowed people, products and ideas. They were an integral part of the ancient landscape, both physical and mental. To paraphrase Butzer (2001, 385): For those skilled in their ways, the deserts are worlds of opportunity.

Bibliography

Bergmann C and Kuhlmann K P, 2001. Die Expedition des Cheops. *Geo Special* 5 (Oct/Nov 2001): 120–7.

Butzer K W, 2001. Desert Environments. In D B Redford (ed.), *Oxford Encyclopedia of Ancient Egypt*. Vol. 1. Oxford: 385–9.

Kaper O E (ed.), 1998. *Life on the Fringe. Living in the Southern Egyptian Deserts during the Roman and early-Byzantine Periods*. CNWS Publication 71. Leiden.

Acknowledgements

For the production of this volume I am indebted to the skills of Dr Nigel Strudwick, who has been responsible for its format and layout, and to Colin Grant of British Museum Press who has overseen its progress to final publication. I am also grateful to Vivian Davies, Claire Thorne, Suzanne Woodhouse, Alison Cameron and Stefan Kröpelin for their invaluable editorial and technical assistance. I would like to reserve special thanks for Tom and Linda Heagy, who made my work on this publication possible.

Routes and Roots in Egypt's Western Desert:
The Early Holocene Resettlement of the Eastern Sahara

Rudolph Kuper

The following paper reflects a double fascination: that of archaeology and that of the desert. Both of them require complete dedication and together they provide multiple satisfaction. The unexplored realms of the desert hold answers to many questions regarding the development of human civilisation in general and Egypt's past in particular. They also provide the archaeologist with the unique opportunity to add still, at the change of the millennium, to an unwritten chapter in the history of humankind.

When dealing with desert archaeology, one has to be aware that all evidence of human activity, be it 10,000 or just 10 years old, is concentrated on the present-day surface, as a result of wind erosion. This state of affairs causes problems for prehistoric chronology while at the same time providing an attraction for tourists. The simple question that you ask yourself about the remains at some remote place in the middle of nowhere – 'Who was here before?' – refers as much to the stone age hunter as to the colonial officer. So one might perhaps understand that within the framework of the main topic of this paper, the early Holocene resettlement of the Eastern Sahara, reference will occasionally be made to some of those who, long before us, left their tracks in the sands of the Libyan Desert.

In particular, mention must be made of the many desert comrades, most of them based in the Royal Geographical Society, whom I never met in person, but came to know in the remote places where they worked and camped. They felt the hardship and the enjoyment of the desert like us and revealed a great part of a previously unknown world. There were men like Ralph Bagnold (**Plate 1**), whose camp of 2 November 1930 we found in the Selima Sandsheet within a barchan dune (which in the ensuing 50 years had moved about 60 m); Pat Clayton (**Plate 2**), to whom we owe the mapping of major parts of Egypt's deserts and the discovery of the Libyan Desert Glass in 1932 (the place where he camped in 1934 with the Keeper of Minerals of the British Museum, Dr Spencer, is still visible); Bill Shaw, who also in 1932 discovered a rich archaeological site at his camp 49 in northern Sudan (identified by a lost teaspoon) in a wadi that now bears his name; and Guy Prendergast, whose route markers of 1936, composed of empty petrol tins set up on posts, led us safely to the oasis of Merga 44 years later.

The desert keeps it all: their remains and ours, as well as the evidence of millennia of earlier human activities, which is omnipresent. This wealth of archaeological material today provides an attraction for many tourists, and before I come to speak about what it can tell us about Egypt's past, I would like to quote a text of the great Ralph Bagnold (1982, vii), who, in wonderful words, expressed his concern about this Saharan heritage.

He states how vulnerable the desert is and continues:

… human nature is such that the temptation to pick up and remove ancient artifacts seen lying on the ground is almost irresistible. Even now the original statistical pattern of artifact distribution must in some places have already been spoilt. … There is in this wonderful desert, unlimited scope for many more scientific expeditions … But for the sake of posterity it is to be hoped (I fear probably in vain) that mankind's craving for exploitation will not lead to the exhaustion of the accumulated past, whether of water or of archaeology, in the same way as is now happening in the case of fossil fuels.

It is a tragic coincidence that at the same time that we are finally learning to read the book of Saharan history more and more of its pages are being lost forever.

In spite of the fact that the rich archaeological evidence within the Sahara has been known from the earliest days of exploration (for example, in 1850 Heinrich Barth [1857, 210–17] discovered the first rock pictures in the Fezzan and had already discussed their ecological significance), the importance of this prehistoric heritage for an understanding of the history of the African continent has long been disregarded or misinterpreted. In 1955 Elise Baumgartel asked, 'Where did the Egyptian Civilisation originate?' and answered the question by stating that she 'does away with the story of hordes roaming through North Africa and eventually settling in the Nile Valley because the desiccation of the Sahara had made human life impossible there.' She concluded that such hoards 'were not the ancestors of Predynastic Egypt' (Baumgartel 1955, 19).

Nevertheless, there were other (more informed) opinions, some of them already much earlier than that of Baumgartel. In 1934 Lazlo Almásy (**Plate 3**), the Hungarian pioneer explorer of the Eastern Sahara, who has recently become popular as the 'English Patient', asked in the first, Hungarian, edition of his book *Unbekannte Sahara* (1939; 1997, 224), 'Is it possible that people from one day to the next start their development with monuments like the pyramid of Sakkara? Those who built such buildings, and who painted such frescoes, must have built and painted before.' He theorised that people from the west migrated into the Nile Valley, where they perhaps met others coming from Mesopotamia, and laid the foundation of Egyptian civilisation. And he continues:

Obviously the Libyan Desert then – 8000 to 10,000 years ago – still provided suitable living conditions for the herding and hunting people living at the foot of the Gilf Kebir, in Uweinat and in Southern Libya, as in Nubia, while at the same time the Nile Valley was probably moist and unsound. So it would be possible that the Libyan Desert was the cradle of the ancient Egyptian culture, ... however, we are still far from being able to describe the relations between the pharaonic pyramids and the rock art of the desert mountains with any certainty (Almásy 1997, 225).

This last statement still holds true today, but these sentences were written 64 years ago, long before radiocarbon dating became a common method in prehistory and before the first archaeological expedition into the Libyan Desert had taken place. What have we accomplished in the meantime? What is the state of research with which we can discuss these questions today?

By 'we' I refer only to the brave few who regularly undertake archaeological fieldwork in the Western Desert. There is Fred Wendorf's Combined Prehistoric Expedition (CPE), whose continuous work in the Eastern Sahara started over 30 years ago and has resulted in outstanding discoveries concerning the economic and social development of Holocene societies in the Western Desert and the establishment of the chronological and climatological framework to which we all can refer (Wendorf et al. 1984; 1998; Wendorf and Schild 1998; this volume; Schild and Wendorf this volume; Close 1992); the Dakhleh Oasis Project (DOP), led by Anthony Mills, which has allowed us to reflect desert developments against the environmental background of the oasis (Churcher and Mills 1999; McDonald 1998; Hope this volume); Barbara Barich and Fekri Hassan, active now for several years in the Farafra area (Barich 1996); and in the Eastern Desert the Belgium team led by Pierre Vermeersch, which has provided remarkable results regarding the Neolithic developments in that area (Vermeersch et al. 1994). Finally there are our own BOS and ACACIA projects, to which I now will mainly refer when trying to give a short overview of the state and perspectives of archaeological research in the Western Desert.

The BOS project—*Besiedlungsgeschichte der Ost-Sahara* (History of Settlement in the Eastern Sahara)—has been financed by the German Research Council (DFG) since 1980 (Kuper 1981; 1995). It has involved long-range surveys and numerous excavations that were organised along a transect some 1200 km long, running from the Mediterranean area down to the sahel zone. The main interest of the project concerns the interdependence between man's cultural and economical development and the changing climate during the last 10,000 years. Essential topics of research also include the beginning of what is called the 'Neolithic' way of life in that area and the relationship between the desert and the Nile Valley during Predynastic and Dynastic times.

The transect connects the area of winter rain in the north with that of possible summer rains in the south and includes, at its centre, the largest zone of highest aridity in the entire Sahara (**Plate 4**). Within this transect we have investigated seven areas in detail, each of which displays different geographical and ecological conditions: Siwa and the fringes of the Qattara Depression (Cziesla 1989; 1993); the

Great Sand Sea with its giant dunes (Klees 1989; Kuper 1988); the open landscape along the Abu Ballas scarp (Kuper 1993); the mountainous Gilf Kebir Plateau (**Plate 5**)(Schön 1996); the vast plains of the Selima Sandsheet (**Plate 6**) (Schuck 1993); the shallow valley of Wadi Shaw in the Laqiya area (Schuck 1988); and finally the Wadi Howar, where even today some nomadic families still manage to survive (Gabriel et al. 1985; Keding 1997; 1998; Kröpelin 1993a; Richter 1989). Since 1980, over the course of eight expeditions, more than 500 archaeological sites have been recorded and excavations have been made at about 200 of them. Most of the work has taken place in remote, waterless parts of the desert, up to 500 km away from the next oases. This work has required extensive logistical efforts and prevented, for instance, the employment of workmen to undertake the excavations. Technical equipment therefore included a mechanical excavator mounted on an Unimog (see **Plate 13**), which proved very useful for investigating sedimentological and stratigraphical questions.

This project has now become the backbone of another long-term multidisciplinary project composed of anthropologists, geographers, linguists, botanists, historians, egyptologists and prehistorians from the University of Cologne, which started its work five years ago in Egypt, Sudan and Namibia. Its main target is an interregional and transcontinental comparison of human adaptation to arid environments. Thus its acronym is ACACIA—*Arid Climate Adaptation and Cultural Innovation in Africa*. One of the main adaptation and survival strategies on the continent is pastoralism and still today in major parts of Africa, especially in its arid regions, human life is based on the herding of cattle, sheep and goat.

The circumstances and consequences of the rise and spread of pastoralism throughout the African continent are thorny issues, and not only for African prehistorians. On the basis of the available data, the earliest regional appearance of domestic animals suggests a rather diffusionistic distribution pattern with the oldest dated examples in the northeast and the most recent ones, dating at least 6000 years later to around the beginning of our era, in the southernmost part of the continent. According to this picture it is obvious that northeastern Africa is a crucial area for understanding the development of the Neolithic tradition in general and the spread of domestication in particular. Regarding the latter it has been suggested that cattle had already been domesticated locally in the Eastern Sahara more than 10,000 years ago. I will come back to this later. In contrast, wild species of sheep and goat are not endemic in Africa and therefore must have been introduced from Western Asia, most probably through the northeastern corner of the continent, from whence they found their way down to the Cape. This scenario gives rise to three major questions:

1. To what extent has human adaptation to a new way of life been caused by ecological changes, in particular by the desiccation of the Sahara?

2. To what extent did these processes influence the distribution of people and languages throughout the African continent such as we find them today?

3. What contribution did they make to the rise of Egyptian civilisation?

A possible answer to these questions may be contained in the hypothesis that the desiccation of the Sahara was the driving force of African history. As the ACACIA project is scheduled for 12 to 15 years of funding by the German Research Council, we look forward to finding more evidence to support this theory and provide a better understanding of the historical role of northeast Africa during this period and its dependence on the changing environmental background.

The early Holocene settlement of the Eastern Sahara has generally been identified with a period commonly called 'The Neolithic Wet Phase'. In actuality, this period, at least in major parts, was neither wet nor Neolithic. Nevertheless, it represents one of the most fascinating epochs in prehistory. After tens of thousands of years of hyper-aridity during the last ice age, when the Sahara extended much further south than it does today (Vernet 1995), about 12,000 years ago environmental conditions changed. Man returned and wrote a chapter of prehistory before the desert reclaimed what it had granted only as a loan for four to five thousand years. This climatic situation provides us with the unique chance to view the cultural development from the Late Palaeolithic to the beginning of written history within a clearly defined chronological framework. It puts the archaeologist into the role of a lucky biologist able to observe a volcanic island being born from the sea and to study how incipient life begins and develops. Moreover in our case we, as archaeologists, have the opportunity to study the end of the story as well.

During the period in question one of the most momentous events in later prehistory took place: the transition from hunter-gatherer to farmer and cattle breeder, an essential step that Gordon Childe (1957) called the 'First Revolution' in the history of mankind. The origin of this new way of life and its accompanying technological achievements, such as the production of pottery, was identified in the Near East, in the so-called 'Fertile Crescent', an area that originally was thought to include Egypt. In the 1970s the situation was viewed in a somewhat different manner and Egypt and the Sahara were instead considered as receiving areas of this new lifestyle (Quitta 1971, 47). However at the same time a map was published displaying some of the findspots of pottery in the central Sahara, and these were dated as early as those in the Near East (see Fig. 1), yet in Egypt nothing older than 4000 BC was known (Quitta 1971, 46).

On the basis of growing evidence from the Sahara, Gabriel Camps in 1974 was able to distinguish two Neolithic families in the western Sahara: the Neolithic of Capsian Tradition, characterised mainly by pointed-based vessels and decorated ostrich eggshell; and the Saharan-Sudanese Neolithic, for which bone harpoons and particularly globular pots with overall decoration in the Khartoum or Wavy Line style are typical (Camps 1974, 219). When seeking an explanation for these two clearly defined groups, a look at a regional climatic map of the Eastern Sahara was of use (Walter et al. 1975). Such a map showed that the distribution of average annual temperature and rainfall clearly falls to either side of the central Libyan Desert, the area of highest aridity with almost no precipitation. Looking at it in

more detail, it became obvious that when it rains in Kufra Oasis it is winter and when it rains at Wadi Halfa it is summer. As the boundary between the two climatic regimes is located in the far southern part of Egypt, the border between the two cultural groups may be found there as well. However, it is still an open question whether or not the climatic situation was the same at the beginning of the Holocene, when the rains returned to the Sahara. Determining this is essential for answering the crucial question: From which direction did man re-enter the desert?

Today all palaeo-climatological evidence indicates that the early Holocene wet front came from the south and monsoon rains reached as far north as the latitude of Dakhleh Oasis (Kröpelin 1993ab). From the northern part of our transect corresponding evidence is so far missing. Reconstruction of the vegetation in the desert during the middle Holocene, between 7000 and 6000 years bp, is based on the identification of charcoal from prehistoric fireplaces. This evidence shows a northward shift of the vegetation zone of more than 800 km (Plate 7) (Neumann 1989a, fig. 37; 1989b). At the same time it demonstrates that there never was a really 'Green' Sahara in the Western Desert of Egypt. Instead it was rather a sahelian environment, perhaps similar to the acacia desert scrub around Khartoum at present (see also Schild and Wendorf this volume).

Within these semi-arid environments there also existed, as there does today, favoured areas where, after the rainy season, temporary lakes became the centre of life. These are mainly represented by the so-called 'playa deposits' that can be found in open plains as that near Gebel Nabta (Wendorf et al. 1984; Wendorf and Schild this volume), or up to 9 m above the surrounding plain in mountain gorges like Wadi Bakht in the Gilf Kebir Plateau (Plate 8)(Kröpelin 1987). In addition to this, recent space shuttle radar images have detected systems of rivers that ran down the mountains during the rainy season, their beds now hidden under perhaps only two metres of sand. This, for instance, is the case in front of the southwestern cliff of the Gilf Kebir near Wadi Sura, a place that has recently become world famous for its rock paintings.

It was Patrick Clayton in 1931 who discovered some engravings of giraffes here, and it was Lazlo Almásy in 1933 who, during an expedition with Leo Frobenius, Elisabeth Pauli and Hans Rhotert, found two caves with several panels of very fine rock paintings (Almásy 1997, 132; Rhotert 1952, 2). It was also during this same year that Pat Clayton crossed the Great Sand Sea to Siwa (Clayton 1998, 55ff) together with Lady Dorothy Clayton East, the woman who became the model for Catherine Clifton in *The English Patient*. The paintings in the caves represent cattle in different styles, people with bows executed in a very elegant and vivid manner, and hand prints. There were also people depicted wearing various types of clothing and body paint—some of them with crossed bands over the chest like the distinctive dress of Libyans in ancient Egyptian representations. Finally there was also a long row of about sixteen figures that gave the place its name: the 'Cave of Swimmers' (Plate 9). It may be a matter of dispute whether or not the attitude of the figures really depicts that of swimming, as some rock art spe-

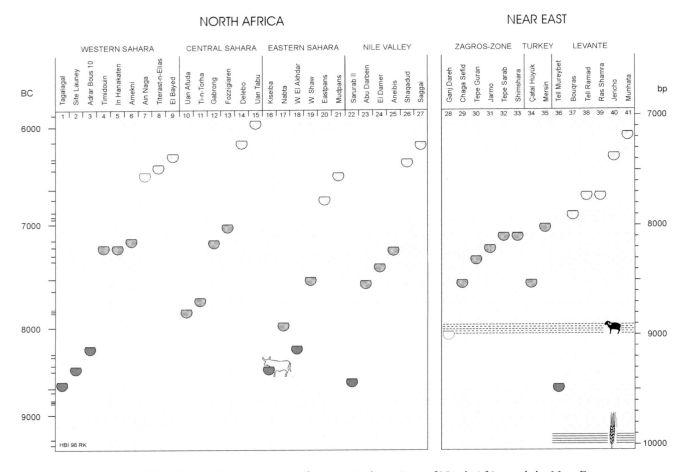

Fig. 1   Comparative table of the earliest appearance of pottery in the regions of North Africa and the Near East.

cialists will argue that they could instead be moving in trance-like meditation into another world. However, standing in front of the pictures one prefers the simple positivistic interpretation, especially since this idea is strengthened by the investigations of the geomorphologist, who has reasons to reconstruct extended pools immediately in front of the caves (Kröpelin, pers. comm.).

Almásy must have loved this place. He copied many of the pictures himself (Almásy 1939, 136 ff). This is a good point at which to insert some words about a more recent chapter of desert history, a time when desert comrades found themselves on opposing sides. In 1942 Almásy had the opportunity to return to the Gilf Kebir when he agreed to take two German spies behind British lines from Libya to the Nile. The area was, of course, under the control of the British forces, especially the Long Range Desert Group, which had been founded by men like Bagnold, Clayton, Shaw, Prendergast and other desert enthusiasts from the good old pre-war days.

On this spectacularly risky venture Almásy did not hesitate to visit Wadi Sura, as is proven by a photograph that surprisingly appeared recently in an Italian journal (**Plate 10**). It was taken right in front of the Cave of Swimmers, and it is amusing to quote from the diary of a German sergeant who also visited the cave: 'Something as beautiful as that in this boring desert!'

Let us now return from these late records of the desert back to some of the earliest, some 10,000 years ago. The earliest evidence for the return of human life into the Western Desert comes from the area of Bir Kiseiba and Gebel Nabta, located c. 100 km west of Lake Nasser. Here Fred Wendorf and his associates have excavated several sites of what they have named the El Adam phase, dated by a broad base of radiocarbon dates to between 9500 and 8900 bp (Wendorf et al. 1984, 7; Schild and Wendorf this volume, **Fig. 2**). They have found decorated pottery as well as cattle bones that probably belong to domesticated animals since the reconstructed environment, with only a maximum of 200 mm of precipitation per year, would not have supported wild cattle. The question of whether these new features were developed locally or whether they were introduced from the Nile Valley, however, is still a matter of discussion (Wendorf and Schild 1994; this volume).

With regard to pottery, there is a new date for some Wavy Line sherds from the Gilf Kebir in the remote southwestern corner of Egypt. The southern and eastern parts of this sandstone plateau, stretching some 80 × 50 km, are dissected by numerous gorges, one of which is the Wadi el-Akhdar (Kröpelin 1989, 262ff; Schön 1996). In its upper part there is an amphitheatre-shaped basin, 2.5 km in diameter, where we focussed our work for several field seasons from 1980 onward. The entrance to this wadi is almost completely blocked by a dune located between two steep slopes. A similar dune also existed in this spot in the early Holocene, and this prevented the sediments brought down by rains from the plateau being swept further downstream. Up to 6 m of these deposits are now exposed and embedded remains of human occupation from different periods are visible (**Plate 11**).

The pottery under discussion comes from a spot just above the entrance, between huge rocks, a situation that made the excavation work quite difficult. Most of the sherds are relatively thick and bear a Wavy Line decoration (**Plate 12**) that finds its closest parallels along the Nile near Khartoum. The original pot had a diameter of 40 to 50 cm and may have weighed 7 to 10 kg. It is hard to imagine that it could have been brought from far away by nomads without pack-animals. The AMS date of 9080 ± 50 bp or 8059 ± 33 cal BC (UtC 6536) comes from the sherd itself and places this pottery among the oldest known from the Sahara, or elsewhere for that matter.

Comparing the appearance of ceramic technology in the Near East with that in the Sahara (**Fig. 1**), it becomes evident that during the ninth millennium BC well-made pottery is far better represented in the Sahara than in Western Asia, where the only known examples from Tell Mureybet consist of roughly made, small, undecorated vessels. Taking into account that many more excavations have been carried out in the Near East than in the Sahara, an autochthonous development of ceramic technology along the southern fringes of the Sahara seems quite probable. Here the cultural element of pottery, which from the European point of view has generally been regarded as a characteristic of the Neolithic way of life, can be found in its earliest manifestation in a context with bone harpoons and the remains of fish, hippopotamus, crocodile and other amphibious animals, thus representing relatively sedentary hunting and fishing communities living along the shores of permanent lakes. How these people changed their economy and their lifestyle when they moved northward with the rains is a matter for further research.

This question becomes even more exciting in view of the fact that the reoccupation of the Eastern Sahara obviously took place over a relatively short space of time. Recent excavations in the Great Sand Sea have provided some dates earlier than 9000 bp. They come from the area of Regenfeld, 300 km to the north of Bir Kiseiba (**Plate 13**). Here, alongside a dune corridor, several concentrations of Epi-Palaeolithic artefacts have been investigated. These were situated on top of a former whale-back dune between an active seif dune and several playa lakes that once filled the dune street east of it. Test excavations were carried out on several of the concentrations and a 40 m long trench was dug in order to clarify the geological relationship of the playa and the dune (Besler 1997). The lithic assemblages are based on a blade and bladelet technology (**Fig. 2**). Characteristic tools are straight-backed pointed bladelets and other microliths, such as elongated triangles and trapezes (Riemer 2000). Unlike the contemporary El Adam sites near Bir Kiseiba, there was no pottery immediately associated with these lithic artefacts, but some sherds have been found at concentration 4. They are undecorated and coarse-tempered, and obviously represent a completely different ceramic tradition. Such pottery is known from several other sites in the Great Sand Sea and might be the result of cultural inflow originating from the Near East.

The earliest evidence for this type of undecorated pottery comes from the Gilf Kebir and from Mudpans near Abu Ballas and is dated to the so-called 'Middle Neolithic', around 7500 bp. It appears together with new elements in the stone artefact assemblage and a new social structure in the settlements (Kuper 1995). With regard to the origin of these new ceramic forms there are three alternative models to discuss. After having moved northward with the Holocene wet front the makers of Khartoum-style ceramic either: a) met with and were influenced by a non-decorated pottery tradition (wherever the origins of this are to be found); b) generated of themselves a facies that gave up the usual mode of decoration; or c) stimulated people so far without pottery to adopt ceramic technology, who, however, preferred not to ornament their pots. Which of these three possibilities will be substantiated is a key issue for future research, especially as this pottery may be linked to 'Neolithisation' in the Near Eastern sense, that is, the introduction into that region of a productive economy that included the herding of sheep and goat.

This is not the place to plunge deeper into the details of a possible influx from the Near East. The actual state of research is reflected by our chronological results which—together with the radiocarbon dates from Fred Wendorf's CPE and other desert colleagues – reveal some informative patterns that obviously mirror the human occupation of the different regions of the Eastern Sahara.

Some of the observations worth noting in this context include the following (see **Plate 7**):

1. The general arrangement of the older radiocarbon dates in the north and the bulk of the younger ones in the southern part of the desert suggests a retreat of human settlement over time in a southerly direction.

2. There is a clear contrast between the well-documented human presence in the desert and the dearth of early Holocene data from the Nile Valley, whether due to ecological reasons or insufficient research remains unknown.

3. There is an obvious break in the settlement record of the Western Desert at around 6000 bp, after which time life could only go on in some ecologically favoured places like the Gilf Kebir, while in the Nile Valley the Neolithic and Predynastic cultures began to flourish.

The appearance of undecorated pottery in the Eastern Sahara around 7700 bp or 6500 BC seems to correlate with a new stone tool technology: bifacial flint working. This is the technique typical of the Predynastic cultures in the Nile Valley, but dates by which to secure its chronological relationship with this same cultural component in the desert have long been missing. Now, in addition to results from the Dakhleh Oasis (McDonald 1998; Hope this volume), further evidence has recently come from an extraordinary desert site that is related to the early exploration of the Eastern Sahara in a very special way.

It is a place called Djara and it is situated in the middle of

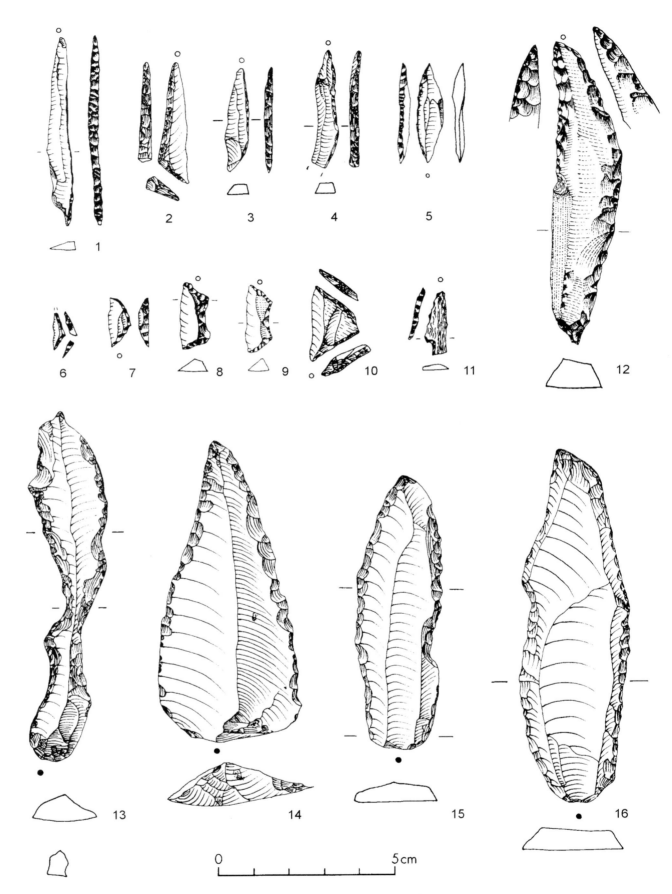

Fig. 2   Epi-Palaeolithic artefacts from Regenfeld site 96/1 in the Great Sand Sea.

the so-called 'Libyan' or 'Abu Muharik' Plateau between the Egyptian oases and the Nile (**Plate 14**). In spite of the fact that the area lies relatively close to the Nile Valley, or perhaps for this reason, it has not hitherto attracted the attention of recent scientific expeditions, which from the early days of Ball and Bagnold up to Wendorf and ourselves have preferred more remote areas like the Gilf Kebir or the Great Sand Sea. However 120 years ago it was part of the exploratory work of the first and, for the next hundred years, the only interdisciplinary expedition carried out in this part of Egypt. It was headed by Gerhard Rohlfs who gave a general description of the results in his book *Drei Monate in der Libyschen Wüste* (1875).

The main goals of this unique enterprise, and the reason for its financial support by the Khedive Ismail of Egypt, were to reach Kufra Oasis and especially to find a solution to the so-called *'Bahr-bela-ma* problem': the question of the existence of a former Nile bed in the Western Desert. It was hoped that this former river bed would be suitable for land reclamation, already at that time seen as a solution for the over-population of the Nile Valley. With regard to the chronological relationship between the two river beds, during a session of the *Institut Égyptien* directed by Mariette Bey, Rohlfs was also asked to pay special attention to 'worked stone fragments' as indications of a formerly moister climate.

The extensive logistical preparations of this journey included 500 iron water tanks, each able to hold 50 litres, made in Germany and brought to Egypt. To the technical equipment the Khedive added one of his comfortable travelling kitchens including porcelain and crystal glassware, the daintiest foods and different varieties of wine, beer, liquor and champagne. The expedition left Assiut on 18 December 1873 with 100 camels and reached Farafra 12 days later. In his description of this route Rohlfs mentions that on Christmas evening 1873 they made camp near a place called 'Djara', which he describes as a spacious drip-stone cave with beautiful stalactites. No further details were given and later researchers seem not to have taken this report seriously since for nearly 120 years—in contrast to the other results of the expedition—the cave appears to have been ignored.

Rohlfs' team comprised ten members from Germany who left their names on a pillar of the temple of Deir el-Hagar in the Dakhleh Oasis (**Plate 15**). In the left column were the names of the masters, in the right their respective German servants. We see Gerhard Rohlfs, who was a doctor; Georg Zittel, Professor of Geology; Wilhelm Jordan, a geographer; Paul Ascherson, a botanist; and finally and most remarkably a photographer, Philipp Remelé. Not only did he take the earliest photographs of this temple, but also carried out extensive excavations there—surely not to the pleasure of the DOP team who have recently done this yet again. However, it is for his photography that he should be remembered.

At el-Qasr in Dakhleh Oasis the inhabitants welcomed the expedition much more warmly than the people of Farafra and offered them a roomy house that served for weeks as a base for their march westward into the Great Sand Sea towards Kufra. Remelé's photograph shows the whole expe-

dition in front of this house (**Plate 16**). The house no longer exists in its original shape, but its location can be identified thanks to the fact that even at that time Sahara expeditions liked to employ the latest technology. In the *Bulletin de la Société Khédiviale de Géographie* for 1876 one can find a complete plan of the oasis published by Jordan, the geographer of the expedition, who constructed it by means of photogrammetry, a method that had been developed only a few years earlier. All the details of the village and its surroundings are given and these can be compared with the present day appearance of the oasis to show very little has actually changed.

Rohlfs' original plan to reach Kufra eventually had to be abandoned. The expedition had advanced 150 km into the Great Sand Sea when they experienced two days of continuous rainfall, lasting from 2 to 4 February 1874. As a result, in a message placed in a bottle and left inside a cairn of cobbles, they named the site 'Regenfeld' (Rainfield). Here the giant dunes that became progressively higher the further west they went turned out to be impassable for the camels and their plans had to be changed. From Regenfeld the expedition headed northward for Siwa, which they reached two weeks later. From there they returned to Dakhleh and then via Kharga to Cairo.

Except for the failure to reach Kufra the scientific results of the expedition were of great importance for all the participating disciplines. The first geological map of Egypt, published by Zittel, was for nearly one hundred years the basis of the geology of Northeast Africa. Only their archaeological results seem to have had only minor impact—until recently. In 1989 Dr Carlo Bergmann, a German camel nomad, who treks every winter with his camels for hundreds of kilometres through the desert, re-discovered the dripstone cave marked by Rohlfs on his route to Farafra. He not only found Rohlfs' description fully confirmed, but additionally reported rich prehistoric remains in the immediate surroundings of this cave. Indeed, if we look at Rohlfs' map, we find the word *Feuersteinsplitter*—stone splinters—close to the name Djara.

As a consequence of Bergmann's publication we knew that tourists would be attracted to the site. In order to salvage this unique natural and cultural resource, we visited the cave for the first time in November 1990 (Kuper 1996). Coming from the north one meets the broad camel route that Rohlfs used and this can be followed westward. Well-preserved, it clearly showed no earlier car tracks. The entrance to the cave lies in the centre of a featureless, flat depression; a plain hole in the ground, where only at close view does the earth open up. A filling of wind-blown sand has left only a narrow entrance. Sliding down the sand slope a few metres into the cave one meets a great stalagmite covered with engravings. It was not possible to remove the sand to its base, but the stalagmite as it stands displays a great number of figures on all sides, partly overlapping and executed in varying techniques. Only animals appear: ostriches, addax, antelope and a great number of other bovids and quadrupeds, some of them obviously representations of goats.

From here one slides another 10 m deeper into a great

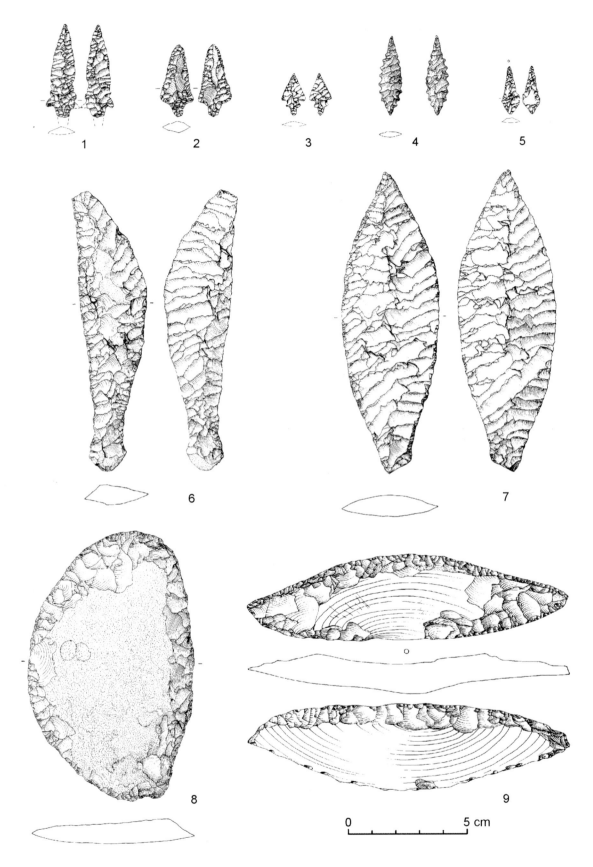

Fig. 3   Lithic artefacts from the prehistoric settlement around Djara cave. Nos 2, 3 and 5 have been directly dated to older than 5500 cal BC.

hall that extends over 50 m. Impressive stalactites hang from the roof while the floor is covered with sand (**Plate 17**). We were intrigued to learn how deep this sand layer might be, as it seemed that for thousands of years a cavern of this type would have served as a sediment trap for microfossils as well as for human debris. The foliate structures on the surface were clear evidence that water had quite recently been standing on the sand for some time. There seemed little doubt that such a place would have been quite attractive to prehistoric settlers. In a following campaign cores were taken from several places within the cave, yet they revealed nothing but fine white sand down to more than six metres!

More interesting finds were made outside the cave where the surface is scattered with lithic artefacts, mainly concentrated in an area of 300 × 200 m immediately north of the entrance. At first glance there are no visible stone structures, but large areas are densely covered with artefacts indicative of the intensive working and use of flint. Beside some microlithic elements, the tool kit is dominated by large, bifacial pieces showing a fine pressure flaking technique that produced parallel ripples and additional sharpening of the edges (**Fig. 3.7**). The spectrum also includes forms with partly parallel edges whose shape suggests the term 'knife' (**Fig. 3.6**). Most seem to be made of tabular flint. Common items on the site are planes or tranchets, predominantly made from natural flint fragments. The smaller artefacts are comprised of carefully worked points and arrowheads that are quite varied in size and shape (**Fig. 3.1–5**), as well as so-called 'side blow flakes' (**Fig. 3.9**), a characteristic tool of the Late Middle Neolithic and the Late Neolithic in the Western Desert. They occur in the Bashendi Cultural Unit of Dakhleh Oasis (McDonald 1991, fig. 5) and also in the Fayum culture (Caton-Thompson and Gardner 1934, pl. XLIV).

When seeking parallels for the assemblage from Djara, it must be kept in mind that it may be a composite of several occupations, in spite of the relatively uniform impression it gives at first glance. If one looks to the Nile Valley, the site of Badari, for instance, lies only 200 km east of Djara and the Fayum with its characteristic bifacial tools is not very far away. Within the regions investigated by the BOS project, the Sitra area as well as the eastern Great Sand Sea have produced comparable inventories (Cziesla 1989; Klees 1989). Here especially the site of Lobo, near Abu Minqar should be noted, as scarce, but characteristic, undecorated ceramics were found that are comparable to the pottery from the Fayum. Many parallels can also be detected within the Bashendi groups of the Dakhleh Oasis (McDonald 1991; Hope this volume) and in the material from the prehistoric excavations in the Farafra area (Barich 1996).

In order to understand the direction of possible influences, the dating of the Djara assemblage is of special importance. As luck was with us, a small test excavation near the entrance of the cave uncovered two fireplaces, both of which contained bifacial lithic pieces. Four radiocarbon dates place them between 6800 and 6500 bp, several hundred years before comparable occurrences of similar cultural material in the Fayum and the Nile Valley. Another group of dates obviously associated with a bladelet complex, excavated at another spot, provided proof of an even earlier occupation. It is hoped that further excavations will reveal well-preserved bone and plant remains that will allow us to formulate some insights into the economic structure of the settlement, its relation to the changing environment and its role in the prehistoric development of the Sahara and the Nile.

Following the increasing aridity after 6000 bp the desert became more and more depopulated, and with the development of Dynastic Egyptian culture, desert and Nile grew further and further apart. 'Desheret', the 'Red Land', became the land of evil and the dead. Even today Bagnold's (1937, 265) remark still proves true: 'By Egyptian standards there was no water west of the oases and the world ended.' But there have always been exceptions, like the desert traveller Harkhuf, governor of Aswan, who, in the Sixth Dynasty, around 2225 BC, travelled along the 'oasis-route' to a land called 'Yam', which can perhaps be located in the area of Dongola in the Sudan. As many of the papers in this volume show, the bonds between the desert and the valley that were formed in Neolithic times were never severed completely. The pharaonic monuments in the oases are not the only evidence for this. Far reaching relations with the Nile Valley are also suggested by small finds in the desert itself like, for example, a fragment of a so-called Meidum bowl from the Fourth Dynasty that was found in Wadi Shaw in northern Sudan (Kuper 1995, fig. 7).

In this particular case it remains an open question whether Egyptians themselves were in that area or not, but there is evidence from other places that shows quite convincing proof of the long range desert activities of the ancient Egyptians. The most prominent place is Abu Ballas, a small conical hill about 500 km west of the Nile, which curiously enough can be found even on large scale maps. Among thousands of similar hills it has the distinction of having been named by John Ball, who in 1918 during a geological survey passed through this practically unknown part of the Libyan Desert. At the foot of this inconspicuous sandstone cone, approximately 200 km southwest of Dakhleh Oasis, he discovered about one hundred large jars, and these led him to name the site Abu Ballas, 'Father of Jars' or 'Pottery Hill'. Fifteen years later the Frobenius Expedition of 1933 found the original arrangement of the pots already in an advanced state of destruction (Rhotert 1952, fig. XXXVI). This was even more the case when the BOS expedition visited in 1981. Photographs demonstrate to what extent the site had been looted between 1933 and 1985 (**Plate 18** and **Plate 19**). Fortunately there are still a few vessels with potmarks, some of which seem to resemble hieroglyphs. Moreover, the specific shape of the rim on some of the vessels allows them to be dated by parallels from Elephantine to between the Sixth Dynasty and the Middle Kingdom.

Into this chronological framework also fit some rock engravings from below the top of the hill discovered by Prince Kemal el Din in 1923 and later recorded by Hans Rhotert in his book *Libysche Felsbilder* (1952). The first one depicts a cow, obviously carved by a skilled hand, suckling its calf, a motif quite popular in early Dynastic Egypt. The other drawing depicts a hunter taking aim at a gazelle that has just been hit by his arrow as well as being attacked by his two dogs (**Plate 20**). This scene is closely paralleled by a painted bowl from the Nile Valley (**Plate 21**) that shows a man in the same costume with the Libyan feather on his head, holding his bow and bundle of arrows in the same manner. The bowl comes from Qubbet el-Hawa near Aswan, 550 km to the east, where it has been dated to the Sixth Dynasty.

This is also the time when the governors of Ayn Asil near Balat in the Dakhleh Oasis built their impressive mastabas, constructions that may be regarded as local symbols of kingship (see Mills; Kaper and Willems this volume). Excavations carried out there by the French Institute of Archaeology revealed some clay tablets worth mentioning for our purposes (Posener-Krieger 1992). The writer, who is not in Ayn Asil, but at a place named *Rwdjet,* complains that 'the pottery intended to prepare the way' for the governor from a place named 'Demy-iu' has not yet arrived at its destination. We do not know where the mentioned localities are, but it seems clear that the pots were to transport provisions for a longer desert journey.

A recent discovery from the open desert southwest of Dakhleh can perhaps add to this discussion. At a conspicuous rock, one that might well have served as a landmark, beside some older engravings of wild animals, a hieroglyphic inscription has been detected (**Plate 22**). Arranged within two lines, the text has been transcribed and translated as follows (Burkard 1997): 'Regnal year 23 (we do not know of which king): The steward Meri, he goes up to meet the oasis-dwellers'. For several, mainly palaeographic, reasons, the inscription can be dated to the Sixth or the Twelfth Dynasty, but the latter date seems more probable. Certainly the most intriguing question is: Where did Mr. Meri intend to go? Since he came from Egypt we should search for his 'oasis-dwellers' in a southwestern direction where only two reasonable destinations can be recognised: Gebel Uweinat, at a distance of 500 km through barren desert, or slightly more westward, at Abu Ballas some 150 km away.

At this point one cannot but pay tribute to a topic that so often has been the subject of discussion in different circles especially in London: Zerzura. It is not my intention to add to Ralph Bagnold's article 'The last of the Zerzura legend' in the *Geographical Journal* of 1937 an addendum entitled perhaps 'The very last of the Zerzura legend'. Certainly he was right in his opinion that this 'lost oasis' can never be found, since it exists in the heads and in the hearts of people as long as any part of the world remains to be discovered (Bagnold 1935, 283).

Instead I wish to refer here to Almásy's personal Zerzura, which he was convinced he had found in the three valleys in the northwestern Gilf Kebir, discovered from the air together with Pat Clayton in 1932. Today these valleys still support some vegetation. Aligning them with Balat in Dahkleh Oasis, Meri's rock and Abu Ballas, they might well have served as relay stations on a route between Dakhleh and Kufra Oasis (**Plate 23**). In contrast to the course that forced Rohlfs to give up his attempt to reach Kufra, this route avoids the dunes of the Great Sand Sea and could, in stages of 210 km, perhaps also be mastered with donkey caravans,

but only if we follow Almásy's idea of an artificial, man-made, oasis at Abu Ballas. The recent discoveries and new dates help to support his speculations concerning the archaeology of the desert and surely give us more reason to remember him than the fiction of a film.

Not long after the lecture on which this paper is based, Carlo Bergmann set out from Dakhleh with his camels towards Abu Ballas in search of this alleged route. Between March 1999 and March 2000 he discovered nearly 30 stations arranged like a string of pearls from Balat via Abu Ballas to as far as the cliffs of the Gilf Kebir. From there, where this route may lead is as yet unknown. Many of the sites contain large amounts of pottery dating from the Old Kingdom up to the Ptolemaic period, thus proving traffic on the 'Abu Ballas Trail' for more than 2000 years (Kuper 2001).

Although we can only speculate on certain details of the history of the desert and its relationship with the Nile Valley over time, we can summarise the main aspects of 5000 years of settlement in the Eastern Sahara as they are compiled in the somewhat hypothetical table in **Plate 24**:

With the onset of the monsoon rains before 9000 years bp the first re-occupants of the southern Sahara—possibly from the Nile Valley—brought with them quite advanced ceramic technology and perhaps already domesticated cattle. At the same time in the north, where surprisingly even the Great Sand Sea was rather quickly reoccupied, a spectrum of stone inventories provide evidence of Epi-Palaeolithic foragers, while pottery appears only later. This pottery was generally undecorated and probably originates with an influx of people or influences from the Near East. The introduction of sheep and goat may also have been part of this same movement that took place between 7500 and 6500 bp. Bifacial flint technology also appeared at this time and later continued to dominate the Predynastic industries of the Nile Valley.

Before 6000 bp—or in calibrated years 5000 BC—when the desert started to reclaim its land, at sites like Fayum and somewhat later at Merimde, a fully Neolithic way of life developed that included the cultivation of wheat and barley. Meanwhile people in the desert still relied on the collection of the wild grasses that were surely the main attraction of the Saharan savannas in the Early and Middle Holocene. On the other hand, as the evidence of the Late Neolithic megaliths at Nabta suggests (see Wendorf and Schild this volume), there was more between the desert and the Nile than simply similarities in material culture as they can be traced, for example, from the pottery tradition in the Gilf Kebir to the A-Group in Nubia. The evidence from Nabta suggests that the desert, more than previously realised, contributed to the intellectual background and the ideas that made the pyramids possible. Perhaps Horus and Seth in the well-known pharaonic image are not only knotting together the Lily and the Papyrus, the symbols of Upper and Lower Egypt, but are also tying together Epi-Palaeolithic and Mediterranean roots with Khartoum and Sudanic traditions, thus symbolizing Egypt's role as a transmitter between Africa and the Old World.

One hundred and twenty years ago Georg Zittel, the

geologist in Rohlfs' team, opened his essay 'Über den geologischen Bau der libyschen Wüste' with a sentence especially remarkable for its time (Zittel 1880, 1): 'On the southern shores of the Mediterranean, in the sunny Nile country stands the cradle of European culture'. Most Europeans

learn in school that the cradle of their culture stands in Rome and Greece, and until now Zittel's statement from 1880 has found only limited echo. Yet, as work in the desert continues, the reverberations of that sentence become ever stronger.

Bibliography

Almásy L E, 1936. *Récentes explorations dans le désert libyque.* Cairo.

Almásy L E, 1939. *Unbekannte Sahara.* Leipzig.

Almásy L E, 1997. *Schwimmer in der Wüste* (new edition of *Unbekannte Sahara* completed by chapters from the Hungarian edition of 1934 and documents about Almásy's 'Operation Salam' of 1942). Innsbruck.

Bagnold R A, 1935. *Libyan Sands.* London.

Bagnold R A, 1937. The last of the Zerzura legend. *Geographical Journal* 89: 265–8.

Bagnold R A, 1982. Foreword. In F El-Baz and T A Maxwell (eds), *Desert landforms of Southwest Egypt: a basis for comparison with Mars.* Washington: vii.

Barich B, 1996. Archaeology of Farafra (Western Desert, Egypt). In G Pwiti and R Soper (eds), *Aspects of African Archaeology.* Harare.

Barth H, 1857. *Travels in North and Central-Africa.* London.

Baumgartel E, 1955. *The cultures of Prehistoric Egypt.* London.

Besler H, 1997. Aktuelle und Paläoformung in der Großen Sandsee Ägyptens. *Zeitschrift für Geomorphologie N.F.* Suppl. 111:1–16.

Burkard G, 1997. Inscription in the Dakhla region. Text, Translation and Comments. *Sahara* 9: 152–3.

Camps G, 1974. *Les civilisations préhistoriques de l'Afrique du nord et du Sahara.* Paris.

Caton-Thompson G and Gardner E W, 1934. *The Desert Fayum.* London.

Childe G, 1957. *The Dawn of Civilisation.* London.

Churcher C S and Mills A J (eds.), 1999. *Reports from the Survey of the Dakhleh Oasis. Western Desert of Egypt, 1977-1987.* Oxbow Monograph 99, Dakhleh Oasis Project Monograph 2. Oxford.

Clayton P, 1998. *Desert Explorer. A Biography of Colonel P. A. Clayton DSO, MBE, FRGS, FGS. 1896 to 1962.* Cargreen, Cornwall.

Close A E, 1992. Holocene Occupation of the Eastern Sahara. In F Klees and R Kuper (eds), *New Light on the Northeast African Past.* Africa Praehistorica 5. Köln: 155–83.

Cziesla E, 1989. Sitra and related sites at the western border of Egypt. In L Krzyzaniak and M Kobusiewicz (eds), *Late Prehistory of the Nile Basin and the Sahara.* Poznan: 205–14.

Cziesla E, 1993. Investigations into the archaeology of the Sitra-Hatiyet, northwestern Egypt. In L Krzyzaniak, M Kobusiewicz and J Alexander (eds), *Environmental Change and Human Culture in the Nile Basin and Northern Africa until the Second Millennium B.C.* Poznan: 185–97.

Gabriel B, Kröpelin S, Richter J and Cziesla E, 1985. Parabeldünen am Wadi Howar. *Geowissenschaften in unserer Zeit* 3,4: 105–12.

Keding B, 1997. *Djabarona 84/13.* Africa Praehistorica 9. Köln.

Keding B, 1998. The Yellow Nile: New Data on Settlement and Environment in the Sudanese Eastern Sahara. *Sudan & Nubia* 2: 2–12.

Klees F, 1989. Lobo: a contribution to the prehistory of the eastern Sand Sea and the Egyptian oases. In L Krzyzaniak and M Kobusiewicz (eds), *Late Prehistory of the Nile Basin and the Sahara.* Poznan: 223–31.

Kröpelin S, 1987. Palaeoclimatic evidence from early to mid-Holocene playas in the Gilf Kebir (Southwest Egypt). *Palaeoecology of Africa* 18: 189–208.

Kröpelin S, 1989. Untersuchungen zum Sedimentationsmilieu von Playas im Gilf Kebir (Südwest-Ägypten). In R Kuper (ed.), *Forschungen zur Umweltgeschichte der Ostsahara.* Africa Praehistorica 2. Köln: 183–305.

Kröpelin S, 1993a. *Zur Rekonstruktion der spätquartären Umwelt am Unteren Wadi Howar (Südöstliche Sahara / NW-Sudan).* Berliner Geographische Abhandlungen 54. Berlin.

Kröpelin S, 1993b. Geomorphology, Landscape Evolution and Paleoclimates of Southwest Egypt. In B Meissner and P Wycisk (eds), *Geopotential and Ecology of the Western Desert, Egypt.* Catena Supplement 26: 31–66.

Kuper R, 1981. Untersuchungen zur Besiedlungsgeschichte der östlichen Sahara. *Beiträge zur Allgemeinen und Vergleichenden Archäologie* 3: 215–75.

Kuper R, 1988. Neuere Forschungen zur Besiedlungsgeschichte der Ost-Sahara. *Archäologisches Korrespondenzblatt* 18: 127–42.

Kuper R, 1993. Sahel in Egypt: environmental change and cultural development in the Abu Ballas area, Libyan Desert. In L Krzyzaniak, M Kobusiewicz and J Alexander (eds), *Environmental Change and Human Culture in the Nile Basin and Northern Africa until the Second Millennium B.C.* Poznan: 213–23.

Kuper R, 1995. Prehistoric Research in the Southern Libyan Desert. (Actes de la VIIIe Conférence Internationale des Études Nubiennes, Lille 1994). *Cahier de Recherches de l'Institut de Papyrologie et d'Égyptologie de Lille* 17: 123–40.

Kuper R, 1996. Between the Oases and the Nile–Djara: Rohlfs' Cave in the Western Desert. In L Krzyzaniak, K Kroeper and M Kobusiewicz (eds), *Interregional Contacts in the Later Prehistory of Northeastern Africa.* Poznan: 81–91.

Kuper R, 2001. By Donkey Train to Kufra? – How Mr. Meri went west. *Antiquity* 75: 801–2.

McDonald M M A, 1991. Origins of the Neolithic in the Nile Valley as seen from Dakhleh Oasis in the Egyptian Western Desert. *Sahara* 4: 41–52.

McDonald M M A, 1998. Early African Pastoralism: View from Dakhleh Oasis (South Central Egypt). *Journal of Anthropological Archaeology* 17: 124–42.

Neumann K, 1989a. Zur Vegetationsgeschichte der Ostsahara im Holozän. Holzkohlen aus prähistorischen Fundstellen. In R Kuper (ed.), *Forschungen zur Umweltgeschichte der Ostsahara.* Africa Praehistorica 2. Köln: 13–181.

Neumann K, 1989b. Holocene vegetation of the Eastern Sahara: charcoal from prehistoric sites. *The African Archaeological Review* 7: 97–116.

Posener-Krieger P, 1992. Les tablettes en terre crue de Balat. In É Lalou (ed.), *Les tablettes à écrire de l'antiquité à l'époque moderne.* Turnhout: 41–52.

Quitta H, 1971. Der Balkan als Mittler zwischen Vorderem Orient und Europa. In F Schlette (ed.), *Evolution und Revolution im Alten Orient und in Europa.* Berlin: 38–63.

Rhotert H, 1952. *Libysche Felsbilder.* Darmstadt.

Richter J, 1989. Neolithic sites in the Wadi Howar (Western Sudan). In L Krzyzaniak and M Kobusiewicz (eds), *Late Prehistory of the Nile Basin and the Sahara*. Poznan: 431–42.

Riemer H, 2000. Regenfeld 96/1 – Great Sand Sea and the question of human settlement on whaleback dunes. In L Krzyzaniak, K Kroeper and M Kobusiewicz (eds), *Recent Research into the Stone Age of Northeastern Africa*. Poznan: 21–31.

Rohlfs G, 1875. *Drei Monate in der libyschen Wüste*. Kassel. (Africa Explorata 1, Reprint Köln 1996).

Schön W, 1996. *Ausgrabungen im Wadi el Akhdar, Gilf Kebir (SW-Ägypten)*. Africa Praehistorica 8. Köln.

Schuck W, 1988. Wadi Shaw–Eine Siedlungskammer im Nord-Sudan. *Archäologisches Korrespondenzblatt* 18: 143–53.

Schuck W, 1993. An archaeological survey of the Selima Sandsheet, Sudan. In L Krzyzaniak, M Kobusiewicz and J Alexander (eds), *Environmental Change and Human Culture in the Nile basin and Northern Africa until the Second Millennium B.C.* Poznan: 237–48.

Vermeersch P M, Van Peer Ph, Moeyersons J and Van Neer W, 1994. Sodmein Cave Site, Red Sea Mountains (Egypt). *Sahara* 6: 31–40.

Vernet R, 1995. *Climats anciens du nord de l'Afrique*. Paris.

Walter H, Harnickell E and Mueller-Dombois D, 1975. *Climate-diagramm Maps*. Berlin.

Wendorf F and Schild R, 1994. Are the Early Holocene Cattle in the Eastern Sahara Domestic or Wild? *Evolutionary Anthropology* 3 (4): 118–28.

Wendorf F and Schild R, 1998. Nabta Playa and Its Role in Northeastern African Prehistory. *Journal of Anthropological Archaeology* 17: 97–123.

Wendorf F, Schild R and Close A E (eds), 1984. *Cattle-Keepers of the Eastern Sahara: The Neolithic of Bir Kiseiba*. Dallas.

Zittel K, 1880. *Ueber den geologischen Bau der libyschen Wüste*. München.

Implications of Incipient Social Complexity in the Late Neolithic in the Egyptian Sahara

Fred Wendorf and Romuald Schild

Introduction

The Western Desert of Egypt is not a place where one would expect to find evidence for early complex cultural or social developments. It is one of the driest places on earth, receiving less than 1 mm of precipitation per year. A seemingly lifeless desert, it lacks people and supports only a few desert-adapted animals, such as lizards, gerbils, snakes, and small gazelle. There is almost no vegetation. The few existing plants occur in those rare places where ground water comes near the surface or as patches of 'accidental vegetation', consisting of a few bushes or clumps of dry grass that grow where water from the very rare rains happened to accumulate. In truth, the area would seem to have few redeeming qualities.

Despite this forbidding appearance, there is a long history of human use of this desert, and a brief summary of this history provides a useful background for the emergence of the initial expressions of social complexity in the Egyptian Sahara. These phenomena offer an insight into how the first manifestations of social differentiation in Egypt may have looked because they seem to have begun prior to the appearance of similar developments in the adjacent Nile Valley.

Background and Earlier Occupations

Although the Western Desert today is a rainless desert it was not always this dry. There is good evidence that at several times in the past this area received as much as 500 mm of precipitation per year, at which times there were permanent lakes, large springs and at least seasonal streams (Wendorf *et al.* 1993a). These wet intervals have an approximate correlation with the onset of interglacials and interstadials. The most recent of these wet periods occurred during the Last Interglacial, and is dated between 130,000 and 70,000 years ago by several radiometric techniques. During this time the area was a thornbush savanna and supported numerous large animals such as extinct buffalo and camels, large giraffes, and several varieties of antelope and gazelle.

There are numerous Middle Palaeolithic sites associated with the lake and spring sediments of this period (Caton-Thompson 1952; Wendorf *et al.* 1993). Even earlier Middle Palaeolithic, Final and Late Acheulean, and perhaps Middle Acheulean artefacts are associated with deposits of wet periods prior to the Last Interglacial (Schild and Wendorf 1977; Wendorf and Schild 1980; Wendorf *et al.* 1987a; McHugh *et al.* 1988a; 1988b; 1989).

Early Holocene Occupations

After the Last Interglacial there followed a long period of hyper-aridity when Egypt was at least as dry as today, and perhaps drier. Around 12,000 years ago the summer rains of tropical Africa began to move northward again. This increase in rainfall marks the onset of the early Holocene in the Eastern Sahara. The desert, however, was not as wet as during the earlier interglacials. Even with the rains, the Western Desert was still very dry. The annual rainfall has been variously estimated, based on the identifications of wood charcoal, to have been between 50 and 100 mm per year (Neumann 1989; Barakat 1995), and on the basis of associated fauna between 100 and 200 mm per year (Wendorf and Schild 1980, 236). Some interpretations based on sediments place the rainfall at similar levels, around 100 mm per year (Kröpelin 1993). Whatever the amount, the precipitation was limited and highly seasonal; both plants and animals indicate that most of the rain fell during the summer months. The rains did provide sufficient moisture to support a wide variety of sahelian grasses, trees and bushes. Also present were several kinds of small animals, mostly hares and small gazelle, but also a few small carnivores, such as foxes. Humans were also present, and they brought with them domestic cattle. The climate in the early and middle Holocene, however, was unpredictable, with numerous droughts, some of which caused the desert to be abandoned for lengthy periods.

Nabta Playa

One of the best places to study the Holocene in the Western Desert is Nabta Playa, an unusually large internally drained basin located 100 km west of Abu Simbel, in southernmost Egypt (**Fig. 1**). During the early and middle Holocene, from around 12,000 to 7300 radiocarbon years ago (these and all other dates in this paper are uncalibrated), a seasonal lake, or playa, developed in the basin. The drainage area for the basin was enormous, estimated at around 1500 square kilometres, and after the rains the resulting seasonal lake was very large and deep. For this reason, Nabta Playa was an unusually attractive locality for these Holocene pastoralists, and numerous archaeological sites occur here, often imbedded in the lacustrine sediments that filled the lower part of the basin. Nabta is also of particular interest because it has one of the longest and most complete sequences of Holocene occupations known in the Sahara.

Our research group, identified as the *Combined Prehis-*

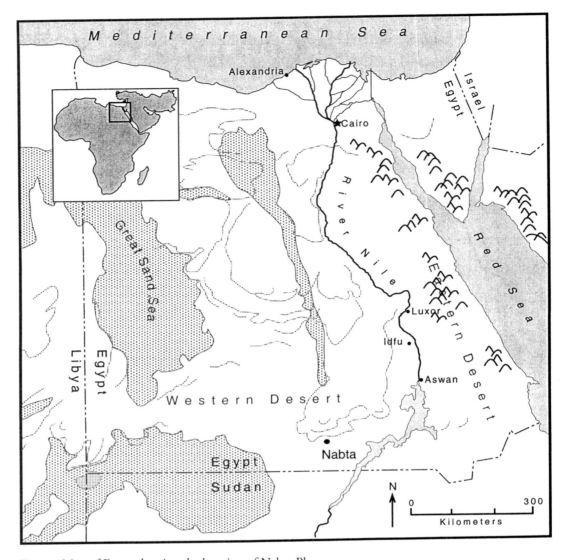

Fig. 1   Map of Egypt showing the location of Nabta Playa.

toric Expedition, began studying the Holocene archaeology at Nabta in 1974, 1975 and 1977 (Wendorf and Schild 1980, 82–165). More recently, additional excavations were undertaken in 1990–92, 1994, and 1996 through 2000. The work since 1990 has recently been published (Wendorf, Schild and Assoc. 2001), and several short papers have also appeared that discuss some of the more interesting features found at Nabta. These include Dahlberg *et al.* 1995; Gautier *et al.* 1994; Kubiak-Martens and Wasylikowa 1994; Wasylikowa and Kubiak-Martens 1995; Wasylikowa *et al.* 1993; 1995; 1996; Wendorf *et al.* 1991; 1992; 1993; 1996; Wendorf and Schild 1994; 1995/1996; 1998.

The earliest (9500–8700 bp) settlements at Nabta are identified as El Adam Early Neolithic. They were small seasonal camps of cattle-herding and ceramic-using people. The cattle in these early sites are regarded as domestic, largely on the basis of ecological arguments, and less firmly on metrical evidence (Gautier 1980; 1984). This conclusion suggests an early and independent centre of cattle domestication in Africa separate from that of Southwest Asia (Wendorf and Schild 1994). Our interpretation of the cattle

remains in the Western Desert has been highly controversial (Smith 1984; 1992; Clutton-Brock 1989; 1993; Muzzolini 1989; but also see Wendorf *et al.* 1987b). The objections to the hypothesis of an early and separate centre of cattle domestication have been considerably weakened, however, by recent mitochondrial DNA analyses of African, Eurasian and Indian cattle. These studies indicate that modern African and Eurasian cattle have been genetically separate populations for over 25,000 years, and that Indian cattle have been separate from the other two even longer. The genetic signals attributed to domestication also occur earlier in African cattle (Bradley *et al.* 1996).

It is believed that the cattle were brought into the desert after the summer rains to graze on the new grasses, and the cattle in turn may have provided milk and blood as dependable sources of food in this harsh environment. Where these early pastoralists originated is unknown; they may have come from the adjacent Nile Valley near Wadi Halfa where lithic assemblages similar to those in the early camps also occur (Schild *et al.* 1968), or from farther south in northern Sudan. Whatever their source, it may have been in the Western Desert, or a similar area farther west, that the African pattern of cattle herding developed, with cattle serving as a 'walking larder', and rarely used for meat. Most African cattle pastoralists kill cattle only on ceremonial occasions, such as a marriage or the death of a leader. Among these groups cattle are the economic basis for power and prestige.

Pottery is very rare in these earliest Nabta sites, but it occurs at most and has its own distinctive character (Close 1995). The vessels are usually well-made, small open bowls, decorated over the entire exterior with complex patterns of stamped impressions applied with a comb using a rocking motion. This pottery is probably locally made, and it is among the oldest known in Africa (Roset 1987). It is considerably older than pottery in the Nile Valley or in Southwest Asia (see Kuper this volume, Fig. 1)

Around 8000 years ago, during the El Nabta Early Neolithic, there was a change in the settlement system. Almost all sites now have large, deep wells, and these made it possible for the groups to live in the desert during the dry season, and perhaps throughout the year. The excavation of the wells required a group effort, which may indicate some leadership with incipient control over labour for community projects. The settlements also became much larger, some of them with 18 to 20 simple brush or mat-walled houses or huts in round or elongated shape (Figs 2–3), although perhaps not all were occupied at the same time (Schild et al. 1996). Beside each house there were one or more bell-shaped storage pits, suggesting seasonal surpluses of some foods that were stored for later use. The likely identity of this surplus food is indicated at one site that yielded over 20,000 carbonised remains of edible wild plants, including sorghum, millets, legumes, tubers and fruits (Wendorf et al. 1992; Wasylikowa et al. 1993; 1995). This may have been a specialised plant-harvesting site, which was perhaps used on a seasonal basis by groups who were otherwise cattle pastoralists (Harlan 1989).

Pottery for the first time becomes abundant in the Western Desert around 7800 years ago, during the Al Jerar Early Neolithic. The designs on this more abundant pottery are slightly different from those used earlier, but executed in the same manner. The vessels are also larger, which may indicate a new method of cooking and storage, or it may be a reflection of increased sedentism, or both. The pottery is now clearly locally made because firing failures have been found in the sites and the temper used in the pots is closely similar to sand from the nearby washes.

The desert appears to have been abandoned during a major period of hyper-aridity between 7300 and 7100 years ago, during the Post-Al Jerar Arid Phase. When the people returned they brought with them the first sheep and goats. These were almost certainly introduced from Southwest Asia, where domestic caprovids by then had been known for over 2000 years. In addition to introducing caprovids, this new population had a different way of decorating their pottery. They still used impressed rocker stamped designs, but the combs had larger teeth and the resultant larger stamped impressions were almost completely obliterated while the clay was still soft, leaving a rough exterior surface. These new groups are identified as Middle Neolithic, but sites are very few, with only one large settlement of this period known at

Nabta, located where water could be obtained because of a perched water table. It must have been a relatively dry period; playa deposition occurred only at the mouths of major wadis where they entered the basin.

There was another episode of hyper-aridity between 6700 and 6500 bp and the desert was again abandoned. When the rains returned, the groups who reoccupied Nabta brought with them a social system very different from that evident earlier. These new groups are identified as Late Neolithic. There are numerous radiocarbon dates that place the beginning of the Late and Final Neolithic at around 6500 bp and put the end at about 4800 bp, when the desert was abandoned (see Schild and Wendorf this volume, Fig. 2). These dates suggest that the Saharan Late Neolithic began slightly before the earliest known Neolithic in the Nile Valley, and was otherwise generally contemporary. The pottery in these Late Neolithic sites is now burnished on the exterior, and bowl interiors are also burnished and frequently smudged, closely resembling some Badarian, Abkan and other early Neolithic ceramics found in the Nile Valley.

There is also strong evidence that these Late Neolithic groups had a social system that involved a level of organisation and control not previously seen in Egypt. They built crude, but impressive, public works and expressed their religious beliefs in ways previously unknown.

The Nabta Regional Ceremonial Centre and Incipient Social Ranking

In addition to several Late Neolithic living sites at Nabta, there are also a number of localities with unusual architectural features that presumably had ceremonial functions. They include three groups of megalithic alignments, a 'calendar circle', and eight stone-covered tumuli containing the remains of cattle, one of which was in a clay-lined subsurface chamber. There are also thirty 'complex structures', which involve both surface and subsurface architecture constructed with large, shaped and unshaped stones. One of these held a very large shaped stone that may well be Egypt's earliest sculpture.

Many of the major basins in the Egyptian Western Desert have been surveyed and no other locality has yielded any evidence of a similar complex of unusual architectural features like those found at Nabta. For this reason it is possible that Nabta had a unique and very specialised function as a regional ceremonial centre during the Late Neolithic, although there may have been other ceremonial centres elsewhere in the Western Desert. Even if others exist, however, it is likely that they and Nabta functioned in a fashion similar to regional ceremonial centres still used today by many sahelian and sub-Saharan pastoralists.

The modern regional ceremonial centres are places where related but geographically dispersed groups can gather periodically to conduct ceremonies and reaffirm their social and political solidarity. They serve as foci of religious, political and social functions for large social units. It is suggested that Nabta may have been a regional ceremonial centre for the pastoralists who were widely dispersed across the southwestern portion of the Egyptian and the adjacent Sudanese/ Nubian Western Desert.

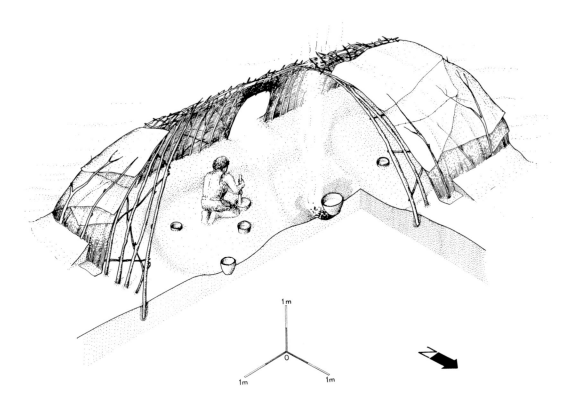

Fig. 2   Reconstruction of an elongated hut of the Early Neolithic period. Measuring about 7 m long, the hut had a slightly sunken floor with three depressions possibly for sleeping (artist: Marek Puszkarski 1992).

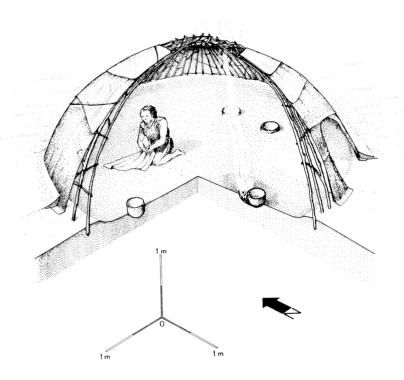

Fig. 3   Reconstruction of a round hut of the Early Neolithic period. The huts were most probably made of tamarisk branches covered with animal hides (artist: Marek Puszkarski 1992).

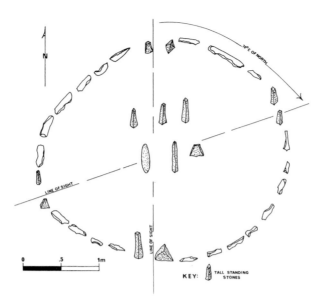

Fig. 4   A reconstructed plan of the 'calendar circle' before it was damaged, showing the alignments of the gates.

The emergence of Nabta as a regional ceremonial centre seems to coincide with the beginning of the Late Neolithic, although dates for the various components are not very strong. The first in order of discovery, but not necessarily the earliest, are three alignments of large (ranging from 3 × 2 × 0.5 m to 1.5 × 1 × 0.35 m) quartzitic sandstone slabs set upright in the playa basin on a large remnant of Early Neolithic playa sediments (Malville *et al.* 1998). The largest group has ten slabs; the others have eight and six slabs (**Plate 25**). Not all of the slabs are in perfect alignment, some are slightly offset and in positions that may have astronomical implications. A few are still partially imbedded in playa sediments (**Plate 26**). The slabs were unshaped, and many of them are now broken into large blocks. The aligned slabs were probably quarried nearby, because outcrops of similar sandstone occur in the vicinity, some only a kilometre or so from the alignments.

About 300 m beyond the north end of the Nabta alignment is a 'calendar circle' consisting of a series of small sandstone slabs arranged in a circle about 4 m in diameter (**Fig. 4; Plate 27**). Within the ring of stones are four pairs of larger stones, each pair set close together and separated by a narrow space, or gate. The gates of two opposing pairs align generally north–south, the gates of the other two form a line running 70° east of north, which aligns with the calculated position of sunrise at the summer solstice 6000 years ago (Malville *et al.* 1998). In the centre of the circle are six upright slabs arranged in two east–west lines. The astronomical functions of the centre stones are not evident. Charcoal from one of the numerous hearths around the 'calendar' dated to 6000 ± 60 years bp (CAMS-17287).

Another 300 m to the north of the calendar circle was a tumulus, which when excavated was about 5 m in diameter and 1 m high, made of large, roughly broken and unshaped sandstone blocks (**Plate 28**). Under the pile of sandstone blocks was a chamber containing the remains of a complete, articulated young adult cow. The chamber had been dug into the floor of the wadi and surrounded by a clay collar 25 cm wide. The cow was then placed on the floor of the chamber (**Plate 29**). The chamber was roofed with limbs of tamarisk and clay and the mound of rocks was then piled over it. A piece of wood from the roof yielded a radiocarbon date of 6470 ± 270 years bp (CAMS-17289). In the same area seven other similar stone tumuli containing the remains of cattle were excavated, but none of them had subsurface chambers; instead, the bones of the cattle, a few of which were partially articulated, were simply placed among the stones.

Another interesting group of Late Neolithic architectural features at Nabta is the approximately thirty 'complex structures' located on a remnant of playa about 500 m southwest of the largest megalithic alignment (**Plate 30**). Most of these structures occur in an area about 500 m long and 200 m wide, but five others are located on a smaller playa remnant located 300 m to the east of the main group. The sediments underlying both groups were deposited during the final phase of the El Nabta/Al Jerar Humid Interphase. Most of these playa sediments accumulated at the onset of the hyper-arid period that began around 7300 bp. This provides a basal date for these features.

These complex structures consist of isolated groups of large, elongated, roughly shaped or unshaped sandstone blocks, set upright to frame an oval area between 5 and 6 m long and 4–5 m wide, oriented slightly northwest–southeast (**Plate 31**). In the centre of the oval there is one, sometimes two, very large flat slabs laid horizontally, and similarly oriented. Two of these structures have been excavated, a third has been tested, and drill-holes have been dug to bedrock at two others. They are all basically similar, although they differ in some details. The excavated and tested structures were built over large table rocks around 4 to 5 m in diameter, and from 3 to 4 m below the surface, buried under heavy playa clays and silts.

These table rocks are hard, quartzitic lenses in the underlying soft shale bedrock that had been isolated from the surrounding softer deposits by wind erosion, probably during the Late Pleistocene period of deflation that formed the Nabta basin. A large area of similar table rocks may be seen on a hill slope about 2 km to the south. They were probably a prominent part of the Neolithic landscape, but it is not clear why the table rocks were sought below the thick playa sediments, or how they were located.

Although basically similar in their construction, the two completely excavated complex structures are different in some details. At the first and largest of the studied complex structures (A)(**Plate 31**), the construction of the feature had begun by digging a pit 6 m in diameter and about 4 m deep to expose a large table rock about 4 m in diameter. The table rock was then shaped by removing the irregular edges to produce a convex perimeter on three sides. On the fourth side, on the north, the end of the table rock was worked by flaking to form a straight edge. The top of the table rock was also smoothed (**Plates 32–33**).

After the table rock was shaped, the pit was partially refilled, using some of the playa sediments previously removed, to a level about 50 cm above the top of the table rock. A large (c. 3 to 4 tons), carefully shaped stone was then brought in, set upright and held in position by two small slabs wedged at the base. The base of the shaped stone was 2.5 m below the surface (**Plate 34**). What this 'sculpture' represents is not clear; it is shaped on only two sides, and the natural bedding in the rock was used to achieve a wide, curved surface, which was then smoothed. In some views the stone vaguely resembles a large animal, possibly a cow (**Plates 35–36**).

After the shaped stone was placed in position, the pit was backfilled completely. The surface architecture of large upright stones and two large horizontal central stones was then erected directly over the table rock (**Plates 31 and 37**).

The other excavated complex structure had also been erected over a table rock, but unlike the first structure, the table rock was unshaped. Weathering had caused the rock to look like two stones, one above the other, but the only work on that stone comprised a few flakes removed from one end.

A third complex structure was tested. It was also different in that it was one of eight similar structures that were tightly clustered and interlocked together. All of the individual units in this group were small, in plan about 2 × 3 m, and constructed of smaller stones, but each of these small structures had the same surface configuration of an oval with one or two large horizontal central stones. Drill tests indicated the presence of a table rock near the centre of the cluster, but it was not exposed in the test excavations. Charcoal, recovered from a shelf on the edge of the pit under the tested structure, yielded a radiocarbon age of 4800 ± 80 years bp (DRI 3358). This is the only date available for these structures, and it is about 1500 years later than the estimated age based on the stratigraphic evidence from the other two larger structures. There is, however, no reason to reject the date. This linked cluster of small complex structures may relate to a late phase for these phenomena.

Drilling at two other large complex structures showed that they also had been erected over buried table rocks, and it seems likely that most of the other twenty-seven structures were also built over them. These complex structures appear to be unique to Nabta; they are not known in the Nile Valley or elsewhere in the Western Desert. It should be noted, however, that they are difficult to recognise (we regarded them as bedrock outcrops for many years), and may be more widespread in the Eastern Sahara than now believed. If indeed Nabta was a regional ceremonial centre, there may be others in the desert, some of which, like Nabta, not far from the Nile.

Why the Nabta people wanted to find and shape these deeply buried table rocks is not known. Neither is it clear how they managed to find them. We had expected to find burials of elite individuals below the central stones, but no traces of human remains were seen and no secondary chambers or pits were found, although the excavations were carried beyond the limits of the original pits that had been dug to expose the table rocks. They may have functioned as cenotaphs for leaders who died during their seasonal migrations and were buried elsewhere. This, however, is only a hypothesis, and the true function of these complex structures remains unknown.

The Western Desert and the Nile Valley

The Egyptian Sahara has long been regarded as an insignificant factor in the emergence of complex society along the Nile. In part this is because many important features of the Nilotic Neolithic are obviously derived from Southwest Asia, particularly the domestic plants and small livestock. Many scholars have noted, however, that many characteristic features of the Nilotic Neolithic appear to be local developments (see for example, Caton-Thompson and Gardner 1934). Others, such as Frankfort (1978), have seen strong sub-Saharan African elements in both the political structure and ceremonial features of the Old Kingdom.

The suggestion that Neolithic groups in the Western Desert may have been involved in developments along the Nile is not new. Among the first to promote this view were Mond and Myers (1937, 269), who proposed that increased aridity in the Sahara may have forced people to move to the Nile Valley. Childe (1952, 48) also developed this theme in his discussion of the origin of Egyptian civilisation. Nordström (1972, 24) suggested that cattle pastoralism may have been introduced to the Nile Valley from the Western Desert during an arid phase, and Hoffman (1980, 102) and Hassan (1984) also offered similar proposals (see discussion in Holmes 1989, 367–394). Whatever the evidence for these suggestions, all were based on the assumption that the Saharan groups were limited to simple bands, possibly with an agricultural or pastoralist economy, and with no indication of social ranking.

We suggest, however, that the discovery of megalithic alignments, calendar circles, cattle burials, and the enigmatic complex structures at Nabta indicate that a very different kind of society existed in the Western Desert during the Late Neolithic. These Neolithic cattle pastoralists can no longer be viewed as simple bands. Instead, there must have been at Nabta a religious or political authority with control over human resources for extended periods of time. These leaders organised and supported a previously unsuspected, elaborate ceremonial complex involving burial and possible worship of cattle, the use of astronomical observations, the transport and working of large stones, and the construction of elaborate enigmatic structures. It is unlikely that these developments in the desert occurred in a cultural vacuum. They almost certainly had some impact on their Neolithic neighbours living in the adjacent Nile Valley. Were similar or related developments underway at this time in the Nile Valley? Did the presence of incipient social complexity at Nabta play a role in the later emergence of social complexity in the late Predynastic period?

The rise of social complexity in Egypt has always been a topic of considerable discussion. Initially it was believed that Egypt might have been the first to have had a complex society, but radiocarbon dates indicated that it developed earlier in Mesopotamia. It was then assumed that Egypt was the great borrower, and the concepts of complexity spread from Mesopotamia to Egypt. However, it is now generally held that a process like social complexity probably cannot be diffused from one area to another, but rather develops from local causes (Wenke 1991). There are many hypotheses as to why social complexity occurs. One possibility is that it may develop from the interaction of two radically different economic systems in close physical proximity, as is found where agriculturalists with a centralised political system have close relationships with pastoralists. The pastoralists usually live in tense harmony with their village neighbours, and it is in this setting that the Late Neolithic cattle pastoralists and their regional ceremonial centre at Nabta is of particular interest. Did the Saharan pastoralists provide the external differentiation that stimulated the emergence of social complexity in Egypt?

Although little is known about ceremonial life during the Neolithic in the Nile Valley, cattle and cattle imagery appear to play a central role in the Predynastic and Old Kingdom belief systems. Pottery figurines of cattle appear in the Neolithic settlement at Merimde, making cattle one of the earliest dated images recorded in Egyptian art. In the Nile Valley, cattle representations are frequent from Naqada I times onward with symbolic reference to power and strength in general as well as fertility and the regeneration of life. In dynastic times gods and goddesses took on the titles and attributes of cattle, and the bull was one of the favourite animals with which the king identified himself. Among the most important titles of the king was 'Strong Bull, Great of Strength' and 'Bull of Horus'. The bull's tail attached to the king's girdle and possibly even his false beard were all part of his association with the strength and fertility of the bull (Hendrickx 2002).

How did this emphasis on cattle in the belief system of the early Egyptians develop? Frankfort (1978) suggested that the cattle cult was derived from Nilotic pastoralists, like the Dinka, who lived farther south in central Sudan. It is highly likely that had he known cattle pastoralists had been living in the desert adjacent to the Nile for 4000 years before the Predynastic he would have suggested the desert pastoralists as a more likely source.

The evidence to support the Sahara as the source of Egyptian cattle cult obviously remains weak. The available data on the structure of the Saharan pastoral societies is very limited, and the character of the early Neolithic societies in the Nile Valley in Nubia and Upper Egypt is also poorly understood. Despite these reservations, the limited evidence now available suggests that a study of the interaction between the Sahara and the Nile may provide a better understanding of the processes that led to the emergence of Egyptian civilisation.

Bibliography

Barakat H, 1995. *Contribution archeobotanique à l'histoire de la végétation dans le Sahara Oriental et le Soudan Central.* PhD. Thesis. Université de Droit d'Economie et des Sciences d'Aix-Marseille, Faculté des Sciences et Techniques de Saint-Jerome. Aix-Marseille.

Bradley, D G, MacHugh D E, Cunningham P and Loftus R T, 1996. Mitochondrial diversity and the origins of African and European cattle. *Proceedings of the National Academy of Science* 93: 5131-5.

Caton-Thompson G, 1952. *Kharga Oasis in prehistory.* London.

Caton-Thompson G, and Gardner E W, 1934. *The Desert Fayum.* Royal Anthropological Institute. London.

Childe V G, 1952. *New Light on the Most Ancient East.* London. (First published 1928).

Close A E, 1995. Few and Far Between: Early Ceramics in North Africa. In W K Barnett and J W Hoopes (eds), *The Emergence of Pottery: Technology and Innovation in Ancient Societies.* Washington and London: 23-37.

Clutton-Brock J (ed.), 1989. *The Walking Larder. Patterns of Domestication, Pastoralism, and Predation.* London.

Clutton-Brock J, 1993. The spread of domestic animals in Africa. In T Shaw, P Sinclair, B Andah and A Okpoko (eds), *The Archaeology of Africa: Food, Metal and Towns.* London: 71-103.

Dahlberg J A, Evans J, Johnson E, Hyman M, Biehl E and Wen-

dorf F, 1995. Attempts to Identify 8000-BP Sorghum using Image-Analysis, Infrared Spectroscopy, and Biotechnological Procedures. *Acta Palaeobotanica* 35 (1): 167-73.

Frankfort H, 1978. *Kingship and the Gods. A Study of Ancient Near Eastern Religion as the Integration of Society and Nature.* Chicago.

Gautier A, 1980. Appendix 4. Contributions to the archaeozoology of Egypt. In F Wendorf and R Schild, *Prehistory of the Eastern Sahara.* New York: 317-44.

Gautier A, 1984. Archaeozoology of the Bir Kiseiba Region. Eastern Sahara. In F Wendorf, R Schild and A E Close (eds), *Cattle Keepers of the Eastern Sahara: The Neolithic of Bir Kiseiba.* Dallas: 49-72.

Gautier A, Schild R, Wendorf F and Stafford Jr. T W, 1994. One elephant doesn't make a savanna. Palaeoecological significance of 'Loxodonta africana' in the Holocene Sahara. *Sahara* 6: 7-14.

Harlan J R, 1989. Wild-grass seed harvesting in the Sahara and Sub-Sahara of Africa. In D R Harris and G C Hillman (eds), *Foraging and Farming: The Evaluation of Plant Exploitation.* London: 79-98.

Hassan F A, 1984. A Radiocarbon Date from Hamamieh, Upper Egypt. *Nyame Akuma* 24/25: 3.

Hendrickx S, 2002. Bovines in Egyptian early Predynastic and Early Dynastic Iconography. In F Hassan (ed.), *Ecological*

Change and Food Security in Africa's Later Prehistory. New York: 275–318.

Hoffman M A, 1980. *Egypt before the Pharaohs.* London.

Holmes D L, 1989. *The Predynastic Lithic Industries of Upper Egypt: A comparative study of the lithic traditions of Badari, Nagada and Hierakonpolis.* Cambridge Monographs in African Archaeology 33. British Archaeological Reports International Series 469. Oxford.

Kröpelin S, 1993. The Gilf Kebir and Lower Wadi Howar: Contrasting Early and Mid-Holocene environments in the Eastern Sahara. In L Krzyzaniak, M Kobusiewicz and J Alexander (eds), *Environmental Change and Human Culture in the Nile Basin and Northern Africa Until the Second Millennium B. C.* Poznan: 249–58.

Kubiak-Martens L and Wasylikowa K, 1994. Sorgo ze Stanowisak Wczesnoneolity Cznego Nabta Playa w Poludniowym Egipcie. *Polish Botanical Studies, Guide Book Series* 11: 109–19.

Malville J M, Wendorf F, Mazhar A, and Schild R, 1998. Megaliths and Neolithic astronomy in southern Egypt. *Nature* 392: 488–92.

McHugh W P, Breed C S, Schaber G G, McCauley J F and Szabo B J, 1988a. Acheulian sites along the 'Radar Rivers,' southern Egyptian Sahara. *Journal of Field Archaeology* 15: 361–79.

McHugh W P, McCauley J F, Haynes C V, Breed C S and Schaber G G, 1988b. Paleorivers and geoarchaeology in the southern Egyptian Sahara. *Geoarchaeology* 3: 1–40.

McHugh W P, Schaber G G, Breed C S and McCauley J F, 1989. Neolithic adaptation and Holocene functioning of Tertiary paleodrainages in southern Egypt and northern Sudan. *Antiquity* 63: 320–36.

Mond R and Myers O H, 1937. *Cemeteries of Armant I.* Egypt Exploration Society Excavation Memoir 42. London.

Muzzolini A, 1989. La 'neolithisation' du Nord de l'Afrique et ses causes. In O Aurenche and J Cauvin (eds), *Neolithisations.* British Archaeological Reports International Series 516. Oxford: 145–86.

Neumann K, 1989. *Zur Vegetationsgeschichte der Ostsahara im Holozän. Holzkohlen aus Prähistorischen Fundstelle. Mit Einem Exhurs über die Holzkohlen von Fachi-Dogonbolo Niger.* PhD Thesis, University of Frankfurt.

Nordström H-A, 1972. *Neolithic and A-Group Sites.* The Scandinavian Joint Expedition to Sudanese Nubia 3. Stockholm.

Roset J P, 1987. Paleoclimatic and Cultural Conditions of Neolithic Development in the Early Holocene of Northern Niger (Aïr and Ténéré). In A E Close (ed.), *Prehistory of Arid North Africa: Essays in Honor of Fred Wendorf.* Dallas: 211–34.

Schild R, Chmielewska M and Wieckowska H, 1968. The Arkinian and Sharmarkian industries. In F Wendorf (ed.), *The Prehistory of Nubia.* Dallas: 651–767.

Schild R, Hrolik H, Wendorf F and Close A E, 1996. Architecture of Early Neolithic hunts at Nabta Playa. In L Krzyzaniak, K Kroeper and M Kobusiewicz (eds), *Interregional Contacts in the Late Prehistory of Northeastern Africa.* Poznan: 101–14.

Schild R and Wendorf F, 1977. *The prehistory of Dakhla Oasis and adjacent desert.* Polish Academy of Sciences. Warsaw.

Smith A B, 1984. The Origins of food production in Northeast Africa. In J A Coetzee and E M Van Zinderen Bakker (eds), *Palaeoecology of Africa and the Surrounding Islands, Volume 16.* Rotterdam: 317–24.

Smith A B, 1992. *Pastoralism in Africa. Origins and Development Ecology.* Hurst. London.

Wasylikowa K, Harlan J R, Evans J, Wendorf F, Schild R, Close A E and Królik H, 1993. Examination of Botanical Remains from Early Neolithic Houses at Nabta Playa, Western Desert, Egypt, with Special Reference to Sorghum Grains. In T Shaw, P Sinclair, B Andah and A Okpoko (eds), *The Archaeology of Africa: Food, Metal and Towns.* London: 154–64.

Wasylikowa K and Kubiak-Martens L, 1995. Wild Sorghum from the Early Neolithic site at Nabta Playa, South Egypt. In H Kroll and R Pasternak (eds), *Res archaeobotanicaie* (9th Symposium IWGP). Kiel: 345–58

Wasylikowa K, Mitka J, Walanus A, Wendorf F and Schild R, 1996. Distribution of plant macrofossils within a settlement: A case study on plant exploitation manners in a hunter-gatherer site at Nabta Playa, south Egypt. (The XIII International Congress of Prehistoric and Protohistoric Sciences, Forli, Italy, 1996) *Paleoecology:* 47–56.

Wasylikowa K, Schild R, Wendorf F, Królik H, Kubiak-Martens L and Harlan J R, 1995. Archaeobotany of the Early Neolithic Site E-75-6 at Nabta Playa, Western Desert, South Egypt. *Acta Palaeobotanica* 35 (1): 133–55.

Wendorf F, Close A E and Schild R, 1985. Prehistoric Settlements in the Nubian Desert. *American Scientist* 73: 132–41.

Wendorf F, Close A E and Schild R, 1987a. A survey of the Egyptian radar channels: an example of applied archaeology. *Journal of Field Archaeology* 14: 43–63.

Wendorf F, Close A E and Schild R, 1987b. Early domestic cattle in the Eastern Sahara. *Palaeoecology of Africa* 18: 441–8.

Wendorf F, Close A E, Schild R, and Waslikowa K, 1991. The Combined Prehistoric Expedition: results of the 1990 and 1991 seasons. *Newsletter of the American Research Center in Egypt* 154: 1–8.

Wendorf F, Close A E, Schild R, Wasylikowa K, Housley R A, Harlan J R and Krolik H, 1992. Saharan exploitation of plants 8000 years ago. *Nature* 359: 721–4.

Wendorf F, Close A E and Schild R, 1993. Megaliths in the Egyptian Sahara. *Sahara* 5(1992–3): 7–16.

Wendorf F and Schild R, 1980. *Prehistory of the Eastern Sahara.* New York.

Wendorf F and Schild R, 1994. Are the Early Holocene Cattle in the Eastern Sahara Domestic or Wild? *Evolutionary Anthropology* 3 (4): 118–28.

Wendorf F, and Schild R, 1995/1996. Nabta Playa During the Early and Middle Holocene. *ANKH* 4/5: 33–45.

Wendorf F and Schild R, 1998. Nabta Playa and its Role in Northeastern African Prehistory. *Journal of Anthropological Archaeology* 17: 97–123.

Wendorf F, Schild R and Associates, 2001. *Holocene Settlement of the Egyptians Sahara. Volume 1: The archaeology of Nabta Playa.* New York.

Wendorf F, Schild R, Close A E and Associates, 1993a. *Egypt During the Last Interglacial. The Middle Paleolithic of Bir Tarfawi and Bir Sahara East.* New York.

Wendorf F, Schild R and Zedeno N, 1996. A Late Neolithic megalith complex in the Eastern Sahara: a preliminary report. In L Krzyzaniak, K Kroeper and M Kobusiewicz (eds), *Interregional Contacts in the Late Prehistory of Northeastern Africa.* Poznan: 125–32.

Wenke R J, 1991. The Evolution of Early Egyptian Civilization: Issues and Evidence. *Journal of World Prehistory* 5(3): 279–329.

Palaeo-ecologic and Palaeo-climatic Background to Socio-economic Changes in the South Western Desert of Egypt

Romuald Schild and Fred Wendorf

Introduction

Recent excavations at Nabta Playa and near Gebel Nabta conducted by the Combined Prehistoric Expedition since 1990 have yielded a vast amount of geomorphic, stratigraphic, biologic and radiochronologic data that suggest considerable revision of the previous reconstruction of Final Pleistocene and Holocene climates and chronologies. Although the general order of the main climatic phases remain unchanged, a major chronological and palaeo-climatic revision is necessary. It is no longer possible to constrain the evolution of the climates into three major wet episodes called 'Playa I', 'Playa II' and 'Playa III' (Wendorf and Schild 1980, 236; Schild and Wendorf 1984). Instead, we propose here a synopsis of new terminology for and chrono-stratigraphy of the climatic changes in the Final Pleistocene and Holocene of the south Western Desert that, we suggest, arranges the data in a more appropriate fashion.

Chrono-Stratigraphy

Most of the lithostratigraphic signals pertaining to Final Pleistocene/Holocene climates of the south Western Desert of Egypt come from several loci along the Kiseiba Scarp, Nabta Playa, the vicinity of Gebel Nabta and the playas slightly to the north of Nabta Playa (**Fig. 1**). These areas were studied by the Combined Prehistoric Expedition over the course of 15 field seasons. The signals are rather monotonous and limited to the accumulation of suites of clastic sediments in enclosed, internally drained basins by aeolian, lacustrine and alluvial phenomena. The sedimentary depositions may be interrupted by major unconformities caused by aeolian erosion. The periods of accumulation are generally coeval with wet interphases and local rainfall, while the intensive aeolian erosion usually marks hyper-arid phases.

Nearly 150 radiocarbon measurements as well as the association of the deposits with the well-dated prehistoric entities enables relatively precise chronologic placement of the sedimentary signals (**Fig. 2**). The radiochronometric ages of archaeological entities clearly cluster in discrete units with very minor overlapping in some places (**Figs 3–4**). Only the long interphase between the El Nabta and Al Jerar occupations shows a continuum.

Pre-El Adam Humid Interphase

The C^{14} dates for the El Adam variant of the Early Neolithic spread in time from around 9800 years bp (uncalibrated) (SMU-858) at El Adam Playa to around 8850 years bp (SMU-416) at El Kortein Playa, Site E-77-3. The radiocarbon ages of the oldest samples at El Adam have a large standard deviation of up to around 400 years. There is a cluster of samples at around 9400 radiocarbon years bp and therefore it is legitimate to assume an age of about 9500 years bp for the oldest known assemblages of the Early Neolithic El Adam phase.

At El Adam Playa the artefacts of the Early Neolithic El Adam variant occur in the topmost sandy playa deposits. Underneath is a suite of playa sands, almost 5 m thick, with an intervening sandy silt bed suggesting a wetter episode (Schild and Wendorf 1984, 31). The lithostratigraphy of the playa deposits below this occupation is known only from bore holes; therefore, no clear unconformities have been observed. Yet, the possibility of an unconformity above the silty sand cannot be ruled out. At Site E-77-7, at El Gebel El Beid Playa, silts and sands assuming a depth of more than 6 m underlie the late El Adam archaeology (Wendorf and Schild 1980, 102).

A very early playa silt is also observed at Site E-77-1 at the foot of the southeastern slope of the El Nabta Mountain. Here, a phytogenic dune topped by archaeology of the Al Jerar, or late Early Neolithic phase of about 7550–7350 radiocarbon years bp, overlies highly weathered and truncated sandy silt. It is believed that the phytogenic dune is of the same age as that immediately preceding the playa deposits of Early Neolithic age at Nabta Playa. One may also associate with a Pre-El Adam wet interphase the deposition of early lacustrine playa silts interstratified with slope wash sands generated by local rainfall in Wadi Kubbaniya, postdating the Late Palaeolithic Aggradation of the Nile (Schild and Wendorf 1989, 77).

It is not yet possible to assign an age to the water-laid deposits preceding the El Adam Humid Interphase and the subsequent hypothetical dry phase. In addition, it is not clear whether we are here confronted with a single interphase or more. Thick playa sands underlying the El Adam occupations at El Adam Playa and El Gebel El Beid Basin may suggest more than one interphase. One may assume that the interphase is synchronous with the Alleröd Chronozone.

Pre-El Adam Arid Phase

A dry phase is suggested by the considerable denudation and truncation of the conceivable Pre-El Adam playa deposits at the foot of Nabta Mountain, at Site E-77-1. The overlaying Early Neolithic phytogenic dune is most probably of the El Adam Interphase age. Because of the chronology proposed for the El Adam Interphase, the age of this dry phase should be associated with the Younger Dryas.

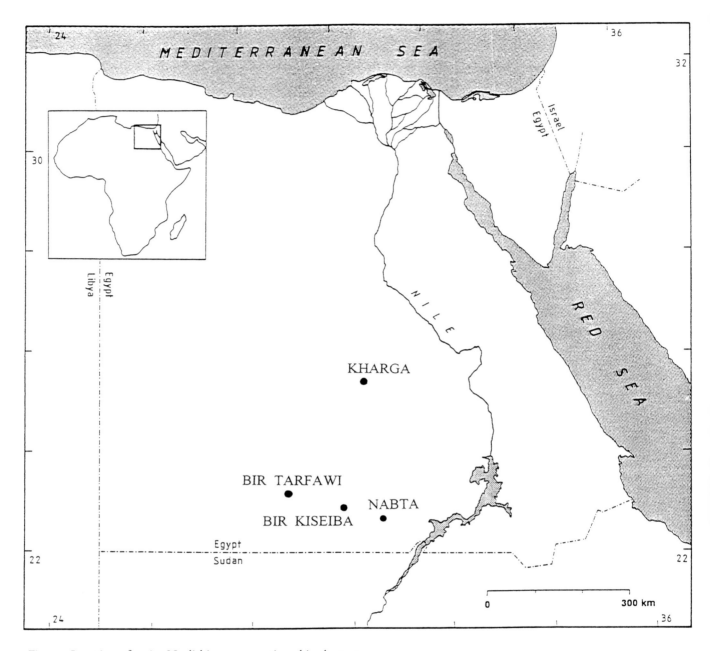

Fig. 1   Location of major Neolithic areas mentioned in the text.

El Adam Humid Interphase

The deposition of playa sediments during this interphase is immediately preceded by the formation of dunes in the basins around the first clusters of vegetation, as a witness to either local rainfall and/or the rise of the water table, heralding the northward movement of the monsoon belt. At El Adam, Nabta and El Gebel El Beid playas, the El Adam variant of the Early Neolithic is contemporaneous with lacustrine deposition in enclosed basins and local rainfall. No evidence suggesting arid phases during the El Adam time has been reported. A conservative, short chronology places the El Adam Humid Interphase between at least 9500 and 8850 years bp.

Post-El Adam Arid Phase

At El Ghorab basin, at the foot of the Kiseiba Scarp (Site E-79-4), an influx of aeolian sand intercalated in the playa deposits immediately beneath a cultural level, which has a radiocarbon age of 8560 ± 140 years bp (SMU-862), may indicate a dry phase preceding the El Ghorab Wet Interphase (Schild and Wendorf 1984, 21). A large standard deviation in the sample does not exclude a slightly younger age for this dry phase.

El Ghorab Humid Interphase

Settlements of the El Ghorab variant of Early Neolithic are

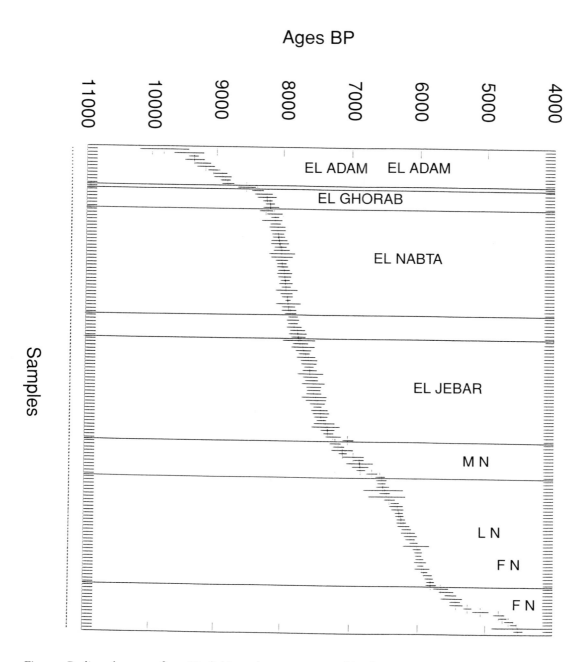

Fig. 2   Radiocarbon ages from Neolithic settlements excavated by the Combined Prehistoric Expedition.

clearly associated with lacustrine deposits and/or sandy beaches interfingering with playa silty sands. A number of radiocarbon ages for El Ghorab occupations securely place them between around 8400 and 8200 years bp. Onset of a dry phase following the El Ghorab rains is seen at El Kortein Playa, Site E-77-6, in the termination of the deposition of lacustrine sediments and the vertisolisation of the cultural layer (Wendorf and Schild 1980, 99).

Post-El Ghorab Arid Phase

An arid interphase post-dating the El Ghorab archaeology and preceding the El Nabta/Al Jerar rains is signalled at El Adam Playa. Here, redeposited, polished El Ghorab lithics

occur in the deposits of a fossil wadi near the centre of the basin (Schild and Wendorf 1984, 29). The wadi is cut into the playa sands of the El Adam Humid Interphase and covered by the silty sands containing El Nabta archaeology; therefore, indicating a deflational lowering of the base level in the basin. Clear influx of aeolian sands in the deposits after El Ghorab archaeology and before the large settlement of El Nabta is also seen at Site E-79-4 in El Ghorab Basin (Schild and Wendorf 1984, 35).

El Nabta/Al Jerar Humid Interphase

A long humid interphase contemporaneous with the El Nabta and Al Jerar late Early Neolithic settlements is best recorded at Nabta Playa, with evidence from Sites E-75-6 and E-91-1. The radiocarbon ages, both for the El Nabta and the Al Jerar Neolithic span from slightly before 8000 to around 7300 years bp (Fig. 2).

The El Nabta/Al Jerar Interphase is characterized by the development of hydromorphic soils around the seasonal lake in the centre of the Nabta Basin as well as by a dramatic decrease in the deposition of clastic lacustrine sediments in the playa. Both are a result of reinforcement by vegetation of the slopes in the entire catchment area. It appears that during the El Nabta and Al Jerar Neolithic the climate in the south Western Desert reaches its Holocene optimum.

The end of Al Jerar occupation at Nabta coincides with the renewal of aeolian deposition. There is also a massive influx of silty sands into the basin grading laterally into thick deltaic alluvium as seen at Sites E-92-7 and E-94-2 along the northern fringes, where major tributary wadis enter the depression from the north and northeast. They herald a dry interphase with receding vegetation and highly seasonal torrential rains. No lacustrine sands and/or silts were laid down in the Nabta Basin after the El Nabta/Al Jerar Interphase.

Post-Al Jerar Arid Phase

Massive deflation marks this new arid phase at Nabta Playa. In the western section of Nabta Playa, at Site E-75-8, a deflational basin of several hundred metres in diameter has formed. The age of this new arid phase, which was accompanied by high winds and heavy sand storms, should be bracketed between the youngest ages for the Al Jerar settlement and the oldest ones for the following Middle Neolithic, that is, most probably between about 7300 and 7200 C^{14} years bp. The radiocarbon ages suggest a very short duration for this phase, but one should not forget the considerable radiocarbon reversals at around 7100 C^{14} years bp.

Middle Neolithic Humid Interphase

New rainfall at Nabta Playa, at Site E-75-8, is heralded by the deposition of aeolian sands interstratified with lamina of silts and the development of phytogenic dunes in deflational hollows. Human occupation appears again in the area and is concentrated on a dune near a deflational hollow with perched water table (Site E-75-8). There is no further lacustrine deposition in the basin. Local rains, however, result in surface wash and the redeposition of the post Al Jerar silts in the local deflational basin. The radiocarbon ages for the lowermost Middle Neolithic cultural deposits in the dune at Site E-75-8 are about 7200 years bp, while the latest ones at the key site E-75-8 are about 6600 years bp.

Post-Middle Neolithic Arid Phase

Massive aeolian erosion during this phase is suggested at the northern fringe of the Nabta Basin, at Sites E-92-7 and E-94-2, where several metres of lacustrine sandy silts and dunes were removed before the deposition of the Late Neolithic Humid Interphase took place. Along the western side of Nabta Playa, at Sites E-92-9, E-94-1 and E-94-3, among others, the deflation created largely modern morphology. At Site E-75-8, the topmost silty sand of the Middle Neolithic age is truncated by deflation. Termination of the phase is placed at around 6550 radiocarbon years bp, the age of the lowermost Late Neolithic occupations at Site E-75-8.

Late Neolithic Humid Interphase

Along the northern fringe of the Nabta Basin, Late Neolithic occupations are embedded in the poorly sorted alluvial sands from the large wadis entering the basin from the northeast and north. The alluvium assumes a maximal depth of about 3 m. At Site E-75-8, the deposition is restricted to the dune and, as during the previous humid interphase, to the older deflational basin. This time, however, the washed-in sediments in the basin are very sandy. A perched water table in the deflational basin at Site E-75-8 is indicated by consecutive wells in the centre. The oldest Late Neolithic hearths in the Nabta Basin provide an age of around 6550 radiocarbon years bp, while the youngest gives a date of about 5800 years bp.

Post-Late Neolithic Arid Phase

In Nabta Playa, at Site E-75-8, the topmost Late Neolithic beds are truncated by deflation. Furthermore, a deflational basin is cut into the Middle Neolithic dune and the post-Al Jerar playa silty sands, which were redeposited during the Middle Neolithic Humid Interphase. These depressions are consequently filled up during the following interphase by the washed-in slope deposits. The age of the phase is constrained, on the one hand, by the latest radiocarbon measurements for the preceding interphase, which are at about 5800 years bp and, on the other, the oldest age of a hearth overlaying the truncation at Site E-75-8 placed at *c.* 5500 years bp.

Final Neolithic Humid Interphase

Two areas at Nabta Playa yield some evidence concerning mineral deposition generated by local rains. One is at Site E-75-8 where stone hearths of Final Neolithic age are embedded in silty colluvial sands of Layer 10. One of them provided a radiocarbon age of about 5500 years bp. In the northern section of the basin, at Site E-92-7 and Site E-94-2, hearths that may be associated with this interphase range in age from about 5650 to 5250 years bp. The samples from the oldest of these hearths, however, show large sigmas of slightly over 100 years. The hearths in the northern section are embedded in alluvial sands.

In the northern Kharga Oasis, at Site E-76-7, a Final Neolithic settlement occurs at the base of fine, laminated silty sands of a small playa immediately underlain by truncated clays of an earlier spring (Wendorf and Schild 1980, 179). A sample of ostrich eggshell gave a corrected radiocarbon age of 5450 years bp (SMU-741). It is a very similar age to the oldest Final Neolithic hearth from Site E-75-8 at Nabta. At Site E-79-9, located in a shallow basin on the

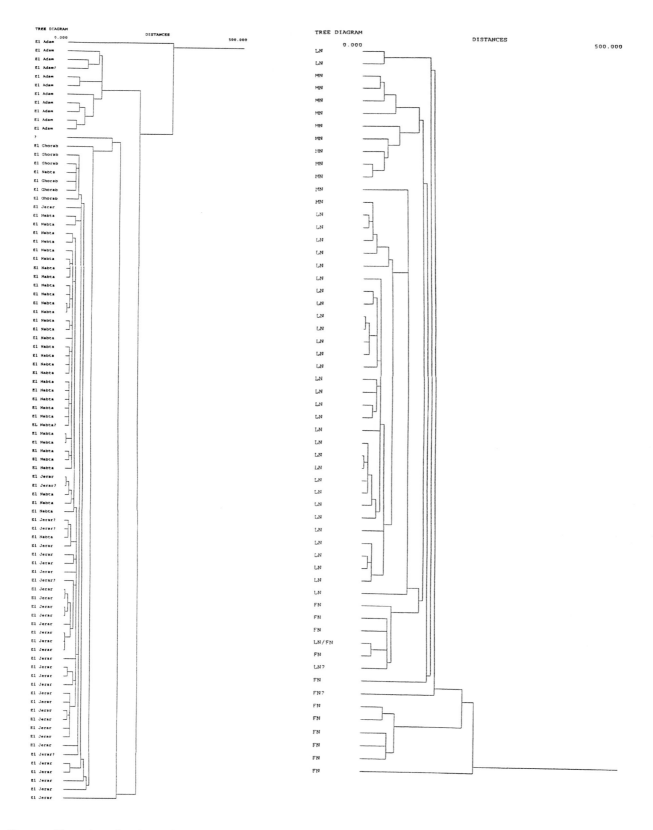

Fig. 3   Clustering of Early Neolithic radiocarbon ages (Euclidean distance, nearest neighbour).

Fig. 4   Clustering of Middle to Final Neolithic radiocarbon ages (Euclidean distance, nearest neighbour).

Kiseiba Plateau, a hearth in a Final Neolithic settlement gave an age of *c.* 5050 years ago (Connor 1984, 352).

There is no clear-cut indication as to when the Final Neolithic Humid Interphase ends. A number of relatively late radiocarbon measurements from archaeological sites in the south Western Desert certainly indicate local rainfall. They range from about 4800 years bp at Megalith E in the Western Graveyard of Nabta Playa to *c.* 4500 bp at Site BT-20 near Bir Tarfawi. It is very unlikely that all these later ages can be associated with the Final Neolithic Humid Interphase, however, most probably Megalith E should fit in. The pits of the megaliths in the Western Graveyard show post-depositional changes related to vertisol phenomena indicating direct rainfall.

Palaeo-climates

The Final Pleistocene and Holocene lithostratigraphy and geomorphology yield only vague signals with regard to the palaeo-climates of the south Western Desert of Egypt. Theoretically, archaeobotany and archaeozoology should provide a better record. However, a limited pollen record exists only in rare biogenic deposits in northern Sudan (e.g., Haynes *et al.* 1989). Elsewhere, it is not available due to the poor preservation of pollen grains in mineral deposits of arid environments.

Floral macro-remains, with the exception of charcoal, are very rare and restricted to the condition and situation of immediate burial. At most sites charred macro-remains were removed after deposition by either wind or water. Although charcoal is rather common in buried cultural deposits, anthracological studies are relatively rare (e.g., Neuman 1989; Barakat 1995a) and limited to only a few sites. Furthermore, they usually yield information confined to a restrained number of taxa. The best record based on charcoal is available for the El Adam, El Nabta/Al Jerar, Middle and Late Neolithic interphases. As for the macro-remains, the El Nabta/Al Jerar flora is exceedingly well documented, particularly at Site E-75-6 at Nabta Playa. Later sites at Nabta yielded only rare macro-remains.

In spite of the fact that the preservation of bone is good at most of the south Western Desert sites, the spectrum of species is not very informative. Megafauna is generally absent, except for the presumably domesticated Bos (Gautier 1984, 69). The omnipresent pair, small gazelle and hare, always dominates the wild assemblage (Gautier 1980; 1984, 68). In short, the faunal spectra indicate the low capacity of the environment and point to semi-arid conditions during humid interphases.

Palaeo-environment of the El Adam Interphase

The floral record from the El Adam interphase is limited to tamarix only, indicating to Hala Barakat (1995a) desert conditions with vegetation contracted to catchment areas, like modern wells in the south Western Desert. However, the accumulation of fine mineral deposits in the playas and the presence of mid-size antelopes, gazelles and hare (Gautier 1984) at El Adam Playa imply a seasonal rainfall and the sta-

bilisation of surfaces in the catchment areas by at least patchy grass cover.

Palaeoenvironment of the El Nabta/Al Jerar Interphase

The macro-remains of as many as 128 plant taxa have been recovered from both the El Nabta and Al Jerar deposits at Site E-75-6 in Nabta Playa (Wasylikowa 1997). The largest assemblage of trees and bushes, counting nine taxa, has also been identified here (Barakat 1996).

Most of the taxa are grasses, legumes and sedges. Almost all are dry soil species, but the presence of *Typha* (Wasylikowa 1997) and *Cyperus rotundus* (Hather 1995), among others, evokes a swamp environment. A water lily, *Nymphea* sp., as well as fully mature water gastropods suggest the presence of small pools of water even in the dry season (Wasylikowa 1997). The size of vermiform trace fossils found in quantities in the hydromorphic soil most likely indicates rhizomes of either *Nymphea* or *Typha* (Gautier, pers. comm.). Among the trees and bushes are acacias *radiana*, *nilotica* and *ehrensbergiana*, and tamarix (Barakat 1996).

To Krystyna Wasylikowa (1997, 144) the plant spectrum at Nabta suggests an ecotone between desert and semi-desert. Hala Barakat (1995b, 164), on the other hand, postulates a contracted, oasis-like desert with sahelian elements. However, the fact that during the El Nabta/Al Jerar time there was almost no mineral deposition in the basin, in spite of unquestionable local rainfall, indicates a relatively dense grass cover over the entire catchment area of about 1500 km^2 and may suggest a vegetation similar to the northern sahelian margin.

Palaeo-environments of the Middle and Late Neolithic Interphases

The limited assemblages of floral macro-remains from Middle and Late Neolithic occurrences at Nabta Playa prevent more elaborate climatic assessments. The few identified taxa belong to *Capparaceae* and *Chenopodiacca*. Charcoal samples, on the other hand, are richer; however, they are limited to tamarix and *acacia nilotica*, *radiana* and *ehrensbergiana* (Barakat 1996, 64). The available floral spectra and particularly the character of mineral deposition announce clear desiccation in relation to the El Nabta/Al Jerar Interphase, and a contracted, groundwater-bound desert vegetation accompanied by erratic and poor rainfall.

Conclusions

The geomorphic and biologic record of the Final Pleistocene and Holocene south Western Desert paints a spectre of an austere desert and semi-desert environment throughout the entire period. Even in the relatively 'lush' climatic optimum of the El Nabta/Al Jerar Interphase, the best that one may envision is the northern margin of the sahelian zone. The climatic pulsations are very short-termed and erratic, yet every interphase brings in a new wave of plant and animal colonisation followed by human settlers. Clearly, the climax of human occupation coincides with the climatic optimum, as shown by the hundreds of settlement units along the shores of the Nabta Lake.

Bibliography

Barakat H, 1995a. *Contribution archeobotanique à l'histoire de la végétation dans le Sahara Oriental et le Soudan Central.* PhD. Thesis. Université de Droit d'Economie et des Sciences d'Aix-Marseille, Faculté des Sciences et Techniques de Saint-Jerome. Aix-Marseille.

Barakat H, 1995b. Charcoals from Neolithic Site at Nabta Playa (E-75-6), Egypt. *Acta Palaeobotanica* 35(1): 163–6.

Barakat H, 1996. Anthracological Studies in the Northeastern Sahara: Methodology and Preliminary Results from the Nabta Playa. In L Krzyzaniak, K Kroeper and M Kobusiewicz (eds), *Interregional Contacts in the Later Prehistory of Northeastern Africa.* Poznan: 61–9.

Connor D R, 1984. The Kiseiba Plateau and Bir Murr Playa. In F Wendorf, R Schild and A E Close (eds), *Cattle-Keepers of the Eastern Sahara: The Neolithic of Bir Kiseiba.* New Delhi: 350–403.

Gautier A, 1980. Contribution to the Archaeozoology of Egypt. In: F Wendorf and R Schild, *Prehistory of the Eastern Sahara.* New York: 317–44.

Gautier A, 1984. Archaeozoology of the Bir Kiseiba Region, Eastern Sahara. In F Wendorf, R Schild and A E Close (eds), *Cattle-Keepers of the Eastern Sahara: The Neolithic of Bir Kiseiba.* New Delhi: 49–72.

Haynes Jr. C V, Eyles C H, Ritchie L A and Rybak M, 1989. Holocene Palaeoecology of the Eastern Sahara; Selima Oasis. *Quaternary Science Reviews* 8: 109–36.

Hather J, 1995. Parenchymatous tissues from Early Neolithic site E-75-6 at Nabta Playa Western Desert, south Egypt. Preliminary report. *Acta Palaeobotanica* 35: 157–62.

Neumann K, 1989a. Zur Vegetationsgeschichte der Ostsahara im Holozän. Holzkohlen aus prähistorischen Fundstellen. In R Kuper (ed.), *Forschungen zur Umweltgeschichte der Ostsahara.* Africa Praehistorica 2. Köln: 13–181.

Schild R and Wendorf F, 1984. Lithostratigraphy of Holocene Lakes Along the Kisseiba Scarp. In F Wendorf, R Schild, A E Close (eds), *Cattle-Keepers of the Eastern Sahara: The Neolithic of Bir Kisseiba,* New Delhi: 9–48.

Schild R, and Wendorf F, 1989. The Late Pleistocene Nile in Wadi Kubbaniya. In F Wendorf, R Schild, A E Close (eds), *The Prehistory of Wadi Kubbaniya.* Dallas: 15–100.

Wasylikowa K, 1997. Flora of the 8000 Years Old Archaeological Site E-75-6 at Nabta Playa, Western Desert, Southern Egypt. *Acta Palaeobotanica* 37(2): 99–205.

Wendorf F and Schild R, 1980. *Prehistory of the Eastern Sahara.* New York.

Human Responses to Holocene Environmental Changes in the Northern Dongola Reach of the Nile, Sudan

Derek A Welsby, Mark G Macklin and Jamie C Woodward

Introduction

In northern Sudan and southern Egypt the River Nile flows through what is today a hyper-arid zone. Where it crosses the eastern edge of the Sahara, the fundamental importance of the river for human settlement is clearly demonstrated by the almost continuous settled zone along its banks, except for the area around Lake Nasser where the transition from lake to desert is abrupt. Many studies have demonstrated that the situation we observe today differed greatly in the past, partly as a result of climatic changes directly affecting these latitudes (Ritchie *et al.* 1985), and partly through climatic variation affecting the major headwater catchment areas of the Nile, particularly the Ethiopian highlands (Williams and Adamson 1980). Both the climatic regime and the River Nile itself are dynamic, and in the marginal zone under consideration even minor fluctuations in rainfall or flood magnitude had a dramatic impact on communities along the river banks (see Hassan 1997; 1998). Recent archaeological work in the Northern Dongola Reach, just upstream of the Third Cataract, has highlighted the close relationship between Holocene environmental change and human activity in the Nubian/Sudanese Nile Valley. In view of this intimate relationship, any investigation of the cultural record must be a multidisciplinary enterprise with a carefully designed geoarchaeological component. Geomorphological and stratigraphic investigations can provide the long-term environmental context for the record of human settlement, while the archaeology provides cultural as well as chronological data for adaptation to changing climatic and fluvial conditions.

The archaeological and geomorphological investigations reported here were conducted under the auspices of the Sudan Archaeological Research Society (SARS) in response to the rapid pace of modern development in the Northern Dongola Reach. Widespread destruction of archaeological sites in the region has been caused by the recent expansion of agriculture. This expansion is evident throughout the area from the Nile to the edge of the bedrock plateau that forms the eastern margin of the Holocene valley floor – a maximum distance of some 18 km. Another major destructive force in the region is aeolian erosion, although this process has been in operation over a much longer time scale, as we discuss further below.

The Northern Dongola Reach

The Nile river is approximately 1847 km long between Khartoum (378 m asl) and Aswan (91 m asl), with a mean average gradient of 0.154 m km^{-1}. This stretch of the Nile comprises two great structurally controlled bends and traverses the six major cataracts where the channel gradient increases markedly (Said 1993). The steepest reach downstream of Khartoum is just upstream of Merowe, along the Fourth Cataract, where the channel falls some 53 m over a distance of *c.* 110 km. The great cataracts are separated by much longer reaches of lower gradient where large volumes of fine-grained alluvial sediments have been deposited during the Holocene and earlier periods. Upstream of the Third Cataract lies the broad alluvial plain of the Dongola Reach, which is approximately 313 km in length with an average gradient of 0.083 m km^{-1}. The downstream section of this reach includes the SARS concession where our archaeological and geomorphological investigations have taken place (see Welsby 1995; 2001; Macklin and Woodward 2001; Woodward *et al.* 2001).

The SPOT satellite image of the Northern Dongola Reach in **Plate 38** shows the present channel of the Nile and the major landforms in this part of the valley. It is clear from this image that most of the alluvial plain to the east of the modern Nile is traversed by a series of large palaeochannel belts (Macklin and Woodward, 2001; Woodward *et al.* 2001) and these are discussed in detail below. In the recent geological past the valley floor in this reach contained a series of avulsing channels, which have effected a relatively uniform distribution of predominantly fine-grained alluvial sediment across the valley floor up to the bedrock plateau in the east. Sediment deposition along these channel systems created differences in elevation between the channels and inter-channel zones or flood basins. As the convex channel forms became unstable, flood waters would have shifted into adjacent areas and filled them with sediment. This process has created a relatively flat Holocene valley floor that is bordered to the east by a series of low angle alluvial fans that drain from the bedrock plateau. In many parts of the valley floor the alluvial sediments are overlain by sheets of wind-blown sand that vary in thickness from a few centimetres to several metres. Apart from the isolated sandstone hill, Barqat Kuluf, which attains an elevation of 294 m asl, west of the bedrock plateau the highest relief is provided by active barchan dunes up to 15.5 m in height. Some of these forms are migrating at a rate of more than one metre per year. In the northern part of the concession is a low-lying depression, the Seleim Basin that is contiguous with the Kerma Basin to its north. This area supports a considerable amount of vegetation as well as seasonal lakes and is extensively used for irrigation-based agriculture (**Plate 39**).

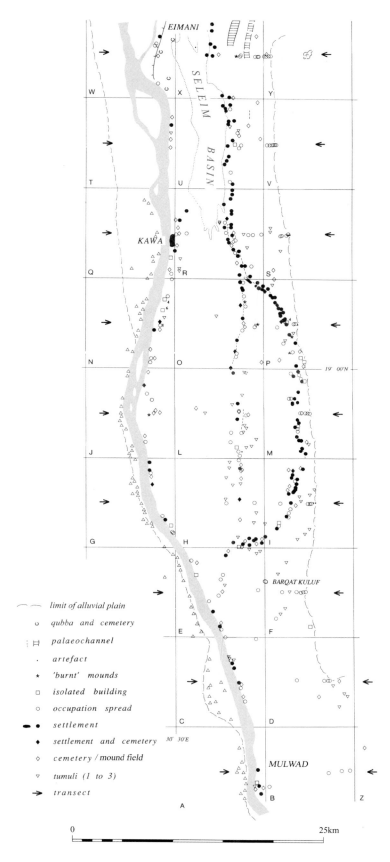

Fig. 1   Map of the SARS concession with sites of all periods (data on left
bank sites courtesy of Stuart Tyson Smith).

The Archaeological Survey

The SARS concession lies to the east of the Nile and extends over a distance of some 80 km from Mulwad downstream to Eimani and included the only major archaeological site hitherto known in the area, Kawa (N 19° 7.350' / E 30° 2.801') (**Fig. 1**). Kawa was first investigated by the Oxford Excavation Committee in 1929–31 and 1935–6, during which time several temples were excavated yielding evidence of occupation from the middle of the second millennium BC into the third century AD (Macadam 1949; 1955). The area to the north of Eimani has been extensively investigated for over a decade by the French Section of the Sudanese National Corporation for Antiquities and Museums, under the direction of Jacques Reinold (1993; 1994). Large palaeochannel systems have also been reported in this part of the Northern Dongola Reach (Marcolongo and Surian 1993; 1997). The urban sites at Tabo on Argo Island (Jacquet-Gordon 1999; Jacquet-Gordon et al. 1969; Maystre 1967–68; 1969) and at Kerma have been examined by missions from Switzerland. Another French mission is currently excavating rural settlements immediately to the north of the SARS concession. To the south, the Royal Ontario Museum has surveyed as far downstream as Mulwad (Grzymski 1987). Limited survey has also been undertaken along the reach to the west of the present Nile by Jacques Reinold (1993) and by Stuart Tyson Smith.

The SARS Survey

The concession was divided along a grid (**Fig. 1**), each 'square' measuring 5' of latitude by 5' of longitude and labelled A–Z (K was not used). The survey employed a twofold strategy. The systematic component involved the survey of all sites along east-west transects from the plateau to the river through the centre of each grid square, using a combination of a walking survey and site observation from the vehicle. All observed sites were examined in detail, planned where appropriate, and a sample collection of surface material was collected. It soon became clear that sites were concentrated in certain areas and these areas were then subjected to intensive survey. The site locations drew attention to the presence of palaeochannels. These palaeochannels branched off from the present-day river (the Dongola Nile) near the southern end of the survey area and then divided to form the Hawawiya Nile palaeochannel and the Alfreda Nile palaeochannel belts. Downstream, to the southeast of Kawa, these palaeochannel belts join up again and form the Seleim Nile palaeochannel, which flowed due north close to the eastern edge of the Seleim Basin (**Fig. 1**).

In excess of 450 archaeological sites were located in the survey area with sites dating to most periods between the later Neolithic and the present day (**Fig. 1**). The absence of evidence for extensive use of the region before the Neolithic may reflect the generally poor quality of the raw materials available for Palaeolithic tool production (Prof Kobusiewicz and Dr Kabacinski, pers. comm.).

The Neolithic period

During the Neolithic period (fifth–fourth millennia BC), the human population becomes highly visible and evidence for occupation is present throughout the survey area (**Plate 40**). The impression of widespread occupation during this period must, however, be treated with caution as Neolithic settlement sites have suffered extensively from aeolian erosion. This process has concentrated artefacts from different periods at the present-day land surface; nevertheless, it is apparent that there was little nucleation of settlement during this period and Neolithic artefacts are found over much of the survey area, except where wind-blown sand sheets and dunes cover the current surface.

The Kerma period

The evidence for occupation in the succeeding Kerma period (c. 2500–1450 BC) is very different (**Fig. 2**). Approximately 150 settlement sites have been recorded. Many of these are of considerable size and the largest is over 1 km in length. Extensive occupation over a considerable period is indicated by the formation of settlement mounds up to 6.8 m in height (**Plate 41**). The distribution of Kerma sites clearly shows that human settlement patterns changed radically after the Neolithic. Without exception, all the Kerma settlements are located along the margins of a number of well-developed palaeochannels or immediately adjacent to the Seleim Basin, with a much smaller number of sites along the banks of the present river. Although it appears that the preferred area of settlement in the Kerma period was along the palaeochannels, rather than beside the banks of the present Nile, this distribution may partly reflect the processes of site destruction by recent human settlement and sand dune migration.

Environmental Change During the Neolithic and Kerma Periods

Population Growth and Water Demand

Around the time of the development of the Kerma culture, a combination of factors is believed to have enhanced the importance of the palaeochannels for human settlement. These factors may have included a rise in population and therefore a need for a more intensive use of local soil and water resources. This population rise is perhaps associated with the expansion of Kerma, the capital of the first Kingdom of Kush, a little to the north. As the seat of government, Kerma would have introduced a large parasitic population into the region, the support of which would have required the production of a food surplus. The development of more intensive agriculture, coupled perhaps with an expansion into more marginal areas, would have been a logical response to this situation. Intensified agriculture would also have led to a greater degree of sedentism, for which, along with increases in both the area under cultivation and livestock numbers, a ready and copious supply of water would be necessary. Yet these developments coincide with the onset of an increasingly arid phase.

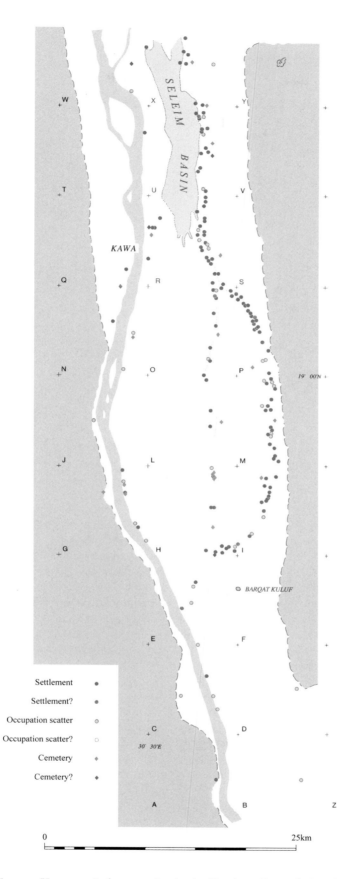

Fig. 2   Kerma period occupation in the Northern Dongola Reach
(data on left bank sites courtesy of Stuart Tyson Smith).

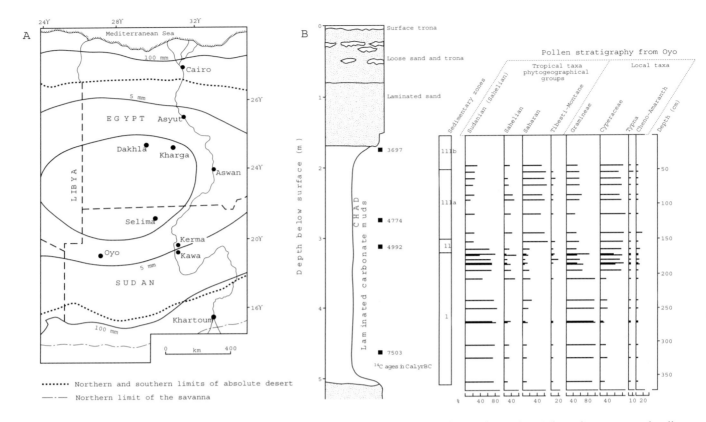

Fig. 3   The Oyo Basin, northwest Sudan. A: Location of the Oyo Basin (after Ritchie *et al.* 1985). B: The sedimentary and pollen record from the Oyo Lake Basin sequence (after Ritchie *et al.* 1985) with calibrated radiocarbon dates after Roberts (1998).

The rising demand for a reliable supply of water in the Northern Dongola Reach–at a time when the region was becoming generally more arid–may have been the critical factor that led to the concentration of human activity along the banks of the palaeochannels. The archaeological model proposed is one in which the settlements were occupied by a significant population on a permanent basis. Although it is likely that animal husbandry was an important component of the Kerma economy – excavations in the necropolis at Kerma have revealed large circular pits of Middle Kerma age (2050 to 1750 BC) in which entire flocks of sheep have been placed to accompany the deceased (Bonnet 1992) and there is evidence that vast herds of cattle were sacrificed on the occasion of a burial – it is likely that crop production would have been the mainstay. To sustain large-scale agriculture in the absence of mechanical water pumps and even before the introduction of the *saqia* (water wheel), surface water and ideally annually-flooded, or *seluka*, land is considered essential.

The Oyo Basin Record, Northwest Sudan

A key record of environmental change spanning the early and mid-Holocene period (*c.* 8050 to 3050 BC) comes from the site of Oyo (N 19°16' / E 26°11') in northwest Sudan. The work at this site, reported by Ritchie *et al.* (1985), provides the first conclusive demonstration of vegetation and

climate change in the early to mid-Holocene of the Eastern Sahara. This site is located in the present hyper-arid core of the eastern Sahara at around the same latitude as the Northern Dongola Reach. It therefore provides a valuable source for comparison with the early part of our cultural and fluvial sedimentary records. The Oyo Depression contains Holocene lacustrine sediments covered by dune sands and these have been cored, analysed for their fossil pollen, and radiocarbon dated. The sequence from the Oyo Basin has been sub-divided into four zones and these are shown in **Fig. 3** with calibrated radiocarbon ages after Roberts (1998). Ritchie *et al.* (1985, 352) describe an early to mid-Holocene humid episode (Zone I) that supported a relatively deep stratified lake surrounded by tropical savanna woodland vegetation. The data from Oyo suggest a humid tropical climate with annual monsoonal rainfall of at least 400 mm for Zone I before about 5000 cal BC. A progressive increase in aridity took place during Zones II and III with mean annual rainfall decreasing from *c.* 300 mm at 4800 cal BC to <100 mm at *c.* 3100 cal BC. The later part of this sequence corresponds to the phase of Neolithic settlement in the Northern Dongola Reach when many sites were located away from the palaeochannels. However, around 3100 cal BC the Oyo Lake system dried out completely and the sediments became dominated by the crudely bedded and bleached aeolian sands of Zone IIIb (Ritchie *et al.* 1985). At this time the desert scrub and grasslands disappeared from

Table 1: The OSL and radiocarbon dates from samples taken from pit sections in the Northern Dongola Reach.

Pit No.	Depth	OSL or C¹⁴ Age	BC/AD	Culture
Seleim Palaeochannel Belt:				
18	1.45 m	2790 ± 100 BP	790 BC	Kushite
18	5.15 m	4500 ± 300 BP	2500 BC	Pre/Early Kerma
Alfreda Palaeochannel Belt:				
23	1.30 m	1490 ± 100 BP	AD 510	Post-Meroitic
14	0.75 m	3190 ± 300 BP	1190 BC	New Kingdom/Kushite
14	4.40 m	4060 ± 300 BP	2060 BC	Early/Middle Kerma
7	1.60 m	5170 ± 530 BP	3170 BC	Pre-Kerma
24	1.55 m	5680 ± 300 BP	3680 BC	Neolithic/Pre-Kerma
4	2.55 m	7060 ± 430 BP	5060 BC	Neolithic
12	1.83 m	5100 ± 80 BP**	4045 to 3705 BC	Neolithic
Hawawiya Palaeochannel Belt:				
5	2.30 m	7100 ± 1090 BP 7490 ± 1120 BP	5100 BC 5490 BC	Neolithic Neolithic
26	1.2 m	3830 ± 50 BP*	2460 to 2140 BC	Early Kerma

See **Plate 38** for the location of key pit and palaeochannel belts. Sample depths are from the top of the logged section (modern land surface). *Note that the date from Pit 26 is a radiocarbon date (BM-3128) that has been calibrated using the curve of Pearson and Stuiver (1986) and the Oxcal v2.18 calibration program. This figure gives a 68% probability that the true calendar date is between 2460 and 2420 or 2400 and 2270 or 2250 and 2200 BC and a 95% probability that it is between 2460 and 2190 or 2170 and 2140 BC (Janet Ambers, pers. comm. 1998). This sample dates to the Early Kerma period. **The date from Pit 12 is also a radiocarbon date on charcoal (Beta 100605). The calibrated age represents a 2 sigma uncertainty and dates to the Neolithic period.

all habitats apart from oases and wadis. During the course of the third millennium BC, the pattern of human settlement in the Northern Dongola Reach changed dramatically as sites became concentrated along the margins of the major palaeochannel belts.

Geomorphological Investigations of the Palaeochannel Systems

Macklin and Woodward carried out geomorphological fieldwork in the SARS concession during the 1995/96 and 1996/97 field seasons. The broad aim of this part of the project was to establish the nature of the valley floor environment during the Neolithic, Kerma and later periods in order to allow a fuller interpretation of the cultural data produced by the SARS survey and excavations. This geoarchaeological component involved documenting the nature of the alluvial sedimentary record preserved in the Northern Dongola Reach and developing a geochronological framework for the major palaeochannel belts associated

with the observed settlement patterns.

Away from the present Nile the modern phase of agricultural activity, which has destroyed many of the archaeological sites in the region, is reliant on groundwater for irrigation. The farmers tap the groundwater supplies using diesel pumps that are installed at the bottom of pits dug into the Holocene alluvium. These groundwater pump pits are normally square (c. 4–5 m wide) and around 4 m deep, although some may exceed 6 m. They are present throughout much of the survey area and provide high-quality three-dimensional exposures of the alluvial sedimentary record. We have observed the alluvial sedimentary record in more than 150 pits in the SARS concession and we have described and sampled 31 of them in detail (Macklin and Woodward 2001; Woodward et al. 2001). All of these sampled pits were spatially referenced using GPS and the placement of four of them (5, 14, 18, 23) is shown in **Plate 38**. Our sampling strategy was partly constrained by the availability of accessible pits (with sides that had not been lined) and this in turn was largely controlled by the distribution of agricultural activity. As the majority of agricultural activity is focused on the major palaeochannels, this allowed us to record the alluvial stratigraphic record in detail (**Fig. 4**) across an area that included the vast majority of the archaeological sites recorded in the SARS survey.

A fundamental requirement of the geomorphological part of the project was to establish the age of the alluvial sediments and associated palaeochannel belts across the SARS concession. We have used Optically Stimulated Luminescence (OSL) dating (n = 10) and, to a lesser extent, radiocarbon dating (n = 2) to develop an independent chronological framework for the alluvial sediments that can be compared to the archaeological record and to Holocene proxy climate data from the region such as the record from Oyo. The OSL method has proved to be especially suitable for the well-sorted fine sands we have sampled. These materials appear to have been partially reworked by aeolian activity prior to burial by later flood sediments and this has ensured effective zeroing of the luminescence signal (Macklin and Woodward 1998; Woodward *et al.* 2001). The OSL and radiocarbon chronology derived from samples collected from the groundwater pump pits is shown in **Table 1**.

Hawawiya Nile Palaeochannel Belt

Pit 5 (N 19° 02.62' / E 30° 33.94')

This pit is located approximately 6 km upstream of the main palaeochannel belt confluence with the Alfreda Nile. It is the most northerly of the sites sampled on the Hawawiya palaeochannel complex. The alluvial sediments in this pit reach a maximum depth of 2.8 m below the modern land surface (**Fig. 4**). Two OSL assays were obtained from a depth of 2.3 m yielding ages of 5100 BC and 5490 BC (**Table 1**). These are the oldest ages so far obtained for alluvial materials in the Northern Dongola Reach. They show that this channel complex was active in the early Holocene and at least part of this sequence can be correlated with Zone I at the Oyo Basin. At this time the Oyo Basin contained a relatively deep stratified lake surrounded by continuous, deciduous savanna vegetation, similar to that found today approximately 500 km to the south (Ritchie *et al.* 1985). Pit 5 is comparatively shallow and the depth of the alluvial sequence in this part of the Hawawiya palaeochannel complex is not known. A significant number of Neolithic sites have been recorded in this area (Welsby 1995).

Seleim Nile Palaeochannel Belt

Pit 18 (N 19° 07' 26.0" / E 30° 33' 09.5")

This pit lies on the right bank of the Seleim Nile palaeochannel system approximately 4 km downstream of the confluence of the Alfreda and Hawawiya palaeochannel belts and about 7 km due east of the modern Nile (**Plate 38**). Reaching a maximum depth of 6.1 m, this pit contains the second deepest exposure recorded in the survey area and Nubian sandstone is visible at its base. The sequence includes over 5 m of well-sorted fine sand units that alternate with units of fine sandy silt. The OSL sample depths and ages are shown on **Table 1** and **Fig. 4**. These data

demonstrate that much of the alluvial sequence at this site within the Seleim Nile palaeochannel belt dates from the beginning of the Early Kerma period until sometime in the early part of the first millennium BC, more than 700 years after the end of the Final Kerma culture (**Table 1**). The lower part of this sequence was deposited several hundred years after the Oyo Lake Basin finally dried out.

Alfreda Nile Palaeochannel Belt

Pit 14 (N 19° 02' 31.4" / E 30° 36' 16.5")

This site is approximately 3.5 km from the bedrock plateau within the Alfreda Nile palaeochannel belt. It contains a 5.7 m exposure of fine-grained alluvial sediments (**Fig. 4**). The sequence is comparable to Pit 18 as it comprises well sorted fine sand units that commonly grade upwards into fine sandy silts of varying thickness. The two OSL ages obtained from this sequence are shown in **Table 1**. The lower part of this sequence yielded an age of 2060 BC, equivalent to Early/Middle Kerma times. The upper part of this exposure (0.75 m from the modern land surface) has been dated to just after the Final Kerma period with an age of 1190 BC. These OSL dates indicate that this channel belt was active throughout the Kerma period.

Pit 23 (N 19° 04' 38" / E 30° 34' 53.2")

Pit 23 was dug into the bed of a well-preserved palaeochannel in February 1997 with the aim of revealing sediments that could be attributed to the last phase of fluvial activity in this channel. This is the only section that was not already exposed in a groundwater pump pit. A section of 1.9 m was exposed and the stratigraphy is shown in **Fig. 4**. A sample for OSL dating was collected from a depth of 1.3 m below the present land surface from the uppermost fluvial silty sand unit in the sequence. This yielded a date of AD 510 (**Table 1**) for the last time there was significant flow in this channel. Very thin layers of fluvial silt are present above this level and these represent only very shallow and intermittent channel flows. The transition from riverine to aeolian facies was observed in section and the upper part of this exposure comprised 30 cm of medium to coarse-grained aeolian sands (Macklin and Woodward 2001). Recent data produced by the UK Natural Environment Research Council's Tigger Project (Terrestrial Initiative in Global Environmental Research) have shown that a major shift to a more 'drought-ridden' regime occurred in the sub-Saharan Sahel during the first millennum AD (Chaloner 1997).

Agriculture and Water Resource Management Strategies during the Kerma Period

Most, if not all, of the settlements occupied during the Kerma period remained in use as least as late as the Kerma Classique (1750–1550 BC). However, by the middle of the first millennium BC, all permanent settlement had relocated or, perhaps more correctly, had become concentrated, along the banks of the present-day river. A number of factors may have been responsible for this new settlement distribution.

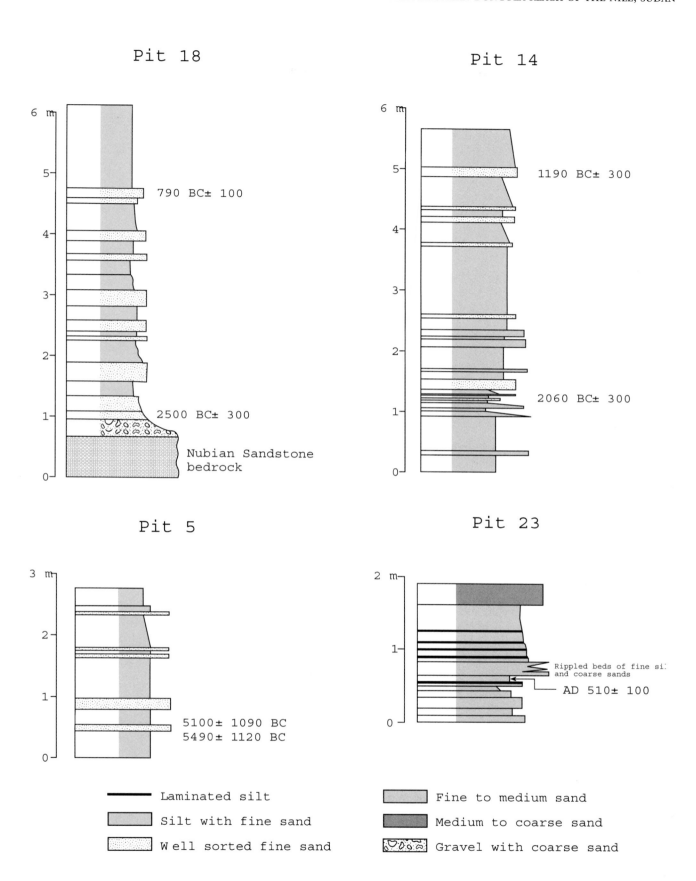

Fig. 4   Schematic stratigraphic logs and Optically Stimulated Luminescence (OSL) ages from four pits in the Northern Dongola Reach. The pit locations are shown on **Plate 38**.

The most probable cause was a decrease in effective local rainfall and the desiccation of the land away from the riparian zone. The flood waters of the Nile were now largely concentrated in the present channel of the Nile and the palaeochannels conveyed water much less frequently than during the Kerma period. Although we have no direct evidence for salinisation, the decrease in rainfall may have created this problem away from the present course of the Nile where irrigation waters were not plentiful enough to flush salts from the upper soil. The importance of purely economic factors is difficult to assess, but in the post-Kerma period the decline in the region's political prominence may have reduced the size of the parasitic population and therefore the need for surplus food production. This would have encouraged the abandonment of more marginal land, particularly as the climate became drier.

The archaeological remains indicate that there may have been a long period, perhaps between c. 1500 BC and the early first millennium BC, when the population sought to adapt to the worsening conditions by various expedients; a battle that in the end was lost. We have extensive archaeological evidence for two types of water management installations that can be related to this phase, and these are wadi walls and wells.

Wadi Walls

Wadi walls are a feature of many arid zones and are designed to make the maximum use of limited water resources, particularly runoff following local flash floods (Gilbertson and Hunt 1996). They are designed to slow down the runoff, thereby allowing it to percolate into the soil, and also to reduce the erosive potential of the waters that might otherwise strip off the fertile topsoil. Towards the southern end of the Alfreda Nile palaeochannel system several parallel stone walls survive that run across the depression of the palaeochannel. Although the identification of these walls as part of a water management system seems likely, the local topography appears far from ideal. There is only very limited relief and the low gradients would not have led to the concentration of runoff resources that one usually associates with such systems. It is possible that these walls were associated with seasonal discharges in the palaeochannel itself, and we have evidence from Pit 23 of a decline in the magnitude of channel flows in the Alfreda Nile palaeochannel after AD 510 (Woodward et al. 2001).

Wells

In many areas of the concession, dense concentrations of mounds covered in brown quartzite pebbles (**Plate 42**) are closely associated with the palaeochannels. When these features were first observed, they were recorded as tumuli, as similar features had previously been observed in the eastern cemetery at Kawa (Welsby 1993). Excavation of one of these features at Kawa revealed a primary burial and a number of secondary interments (Salih 1994). However, close examination of the mounds within the survey areas in what we referred to as 'mound fields' indicates that they had a rather different origin.

Two of these features were partly excavated at site P17

and another was investigated at site P1. Although the two mounds at P17 had small pits dug into their surface, a grave was not found. A grave was not found at P1 either. At site H10 circular settings of red bricks were set into four or possibly five mounds. These features looked more like well shaft linings than anything one would expect in a funerary context. Another similar mound at site E12 had a pit in its centre, 4.55 m in diameter, the edges of which were heavily burnt, suggesting that it had functioned as a kiln. At least one other structure of this type was noted at that site.

During the 1996/97 field season the opportunity was taken to examine in detail a number of these mounds at Site P1. One of the five mounds that were investigated was not associated with any cultural features and its interpretation is problematic. The others contained wells. The well in mound 13 had a shaft 1.03 to 1.1 m in diameter, and was excavated to a maximum depth of 6.5 m, at which point it became too dangerous to continue. In the walls of another, well-preserved hand and foot holes used to climb in and out of the shaft were present. The sides of this shaft were perfectly preserved up to current ground level, suggesting that the upper part of the shaft and any above-ground well-head installations had been removed. There is extensive evidence for severe erosion by aeolian action in the Northern Dongola Reach and it seems likely that this process was responsible for the loss of the upper parts of the well shafts.

One might logically assume that the mounds, in which the wells lie, were formed from the material derived from their excavation. However, stratigraphic observations make it clear that the well shafts were actually cut through the sediments that today form the mounds. At a depth of 5.7 m in mound 13, the well shaft, which down to that level was cut through alluvium, cuts through a layer of well-rounded quartzite gravels in a matrix of coarse sand. Similar deposits of gravel have been noted in the modern groundwater pump pits elsewhere in the concession. These gravels form a distinctive bed up to c. 2 m in thickness that lies immediately above the Nubian sandstone bedrock. During the excavation of the wells these gravels would have been brought up to the surface and presumably discarded immediately adjacent to the well-head along with the silts. These gravels subsequently offered some protection from aeolian erosion to the ground surface beneath them, while the silts from the well upcast were blown away. Thus, the mounds in the mound fields appear to be residual features that have been protected from the aeolian erosion that has lowered the inter-mound areas and surrounding ground surfaces.

Although not all of these mounds are associated with wells, the available evidence indicates that many of them are, and in the Northern Dongola Reach there are up to 400 at any one site. Moreover, there are very good ethnographic parallels from elsewhere in the Sudan for this close arrangement of wells in dryland environments. For example, close to the dry season camps of the Kababish Arabs of northern Kordofan at the southern end of their annual migration route, there are concentrations of between 6 and 200 wells, and these are usually dug in the beds of wadis (Asad 1970). They are set only far enough apart so as to allow unimpeded access to each well by the well owner's flock. These well fields or *mushra'* range from 50 to 1000 m in length (Asad 1970, 25). Another well field was observed in operation at Gebel Fau between Wad Medani and Gedaref in March 1999 (see Vila 1979, fig. 89). This was very similar in layout to the well fields of the Kababish. Next to each well-head was a trough from which the animals could drink (**Plate 43-44**).

The similarities between these modern well fields and the ancient mound fields in the Northern Dongola Reach is striking, but particularly interesting is the difference in location. All modern examples lie at least 400 km to the south of the Northern Dongola Reach, well within the regions affected by the annual summer rains. The presence of similar installations in the Northern Dongola Reach must represent a stage in the utilisation of the area when there was sufficient rainfall to make the grazing of considerable flocks (presumably of caprines) possible. Although the mound fields are not closely dated, a number of them lie in the bed of the palaeochannels and must date to a time when the channels were inundated only on a seasonal basis. The well fields, and the economic activity with which they were associated, may represent the last phase of utilisation of the areas away from the course of the modern river. Following the demise of that economic system, probably in the early to mid first millennium BC, all the evidence suggests that human activity was confined to the banks of the present-day river.

Conclusions

Archaeological evidence in the Northern Dongola Reach illustrates a process of human adaptation, largely conditioned by natural factors, to a changing climatic and river regime. The inexorable, but by no means linear, progression towards greater aridity was tempered to some extent by the presence of the Nile. However, a climatic deterioration around 1000 BC, coinciding with the demise of the two eastern palaeochannels of the Nile, greatly reduced the carrying capacity of the region and robbed it of those special factors that may have made it, for a period of over 1000 years, the bread-basket of the first Kingdom of Kush.

The potential fertility of the area is once again being demonstrated by modern developments. High capacity diesel water pumps, tapping the aquifers fed by the Nile, are allowing large tracts of the Northern Dongola Reach once again to be settled and farmed. The preferred areas for this farming are the levées alongside the palaeochannels where the fertile alluvium lies at the present land surface. Although such development is to be welcomed, the juxtaposition of the modern farming activities and those of the farmers living in the area 4000 years and more before is taking a heavy toll on the archaeological remains. The present project is an attempt to document and understand the interactions between these early farmers and their environment before further evidence is lost.

Acknowledgements

The project has been funded from a number of sources, among them The Bioanthropology Foundation, The British Museum, The British Academy, The Society of Antiquaries of London, the University of Newcastle upon Tyne and the University of Leeds. We are most grateful for the generous assistance extended to the project by the staffs of the National Corporation for Antiquities and Museums, The British Council and the British Embassy in Sudan. **Plate 38** and **Figs 3** and **5** were prepared by David Appleyard of the Graphics Unit, School of Geography at the University of Leeds.

Bibliography

Asad T, 1970. *The Kababish Arabs. Power, Authority and Consent in a Nomadic Tribe.* London.

Bonnet C, 1992. Excavations at the Nubian royal town of Kerma: 1975–91. *Antiquity* 66: 611–25.

Chaloner W, 1997. Global change: the time dimension. *NERC News* Autumn 1997: 14–5.

Gilbertson D D and Hunt C O, 1996. Romano-Libyan Agriculture: Walls and Floodwater Farming. In G Barker (ed.), *Farming the Desert. The UNESCO Libyan Valleys Survey Volume One: Synthesis.* Paris, London: 191–225.

Grzymski K A, 1987. *Archaeological Reconnaisance in Upper Nubia.* Toronto.

Hassan F A, 1997. The dynamics of a riverine civilization: a geoarchaeological perspective on the Nile Valley, Egypt. *World Archaeology* 29: 51–74.

Hassan F A, 1998. Climatic change, Nile floods and civilization. *Nature and Resources* 34: 34–40.

Jacquet-Gordon H, 1999. Excavations at Tabo, Northern Province, Sudan. In D A Welsby (ed.), *Recent Research in Kushite History and Archaeology: Proceedings of the Eighth International Conference of Meroitic Studies.* London: 257–64.

Jacquet-Gordon H, Bonnet C and Jacquet J, 1969. Pnubs and the Temple of Tabo on Argo Island. *Journal of Egyptian Archaeology* 55: 103–11.

Macadam M F L, 1949. *The Temples of Kawa I: The Inscriptions.* London.

Macadam M F L, 1955. *Temples of Kawa. II. History and Archaeology of the Site.* Oxford.

Macklin M G and Woodward J C, 1998. Alluvial architecture and luminescence dating of Holocene palaeochannels in the Northern Dongola Reach of the Nile. *Sudan & Nubia* 2: 21–5.

Macklin M G and Woodward J C, 2001. Holocene alluvial history and the palaeochannels of the Northern Dongola Reach of the Nile. In D A Welsby, *Life on the Desert Edge: 7000 years of settlement in the Northern Dongola Reach, Sudan.* Sudan Archaeological Research Society Publications 7. London: 7–13.

Marcolongo B and Surian N, 1993. Observations préliminaires du contexte gémorphologique de la plaine alluviale du Nil en amont de la IIIᵉ cataracte en rapport avec les sites archéologiques. *Genava* n.s. 41: 33.

Marcolongo B and Surian N, 1997. Kerma: Les sites archéologiques de Kerma et de Kadruka dans leur contexte géomorphologique. *Genava* n.s. 45: 119–23.

Maystre C, 1967–68. Excavations at Tabo, Argo Island: Preliminary Report. *Kush* 15: 193–9.

Maystre C, 1969. Les Fouilles de Tabo. *Bulletin de la Société française d'Égyptologie* 55: 5–12.

Reinold J, 1993. Section française de la Direction des Antiquités du Soudan. Preliminary Report on the 1991/92 and 1992/93 Season in the Northern Provinces. *Sudan Archaeological Research Society Newsletter* 5: 33–43.

Reinold J, 1994. Le Cimitiere Néolithique Kdk.1 De Kadruka (Nubie Soudanaise): Premiers Résultats et Essai de Corrélation avec les Sites du Soudan Central. In C Bonnet (ed.), *Études Nubiennes* II. Geneva: 93–100.

Ritchie J C, Eyles C H and Haynes C V, 1985. Sediment and pollen evidence for an early to mid-Holocene humid period in the eastern Sahara. *Nature* 314: 352–55.

Roberts N, 1998. *The Holocene: An Environmental History.* Second edition. Oxford.

Said R, 1993. *The River Nile; Geology, Hydrology and Utilization.* Oxford.

Salih F A, 1994. The excavation of tumulus (KE5) at Kawa, Sudan. *Sudan Archaeological Research Society Newsletter* 7: 26–30.

Vila A, 1979. *La prospection archéologique de la vallée du Nil au sud de la cataracte de Dal 11. Récapitulations et conclusions. Appendices.* Paris.

Welsby D A, 1993. Kawa Survey Project. *Sudan Archaeological Research Society Newsletter* 4: 3–7.

Welsby D A, 1995. The Northern Dongola Reach Survey. The 1994/5 season. *Sudan Archaeological Research Society Newsletter* 8: 2-7.

Welsby D A, 2001. *Life on the Desert Edge. 7000 Years of Settlement in the Northern Dongola Reach, Sudan.* Sudan Archaeological Research Society Publications 7. London.

Williams M A J and Adamson D A, 1980. Late Quaternary depositional history of the Blue Nile and White Nile rivers in central Sudan. In M A J Williams and H Faure (eds), *The Sahara and The Nile: Quaternary Environments and Prehistoric Occupation in Northern Africa.* Rotterdam: 281–304.

Woodward J C, Macklin M G and Welsby D A, 2001. The Holocene fluvial sedimentary record and alluvial geoarchaeology in the Nile Valley of Northern Sudan. In D Maddy, M G Macklin and J C Woodward (eds), *River Basin Sediment Systems: Archives of Environmental Change.* Rotterdam: 327–56.

Early and Mid-Holocene Ceramics from the Dakhleh Oasis: Traditions and Influences

Colin A Hope

During the last few decades an increasing number of scholars have expressed the opinion that the development of the earliest agricultural communities within Egypt and Nubia was influenced to varying degrees by Saharan traditions, and further, that domesticated cattle and goats and aspects of agriculture practice may have been introduced into the Nile Valley from the Western Desert. This influence has been postulated for communities throughout the lower and middle Nile, different parts of which, it has been suggested, shared different cultural traits with various parts of the desert to the west. In general it is thought that the Delta and Fayum may have been influenced by groups from the northern part of the desert in the vicinity of the Great Sand Sea (see Kuper this volume); that Upper Egypt came under the influence of cultures at home in the Kharga and Dakhleh Oases; and Nubia was influenced from the region of Nabta Playa.[1] This pattern is complicated by suggestions of less direct transfers of traits, possible influences and similarities. Thus it has been suggested that Merimde II was influenced from both the Sahara and Nubia (Eiwanger 1988, 52; Hayes 1965, 108, 114–5, 136) and Dakhleh (McDonald 1991a, 48); Fayum A from Uweinat (Banks 1980, 311), Nabta (Kozlowski and Ginter 1989, 176, 178), Dakhleh (McDonald 1991a, 48), Kharga (Hayes 1965, 101), regions further west (Arkell and Ucko 1965, 146–7), the Khartoum Neolithic (Arkell and Ucko 1965, 148–50) or from a mixture of these (Wenke 1999, 315); el-Omari from Dakhleh (McDonald 1991a, 48); the Badarian and early Naqada sites in the Khattara region from Nubia/Sudan (Friedman 1994, 519–23; Hays 1984, 217–8) and Saharan groups (Kaiser 1985; Friedman 1994, 20); the Abkan and Khartoum Variant from the Wadi Bakht (Banks 1984, 160); the Khartoum Variant from Kharga (Nordström 1972, 8–12); and finally Shaheinab from Dakhleh (McDonald 1991a, 49; 1992). That this situation resulted from the movement of peoples from the Sahara into the Nile Valley is generally gaining acceptance, the motivation for such transhumance being seen in the increasing aridity that occurred in the Sahara (Hassan 1986a; McDonald 1991a) especially coincident with the end of the seventh millennium bp (McDonald 1992, 65–6). The material discovered at Armant by Mond and Myers in the early 1930s, for example, may represent a settlement of these Saharan peoples on the edge of the cultivation (Myers 1937, 267–77; Hayes 1965, 102; Hoffman 1980, 227–43; D Darnell this volume).

The case for a significant role having been played by Dakhleh Oasis during the Holocene because of the favourable habitat that it provided has been argued by McDonald on various occasions (1991a; 1991b; 1992; 1998; 1999a; 1999b; 2001). In these discussions she has suggested that

cultural traits that are found throughout the lower and middle Nile occurred in Dakhleh considerably earlier and that their development can be documented in the oasis over several millennia. These traits include general aspects and details of the lithic technology, items of personal adornment, architecture and subsistence patterns (McDonald 1991a; 1992). Thus the cultural units of Dakhleh may have had a significant influence on neighbouring regions.

This idea was challenged some years ago by Tangri, who, in the late 1980s and early 1990s, studied the ceramics of the Holocene cultural units of Dakhleh under my supervision. Both in an undergraduate thesis presented at the University of Sydney (Tangri 1989) and a subsequent article (Tangri 1992), he attempted to refute McDonald's position and the suggestion that desertification prompted the movement of people into the Nile Valley from the west, thus denying any Saharan impact on the evolution of Nile Valley cultures within Egypt. A major element within his argument was that the ceramics from Dakhleh bore little resemblance to those of the earliest Egyptian communities. Unfortunately, Tangri appears to have confused material from the different cultural units. Further, when he wrote, the detailed radiocarbon chronology that now exists for the Dakhleh units (McDonald 2001) had not been established.[2] It is the purpose of the present paper to re-examine the ceramic data in the light of this chronology with the specific intention of determining whether it does confirm McDonald's theories.[3] I shall take the opportunity to present a characterisation of the material and also to identify imports into the oasis that might indicate the range of contacts the early oasis dwellers maintained. This reassessment has benefited from discussion with Rudolph Kuper and members of his *Besiedlungsgeschichte der Ost-Sahara* (BOS) project and, of course, Mary McDonald, who has patiently answered my numerous enquires.[4] I am most grateful to them all. A discussion of the composition of the ceramic materials used in the manufacture of the early and mid-Holocene Dakhleh material is presented by Mark Eccleston in the following paper.

I Traditions in the Early and Mid-Holocene Ceramics of Dakhleh Oasis

I.1 Early Holocene Masara Unit

The Masara Cultural Unit is the earliest to have been identified and it is dated between 9200–8500 bp on the basis of 18 uncalibrated radiocarbon dates (McDonald 2001; in press). It has been divided into three sub-units termed A–C, which appear to be contemporary (McDonald 1991b; 1991c; 1992; 1999; 2001; in press). Masara A and B sites are comprised of scatters of lithics associated with hearths, while Masara C sites contain clusters of hut foundations made of stone slabs with a rich assemblage of artefacts. Aspects of its lithic technology also distinguish Masara C from the other sub-units. It is suggested that Masara C sites indicate increased sedentism within the oasis, though these sites yield no definite evidence of herding or the cultivation of crops, while Masara A and B sites are those of specialist activity groups.

A distinctive pottery fabric profusely tempered with shale (Eccleston's Coarse Shale Fabric I) occurs on a few Masara A and B sites (*contra* McDonald 1998, 131); it is noticeable by its absence from Masara C sites. Sherds are fired a wide range of colours including greyish-green, brown, yellow, pink and black, often with numerous colours on the same sherd, and may be grey-black on the interior. The fabric has uncoated compacted surfaces and is fairly resistant to abrasion (Mohr 4.5–6.5). These features may have resulted from exposure to sand and wind blasting, phenomena that complicate the identification of original surface treatments on this and all early and mid-Holocene ceramic material, the vast majority of which comes from surface collections. This ware was used to manufacture thin and thick-walled, coil-built vessels (4–14 mm). No diagnostic pieces have been found but the vessels all appear to have been open forms. This fabric has been found on the surface of the following sites:[5]

Masara A: Loc. 259:   9 sherds
Masara B: Loc. 200:   5 sherds

In addition, considerable quantities were collected 200 m east of the Bashendi B site Loc. 271. Three collections from this site are comprised of the following: 12 sherds from one vessel with a wall thickness varying from 5.5 to 14 mm, with one sherd having a variation of 7.5–10.5 mm; 15 sherds from one vessel with noticeable inclusions of red pebbles; and 87 sherds possibly from the same vessel or several vessels with very similar firing patterns.

The only other Masara site to have yielded pottery is Loc. 76, located on the plateau above Maohub at the western end of the oasis. It is a Masara A site. Two sherds were found there, both in a distinctive fabric tempered profusely with quartz grains and pebbles of various colours up to 7 mm in length (Eccleston's Coarse Grit Fabric II). The surfaces of both are rough through erosion and they are fired light brown throughout. This fabric is not encountered on later sites. Some of the inclusions have been identified as possibly igneous in origin (see Eccleston this volume). If this is correct, then these sherds represent imports into Dakhleh from an as yet unidentified region.

The profusion and size of the inclusions in the coarse shale fabric may in themselves indicate production by a group experimenting with ceramic manufacture and one that had not yet discovered the benefits of levigating the clay body. This fabric may also be indicative of manufacture by people not permanently resident in the oasis, a scenario suggested for the Masara Unit folk in general, who were either unaware of, or who did not have the time to exploit, finer clay deposits. Interesting though such speculation may be, it should be pointed out that amongst the ceramic bodies utilised by the occupants of the oasis in the Old Kingdom there

was also a coarse shale-tempered fabric and its makers were experienced potters (Hope 1999). The two shale fabrics are quite distinct in terms of hardness, thickness and surface treatment. It has, however, been suggested (Ballet and Picon 1990, 80; Friedman 1994, 154–5, 631–2) that the quantity of shale inclusions helped such fabrics withstand thermal shock and made them suitable for the manufacture of cooking vessels.

Occasionally sherds of the coarse shale-tempered fabric are found on sites of later cultural units, namely:

Bashendi A:	Loc. 196	2 sherds
Bashendi B:	Loc. 252	1 sherd
	Loc. 257/257b	2 sherds
Sheikh Muftah:	Loc. 72	4 sherds
	Loc. 135	1 sherd
	Loc. 136	1 sherd

Similarly, sherds typical of later cultural units are occasionally found on Masara sites: at Loc. 243 and in its basin four Bashendi A–B sherds were found, and a single sherd of the same fabric was found at Loc. 259. The infrequency with which the shale-rich fabric occurs on sites of later date indicates that it is not to be attributed to these units. In addition, it should be emphasised that the coarse shale fabric was the only fabric noted at three separate places on Loc. 271 and also on Loc. 259. These factors appear to confirm its identification as an early Holocene manufacture and serve as another indication of the exceptional character of the Masara Unit. It seems to be the only early Holocene cultural unit noted to date north of the Salima Sandsheet, Kiseiba and Nabta, which is ceramic-producing, though contemporary and earlier groups further south in the Laqiya region (Kuper 1995, 129–30; this volume) and elsewhere in northeast Africa manufactured pottery from possibly as early as 10,060 ± 150 bp (Close 1995).

1.2 Mid-Holocene Bashendi Unit

On the basis of differing assemblages of artefacts the Bashendi Cultural Unit has been divided into two sub-units: A and B, the former further divided into Early A and Late A. The Bashendi A people appear to have been nomadic hunters, though at the end of Late Bashendi A pastoralism may have appeared during a phase of increased sedentism. The Bashendi B people were pastoral nomads (McDonald 1990, 38–9; 1991a, 43–8; 1998, 131–7; 1999b, 120–1, 127–8). The following time frames have been established for the phases of the Bashendi Unit on the basis of some 60 individual radiocarbon dates (McDonald 2001):

Bashendi A = 7600–6800 bp with clusters around 7300 and 6900 bp = Early A and Late A

Bashendi B = 6500–5200 bp with half of the dates falling between 6400–6100 bp.

Early Bashendi A does not have ceramics; they begin in Late A and become more common in B. Several Late A localities, however, have yielded dates in the mid- to late eighth millennium bp, raising the possibility that the two sub-units, distinguished on the basis of differing cultural traits, may have been in part contemporary.

I.2.1 Late Bashendi A

Ten Late Bashendi A sites have yielded ceramics.[6] The quantity on each site is small. I have examined a total of only 71 sherds, though the actual number may be slightly in excess of this figure.[7] The maximum number of sherds found on a site is five with the exception of Loc. 307,[8] from which I have examined 14 sherds, and Loc. 275[9] with 31 sherds. The latter were probably not made in Dakhleh and thus the total of oasis-manufactured sherds is approximately forty. The majority of these pieces are surface finds. Loc. 270 has yielded the only excavated sherd found to date; this derives from a sealed deposit in Grid B, feature 3, stratum 3 in Square J11d. Two samples from within feature 3 have yielded radiocarbon dates of 7120 ± 90 bp and 7110 bp. There are a total of 12 dates from this site commencing in 7340 bp and extending for a thousand years. The excavated sherd is small, eroded and affected by salt; the original shape cannot be determined. The fabric is extremely fine clay with a close-grained matrix and few visible inclusions other than fine quartz. It is fired brown (7.5YR 5–6/4) and has compacted surfaces.

This fabric, attested by only nine sherds,[10] represents a finer version of a fabric known from 25 sherds from this and other localities.[11] This has a fine-grained, close matrix that contains significant amounts of small inclusions of fine quartz and shale and is Eccleston's Fine Quartz and Shale Fabric IV (**Plates 45–46** [examples from Bashendi B Unit]). It is fired light grey-brown, with light brown exterior surfaces, occasionally with a yellowish (**Plate 47**) or reddish hue and grey interior surfaces; zoning is uncommon. The surfaces are normally uncoated, but all are lustrous and appear to have been compacted both inside and out. Some sherds display a rippled effect on their exterior (**Plate 47**, centre), but this seems to be the result of surface erosion. Indeed, it is uncertain how much of the compaction results from exposure to wind and sand.

Most of the surviving pieces are small and no diagnostics have been recovered, but the fabric was used for thin and medium thick-walled (3–8 mm), coiled, well-constructed vessels, probably mostly open bowls. One sherd from Loc. 174 may attest to the existence of a restricted form with thin walls (3.5–4 mm). An interesting feature of several sherds in this fabric is the occurrence of a deliberate blackening of the upper exterior (**Plate 47**, centre; **Plate 48**, lower left). A few display vertical and/or oblique short lines incised prior to firing (**Plate 48**, upper left).

Other fabrics are rare. Loc. 103 yielded four sherds in an uncoated quartz- and straw-tempered, brown-fired ware, which resembles that used for the impressed sherds found on the Bashendi B site Loc. 212 (discussed below), and a single sherd in an uncoated, quartz-rich fabric with little shale, which in turn recalls the fabric of 31 sherds found on Loc. 275 (discussed below). One sherd from Loc. 174 attests to a quartz-rich fabric which also contains white and opaque inclusions that are identified as gypsum and possibly microfossils (Eccleston's Coarse Calcareous Fabric V) (**Plate 48**, upper right). It is uncoated and fired light orange-brown. Fabrics possibly similar to this are known from Kharga and Bir Tirfawi (Banks 1980, 309, 313–4).

An extremely important collection of sherds originates from Loc. 275. Thirty-one pieces in all have been found in small clusters on various parts of the site. They are of a distinctive quartz-rich fabric that also contains small black, red and white pebbles (**Plate 49**; Eccleston's Coarse Quartz Fabric III). These sherds have a medium wall thickness of 6–8 mm, and a zoned firing pattern with brown (5YR 5/6–7.5YR 5–6/2–4) to reddish (2.5YR 5/6) surfaces. Six of these sherds have overall punctate decoration in rows, two have rows of punctates and incised lines, one has crescentic rows of punctates and one has festoons and rows of punctates (**Plates 50–51**). The fabric may indicate that these pieces were not manufactured in Dakhleh as such quartz-rich fabrics without shale are not a general characteristic of the ceramics found on other mid-Holocene sites in the oasis. Further, the decoration is clearly of the impressed, dotted-wavy line type belonging to the so-called Saharo-Sudanese horizon. Material decorated with similar motifs has been found in varying quantities from Shabona in the Sudan to Niger and north into Algeria and Libya, and within Egypt as far north as Farafra (Arkell 1949; Banks, 1980, 1984; Barich and Hassan 1990, 60; Close 1995; Kuper 1995, 129; Richter 1989). Some pieces from the region of the Gilf Kebir and Abu Ballas, however, are made in a quartz and shale-tempered fabric similar to that of the typical Late Bashendi A material (R Kuper, pers. comm. 1998). Whilst it has been shown that sherds from different localities within the area over which this decorative style occurs are made in different ceramic bodies (Hassan and Hays 1974; Hays 1975, 200; Francaviglia and Palmieri 1983), quartz-rich fabrics are ubiquitous in the region and thus the possible origin of the Dakhleh pieces cannot be determined. The presence of this pottery at Dakhleh and in Farafra (Barich and Hassan 1990, 60) suggests that people came to these oases who were from the south and/or southwest. Thus these oases shared in the extensive network of cultural exchange to which the wide distribution of this decorated pottery bears witness.

I.2.2 Bashendi B

Sherds have been retrieved in greater number from sites of the Bashendi B phase and there are in excess of 215 examples from 20 sites.[12] The dominant fabric continues to be the fine quartz- and shale-tempered fabric (**Plates 45–46**) used in the Late Bashendi A Unit, almost invariably with highly compacted surfaces (**Plate 47**). A few sherds display burnishing marks but most have an overall lustre that was probably produced by polishing. The firing pattern shows some zoning with grey cores and lighter red or brown surface zones, though the sections often display a grey inner zone and a brown outer zone. A few are fired light grey (**Plate 52**, upper row; **Fig. 1** n–o). Many pieces have an exterior surface that displays various colours, predominantly brown or reddish-brown, and some have black or grey patches. Such surfaces are darker than the body and appear to result from a self-slip. Whilst some sherds are hard, the majority are quite soft and easily broken. Wall thickness varies from 3.5–7 mm but is mostly within the range of 3.5–5 mm; thicker sherds originate from near the base of the vessel. Other surface treatments encountered with this fabric are a red-coated

Table 1: Frequency of fabric and surface treatments in Bashendi B ceramics.

Fabric Group (after Eccleston this volume)	Uncoated	Self-slipped & compacted	Red-coated & compacted	Black-topped	Decorated
IV: Quartz and Shale		126	14	6	12
IV: Finer version		14			
V: Gypsum and Quartz	36				
–: Quartz and Straw					6
IX: Quartz					1

and compacted exterior surface and a black-topped, compacted exterior. Vessels are again coil built.

Other fabrics also occur, all of which are found on Late Bashendi A sites as well. They include: the finer version of the common quartz- and shale-tempered fabric again with compacted surfaces; the sandy, gypsum-tempered fabric that also contains microfossils (Eccleston's Coarse Calcareous Fabric V); the quartz- and straw-rich fabric; and a quartz-rich fabric (Eccleston's Coarse Quartz Fabric III). The sherds in the gypsum-tempered fabric are all eroded so it is not possible to determine the original nature of their surfaces; this fabric is most common on Bashendi B sites. The sherds in the straw-rich fabric all preserve impressed decoration, while the one sherd in the quartz-rich fabric has black-fired surfaces and incised rim decoration. These decorative elements will be discussed further below. The frequency of the different fabrics is summarised in **Table 1**.

The count in **Table 1** does not include the intact jar illustrated in **Fig. 1** t. With regard to the distribution of these fabrics, Group IV has been found on 19 sites, and its finer version has been found on four sites.[13] Fabric Group V occurs on five sites[14] and the final two fabrics have been recovered on one site each.[15] There is only one Bashendi B site that has not yielded an example of Fabric Group IV, namely Loc. 200W, but a single sherd of Fabric Group V was found there. The majority of sites have yielded less than 15 sherds each, and many less than five. Localities 212 and 254 are exceptional in this regard as some 80 sherds have been found at Loc. 212 and 40 at Loc. 254; thus they account for approximately half of the entire collection.

As a result of the fragmentary nature and size of most of the finds it is not possible to identify with certainty the shapes in which the various wares occurred. Fortunately a number of diagnostics have been recovered. These show that the shape repertoire was dominated by deep, open and slightly-restricted bowls, some quite large, and that jars were uncommon (**Figs 1–3**). Naturally, the majority of the forms illustrated occur in the self-slipped and compacted, fine quartz- and shale-tempered fabric (Group IV). The bowls illustrated in **Fig. 2** m-n, with their distinctly modelled rim formation, are made in the gypsum-tempered fabric (Group V); those illustrated in **Fig. 1** t and **Fig. 2** p are made in the quartz- and straw-tempered fabric, while that in **Fig. 1** h is made in the quartz-tempered fabric (Eccleston Group X).

Amongst the shapes of these undoubtedly local manufac-tured vessels, those shown in **Fig. 2** b and **Fig. 3** a are of particular interest as they are the only definite jars in Fabric Group IV. The jar in **Fig. 2** b has a dark brown-fired surface, probably a self-slip, with a distinct black top, while that in **Fig. 3** a is also brown-fired and has irregular dark grey to black patches on its exterior. The more open vessel illustrated in **Fig. 2** a is made in a similar ware, though the lowest part of the body is fired red. The site from which the latter originates (Loc. 104) yielded many small sherds probably from a few vessels, including at least one other black-topped bowl. The bowls in **Fig. 2** k and **Fig. 3** c are also brown-fired with compacted surfaces.

Decoration on Dakhleh-made ceramics of the Bashendi B Cultural Unit is rare. Two bowls have pre-firing, rim-top incisions (**Fig. 1** o-p; **Plate 52**), one of which has in addition light, oblique grooves in its surface (**Fig. 1** o; **Plate 52**, upper right). These grooves also occur on another rim sherd from a bowl of the same shape (**Fig. 1** n) and on a body sherd (**Fig. 3** e). The two bowls with oblique grooves are fired light grey, as is another sherd, probably also from the same shape and from the same site, which also has these grooves (**Plate 52**, upper left). Vertical or oblique rows of fingernail incisions made before firing occur on a few sherds as they do in the Late Bashendi A Unit. One sherd, a rim from a coiled bowl (**Fig. 2** f), has very shallow oblique lines that are barely visible. Repair holes occur infrequently (**Fig. 1** i and r).

More elaborate decoration occurs on seven sherds from Loc. 74 (**Fig. 1** a–f; **Plate 53**). These sherds preserve a motif of incised triangles filled with vertical or horizontal rows of impressed dashes or dots, apparently arranged in several rows between incised lines. One sherd also has short oblique dashes incised on its interior (**Fig. 1** a). These examples are all made in the typical fine quartz- and shale-tempered fabric but with uncompacted, blackened or greyed surfaces. Parallels for these decorated sherds may exist at Nabta Playa (Banks 1980, 306), Gebel Uweinat (Banks 1980, 311–3), Wadi Bakht (McHugh 1975, 53–4; Banks 1984, 156–60) and Wadi el-Akhdar (Kuper 1981, 250). Material reported by Arkell (1949, 93–4) from Khartoum is not dissimilar, especially as the pieces have decoration both inside and out.

Rim notches occur over a wide area at various times: e.g., from the Khartoum Mesolithic (Arkell 1949, 84); amongst A-Group material (Nordström 1972, pl. 24); on Badarian and early Naqada sites (Friedman 1994, 199); at Abu

Locality 74: (31/420-C10-2)

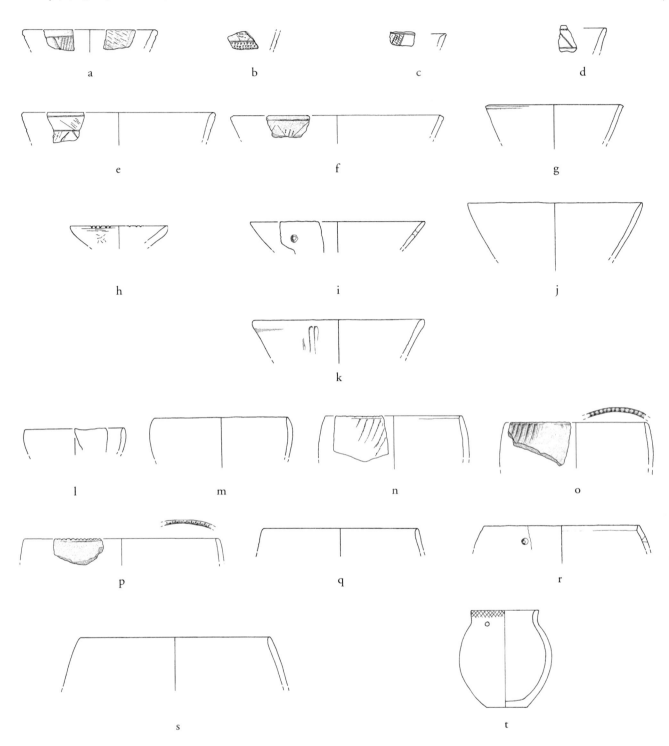

Fig. 1   Ceramics of the Bashendi B Cultural Unit, Dakhleh Oasis. Scale 1:4.

Munqar and in the region of the Gilf Kebir (Kuper 1995, 129–30); and in the Great Sand Sea (Kuper 1989, 200). None of this material, however, has exactly the same triangular motifs as the Dakhleh sherds. This motif may indicate that these vessels were locally manufactured; the fabric in which they are made would also tend to confirm this, though quartz- and shale-tempered fabrics are also found in the

regions to the south of Dakhleh (R Kuper, pers. comm. 1998).

The site from which most of this decorated material comes, Loc. 74, has also yielded the only example from Dakhleh of a short-necked jar with flat base and incised decoration on the upper exterior of the neck (**Fig. 1** t). Unlike the material just described, it is probably not a Dakhleh

Locality 104: (31/420-M9-2)

Locality 116: (31/435-A6-3)

Locality 212: (30/450-C6-1)

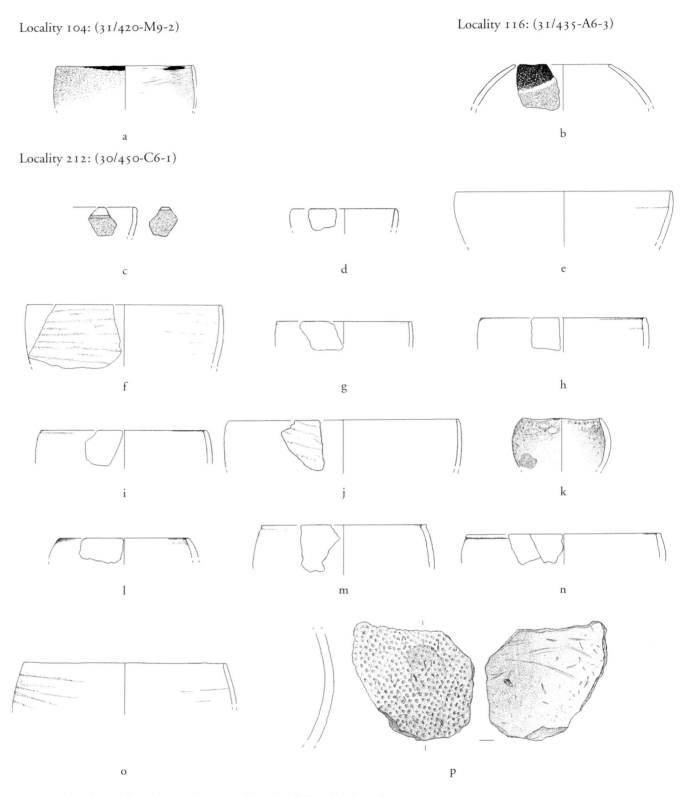

Fig. 2   Ceramics of the Bashendi B Cultural Unit, Dakhleh Oasis. Scale 1:4.

manufacture. It is 103 mm high and has a rim diameter of 69 mm; the surface is fired light red with grey patches and there are straw impressions on the surface.[16] Two opposing holes perforate the upper body. The use of straw as a temper is not typical of early to mid-Holocene ceramics from the oasis. The shape can certainly be paralleled amongst the

wide range of small jars from Ma'adi of type 5a, which are mostly made in a grit-tempered fabric with some organic material, and fired either black or reddish-brown (Rizkana and Seeher 1987, 23–6). None of the published jars from Ma'adi has the same decoration as the Dakhleh jar. If this jar is a Ma'adi ware, then it would most likely be intrusive to

Locality 254: (30/450-B10-1)

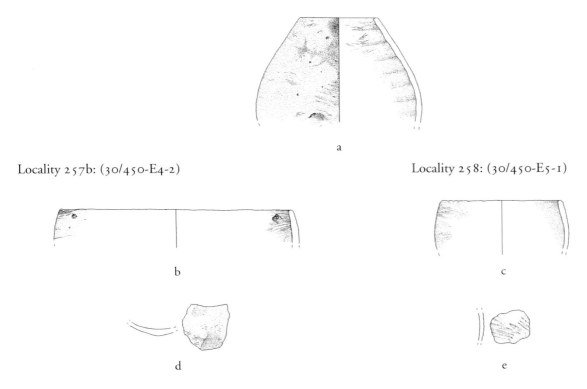

Locality 257b: (30/450-E4-2)

Locality 258: (30/450-E5-1)

Fig. 3   Ceramics of the Bashendi B Cultural Unit, Dakhleh Oasis. Scale 1:4.

Loc. 74, as the site of Ma'adi appears to post-date the Bashendi B Cultural Unit. Similar decoration does, however, occur on some Khartoum Variant pottery (Nordström 1972, 76 type RB 14, pls 24 and 121.12–3).

Another interesting find from Loc. 74 is a rim sherd probably from a shallow bowl (**Fig. 1** h), though there is some uncertainty about this due to the small size of the piece. It is made in a quartz-rich fabric, fired grey-black throughout, with black surfaces (Eccleston's Quartz-tempered Fabric IX; Eccleston's Sample 20). The rim is notched. The surfaces are uneven though the exterior may have been polished. At first glance it resembles the more elaborately-decorated sherds from the same site in terms of its fired colour, but the quantity of quartz temper it contains distinguishes it from them and most other Dakhleh fabrics, and indicates that it is probably an import. The size of its rim notches also differs from those on locally-made vessels. Despite its small size, it is tempting to attribute this sherd to the Khartoum Variant or Abkan traditions of Lower Nubia, with a preference for the former (Nordström 1972, 48–50, 57–60; pl. 121. 22–3, 25–31 and pl. 141.2).

The final pieces to be discussed here come from Loc. 212, and are all made in a sandy, straw-rich fabric. There are six sherds, all of which bear an overall impressed design (**Fig. 2** p; **Plate 54**) that has been interpreted as indicating that the vessel from which they originate, assuming that they all come from the same one, was made inside a woven basket (Tangri 1991). Whilst the impressions certainly resemble basketry, a close study of the pieces indicates that the decoration was impressed with a tool and there are irregularities

in the directions of the impressions that are inconsistent with basket weave. The design is best characterised as imitation basketry or woven mat. The fabric is very distinctive and clearly not local. There is a large quantity of quartz grains of various sizes and numerous impressions from organic material; these are predominantly long and thin, with one 80 mm in length (**Fig. 2** p). Wall thickness varies from 6 to 10 mm. The sherds are fired with a grey core, have brown and red zones, and brown surfaces. Designs in imitation of basketry have been recorded from various sites in the Nile Valley and Sahara, often on organic-tempered pottery, of widely varying dates. From regions west of Tibesti it occurs on several sites from the second half of the tenth millennium bp (Roset 1987; Smith 1980, 452) until the mid-fifth millennium (Gabriel 1981, 203; Smith 1980, 455; Vita-Finzi and Kennedy 1965, 198, 203). From the mid-eighth millennium onwards the motif is known from Gebel Uweinat (Banks 1980, 311), Wadi Bakht (Banks 1984, 159), Nabta Playa (Banks 1980, 304) and Bir Tirfawi (Banks 1980, 313–4). It occurs on Khartoum Mesolithic (Arkell 1949, 82–3, 87–8)[17] and Khartoum Variant pottery (Nordström 1972, pls 60 and 122).

1.3   The Sheikh Muftah Unit

Only two reliable dates are available for the final mid to late Holocene cultural unit from Dakhleh: 5070 and 4310 bp. These can only serve, therefore, as a rough indication of the temporal duration over which the Sheikh Muftah Unit lasted. This is particularly so of its commencement and it is possible that it developed out of the Bashendi B or was coexistent with its final stages. A certain overlapping with Bashendi B is indicated by the similarity in the ceramics and also by the discovery of what may be Badarian-related material on some Sheikh Muftah sites.[18] Archaeological evidence indicates that the Sheikh Muftah Unit survived until the late Old Kingdom. Several Sheikh Muftah sites lie adjacent to contemporary sites that display an entirely Egyptian, that is Nile Valley, material culture. On the basis of artefactual assemblages it is possible to distinguish an early or transitional phase from a later one within this unit: the former possibly contemporary with the late Badarian to Naqada IIc of the Nile Valley and the latter with Naqada IIc/d[19] to Dynasty VI. After that time evidence for a distinctive Dakhleh material culture is non-existent. In both phases pottery was certainly far more common than in earlier cultural units and it occurs on all Sheikh Muftah Cultural Unit sites of which there are more than seventy.

I.3.1 Early Sheikh Muftah

Seven sites only are tentatively ascribed to an early phase within the Sheikh Muftah Cultural Unit based upon both the characteristics of the lithic technology and also the ceramics, which display features in common with those of the Bashendi B Cultural Unit. Thus, the fine quartz- and shale-tempered fabric known from both phases of the Bashendi Cultural Unit occurs, employed in the manufacture of thin-walled, coil-built vessels with compacted surfaces, the shapes of some of which resemble those of the earlier unit. Associated with such material is a coarser quartz- and shale-tempered fabric often with striated surfaces, occasional blackened rims and smoke patches, which eventually became the dominant material on later Sheikh Muftah Unit sites. The striations (rilling/finger tracks) appear to result both from brushing with reeds and pressure from the potters' fingers. The fabric is defined as coarse because it contains larger, more frequent quartz grains and a rougher surface; however, the basic clay body is very similar to that of the fine quartz- and shale-fabric.

Of the seven early sites (Locs 35, 72, 118, 135, 138, 221 and 381), a selection of the pottery from two (Locs 35 and 135) is illustrated here (Figs 4–5). These two sites have yielded the most significant collections and include examples of all of the characteristic types. The ceramic repertoire at Loc. 35 (Fig. 4; Plate 55–56) includes open bowls (Fig. 4 a-f, i) and small to large jars (Fig. 4 l-r) in the fine quartz- and shale-tempered fabric. Amongst both shape groups are examples with red-coated, compacted surfaces and blackened rims and some with brown rather than red surfaces (Fig. 4 a, i, m-q; Plate 55). The bowls also have compacted interiors.

Decoration is restricted to rim notches (Fig. 4 b, d-f, r), occasional controlled oblique or vertical ridges (Fig. 4 r; Plate 55, top right), and incised lines (Plate 56, bottom). There is one sherd only with a closely spaced, incised design of zigzags that may have been executed in a rocker technique (Fig. 4 t; Plate 56, top left). A single sherd from Loc. 24 (Fig. 6 n) preserves a motif executed in a similar technique. A few sherds preserve vertical rows of fingernail incisions, examples of which occur at Loc. 381 also. One sherd (Fig. 4 s; Plate 56 top right) has a more elaborate incised design of

triangles filled with lines; the exterior surface has a red coating. This motif occurs on A-Group pottery (Nordström 1972, 76, pl. 25, Group 2 no. 11); however, the fabric of the sherd from Loc. 35 is fine quartz- and shale-tempered and appears local to Dakhleh or this part of the Western Desert. Parallels to the rocker design of zigzags are also encountered within A-Group and Abkan material (Nordström 1972, 76, pl. 25, Group 1 nos 16–19), and in the Wadi Shaw (Schuck 1989, 426).

Forms occurring in the coarser quartz- and shale-tempered fabric are all bowls (Fig. 4 g-h, j-k). These display a rough, striated surface and some have blackened rims. The walls of such vessels tend to be thicker than those of similar form in the finer version of the fabric.

The repertoire at Loc. 135 comprises, in general, a similar selection of material to that found at Loc. 35; the illustrations included here (Fig. 5 c-h, j-p; Plate 57) have been selected to show the forms that differ from those illustrated from Loc. 35 and those that occur mostly in the coarser quartz- and shale-tempered fabric. Examples from specific clusters on the site are marked accordingly within the figure. The examples illustrated in Fig. 5 e-f, m, o (Plate 57 upper right) are red-coated, compacted and have blackened rims. The vessel shown in Fig. 5 l is in a similar ware but has random blackened areas. This vessel introduces a type that occurs regularly on Sheikh Muftah sites: its shape resembles that of an inverted, truncated cone and it is open at both ends. Its function has yet to be determined, but it is undoubtedly connected with the perforated ceramic disks (Fig. 5 p) regularly found on the same sites, examples of which have been found inside them in regions south of Dakhleh (R Kuper, pers. comm. 1998). Very similar forms have also been found in the Eastern Desert (Murray 1939),[20] and perforated disks occur over a wide area (Caton-Thompson 1952, 43; see D Darnell this volume).

Amongst the material from the other early Sheikh Muftah sites (not illustrated), a few of the more interesting pieces may be noted. Loc. 72 yielded numerous sherds from a conical bowl with a pointed base, a pinched tapering rim only 4 mm thick, and a shallow rippled/rilled exterior surface that was fired light brown to reddish-brown. Its shape resembles that of later Sheikh Muftah Unit bowls (e.g., Fig. 8 a) but the fabric is low-fired and contains fine quartz and shale; thus it is similar to the Bashendi B Unit material. One other sherd in the same fabric, fired grey, is decorated with small impressed circles probably made with a hollow reed, possibly within triangles, below a continuous band of similarly-executed circles; it may have come from a closed vessel.

Localities 35, 72 and 135 have all yielded imports from the Egyptian Nile Valley. From Loc. 35 come three sherds in Nile B1 fabric (Nordström and Bourriau 1993, 171); two have reddish-brown compacted surfaces and one a red, compacted surface below a blackened area (i.e., Petrie's Black-topped Red ware). The former are apparently compacted on the interior and thus derive from bowls while the latter is probably from a small ovoid jar of early Naqada type. The identity of these three sherds as Nile Valley products has been confirmed by X-Ray Diffraction (XRD) (Segnit 1987).

Locality 135 has yielded two sherds of the same material;

Locality 35: (31/405-G6-1)

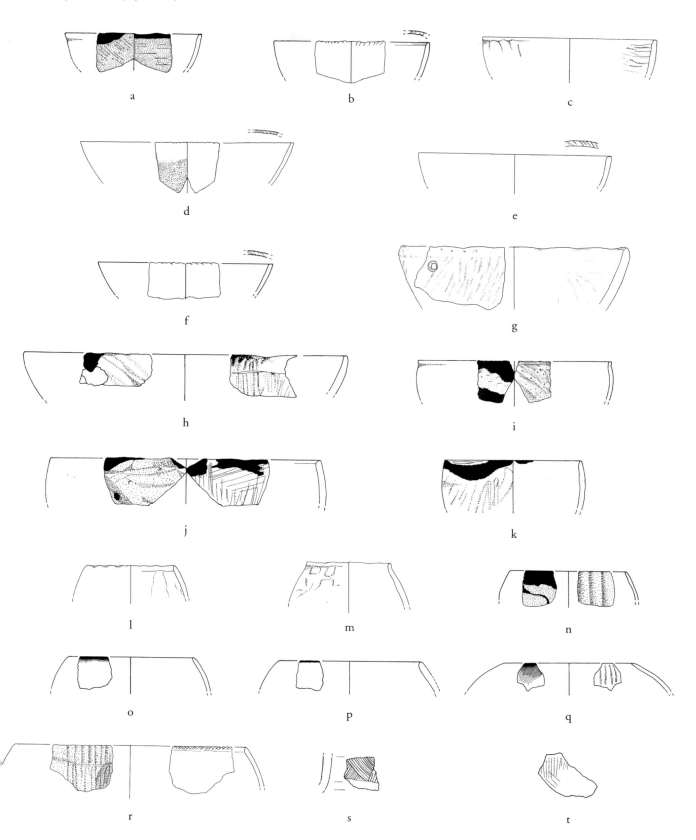

Fig. 4 Ceramics of the Early Sheikh Muftah Cultural Unit, Dakhleh Oasis. Scale 1:4

one is a body sherd from a closed form and the other is a rim from a small restricted bowl (**Fig. 5** i; **Plate 57** bottom right). The exterior surface is eroded but clearly once had a compacted black section at the rim above a brown, possibly compacted body; the interior of the fragment is black fired and burnished.[21] This piece resembles Badarian Black-topped Brown ware, Brunton and Caton-Thompson's (1928, pl. XIV) type BB57E, though the fabric is coarser than that normally employed for Badarian pottery with much quartz and straw, especially visible on the eroded exterior (cf. Eccleston's Fabric VI, Sample 15). For the moment no certain identification can be made of the piece and it may prove to be of later date or from Nubia. It is of interest to note that Badarian pottery has recently been found on the desert routes leading into Kharga (D Darnell this volume). From Loc. 135 also comes a ceramic 'spoon' (**Fig. 5** a) in a compacted, brown-fired, fine Nile silt fabric similar to examples from Mostagedda (Brunton 1937, pl. XVIII, 36–7).

Locality 72 has produced two sherds in a very distinctive fabric attesting to another import from the Nile Valley. These sherds are fired dull brown with grey to black cores and profusely tempered with crushed gypsum and thin organic material (Eccleston's Straw- and Gypsum-tempered Fabric, VIII). The fabric has parallels from Hierakonpolis, and may be equated with Petrie's Rough Ware (see Eccleston this volume).

The final piece to be mentioned here is a small sherd from a so-called Tasian beaker (**Fig. 10** c), which was found near Loc. 304, southeast of Teneida in an area with numerous rock art sites. Loc. 304 has a general scatter of Bashendi B material but whether the beaker sherd can be associated with this is uncertain, though chronologically possible.[22] The sherd is brown-fired with a black surface and carries an incised design of triangles.[23] Tasian material has also recently been found in the region west of Thebes on the Farshût Road (D Darnell this volume), whence depart routes leading out into the Western Desert, indicating possible contact between this ill-defined group and the latter region.

A further import from Loc. 135 is illustrated in **Fig. 5** b and **Plate 58**. Although only partly reconstructed, the vessel form is quite distinctive, being almost globular with a short everted neck, thickened rim, and round base. The fabric is hard and well-fired with brown surfaces and a grey core; it is tempered with quartz and straw. The body is covered with an impressed design imitating a basket weave. In terms of decoration and temper this vessel recalls the sherds found on the Bashendi B site Loc. 212 mentioned above (**Fig. 2** p), but in contrast, its fired colour, hardness and wall thickness are quite different. A similar provenance can, however, be suggested, but from a later culture contemporary in part with the Sheikh Muftah, namely the Tenerian of Central Niger, which produced thin-walled globular jars with everted necks and impressed decoration in straw/grass-tempered hard fabrics (Smith 1980, 455, fig. 18.6, photos 18.3 and 18.5). It may be noted that a few fragments possibly from jars of a similar shape, though with flat bases, also decorated in imitation of basketry have been found at Ain en Raml in Farafra. The fabric contains seeds. The date of the pieces is, however, uncertain (M Gatto, pers. comm. 1999).

I.3.2 Late Sheikh Muftah

The ceramics of the later Sheikh Muftah Cultural Unit are characterized by the dominant use of a coarser version of the quartz- and shale-tempered fabric, which was in use throughout the Bashendi Cultural Unit until the early Sheikh Muftah (Eccleston's Fine Quartz and Shale Fabric, IV).[24] In this coarser version, the inclusions occur in larger sizes and possibly greater frequencies than previously, and the surface has a gritty texture and is mostly uncoated and neither compacted nor burnished. The colour of the fired surface varies considerably from grey to red even on the same vessel, indicating firing in bonfire conditions; blackened patches occur regularly. This fabric is employed for a range of open to slightly restricted, small to large bowls (**Figs 6–11** from various sites). The sides are always convex, the bases round or slightly pointed, and the rims direct. The vessels are coil-built with the coil junctions clearly visible in many cases. The walls tend to be thicker than on vessels of the Bashendi Cultural Unit.

The occurrence of vertical and oblique, sometimes random rilling is extremely common. This normally occurs on the exterior only, though there are a few vessels that display vertical grooves produced by the fingers on the interior (**Fig. 10** b). Decoration is rare and restricted to occasional rim notches and incised lines (**Fig. 6** a-b), unless, of course, the rilling is to be considered a decorative effect, which, given its frequency, is quite possible. Horizontal rows of fingernail incisions occur (**Fig. 6** l, **8** e), but whether this is a deliberate decorative effect is uncertain. The same uncertainty applies to the undulating rim tops of some vessels (**Figs 7** g, **8** a, **9** c-e and **10** e), which may simply be a result of careless manufacturing techniques. In general, pottery of this phase of the Sheikh Muftah Unit presents a much rougher appearance than that of the preceding phase and the Bashendi Cultural Unit.

The unusual vessels open at both ends and the perforated disks, noted first in the earlier phase of the Sheikh Muftah Unit, appear more frequently in this later phase (**Figs 7** d-e, g, and **11** a). Vessels of this phase regularly have post-firing perforations in the upper wall (**Figs 8** d, **9** e, **10** a-b). Whether they represent ancient repairs or holes for suspension is uncertain.[25] It is conceivable that in some cases they were for the attaching of lids, though no fragments of such have been identified.

Two other characteristics of the Late Sheikh Muftah Cultural Unit distinguish it from proceeding periods. First, the compacted, brown-fired, fine quartz and shale ware, which was used for thin-walled vessels, is no longer encountered. Thus came to an end a tradition that is the most characteristic of ceramic manufactures in Dakhleh and one that had been dominant for over two thousand years. The reason for this and the precise time of its disappearance is as yet unknown. Second is the use of a coarse shale-tempered fabric. This fabric resembles the Coarse Shale Fabric of the Masara Cultural Unit but it is not so hard and the walls of vessels made in this fabric are generally thinner than those of the Masara Unit. Whilst the dominant fabrics of the Bashendi Cultural Unit contain shale, it is in small sizes that do

Locality 135: (30/450-B4-1)

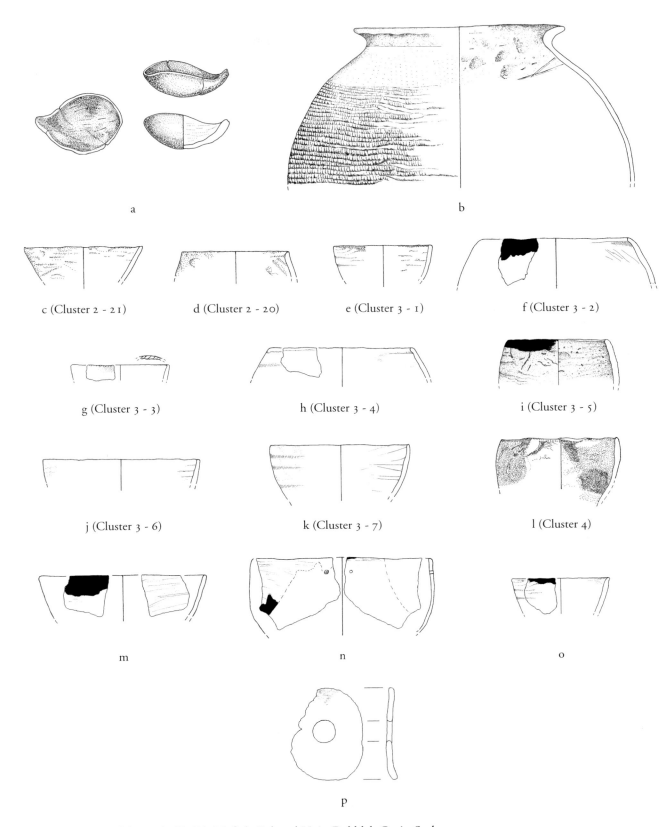

a

b

c (Cluster 2 - 21)

d (Cluster 2 - 20)

e (Cluster 3 - 1)

f (Cluster 3 - 2)

g (Cluster 3 - 3)

h (Cluster 3 - 4)

i (Cluster 3 - 5)

j (Cluster 3 - 6)

k (Cluster 3 - 7)

l (Cluster 4)

m

n

o

p

Fig. 5   Ceramics of the Early Sheikh Muftah Cultural Unit, Dakhleh Oasis. Scale 1:4.

Locality 2: (33/390-I9-1)

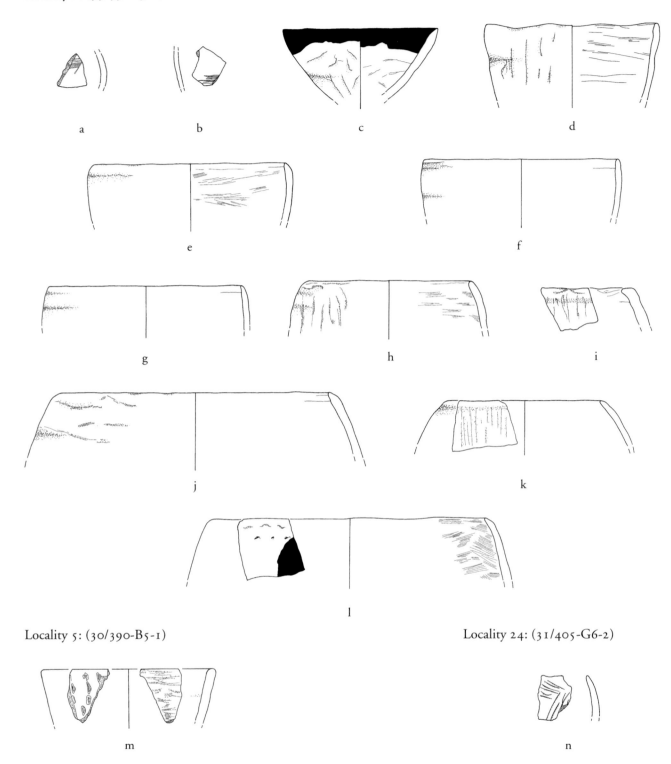

Locality 5: (30/390-B5-1)

Locality 24: (31/405-G6-2)

Fig. 6   Ceramics of the Late Sheikh Muftah Cultural Unit, Dakhleh Oasis. Scale 1:4.

not affect the texture and fired appearance of the fabrics. The use of coarse shale-tempered fabrics during the earlier part of the Late Sheikh Muftah Cultural Unit is shown by sherd material from various sites and a finely-constructed and finished bowl from Loc. 222 (**Fig. 10** a and **Plate 59**). The surface of this vessel is fired a variety of colours from orange to red and brown, and the exterior is compacted and displays controlled rilling. A 'mosaic' fired appearance is typical of the shale fabrics.

During what may be the later part of the Late Sheikh Muftah Cultural Unit a red-coated and compacted, coarse shale-tempered ware is regularly used for large bowls. It is uncertain whether this should be assigned exclusively to the Sheikh Muftah people as it is common on Egyptian sites of late Old Kingdom date within the oasis in similar shapes (Ballet and Picon 1990; Hope 1999). Sites of both the Sheikh Muftah and Egyptian groups are found in close proximity and it is possible that the use of shale wares on Egyptian sites was inspired by the Sheikh Muftah potters.

Sites of the Late Sheikh Muftah Cultural Unit have yielded a small number of sherds that attest to imports from the Nile Valley. Three sherds in the gypsum- and straw-tempered fabric (Eccleston's Fabric VIII), first noted on Loc. 72 of the earlier Sheikh Muftah, have been found, one on Loc. 69 and two on Loc. 100 (one is Eccleston's Sample 11). Two are rims from deep bowls and the other is a body sherd (**Plate 60**).

A body sherd from a restricted vessel with a row of short vertical incisions (**Fig. 7** c) found on Loc. 69 is probably also an import; the fine fabric contains fine organic temper. The shape recalls that of the small jars of type 5a from Ma'adi, which were sometimes decorated with a single row of impressed dots on the shoulder (Rizkana and Seeher 1987, 39; pls. 34–5). These jars are often made in a red burnished ware, tempered with quartz and sometimes crushed limestone (Ma'adi Ware II). Although similar, the Dakhleh sherd differs from them in the placement of the decoration, its type (dashes not dots) and its ware. Closer similarities may exist with Petrie's (1921, pl. XIII) P76 series, a Lower Egyptian type closely associated with Buto.[26] Such jars are regularly made in what Köhler (1998, 10–11) has termed fibre-ware, and have incised decoration of varying complexity executed in dashes, a decorative effect that also occurs on larger vessels and is known from Buto Schicht I and especially Schicht II (von der Way 1997, 99–100, 189–91, pls. 41–2). If the identification of the sherd from Loc. 69 as being from one of these Buto vessels is correct then this provides a valuable indication that the late phase of the Sheikh Muftah Cultural Unit had developed by Naqada IIc-d1, with which Schicht II at Buto was contemporary (von der Way 1991; 1992; Faltings 1998).

From Loc. 69 also come three rim sherds from jars with distinct modelled rims and short, wheel-turned necks, made in a fine Marl A fabric tempered with limestone, one of which is red-coated. They are clearly from Early Dynastic storage jars. Sherds in the same fabric (Eccleston's Fabric XI) have been found at Loc. 59 (see Eccleston's discussion of two from this site, Samples 2–3), Loc. 170, near sites with petroglyphs, and as isolated finds. A few of these sherds have incised marks, a feature not encountered on locally-manufactured pottery. Further examples of this type of pottery have recently been discovered on routes leading into Kharga (D Darnell this volume). At Loc. 170 sherds in this fabric occurred with others in Nile silt fabrics, further examples of which have been found at Locs 136, 139, 256 and 382. Of these, two have profuse straw-temper and also quartz. One, from Loc. 139, located atop the escarpment near Teneida, is from the base of a restricted vessel, probably a jar; it has a brown-fired exterior with vertical streak burnish. Another piece, from Loc. 136, is the rim and wall from a bowl with a deep red-coated exterior surface and compacted exterior and interior.

Two final sherds remain to be mentioned. One (**Plate 61**) is a small sherd from Loc. 48, which is made in a hard-fired fabric with inclusions of limestone (Eccleston's Limestone-tempered Fabric VII) and a distinct greyish-brown core and red zones. The surfaces are grey and the exterior is covered with impressed, irregularly-shaped depressions resembling a basketry design similar to that on the large jar from the early, or transitional, Sheikh Muftah Unit Loc.135 (**Fig. 5** b). The fabric is distinct from that of this earlier example. Because of its small size, the shape of the vessel from which the Loc. 48 sherd derives cannot be determined. For the same reason it is not possible to determine the technique in which the decoration was executed. As woven-basket motifs occur over a wide geographic distribution,[27] it is not possible to suggest a provenance.

The other piece is also somewhat enigmatic. It is an isolated find on a Middle Palaeolithic site, Loc. 5, and thus the find context provides no assistance with its dating. The fragment is a rim sherd from a deep bowl with slightly everted sides and a rounded, direct rim (**Fig. 6** m; **Plate 62**). It is fired grey throughout and originally had black compacted surfaces; the fabric is fine-grained, silty and contains quartz and possibly ash temper (Eccleston's Ash-tempered Fabric X). The exterior preserves vertical impressions that were made with either a fingernail of the potter's left hand or with a two-toothed implement. The fabric resembles Nordström's (1972, 51) Fabric IIA, and the fired colour and surface treatment resembles his Ware Group H3, possibly Ware H3.01 belonging to the A-Group (Nordström 1972, 62–3). The shape of the Dakhleh piece, however, is dissimilar to those published by Nordström for this ware, although it does resemble one that occurs in a brown and black polished ware (H4.01), which employs Fabric IIA, with quite different decoration (Nordström 1972, 87 Type AVIIA, pl. 41). Similar decoration does occur on a few sherds from the A-Group site 430, made in different fabrics (Nordström 1972, 236, pl. 137 nos 1–3 and 7). It should be noted that ash-tempered pottery has also been recorded at Nabta Playa in Late Neolithic contexts (R Friedman, pers. comm 1998).

I.4 Comments

In relation to what is known of the trends in the manufacture of ceramics during the early and mid-Holocene in northeast Africa those from Dakhleh Oasis present some interesting variations. Early Holocene ceramics in Dakhleh are undecorated unlike those from elsewhere (Close 1995; Kuper this volume). The mid-Holocene ceramics are characterized by thin-walled vessels with compacted or burnished surfaces, and the majority is also undecorated. Ceramics decorated in the techniques and motifs known from early Holocene traditions elsewhere to the south and west (Saharo-Sudanese decorative horizon) only occur in the mid-Holocene Late Bashendi A Cultural sub-Unit and are imports. Fine, undecorated and compacted wares apparently occur much earlier than in other parts of the region, from at least 7380 ± 120 bp at the Late Bashendi A site Loc. 261 for example, rather than circa 6000 bp as has been noted elsewhere (Close 1995, 26; Kuper 1995, 130). From Late Bashendi A the potters of Dakhleh occasionally produced

Locality 39: (31/405-E8-1)

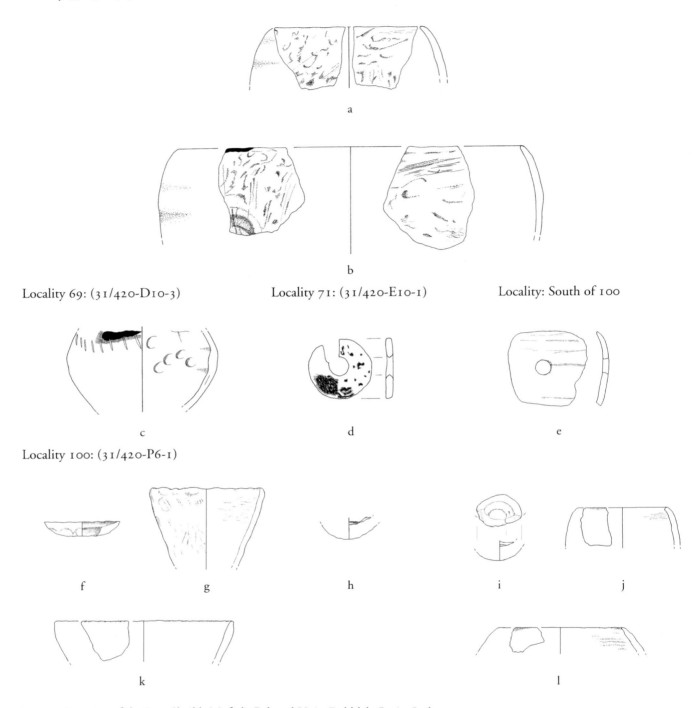

Locality 69: (31/420-D10-3)   Locality 71: (31/420-E10-1)   Locality: South of 100

Locality 100: (31/420-P6-1)

Fig. 7   Ceramics of the Late Sheikh Muftah Cultural Unit, Dakhleh Oasis. Scale 1:4.

black-topped wares. In general, the mid-Holocene ceramics of Dakhleh Oasis appear to resemble those from the Gilf Kebir more so than elsewhere (Kuper 1995, 129), and the repertoire is dominated by bowls. Ceramics indicate that the Dakhleh occupants maintained contacts with regions far to the west, to the south and southeast during the Bashendi B and early Sheikh Muftah Cultural Units, while imports from the Predynastic cultures of Egypt occur from the early phase of the Sheikh Muftah Cultural Unit onward in small numbers.

The growing frequency of pottery from the Masara Unit through the phases of the Bashendi and into the Sheikh Muftah Unit may be linked with the increased level of sedentism amongst these Dakhleh groups. This is a relationship that is considered to hold true in other ceramic-producing cultures throughout North Africa (Close 1995). As in those regions also, the development of pottery cannot be linked directly with sedentism,[28] agriculture or pastoralism, though both of these subsistence mechanisms were relied upon with growing frequency commensurate with the quantity of pot-

Locality 143: (30/435-B6-1)

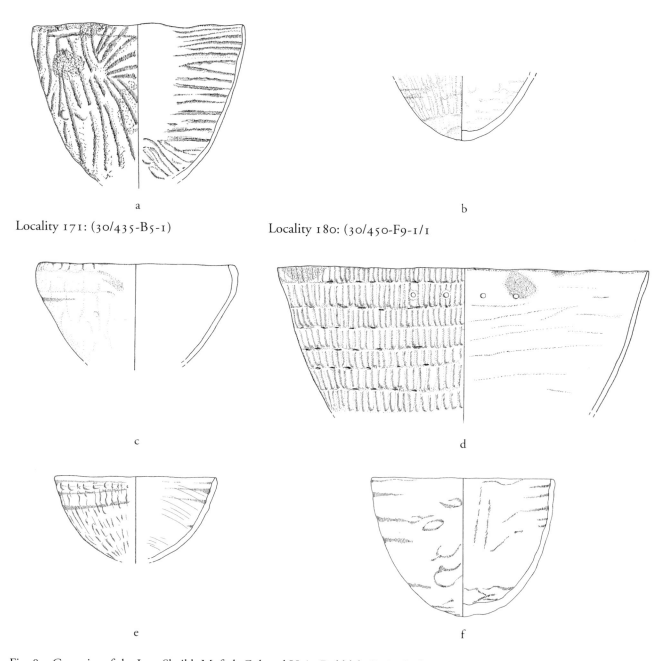

Locality 171: (30/435-B5-1)   Locality 180: (30/450-F9-1/1)

Fig. 8 Ceramics of the Late Sheikh Muftah Cultural Unit, Dakhleh Oasis. Scale 1:4.

tery that survives. During the Sheikh Muftah Unit, which was apparently confined to the oasis, pottery was certainly used within a domestic context. Whether this was also the case in the Bashendi Unit is not certain as sherds are not present on all sites and their quantity is sometimes small. Of the 16 Bashendi A sites, 10 have yielded pottery; of the 22 Bashendi B sites, 20 have ceramics.[29] The paucity of sherds on Masara Unit sites (three out of 36)[30] would seem to indicate that pottery was not of common domestic use, but whether it belonged to what Close (1995, 28) has termed 'social and symbolic spheres' is uncertain. Its absence from the hut circles of the Masara Cultural sub-Unit C is perplex-

ing as it is here that ceramics might have been expected, these sites showing the greatest tendency towards some degree of sedentism within the Masara Unit.

In the discussion of the manufacture of ceramics in Dakhleh during the early and mid-Holocene what has been said above must be regarded as provisional as most of the archaeological exploration has taken place in the eastern part of the oasis and to a lesser extent in the central region. Detailed study of the remaining sites in the central and western sectors may change the picture considerably. One of the significant outcomes of the study, however, is to show that pottery was manufactured in Dakhleh long before its first,

Locality 222: (30/435-J6-2)

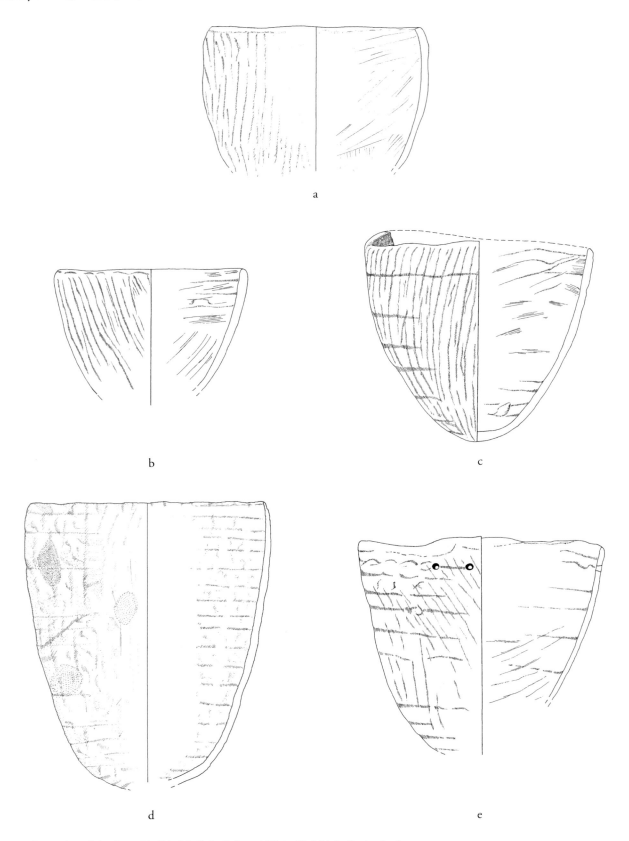

Fig. 9   Ceramics of the Late Sheikh Muftah Cultural Unit, Dakhleh Oasis. Scale 1:4.

Locality 222: continued

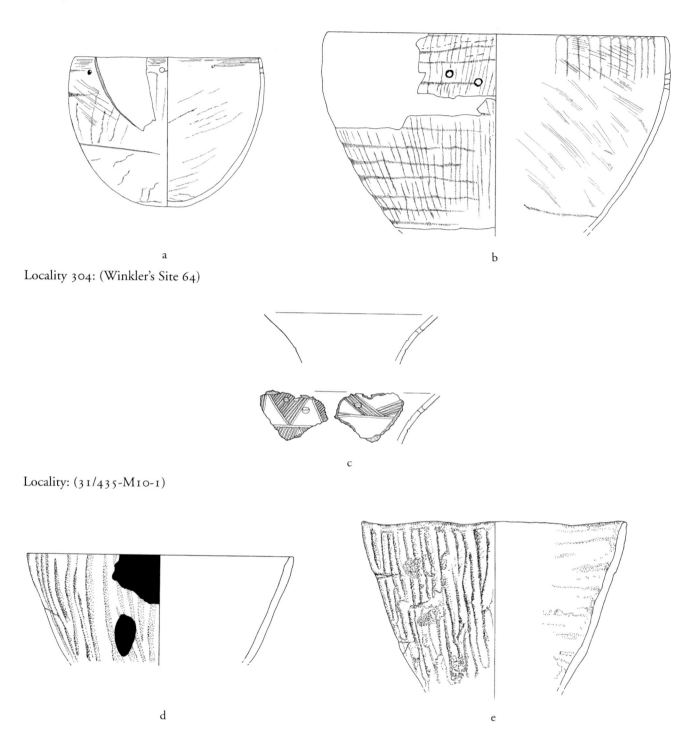

a

b

Locality 304: (Winkler's Site 64)

c

Locality: (31/435-M10-1)

d

e

Fig. 10 Ceramics of the Late Sheikh Muftah Cultural Unit, Dakhleh Oasis. Scale 1:4.

Locality: (30/435-I3-2/1)   Site unknown

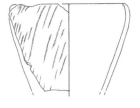
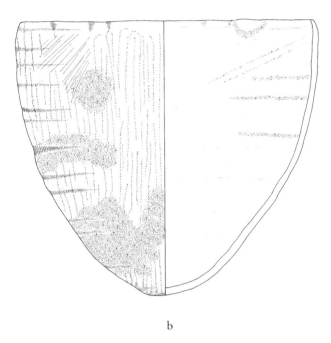

a   b

Fig. 11   Ceramics of the Late Sheikh Muftah Cultural Unit, Dakhleh Oasis. Scale 1:4.

currently-documented, occurrence in the Nile Valley in the third quarter of the seventh millennium bp on sites of the Tarifian culture (Ginter and Kozlowski 1984; Ginter *et al.* 1985, 27–8).

II   The Interaction between Dakhleh and the Nile Valley as Reflected by the Ceramics

In the only previous discussion to consider the ceramic data from Dakhleh in relation to possible influence from that area upon the evolution of the Predynastic cultures of Egypt, Tangri (1992, 117–120) concluded that the limited range of shapes and surface treatments he had identified amongst the material could not have influenced the development of the ceramic traditions of Egypt. As I have indicated above, Tangri's discussion cannot be regarded as reliable as it confuses material of the various cultural units and was produced before a clear idea had been gained of the temporal locations of the units. Furthermore, he clearly expected to find a wholesale transferral of traits from one region to the other, and I doubt whether such would have occurred. It cannot be denied that the repertoire of shapes documented so far in Dakhleh is limited, and it is dominated by bowls. While a major difference can be seen between the Dakhleh assemblages and the diversity seen within the cemeteries in Egypt, this is less evident when comparison is made with settlement material (for convenience compare with Friedman 1994, Figs 10.1–3, 7–11). As will be clear from the discussion above, some features are remarkably similar.

In attempting to define a link between the two regions based upon ceramics we must acknowledge from the outset that the picture we have from Dakhleh is incomplete. The

collections are small and many are from the surfaces of sites that have been badly affected by deflation. Present data pertains really only to the eastern part of the oasis and much of that comes from the region termed the South-Eastern Basin by McDonald (1991a, 1998). Much of the material is extremely fragmentary. It should be emphasised, however, that despite these limitations the characteristics of the ceramics from the different Holocene cultural units described above have been confirmed consistently throughout the fieldwork. Although essentially surface collections, certain distinct ceramic types always occur in combination with particular lithic assemblages and other cultural traits, which are distinct enough for there to be no doubt about their contemporaneity. Whilst some sites do show occupation by several cultural groups, there is a sufficient number that do not to enable the material to be distinguished, and there is an ever-increasing amount of material from excavated contexts of the Sheikh Muftah Cultural Unit to facilitate the task.

A wide variety of factors will have determined the particular features of ceramic manufacture in each area, notably the nature of the available raw materials, functional requirements, the range of uses to which such material was put, degrees of sedentism within the communities, the amount of material required determined by the size of the communities and their cultural attitudes. The impact of one tradition upon the development of another does not, quite clearly, have to result in the adoption by the latter of all of the features of the former; it can serve as a stimulus for development. It is in this manner that I would see the ceramics of Dakhleh impacting on those of Neolithic and Predynastic Egypt.

In examining this we can look at both general and specific features. One aspect that potentially could have shed much light on this topic is morphology, but when comparing the range of shapes that were manufactured in Dakhleh with those from the Nile Valley, the general simplicity of the former renders detailed comparison hazardous. As mentioned, Dakhleh pottery is dominated by forms of simple profile, predominantly open and slightly restricted bowls with convex-sides, round or pointed bases and direct rims. Similar shapes can certainly be found amongst the pottery from the Nile Valley, but also throughout Northeast Africa and elsewhere and I feel that these features are so basic that their occurrence cannot be used to indicate any definite contact between regions in which they occur. Bearing this reservation in mind, the similarity in the range of deep bowls between those of Bashendi B and early Sheikh Muftah with those from Merimde II-III, the Fayum, Badarian and Tasian, and early Naqadan from the Luxor region can be noted. Care must be exercised also in relation to the use that can be made of certain surface treatments to indicate contact between various cultural groups, or the impact of one ceramic tradition upon another. The application of coatings to reduce the permeability of the fabric, change its surface colour, produce a more even surface or provide a contrasting base colour upon which to apply painted decoration in another colour/colours, and also the use of compaction and polishing for some of the same purposes are techniques ubiquitous amongst potters in a variety of places and at different times and may be regarded almost as intrinsic to the craft. It is only when we encounter specific and recurrent combinations of a range of ceramic traits in regions, which are in reasonable proximity, that cultural contact and impact can really be postulated.

In characterizing the pottery of the Bashendi Cultural Unit made in Dakhleh from the later eighth millennium until the late sixth millennium, we can note the use of finely-tempered clay bodies lacking organic material for thin-walled vessels that were evenly fired. The surfaces of these vessels were compacted and regularly fired brown; sometimes a thin layer, possibly resulting from a self-slip, coats the surface. Deliberately blackened tops occur on some pieces that also have darkened interiors, though their paucity warns against assuming that they attest to a black-top tradition; some have black patches on the body. Decoration is minimal; there are a few sherds with impressed designs in triangles, others with incisions in the rim top, a few with vertical rows of fingernail incisions and some with a controlled ridging of the surface produced by the fingers.

If we then compare these features with the earliest products from Egypt some interesting correlations occur. Amongst pottery of the Tarifian one group is described as: '...fragments of thinner vessels (up to 0.5 cm), made from clay with a fine mineral admixture (quartz, mica), with a smooth brown surface' (Ginter *et al.* 1979, 96).[31] Badarian ceramic manufacture is characterized by various surface treatments including black-topped brown or red with rippling or combing, smooth brown surfaces, polished surfaces, and vessels with thin walls made in fine Nile silt clays (Ghaly 1986, 84–91, 118–9). Like the Dakhleh material, Badarian

vessels mostly have direct rims (Brunton and Caton-Thompson 1928, 24). Amongst the Rough Brown class, Brunton and Caton-Thompson (1928, 23) noted: '...sometimes there is a vague rippling as if the fingers had been used for smoothing' (compare also Brunton 1937, pl. XIX, RB9M, pl. XX, RB26E, pl. XXI, RB43M). Rippling of the surface is also recorded on Tasian vessels (Brunton 1937, 28; Friedman 1994, 14), early Naqadan ceramics from the Luxor region (Ginter *et al.* 1985, 36–40; Ginter *et al.* 1986, 61, 65; Ginter and Kowzlowski 1994, 74–81), and from Hemamieh and Khattara in Badarian and Amratian contexts (Friedman 1994, 196–7, 325, 402–3). The Badarian Smooth Brown ware continued to be manufactured into the Amratian (Friedman 1994, 402–5). Rim-top decoration occurs intermittently from the Badarian onwards (Friedman 1994, 199, 331, 391–2, 402, 407; Ghaly 1986, 62–3), most commonly at sites in the Khattara region (Friedman 1994, 502–3). Impressed designs on Upper Egyptian sites of the early Predynastic mostly occur on imported Nubian material but some examples are suggested to be of Saharan origin with parallels at Nabta Playa and in the Wadi Bakht (Friedman 1994, 197–8, 331–2), to which Dakhleh might be added.

One particular shape from Loc. 254 requires comment (**Fig. 3** a). This is a restricted jar with wide convex body and a direct rim. Whilst the features of this form may be thought quite simple, it stands out amongst the Dakhleh ceramics as the most elaborate jar type. It is made in a fine quartz- and shale-tempered fabric typical of the Bashendi Cultural Unit, with a brown compacted surface that has some black patches on the exterior. The shape of the base is uncertain. Amongst Badarian pottery similar shapes occur in both Black-topped Brown and Black-topped Red wares (Brunton and Caton-Thompson 1928, pl. XIII, BB77 and pl. XV, BR43F), both with round bases. It also has parallels in the north at Ma'adi where it occurs in local black-topped ware but with a thicker wall and a flat base (Rizkana and Seeher 1987, pl. 71.7; pl. 9; Jar 8b). At el-Omari it occurs also with a flat base, in Group IIIa, made in a straw-tempered fabric, which is predominantly fired brown with polished surfaces (Debono and Mortensen 1990, 28, pl. 2.13). These authors note the occurrence of similar forms at Merimde in phases II-III and at Sedment. From regions to the south the shape occurs with a round base later amongst A-Group ceramics (Nordström 1972, pl. 44 AXa.13) in Black-topped Brown ware. It may be noted that specific similarities between Dakhleh ceramics and those of Lower Egypt are, in general, few and the use of straw-tempered fabrics and black-fired wares in that region distinguishes its manufactures from those of the oasis. That contact between the two areas did occur may be indicated by two finds in Dakhleh (**Figs 1** t and 7c; see discussion above).

The features of Bashendi ceramics continued into the early Sheikh Muftah Cultural Unit when rippled surfaces produced by the potters' fingers and also by brushing with reeds became more common. Contact with the cultures of the Nile Valley in Egypt is clearly indicated by the discovery in Dakhleh of ceramics from the valley. It is possible that some impact from that region on the Dakhleh potters may be detected in the manufacture of black-topped red-coated wares and small ovoid jars with direct or modelled rims (**Fig. 4** l-m). A characteristic of Sheikh Muftah Unit ceramics is its tendency to use fabrics with greater quantities of shale inclusions. This material occurs in the majority of Bashendi Cultural Unit pottery but in small sizes. The use of shale-tempered fabrics amongst the cultures of Upper Egypt and Hierakonpolis in particular has been discussed by Friedman (1994, 154–5, 504–5, 517–8, 630–2, 669, 718, 735–6), who sees in this a connection with the Western Desert, but as this material is found over a wide area from Dakhleh into Upper Egypt its use in both regions is understandable and need not imply contact between the two.

There are certainly similarities between the ceramics of Dakhleh and the desert regions to the south and southeast from what Kuper (1995) has termed the Middle Ceramic onwards, variously in terms of the lack of decoration, wall thickness, surface treatment, fabric range and morphology. This may be seen to extend into Upper Nubia with the Abkan Tradition (Nordström 1972, 14, 58–60; Wendorf and Schild 1998, 108) and the Khartoum Neolithic of the Sudan (Arkell 1953, 68–77), though the latter had far more decorated pottery. It is from this general region that some scholars have suggested the major influence upon the evolution of Badarian ceramics came, particularly in relation to the use of black-topped wares (Arkell and Ucko 1965, 151; Hays 1984, 217–8; Friedman 1994, 522–3; Needler 1984, 20; *contra* Holmes 1989). Arkell and Ucko (1965, 149) have even suggested that the potters of the Khartoum Neolithic were on the verge of developing rippled surfaces, a feature regarded as typical of Badarian ceramic manufacture.

I suggest that we now need to consider Dakhleh Oasis and regions to the south in the Egyptian Sahara as possible sources of various features of Nile Valley ceramics. This certainly seems likely given their earlier occurrence and consistent use there, particularly in Dakhleh Oasis, until they first appear in Egypt and Nubia. The picture which emerges from the study of the Bashendi Cultural Unit material as a whole certainly supports this suggestion, and is particularly true of the Bashendi B Cultural Unit. These people seem to have been fairly mobile, ranging widely across the Western Desert and they were in part contemporary with the Badarian. Ceramic data seems to indicate greater contact with the peoples of Upper rather than Lower Egypt.

Acknowledgments

I am grateful to Vivian Davies and Renée Friedman for accepting this contribution for inclusion in the present volume, and to Barbara Adams, Christiana Köhler and especially Renée Friedman for their extremely useful comments on the original manuscript. Bruce Parr kindly prepared the line drawings that illustrate this article; original drawings are by the author, Amanda Dunsmore, Alan Hollett, Johnothan C. Howell, Caroline McGregor, John O'Carroll, Bruce Parr and Anna Stevens. The colour photography was done by Janelle Jakowenko and Shannon Matheson of Monash University, and the black and white photography by various members of the Dakhleh Oasis Project, including Alan Hollett and Mark Eccleston.

Notes

1. The published data are considerable: Adams 1997, 12; Banks, 1980 and 1984; Butzer 1976, 4–11; Caneva 1993, 410; Friedman 1994, 886–901, 927 n.10; Hassan 1986a, 70–1; 1986b, 92; 1988, 144–5; 1989, 327–8; Hassan and Holmes 1985; Hays 1975, 200; 1984, 217; 1992; Holmes 1989, 381–4; Klees 1989, 229–31; Nordström 1972, 8–17; Smith 1989, 74–5; Wendorf and Schild 1984, 428; Wenke 1989, 136; Wenke and Casini 1989, 149. The evidence is briefly reviewed in McHugh 1990, 275–6, a study in which he draws attention to an interesting parallel between the decoration on an object reputedly of Naqada II date and rock art in the Gebel Uweinat.

2. It must be pointed out that the radiocarbon dates established for samples from particular sites should be regarded as indications of the general period during which the site was occupied and thus when the ceramics were manufactured; rarely are the dated samples derived from a specific sealed context that also yielded potsherds. The majority of the latter are surface finds.

3. A shorter version of this paper has been published elsewhere, see Hope 1998; and another discussion appeared in Hope 1999. The information provided here supercedes that provided in all other previous studies of the Dakhleh Holocene ceramics. The study of the ceramics has been the responsibility of the writer in collaboration with Daniel Tangri for several years. Preliminary reports by Hope in which Holocene ceramics are discussed appear in the *Journal of the Society for the Study of Egyptian Antiquities* (JSSEA) volumes 9–12 (1979–81) and an overview of the work appears in Hope 1999. The JSSEA articles are republished together with others, including one dealing with the mid-Holocene ceram-

ics by Edwards and Hope in Edwards *et al.* 1987. For another report on the material see Edwards and Hope 1989.

4. McDonald has published the results of her study of the Holocene cultural units in numerous articles with a series appearing in the *Journal of the Society for the Study of Egyptian Antiquities* Volumes 10 (1980) to 20 (1990); an overview of the results appears in McDonald 1999.

5. McDonald employs a consecutive numbering system to reference the Holocene sites. The sites are termed localities, abbreviated here as Loc. Many of these same sites also have a number in the format employed for historic period sites by the Dakhleh Oasis Project (DOP), which includes map and grid references and a sequential number relating to the sites within a specific grid. As McDonald employs her system in published reports I shall follow suit here; a concordance of locality numbers and DOP numbers can be found in Churcher and Mills 1999.

6. Locs 103, 174, 254, 261, 270, 275, 278, 306A, 307 and in the vicinity of Locs 174–181 (Rock Art Basin).

7. From Loc. 307 I have seen only 14 sherds but McDonald (1998, 133) reports 20, while from Loc. 270 I have seen only one sherd but McDonald (1998, 133) reports several.

8. A sample from this site has yielded a date of 7260 ± 90 bp.

9. Two dates are available from this site: 7450 ± 60 bp and 6990 ± 70 bp.

10. Six from Loc. 261 and one each from Locs 270, 278 and 306A.

11. Fourteen from Loc. 307, five from Loc. 174, two each from

Loc 254 and near Locs 174-181, and one each from Locs 278 and 306A.

12. The figure is again approximate as there is a slight discrepancy between the number of sherds I have seen and that recorded by the discoverer, and a total count of fragments originating from a single vessel has not been included.

13. Locs 212, 257, 257B and 304.

14. Locs 184, 200W, 212, 252 and 254.

15. Locs 212 and 74 respectively.

16. I have not examined this vessel. It is now in the Royal Ontario Museum, no. 983.25.236.

17. It should be noted that Arkell (1949, 88) wondered if some of the quartz- and straw-tempered pottery with basket-like impressions was imported.

18. The limited data available at present from which to determine the date of the Badarian would indicate that it was under way at least by the mid-fifth millennium BC (mid–sixth millennium bp) (Hassan 1985, 106–7; Holmes 1996, 188); this would indicate that the early Sheikh Muftah Cultural Unit might have commenced by this date also.

19. The evidence for this is tenuous, see the discussion of the body sherd shown on **Fig. 6** c from Loc. 69 in the section on the Late Sheikh Muftah.

20. I am grateful to Deborah Darnell for this reference.

21. The drawing illustrated here (**Fig. 5** i) is misleading; the blackened area on the exterior extended to near the lower edge of the sherd, further than is indicated.

22. Friedman (1994, 15; 1999, 633; Friedman and Hobbs this volume) has expressed the opinion that the Tasian represents a non-chronological variant, being possibly a nomadic group interacting with both the Badarian and Amratian that originated possibly in the Eastern Desert.

23. I have not examined this sherd and so cannot identify its fabric more precisely.

24. No examples of this coarser version have been analysed recently but samples were included amongst earlier data sets and its similarity to the Fine Quartz and Shale Fabric cannot be doubted.

25. Whilst I am not aware of any representations of ceramics amongst the petroglyphs recorded so far in Dakhleh, others from Gebel Uweinat include depictions of containers (ceramic, woven or wooden?) suspended from poles, see Winkler 1939, pl. XXII.2; van Noten, 1978, figs 138–9. For reports on Dakhleh rock art see Krzyzaniak and Kroeper, 1985; 1987.

26. This has been drawn to my attention by Renée Friedman, who also supplied information on the fabric in which such jars occur.

27. See the references above in the discussion of the sherds with this motif from the Bashendi B Cultural Unit Loc. 212 and the Early Sheikh Muftah Unit Loc. 135.

28. For a discussion of the early development of pottery manufacture see now Rice 1999; I am grateful to Mary McDonald for bringing this article to my attention.

29. There are a number of other sites that can only be attributed to the Bashendi Cultural Unit with no sub-unit identifications because of the small size of the artefact collections.

30. It should be remembered that various later sites have yielded ceramics of the Masara Unit type, see above.

31. For detailed characterization of the ceramic bodies see Kozlowski and Pawlikowski 1998, 32–8.

Bibliography

Adams B, 1997. Petrie at the cult centre of Min at Koptos. In J Phillips, L Bell, B B Williams, J Hoch and R J Leprohon (eds), *Ancient Egypt, The Aegean and the Near East: Studies in Honour of Martha Rhoads Bell*. Volume I. San Antonio: 1–16.

Arkell A J, 1949. *Early Khartoum*. London.

Arkell A J, 1953. *Shaheinab*. London.

Arkell A J and Ucko P, 1965. Review of the Predynastic Development in the Nile Valley. *Current Anthropology* 6.2: 145–66.

Ballet P and Picon M, 1990. Étude de la Céramique. In G Soukiassian, W Wuttmann and L Pantalacci, *Balat III. Les ateliers de potiers d'Ayn Asîl*. Fouilles de l'Institut français d'archéologie orientale 34. Cairo: 75–165.

Banks M, 1980. Ceramics of the Western Desert. In F Wendorf and R Schild (eds), *Prehistory of the Eastern Sahara*. New York: 299–315.

Banks M, 1984. Early Ceramic-bearing Occupations in the Egyptian Western Desert. In L Krzyzaniak and M Kobusiewicz (eds), *Origins and Early Development of Food-producing Culture in North-Eastern Africa*. Poznan: 149–61.

Barich B and Hassan F, 1990. Il Sahara e le oasi: Farafra nel Deserto Occidentale Egiziano. *Sahara* 3: 52–62.

Brunton G, 1937. *Mostagedda and the Tasian Culture*. London.

Brunton G and Caton-Thompson G, 1928. *The Badarian Civilisation and Predynastic Remains near Badari*. London.

Butzer K, 1976. *Early Hydraulic Civilization in Egypt*. Chicago.

Caneva I, 1993. Pre-pastoral Middle Nile: local developments and Saharan contacts. In L Krzyzaniak, M Kobusiewicz and J Alexander (eds), *Environmental Change and Human Culture in the Nile Basin and Northern Africa until the Second Millennium B.C.* Poznan: 405–11.

Caton-Thompson G, 1952. *Kharga Oasis in Prehistory*. London

Churcher C S and Mills A J (eds.), 1999. *Reports from the Survey of the Dakhleh Oasis. Western Desert of Egypt, 1977-1987*. Oxbow Monograph 99, Dakhleh Oasis Project Monograph 2. Oxford.

Close A, 1995. Few and Far Between: Early ceramics in North Africa. In W K Barnett and J W Hoopes (eds), *The Emergence of Pottery*. Washington: 23–37.

Debono F and Mortensen B, 1990. *El Omari, A Neolithic Settlement and other Sites around Wadi Hof, Helwan*. Archäologische Veröffentlichungen, Deutsches Archäologisches Institut Abteilung Kairo 82. Mainz am Rhein.

Edwards W I, Hope C A and Segnit E R, 1987. *Ceramics from the Dakhleh Oasis: Preliminary Studies*. Burwood.

Edwards W I and Hope C A, 1989. A note on the Neolithic ceramics from the Dakhleh Oasis (Egypt). In L Krzyzaniak and M Kobusiewicz (eds), *Late Prehistory of the Nile Basin and the Sahara*. Poznan: 233–42.

Eiwanger J, 1988. *Merimde-Benisalame II. Die funde der mittleren Merimde-kultur*. Archäologische Veröffentlichungen, Deutsches Archäologisches Institut Abteilung Kairo 51. Mainz am Rhein.

Faltings D, 1998. Recent Excavations in Tell el-Fara`in/Buto: New Finds and their Chronological Implications. In C J Eyre (ed.), *Proceedings of the Seventh International Congress of Egyptologists*. Leuven: 365–75.

Francaviglia V and Palmieri A M, 1983. Petrochemical analysis of the 'Early Khartoum' pottery: a preliminary report. *Origini* 12: 191–205.

Friedman R F, 1994. *Predynastic Settlement Ceramics of Upper Egypt: A Comparative Study of the Ceramics of Hemamieh,*

Nagada and Hierakonpolis. PhD Thesis. University of California, Berkeley. University Microfilms International, Michigan.

Friedman R, 1999. Pottery, prehistoric. In K A Bard (ed.), *Encyclopedia of the Archaeology of Ancient Egypt.* London and New York: 632–6.

Gabriel B, 1981. Die östliche Zentralsahara im Holozän–Klima, Landschaft un Kulturen (mit besonderer berucksichtung der Neolithischen Keramik). In *Préhistoire Africaine.* Paris: 195–211.

Ghaly H, 1986. *Pottery of the Prehistoric Settlement Hemamieh in Middle Egypt: Classification and Fabrics.* PhD Thesis, University of Vienna.

Ginter B and Kozlowski J K, 1984. The Tarifian and the origins of the Naqadian. In L Krzyzaniak and M Kobusiewicz (eds), *The Origin and Early Development of Food-producing Cultures in North-Eastern Africa.* Poznan: 247–60.

Ginter B and Kozlowski J K, 1994. *Predynastic Settlement near Armant.* Heidelberg.

Ginter B, Kozlowski J K and Silwa J, 1979. Excavation Report on the Prehistoric and Predynastic Settlement in El-Tarif during 1978. *Mitteilungen des Deutschen Archäologischen Instituts Abteilung Kairo* 35: 87–102.

Ginter B, Kozlowski J K and Pawlikowski M, 1985. Field report from the Survey Conducted in Upper Egypt in 1983. *Mitteilungen des Deutschen Archäologischen Instituts Abteilung Kairo* 41: 15–41.

Ginter B, Kozlowski J K and Pawlikowski M, 1986. Investigations into Sites MA 6/83 and MA 21/83 in the Region of Qurna-Armant in Upper Egypt. *Mitteilungen des Deutschen Archäologischen Instituts Abteilung Kairo* 43: 45–66.

Hassan F, 1985. Radiocarbon Chronology of Neolithic and Predynastic sites in Upper Egypt and the Delta. *The African Archaeological Review* 3: 95–116.

Hassan F, 1986a. Desert Environment and Origins of Agriculture in Egypt. *Norwegian Archaeological Review* 19:63–76.

Hassan F, 1986b. Chronology of the Khartoum 'Mesolithic' and 'Neolithic' and related sites in the Sudan: statistical analysis and comparisons with Egypt. *The African Archaeological Review* 4: 83–102.

Hassan F, 1988. The Predynastic of Egypt. *Journal of World Prehistory* 2: 135–85.

Hassan F, 1989. Desertification and the Beginnings of Egyptian Agriculture. In S Schoske (ed.), *Akten des vierten internationalen Ägyptologen Kongress.* Band 2. München: 325–31.

Hassan F and Hays T R, 1974. Mineralogical analysis of Sudanese Neolithic Ceramics. *Archaeometry* 16: 71–9.

Hassan F and Holmes D, 1985. *The archaeology of the Umm el-Dabadib area, Kharga Oasis, Egypt.* FRSU Research Report 82035. Cairo.

Hays T R, 1975. Neolithic Settlement of the Sahara as it Relates to the Nile Valley. In F Wendorf and A E Marks (eds), *Problems in Prehistory: North Africa and the Levant.* Dallas: 193–204.

Hays T R, 1984. Predynastic Development in Upper Egypt. In L Krzyzaniak and M Kobusiewicz (eds), *Origin and Early Development of Food-producing Cultures in North-Eastern Africa.* Poznan: 211–19.

Hays T R, 1992. Neolithic Chronology in the Sahara and the Sudan. In R W Ehrich (ed.), *Chronologies in Old World Archaeology.* Vol. 1, 3rd edition. Chicago: 309–16.

Hayes W C, 1965. *Most Ancient Egypt.* Chicago.

Hoffman M A, 1980. *Egypt before the Pharaohs.* London.

Holmes D, 1989. *The Predynastic Lithic Industries of Upper Egypt.* British Archaeological Reports International Series 469. Oxford.

Holmes D, 1996. Recent investigations in the Badari region (Middle Egypt). In L Krzyzaniak, M Kobusiewicz and K Kroeper (eds), *Interregional Contacts in the Later Prehistory of Northeastern Africa.* Poznan: 181–91.

Hope C A, 1998. Early Pottery from the Dakhleh Oasis. *The Bulletin of the Australian Centre for Egyptology* 9: 53–60.

Hope C A, 1999. Pottery Manufacture in the Dakhleh Oasis. In C S Churcher and A J Mills (eds), 1999: 215–43.

Kaiser W, 1985. Zur Südausdehnung der vorgeschichtlichen Deltakulturen und zur frühen Entwicklung Oberägyptens. *Mitteilungen des Deutschen Archäologischen Instituts Abteilung Kairo* 41: 61–87.

Klees F, 1989. Lobo: a contribution to the prehistory of the Eastern Sand Sea and the Egyptian oases. In L Krzyzaniak and M Kobusiewicz (eds), *Late Prehistory of the Nile Basin and the Sahara.* Poznan: 223–31.

Köhler E C, 1998. *Tell el-Fara'in. Buto III. Die Keramik von der späten Naqada-Kultur bis zum frühen Alten Reich (Schichten III bis VI).* Archäologische Veröffentlichungen, Deutsches Archäologisches Institut Abteilung Kairo 94. Mainz am Rhein.

Kozlowski J K and Ginter B, 1989. The Fayum Neolithic in the light of new discoveries. In L Krzyzaniak and M Kobusiewicz (eds), *Late Prehistory of the Nile Basin and the Sahara.* Poznan: 157–79.

Kozlowski J K and Pawlikowski M, 1998. Tarifienkeramik. In B Ginter, J K Kozlowski, M Pawlikowski and J Sliwa, *Frühe Keramik und Kleinfunde aus El-Târif.* Archäologische Veröffentlichungen, Deutsches Archäologisches Institut Abteilung Kairo 40. Mainz am Rhein: 32–8.

Krzyzaniak L and Kroeper K, 1985. Report on the Reconnaisance Season of the Recording of Petroglyphs, December 1985. *Journal of the Society for the Study of Egyptian Antiquities* 15: 138–9.

Krzyzaniak L, 1987. Interim report on the First Season of the Recording of Petroglyphs, January–February 1988. *Journal of the Society for the Study of Egyptian Antiquities* 17: 182–91.

Kuper R, 1981.Untersuchungen zur Besiedlungsgeschichte der östlichen Sahara: Vorbericht uber die Expedition 1980. *Beiträge zur Allgemeinen und Vergleichenden Archäologie* 3: 215–75.

Kuper R, 1989. The Eastern Sahara from North to South: data and dates from the B. O. S. Project. In L Krzyzaniak and M Kobusiewicz (eds), *Late Prehistory of the Nile Basin and the Sahara.* Poznan: 197–203.

Kuper R, 1995. Prehistoric research in the South Libyan desert: a brief account and some conclusions of the B.O.S. project. *Cahier de recherches de l'Institut de Papyrologie et d'Égyptologie de Lille* 17: 123–40.

McDonald M M A, 1990. Dakhleh Oasis Project: Holocene Prehistory: Interim report on the 1988 and 1989 Seasons. *Journal of the Society for the Study of Egyptian Antiquities* 20: 24–53.

McDonald M M A, 1991a. Origins of the Neolithic in the Nile Valley as seen from Dakhleh Oasis in the Egyptian Western Desert. *Sahara* 4: 41–52.

McDonald M M A, 1991b. Technological organization and sedentism in the Epipalaeolithic of Dakhleh Oasis, Egypt. *The African Archaeological Review* 9: 81–109.

McDonald M M A, 1991c. Systematic Reworking of Lithics from Earlier Cultures in the Early Holocene of Dakhleh Oasis, Egypt. *Journal of Field Archaeology* 18: 269–73.

McDonald M M A, 1992. Neolithic of Sudanese Tradition or Saharo-Sudanese Neolithic? The View from Dakhla Oasis, South Central Egypt. In J Sterner and N David (eds), *An African Commitment: Papers in Honour of Peter Lewis Shinnie.* Calgary: 51–70.

McDonald M M A, 1998. Early African Pastoralism: View from Dakhleh Oasis (South Central Egypt). *Journal of Anthropological Archaeology* 17: 124–42.

McDonald M M A, 1999a. Dakhla Oasis, prehistoric sites. In K A Bard (ed.), *Encyclopedia of the Archaeology of Ancient Egypt*. London and New York: 226–9.

McDonald M M A, 1999b. Neolithic Cultural Units and Adaptations in Dakhleh Oasis, Egypt. In C S Churcher and A J Mills (eds) 1999: 117–32.

McDonald M M A, 2001. The Late Prehistoric Radiocarbon Chronology for the Dakhleh Oasis within the wider Environmental and Cultural Setting of the Egyptian Western Desert. In M Marlow (ed.), *Proceedings of the First International Dakhleh Oasis Project Seminar, July 5–9, 1994*. Oxford.

McDonald M M A, in press. Holocene Prehistory: Preliminary Report on the 1997–1998 Field Season. In G E Bowen and C A Hope (eds), *Dakhleh Oasis Project: Preliminary Reports on the 1994–1995 to 1998–1999 Field Seasons*. Oxford.

McHugh W P, 1975. Some Archaeological Results of the Bagnold-Mond Expedition to the Gilf Kebir and Gebel 'Uweinat, Southern Libyan Desert. *Journal of Near Eastern Studies* 34: 31–62.

McHugh W P, 1990. Implications of a Decorated Predynastic Terracotta Model for Saharan Neolithic Influence in the Nile Valley. *Journal of Near Eastern Studies* 49: 265–80.

Murray G W, 1939. An Archaic Hut in Wadi Umm Sidrah. *Journal of Egyptian Archaeology* 25: 38–9.

Myers O H, 1937. A Saharan Culture. In R Mond and O H Myers, *Cemeteries of Armant I*. London: 267–77.

Needler W, 1984. *Predynastic and Archaic Egypt in the Brooklyn Museum*. Brooklyn.

Nordström H-Å, 1972. *Neolithic and A-Group Sites*. Stockholm.

Nordström H-Å, and Bourriau J, 1993. Ceramic Technology: Clays and Fabrics. In Do Arnold and J Bourriau (eds), *An Introduction to Ancient Egyptian Pottery*. Fascicle 2. Mainz am Rhein.

Petrie W M F, 1921. *Corpus of Prehistoric Pottery and Palettes*. London.

Rice P, 1999. On the Origins of Pottery. *Journal of Archaeological Method and Theory* 6.1: 1–54

Richter J, 1989. Neolithic sites in the Wadi Howar (Western Sudan). In L Krzyzaniak and M Kobusiewicz (eds), *Late Prehistory of the Nile Basin and the Sahara*. Poznan: 431–42.

Rizkana I and Seeher J, 1987. *Maadi I: The Pottery of the Predynastic Settlement*. Archäologische Veröffentlichungen, Deutsches Archäologisches Institut Abteilung Kairo 64. Mainz am Rhein.

Roset J-P, 1987. Paleoclimatic and Cultural Conditions of Neolithic Development in the Early Holocene of Northern Niger (Aïr and Ténéré). In A Close (ed.), *Prehistory of Arid North Africa*. Dallas: 211–35.

Schuck W, 1989. From lake to well: 5,000 years of settlement in Wadi Shaw (Northern Sudan). In L Krzyzaniak and M Kobus-iewicz (eds), *Late Prehistory of the Nile Basin and the Sahara*. Poznan: 421–29.

Segnit E R, 1987. X-Ray Diffraction Examination of some Sherds and Clays from Dakhleh Oasis and the Nile Valley. In W I Edwards, C A Hope and E R Segnit, *Ceramics from the Dakhleh Oasis: Preliminary Studies*. Burwood: 6–7.

Smith A B, 1980. The Neolithic tradition in the Sahara. In M A J Williams and H Faure (eds), *The Sahara and the Nile*. Rotterdam: 451–65.

Smith A B, 1989. The Near Eastern connection: Early to Mid-Holocene relations between North Africa and the Levant. In L Krzyzaniak and M Kobusiewicz (eds), *Late Prehistory of the Nile Basin and the Sahara*. Poznan: 69–77.

Tangri D, 1989. *Pottery from the Dakhleh Oasis*. Unpublished B A (Honours) Thesis, University of Sydney.

Tangri D, 1991. Neolithic basket-impressed pottery from Dakhleh Oasis, Egypt. New Evidence for regionalism in the Eastern Sahara. *Sahara* 4: 141–3.

Tangri D, 1992. A Reassessment of the Origins of the Predynastic in Upper Egypt. *Proceedings of the Prehistoric Society* 58: 111–25.

van Noten F, 1978 *Rock Art of the Jebel Uweinat*. Graz.

Vita-Finzi C and Kennedy R A, 1965. Seven Saharan Sites. *The Journal of the Royal Anthropological Institute of Great Britain and Ireland* 95: 195–213.

von der Way T, 1991. Zur Herkunft keramischer Dekorationen des spätvorgeschichtlichen Unterägypten. *Cahiers de la Céramique égyptienne* 2: 1–9.

von der Way T, 1992. Excavations at Tell el-Fara'in / Buto in 1987–1989. In E C M van den Brink (ed.), *The Nile Delta in Transition: 4th–3rd Millennium B.C.* Tel Aviv: 1–10.

von der Way T, 1997. *Tell el-Fara'in. Buto I*. Archäologische Veröffentlichungen, Deutsches Archäologisches Institut, Abteilung Kairo 83. Mainz am Rhein.

Wendorf F and Schild R, 1984. Conclusions. In F Wendorf, R Schild and A E Close (eds), *Cattle-keepers of the Eastern Sahara: The Neolithic of Bir Kiseiba*. Dallas: 404–28.

Wendorf F and Schild R, 1998. Nabta Playa and its Role in Northeastern African Prehistory. *Journal of Anthropological Archaeology* 17: 97–123.

Wenke R, 1989. Egypt: Origins of Complex Societies. *Annual Review of Anthropology* 18: 129–55.

Wenke R, 1999. Fayum, Neolithic and Predynastic sites. In K A Bard (ed.), *Encyclopedia of the Archaeology of Ancient Egypt*. London and New York: 313–6.

Wenke R and Casini M, 1989. The Epipalaeolithic-Neolithic transition in Egypt's Fayum Depression. In L Krzyzaniak and M Kobusiewicz (eds), *Late Prehistory of the Nile Basisn and the Sahara*. Poznan: 139–56.

Winkler H A, 1939. *Rock Drawings from Southern Upper Egypt II*. Archaeological Survey of Egypt 27. London.

Early and Mid-Holocene Ceramics from the Dakhleh Oasis: Macroscopic, Petrographic and Technological Descriptions

Mark A J Eccleston

Introduction and Methodology

As part of the 1997/8 and 1998/9 field seasons of the Dakhleh Oasis Project (DOP), a thorough re-examination of the entire corpus of early to mid-Holocene ceramics was made in light of recent advances in the refinement of the dating of these periods by McDonald (Hope 1998; McDonald 2001). Previous analytical data were also reviewed and new analyses of the ceramics undertaken. The following is a preliminary report on this work.

This paper is divided into two major sections. The first is a macroscopic description of each fabric with a short comment. It is anticipated that the first section may be more useful as a guide to assigning preliminary identification to ceramics collected in the field. The second section is a discussion of the analytical results and conclusions, which is separated further into those concerning Dakhleh-products and imported material. This section is intended as a more detailed discussion of the post-excavation analysis of the material, with reference to some of the practical and methodological problems that have been encountered in the study of these ceramics from Dakhleh.

Macroscopic observations of the most common fabrics were made in the field using a combination of hand lens (× 10) and binocular microscope (× 6.7–× 40). In addition to the most commonly occurring fabrics, a selection of other individual pieces of interest was examined and these are also included in this discussion. It must be stressed, however, that this is not a comprehensive examination of all of the fabrics that are known in Dakhleh from the period with which we are concerned here.

During the course of the study of ceramics found in Dakhleh since 1979, a number of different types of analysis have been carried out. In the early 1980s Hope had 156 samples of pottery dating from the Sheikh Muftah Cultural Unit to the fifth century AD analysed by Neutron Activation Analysis (NAA). These results were later re-examined (Eccleston 1997) in light of further advances in the study of Dakhleh ceramics. In addition to this, NAA of 22 early and mid-Holocene sherds was undertaken for Tangri as part of his study of the early ceramics during the late 1980s and early 1990s (Tangri 1989; 1991; 1992). The test results from the majority of this set are presented here as Samples 1 to 22 (see **Table 3** for full results).[1]

Some thin section and X-ray Diffraction (XRD) analysis of relevant ceramics was undertaken in 1989, however, the results were never published.[2] Although thin section analysis of ceramics of later periods from Dakhleh has been undertaken on material recently exported (Eccleston 1998), this group of material did not include examples of early and mid-

Holocene ceramics. Therefore thin sections were made from some of the sherds sampled for NAA by Tangri.[3] Thin section analysis of these sherds has helped to substantiate certain conclusions that are drawn in this study.

The descriptions of the more common fabrics were made with reference to the entire corpus of each fabric in storage in Dakhleh. These include Coarse Shale Fabric, Coarse Quartz Fabric, Fine Quartz and Shale Fabric, and the Coarse Calcareous Fabric. The other fabrics were described using only single examples that were exported for analysis and are now stored at Monash University, Australia. A list of the find context and date of the samples that are discussed specifically in the text is given in **Table 2**. In addition to this information, the macroscopic fabric and the NAA groups to which the sherds have been assigned are also listed for cross-reference.

The majority of the eleven descriptive terms and all of the fabric numbers that are used here were created specifically for this paper. Some of these terms do relate to those used in the DOP recording system, and some have been published previously by Hope (1998); others are names commonly used in the study of ceramics from the Nile Valley. Until a comprehensive final publication of the entire corpus is prepared, it was thought more useful to use descriptive terms rather than introduce a fabric reference system that may have to be modified in light of future work.

The macroscopic descriptions of these fabrics were made using a binocular microscope (× 6.7–× 40) on sherds with fresh breaks perpendicular to the manufacturing marks where possible. The descriptive terms for the size of inclusions follows that of Nordström and Bourriau (1993, 162–7). Petrographic descriptions and identifications were made using a polarising microscope (× 20–× 400) on thin sections prepared to a thickness of 30 microns.

Early and Mid-Holocene Fabric Descriptions

The fabrics discussed specifically in this paper are given in **Table 1**.

I: Coarse Shale Fabric

The Coarse Shale[4] Fabric is thought to be restricted to the Masara unit, the earliest of the Dakhleh Holocene Cultural Units, dated by McDonald (2001) to *c.* 9200–8500 bp. Sites of this period have yielded very little ceramic evidence (see Hope this volume, section I.1 for full discussion), but of those sherds that have been found, all but two occur in this same distinctive fabric.

Table 1: Fabrics discussed in this paper

	Fabric	Date Range
I.	Coarse Shale Fabric	Masara Unit
II.	Coarse Grit Fabric	Uncertain
III.	Coarse Quartz Fabric	Bashendi A Unit
IV.	Fine Quartz and Shale Fabric	Bashendi A- Sheikh Muftah Unit
V.	Coarse Calcareous Fabric	Bashendi A- Bashendi B Unit
VI.	Nile Silt B1	Badarian- Naqada I=Sheikh Muftah Unit
VII.	Limestone-tempered Fabric	Sheikh Muftah Unit
VIII.	Straw-and Gypsum-tempered Fabric	Naqada II-III=Sheikh Muftah Unit
IX.	Quartz-tempered Fabric	Sheikh Muftah Unit
X.	Ash-tempered Silt	Uncertain
XI.	Marl A1	Early Dynastic

Macroscopic Description

This is a medium-dense bodied, coarse-textured fabric. The predominant surface colours of this fabric are pink/brown and grey/brown. Some sherds have black marks on the surface that could have been produced as a result of fire or smoke clouding during the firing process. The colour of the groundmass is light brown/grey throughout the section.

Macroscopically-visible inclusions in this fabric include frequent, coarse platey shale and common medium quartz. The colour of the shale laths ranges from red/brown to very dark brown/black to light grey/brown; their size can be up to *c.* 8 mm in length.

Comments

Some sherds have the characteristic marks of coil built vessels whose surfaces have been smoothed over before firing. The surface colours, the presence of fire-clouding on the surface and the colour of the groundmass are indicative of firing in a bonfire with a mixed reducing and oxidising atmosphere. The sherds have quite hard surfaces that could be an indication of a relatively high firing temperature, however, this could also have resulted from extended exposure to wind.

Sample number: 16

II: Coarse Grit Fabric

Macroscopic Description

This is a medium-dense bodied, coarse-textured fabric. The interior and exterior surfaces are both light brown in colour. The surfaces are very rough and are quite heavily wind eroded. The colour of the groundmass is light brown throughout.

Macroscopically-visible inclusions in this fabric include frequent coarse rock fragments, and common medium quartz. The size of the rock fragments can be up to *c.* 9 mm by *c.* 4 mm; their colours include black, grey, and orange/brown.

Comments

The various rock fragments in this fabric differ in size, shape and colour and may represent different geological types. Some of the fragments have the appearance of being igneous, however, it was not possible to identify them macroscopically. The rock fragments in the Coarse Grit Fabric do not occur in any other Dakhleh-produced fabric and, if igneous, are not compatible with a Dakhleh provenance.

Sample number: 6

III: Coarse Quartz Fabric

Macroscopic Description

This is an open-bodied, coarse-textured fabric. The exterior surface colour is generally pale brown and the internal surface colour is orange/brown; most sherds are decorated with various impressed designs (see **Plates 50–51** and **Plate 49**). The groundmass has two zones of firing colours. The zone closest to the exterior surface is grey/brown and the zone closest to the interior surface is orange/brown.

Macroscopically-visible inclusions in this fabric are dominated by large, rounded, coarse quartz/sand grains, rare to very rare medium to coarse limestone, and very rare medium lath-like, reflective inclusions, which could be a form of mica. The colour of the quartz grains includes transparent green and some black. The quartz grains are generally 1–2 mm in diameter, with some as large as 3 mm. Until thin section analysis is undertaken it is not possible to identify positively the apparent micaceous inclusions.

Comments

This fabric is unlike that of any of the other Bashendi A sherds thought to have been produced in Dakhleh. The main macroscopic difference in the fabric is the amount, size and distribution of quartz grains in the matrix, as well as the reflective, mica-like inclusions, which are not typical of Dakhleh fabrics of any period. The impressed decoration is atypical of the corpus of Dakhleh-produced wares of this period. Therefore, vessels of this fabric are unlikely to have been made in Dakhleh and could have originated in desert areas to the west or south, where similarly decorated sherds and coarse fabrics are common (see Hope this volume, section I.2.1 for a discussion of possible provenance).

IV: Fine Quartz and Shale Fabric

Macroscopic Description

The fine quartz and shale fabric is usually an open-bodied, medium-textured fabric. The exterior surface is generally light brown in colour with grey/brown, brown and orange/brown also occurring. The interior surface colour can be black to black/grey, grey or light brown. Certain examples also have blackened areas that could have been produced as a result of fire-clouding during firing. Some sherds have what appear to be fingernail incisions on their external surface. In many of the mid-Holocene examples these incisions appear to have been produced in deliberate rows, however, in others they are more random and may have been made accidentally by the potters during surface smoothing. The colour of the groundmass can be brown/grey, grey or grey/black throughout, or zoned brown and black/grey. The weathered edges of sherds are usually a light brown colour, regardless of the actual colour of the groundmass.

Macroscopically-visible inclusions in this fabric include frequent to common medium platey shale, frequent to common fine sand/quartz, few to absent, fine to coarse red/brown clay pellets, very rare to absent medium limestone, and possibly very rare to absent fine calcareous microfossils. The colour of the quartz grains varies; transparent green being by far the most common and black occurring occasionally (see **Plate 45–46**).

Comments

All of the vessels produced in this fabric during the Bashendi A and B periods were almost certainly coil-built. The external and internal surfaces are generally smoothed, sometimes to the point of a streaky burnish, thus superficially masking the marks left as a result of coil building. These marks are more obvious on some sherds than others, however, upon close examination they are always extant. Variants of this fabric existed during the Bashendi A and Bashendi B periods that were more quartz-rich or more shale-rich than is normal. Although these fabrics may indicate the exploitation of different clay beds throughout the oasis, they are sufficiently similar macroscopically to be considered the same basic fabric.

The ceramic type that characterises the Bashendi B period is a thin-walled (c. 2–4 mm) and probably low-fired variant of this fabric. Some sherds are so brittle that they can be broken easily by hand and almost have the appearance of being sun-dried rather than fired. Surface colours of these sherds are predominately black or brown.
Sample numbers: 1, 4, 5, 7, 8, 9, 12, 14, 21, 22.

V: Coarse Calcareous Fabric

This fabric is unique to the Bashendi A and B Cultural Units in the Dakhleh Oasis, with the majority of examples occurring on Bashendi B sites. There are no other fabrics in Dakhleh from any other time periods that it resembles.

Macroscopic Description

This is a medium-dense bodied, coarse-textured fabric. The exterior surface of sherds of this fabric is uniformly orange/brown in colour and the interior surface is light brown. The exterior has a high concentration of visible coarse (up to c. 5 mm) white or transparent inclusions. Less of these inclusions are visible at the internal surface, however, they are still clearly present there and in the section. The surfaces have only been roughly smoothed, with various marks visible on the exterior surface. The groundmass is orange/brown to brown in colour. There is some evidence of zoning with an orange/brown zone at the exterior surface and a grey/brown zone at the interior surface.

Macroscopically-visible inclusions in this fabric include frequent fine-medium quartz/sand, common coarse white or transparent, possibly calcareous inclusions, and common fine to medium platey shale inclusions.

Comments

Thin section analysis has shown that the coarse calcareous inclusions are a combination of primarily limestone with some gypsum or anhydrite. Results of the NAA of a sherd of this fabric supports the identification of the white inclusions as being calcareous, with a value of 10.5% for calcium. However, as it is a bulk analytical method, it is virtually impossible to use the results of NAA alone to identify individual mineralogical components of ceramics. It is possible that during the Bashendi A and B Cultural Units a clay resource was exploited that was not used during any other period. This resource may have been abandoned for a number of reasons, but one might suggest that due to the high proportion of large calcareous inclusions in the clay, it was not suitable for firing at the higher temperatures used during later periods.
Sample number: 13

VI: Nile Silt B1

This sherd is the only definite example of Nile silt, Badarian Black-topped Brown ware from Dakhleh to date. It was found at site Loc. 135 (30/450-B4-1), which has been assigned by McDonald to the Sheikh Muftah Cultural Unit.

Macroscopic Description

This is a medium-dense bodied, fine-textured fabric. The colour of the exterior surface is brown, except around the top of the vessel, where there is a black/grey band approximately 1 cm wide (see Hope this volume, **Fig. 7i**, **Plate 57**, bottom right). The interior surface of the sherd is uniformly black/grey. Small marks left by straw are visible on the exterior surface, some of which may contain the silica skeletons noted by Nordström and Bourriau in Nile B1 (1993, 171). The groundmass is zoned, with a large (c. 90%) black/grey core and narrow, brown surface zones. Macroscopically visible inclusions in this fabric include frequent fine to coarse sand/quartz, few fine reflective lath-like inclusions that could be mica, very few fine limestone and voids left as a result of burnt-out straw.

Sample number: 15

VII: Limestone-Tempered Fabric

Macroscopic Description

This is a dense-bodied, medium-textured fabric. The exterior and interior surfaces are grey/black in colour. The exterior has been covered in a punctate design, with rows of circular and squarish impressions present (see **Plate 61**). The groundmass of this fabric has a central brown/grey core with orange/brown surface zones. The larger, elongated voids seem to have a preferred orientation parallel to the vessel walls.

Macroscopically-visible inclusions include common medium quartz/sand, common fine to medium red/brown clay pellets, common fine to coarse limestone and very rare fine calcareous microfossils.

Comments

There is a relatively high proportion of what appear to be limestone inclusions in this fabric. These include one very large piece that is *c.* 5 mm in diameter and could possibly be a type of sandstone. Some of the limestone in this fabric has spalled or decomposed, indicating a firing temperature of at least 750-800°C. The colour zoning of the groundmass indicates that it was fired in a kiln with a predominately oxidising environment. Given the grey/black surface colours, it was almost certainly exposed to a controlled reducing atmosphere at some stage of the process. It appears that the vessel from which this sample originated was fired with a much higher degree of control than is normally the case with Dakhleh ceramics of the period. The general mineralogy of the clay used to produce this vessel, however, could be consistent with an origin in Dakhleh. Based on other factors such as decoration and firing, it is suggested that it represents an import from the west into the Dakhleh Oasis (see Hope this volume, section I.3.2 for a more detailed discussion of possible provenance).

VIII: Straw- and Gypsum-Tempered Fabric

Macroscopic Description

This is an open-bodied, coarse-textured fabric. The exterior and interior surfaces are brown. Both surfaces have small, rectangular impressions in a random arrangement, which were almost certainly made by some type of vegetal material such as fine straw (see Hope this volume, **Plate 60**). The groundmass has a wide, grey central core with brown zones on either side.

Macroscopically-visible inclusions include frequent coarse white/clear limestone and gypsum fragments, common medium to coarse sand/quartz, few fine reflective, lath-like inclusions that are possibly mica and the remains of burnt-out straw/vegetal material.

Comments

This fabric is almost certainly a Nile silt fabric that is similar to Petrie's Rough ware. Recent descriptions of several fabrics are similar to this sherd, namely Hierakonpolis Fabric/temper class 1: Straw tempered Nile Silt (Friedman 1994, 141–7), Hierakonpolis Fabric/temper class 4: Straw and Stone tempered Nile Silt (Friedman 1994, 147–8), and Naqada Fabric/temper class 1: Straw tempered Nile silt (Friedman 1994, 506). Friedman's description of Hierakonpolis Fabric/temper class 4: Straw and Stone tempered Nile Silt most closely resembles this fabric. She notes (1994, 147) that well distributed 'stones' or white-grey minerals, rounded to sub-angular in shape and ranging in size from 2–4 mm are characteristic of this fabric. The colour of this fabric is the same as that of the Hierakonpolis fabric. It has the similar dark grey core zones with brown margins (Friedman 1994, 147) and a brown surface colour, possibly the result of self-slipping (Geller 1984, 66).

Sample 11, an example of this fabric, is almost certainly a piece of standard Predynastic Rough ware rather than specifically a Hierakonpolis product. The descriptions in Friedman (1994) and Geller (1984) are, however, the most detailed comparative materials available to date.

Sample number: 11

IX: Quartz-Tempered Fabric

Macroscopic Description

This is an open-bodied, medium-textured fabric. The external and internal surfaces of the sherd are black/grey. Neither surface appears to have been carefully smoothed or polished. The rim has incisions spaced at approximately 5 mm intervals running across it (see Hope this volume, **Fig. 1h**). The groundmass of the sherd is brown/grey throughout.

Macroscopically-visible inclusions include frequent medium to coarse sand/quartz, common medium limestone and few fine to medium clay pellets. The colour of the quartz includes opaque white, transparent green and black, while the clay pellets are orange/brown and red/brown. Some of the limestone has spalled during firing leaving the characteristic reaction rims.

Comments

The colour of the surfaces and the groundmass indicate that this sherd was fired in a predominantly reducing environment. Macroscopically, this fabric does not resemble any other Dakhleh fabric of the period as the sand/quartz occurs in greater quantities and larger sizes than is generally the case. The size and distribution of the quartz grains is similar to that of the Coarse Quartz Fabric, however, the presence of the clay pellets clearly differentiates it. It is possible that these two fabrics may be related, but unfortunately analysis of Coarse Quartz Fabric sherds was not possible for this study to be able to confirm this. Given the fact that its chemical composition is quite different from the known Dakhleh material, a provenance somewhere to the southeast of Dakhleh is suggested on the basis of the fabric (see Hope this volume, section I.2.2 for a more detailed discussion of the provenance of this type based on published stylistic parallels).

Sample number: 20

X: Ash-Tempered Silt

Only one sherd of this ware has been recovered in Dakhleh, at site 33/405-B5-1 (Loc. 5). This site was found during the second year of the survey of the oasis undertaken in 1979 and, based on the amount of surface debitage, was reported as having evidence of large-scale lithic production (Mills 1980, 255; McDonald 1980, 317–9). McDonald's report (1980, 317) indicates that in addition to this isolated, hand-made sherd, 'some Roman and Islamic pottery' was also found. Recent re-examination of the lithics at this site has shown that they date to the Middle Stone Age (McDonald, pers. comm. 1999). Given the probable date of the other scattered ceramics, this sherd should be seen as an isolated surface find, with no date attributable on the basis of association with other material at the site.

Macroscopic Description

This is a medium-dense bodied, fine-textured fabric. The external and internal surfaces are black in colour. The external surface of the sherd has what appear to be deep fingernail impressions running down the body, perpendicular to the rim. Both surfaces have the appearance of having been either burnished, polished or scraped, although the exterior surface is quite weathered (see Hope this volume, **Fig. 6** m and **Plate 62**).

Macroscopically visible inclusions include frequent fine to medium sand/quartz, few fine reflective, lath-like inclusions that are possibly mica, very few fine to medium limestone, very few fine white/grey inclusions that are possibly ash and very rare vegetal/straw/charcoal.

Comments

This vessel was probably coil built, with the manufacturing marks masked by the surface treatment applied to the vessel walls. It appears that it was made from a silt clay that was highly polished and decorated with fingernail incisions prior to firing in a fully reducing atmosphere.

XI: Marl A1

Several sherds from sites dated to the Sheikh Muftah Cultural Unit or the Old Kingdom resemble the marl fabric of some of Petrie's Late ware. Two of these sherds from 31/405-M10-3 (Loc. 59) were analysed by NAA (Sample numbers 2 and 3), however, statistical analysis of the NAA results of these sherds has grouped them with sherds known to have been produced in Dakhleh. A discussion of the problems associated with this is provided below.

Macroscopic Description

This is a medium-dense to dense-bodied, medium to fine-textured fabric. The external and internal surfaces are orange/brown in colour. There are possible signs of an original plum or red slip on the external surface of Sample 3.

There are also possible signs of straw impressions on the surface with remains of silica being visible in some of them. The groundmass is orange/brown throughout.

Macroscopically visible inclusions include common, fine to medium limestone, common fine sand/quartz, few fine reflective, lath-like inclusions that are possibly mica, very few fine red/brown clay pellets, and the remains of straw.

Comments

Macroscopically this fabric resembles Marl A1 fabric (Nordström and Bourriau 1993, 176) of an Early Dynastic vessels, part of Petrie's Late ware. Given the date of the site from which the samples come, an Early Dynastic date is not at all problematic.

Sample numbers: 2 and 3

Discussion of Results from NAA and Thin Section Petrology

Macroscopic examination of the entire corpus of early and mid-Holocene ceramics from Dakhleh has shown that by far the most common fabric of this period is the Fine Quartz and Shale Fabric. The raw material used in the production of virtually all vessels of the early and mid-Holocene is almost certainly the shale and/or mudstone clays common within Dakhleh. Geologically, the majority of Dakhleh is covered by the Quseir formation. This consists primarily of claystones, siltstones and sandstones that overlie the sandstones of the Taref formation (Hermina 1990, 271). Unfortunately, these shale formations extend through Kharga, Aswan and into parts of Nubia (Said 1962, 133). This fact makes it difficult to rely on any one method of analysis alone when attempting to assign a definite provenance to these ceramics.

Limestone and chert pediments and gravels also occur throughout Dakhleh (Kleindienst et al. 1999). Kleindienst et al. (1999) have noted the presence of many Ferruginous Sandy Sediment (FSS) and Calcareous Silty Sediment (CSS) deposits throughout Dakhleh that are made up of several units of claystone derived muds. These clays are known to contain calcareous sediments, sandstone and quartzite gravel, chert and ironstone. These FSS and CSS deposits were possibly exploited for clay by potters in antiquity as they are by the potters working at el-Qasr (Henein 1997) and Zukheir[5] today (Eccleston 1998).

Recently it has been possible to prepare thin sections of a selection of the sherds analysed previously by NAA plus two more that were not analysed. This selection included Sample numbers 1, 2, 4, 7, 9, 11, 13, 15, 16, 22, the Limestone-tempered Fabric and the Ash-tempered Fabric as listed in **Table 2**. These sherds are as representative as possible of the different chronological periods and fabric groups, given the size of the sherds remaining after being sampled for NAA.

Dakhleh Fabrics

Thin section analysis of Sample numbers 1, 4, 7 and 22 of the Fine Quartz and Shale Fabric showed a similar mineral-

Table 2: Samples discussed specifically in the text

Sample	DOP Site Number	Loc. Number	Cultural Unit (Based on lithics)	Macroscopic Group	NAA Cluster
1	30/450-C6-1	212	Bashendi B	IV	1
2	31/405-M10-3	59	Sheikh Muftah	XI	1
3	31/405-M10-3	59	Sheikh Muftah	XI	1
4	30/450-B10-1	254	Bashendi B	IV	1
5	Unknown	Unknown	Bashendi B?	IV	1
6	Plateau-Mauhoub	76	Masara A	II	1
7	30/405-B10-1	254	Bashendi A	IV	1
8	30/450-B4-1	135	Sheikh Muftah	IV	1
9	30/450-C6-1	212	Bashendi B	IV	1
11	31/420-P6-1	100	Sheikh Muftah	VIII	2
12	30/450-C6-1	212	Bashendi B	IV	1
13	30/450-C6-1	212	Bashendi B	V	1
14	30/450-B4-1	135	Sheikh Muftah	IV	3
15	30/450-B4-1	135	Sheikh Muftah	VI	2
16	30/430-D7-1	259	Masara	I	4
20	31/420-C10-2	74	Sheikh Muftah	IX	5
21	30/450-B4-1	135	Sheikh Muftah	IV	1
22	30/450-C6-1	212	Bashendi B	IV	1
L.T.F.	31/405-K10-5	48	Sheikh Muftah	VII	Not Analysed
A.T.S.	33/405-B5-1	5	Sheikh Muftah?	X	Not Analysed
C.Q.F.	30/435-P10-1	275	Bashendi A	III	Not Analysed

L.T.F. = Limestone-tempered Fabric
A.T.S. = Ash-tempered Silt
C.Q.F. = Coarse Quartz Fabric

Masara Unit: *c.* 9200–8500 bp
Bashendi A Unit: *c.* 7600–6800 bp
Bashendi B Unit: *c.* 6500–5200 bp
Sheikh Muftah Unit: *c.* 5070–4310 bp

ogy to the samples that form what I have elsewhere defined as the Coarse Ferruginous Fabric (Eccleston 1998, 29–33, 49–51, figs 8–12). This includes the macroscopically-defined fabrics A1, A2 and A29 of the Dakhleh fabric typology for the Pharaonic and Roman periods (Hope *et al.* 2000). This fabric is characterised by dominant to frequent elongated ovoid ferruginous features and monocrystalline quartz, few to absent micritic limestone, very few clay pellets, very few to absent chert, rare to very rare polycrystalline quartz and opaques (iron oxide), rare to absent foraminifera, and very rare to absent sandstone, dolomite, plagioclase feldspar, alkali feldspar, microcline, amphibole, biotite mica, clinopyroxene and epidote.[6]

Photomicrographs of the thin sections of early and mid-Holocene sherds prepared by Hughan and Segnit (1989) show the same fabric that was observed in the recently-made thin sections. Mineral types noted were the elongated shaley fragments, quartz, chert, feldspars, haematite (iron oxide), shale and flint. All these minerals are mineralogically com-

patible with a sedimentary deposit such as the FSS deposits in Dakhleh (Hermina 1990; Kleindienst *et al.* 1999).

The apparent macroscopic differences between the fabrics of the early and mid-Holocene and the ferruginous fabrics of the later periods are likely to be a result of the differences in clay preparation techniques and firing technology, rather than a difference in the type of raw clay used. No evidence of fixed firing structures have been found at sites of the early to mid-Holocene, and it has been postulated that pottery from this period was fired in bonfires or in what Edwards termed 'proto-kilns' (Edwards and Hope 1989, 4). However, hearths are commonly encountered on the sites and could possibly have been used for firing pottery.

Hughan and Segnit (1989) have reported that in thin section the groundmass of the Fine Quartz and Shale Fabric is optically active. The recent thin section samples are also optically active, supporting Hughan and Segnit's earlier observations. This type of groundmass is usually indicative of a low firing temperature, probably below 700°C. Examples of ferruginous fabrics of later date examined in thin section are optically inactive, indicating a firing temperature of at least 800-850°C (Eccleston 1998, 30). It is possible that this higher firing temperature would cause the clay to sinter and vitrify further, so it would appear macroscopically to be a denser fabric.

Samples 12 and 22 were discovered to have originated from the same vessel after the analysis was undertaken. During the recent re-examination of this material they were loosely grouped together on the basis of chemical analysis alone before a close macroscopic comparison was made. This example highlights the problems associated with using chemical analysis alone in a ceramic study such as this. Visual comparison of the results of the chemical analysis of these sherds shows that while they are similar, there is still a fair degree of heterogeneity in the fabric of any one ceramic vessel and that one should be wary of relying solely on the results of chemical analysis.

Sample 9 was identified with a hand lens as a Fine Quartz and Shale Fabric, however, in thin section its texture is visually different to the previous four samples. This sample is consistent with Eccleston's (1998, 52–54) Fine Ferruginous Fabric, which has an almost identical mineralogy to the Coarse Ferruginous Fabric except for the presence of the distinctive elongated, ovoid ferruginous features. It is possible that the two clays used to make these fabrics are versions of the same geological deposit, however, until further sampling and more extensive ceramic analysis is undertaken, it is not possible to comment further on this.

Macroscopically, Sample 14 resembles a shale-rich, coarse variant of the Fine Shale and Quartz Fabric. Statistical grouping of the results of NAA on this sherd, however, shows that it stands alone and away from the other Dakhleh produced samples (**Table 4**, Cluster 3). Given that the sherd is typologically and macroscopically compatible with its Sheikh Muftah find context, it is suggested that this sherd was produced in Dakhleh during the Sheikh Muftah period, rather than being an import, as the NAA results alone might have suggested.

The possible Masara Unit sherds give some of the most perplexing results of this study. Sample 16 groups alone on the basis of chemical composition, but definitely appears to be a locally-produced Coarse Shale Fabric. Sample 6 is in fact quite different. The large rock fragments that occur have the appearance of being igneous, however, it is far from certain that this is the case. If they are igneous, it would preclude Dakhleh as a provenance for this fabric based on the geology of the region (Kleindienst *et al.* 1999). Yet the chemical composition of Sample 6 is similar to the majority of the other Dakhleh pieces that group in Cluster 1 of **Table 4**.

Sample 13 of the Coarse Calcareous Fabric contains frequent quartz, frequent limestone, few gypsum, very few opaques (iron oxide) and very few clay pellets. The groundmass of the sample appears to have frequent, small limestone inclusions scattered across the entire section. This, along with the large fragments of limestone and gypsum present, explains the 10.5% calcium content in this sherd.

All of the fabrics discussed above, with the exception of Sample 6, have a mineralogy that is consistent with an origin in the Dakhleh Oasis. This, combined with the above discussion by Hope, provides the basis of our hypothesis that these fabrics were produced in Dakhleh during the early to mid-Holocene.

Imports

The majority of fabrics discussed in this part of the study represent imports into Dakhleh during the early and mid-Holocene, although they only form a small percentage of the total assemblage. The identification of imported ceramics is an important facet for the study of this period. Such ceramics show us quite clearly that long distance movement of material culture was occurring in the region at this time.

Multivariate statistical analysis of the NAA data shows that the majority of samples, most of which are thought to have been produced locally, have a sufficiently similar chemical composition to be grouped together (**Table 4**, Cluster 1).[7] The date of this material ranges from the Masara to Sheikh Muftah and includes sherds from four of the local fabric groups. The most problematic part of this cluster is the inclusion of Samples 2 and 3, which implies that they are chemically similar to ceramics produced in Dakhleh.

Samples 2 and 3 were both identified macroscopically in the field as being a Nile Valley Marl A1 fabric and part of the group of vessels included in Petrie's Early Dynastic Late ware.[8] Petrographic analysis of Sample 2 seems to confirm this identification, with quartz, limestone, biotite mica, muscovite mica, plagioclase feldspar, pyroxene, opaques (iron oxide) and clay pellets being present. This is consistent with Nicholson's descriptions of Marl A fabrics from later periods at Memphis/Saqqara and Amarna (Nicholson and Rose 1985; Bourriau and Nicholson 1992) and is not consistent with the petrology of ceramics from Dakhleh (Eccleston 1998, 48–71).

Previous work on the results of NAA of 156 samples of ceramics of the Sheikh Muftah Cultural Unit to the fifth century AD from Dakhleh also resulted in a Marl A1 sample grouping with locally-produced Dakhleh material (Eccleston 1997, 32, 89). The sample was taken from a sherd that was identified by Hope as being from an Old Kingdom Meidum bowl manufactured in the Nile Valley. These two independent studies show that there is a problem in using chemical composition alone in assigning provenance to ceramics. It also raises an interesting question for future consideration regarding the apparent chemical similarity of Marl A1 to ceramics from Dakhleh.

Samples 11 and 15 are both identified macroscopically as being possible Nile silts. They are loosely grouped together on the basis of chemical composition (**Table 4**, Cluster 2), independent from Cluster 1. Petrographic analysis of these samples has confirmed their macroscopic identification as Nile silts and explains their clustering away from Dakhleh samples on the basis of chemical composition. The major difference in the chemical composition of these samples is in calcium, with Sample 11 containing 7.97% and Sample 15 containing 3.20%. Petrographically, Sample 11 contains common quartz, common biotite mica, few gypsum or anhydrite, very few muscovite mica, very few limestone, very few plagioclase feldspar, rare opaques (iron oxide), rare voids produced from burnt-out straw, very rare pyroxene and very rare hornblende. This is consistent with other petrographic descriptions of Nile Silt B1 (Bourriau *et al.* 2000) and Geller's description of Rough ware from Hierakonpolis (Geller 1984, 65), with the exception of the gypsum. It is possible that this was added intentionally to the paste as a filler by the potter during the preparation process. Mineralogically, Sample 15 is similar to Sample 11, except for the presence of the large, angular gypsum/anhydrite fragments. It also appears to have slightly more biotite mica and to be a better-sorted and finer fabric. The presence of the gypsum/anhydrite in Sample 11 explains the difference in calcium content and is an example of how macroscopic, microscopic and chemical analysis can be used in conjunction to assist in confirming provenance and technology.

The chemical composition of Sample 20, taken from a very small rim sherd of the Quartz-tempered Fabric, is unlike any other in this sample set. This is reflected in it clustering alone and away from all other samples (**Table 4**). On the basis of chemical composition alone, it is unlikely that this fabric originated in either Dakhleh or the Nile Valley. The incised decoration on the rim is not common in the Dakhleh tradition and it has been suggested that it could have come from the desert area to the southeast of Dakhleh (Hope this volume). As the size of the sherd was very small and this is the only known example of a vessel of this type in Dakhleh, it was decided not to make a thin section from it.

It also proved difficult to assign a precise provenance to the Ash-tempered sherd on the basis of both thin section analysis and stylistic parallels. Nordström's (1972, 51–53) Fabric Group II (Ferruginous Fabrics with Organic Temper) seems to be the closest macroscopic parallel. He reports (1972, 62) that the Black Polished Group (H3) appeared most commonly in Fabrics IIA or IIB. The most likely parallel with our sherd is Fabric IIA, which is described as a low to medium-grade fabric with ash-tempered paste (Nordström 1972, 51). Although this fabric seems harder and not as crumbly as Nordström's description, it is possible that it is a slightly different variant. The small white/grey inclusions that were noted macroscopically in the Dakhleh sherd may be ash, which would be consistent with this fabric.

A thin section has been made of the Ash-tempered Silt sherd in an attempt to assist in determining its provenance. This analysis revealed that it has common monocrystalline quartz, few plagioclase feldspar and biotite mica, very few hornblende, pyroxene and limestone, and very rare calcite. Unfortunately, these results do not suggest anything more than that it is made from a clay with a similar mineralogy to a standard Nile silt. Nordström (1972, 51) reports that

quartz, plagioclase feldspar, mica and high relief minerals have been noted in thin section analysis of Fabric IIA from Neolithic and A-Group sites in Nubia. With the exception of the calcareous inclusions, the mineralogy seems to be consistent, although it would also be consistent with a Nile silt clay from many locations in the Nile Valley.

The final sherd to be discussed is the Limestone-tempered Fabric sherd from Loc. 48. Stylistically this sherd has many parallels in the desert regions west of Dakhleh. Thin section analysis did not provide any useful results, revealing a mineralogy that is compatible with an origin in any number of areas in the vicinity. Without further information, the exact provenance of the Ash-tempered Silt and Limestone-tempered Fabric sherds remains problematic.

Conclusions

Samples 14 and 16, two examples of what are thought to be Dakhleh manufactures, raise an interesting methodological problem regarding the use of chemical composition alone in assigning provenance to ceramics without reference to other types of analysis. The results of this study show that until further surveying and analysis of clay beds in Dakhleh is carried out, it is not possible to say how much chemical variation is present in different clays within Dakhleh. Thus it is difficult to use bulk chemical analysis alone as a method of identifying Dakhleh manufactures amongst large collections of material found outside the oasis.

Attempting to locate clay deposits exploited by potters in antiquity and taking samples from them will form a component of future field seasons of the DOP. It is anticipated that this work and subsequent thin section and chemical analyses of ceramics from all periods will allow us to quantify some of the macroscopic differences in the fine and coarse variants of some fabric types, especially the Fine Quartz and Shale Fabric. It may also eventually be possible to discover long-term patterns of resource exploitation and clay preparation techniques of potters within Dakhleh and intra-oasis differences in the composition of superficially similar clay beds and the ceramics produced from them.

Examination and analysis of the early and mid-Holocene ceramics from Dakhleh have shown that it is generally possible to identify locally-produced ceramics macroscopically with the aid of a hand lens and/or a relatively low magnification binocular microscope. Use of thin section analysis, and to a lesser extent NAA, has allowed the early and mid-Holocene ceramics to be related mineralogically to the local geology and ceramics of later periods, and to be differentiated from ceramics produced outside Dakhleh. The cases where the results are inconclusive are rare and further research in Dakhleh and the surrounding desert areas may soon help to resolve the problems they raise.

Notes

1. Samples 17, 18 and 19 are not included as they were subsequently re-identified as dating to the Roman period. No results were provided for Sample 10 or a sherd so labelled present among the samples. There were two results for Sample 2 numbered Sample 2A and 2B.

2. Unpublished report Hughan and Segnit 1989.

3. All thin sections were produced by the author in the normal way to a thickness of thirty microns and were examined on a standard petrographic microscope at magnifications predominantly of ×50 and ×100 using both plane and cross-polarised light.

4. In macroscopic descriptions previously published by a number of authors, the word 'shale' has commonly been used to refer to the platey, lath-like and pellet inclusions of clay common in Dakhleh ceramics of all periods. The use of the word 'shale' in describing these inclusions is probably technically incorrect, as the inclusions are shale, mudstone or claystone. To facilitate interpretation and until further detailed geological and petrographic analysis is undertaken, use of the word 'shale' to describe the platey inclusions of this type will be adopted for convenience. The term 'clay pellets' will be used to describe the more rounded inclusions that are almost certainly the same basic material.

5. Zukheir is a small village located in the east of the Dakhleh Oasis, approximately 5 km to the south of Bashendi.

6. A full petrographic description of this fabric and colour plates appear in Eccleston 1998 (29–33, 49–51, figs 8–12). They are also published by Eccleston as part of 'Appendix 1: Macroscopic and Petrographic Descriptions of Late Period Keg and Flask Fabrics' in Hope *et al.* 2000.

7. This conclusion is also supported by the results obtained on ceramics of later periods (Eccleston 1997).

8. The initial macroscopic identification of these fabrics was made by Hope.

Bibliography

Bourriau J D and Nicholson P T, 1992. Marl Clay Pottery Fabrics of the New Kingdom from Memphis, Saqqara and Amarna. *Journal of Egyptian Archaeology* 78: 29–91.

Bourriau, J D, Smith L, and Nicholson P T, 2000. *Nile Clay and Mixed Nile/Marl Clay Pottery Fabrics of the New Kingdom from Memphis and Amarna.* London.

Eccleston M A J, 1997. *Provenance Study of Ceramics from the Dakhleh Oasis, Egypt.* Unpublished BA (Honours) thesis. Department of Classics and Archaeology, Monash University, Melbourne.

Eccleston M A J, 1998. *Petrographic Study of Locally Produced Ceramics from the Dakhleh Oasis, Egypt.* Unpublished MSc thesis. Department of Archaeology and Prehistory, University of Sheffield, Sheffield.

Edwards W I and Hope C A, 1989. A Note on the Neolithic Ceramics from the Dakhleh Oasis (Egypt). In L Krzyzaniak and M Kobusiewicz (eds), *Late Prehistory of the Nile Basin and the Sahara.* Poznan: 233–42.

Friedman R F, 1994. *Predynastic Settlement Ceramics of Upper Egypt: A Comparative Study of the Ceramics of Hemamieh, Nagada and Hierakonpolis.* PhD Thesis. University of California, Berkeley. University Microfilms International, Michigan.

Geller J R, 1984. *The Predynastic Ceramics Industry at Hierakonpolis, Egypt.* MA thesis. Washington University, St. Louis. University Microfilms International, Michigan.

Henein N H, 1997. *Poterie et Potiers d'al-Qasr.* Cairo.

Hermina M, 1990.The Surroundings of Kharga, Dakhla and Farafra Oases. In R Said (ed.), *The Geology of Egypt.* Rotterdam: 259–92.

Hope C A, 1998. Early Pottery from the Dakhleh Oasis. *The Bulletin of the Australian Centre for Egyptology* 9: 53–60.

Hope C A, Eccleston M A J, Kaper O E, Marchand S, and Darnell D, 2000. Kegs and Flasks from the Dakhleh Oasis. *Cahiers de la Céramique Égyptienne* 6: 189–234.

Hughan R R, and Segnit E R, 1989. *Examination of Dakhleh Sherds.* Unpublished Report. The Research and Consulting Company of Victoria College, Melbourne.

Kleindienst M R, Churcher C S, McDonald M M A, and Schwarcz H P, 1999. Geomorphological Setting and Quaternary Geology of the Dakhleh Oasis Region: Interim Report. In C C Churcher and A J Mills (eds), *Reports from the Survey of the Dakhleh Oasis, Western Desert of Egypt, 1977-1987.* Oxbow Monograph 99, Dakhleh Oasis Project Monograph 2. Oxford: 1–54.

McDonald M M A, 1980. Preliminary Report on Lithic Industries in the Dakhleh Oasis. *The Journal of the Society for the Study of Egyptian Antiquities* 10: 315–29.

McDonald M M A, 2001. The Late Prehistoric Radiocarbon Chronology for the Dakhleh Oasis within the wider Environmental and Cultural Setting of the Egyptian Western Desert. In M Marlow (ed.), *Proceedings of the First International Dakhleh Oasis Project Seminar, July 5–9, 1994.* Oxford.

Mills A J, 1980. Dakhleh Oasis Project: Report on the Second Season of Survey September–December 1979. *The Journal of the Society for the Study of Egyptian Antiquities* 10: 251–82.

Nicholson P T and Rose P, 1985. Pottery fabrics and ware groups at el-Amarna. In B J Kemp (ed.), *Amarna Reports II.* Cambridge: 133–74.

Nordström H-Å, 1972. *Neolithic and A-Group Sites.* Stockholm.

Nordström H-Å, and Bourriau J, 1993. Ceramic Technology: Clays and Fabrics. In Do Arnold and J Bourriau (eds), *An Introduction to Ancient Egyptian Pottery.* Fascicle 2. Mainz am Rhein.

Said R, 1962. *The Geology of Egypt.* New York.

Tangri D, 1989. *Neolithic Pottery from the Dakhleh Oasis.* Unpublished BA (Honours) thesis. Department of Archaeology, University of Sydney, Sydney.

Tangri D, 1991. Basket-Impressed Pottery from the Dakhleh Oasis. *Sahara* 4: 141–3.

Tangri D, 1992. A Reassessment of the Origins of the Predynastic in Upper Egypt. *Proceedings of the Prehistoric Society* 58: 111–25.

Table 3: Neutron Activation Analysis Results of Early to Mid-Holocene Sherds

	Sample 1	Sample 2	Sample 2A	Sample 3	Sample 4	Sample 5	Sample 6	Sample 7	Sample 8	Sample 9
Na	6960	8040	8230	6590	4430	5520	5640	4330	6350	5920
Mg	1.4	2.8	2.3	1.6	1.4	1.3	1.3	1.7	1.2	1.1
Al	7.3	7.2	7.4	8.2	9.3	5.7	5.4	9.7	11.3	4.5
Na2	6610	8570	8670	6640	4430	5490	6160	4350	6560	6050
Na3	7250	8650	8760	6910	4520	5510	6130	4240	6470	6470
Cl	4000	1790	1820	420	280	880	790	1460	870	2290
K	1.15	1.22	1.19	1.26	1.44	1.08	1.13	1.19	1.56	1.14
Ca	3.82	8.63	8.08	8.33	2.59	9.54	11.5	3.88	3.59	17.2
Sc	16.1	15.6	15.7	17.7	17.2	10.1	10.9	17.9	20.3	9.75
Ti	3850	4420	4900	5370	5020	3960	3650	4970	4710	4070
V	156	114	110	113	166	88	80	184	195	68
Cr	131	154	160	178	160	105	110	173	193	90
Mn	364	647	681	739	502	426	478	432	384	565
Fe	5.52	4.40	4.66	5.12	5.17	3.06	3.20	5.16	5.69	3.03
Co	15.2	19.4	20.5	23.1	17.0	11.9	12.4	16.0	18.6	13.0
Ni	≤36	≤32	≤34	≤35	≤45	≤33	≤35	≤37	≤45	≤31
Sc2	15.3	15.3	16.2	18.2	17.5	10.8	10.9	18.1	19.1	10.9
Ga	≤16	≤16	≤16	≤16	≤17	≤16	≤17	≤13	≤19	≤15
As	8.9	5.9	5.7	5.6	6.8	3.4	3.1	8.7	10.9	8.9
Br	≤0.9	2.0	1.9	≤0.9	2.1	3.0	≤0.9	≤0.8	2.2	2.9
Rb	40	47	52	63	43	40	42	48	55	65
Sr	370	510	490	540	360	440	530	390	550	430
Sb	0.34	0.39	0.36	0.46	0.32	0.29	0.33	0.27	0.38	0.22
Cs	1.1	2.1	2.0	2.4	1.4	1.3	1.5	2.0	2.4	2.5
Ba	450	490	330	300	620	280	330	340	270	310
La	38.2	36.4	36.9	41.2	39.0	29.6	32.3	39.8	47.8	23.7
Ce	66.7	67.3	71.7	81.5	73.8	61.3	61.1	74.9	83.6	52.0
Nd	33	32	29	37	34	28	29	31	40	22
Sm	7.21	6.87	6.93	7.66	6.84	5.44	5.82	6.78	8.24	4.77
Eu	1.66	1.46	1.66	1.54	1.68	1.58	1.28	1.70	2.04	1.44
Eu2	1.66	1.66	1.67	1.94	1.70	1.26	1.25	1.64	1.80	1.25
Tb	0.87	1.06	1.02	1.09	1.06	0.84	0.75	0.81	1.28	0.91
Dy	3.7	3.5	3.4	3.8	3.6	3.3	3.2	3.5	4.1	3.2
Yb	2.88	3.18	3.10	3.34	2.56	2.74	2.47	2.63	3.17	2.54
Lu	0.41	0.45	0.46	0.50	0.45	0.45	0.41	0.39	0.42	0.43
Hf	3.47	4.80	5.20	5.79	5.40	9.97	7.34	4.40	4.24	5.54
Ta	0.95	1.28	1.33	1.45	1.27	1.24	1.20	1.35	1.41	1.22
Th	7.80	7.80	8.56	5.79	9.82	8.23	7.82	10.1	11.3	4.94
U	3.8	5.2	3.7	6.9	3.0	4.7	3.2	5.3	4.5	3.9

Table 3: Neutron Activation Analysis Results of Early to Mid-Holocene Sherds (continued)

	Sample 11	Sample 12	Sample 13	Sample 14	Sample 15	Sample 16	Sample 20	Sample 21	Sample 22
Na	11000	5900	3050	11000	12200	2720	10000	5570	4650
Mg	1.3	1.6	1.1	1.2	1.7	1.0	≤2.7	1.1	1.0
Al	6.4	10.7	6.75	10.2	7.00	13.5	6.8	5.4	8.7
Na2	11400	6040	2990	11800	12800	2780	10600	5900	4730
Na3	10900	6200	3280	12100	12300	3350	10000	5820	4560
Cl	7550	1500	770	10600	2120	160	11300	720	570
K	1.17	1.19	1.30	1.17	1.18	1.21	1.21	1.29	1.41
Ca	7.97	2.74	10.5	3.83	3.20	1.00	2.50	9.12	3.49
Sc	18.6	20.1	12.7	19.7	19.7	25.5	14.4	10.3	16.2
Ti	8270	5720	5480	4470	9640	6240	10700	4190	4620
V	142	210	96	180	188	299	≤160	91	152
Cr	143	209	108	211	158	250	146	101	151
Mn	854	362	556	298	1080	86	10900	435	477
Fe	5.94	6.05	4.08	5.67	6.59	4.97	5.24	3.24	4.83
Co	27.1	19.9	13.7	19.6	29.7	14.5	99.6	12.0	16.5
Ni	≤44	≤50	≤36	≤38	≤35	≤43	107	≤34	≤30
Sc2	19.2	20.9	12.5	20.6	19.8	26.0	14.9	10.3	16.3
Ga	≤22	≤18	≤13	≤21	≤18	39±4	≤18	≤17	≤14
As	2.0	11.5	4.7	9.2	3.1	10.1	18.6	3.5	6.9
Br	≤1.0	≤1.4	≤1.0	2.3	≤1.0	≤1.1	2.6	4.2	2.1
Rb	54	52	44	43	52	57	43	34	39
Sr	370	370	310	510	360	220	390	390	290
Sb	0.23	0.38	0.42	0.45	≤0.14	0.33	0.33	0.31	0.30
Cs	1.0	2.7	1.9	2.3	1.3	3.4	1.3	1.2	1.3
Ba	630	270	470	260	480	200	1900	250	460
La	28.0	46.9	40.9	47.2	31.2	49.4	31.4	31.5	32.3
Ce	58.8	94.3	77.9	95.2	65.9	92.1	68.5	61.8	74.0
Nd	25	53	27	42	26	32	18	18	32
Sm	6.07	8.00	7.67	8.01	6.78	6.65	5.63	5.63	6.55
Eu	1.62	1.52	1.62	1.90	1.78	1.40	1.56	0.99	1.56
Eu2	1.69	1.84	1.59	1.80	1.78	1.52	1.42	1.22	1.43
Tb	1.05	0.97	0.92	0.85	0.74	0.52	0.72	0.73	0.74
Dy	3.4	4.2	4.2	3.6	4.1	2.6	6.7	2.9	3.5
Yb	2.82	2.97	3.39	2.63	3.18	2.05	1.94	2.48	2.57
Lu	0.41	0.47	0.54	0.45	0.48	0.35	0.31	0.41	0.40
Hf	1.62	4.50	8.79	4.82	7.87	4.09	2.93	9.62	4.82
Ta	—	1.53	1.32	1.61	2.07	1.85	1.30	1.28	1.13
Th	5.69	12.4	9.81	12.9	6.68	15.8	8.8	7.8	9.61
U	3.0	5.4	4.2	5.1	4.4	3.3	12	2.9	4.7

Table 4: Near Neighbour Clustering of Dakhleh Early to Mid-Holocene Sherds

Distance Measure: Average Distance
Number of Neighbours Considered: 6

Number of Shared Near Neighbours

Cluster 1: Samples 1, 2, 2A, 3, 4, 5, 6, 7, 8, 9, 12, 13, 21, 22

Cluster 2: Samples 11, 15

Cluster 3: Sample 14

Cluster 4: Sample 16

Cluster 5: Sample 20

Another Old Kingdom Site in the Dakhleh Oasis

A J Mills

The Dakhleh Oasis is a large oasis – today shrunk to just over 2,000 km² in total area and centred on 25° 30' N and 29° 15' E (**Fig. 1**). The present-day oasis is about 80 km long and up to 25 km wide, and consists of a flat plain of rich clay soil, bounded on the north and east by a 350 m escarpment and on the south by the sand and stone wastes of the Sahara. There is virtually no mineral or other resource, only the rich clay soil, and agriculture is the foundation of the economy and society of the oasis. The climate is hyper-arid and irrigation is effected from the several hundred wells and springs. All man's needs for water are met from under-ground aquifers, which feed to the surface either under artesian pressure or are pumped. The present population of about 75,000 is settled in some thirty towns and villages. The largest, Mut, at the centre of the region, is the capital. The nearest neighbour to Dakhleh is the Kharga Oasis, some 175 km distant.

The oasis farmers are self-sufficient and each household produces enough cereals (wheat, barley and rice are the major crops), vegetables and fruits to feed itself, with a little surplus. Every family also has a small flock of sheep and goats, a cow or two, and the ubiquitous donkey. Dates are the major cash crop of the region, supplemented by some olives and apricots.

This basic scenario has obtained for the last four thousand years or so. There has been no significant climatic alteration in that time and the configuration of the land is the same. It has been argued elsewhere (Mills 1999) that the arrival of the Pharaonic Egyptians from the Nile Valley in the late Old Kingdom introduced major changes to the oasis. The appearance of the present-day Dakhleh Oasis, with irrigation channels running to a pattern of small field enclosures, is a direct result of those land reforms. Gravity-fed flood irrigation is the usual pattern both in the Nile Valley and in the oasis. The introduction of this technology, well understood by them, allowed the Egyptians to feed themselves in this remote region.

Since the beginning of the Holocene, there has been a general trend of a gradually increasing and diverging use of the Dakhleh Oasis region. Aggregation was already taking place 9000 years ago during the period of the Masara Unit (McDonald 1986; 1990) and there are a number of sites with hut circles present. As climatic conditions in the Western Desert became progressively less humid, the palaeoasis area contracted and, at the same time, there was an increasing dependence on the oasis resources. Just prior to about 2200 BC, there was a settled local population in the oasis region of a late Neolithic culture known as the Sheikh Muftah (McDonald 1999).

We are particularly interested in the immigrant Egyptian population here. The work of the French Institute team at Ayn Asil, at Balat in eastern Dakhleh, is well known. They are painstakingly revealing what may be the best preserved Old Kingdom settlement in Egypt. The site is large, appears to have been at least initially fortified, and was overseen by royal officials as governors, several of whom are buried nearby in huge mastaba tombs (e.g., Soukassian *et al.* 1990; Valloggia 1986). The French have exposed the governors' palace, a pottery atelier, large heavy defence works, and a variety of other buildings and structures (see also Kaper and Willems this volume for overview). The mastaba tombs have yielded fine objects, interesting stelae and wall decoration. The site is a real provincial centre of the late Old Kingdom period and was the capital of the Dakhleh Oasis at that time. The complex tells us a great deal about the history of the oasis region and its relationship with the Nile Valley. During our archaeological survey the Dakhleh Oasis Project (DOP) located a total of 51 sites (Churcher and Mills 1999, Appendix 2) across the entire oasis area, bearing evidence of Old Kingdom activity. This includes the site under consideration below. The whole region was subjected to immigration and settlement, and not just a single centre at Balat. The reasons for this extensive commitment are as yet unclear.

As in Lower Nubia, the arrival of the Egyptians has left no evidence for having caused any particular problem for the locals and there are no certain indications of conflict between the newcomers and the indigenes. There was a co-occupation in the Dakhleh Oasis that probably lasted for about a century, after which both populations dwindled. The succeeding two millennia, as witnessed in the archaeological evidence, saw only a 'token' population in the Dakhleh Oasis, although it does seem that there were always some inhabitants.

At Ein el-Gezareen is another Old Kingdom site, located within the modern district of Mushia, about half-way along a major line of spring mounds that lies north to south between the western towns of el-Qasr and Gedida. It is 42 km northwest of Ayn Asil and some 15 km south of the escarpment, close to the southern end of the major Roman period settlement at Amheida. The site was originally tested by R A Frey and indexed as 32/390-K2-2 by the Dakhleh Oasis Project in 1979 (Mills 1980, 257–8). Situated on slightly rising ground, the surface of the site is sandy, with a concentrated litter of chipped stone, potsherds, considerable evidence of burning, and, most noticeably, thousands of fragments of animal bone. The name 'Ein el-Gezareen' means 'the Spring of the Butchers', which must relate to this latter aspect of the site's surface. Obviously, there has been an extensive knapping industry on the site, and the amount of chipped stone on the surface is far greater than past pub-

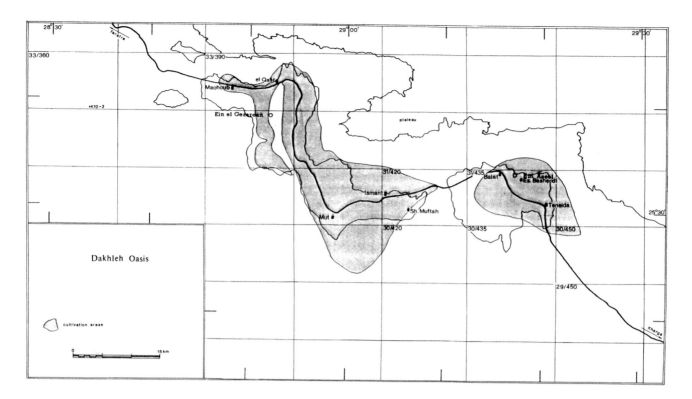

Fig. 1   Map of Dakhleh Oasis showing areas of present cultivation, various towns, and sites mentioned in the text.

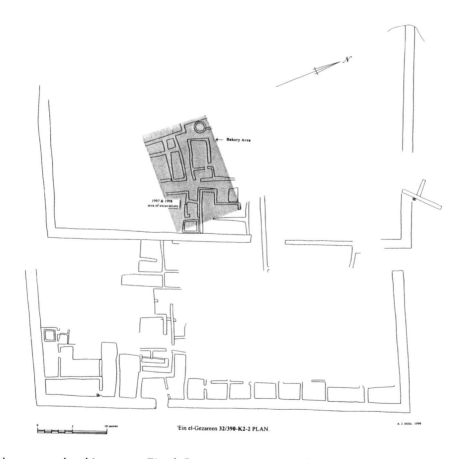

Fig. 2   Plan of the excavated architecture at Ein el-Gezareen. Area excavated in 1997 and 1998 is shaded.

lication of Pharaonic flints would lead one to expect. Surface ceramics include a great number of bread moulds, as might be expected on any Old Kingdom site: considerable numbers of the so-called 'Meidum Bowls', the shallow, red polished bowls with carinated rims that are so typical of the Fourth to Sixth Dynasties; plenty of hand-made pieces, including a number of the local Sheikh Muftah typical coarse pottery (Hope 1999, 217–25; this volume). Other surface features of the site include several areas where mud-brick construction is visible as well as hints of ash concentrations, the quantity of which suggest some industrial activity. The appearance of the surface gives the impression of an archaeologically rich site.

These are all good reasons for opening work at the site. As a complement to the work of the French, we considered it important to investigate a site without obvious official political connections, and to be able to concentrate on the archaeology of a settlement where it appeared that the chief occupation was agriculture, but where there was the possibility of investigating industrial activity as well. The environmental information contained in faunal remains, so visible on the surface, and possible floral remains could be used to reconstruct the environment of the oasis at this period. The chipped stone industry was available here for analysis and description for the first time in Pharaonic investigations. Finally, as the Dakhleh Oasis Project has primarily concentrated its attention on Prehistoric and Roman period remains, both of which are so commonly found in the oasis, it was felt that it was time to fill in the rather long temporal gap of the second and first millennia BC.

Ein el-Gezareen has met all our expectations in the past three seasons. Work began by investigating a 10 m × 10 m test square in 1997 (designated H.13), excavating in 10 cm layers and sieving all removed debris (**Fig. 2**, shaded area).

The test square was excavated to about a 30 cm depth. It revealed mud-brick architecture and an unbroken fill, without flooring or separate occupation layers, but with a relatively even vertical distribution of artefacts and midden remains. In addition to all the various surface materials, the fill revealed substantial deposits of ash and charcoal. During the 1998 season, an extension of the test was made into an adjacent square (I.13), providing a test area of 10 m × 15 m. Not least among the reasons for the extension was that only one complete but rather small architectural space had been defined in the previous exposure. Excavation throughout this area was taken down to a depth of about 1.00 m. In addition, a 1 m² pit was excavated to bedrock clay soil. From this we now understand there to be a depth of 2.96 m from the surface in the area of the test square. Artefacts, bone fragments and charcoal were found at all depths. Interestingly, no single lenses or floors could be discerned within the baulks of this pit. Below the level of about one metre, the artefactual content of the soil may, however, be attributed to the vertical movement of individual pieces along the cracks, which readily form in the clay, and may not represent the actual depth of occupation.

The quantity of materials coming from the test square was great and a particularly large amount of environmental material was recovered. Although considerable data on the

Romano-Byzantine period from Ismant el-Kharab and on a succession of changing environments from the earlier parts of the Holocene have been collected, we still have a gap in our knowledge with regard to the landscapes throughout the Pharaonic occupation of the oasis. Now we can begin to fill this gap. The quantities of ash and charcoal recovered were examined by Johannes Walter, under the supervision of Dr Ursula Thanheiser, with the following preliminary results (U Thanheiser, pers. comm. 1998). Barley (*Hordeum vulgare*) is dominant; grains occur in all samples, rachides in high numbers but in a few samples only. Of emmer wheat (*Triticum dicoccum*), the traditional wheat of Pharaonic Egypt, grains occur in a few samples only, while spikelet forks are present in almost all samples. Pulses and other cultivated food plants are completely absent. There are hardly any weeds – both the recovered taxa and the number per taxon are very small. Many samples contain small twigs and charcoal from tamarisk (*Tamarix* sp.) and Nile acacia (*Acacia nilotica*), of which pods and seeds have also been found.

Faunal materials, due to the extensive surface deposit, are even more prolific. C S Churcher reports (pers. comm. 1998) that from the test area the identified animals present include: cattle (*Bos*), goat (*Capra*), Dorcas gazelle (*Gazella dorcas*), duck (*Anas*), goose (*Anser*), ass (*Equus asinus*), rabbit (*Oryctolagus*), and possibly pig (*?Sus*); and the wild or commensuals are pigeon (*Columba*), hare (*Lepus*), fennic fox (*Fennicus*), fox (*Vulpes*), hartebeest (*Alcelaphus*), ostrich (*Struthio camelus*), as represented by many eggshell fragments, catfish (*Clarias*), and several species of mollusca and rodents. It is interesting to record here that no horn cores or horns of sheep (*Ovis*) were observed in the sample, while more than 24 of goat were identified. The horns or horn cores being the only certain criteria for differentiating goats from sheep, sheep do not appear to have been present during the occupation of the site. The material from cattle, goats and gazelles far outweighs and outnumbers that of all the remainder and it is likely that these taxa were the major protein sources.

The ceramics so far identified at the site, apart from the rather small number of 'Sheikh Muftah' vessels, all date to the late Fifth and Sixth Dynasties. There is nothing later (C A Hope, pers. comm. 1999). Analysis is as yet in its earliest stages here, but some data can be related. There is a great quantity of the heavy bread moulds of the Old Kingdom type, with a conical interior and wide mouth. These far outnumber other vessels from the surface and from the test excavations. There are red polished vessels of various shapes, from carinated bowls to larger close-mouthed pots. There are large, brown storage vessels, various hand-made shapes, and tiny jars that were perhaps for precious commodities.

The lithics from the site[1] are another major element of the artefactual remains. There are heavy concentrations on the surface, which probably represent knapping areas. The discovery of a deposit of short blade flakes in the test square, as well as a number of more specialised tools like arrowheads and knives gives credence to the industry as a part of the site's normal functioning. Rectangular scrapers on tabular chert are as common here as on other Old Kingdom sites. As well as the chipped stone, there is a great quantity of grinding equipment, both on the surface and from the excavated area. There are both saddle-shaped querns, principally made from a locally sourced coarse sandstone, and the upper, or hand, rubbing stones, which are in a variety of finer materials. An idea of the quantities of these stones can be gained from the statistics of the 5 m × 10 m test square extension – 64 grindstones and 38 handstones were counted.

One interesting group of artefacts that has come from the test excavation are 22 seal impressions (O E Kaper, pers. comm. 1999). Some are on pottery bread moulds, others are on seals for bags or other small objects. There are nine seal impressions on bread moulds, made prior to the firing of the vessel. Five of these have a diameter of 2.7 cm and show two birds, an 'ankh, and a fallen enemy figure. The other seal impressions are round, oval and rectangular; most are small. Motifs include geometric designs and a lizard, and three are from cylinder seals. The seal impressions found at this site are closely comparable to the impressions found by the excavators at Ayn Asil (according to a verbal communication from L Pantalacci, whom we thank). The occurrence of the large impressions on the bread moulds is a remarkable feature, hitherto encountered only in the palace area at Ayn Asil. This may betray the presence at Ein el-Gezareen of high ranking officials, for whom the impressed bread moulds were produced. However, other interpretations are also being considered, for example, whether these impressions denote a standard measure or a particular quality of bread.

The test area was most probably a bakery or part of a bakery. The evidence for this includes the great quantity of bread moulds, the large number of grinding stones, the storage facilities, and the heavy deposits of charcoal and ash and the botanical evidence contained within them.

The conclusion drawn from the botanical evidence is that wheat and barley were processed at the site. One possibility is that the cereals were threshed, winnowed and coarse sieved somewhere else and then placed in storage. The stored cereals would then have been taken from the granaries as needed and further processed: emmer was pounded to break the glumes and release the grains, winnowed, fine sieved and milled. Certainly, there are plenty of grindstones in the test area. It is certain that Old Kingdom bakers used an open fire, and again, the botanical evidence of twigs of tamarisk and acacia suggests a high heat from a rapid brush fire. The bread moulds are extremely heavy and would have quickly absorbed considerable heat. The bread would bake while the bread mould cooled, over perhaps an hour. The Sakkara tomb of Ti (Steindorff 1913, pls 43, 83–6, 99) contains a famous series of scenes depicting the production of bread, including grinding the grain and firing the filled moulds on an open fire.

The 1998/1999 season commenced with a geophysical survey[2], which covered some 2.4 hectares of the surface, about one-half of the site area. The area surveyed lies at the southern part of the site and almost completely covered an east-west slice. The major feature revealed was a series of heavy walls, with lesser structures adjacent to them (**Fig. 2**). The heavy walls form a large rectangular enclosure, some 80 m × 55 m, with an attached enclosure at the east side measuring 25 m × 55 m. There are structures apparent both within and outside the enclosures. It became the archaeolog-

ical task of the season to confirm and explore the results of the geophysical survey.

The outer mud-brick wall is some 1.45 m thick and is very well-built. Time did not permit the tracing of its complete extent. Only a part of the eastern enclosure, and the extent of the main walls up to a point where a later well had been dug into the site, were followed. Preservation is up to a metre in height along the eastern wall, which was generally well built, with good rectangular corners. There is a single entrance to the eastern enclosure, about one-third of the way along from the south corner. The north and south walls of the two enclosures are not in alignment and do not meet. It is not yet certain which of the two enclosures was built first.

Rooms were built adjacent to the wall of the eastern enclosure and were contiguous with one another. The rooms are similar in construction to those of the bakery area, with a maximum thickness for the walls of 1.5 bricks, but often just a single brick. Corners and angles were not rectangular and the construction looks as if it had grown in a haphazard fashion. Packed mud floors were found only in a couple of places. However, it is perhaps a little early to expand on a description of the architecture as excavation has only attained a depth of 30 cm. The entire length of the eastern wall and the rooms adjacent to it have been exposed as well as a group of rooms linking the eastern enclosure wall with the east wall of the larger enclosure. No real sense of a planned community has been obtained, despite the formal appearance of the main walls. No streets have yet been discerned within the enclosures, nor have separate districts been identified. Apart from the bakery rooms of the initial test area, which are within the larger western enclosure, no specific areas of activities have been identified. Finds from the newly exposed rooms are predominantly sherds, although small finds of various kinds and the environmental components of the fill are present.

The results have completely altered our perspective of the site. Initially, as a working hypothesis, Ein el-Gezareen was seen as a large village with a farming community in residence, working the adjacent arable areas watered from local wells or springs. It was expected to have had an official connection with the governorate at Ayn Asil, but would be largely independent and self-sufficient. Now, with its heavy enclosing walls, it would seem that perhaps there is some real influence from the governorate in its placement and planning. Giddy (1987, 185–6) reports a massive walled enclosure at Ayn Asil at the early stage of the establishment of the site. Possibly, Ein el-Gezareen was similarly established initially as a defended community and grew outside its walls once the perceived danger, whatever that was, had been put to rest in the minds of the inhabitants. The growth at Ayn Asil seems to have followed this pattern (see also Kaper and Willems this volume). What it does mean for Ein el-Gezareen is that it was probably established as a satellite of the governorate and so had a formal, rather than a casual, connection with the central site.

In conclusion, in pondering the title of this colloquium, I wonder whether the Dakhleh Oasis, as we know it today, and from the Old Kingdom onwards, is in fact a gift to the desert from the Nile Valley instead.

Notes

1. Dr M M A McDonald is undertaking the study of this material as well as that of the Holocene Cultural Units.

2. The geophysical surveys were undertaken by Dr T Smekalova, Physical Institute of St. Petersburg State University, and Dr T Her-bich, Polish Centre of Mediterranean Archaeology, Cairo. The instruments used were an Overhauser gradiometer GSM-19WG of Gem Systems, and a fluxgate gradiometer FM-36 of Geoscan Research.

Bibliography

Churcher C S and Mills A J (eds.), 1999. *Reports from the Survey of the Dakhleh Oasis. Western Desert of Egypt, 1977-1987*. Oxbow Monograph 99, Dakhleh Oasis Project Monograph 2. Oxford.

Giddy L L, 1987. *Egyptian Oases. Bahariya, Dakhla, Farafra and Kharga during Pharaonic Times*. Warminster.

Hope C A, 1999. Pottery Manufacture in the Dakhleh Oasis. In Churcher and Mills (eds) 1999: 215–43.

McDonald M M A, 1986. Dakhleh Oasis Project: Holocene Prehistory: Interim Report on the 1987 Season. *Journal of the Society for the Study of Egyptian Antiquities* 16: 103–13.

McDonald M M A, 1990. The Dakhleh Oasis Project: Holocene Prehistory: Interim report on the 1988 and 1989 seasons. *Journal of the Society for the Study of Egyptian Antiquities* 20: 24–53.

McDonald M M A, 1999. Neolithic Cultural Units and Adaptations in Dakhleh Oasis, Egypt. In Churcher and Mills (eds) 1999: 117–32.

Mills A J, 1980. The Dakhleh Oasis Project. Report of the Second Season of Survey. September–December 1979. *Journal of the Society for the Study of Egyptian Antiquities* 10: 251–82.

Mills A J, 1999. Pharaonic Egyptians in the Dakhleh Oasis. In Churcher and Mills (eds) 1999: 171–8.

Soukiassian G, Wuttmann M and Pantalacci L, 1990. *Balat III. Les ateliers de potiers d''Ayn Asîl*. Fouilles de l'Institut français d'archéologie orientale du Caire 34. Cairo.

Steindorff G, 1913. *Das Grab des Ti*. Leipzig.

Valloggia M, 1986. *Balat I. Le Mastaba de Medou-Nefer*. Fouilles de l'Institut français d'archéologie orientale du Caire 31. Cairo.

Policing the Desert: Old Kingdom Activity around the Dakhleh Oasis

Olaf E Kaper and Harco Willems
With an appendix by Mary M A McDonald

In memoriam Carla van Battum

Introduction

In January 1947 a severe sandstorm exposed some architectural remains of an ancient town to the east of the village of Balat in the Dakhleh Oasis (Osing *et al.* 1982, 14). After a delay of some decades, this discovery overturned many of our views on the administration of Egypt in the Old Kingdom. These had previously been based almost exclusively on texts, which gave an impression of the administrative hierarchy, but not really of the actual context in which the administrators worked. Moreover, it was widely assumed that Egyptian government was largely confined to the Nile Valley and the Delta. For instance, the important studies by E Martin-Pardey (1976) and N Strudwick (1985) make hardly any mention of Egyptian involvement in the deserts around the Nile basin.

In the meantime, the picture has changed significantly, as the present volume amply demonstrates. The excavations of the IFAO near Balat, which have been on-going without interruption since 1977, have produced the most impressive evidence for Egyptian presence in the deserts so far: a complete town of Old Kingdom date at Ayn Asil and its cemetery at Qila ed-Dabba. In addition, L Giddy and A Minault-Gout recorded some twenty petroglyphs of Old Kingdom date in two locations northeast of Ayn Asil and southeast of Teneida (Giddy 1987, 253–7, 275–89; Minault-Gout 1985).

The investigations by the Dakhleh Oasis Project (DOP) place the evidence from Balat in a wider perspective. An archaeological survey has revealed the presence of numerous other sites in the oasis, both settlements and cemeteries that can be dated to the Old Kingdom (Churcher and Mills 1999, 175–6, 258–9). Since 1988, L Krzyzaniak and K Kroeper have undertaken a systematic survey and study of the petroglyphs in the entire Dakhleh region and they include many Old Kingdom examples (Krzyzaniak 1987; 1990; Krzyzaniak and Kroeper 1990). In recent years, A J Mills has started excavations at a large Old Kingdom settlement in the west of the oasis on which he reports in the present volume. The important work carried out on the prehistoric cultures of Dakhleh by M McDonald are discussed below and also in Hope and Eccleston in this volume. Before embarking on a presentation of the first results of our own investigations for the Dakhleh Oasis Project, however, it will be useful to recapitulate some of the results of the French project.

The central part of the city of Ayn Asil is still mostly unexcavated. It has a squarish outline and is surrounded on all sides by a thick enclosure wall. The sides are approximately 170 m in length and the corners have been provided with towers. Smaller towers protected the gates to the city, of which one in the north and one in the south have been unearthed.[1]

Originally, habitation seems to have been confined to the walled city, although a potter's workshop was already established at an early date to the southwest of the town (Soukiassian, Wuttmann and Pantalacci 1990). In recent years, archaeological activity has concentrated on the southern extension of the town where the well-preserved remains of a governor's palace have come to light.[2] This palace seems to have been in use throughout the reign of Pepi II.

The excavators have reconstructed the growth of the entire settlement as follows (the numbers here attributed to the various phases differ slightly from those in Soukiassian, Wuttmann and Schaad 1990):

Phase 0. Foundation of the settlement at an uncertain date, perhaps prior to the beginning of the Sixth Dynasty. In the northern city the deepest levels of the occupation have not yet been reached, so it is uncertain how long before phase I the city may have been founded.

Phase I. The northern city existed within a circular wall. This wall itself has not yet been investigated, but the lowermost levels in the excavators' *sondage nord* have revealed the tops of walls in positions, which suggest that the city wall as known in the later phases was already in existence.[3] The area of the later south city was still largely uninhabited.

Phase II. The walls of the north city were provided with defensive towers. The early phase of the potter's workshop dates to this period. The area to the south was still largely uninhabited.

Phase III. Extensions of the city gradually began south of the city wall and the early phase of the governor's palace was built. It is important to note that this building was initially located in the open space south of the first precinct and that it apparently had no defensive walls.

Phase IV. The quarter around the governor's palace expanded and was surrounded by a wall (plan in Cherpion 1999, fig. 2b). However, there are no indications that this wall, which was relatively thin and had no defensive towers, had a military purpose. A further quarter was added to the west of the governor's palace.

Phase V. A deliberate fire ruined the governor's palace and at least part of the north city. The destruction layer can be dated to the end of the reign of Pepi II.[4]

Phase VI. The town was reconstructed on roughly the same plan as the earlier one, although the palace was not rebuilt. The partly ruined city wall was integrated into the

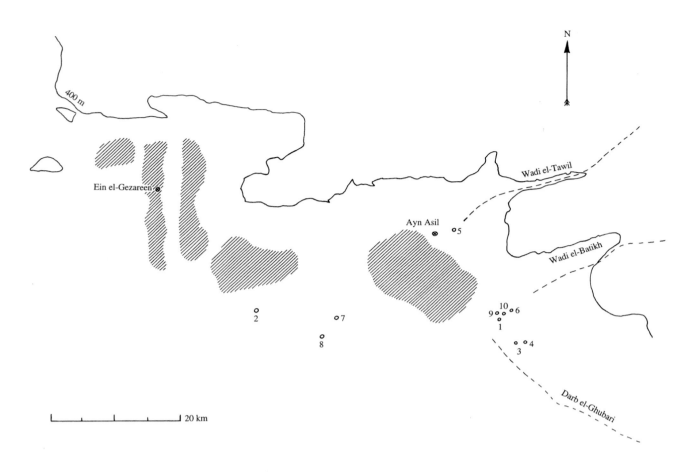

Fig. 1   Map of the Dakhleh Oasis indicating the position of the hilltop sites.

houses built in the area, so it could no longer have served its original purpose.

Phase VII. The town was rebuilt again in the First Intermediate Period. In several places, massive volumes of filling material were used to raise the floor level to the top of the former city walls. This town does not seem to have had a wall (Soukiassian, Wuttmann and Schaad 1990, 355–8; Soukiassian 1997, 15–7).

A remarkable feature in the above survey is that the expansion of the city is inversely proportional to the importance of the defensive system. In phases I and II, the settlement was still largely confined to the area within the city walls, and these walls were even strengthened in phase II. With the beginning of the expansion of the settlement in phase III, no further defences were built. The construction of the palace, which marks the beginning of phase III, is probably datable to the early reign of Pepi II or perhaps slightly earlier (Soukiassian 1997). The decision not to provide the phase III city with a protective wall suggests that the oasis was now a less dangerous place than it had apparently been in the first period of the city's existence, a period that corresponds to the early Sixth and perhaps the end of the Fifth Dynasty.

This account of the city's history for the most part follows the views propounded so far by the French excavators of the site, but in a recent article M Ziermann (1998) seeks to demonstrate that the early development of the city followed a slightly different track. In his view, the *sondage nord* excavated by Giddy did not reveal the original north gate of the walled town, but rather the south gate of a smaller fortification that had been founded much earlier. In his interpretation, this early gate was defended by two semicircular towers. This would fit in well with the excavators' conclusion that the early town at Ayn Asil was constructed under conditions that necessitated strong fortifications. Ziermann suggests that the earlier northern fortress extended as far back in time as the Fourth Dynasty.

Against these views one must point out that there is not a single reliable piece of evidence for this early date. Moreover, Ziermann's interpretation of the stratigraphy is questionable. He believes that the alleged north town was abandoned when it was covered by windblown sand, forcing the inhabitants to leave the northern settlement and to resettle further south in the central city (Ziermann 1998, 350–7). In view of the prevailing direction of the wind, it is highly unlikely that they would have moved in this direction, as the central city itself would also have been threatened by the wandering dunes. We are therefore disinclined to accept his theory. Our conclusion remains that the town of Ayn Asil was founded at some unspecified point in time before the beginning of the Sixth Dynasty and that it had a defensive function before the reign of Pepi II.

It is important to note the completely Egyptian nature of the settlement and its cemetery. The administrative system and the names encountered in the documentation from Ayn Asil are Egyptian (Pantalacci 1997; 1998), and during a visit paid by the authors to the site in December 1998, G Soukiassian pointed out that the same applies to the material remains being unearthed there.[5]

The Indigenous Population of Dakhleh

As mentioned above, the Dakhleh Oasis Project has discovered numerous other sites attesting to the presence of Egyptians in the oasis. Moreover, it has found evidence for a sizeable non-Egyptian population that inhabited the oasis before the arrival of the Egyptians.

The Neolithic cultures in the oasis are being studied and classified by Mary M A McDonald. From her work it emerges that the oasis was inhabited by the Sheikh Muftah Cultural Unit from some time before 3000 BC, and that this unit presumably survived into late Old Kingdom times, around 2200 BC.[6] The sites of this prehistoric group are situated within and just beyond the limits of the present-day oasis (map in McDonald 1999, 125). More than 70 sites have thus far been located in the eastern half of the oasis. Unfortunately, these are all much deflated and disturbed by subsequent occupation. The sites consist of hearth mounds, fire pits and ashy layers, none of which have thus far been excavated. No architecture is known from these sites. The population was pastoral, depending to some degree on domestic herd animals, such as cattle and goats, which were held as property (McDonald 1998). The use of grinding stones and sickle blades shows that plant food was collected. The chipped stone tool kit of the Sheikh Muftah Unit included piercers, denticulates, scrapers, arrowheads, picks, sickles and bifacial knives. There are occasional finds of copper at these sites, while the pottery, principally in the form of bowls, is abundant and varied. The few imported vessels from the Nile Valley can be ascribed to the period from at least Naqada III into the First Dynasty (Edwards and Hope 1987, 1–10; Hope 1999, 217–12, 239; this volume).

Thus, the Egyptians came to settle in an environment that had a sizeable indigenous population with its own distinct culture. The evidence so far suggests that the Sheikh Muftah Cultural Unit occupied both the lowlands of the oasis and the basins surrounding these in the east, whereas the Egyptians seem to have settled mainly in villages in the lowlands of the oasis where there was abundant spring water to support agriculture (McDonald 1985, 133). Some sites in the oasis have yielded a mixed ceramic assemblage of Egyptian and Sheikh Muftah material, which may point to a peaceful symbiosis of the two cultures (McDonald 1986, 112). The ceramic finds from late Old Kingdom sites in the oasis demonstrate that the local ceramic traditions continued during the Egyptian occupation despite the introduction of Egyptian style ceramics (Hope 1999, 221). By the end of the Old Kingdom this local culture had completely disappeared in favour of the Egyptian culture.

In 1988, McDonald excavated one of three huts found on the hilltop site 30/450-G8-2 (229), which lay outside the lowlands of the oasis. The surface finds at this site revealed a mixed assemblage of Sheikh Muftah and Old Kingdom ceramics. The aims of this excavation were to establish the function of this type of site, of which four other examples were known at the time, and to investigate the question of the relationship between the Sheikh Muftah Unit and the Egyptian settlers. Even though the results of her excavation were important (see the description below), it left a number of questions unanswered with regard to the nature of the occupation and ethnic origin of the inhabitants of this hill. McDonald (1990a, 50) concluded that 'the testing of more of these hut circles might help clarify the matter'.

Since 1988 similar Old Kingdom hilltop sites have been discovered during surveys of the desert conducted by M R Kleindienst and C S Churcher (Kleindienst *et al.* 1999, 42– 3). In 1998 we decided to undertake a study of these sites as a group with the aim of determining the role played by the hilltop sites in the context of the Egyptian occupation of the Dakhleh Oasis.

The Hilltop Sites

The following ten sites are now known to belong to the group under study and are listed in the order of their discovery. The site numbers indicated are usually those of the DOP, the numbers between brackets are those of McDonald's parallel numbering system for localities yielding stone tools, which include the Sheikh Muftah sites. The position of the sites is indicated on the map in **Fig. 1**. The ceramics from all hilltop sites were examined by C A Hope.

1. Winkler's site 68 (Winkler 1939, 8, 15–6). This site was discovered during a survey for petroglyphs undertaken in 1937–1938 by H A Winkler. It was relocated in 1988 during the survey conducted by L Krzyzaniak and K Kroeper for the DOP (McDonald 1990b, 55 [map], 63, Krzyzaniak and Kroeper 1990, 78). It lies on the western edge of the Southeast Basin, and Winkler termed it a 'watchpost' because of its splendid view. Finds include ceramics, chipped stone, and petroglyphs showing hieroglyphs, animals (gazelle, ibex, hare and bird), men, some with a feather on their head, women, vulvae, sandals, and many outlines of feet. The hill also bears an inscription that may date to the Middle Kingdom (Osing 1986, 82).

2. Site 30/405-L1-1 (057). This hill, located only a few kilometres southeast of the town of Mut, was found during the DOP survey in 1980 and was tested by R A Frey (Mills 1981, 180). There are two huts on top of this hill, both open to the east. The finds include pottery, among which are the remains of many bread moulds, a spindle whorl, some chipped stone and petroglyphs mainly of feet and animals (Mills 1981, pl. 13b). The principal view from this hill is to the south.

3. Site 30/450-F9-1 (180). A large hill with 'a score of hut circles' was located by McDonald in 1987 (map in McDonald 1990a, 25). One of the huts was examined archaeologically, but proved to be 'clean but for wind-blown sand' (McDonald 1986, 112; 1990a, 46). The ceramics from this site date to the Old Kingdom.

4. Site 30/450-G8-2 (229). The site is situated in Rock Art Basin (McDonald 1990a, 25 [map], 45), which lies southeast of the Southeast Basin in McDonald's terminology. One of the three huts on this hill was excavated by McDonald in 1988 (McDonald 1990a, 46–50). Several pieces of rock art were found on the stones of the hut, including animals and a man leading a bull (Krzyzaniak 1987, pl. 18a; 1990, 96–7; Krzyzaniak and Kroeper 1990, 78, fig. 8). The excavations revealed 30 cm of deposit inside the western chamber of the hut, which contained a wide range of artefacts and organic materials. Apparently reed mats had covered the floor and at one stage the floor had been paved with flat stone slabs over which another layer of reeds had been placed. The eastern chamber of this hut was found to contain only a shallow layer of deposit, c. 10 cm in depth, which preserved an earlier layer of matting and a later paved floor. The items recovered from this hut include grinding stones, lumps of ochre and rope. The surface scatter of the hut yielded pottery from both cultural units, i.e., Egyptian ceramics, such as fragments from Meidum bowls, as well as Sheikh Muftah products. The chipped stone assemblage was mainly produced from a grey-brown nodular chert in which piercers predominate, including drill bits and points (see the appendix below). Sections of small wooden sticks seem to have belonged to arrow shafts. The presence of several seal impressions indicates contact with the administrative centre of the oasis. An interesting feature was also the presence of strips of raw gazelle hide and finished leather, which seem to have been processed on the hill itself. The ochre and stone scrapers found within the hut could have been used in this craft.

5. Site 32/435-L10-3 (235). This site consists of at least two adjacent hills inside the basin northeast of the village of Bashendi (McDonald 1990a, 46). From these hills, a view to the northeast over the Darb el-Tawil is possible. There are hut circles on top of both hills, and Old Kingdom ceramics were collected from the top of one of them in 1998.

6. Site 30/450-E4-1 (256). This is a prominent hill located at the northern end of the Southeast Basin (map in McDonald 1990a, 55). It is reported to have hut circles, Old Kingdom artefacts and petroglyphs that include depictions of cattle, a donkey and perhaps a dancing girl (McDonald 1990b, 63).

7. Site 30/420-H3-1. This is a prominent hill lying isolated in the desert southeast of the village of Sheikh Muftah. During our visit to this site in 1998, we noticed the remains of at least one hut of Old Kingdom date that has been destroyed by the insertion of a metal surveying stake in the 1930s. This hut once contained several stones with petroglyphs, which were found scattered on the surface around the stake. Apart from Old Kingdom ceramics, this hill also yielded evidence from later periods. A fragment of a demotic stela from the area of the hut probably dates to the late Ptolemaic or Roman period.[7] Post-Old Kingdom graffiti on the hill include two incised *senet* board games and a stylised horned altar.

8. Site 30/420-F3-1 (**Plate 63**). Lying due south of the village of Sheikh Muftah, this hill commands a wide view towards the south. From its apex, the site of Ayn Asil cannot be seen, but direct eye contact was possible with occupants of the large hill 30/420-H3-1 (no. 7 above). There are two huts on top of this hill (**Plate 64**), inside which several pieces with petroglyphs were found showing hunting scenes (cf. Kleindienst *et al.* 1999, 43, fig. 1.47), birds and foot impressions. The scenes were removed for safekeeping. The interior dimensions of the two huts are similar; they measure 3.40 × 1.10 m and 3.70 × 1.70 m respectively. A third hut, composed of two rooms, is located at the base of the hill. The ceramic finds include fragments from a 'beer jar' and of a small globular jar, both of Old Kingdom date. A fragment of a water keg dated to the Twenty-Seventh Dynasty indicates a later human presence upon this hill.

9. Site 30/450-C4-1. There are two small huts on top of this hill and a large one at a slightly lower level. The hill forms part of the northeastern ridge bordering Camel Thorn Basin to the east of present-day Dakhleh. The view from this site is principally toward the south and west, overlooking Camel Thorn Basin. Its petroglyphs include animals, outlines of feet and rows of notches. The abundant ceramic finds on the surface date to the Old Kingdom but a few pieces are made in later, perhaps Roman, wares.

10. Site 30/450-D4-2 (386) (Nephthys Hill). The discovery of this hilltop site, on the northeastern edge of the Southeast Basin, was made by M Kleindienst in 1997. The abundance of ceramics and chipped stone as well as petroglyphs made this hill a promising site for detailed investigation, especially as no later material seemed to occur on the site. A detailed description is given below.

On the basis of these ten hilltop sites, some general characteristics can be defined as follows:

1) The sites are located on prominent hills that offer a good view over the surrounding desert.

2) There are usually several stone hut circles on top of the hill, two or three as a rule, and occasionally there is another hut at the base of the hill. The huts are spread evenly over the surface of the hilltop.

3) The huts are constructed from local stones of varying sizes and have a rectangular or horseshoe-shaped plan with an opening to the south or southeast. There is no evidence that they were ever roofed and their primary purpose appears to have been to provide protection from the wind.

4) The hills were inscribed with petroglyphs, among which the following elements are regularly present: sandals, human feet, hunting scenes, mammals, birds, men and pubic triangles. Another recurring element among the petroglyphs is rows of notches carved in the rocks, a feature discussed further below.

Nephthys Hill

The hilltop site 30/450-D4-2 (termed by us 'Nephthys Hill' because of the petroglyphs reproduced in **Figs 5–6**) was chosen as a type-site for the entire group of hilltop sites. Its excellent state of preservation and wide range of material made this hill particularly suited for that purpose. A survey and excavation season was carried out in January and December of 1998. A detailed report of this excavation will

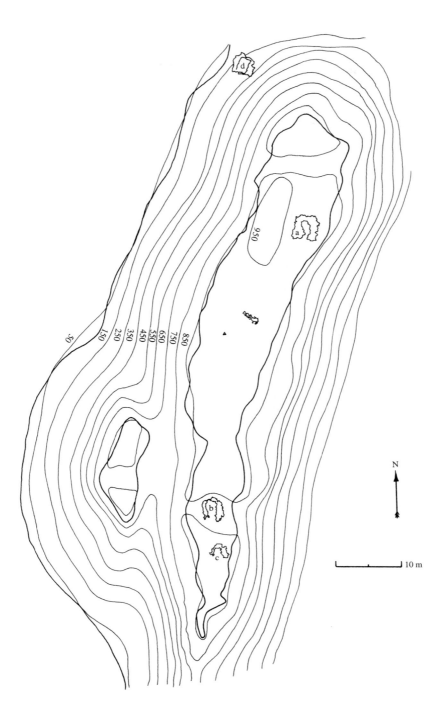

Fig. 2   Map of Nephthys Hill showing the positions of its four Huts A-D (surveyed by A Hawkins).

appear elsewhere;[8] here we will only refer to the principal results.

The hill itself (**Fig. 2**) measures *c.* 8 m in height and is situated among a range of similar hills, of which it is only barely the highest, at the northwestern edge of the Southeast Basin. There are four huts at this site, three of which lie on top of the hill (designated A, B, and C from north to south), and one at the base (D). Three huts (A, B and C) were excavated in 1998. The largest, Hut A (**Plate 65, Fig. 3**), consists of a single horseshoe-shaped structure with an addi-

tion to its western side that was intended as a small sheltered storage space. It is situated on the highest point of the hill. The interior of the hut was paved with irregularly shaped flat slabs of local sandstone. Underneath this pavement was a layer of sand mixed with patches of ash and some straw. It is clear that there was no major fireplace in this hut, and only incidental fires occurred. In front of Hut A and inside its entrance was a dense scatter of flint chips and some tools. The largest quantity of potsherds was also recovered from this area, as was the largest number of petroglyphs. This evi-

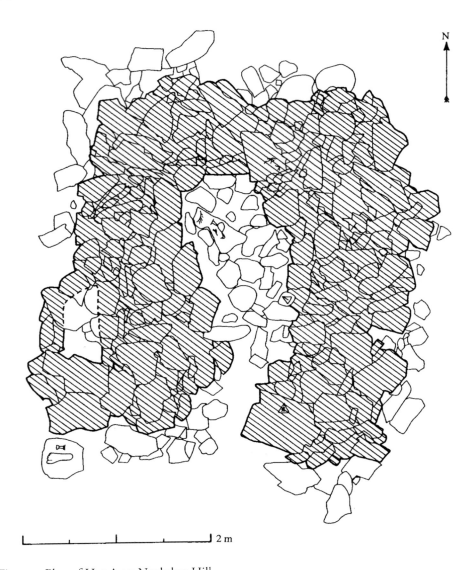

Fig. 3   Plan of Hut A on Nephthys Hill.

dence shows that Hut A functioned as the principal shelter for the occupants of the hill.

Hut B (**Plate 66**) lies in a slight depression on the top of the hill and is, therefore, better shielded from the wind than is Hut A. Its walls were built from large slabs of local stone that were placed around the sides of a shallow pit dug into the surface of the hill. A layer of compacted earth in the northwestern corner of the hut indicates the place where the inhabitant(s) sat and slept. This is the most sheltered spot on the hilltop and the northwesterly winds are most successfully kept out. There was a thick ash layer at the entrance to the hut where bonfires had been placed. Other finds in this hut were rare, in sharp contrast to the rich find context of Hut A.

At the base of the hill, Hut D was also examined. This hut resembles Hut B in the sparseness of its contents, in the compacted earth along its northwestern wall and the thick ash deposits along its eastern wall. A hole in the middle of the hut may have contained a storage vessel of some kind. Remarkably, as in Hut B, almost no artefacts were found, nor were there petroglyphs or botanical remains inside.

More than 25 petroglyphs were found on the hill. Nearly all of these were located in the floor and the walls of Hut A. Some of the stones had been used as building blocks after they had been inscribed. To the west of Hut A was a flat stony area with a commanding view, and on the surface of this spot a large number of images had been incised. Several slabs with petroglyphs were also found upon the slope of the hill. The most notable among the petroglyphs depict men, foot outlines, pubic triangles, animals (birds, cattle and a lion), a hunting scene and a portrait of a soldier with his equipment (described below).

Botanical samples from the hill are few. The excavations within the huts yielded only pieces of charcoal, which have been identified for us by U Thanheiser as acacia (including *Acacia nilotica*) and tamarisk (*Tamarix* sp). Acacia did not grow near the site, and this wood must therefore have been brought in. The faunal remains from the site are likewise few in number and have as yet only partly been analysed by C S Churcher. These include a cow's lower molar that was found halfway up the hill, and the bones of a hare (or the like) from inside Hut A.

Fig. 4   Stone slab with the depiction of a soldier and his gear.

The ceramic finds consist of more than fifty small sherds from a large number of different vessels. Among them no wares or shapes suggest a date later than the Old Kingdom. Distinctive Old Kingdom shapes present in the assemblage are Meidum bowls (see the comments on **Fig. 11** below) and a small carinated bowl with a low modelled rim (as in Hope 1979, pl. 20.11). No distinctive Sheikh Muftah pottery was found.

Nearly all of the chipped stone tools and debitage was found at surface level directly in front of Hut A. This material is described by M McDonald in the appendix below.

The Portrait of a Soldier (Plate 67; Fig. 4)

We would like to discuss one of the petroglyphs here at some length because it provides evidence regarding the occupants of Nephthys Hill. It was found inside Hut A on the reverse of a paving slab that had been decorated again on the obverse with a pair of birds (see **Fig. 3**, centre).

The reverse surface of the stone was entirely taken up by a series of individual images (**Fig. 4**). The two ends of the slab contain the outlines of a right foot, *c.* 24 cm long, and a small left hand, *c.* 17.5 cm in length. The depiction of a foot as a form of signature is well known from later times and has been found throughout the Mediterranean region, dating especially from the Graeco-Roman period. Old Kingdom foot graffiti are rare, and generally such drawings have been taken as a dating criterion for much later times (e.g., especially Verner 1973, 25–7, 44; Huyge 1998, 1386, n. 26). However, Winkler (1939) had already noted that in the Western Desert foot drawings are grouped together with material of definite Old Kingdom date (dismissed by Verner 1973, 107), and the present piece is another case in point.[9] Two other comparable depictions of feet were found on Nephthys Hill (**Figs 5–6**), one of which (**Fig. 6**) was found reused in the masonry of Hut A. These two petroglyphs depict the right foot of the same person, who has added a sign resembling a later hieroglyph used to write the name of

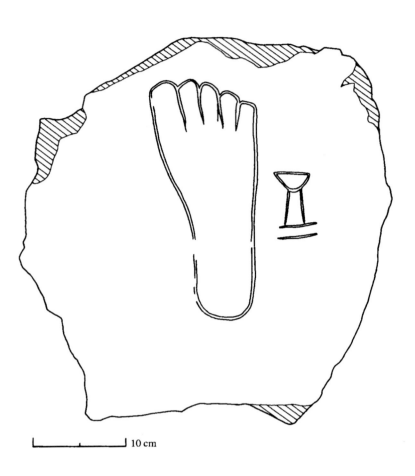

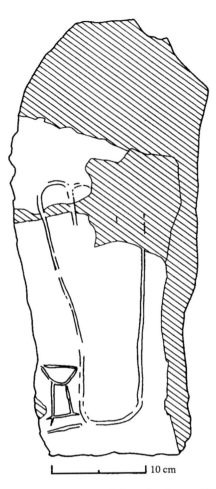

Fig. 5   Foot petroglyph found on a building block within the walls of Hut A on Nephthys Hill.

Fig. 6   Foot petroglyph found in front of Hut A on Nephthys Hill.

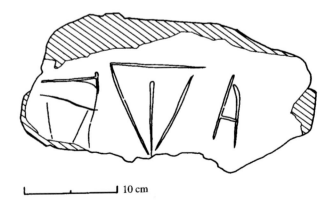

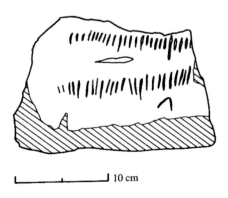

Fig. 7   Portable piece of rock art with a pubic triangle and the *mr*-hieroglyph

Fig. 8   Portable stone with a 'mute account' from Hut A on Nephthys Hill.

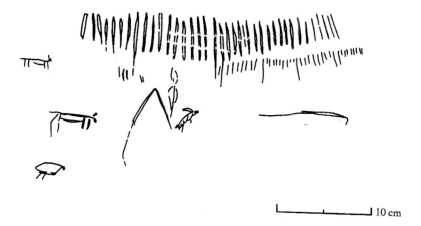

Fig. 9   Rows of notches upon the wall of Hut A (detail) together with the numeral 'ten' and some animal figures.

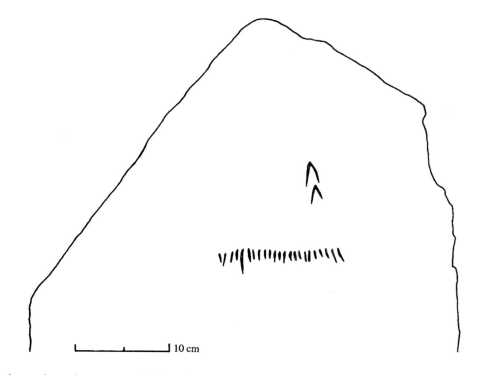

Fig. 10   Notches and numbers upon a slab found in Hut B (detail).

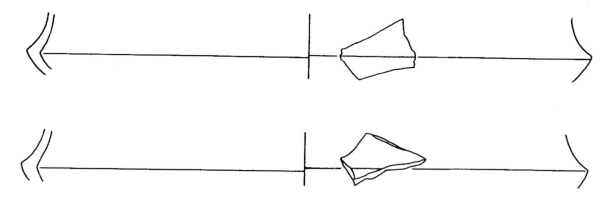

Fig. 11   Two fragments of Meidum bowls found at Nephthys Hill. Scale 1:2.

the goddess Nephthys (*Nbt-Ḥwt*) or, perhaps more likely, a pot on a stand. However, neither suggestion accounts for the horizontal line beneath the sign. The signs probably identify the person who made the drawing, but the true reading of this name remains unclear. A similar sign is known from Nubia, purportedly in C-Group context (Bates 1914, 248–9, fig. 95b). Foot outlines are common among the petroglyphs of the hilltop sites discussed in this paper.

The space between the hand and the foot has been taken up by a full-length depiction of a standing male wearing a triangular apron. His face is stylised with only the hair and mouth indicated. There seems to be a small beard on his chin. The chest is crossed by two bands and upon his head is perhaps a feather. The man holds a lotus flower with a long stem in his left hand and a small horizontal object (unidentified) in his right.

The man's costume might be compared with that of Egyptian soldiers and hunters in some representations. H G Fischer (1961, 66) has argued that the cross bands in these depictions may originate in the dress of Egyptian field workers in the Old Kingdom and he refers to Middle Kingdom instances showing military men with the same costume. However, military men are already represented in the same costume before the Middle Kingdom, as shown by a painted bowl from Qubbet el-Hawa (see **Plate 21**), now kept at the Egyptological Seminar of the University of Bonn (no. 0/1257; Decker and Herb 1994, pl. CXLII). It shows an archer with cross bands and a feather on his head, dogs and desert game, a fish and an unidentifiable object. His black skin suggests that this man was a Nubian. Similar figures, also with black skin, appear in the processions of soldiers depicted in the unpublished tomb of Setka at Qubbet el-Hawa, which dates to a period just after the Sixth Dynasty, although these men have only a single band across their chests. One might also compare the First Intermediate Period examples of the hieroglyph for 'soldier' (Fischer 1962, 50–2). Although no cross-bands are visible, the men are in many cases shown wearing a feather on their heads.

Behind the man are three items of equipment. Above is a life-size rendering of a leather wrist-guard, some actual examples of which derive from Pan Grave cemeteries of the Second Intermediate Period.[10] The decoration and shape of the wrist-guard compares well with the other known examples and it seems that the date for the introduction of this type of object has to be revised as a result of this depiction in a clearly Old Kingdom context. Below this wrist-guard is a bow with five arrows. One arrow is placed in the bow. The shape of the bow is not unusual in First Intermediate Period representations (Fischer 1962; Valloggia 1985). Below this is a square object that has a second square set inside it and two projections at its lower end. The only possible identification for this object that comes to mind is the rucksack depicted on a wooden statue from Meir, dating to the reign of Pepi I (Cairo Museum JE 30810, CG 241, illustrated in Tiradritti 1999, 100). This explanation would perhaps also account for the line extending upwards from it toward the man's waist, as a strap that could be the carrying band of this rucksack.

In front of the man is a sign that should perhaps be interpreted as the ꜥnḫ-hieroglyph. It could then be a spelling of the word ꜥnḫ, 'soldier', that occurs in the clay tablets at Ayn Asil (Posener-Kriéger 1992, 47). There is more evidence to show that the inhabitants of Nephthys Hill had at least a limited knowledge of the hieroglyphic script. In **Fig. 7** we depict a portable piece which shows a pubic triangle next to a *mr*-hieroglyph, and there are several occurrences of the numeral ten written in its hieroglyphic form (see below). The case of the so-called Nephthys-hieroglyph in **Figs 5–6** is not as clear. It probably depicts a vase on a stand, but whether it was intended as writing cannot be determined at this juncture.

We conclude that the image was made by a soldier who depicted himself full-length together with his hand and foot and with the entire range of equipment he possessed. The possible ꜥnḫ-sign next to him may indicate that he formed part of the military forces in the oasis.

The Mute Accounts

In connection with writing, we would also like to refer to the rows of notches frequently found on the walls of the huts on this and the other hilltop sites. These notches employ a notation system in which the tenth notch in every row should be drawn slightly longer than the rest. The fragment shown in **Fig. 8** and in **Plate 68** is broken on the right. It was found reused as a paving stone inside Hut A on Nephthys Hill. The first line seems to have numbered 30 strokes (25 of which remain), the second line is complete and numbers 25. Below the notches is the hieroglyphic numeral ten. The large slab in **Fig. 9** lined the northern interior wall of Hut A. It shows 37 large strokes in the first line, 39 smaller ones in the second, and here again a single number ten has been added below. In the first line (reading right to left), every tenth stroke is drawn longer than the others except for the first one. In the second line the longer strokes fall on notches number 9, 10, 19, 29, and 37. It appears there was some confusion here, with the first nine strokes counted as ten and the ninth drawn longer. Consequently the nineteenth and twenty-ninth strokes count as the twentieth and thirtieth. The mistake was realised at some stage and the actual tenth stroke was then extended. The reason why stroke number 37 in this row was drawn longer is not obvious, but the intended total number of this counting should, therefore, be considered to be 40 rather than 39.

Another large slab (**Fig. 10**) was found lying face down in Hut B, where it must once have formed part of the interior wall. It bears the number twenty in hieroglyphs and a row of 23 strokes of which the nineteenth is drawn longer.

The same counting procedure is also known from the clay tablets at Ayn Asil, in the tablets classified as 'mute accounts' by Pantalacci (1996, 364, 'comptabilités muettes'). Two such tablets have been published thus far. The first, tablet 3446, was published by Posener-Kriéger (1992, 49, fig. 3, shown upside down). It bears four rows of notches on its recto numbering 30, 40, 40 and 30 respectively, in which every tenth stroke is drawn longer. The verso is described as bearing the number ten several times (Pantalacci 1996, 264, n. 23). Another example, tablet 5375, simply bears four hieroglyphic notations of the number twenty (Valloggia 1998, 88, pl. 76C). Another fragment of a 'mute account' on a tablet has recently been found at Ein el-Gezareen (see Mills this volume), but its preserved numbers do not include hieroglyphs and the rows of notches do not exceed seven, so we cannot conclude anything from its contents.

When all the evidence is considered as a whole, it appears that in the system of 'mute accounts', every tenth line is drawn slightly longer at its bottom end, although mistakes in counting are attested twice at Nephthys Hill (Figs 9–10). The emphasis on the numeral 'ten' is also borne out by cases where the notches are accompanied by the hieratic sign for 'ten' singly or in groups, or where groups of such signs occur without notches being present. The notches were written in horizontal lines running from right to left.

The use of this system upon Nephthys Hill does not prove that its inhabitants were fully literate, but it does help demonstrate a certain background in the Egyptian administrative and educational system. It is remarkable that this type of notation is not known from other sites in Egypt. A series of twenty-three strokes was found upon the pyramid stones of Senwosret I at Lisht (F Arnold 1990, 136, E22a.2), but these are all of equal length.

Conclusions

The date of Nephthys Hill can be most securely established on the basis of the ceramic assemblage, which includes several small sherds from Meidum bowls (Fig. 11). They are sharply carinated with tall sides, and have an aperture that appears to be narrower than the shoulder. It is interesting to note that this type does not occur in P Ballet's (1987) classification of the Meidum bowls from the *sondage nord* at Ayn Asil, nor in the pottery workshop of the city or the tombs at Qila ed-Dabba (as far as those have been published). The closest parallels from datable contexts all seem to date to the Fourth and early Fifth Dynasties.[11] Unlike the Meidum bowls found at Ayn Asil, the sherds from Nephthys Hill have not been made from local clays, but from a Nile fabric. None of the other ceramic finds, as mentioned above, contradict an Old Kingdom dating (several samples taken from the site for C14 dating have not yet been processed).

The date of the rock art found on the entire range of hilltop sites will be the subject of further study in the years to come, but so far the impression gained is one of strong homogeneity. Similar hunting scenes occur on the various desert watch posts, as well as typical fixed combinations of themes such as human feet, vulvae and rows of notches. A concurrent study of the Middle Kingdom rock art found on the eastern outskirts of the oasis will assist in defining the variables within the different periods. It has already become clear that the Middle Kingdom petroglyphs in Dakhleh include coherent hieroglyphic inscriptions rendering names and titles and even longer messages (e.g., Burkard 1997) not yet encountered among the older material.

The nature of the occupation on the hills was first suggested on the basis of their position. Winkler labelled his site 68 as a watch post, a qualification that is apt for all of the sites inspected by us so far. McDonald found arrow shafts on

Site 30/450-G8-2 (229), but the mixture with other types of material did not clarify the nature of the occupation. However, the seal impressions recovered from this site suggest that the occupants were integrated into an administrative system of Egyptian type. The petroglyph from Nephthys Hill, which probably depicts a soldier (**Fig. 4**), suggests that watch posts formed part of the military infrastructure of the region.

The location of Nephthys Hill and the other hill sites (cf. **Fig. 1**) can be correlated to the access points into the Dakhleh Oasis. The sites are principally grouped around the eastern access to the oasis where both the Darb el-Ghubari and the Wadi el-Batikh converge. In many periods the Wadi el-Batikh served as an important access route up the escarpment. It was considered the shortest route between Dakhleh and Kharga, and beyond to the Nile Valley. The Darb el-Ghubari, which avoids the steep climbs that the other route entails, is a slightly longer way to Kharga, but this road is more direct when one is travelling to the southern part of that oasis. Several Old Kingdom campsites have been found on the floor of the Southeast Basin, and McDonald (1990b, 63) has already suggested that the basin may have served as a 'staging area' for a trip up the escarpment. It is interesting to observe how the hilltop sites cluster around the Southeast Basin. It is clear that several sites were in eye contact with one other, and in combination the staff could easily have been able to keep an eye on possible intruders or on caravans entering or leaving the oasis.

Other hilltop sites controlled the access to the oasis from the south. The wide view from the southern hills indicates that their principal purpose again lay in the control of approaching traffic.

The assumption that the hilltop sites did not function independently is confirmed by the lack of food remains on Nephthys Hill. As has been remarked above, the analysis by Thanheiser of the ashes from the fireplaces has revealed the presence of acacia and tamarisk, but besides this combustible material no trace of burnt food has been found. This suggests that the fires on the site were not used for cooking meals. All foodstuffs were apparently brought to the hill from a kitchen elsewhere, which perhaps serviced the soldiers upon several hills. However, other sites, such as hilltop sites nos 2 and 4 in the list above, have yielded sherds from bread moulds that indicate cooking took place on some of them.

The question remains as to what it was exactly that the soldiers upon Nephthys Hill and the other hilltop sites were counting. At Ayn Asil and Ein el-Gezareen the purpose of the 'mute accounts' is equally obscure. They might have indicated product deliveries, people, or even days. From the New Kingdom, we know of an army scribe in the reign of Thutmose I who had to count (*ip*) passing ships on the Nile (Hintze and Reineke 1989, 171–2, no. 561).[12] Similarly, it is conceivable that the passing travellers to and from Dakhleh were checked and counted by the soldiers on the hilltop sites. The fact that most of the longer counts are divisible by ten and that the hieroglyph for ten itself frequently occurs suggests that the measured items occurred in groups of ten. It is tempting, therefore, to think of the days of a week. The notches could record, for instance, the number of days in a shift. Until better evidence comes to light, however, this remains a mere hypothesis.

The exact date of the watch posts is admittedly vague, but some may be of an earlier date than the earliest phases of the city of Ayn Asil presently known. It was noted at the beginning of this article that until phase III (early in the reign of Pepi II) the governor's city was provided with a defensive system. We do not know yet how far back the town extends in time. The occurrence of the mute accounts both at Ayn Asil and on the desert watch posts suggests, however, that elements of the same administrative system were operative in both. It is conceivable that the early fortress near Balat and the desert watch posts formed part of a single military infrastructure. The circumstances that urged the Egyptian colonists at Ayn Asil to fortify their settlement might well have been related to the desire to control the access roads to the oasis.

The clay tablets from Ayn Asil prove that there was still a military garrison there in the Sixth Dynasty. The soldiers (ꜥnḫw) stood under the command of a sꜣtw wḥꜣt (commander of the oasis) who is mentioned on one of the clay tablets (Posener-Kriéger 1992, 47). Pantalacci (1997, 345) has established that the governors of Balat held power over an area wider than Dakhleh itself. In the mastaba of Khentika (Dakhleh) inscriptions record connections with Bahariya (Ḏsḏs) in the north. Future surveys around the oasis may demonstrate whether the Egyptian military presence was indeed spread over such a wide region.

The establishment of an Egyptian territorial entity in Dakhleh in the Fifth Dynasty (?) may not be an isolated phenomenon. It has recently been argued that the colonisation of Nubia did not begin in the Middle Kingdom, as is generally believed, but that there were state-planned Egyptian settlements in that region as early as the Fifth Dynasty and perhaps before. However, unlike the situation in Dakhleh, these Egyptian towns were no longer in evidence during the Sixth Dynasty (Gratien 1995, 45–9). It would thus appear that Egypt was, already at this early date, deploying an active

policy of safeguarding its trade routes both in Nubia and in the Western Desert. The fact that they did so proves that considerable interests must have been involved.

One of the major points of concern in Dakhleh must have been the safety of trade caravans. The famous 'Oasis Road', on which Harkhuf travelled at the end of the Old Kingdom, must have passed through Dakhleh (Valloggia 1981; Pantalacci 1997, 345; Kuper this volume, **Plate 23**). Several roads must have led from the oasis further to the south. In the case of Harkhuf, the road led him to Yam, which is possibly to be identified as Kerma (Bonnet 1996, 89). Another direction in which one travelled was to the southwest, past the water point of Abu Ballas, where many large water jars of Old Kingdom date have been found (cf. Sers 1994, 198–207; Kuper this volume **Plates 18–19**), as well as petroglyphs from this period (Sers 1994, 82–5). The recent find of Old Kingdom ceramics in the northwestern Sudan (Lange 1998) may be interpreted as an indication that this route continued further southwards. These ceramics have not yet been published, and M Lange states that they include parts of a Meidum bowl of the Fourth or Fifth Dynasty, but according to C A Hope (pers. comm. 1999), the fragments should be dated later in the Old Kingdom.

It has been noted above that the Meidum bowls from Nephthys Hill were made of an imported Nile fabric. This intriguing finding implies that the occupants on the hill received a fragile part of their equipment from a source in the heartland of Egypt. This would be astonishing if an Egyptian pottery workshop were already functioning in the oasis. It should be borne in mind that Meidum bowls were the most common type of ware for daily use: in the *sondage nord* at Ayn Asil 33–51% of the pottery was of this type (Ballet 1987, 3). It is known that in the early stages of the occupation of the oasis basic commodities like these still had to be brought in from the Nile Valley to provision the settlers (Hope 1999, 221–2). We may conclude that Nephthys Hill is likely to have functioned as a watch post during an early stage in the development of a network of trading posts in the deserts around Egypt.

Addendum 2001

Since the above was written, continuing surveys by the authors have added four further hilltop sites to our list, numbered as 11 (30/450-D4-6), 12 (no DOP number yet assigned), 13 (31/20-H10-3) and 14 (30/420-G2-1). Several sites have been recorded more fully (sites 7, 9, 12 and 13 of the extended list), and the conclusions reached in this paper have been corroborated by new evidence. Most notably, the Meidum ware ceramics recovered from these new sites have generally shown the characteristics of a pre-Sixth Dynasty date, confirming the conclusions based on the scant ceramics from Nephthys Hill.

Hilltop site 12 has added an important new aspect to our study. This site is situated to the northeast of the oasis in direct association with a caravan route between Dakhleh and

Kharga and the Nile Valley. The ceramic finds show that this caravan route was used extensively during Old Kingdom times and again in the Late Period, but not much thereafter. A relationship between the hilltop sites and the entrance routes into the oasis has thus become more plausible. No further artefacts of the Sheikh Muftah culture have been found on the hilltop sites, which futher strengthens our view that these sites formed part of the Egyptian occupation strategies in the region. M McDonald has recently excavated at a number of Sheikh Muftah sites in Dakhleh and important new information on this cutlure is emerging that will complement the work done on the pharaonic involvement in the oasis.

Appendix: The Chipped Stone from Nephthys Hill, Locality 386

Mary M A McDonald

Nine hundred and sixty-eight pieces of chipped stone were collected at Site 30/450-D4-2 or Locality 386, Nephthys Hill.[13] Of these, nearly two-thirds, those >15 mm, were selected out by the excavator, while the remaining 365 pieces were numbered and given to McDonald for examination. The collection includes 50 formal tools,[14] 24 tool fragments, 26 items bearing some use retouch, 10 cores, 5 core fragments, 111 flakes, 4 blades, 59 fragments and 13 chunks. Sixty-three heavily patinated pieces perhaps date from the Middle Stone Age (MSA). A few of these had been cracked open at Loc. 386, but were otherwise largely unmodified.

It is unclear from where the raw materials for the industry came. The materials include nodular grey-brown chert, a whitish, coarse-grained chertball (CBS) material, a bit of yellowish quartzite, and the patinated MSA lithics from which fully 35% of the tools were fashioned. M Kleindienst, who has studied chipping stone distribution around Loc. 386 and in eastern Dakhleh generally (Kleindienst *et al.* 1999), reports that all three major groups would have been extremely rare, at least within a radius of a few kilometres of the site (pers. comm. June 1999). The inhabitants may have brought a supply of chipping stone with them from their base, arguably in the vicinity of Ayn Asil, where such materials are more abundant. If so, however, it is odd that they did not choose any of the good quality caramel-coloured tabular chert that is such an important component of the chipped stone collections in the Central Lowlands. At the town site of Ayn Asil, for instance, 43% of tools are made of

this material (Midant-Reynes 1998), while the percentage can be even higher at other lowland Old Kingdom sites (McDonald 1983, table 1). Even Locality 229, another excavated hut circle site in southeastern Dakhleh (number 4 in the list above), had some tools fashioned in the tabular chert (McDonald 1990a, 49).

The chipped stone industry of Nephthys Hill has a pronounced *ad hoc* or expedient look about it; the raw materials seem to be quite small, the industry heavily flake-based and quite informal. Aside from the bipolar element, the ten cores average 29.0 × 34.2 × 22.5 mm in size, the largest dimension on any of them being 56.0 mm. Four of them are single-platform cores, while the rest show a change of orientation, four of the latter to a radial pattern. The sampled flakes were also small, averaging 25.0 × 25.0 × 7.5 mm, even after all items under 15.0 mm had been removed. The flakes of grey-brown chert (72% of the total) were on average slightly larger than those of CBS material.

Table 1 lists the formal tool types at Loc. 386 (Nephthys Hill) and compares the tool assemblage to that of the hut circle Loc. 229 (hilltop site no.4) and the two Central Lowland town sites of Ein el-Gezareen (32/390-K2-2, Loc. 383) and Ayn Asil. Of the four, the collection from Loc. 386 is the smallest and the least diverse. The most notable difference from the town sites is the absence of sickle elements and knives, a trait Loc. 386 shares with 229. This trait is no doubt a reflection of the specialised nature of these hilltop sites, which are well away from the cultivation. Both sites

Table 1: Percentage frequencies of major tool classes at Loc. 386 and three other Old Kingdom sites in the Dakhleh Oasis

	Loc. 386 'Nephthys Hill'	Loc. 229 30/450-G8-2	Loc. 383 Ein el-Gezareen	Ayn Asil
Notches	6	4.9	7.8	4.5
Denticulates	36	13.3	18.3	5.4
Piercers	12	39.4	7.8	1.2
Scrapers	2	7.9	16.5	59.4
Combinations	20	9.1	18.3	
W/ retouch	10	2.4		10.6
Sickles			13.9	15.4
Lunates		1.2		
Knives			2.8	
Varia				1.8
Scaled	14	21.8	7	
Total number	50	165	115	1551

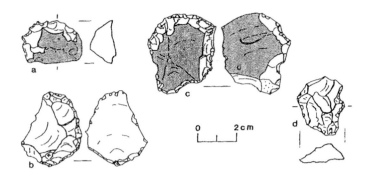

Fig. 12 Chipped stone artefacts from Nephthys Hill, Loc. 386: ab, denticulates; c, combination tool (scraper-denticulate); d, piercer. Shaded areas represent old surfaces of reworked or double patinated artefacts.

also show a higher proportion of piercers and a lower proportion of scrapers than the lowland sites. The two hilltop localities themselves show an interesting contrast in the proportions of denticulates and piercers, Loc. 386 with a preponderance of the former, Loc. 229 of the latter. Loc. 386 also has higher proportions of combination tools and retouched items than 229, but fewer scrapers.

The denticulate is the dominant tool in the industry at Loc. 386 (**Fig. 12** ab). Besides the 18 formal items, there are 15 informal denticulates and tool fragments, while 6 of the 10 combination tools have a denticulated edge as one component (**Fig. 12** c). Like the rest of the assemblage, the formal denticulates are quite small, but they are relatively thick-sectioned (mean dimensions 28.5 × 27.3 × 11.5 mm) with quite steep working edge angles. Fully half are fashioned on MSA flakes, which are normally fairly thick. Half the denticulates bear the retouch along one side, and most of the others along one side and an end.

The six piercers at Loc. 386 (**Fig. 12** d) (and an additional four amongst the combination tools) tend to have small, stubby points (although there are three fragments that might come from more pronounced points). In contrast, in the much larger collection from Loc. 229, over one third of the piercers have fairly large, well-developed points, and there are 12 drill bits as well. Scrapers are poorly represented at 386, with one c-nosed scraper and two or three scraper-denticulates. The retouched items show no real patterns as to blank form or location of retouched edge.

To conclude, the knappers at Loc. 386 used nodular chert or patinated material from earlier cultures to produce a limited variety of small stone tools. The contrast with the chipped stone assemblages from lowland Old Kingdom town sites is not surprising. More interesting, perhaps, are the differences between the collections from Locs 386 and 229. The well-preserved deposits within the hut circle at Loc. 229 contained evidence of a range of activities, notably leather-working, with gazelle hides being tanned and perhaps sewed into clothing on the site (McDonald 1990a). At hilltop site Loc. 386, preservation of organics was not nearly as good. Moreover, there is a danger in generalising from such a small lithic sample. Still, the rather different lithic industry at this site, with scrapers and awl-like tools poorly represented and with its emphasis on denticulates may reflect a different, and perhaps more restricted, range of activities at the hut circles of Loc. 386.

Acknowledgements

We are grateful to Renée Friedman for welcoming us in this volume, to Alicia Hawkins for preparing the map in **Fig. 2** and to Lucia Kuijper for assistance in the field. We have benefited from comments made by Colin Hope, Georges Soukiassian, Anthony Mills and Julia Harvey who have read the manuscript, although we retain full responsibility for the views expressed herein. Olaf Kaper was supported by a fellowship of the Alexander von Humboldt-Stiftung, Bonn.

Notes

1. The excavations in this part of the city have not yet been published, but extensive preliminary reports have appeared in the *Bulletin de l'Institut français d'archéologie orientale* (BIFAO) The best survey of the results can be found in Soukiassian, Wuttmann and Schaad (1990). For more recent results see the annual reports of the director of the IFAO in BIFAO. For the southern gate see Soukiassian, Wuttmann and Schaad 1990, 350–1; for the northern gate see Giddy 1980 and 1983.

2. Since Soukiassian, Wuttmann and Schaad (1990) no preliminary reports have been published about the on-going excavation, but there is the brief article by Soukiassian (1997).

3. See Giddy 1983, 104 and fig. 1. In the part of this figure furthest to the right, the tops of the walls of phase I can be seen in the floors of phase IIa in rooms F, H and I.

4. The excavators earlier expressed the view that the fire had been caused by an accident (see Soukiassian, Wuttmann and Schaad 1990, 356–7), but they now believe it to have been intentional (Soukiassian 1997, 17). No evidence for this has so far been published.

5. Valloggia (1996) seems to express the view that the community was basically non-Egyptian, although governed by Egyptian administrators. The evidence, however, suggests that the material culture at Ayn Asil was fundamentally Egyptian, even when locally produced.

6. In fact, the Sheikh Muftah Unit is the youngest of three major Neolithic cultural units of Dakhleh, the earliest remains of which are dated to the ninth millennium bp. See the overview in McDonald 1999 and Hope this volume.

7. We are grateful to Joachim Quack for his comments on a photograph of this piece. Its inscription is of a religious nature (reading *rn=f mn...*) and suggests the presence of a sanctuary on this hill.

8. This is to be published in the publication series of the Dakhleh Oasis Project.

9. We have discussed some of the petroglyphs from Nephthys Hill with D Huyge, who believes that they closely resemble Old Kingdom rock art from Elkab and Hosh.

10. This identification was first suggested to us by John Darnell. The known examples of wrist-guards have been collected and studied by Müller (1989, 5–9). Two additional instances not taken into consideration in that book were found in Mirgissa cemetery MX, dating to the late Middle Kingdom (Vercoutter 1975, 162, 159, fig. 62A.a). Although Müller considers the find context of the known examples to be a strong indication that this type of object should be attributed to the Second Intermediate Period, the instances are small in number and the find context of many unknown. The Egyptian-style iconography on the wrist-guards suggests that they do not have a background in the Pan Grave culture, but rather an Egyptian origin (thus already Brunton 1937, 128).

11. From Giza: Junker 1929, abb. 12.7–14; Reisner 1942, fig. 242, nos 13.11-76; Kromer 1971, pl. XXIII, 9; Kromer 1978, pl. 21.8. From Dahshur: Stadelmann and Alexanian 1998, Abb. 6, 5–6 and 12–5. From el Tarif: Ginter and Kozlowski *et al.* 1998, 80–2 and abb. 41, 5–6. The determination of the fabric we owe to Colin Hope, the dating to both him and Annelies Op de Beeck, whose MA thesis on Meidum bowls we have consulted with great benefit.

12. We owe this reference to Stephan Seidlmayer.

13. All prehistoric sites in Dakhleh Oasis plus historic sites yielding collections of chipped stone are numbered sequentially in a separate numbering system for ease of reference.

14. Included in this number are seven 'scaled pieces' or products of bipolar knapping, which are, technically speaking, debitage.

Bibliography

Arnold F, 1990. *The South Cemeteries of Lisht II: The Control Notes and Team Marks.* New York.

Ballet P, 1987. Essai de classification des coupes type maidumbowl du sondage nord d'Ayn Asîl (Oasis de Dakhla). Typologie et évolution. *Cahiers de la céramique égyptienne* 1: 1–16.

Bates O, 1914. *The Eastern Libyans: An Essay.* London.

Bonnet C, 1996. Das Königreich von Kerma. In D Wildung (ed.), *Sudan, Antike Königreiche am Nil.* Munich and Paris: 89–118.

Brunton G, 1937. *Mostagedda and the Tasian Culture.* London.

Burkard G, 1997. Inscription in the Dakhla Region, Text, Translation and Comments. *Sahara* 9: 152–3.

Cherpion N, 1999. La statue du sanctuaire de Medou-nefer. *Bulletin de l'Institut français d'archéologie orientale* 99: 85–101.

Churcher C S and Mills A J (eds), 1999. *Reports from the Survey of the Dakhleh Oasis. Western Desert of Egypt, 1977-1987.* Oxbow Monograph 99, Dakhleh Oasis Project Monograph 2. Oxford.

Decker W and Herb M, 1994. *Bildatlas zum Sport im alten Ägypten. Corpus der bildlichen Quellen zu Leibesübungen, Spiel, Jagd, Tanz und verwandten Themen.* Handbuch der Orientalistik. Erste Abt. 14. Leiden.

Edwards W I and Hope C A, 1987. The Neolithic Ceramics from the Dakhleh Oasis. In W I Edwards, C A Hope, E R Segnit, *Ceramics from the Dakhleh Oasis: Preliminary Studies.* Burwood, Australia.

Fischer H G, 1961. The Nubian Mercenaries of Gebelein during the First Intermediate Period. *Kush* 9: 44–80.

Fischer H G, 1962. The Archer as Represented in the First Intermediate Period. *Journal of Near Eastern Studies* 21: 50–2.

Giddy L L, 1980. Balat: Rapport préliminaire des fouilles à 'Ayn 'Asîl, 1979–1980. *Bulletin de l'Institut français d'archéologie orientale* 80: 257–66.

Giddy L L, 1983. Rapport sur la quatrième campagne de fouilles à 'Ayn 'Asîl (Oasis de Dakhleh). *Annales du Service des Antiquités d'Égypte* 69: 103–9.

Giddy L L, 1987. *Egyptian Oases: Bahariya, Dakhla, Farafra and Kharga during Pharaonic Times.* Warminster.

Ginter B, Kozlowski, M P, 1998. *Frühe Keramik und Kleinfunde aus al-Tarif.* Archäologische Veröffentlichungen, Deutsches Archäologisches Institut Abteilung Kairo 40. Mainz am Rhein.

Gratien B, 1995. La basse Nubie à l'Ancien Empire: égyptiens et autochtones. *Journal of Egyptian Archaeology* 81: 43–56.

Hintze F and Reineke W, 1989. *Felsinschriften aus dem sudanesischen Nubien.* 2 vols. Berlin.

Hope C A, 1979. Dakhleh Oasis Project, Report on the Study of the Pottery and Kilns. *Journal of the Society for the Study of Egyptian Antiquities* 9 (1978–1979): 187–201.

Hope C A, 1999. Pottery Manufacture in the Dakhleh Oasis. In C S Churcher and A J Mills (eds), 1999: 215–43.

Huyge D, 1998. Art on the Decline? Egyptian Rock Drawings from the Late and Graeco-Roman Periods. In W Clarysse, A Schoors and H Willems (eds), *Egyptian Religion. The Last Thousand Years.* Part II. Orientalia Lovaniensia Analecta 85. Leuven: 1377–92.

Junker H, 1929. *Giza I.* Vienna and Leipzig.

Kleindienst M R, Churcher C S, McDonald M M A and Schwarcz H P, 1999. Geography, Geology, Geochronology and Geoarchaeology of the Dakhleh Oasis Region: An Interim Report. In C S Churcher and A J Mills (eds), 1999: 1–54.

Kromer K, 1971. *Ausgrabungen im Pyramidendistrikt Giseh. V.A.R.* Österreichische Hochschulzeitung. Vienna.

Kromer K, 1978. *Siedlungsfunde aus dem frühen AR bei Giseh Österreichische Ausgrabungen 1971–1975.* Denkschriften Akademie der Wissenschaften in Wien, philosophisch-historische Klasse 136. Vienna.

Krzyzaniak L, 1987. Dakhleh Oasis Project: Interim Report on the First Season of the Recording of Petroglyphs, January/February 1988. *Journal of the Society for the Study of Egyptian Antiquities* 17: 182–91.

Krzyzaniak L, 1990. Petroglyphs and the Research on the Development of the Cultural Attitude towards Animals in the Dakhleh Oasis. *Sahara* 3: 95–7.

Krzyzaniak L and Kroeper K, 1990. The Dakhleh Oasis Project: Interim Report on the Second (1990) and Third (1992) Seasons of the Recording of Petroglyphs. *Journal of the Society for the Study of Egyptian Antiquities* 20: 77–88.

Lange M, 1998. Wadi Shaw 82/52 – a Peridynastic [sic] Settlement Site in the Western Desert and its Relations to the Nile Valley. In T Kendall and P Der Manuelian (eds), *Ninth International Conference of Nubian Studies, August 21–26 1998. Abstracts of Papers.* Boston: 73.

McDonald M M A, 1983. Dakhleh Oasis Project: Fourth Preliminary Report on the Lithic Industries in the Dakhleh Oasis.

Journal of the Society for the Study of Egyptian Antiquities 13: 158–66.

McDonald M M A, 1985. Dakhleh Oasis Project: Holocene Prehistory: Interim Report on the 1987 Season. *Journal of the Society for the Study of Egyptian Antiquities* 15: 126–35.

McDonald M M A, 1986. Dakhleh Oasis Project: Holocene Prehistory: Interim Report on the 1987 Season. *Journal of the Society for the Study of Egyptian Antiquities* 16: 103–13.

McDonald M M A, 1990a. The Dakhleh Oasis Project: Holocene Prehistory: interim report on the 1988 and 1989 seasons. *Journal of the Society for the Study of Egyptian Antiquities* 20: 24–53.

McDonald M M A, 1990b. The Dakhleh Oasis Project: Holocene Prehistory: interim report on the 1990 season. *Journal of the Society for the Study of Egyptian Antiquities* 20: 54–64.

McDonald M M A, 1998. Early African Pastoralism: View from Dakhleh Oasis (South Central Egypt). *Journal of Anthropological Archaeology* 17: 124–42.

McDonald M M A, 1999. Neolithic Cultural Units and Adaptations in the Dakhleh Oasis. In C S Churcher and A J Mills (eds), 1999: 117–32.

Martin-Pardey E, 1976. *Untersuchungen zur ägyptischen Provinzialverwaltung bis zum Ende des Alten Reiches.* Hildesheimer Ägyptologische Beiträge 1. Hildesheim.

Midant-Reynes B, 1998. *Le silex de 'Ayn-Asil: Oasis de Dakhla-Balat.* Cairo.

Minault-Gout A, 1985. Une inscription rupestre de l'oasis de Dakhla située au débouché du Darb el-Tawil. In F Geus and F Thill (eds), *Mélanges offerts à Jean Vercoutter.* Paris: 267–72.

Mills A J, 1981. The Dakhleh Oasis Project, Report on the Third Season of Survey, September–December, 1980. *Journal of the Society for the Study of Egyptian Antiquities* 11: 175–92.

Müller H W, 1989. *Die «Armreif» des Königs Ahmose und der Handgelenkschütz des Bogenschützen im alten Ägypten und Vorderasien.* Mainz.

Osing J, 1986. Notizen zu den Oasen Charga und Dachla. *Göttinger Miszellen* 92: 79–85.

Osing J, Moursi M, Arnold Do, Neugebauer O, Parker P A, Pingree D and Nur el-Din M A, 1982. *Denkmäler der Oase Dachla aus dem Nachlass von Ahmed Fakhry.* Archäologische Veröffentlichungen, Deutsches Archäologisches Institut Abteilung Kairo 28. Mainz am Rhein.

Pantalacci L, 1996. Fonctionnaires et analphabètes: sur quelques pratiques administratives observées à Balat. *Bulletin de l'Institut français d'archéologie orientale* 98: 359–67.

Pantalacci L, 1997. De Memphis à Balat. Les liens entre la résidence et les gouverneurs de l'oasis à la VIe dynastie. In C Berger, G Clerc and N Grimal (eds), *Études sur l'Ancien Empire et la nécropole de Saqqâra dédiées à Jean-Philippe Lauer.* Montpellier: 341–9

Pantalacci L, 1998. Les habitants de Balat à la VIème Dynastie: esquisse d'histoire sociale. In C Eyre (ed.), *Proceedings of the Sev-enth International Congress of Egyptologists. Cambridge, 3–9 September 1995.* Leuven: 829–37.

Posener-Kriéger P, 1992. Les tablettes en terre crue de Balat. In É Lalou (ed.), *Les tablettes à écrire de l'antiquité à l'époque moderne.* Turnhout: 41–52.

Reisner G A, 1942. *A History of the Giza Necropolis I.* Cambridge Mass.

Sers J-F, 1994. *Sous la direction de Théodore Monod, Désert Libyque.* Paris.

Soukiassian G, 1997. A Governors' Palace at 'Ayn Asil, Dakhla Oasis. *Egyptian Archaeology* 11: 15–7.

Soukiassian G, Wuttmann M and Pantalacci L, 1990. *Balat III. Les ateliers de potiers d'Ayn Asîl.* Fouilles de l'Institut français d'archéologie orientale 34. Cairo.

Soukiassian G, Wuttmann M and Schaad D, 1990. La ville d'Ayn Asîl à Dakhla. État des recherches. *Bulletin de l'Institut français d'archéologie orientale* 90: 347–58.

Stadelmann R and Alexanian N, 1998. Die Friedhöfe des Alten und Mittleren Reiches in Dahschur. Bericht über die im Frühjahr 1997 durch das DAI durchgeführte Felderkundung in Dahschur. *Mitteilungen des Deutschen Archäologischen Instituts Abteilung Kairo* 54: 293–317.

Strudwick N, 1985. *The Administration of Egypt in the Old Kingdom. The Highest Titles and their Holders.* Studies in Egyptology. London.

Tiradritti F (ed.), 1999. *The Treasures of the Egyptian Museum.* Cairo.

Valloggia M, 1981. This sur la route des oasis. *Bulletin du Centenaire, Supplément au Bulletin de l'Institut français d'archéologie orientale* 81: 185–90.

Valloggia M, 1985. La stèle d'un chef d'expédition de la première période intermédiaire. *Bulletin de l'Institut français d'archéologie orientale* 85: 259–66.

Valloggia M, 1996. Note sur l'organisation administrative de l'Oasis de Dakhla à la fin de l'Ancien Empire. *Méditerranées. Revue de l'Association Méditerranées* 6–7: 61–72.

Valloggia M, 1998. *Balat IV: Le monument funéraire d'Ima-Pepy/ Ima-Meryrê.* Fouilles de l'Institut français d'archéologie orientale 38. Cairo.

Vercoutter J, 1975. *Mirgissa II: Les nécropoles.* Paris.

Verner M, 1973. *Some Nubian Petroglyphs on Czechoslovak Concessions: Rock Drawings of (I) Foot and Sandal Prints, (II) Symbols and Signs, and (III) Erotica from the Czechoslovak Concession in Nubia.* Prague.

Winkler H A, 1939. *Rock Drawings from Southern Upper Egypt II.* Archaeological Survey of Egypt 27. London

Ziermann M, 1998. Bemerkungen zu den Befestigungen des Alten Reiches in Ayn Asil und in Elephantine. *Mitteilungen des Deutschen Archäologischen Instituts Abteilung Kairo* 54: 341–59.

Oases Amphorae of the New Kingdom

Colin A Hope[1]

with contributions by Mark Eccleston, Pamela Rose and Janine Bourriau

The study of relations between the Nile Valley and the oases of the Western Desert during the New Kingdom has until recently depended upon a relatively small body of data found in the valley.[2] From the Eighteenth Dynasty this mostly takes the form of references to or depictions of oasis produce in seven Theban tombs of the middle of the dynasty, and in dockets (on these, Tallet 1998b) and jar sealings from amphorae[3] of the later part of the dynasty principally from Malkata and Amarna.[4] The majority of these yield little detail, though a few do provide toponyms within the Southern Oasis (most recently Marchand and Tallet 1999, 312–4).[5] From the Nineteenth and Twentieth Dynasties there are few dockets, though several papyri testify to the interest of the central administration in the various imports from this region. Much of this documentation focuses upon the manufacture and import of wine[6] and its associated commodities[7] into the valley, thus showing its significance within the economy of the oases, at least from the valley perspective.[8] It has been thought that the evidence indicates a degree of control by the Nile Valley administration and, more assuredly, the existence of a ceramic industry in the oasis to provide the necessary containers for the transport of the wine, as Giddy (1987, 75) noted:

> The most prominent export, wine, would necessitate long-term agricultural production, as well as all accompanying installations for the winemaking industry. This could well have also included a complementary pottery industry, as the transport of large empty wine-jars … to what has already been established as a remote region, would surely have been avoided. Such an industry again would have called for a considerable resident population, but a population not entirely occupied with agriculture.

In association with any such industry there were scribes who added the hieratic dockets to some of the jars and who developed some idiosyncratic variations upon the standard formula that was employed (Tallet 1996, 377–8; Marchand and Tallet 1999, 318).

By contrast, the archaeological record within the oases has been comparatively mute; other than a few finds of ceramics, notable exceptions are the tomb of the Governor of Bahariya Amenhotep Huy of the Eighteenth–Nineteenth Dynasty (van Siclen 1981) and four inscribed blocks found by A Fakhry in Dakhleh (Osing *et al.* 1982, nos 30, 38–9, 44; Marchand and Tallet 1999, 308–9). The latter include a stela of the mid-Eighteenth Dynasty and two fragments from door jambs found at Ayn Asil, on two of which a cult installation of the goddess Nerit is attested, and another stela from Mut also of the mid-Eighteenth Dynasty. Whilst the cultivation of vines and the bottling of wine is represented in the tomb of Amenhotep Huy (van Siclen 1981, 8–9, pl. I), from the Southern Oasis, which inscriptional data show was the more important wine-producing region, there is no similar representational evidence.[9]

The range of material available for the study of valley and oases contacts has increased significantly in recent years as a result of detailed studies of the ceramics found in both regions, and the genesis of the present article lies in that work. Intermittently since 1979, throughout the survey of the Dakhleh Oasis, examples of a pottery fabric have been found that bore superficial resemblance to the Nile Valley fabric Marl D of the Vienna System (Nordström and Bourriau 1993, 181). This is termed fabric B23 in the Dakhleh Oasis Project's pottery fabric system. Only a few of the sherds were diagnostics and these preserved rim and base shapes that recalled those of New Kingdom amphorae. In addition, excavations conducted at the cemetery of Ein Tirghi (site no. 31/435-D5-2; see **Fig. 1**) in Dakhleh yielded some examples of this fabric and also vessels that were clearly of New Kingdom date; associated with some of these were other artefacts of the same period. During the study of New Kingdom painted pottery from the excavations at Karnak North conducted by Helen and Jean Jacquet, I was able to examine several fragmentary vessels and various sherds that Helen Jacquet believed to be of oasis provenance. Similarly, while working on such material from Memphis I was shown material Janine Bourriau suspected was also of oasis manufacture. Pottery fabrics had, in the meantime, been identified at other valley sites that were thought to have a Western Desert origin, though this identification was somewhat speculative as no direct comparisons had been made (e.g., Aston 1991, 48; 1992, 77; 1996, 9 and passim; 1998, 73; Hummel and Schubert 1994, 33–4, 73). Then, during the course of 1998, it proved possible to compare directly samples of fabrics identified at Amarna, Karnak North and Memphis with material found in Dakhleh Oasis. This confirmed the similarity of many examples and placed the study of oasis amphora on a firmer footing. At the same time, material excavated at Ayn Asil in Dakhleh by L'Institut français d'archéologie orientale produced a substantial corpus of material identical to that found elsewhere in Dakhleh (Marchand and Tallet 1999),[10] thus confirming the oasis provenance of the fabric termed B23.

The purpose of this article is to present the preliminary conclusions of the comparative study of the material from the Nile Valley with that from Dakhleh and the other oases, to survey the range of find spots of material found in the Nile Valley that has an oasis provenance, and to give an anal-

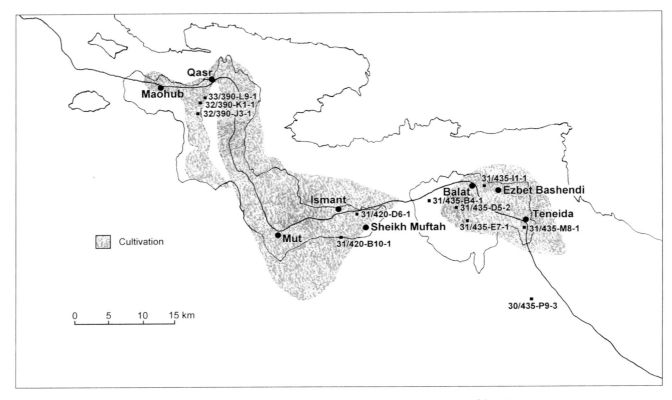

Fig. 1   Location of sites in Dakhleh Oasis that have yielded New Kingdom ceramics in fabric B23.

ysis of the Dakhleh fabric B23 (by Mark Eccleston). The discussion of the distribution of oasis amphorae within the Nile Valley is necessarily of a preliminary nature as it is certain that much remains to be identified.[11] As some of the most important discoveries have been made at Amarna and Memphis, Pamela Rose and Janine Bourriau provide separate discussions of the finds at those sites.

I: Material from the Oases

Dakhleh Oasis

Fabric B23 (Plates 69–72)

The technical description of this fabric is provided below by Mark Eccleston, but a brief description is included here for ease of reference. In general, fabric B23 may be characterised as a medium-fine textured clay that contains numerous inclusions of oxidised limestone of fairly small size, quartz grains of varying sizes, and red particles that may be identified as mudstone; voids of varying sizes and shapes occur. There is the occasional larger piece of limestone. It has a variable firing pattern: there may be a bluish-grey core with oxidised zones coloured light orange to red on either side; two zones, one bluish-grey and the other light orange to red; or it may be fired grey throughout. In all cases the oxidised limestone inclusions are quite distinct. Exterior surfaces may be uncoated and a greyish-brown or red colour, or they may have a red or cream coating; only rarely is any form of compaction attested. This fabric was used in the manufacture of closed forms, predominantly amphorae, one-handled bottles, large jars and flasks (cf. Marchand and Tallet 1999, figs 8–23).

In relation to fabrics identified on Nile Valley sites, it would seem to resemble most closely Amarna fabric IV.3 in the occurrence within the clay matrix of abundant, mainly small white limestone particles, although it may also resemble the finer version of IV.2. The latter has been equated with Memphis fabric P44 and the former with P23; Janine Bourriau (pers. comm. 1998) has noted the similarity of Dakhleh B23 to Memphis fabric P44. B23 is to be identified with fabrics F1G-J of the classification employed at Ayn Asil by the French team (Marchand and Tallet 1999, 335–6).

The Dakhleh finds are characterised by their homogeneity; they lack the variety of fabric types identified upon Nile Valley sites, most notably at Memphis (see Bourriau below). Whether this indicates that those fabrics that are dissimilar to B23 originate either in Kharga, as for example in the case of the coarser, though petrographically similar, Amarna fabric IV.2 and Memphis P45, or the northern oases is uncertain. Sherds recently observed in Bahariya, on sites dating to the Ptolemaic and Roman periods, included examples that resemble Amarna IV.2 and Memphis P45 in containing coarse limestone and mudstone inclusions, while others are similar to various Dakhleh fabrics. It has been established that the fabrics of those periods and of the Late Period (Hope et al. 2000) in Kharga are also indistinguishable from those found in Dakhleh. Further, amongst the latter there is a fabric with large limestone inclusions that is fired grey throughout and resembles the fabric noted in Bahariya. It is clear that much more analysis of samples from the various oases is needed before distinctions can be made with certainty. For the present it may be wisest to note the general similarity of a range of pottery fabrics identified on valley sites with the Dakhleh fabric, and to use this as an indicator of their general provenance, rather than trying to provide exact locations. The difference noted between the oases fabrics identified at Amarna and Memphis also indicates a variety of sources.

Site Material (**Fig. 1**)

In this section I shall present a summary of the discoveries made to date within the Dakhleh Oasis of material manufactured in fabric B23. Unfortunately, the majority of this material is very fragmentary and the dating and morphology proposed are tentative. The designation employed to refer to the sites follows the standard system used by the Dakhleh Oasis Project (Mills 1979, 167–8).[12] The sites will be presented from east to west.

30/435-P9-3 (**Fig. 2**)

This site, discovered in 1999, is located on the western edge of what has been termed the Southeast Basin by McDonald (most recently, 1998), a region that is rich in Holocene sites.[13] It may be identified as a campsite, possibly used in connection with the Darb el-Ghubari route between Dakhleh and Kharga (Giddy 1987, 10–1), and comprises a scatter of surface pottery around sandstone outcrops and a single hearth. No structures could be identified, though it must be noted that the site has not been surveyed in detail. It is clear that many of the clusters of sherds represent individual broken vessels, but restoration work on the material has yet to be undertaken. In addition to vessels in B23, others occur in a coarse straw-tempered fabric and a sand-rich fabric; all forms appear to be restricted jars of various types, predominantly of large size and with relatively thick walls. The assemblage indicates that the site was not one at which diverse activities took place and it may be connected with the transport of commodities between the oasis and Nile Valley.

From this site there are three rim to neck sherds (**Fig. 2** a–c) with distinct modelled rims that probably derive from a type of medium-tall necked amphora, with rounded upper body tapering to a mould-made (?) pointed base. This form evolved during the reign of Amenhotep II and was extremely common during the late Eighteenth–Nineteenth Dynasties, surviving in Upper Egypt to the end of the New Kingdom (Hope 1989a, 93–4, type 1a, figs 1.7–2.8, 3.7; Aston et al. 1998, 165–6; Aston and Pusch 1999, 44–5). The rim types are all paralleled by numerous examples of such a form found upon Nile Valley sites of late Eighteenth Dynasty date (e.g., Malkata), but there are few amongst the Qantir and Theban (Valley of Kings) material of Ramesside date recently published, the necks of which are mostly convex and the modelling of the rims less pronounced on the exterior (Aston 1998, 473, 495–9; Aston et al. 1998, passim; Aston and Pusch 1999, nos 12–15, 49, 71). They are similar to examples from Ayn Asil.

Two body fragments (**Fig. 2**d–e) appear to derive from a type of amphora that possessed a wide rounded or only slightly tapering body and a rounded or carinated base. In the Nile Valley such a form developed during the Nineteenth Dynasty and was manufactured especially in Lower Egypt throughout the remainder of the New Kingdom (Hope 1989a, 94, figs 3.1–2 and 5; Aston and Pusch 1999, 44). The Nile Valley examples possess a convex-sided neck. Given the fragmentary nature of the material from this site, however, it is impossible to be sure of the original complete morphology of the vessels from which these pieces derived, and they may have resembled the amphora found at Karnak North (**Fig. 7** b), possibly dating to the second half of the Eighteenth Dynasty. That type and others of similar date regularly have short necks. The manufacturing process of the base and lower body of such amphorae differs from that illustrated in **Fig. 2** e, which has one finger-modelled section below a wheel-made body rather than the normal finger-modelled base, then a section with distinct vertical grooves, and finally a wheel-made middle and upper body.

A fragment from a tapering base (**Fig. 2** f) with finger-modelled lower part and wheel-made upper section was also recovered. It is possible that this does not derive from an amphora but rather a large necked jar. It is included here because the type may have been an alternative to the amphora in the storage and transport of commodities (especially wine) from the oases as is indicated by other finds in Dakhleh (**Figs 3** i and k) and the Nile Valley (**Fig. 10** b), and in tomb reliefs (van Siclen 1981, 9, pl. 1; Giddy 1987, part II, table VIII).

31/435-M8-1

This cemetery of some 300 graves (Mills 1983, 135) can now be assigned on the basis of the ceramics to the Second Intermediate and Late Periods. It has yielded a single body sherd in B23, 1.8-2.2 cm thick. The form of the vessel could not be determined.

31/435-I1-1: Ayn Asil

In the southern sector of the settlement at Ayn Asil considerable quantities of New Kingdom ceramics have been identified (Marchand and Tallet 1999). The assemblage displays a variety of forms in different fabrics and is the most extensive of this period discovered in any of the oases to date. Amongst this material there is a notable quantity of amphorae sherds made in fabrics F1G-J, which are all variants of the same fabric and clearly identifiable as B23 of the Dakhleh Oasis Project classification.

Two hieratic dockets have been found: one preserves a reference to the 'Southern Oasis' and the other to '...the vineyard of the...' with a possible reference to '...Southern Oasis' (Marchand and Tallet 1999, 318, figs 6 and 7 respectively). These are the earliest references found in Dakhleh to this geographical designation. It has been proposed (Marchand and Tallet 1999, 313–4; Tallet 1999, 171–2) that the toponym *Jw-mrw* (island of the desert) found upon a sherd from an oasis amphora at Deir el-Medina might be an early version of the well-known *Jmrt* of the Roman period (Kaper 1992, 122–4).[14] The term appears to designate a region in the eastern part of Dakhleh, in the vicinity of Balat-Bashendi, wherein lies Ayn Asil and the temple of Ein Birbiyeh, the latter regularly said to be in *Jmrt* (Kaper 1992, 122–4;

1997, 12, 66–7). It is possible that two further toponyms, namely *J3t-t3* and *J3ty* that occur on a late Eighteenth Dynasty docket from Amarna and on an amphora from the tomb of Tutankhamun (Marchand and Tallet 1999, 311–2; see below), may be related to this region as their writings have in common with that of *Jmrt* the element *J3t* (Tallet 1996, 379 and note 48).

Amongst the amphorae sherds that are published by Marchand and Tallet (1999, 318–20, figs 8–17), two distinct groups were identified: one in which the forms copy those of Nile Valley amphorae and the other in which the form is peculiar to the oasis. In the former group, type A1 is a short-necked amphora with modelled rim, and types A2–3 have a taller concave neck (though not a tall neck as implied) also with modelled rim, though they are heavier in many cases than those of type A1. Types A1–3 are assigned to the late Eighteenth Dynasty; this may well be correct, as like those from 30/435-P9-3 (**Fig. 2** a–c) the necks of A2–3 amphorae are concave rather than convex. On the other hand, if we assume that the morphological development of this type of the group 1 amphora paralleled that of the Nile Valley manufactures, the occurrence at Ayn Asil of rounded amphora bases (Marchand and Tallet 1999, figs 15–16) indicates that some should possibly be ascribed to the Twentieth Dynasty (Aston 1998, 472). The lack of necks with convex sides amongst the published selection, if this feature is typical of the assemblage, might, however, serve to indicate that the development in each region was not exactly parallel in all respects.

The second group comprises types A4 and A5 (Marchand and Tallet 1999, figs 10–11). These are quite distinctive and appear to have been made in the oasis only. They have narrow necks, slender bodies, a characteristic narrow button base (compare here **Figs 3** m and **5** a–c), and vary in size (compare **Fig. 5** a–d); some examples carry black-painted, linear decoration on their bodies. This type has been dated by Aston (1992, 76–7) to the Ramesside period, initially to the Twentieth Dynasty, and later also to the Nineteenth Dynasty (Aston 1998, 109, 536–9). The selection of button bases published from Ayn Asil probably derives from this type and not the amphorae of group 1 as the authors suggest (Marchand and Tallet 1999, 319, fig. 14).

East of 31/435-I1-1 (**Fig. 3** a–i)

Amphora fragments were found amongst surface pottery predominantly of Roman date at various localities in the area between Ayn Asil and Bashendi. **Fig. 3** a–b are amphora necks with pronounced modelled rims, and are of the Ayn Asil type A2; **Fig. 3** c–e and possibly **3**h derive from types A4–5. **Fig. 3** f is unusual in having a finger-modelled round base and may not be from an amphora, while the shape and manufacturing technique of **Fig. 3** g is identical to that encountered on many large oasis-made amphorae found in the Nile Valley (compare **Figs 6** b, **7** b, **10** a, also **Fig. 7** a but not shown in the drawing, and examples from Amarna).[15] The lowest section is formed by pushing the clay into a mould, a method encountered regularly with Nile Valley amphorae (Hope 1989a, 93, pl. 5c), but in distinction to the latter, the next section is not wheel-made but

built up from sections that display deep, vertical finger-ridges. The final fragment, **Fig. 3** i, may either be from an amphora or a tall necked jar of the type possibly represented by **Fig. 2** f from 30/435-P9-3 and known from Theban Tomb 253 (**Fig. 10** b).

31/435-E7-1: Ein Dumurrah

This hill contains an active spring, one of the few surviving in Dakhleh, traces of mud-brick walls and a scatter of sherds that are predominantly late Roman in date (Mills 1983, 138). Here two body sherds in B23 with cream-coated surfaces were found; they are probably from amphorae.

31/435-D5-2: Ein Tirghi (**Fig. 3** j–l)

This cemetery contains brick tombs of the Middle Kingdom to Ptolemaic period (Frey 1986; Hope 1983, 144–9; 1999, 229; Mills 1983, 128–9; 1999, 177).[16] Unfortunately the settlement that it served has not been located. Many of the tombs in this cemetery have been considerably reused, yielding collections of artefacts of widely varying dates. Amongst ceramics associated with five tombs there are the following examples in B23:

Tomb 8: A blue-painted, wheel-made amphora (**Fig. 3** j) of Nineteenth Dynasty date was found alongside jars of the Second Intermediate and Persian Periods (Hope 1983, 147–8); its fabric is only tentatively identified as B23. Its morphology is distinct from that of the other oasis amphorae discussed here. The blue pigment upon it has been tentatively identified as calcium copper silicate (frit) and not the cobalt aluminate spinell commonly used in the decoration of blue-painted pottery and also employed on examples found at Ayn Asil (Marchand and Tallet 1999, 323–4). The decorative motifs occurring on this vessel are similar to those upon fragments recently discovered at Ayn Asil (Marchand and Tallet 1999, 323–4), which in their simplicity are more akin to Ramesside material than that of the Eighteenth Dynasty (cf. Aston 1998; Hope 1989b, 56–7, figs 12–19). A date for this amphora within the late Nineteenth to Twentieth Dynasty on the basis of supposed decorative and morphological similarities to material of that time (Aston 1992, 74), which I previously accepted (Hope 1999, 226), must now be rejected, as the motifs are more elaborate than those with which they were compared and the morphology quite different.

Tomb 36: A fragment from the neck (**Fig. 3** l) of either a jar or amphora, with a cream-coated and polished surface, comes from the fill. Also from the tomb is a rim and neck sherd from a jar with a convex-sided neck, decorated with bands and lines in blue, red and black, made in a local iron-rich fabric; it may be Nineteenth Dynasty in date. Other ceramic included three red-slipped bowls of New Kingdom date and a selection of forms of the Second Intermediate Period. Amongst the small finds were hair rings in glass and shell, a fragment of a necklace with polychrome faience cornflower beads, faience olive leaf beads, other beads in faience, carnelian and glass, and a piece from a wooden cosmetic box preserving a representation of a piriform jar. These can all be dated to the late Eighteenth to Nineteenth Dynasty.

Tomb 37: A fragment from the neck of a tall jar (**Fig. 3** k) similar to that from Theban Tomb 253 (**Fig. 10** b) was found as well as other ceramics of Second Intermediate Period date.

Tomb 46: A single small sherd was found near the surface of the tomb.

Tomb 48: Five sherds probably all from amphorae or large jars were found at the surface of the tomb. One has a red exterior coating; two have cream-coated and compacted exteriors; and two have compacted exteriors (for one see **Plate 70**). One of the cream-coated and compacted pieces is from the lower body of an amphora with vertical ridges on the interior. Also from the surface of the tomb came a neck fragment from a small lentoid flask in B23.

Additional New Kingdom material was found in Tomb 26 (three ceramic vessels) and Tomb 38 (scarabs and amulets, one with the prenomen of Thutmose III).

31/435-B4-1

This badly plundered cemetery contains a variety of burial types, including multi-roomed brick structures (Mills 1983, 131). In one of those tested three body sherds in B23 were found (for one see **Plate 69** left). The ceramics from the cemetery indicate that it was in use during the Late to Roman Periods.

31/420-D6-1: Ismant el-Kharab (**Fig. 3** m)

A single base from a slender amphora, cream-coated and compacted outside (**Fig. 3** m), of Ramesside date has been found at this settlement, ancient Kellis, which was occupied during the Ptolemaic and Roman periods (Hope 2001). It was found in surface sand in the southern part of the west court of the Main Temple near to Shrine I (the mammisi); these buildings were erected during the late first or early second centuries AD. Pottery pre-dating this period of occupation has been found associated with various structures, and it is clear from the find contexts that it was brought to the site to be used as chinking sherds in the construction of barrel-vaults. Most common amongst such sherds are those of Late Period date, though a few pieces of Second Intermediate Period material have been found.

31/420-B10-1: Beyout el-Quraysh

The cemetery (Mills 1982, 98) contains nine mud-brick mausolea, subterranean multiple loculi burials opening off single shafts, and graves cut into the slopes of several hills behind the mausolea. No settlement has been located in the vicinity. Ceramics and architectural styles indicate that the cemetery was in use from the Ptolemaic to Roman period. A single sherd from an amphora in B23 was found here (**Plate 69**, centre); it comes from the upper body and preserves part of the handle attachment.

33/390-L9-1: Amheida

This settlement (Mills 1980, 271–2), ancient Trimithis, was undoubtedly occupied mainly in the Ptolemaic to late Roman periods. In its immediate vicinity are several Old Kingdom sites (Mills 1980, 259–60), and thus the discovery of sherds of that date on Amheida is not surprising. Concen-

trated approximately in the centre of the site, at the spot where a temple[17] once stood, sherds of Second Intermediate Period and New Kingdom date have been found. Amongst the latter are a fragment of a cylindrical bread mould of the same type found at Mut el-Kharab (Hope 1999, 226), five fragments from jars with finger-modelled bases and several sherds in B23. In this fabric both types of amphorae occur: those similar to valley types and the distinct oasis version. Of the standard amphora type there is an uncoated rim sherd, a lower body sherd, and a fragment with a cream-coated flat base, both of which show finger modelling on the interior, and a thick (2 cm) sherd from the lower body. Of the oasis type there is a rim sherd (diameter 5.6 cm) and a shoulder fragment with the scar from a handle attachment; there is also a neck and shoulder fragment possibly of the same type as found in Theban Tomb 253 (**Fig. 10** b).

The discovery of this material at Amheida is of great interest in relation to the location of *s3-wḥ3t*, a toponym referring to part of Dakhleh encountered from the reign of Akhenaten into the second century AD (Kaper 1992, 124–9). It is clearly located within the western part of the oasis and contained the Temple of Deir el-Hagar, the cemetery of Muzzawaka and a Temple of Thoth, from which the blocks now at el-Qasr originate; inscriptions from all of these include the toponym. The collection of New Kingdom ceramics, however, confirms that either at Amheida itself or somewhere nearby there was probably a New Kingdom site. This increases the probability that *s3-wḥ3t* could be a designation for the western region of Dakhleh, as Kaper (1992, 128–9) has proposed, rather than Mut.[18] As the capital of the oasis possibly since some time in the New Kingdom, Mut would certainly have had a distinct name (e.g., *Mt/ Mjt/Mjtj*, see Kaper 1992, 130–2; 1997, 60).

32/390-K1-1

This cemetery is probably associated with Amheida (Mills 1980, 256–6) and contains burials from the Ptolemaic period onward (Hope 1999, 230). From within the fill of one grave (no. 2) comes part of the moulded base from an amphora (**Plate 71**).

32/390-J3-1 (**Fig. 3** n–o)

This is a cemetery of Old Kingdom date comprising graves cut into a single hill, but with at least one tomb with a mastaba superstructure and two burial chambers opening off a five metre-deep shaft (Mills 1979, 172; Hope 1979, 192–3). Within the fill of the shaft of the mastaba were two rim sherds from amphorae in B23 (**Fig. 3** n–o; **Plate 69**, right); they have distinct modelled rims and appear to be from a type similar to the Nile Valley standard amphora.

Of the material described above only that from 30/435-P9-3, 31/435-I1-1 (Ayn Asil), 31/435-D5-2 (Ein Tirghi) and 33/390-L9-1 (Amheida) can be regarded as being *in situ* and attesting the location of original New Kingdom sites. To their number can be added ancient Mut (Mut el-Kharab), site 31/405-G10-1, which has also yielded some New Kingdom ceramics (Hope 1999, 226; Mills 1981, 187; 1999, 176–7) and from the vicinity of which derive the two

Dakhleh stela (Gardiner 1933; Janssen 1968). This site has not yielded any ceramics in fabric B23, however. The other discoveries indicate the extent to which individual pieces or small numbers of sherds can move from their sites of origin or use. In some cases, for example at 31/420-D6-1, this resulted from a desire to incorporate potsherds into the barrel vaults of various buildings to aid in their construction and increase their strength, while in others it may have resulted from robbers' activity, as when material of later date is found within earlier graves. The occurrence of New Kingdom sherds on sites of a much later date may be the result of human or natural agency.

Kharga Oasis

To date the only locality within the region of Kharga from which New Kingdom ceramics have been reported lies at Tundaba, east of Kharga, on a probable ancient route into the Thebaid (D Darnell this volume). Amongst the ceramics of this date, which include a variety of valley and oasis manufactures, are fragments from amphorae made in what the excavators describe as oasis fabric that display such distinctive features as moulded bases and pronounced grooves on the interior of the lower bodies.

Bahariya Oasis

Qaret Hilwah

Qaret Hilwah is the cemetery that contains the decorated tomb of Amenhotep Huy, governor of this oasis in the late Eighteenth or Nineteenth Dynasty (van Siclen 1981, 33–4). It was briefly surveyed by Gosline in 1988 (Gosline 1990) and amongst the ceramics he has published are fragments from two types of amphora that were possibly made in local fabrics, though his description of these is inadequate to form more than the basis for speculation. One is a base described as handmade in a red fabric that is uncoated (Gosline 1990, pl. VI.5); it resembles the type of base used upon the slender Ramesside oasis amphora (compare **Fig. 5** b–c) and appears to have been about 8 cm in diameter. The others comprise three examples of an amphora with two vertical handles on an upper body that has a diameter of *c.* 26 cm (Gosline 1990, pl. XIV.3). The fabrics of the pieces are described as light red with a red coating, uncoated grey fabric and a pink fabric with grey core, brown coating and straw impressions.

Qaret el-Tub

During the course of a survey of this Roman fort in 1999 the ceramics from a nearby cemetery were examined by Sylvie Marchand. She identified fragments from the lower parts of amphorae in oasis fabric on the basis of comparison with material excavated at Ayn Asil in Dakhleh (Colin *et al.* 2000, 171).[19] One piece has a flat base approximately 5 cm in diameter and thick walls up to 3 cm. The base has been formed by pushing the clay into a mould; the interior of the lower body to a height of 24 cm has pronounced vertical grooves. It can be compared in morphology and technique to the examples from Malkata, Karnak North and Theban Tomb 253 (see **Figs 6, 7** a–b and **10** a).

II: Finds of Oases Amphorae outside their Place of Manufacture

These discoveries will be presented in summary form as they have either been published in greater detail elsewhere or await publication by their excavators. They will be listed by site from north to south.

Zawiyet Umm el-Rakham

This Ramesside fort/trading post is located some 320 km west of Alexandria and 32 km west of Bates' Island at Mersa Matrouh. The lower part of what was probably an amphora (no. ZUR/G4E/14) has been found there, with a modelled pointed base and distinct oblique finger-grooves in the interior of the lower body. In this respect it resembles the oasis amphora from Karnak North illustrated in **Fig. 7** b, but we should note that similar manufacturing techniques are attested for Nile Valley amphorae (Aston 1998, 475, form 1786). It is made in a uniformly brown-fired fabric with numerous oxidised limestone inclusions of mostly small size, quartz grains and red clay particles; the exterior is cream coated. It contained pieces of yellow ochre. Whilst this mineral undoubtedly originated elsewhere and occurs plentifully in the oases of the Western Desert, the fabric of the vessel bears a superficial resemblance to B23.[20]

Qantir (**Figs 4, 5** a–d)

Oasis-made amphorae from Qantir have recently been published by Aston (1998, 536–9)[21] and fall into two shape categories: those which resemble valley products in their morphology (**Fig. 4**); and the distinctive slender variety, with horizontal handles, a tall neck and button base, which may carry monochrome black linear motifs on its body and neck (**Fig. 5** a–d). Examples of each are made in Aston's Qantir fabrics V.01 and V.02, which shows that both types originate from the same source/sources as the finds in Dakhleh indicate. Aston (1998, 73) relates his fabrics V.01 to Memphis fabric P25 (similar to Memphis P44 and P45; see Bourriau below) and V.02 to Amarna fabric IV.2 (equated with Memphis P45, the finer version is similar to Memphis P44, see Rose below), indicating therefore that they both resemble Dakhleh fabric B23. The date assigned to this material is Nineteenth Dynasty, from the reign of Ramesses I to that of Merenptah (Aston 1998, 109).

Of the former shape category, form 2202 is the most complete (**Fig. 4** a). It has a short concave neck with modelled rim, wide rounded upper body with two vertical handles at the point of maximum diameter, and a long tapering lower body with a narrow base. The wall of the lower body is considerably thicker than the upper body. Unfortunately no details are provided concerning the specific manufacturing techniques of this or other oasis-made amphorae, so it is not possible to comment upon the way in which the base was made. The lower body, however, displays distinct internal vertical grooves. Form 2203 (**Fig. 4** b) is apparently similar to 2202, but would appear to have a wheel-made base and not to possess the internal grooves. It does have two incised undulating lines on the lower body and such marks have also been observed on oasis-made amphorae from Amarna (see Rose below). Form 2218 (**Fig. 4** g) is a neck from a form similar to 2202. Form 2204 (**Fig. 4** c) also has a short neck with modelled rim, but possesses an angular shoulder and the handles are attached higher on the body; form 2206 (**Fig. 4** e) may have resembled form 2204. Form 2214 (**Fig. 4** d) resembles the standard Eighteenth–Nineteenth Dynasty amphora form, and the base sherd, form 2219 (**Fig. 4** h) in fabric V.02, is the moulded base with which it was provided. The neck fragment form 2217 (**Fig. 4** f) recalls those of the Nineteenth–Twentieth Dynasty in being convex.

The distinctive slender amphorae with horizontal handles appear to come in two size classes; small (**Fig. 5** a) represented by form 2208 (plus 2209–12 not illustrated here) and large (**Fig. 5** b–d) represented by forms 2200–2201 and 2215 (plus ?2213 not illustrated here). The bases of forms 2200, 2201 and 2208 all carry incised potmarks. Again no details are supplied concerning manufacture, but compared with the series of bases published from Ayn Asil in Dakhleh (Marchand and Tallet 1999, fig. 14), one might speculate that they were mould-made.

Tell Dab'a

Two base sherds from amphorae made in Qantir fabric V.02 (white coated) and with button-bases (compare **Fig. 5** b–c) were found in a well in Ezbet Helmi area H/V. The well was filled with ceramics of the Twentieth Dynasty (Ramesses III/IV), although some may date back to the time of Ramesses II.[22]

Memphis and Saqqara

The most extensive variety of oasis-made amphora fabrics known to date from the Nile Valley derives from Memphis, from the Egypt Exploration Society's excavations at Kom Rabi'a. The fabrics are described below by Janine Bourriau; they range in date from the early Eighteenth Dynasty (fabric P92) throughout the New Kingdom and their variety suggests exploitation of different clay sources and paste preparations in several of the oases. Until the morphology of the amphorae made in the different fabrics is published little more can be said about their characteristics or evolution. Janine Bourriau (pers. comm. 1998) has informed me that the two distinct types of amphora known from Dakhleh and Qantir are attested. The distinguishing features of those resembling standard valley amphorae are the thickness of the wall of the lower body and the occurrence of vertical finger grooves on the interior of the lower body above the mould-made bases.

From the elite cemetery to the south of the Step Pyramid at Saqqara comes the base of one oasis-made amphora (**Fig. 5** e) of Memphis fabric P25, found in the shaft and chambers B and E of the tomb of Irudef (Aston 1991, 53, type 62),[23] dating to the reign of Ramesses II. It shows the long slender body of Qantir forms 2202–3 and also has an undulating line incised into its lower body; no details of its manufacturing technique are provided.

Amarna

As the discussion by Pamela Rose below indicates, the collection of oasis-made ceramics in her fabrics IV.02, IV.03

and V.10 is comparatively extensive and is dominated by amphorae. Those made in IV.02 and IV.03 display a fairly consistent morphology: short necks with modelled rims, elongated bodies with thick walls and flattened, mould-made bases; handles are mostly vertical and set at the point of maximum diameter (**Fig. 11** a-c). Some of these vessels are larger than others and very slender (**Fig. 12** ab); several have incised marks including undulating lines. A typical manufacturing technique is a mould-made base to which a section with distinct vertical grooves is attached, while the upper body is wheel-made, thus creating three distinct sections. There are only a few fragments in IV.10 and these display variations on the features described for those made in the other two fabrics: in one the mould-made base is attached to a wheel-made section, while in another the handle is horizontal (**Figs 13** e and **12** c). Rose notes below that a hieratic docket recovered during earlier work at the site, referring to 'wine from the estate of the Aten [from] the vineyard of ss-whst' (Fairman 1951, 166 no. 51), occurred upon a fragment of a vessel with horizontal handles, and might therefore be another example of this rare type of amphora.

The mouths of these vessels could be closed with small bowls and sealed with impressed mud stoppers – features typical of Nile Valley practices (Hope 1977) that would have been necessary during the transport of the filled vessels into the valley. Rose (**Fig. 13** a) illustrates one such stamped jar sealing attached to the neck of an oasis amphora from the current excavations at Amarna. This piece raises some interesting questions. The stamps preserve the prenomen of Thutmose IV. Do they allude to an estate of that king that was still producing wine during the reign of Akhenaten, or does the sealing derive from an amphora that brought wine to the valley from the oasis during the reign of Thutmose IV? If the latter, then it was at least 40 years old by the time it was brought to Amarna and might have a role to play in discussions of the ageing or long-term storage of wine in ancient Egypt (most recently Tallet 1996, 370–5). If the former, then it attests to the existence of a royal estate in Dakhleh and is of relevance in discussions of the nature of the wine industry in the oases, which Giddy (1987, 79) has proposed was dominated by the king and the central administration.

Amongst the discoveries made during earlier excavations at Amarna are ostraca (Marchand and Tallet 1999, 311) that indicate an oasis provenance for the content of the amphorae from which they originate. Whilst the study of the fabrics of these is still at a preliminary stage, initial assessment would indicate that several, if not all, have an oasis provenance. Rose has identified one in the British Museum (EA 59379; Fairman 1933, 105 no. 29; Marchand and Tallet 1999, 311 no. 8) as a possible example of her fabric V.10. The fabric of another from Petrie's work now in the British Museum (EA 59950; Petrie 1894, pl. XXV.94; Marchand and Tallet 1999, 311 no. 6) resembles an oasis manufacture, as does that of two others in the same collection from Buhen (EA 65734 and 65736).

An unpublished ostracon from Amarna house Q45.89 now in the Ashmolean Museum (1925.574b=HO 1168; Egypt Exploration Society register number 24-5/76) refers to 'very good quality wine from the Southern Oasis' and its fabric is undoubtedly of oasis provenance (possibly Amarna fabric IV.2). In the same collection there is the body from an amphora (Ashmolean 1893.1-41.268; Hope 1989a, pl. 5a) that is probably an example of Rose's elongated type and comes from Petrie's work. The inscription upon it (Petrie 1894, 32, pl. XXII.28), however, does not refer to the oasis, but only 'very good quality wine from the estate of the Aten, the inspector Tu'. Its fabric is an oasis type.

The Petrie Museum houses several fragments from amphorae (UC 24350, 24381, 46252–7) that display the technological features typical of oasis amphorae and/or are made in fabrics that resemble those of that region, though of the inscribed examples none mentions the oasis. One refers to 'very good quality wine from the tribute of the estate of the High Priest of the Aten Mery-re' and another 'Year 10 (+), very good quality wine of....'. On display in the Amarna Room of the Egyptian Museum Cairo (case I) is another amphora with typical oasis features (JE 62843). It may eventually transpire that the majority of references to oasis produce will be found to be written upon oasis-made vessels, though for an exception see below in the discussion on Malkata.

Luxor

Various sites on the east and west bank at Luxor and in its vicinity have produced finds of oasis amphorae. In the following discussion they will be presented according to type of site: settlement, campsite/trade route, temple and then tomb.

Malkata

From the excavations conducted by Kemp and O'Connor (1974) come two fragments, possibly from the same amphora (**Fig. 6** a–b), in a fabric that closely resembles a hard-fired Dakhleh fabric B23. The morphology, size and technology all conform to what is attested by the finds from Amarna: tall, slender thick-walled body with flat base, and the body manufactured in three distinct sections. The upper section preserves part of a hieratic docket reading 'wine...Huy', possibly with the qualification 'good' (Leahy 1978, 14, no. 66). In addition to these pieces there is a sherd found on the surface of the desert to the west of the site that is in the same fabric, coming from the lower body of a vessel with distinct ridges on the interior. It preserves parts of five lines from the *Instruction of Amenemhat I for his Son* (Leahy 1978, 27–8). A small bowl similar to those found at Amarna in what may be Amarna IV.2 fabric was also found.

The fabrics of three ostraca discovered by the Metropolitan Museum of Art expedition to the site, documenting an oasis provenance for their commodities, have recently been subjected to Neutron Activation Analysis and the results published by McGovern (1997, nos 4, 16 and 28). Two of these (nos 4 and 16) were determined not to be of Nile Valley origin and because the commodity of each originated in an oasis, in one case Kharga and in the other unspecified, McGovern (1997, 95) has assigned the fabrics to the Western Desert. The general thesis of McGovern's study (1997, 84–97), which I find unconvincing, is that Marl D is a Theban product and that commodities brought from vari-

ous parts of Egypt to Malkata for use in Amenhotep III's Sed festivals were re-bottled in locally-made amphorae. That oasis commodities were apparently not re-bottled in such vessels is explained by McGovern (1997, 95) in the following manner: '...royal pottery workshops, with access to good marl clays, might well have been established in the major western oases, in particular Kharga, during the Eighteenth Dynasty'.

Whilst this may be borne out by data presented in this study, none of this material was referred to by McGovern. Such a conclusion therefore based on the analysis of two sherds is somewhat unfounded, even more so as he does not refer to Giddy's (1987) study. He would also appear to be under the impression that the term *wḥзt rsyt* referred specifically to Kharga even though he cites Kaper's (1992) study of the term. A further anomaly may be pointed out: the fabric of the third ostracon referring to an oasis commodity (no. 28) was identified as Marl D and not an oasis type (McGovern 1997, 100) – this is conveniently overlooked! On the basis of examination of colour transparencies showing the sections of each of these ostraca and a small sample from one of them (no. 4),[24] the following identifications might be suggested: no. 4 could be an example of Memphis fabric P25 or P45, whilst no. 16 could be Dakhleh fabric B23.

The Farshût Road

Amongst a collection of Southern Oasis material of various dates that has been found on the roads leading into western Thebes from the desert (Darnell in Hope *et al.* 2000), there is a large body sherd from an oasis amphora.[25] The fabric of this amphora has been identified by Janine Bourriau as Memphis P45 (pers. comm. 1998); the technology of the fragment displays vertical scoring in the lower section of the body and horizontal wheel marks in the upper section. As the routes coming into Thebes from the west would indicate a provenance for this fragment in the Southern Oasis (Dakhleh–Kharga), this might then indicate the probable provenance of Memphis fabric P45. This would receive support from the identification of amphorae in this fabric at Tundaba east of Kharga by the same investigators (see D Darnell this volume).

Karnak North (**Fig. 7**)

From the excavations conducted by Helen and Jean Jacquet at the site of the Treasury of Thutmose I come a variety of fragments of oasis amphorae. There are two main types of vessel: large amphorae with narrow flat bases; and those with rounded bases: these are termed forms 1155 and 430 respectively, the former being more common.[26] There are, in addition, various bases from small vessels with either pointed or narrow flat bases made in oasis clays, the exact original forms of which are uncertain, and hence they are excluded from this discussion. The fabric of several of these closely resembles Dakhleh fabric B23.

Form 1155 (**Fig. 7** a) refers to tall slender amphorae with narrow flat bases and short necks with modelled rims; they have two vertical handles at the point of maximum body diameter. The list of examples includes the following vessels.

A587: This example is used for the type drawing of form

1155 (**Fig. 7** a).[27] It was found in Room 20 in the East Workshops at floor level to the south of a large deposit of ceramic vessels (Jacquet 1983, 86, fig. 19, pl. LVII.C–D). These workshops were constructed after the reign of Thutmose III (Jacquet 1983, 84, 103–4). Within the room was the upper section from a blue-painted Hathor-headed jar (AP 953) and under it was a blue faience lid bearing the cartouche of Hatshepsut (Jacquet 1983, 86). The jar is of a type encountered from the reign of Amenhotep III onward (Hayes 1959, fig. 150; Hope 1989c, figs 10e and 11b; 1991, fig. 7a), and though it continued into the Nineteenth Dynasty (Hope 1989b, 57, fig. 18d), it was certainly less common than in the earlier period. Other than identifying the fabric of this vessel as being from the oasis no further classification is possible.[28]

15/12/86-8 (**Plate 73**; **Plate 76**, centre): This almost complete vessel is made in Memphis fabric P92 (see Bourriau below), a fabric that occurs from the early Eighteenth Dynasty, but is absent from Amarna. It has a greyish-cream surface coating that was applied with a brush, and two holes in the wall, one plugged with plaster. The base has been made in a mould and the lower body displays internal vertical scorings to a height of 42 cm above the base, which is only 5 cm in diameter. It is extremely elongated and recalls vessels of similar size from Amarna (see Rose below). The fragments from which it was reconstructed were found reused in a later wall.

7/2/70-7 (**Plate 74**; **Plate 76**, front right): This fragment from the base of an amphora is made in Memphis fabric P45–Amarna IV.2, a fabric that occurs in all New Kingdom levels at Memphis; it has a smoothed brown exterior. The base is mould-made and the lower wall has internal vertical scorings. It was found high in the debris in the middle of the Treasury.

1/12/88-4 (**Plate 75**): This base fragment is made in Memphis fabric P92 (see Bourriau below). It is mould-made and the lower wall has internal oblique scorings; the exterior preserves a dull cream coating that was applied with a brush.

7/12/89-4: This is the base and lower body from a vessel with an extremely thick and hard wall; it was probably made in Memphis fabric P44, a fabric that is known from the mid- to late Eighteenth Dynasty into the Nineteenth Dynasty. It has a smoothed brown exterior; the manufacturing technology is the same as for other examples of this form.

24/11/75-8: This is a rim sherd in what may be Memphis fabric P45.

2/12/91-2: This is a fragment from a flat base in Memphis fabric P92.

Form 430 (**Fig. 7** b) is distinguished from Form 1155 by its round base, but in other respects it is very similar, though in the example used for the type drawing the shoulder is more distinct and the handles are located higher on the vessel wall.

15/12/75-2 (**Plate 76**, left and **Plate 77**): This example was used for the type drawing; it is reconstructed from fragments. The fabric has light yellowish-brown surfaces and a weak red transition to a blurred light grey core; it contains numerous fine pieces of limestone and quartz, and occasional larger red and black particles. The fabric is crumbly; it recalls Memphis fabric P91. The round base is mould-made and the lower wall displays internal striations that are curved rather than vertical; above this the wall has irregular smoothing marks and only at shoulder level are there obvious throwing marks. The exterior has a greyish-cream coating. It was found outside the northwest corner of the enclosure wall of the Treasury.

6/1/74-8 (**Plate 76**, right): This lower body from an amphora is manufactured in a fabric that most closely resembles Dakhleh fabric B23; it has a cream coating. The base has been made in a mould and attached to a body that is completely wheel made; there are no vertical or oblique finger-ridges on the interior. It was found in Room 32 of the North Workshops (Jacquet 1983, 90–2). The construction of the workshops and the enclosure wall is assigned to the reigns of Hatshepsut and Thutmose III (Jacquet 1983, 103–4) and the deposits within them to the period before Ramesses II, most probably the late Eighteenth Dynasty (H Jacquet-Gordon, pers. comm. 1998).

The Valley of the Kings

KV2: Tomb of Ramesses IV (**Fig. 8** a).[29] This vessel is represented by sherds from the base, body and handles, and its form has been reconstructed on the basis of parallels with Qantir form 2202 (**Fig. 4** a). It is made in an uncoated Memphis fabric P25. Fragments from at least another four such vessels were recovered, as was the base of a black-coated P25 amphora (Aston *et al.* 1998, 158, pl. 33).

KV5: Tomb of Sons of Ramesses II. The occurrence of oasis amphorae amongst the ceramics from this tomb has been confirmed by Kent and Susan Weeks (pers. comm. 1998). No details have been published.

KV8: Tomb of Merenptah. From the well shaft come eight sherds in Memphis fabric P25 and one in Qantir fabric V.02, and from outside the tomb two sherds in Qantir fabric V.02 (Aston *et al.* 1998, 147, 149).

KV9: Tomb of Ramesses VI. From a recent accumulation of material found in a rectangular pit in the floor of the sarcophagus chamber come four fragments of tall-necked, slender amphorae with horizontal handles decorated in black on a cream coating, made in Qantir fabric V.02 (Aston *et al.* 1998, 160, nos 316-9; Aston 1992, 76; compare **Fig. 5** a).

KV62: Tomb of Tutankhamun (**Fig. 8** b).[30] Amongst the collection of amphorae found in this tomb, one from the Annex is quite distinct from the others. It possesses a flat base and two horizontal handles (Holthoer 1993, 54 no. 24, pl. 27 left), and it was closed with a large mud sealing (Hope 1993, 121 no. 22). All other amphorae from the tomb have mould-made pointed bases and two vertical handles. The hieratic docket upon the shoulder of this vessel reads 'Year 10, good quality wine from *J3ty*' and the impressions upon the sealing reads, 'Fruit from the Southern Oasis' (Hope 1993, 121). This indicates that the produce originated in the Southern Oasis in a district named *J3ty* (Tallet 1996, 375–82; see also above discussion of Dakhleh site 31/435-11-1) and that the amphora itself could have a similar provenance. Unfortunately for this discussion, the vessel is intact and its fabric cannot be identified with certainty. Holthoer

(1993, 54) suggested that it was Marl D, while Aston (1997, 235) has proposed the Delta Marl F (on which Aston 1998, 66). The sealing is made from a pink-coloured mud with more straw than is normal (Hope 1993, 121), and in this it resembles the composition of the sealing from Amarna on the neck of an oasis amphora described below by Rose.

Horizontal handles are attested upon oasis-made amphorae (see **Fig. 13** f; Marchand and Tallet 1999, fig. 12 b). The rarity of this feature upon valley-made amphorae can be seen from the fact that in an earlier study, I was able to cite only two fragments from Malkata, a vessel from the Tomb of Kha, a vessel from Amarna and one from the pre-Aye material from Medinet Habu (Hope 1989a, 106, Type 2a). Of these, Rose (below) has raised the possibility of the Amarna vessel being an oasis manufacture, as well as the one from Medinet Habu, judging from the published description of its fabric (Hölscher 1939, pl. 57a). In addition Rose draws attention to another horizontal-handled amphora fragment from Amarna now in Berlin.

The use of flat bases would also seem to be an oasis feature, as can been seen from the numerous occurrences on vessels discussed here. In my earlier study of Egyptian amphorae, I was able to cite only the following examples with this feature: a vessel from the tomb of Meryet-Amun; two from the mortuary temple of Thutmose IV, one from Malkata, two from Amarna, one from Medinet Habu and one from Deir el-Medina (Hope 1989a, 102–4, figs 1.5, 2.2, 3.4). To this list can now be added an amphora found due north of the intersection of the processional route from the Temple of Mut with that from Luxor to Karnak (el-Saghir 1992, fig. 14 centre). Rose (below) has again suggested that one of the Amarna vessels might be an oasis manufacture. When all of these considerations are taken into account, it appears highly probable that the Tutankhamun vessel originated in the oasis region of the Western Desert.

Theban Tomb 99 (**Fig. 9**)

Preliminary analysis of ceramics from the burial chamber of the tomb has yielded many fragments of amphorae of a reddish-brown fabric with a wide grey core, tempered with large quantities of fine and medium-sized white particles, and common sand and grog. Examination under a microscope suggests that it can be identified with Memphis fabric P90 (see Bourriau below). The vessel form is a wide-bodied jar with a short neck and an externally thickened rim; two vertical handles are placed on the maximum diameter (**Fig. 9**). The interior does not show the finger-scoring known from many other oasis amphorae. The vessel has a whitish firing surface. One shoulder fragment in this fabric has a cartouche-shaped stamp on it that reads 'Menkheperre' (N Strudwick, pers. comm.). A few amphora sherds of Amarna fabrics IV.2 and IV.3 have been found in the disturbed deposits in the courtyard of the tomb.

The tomb belongs to Senneferi, an official active in the later part of the reign of Thutmose III; the equipment in the burial chamber belonged to the tomb owner.[31]

The discovery of vessels of this shape and date is of great interest as they are amongst the only examples of an oasis

provenance that can be ascribed to the reign of Thutmose III and they corroborate the data provided by the representations of oasis dwellers bringing tribute into the valley found in Theban tombs of the same period.

Theban Tomb 253 (**Fig. 10**)

This tomb has yielded two vessels that have been identified as of oasis manufacture in a fabric similar to Amarna fabric IV.2 (Rose 1996, 171).[32] One of these (**Fig. 10** a; Rose 1996, 176, Form 125) is an amphora with a flat base, and its manufacturing technology shows the typical three sections used in building up the body as has been noted on other oasis-made amphorae. The other (**Fig. 10** b; Rose 1996, 176, Form 124) is a tall-necked jar; fragments from similar forms have been found on several sites in Dakhleh made in fabric B23 (see **Figs 2**f, **3**i and k). It is suggested that the jar may be ascribed to a slightly earlier period within the Eighteenth Dynasty than the amphora (Rose 1996, 171). The amphora is of a type that may date to the reigns of Thutmose III–IV, differing in its morphology from examples found at Malkata and Amarna (Hope 1989a, 102, fig. 1.5–6).

Deir el-Medina

Three hieratic dockets mentioning an oasis provenance for their commodities are reported by Marchand and Tallet (1999, 311–4), one of which mentions s3-wḥ3t and another Jw-mrw. The latter is from a slender decorated amphora of the type with two horizontal handles and button base (here **Fig. 5** a) and its fabric is identical to Dakhleh fabric B23 (Marchand and Tallet 1999, 335, fig. 73).

Elephantine

Aston (1999, 42) has identified a neck (form 192) made in Qantir fabric V.02 found in the court of Temple Y as originating from a slender amphora with two horizontal handles (compare **Fig. 5** a) and has dated it to the late New Kingdom. Of a similar date, or possibly Twenty-First Dynasty, is the shoulder from an amphora (form 386) in his Oasis Clay 1 (Aston 1999, 7), which was found in deposit 19852A in Temple Y (Aston 1999, 59–60). A third fragment, from the lower body near to the base, displays the manufacturing technique typical of oasis amphorae and is also made in Oasis Fabric 1 (Aston 1999, 100, form 810). This piece comes from Building BC deposit 21865A, which also contained ceramics of the Libyan period; the oasis amphora sherd may be residual.

III: Tentative Conclusions

From the survey of material of oasis manufacture presented above it is possible to draw some preliminary conclusions concerning ceramic production in the Western Desert and trade with the Nile Valley. It is perhaps wise to start with a caveat: only Dakhleh Oasis has been explored fully and little is known of New Kingdom activity in the other oases, thus our evidence is extremely unbalanced. Until this situation is rectified studies such as this one will only indicate the necessity for fuller, systematic exploration of the Western Desert.

The data from Dakhleh show clearly that during the New Kingdom a ceramic industry was well established in the oasis and that one of its principle products was amphorae, though a range of forms were manufactured to cater for a variety of functions (Marchand and Tallet 1999). In general the forms were very similar to those produced in the Nile Valley but the potters did not slavishly copy the latter. This can be seen in relation to the amphorae, characteristics of the morphology, manufacturing technique and decoration of which are quite distinctive. One type, the slender amphora with horizontal handles, button base, and often linear decoration, may well be unique to Dakhleh.

The hieratic dockets upon amphorae found on Nile Valley sites indicate that there were both royal and religious estates within the Southern Oasis, as the evidence from tomb reliefs and other sources suggests. The distribution of New Kingdom ceramics in Dakhleh (**Fig. 1**) would indicate that important sites of that period were located at Ayn Asil (31/435-I1-1), in the vicinity of Ein Tirghi (31/435-D5-2), Mut el-Kharab (31/405-G10-1) and Amheida (33/390-L9-1). The wine of the Southern Oasis is the most frequently alluded to of all oasis wines during the New Kingdom and it was taken into the Nile Valley in locally-made containers on the evidence of the dockets that have been found at various locations in Thebes and at Amarna. Where it has been possible to examine the fabrics from which these vessels are made a limited variety of similar types has been noted. These are generally coarser in appearance than the fabric used for amphora manufacture in Dakhleh and this might indicate that they originate in Kharga. However, the range of fabrics that is ascribed to the oases of the Western Desert on the basis of petrology, and that mostly lack textual confirmation for the suggested provenance, is quite extensive and varied, and examples have been found the length of the Nile Valley in Egypt and into Nubia.[33] This could show that different clay beds in the Southern Oasis were exploited at different times within the New Kingdom or that the other oases provided an equal quantity of wine but in vessels that were less regularly labelled. Wine is certainly known to have been produced in Bahariya[34] and thus we can assume that there was a ceramic industry there that in part provided vessels to contain this valued commodity.

Until we are able to determine the provenances of the fabrics and the range of shapes made in each, it will not be possible to compare the manufactures of the different oases.

In terms of the standard New Kingdom amphora, oasis potters appear to have produced a short-necked, wide-bodied form with a flat base during the mid-Eighteenth Dynasty, with examples known from Theban tomb 99. An elongated variant with a flat base and often very thick walls was in use from the reigns of Amenhotep II–Thutmose IV (Theban tomb 253); some of these were distinctly attenuated by the reigns of Amenhotep III and Akhenaten (Malkata, Karnak North, and Amarna). From the later part of this dynasty come a few amphorae with horizontal rather than vertical handles (Amarna, tomb of Tutankhamun). In the Ramesside period a slightly more traditional form was manufactured, still with a short neck but now with a fuller upper body (Qantir, Saqqara, Valley of the Kings). In terms of documenting any clear morphological development, the well-stratified sequence from Memphis will play a crucial role. It will be interesting to see if variations can be attributed to different oases. In Dakhleh during the Ramesside period a slender amphorae with narrow neck, horizontal handles and button base was manufactured; whether similar types were made elsewhere is uncertain.

From the distribution of oasis amphora sherds at Amarna (Rose below) and their discovery in the artisans' quarter at Memphis, Kom Rabi'a (see Bourriau below), it would seem that such vessels passed well beyond any presumed central control, though whether their contents did also is a moot point. Oasis commodities certainly circulated the length of the Nile Valley, though apparently in comparatively small quantities, or so the material evidence would indicate. The value of the wine from the Western Desert may have been increased by the distance over which it had to be transported and the time such a journey took;[35] its quality was such that it was considered suitable for royal consumption and within temples.

Finally, it should be noted that the identification of New Kingdom ceramics on various sites throughout Dakhleh Oasis indicates that there was more activity there throughout that period than had been surmised (Mills 1999). This situation had been indicated by inscriptional and representational evidence from the Nile Valley. It is impossible to believe that during any period of Egyptian history the oases would not have been exploited and activity there monitored for the benefit of the Egyptian state, particularly in light of the impact of Libyan activity on Egypt's western flank.

Addendum

During the 2000–2001 season several fragments of B23 fabric were found in the Dakhleh Oasis: one futher sherd at 31/420-B10-1, three near the Roman temple at 31/435-K3-1 (Mills 1983, 132), and one at 41/405-M9-1 (Hope et al. 2000, 192–3). More importantly, several fragments were found on the surface of Mut el-Kharab; excavations at this site (the Temple of Seth) revealed in situ desposits of New Kingdom beer jars and some bread moulds in addition to various objects of similar date (sculpture, jewellry and cosmetic items).

Macroscopic and Microscopic Analysis of New Kingdom Dakhleh Oasis Amphorae Fabrics

Mark A J Eccleston

This section will provide macroscopic and petrographic descriptions of Dakhleh fabric B23 and discuss some of the possible relationships between it and the published material from several sites in the Nile Valley, highlighting the difficulty in assigning definite provenances at this point. The ability to identify clearly a source for these fabrics and differentiate them from Nile Valley or other fabrics is of great importance to archaeologists and ceramicists currently working on New Kingdom assemblages. The results of the recent study of three thin sections of fabric B23 have isolated it as a discrete petrographic group within the broader corpus of Dakhleh ceramics; it was earlier termed the 'Quartz and Limestone Fabric' (Eccleston 1998, 39–42, 70–71).

One of the major problems in dealing with the topic of New Kingdom oasis amphora fabrics is that several distinct variants have been identified at Nile Valley sites such as Memphis, Amarna and Qantir, whilst only one main fabric type is attested in Dakhleh. At Memphis the oasis fabrics are designated P23, P25, P44, P45, P90, P91, P92 and P92 (Bourriau below); at Amarna the fabrics are IV.2, IV.3 and V.10 (Rose below); and at Qantir they are V.01 and V.02 (Aston 1998, 73). A possible concordance between all of these fabrics, based on visual comparison of various examples and comparisons published by Aston (1998, 73) and below by Rose and Bourriau (**Table 3**) is also summarised in **Table 1**. It is not my intention to imply that the fabrics in Group 1 and Group 2 directly correlate, but simply that they have been described as being similar or related. Examination of a limited selection of sherds from Nile Valley sites seems to indicate that of these fabrics Amarna IV.3 and Memphis P44 most closely resemble B23. While some of the others are superficially similar, there are some that are visually quite dissimilar to B23.

Description of Fabric B23 (Plates 69-72)

The macroscopic description of Dakhleh fabric B23 was made using a binocular microscope (x6.7-x40) on sherds with fresh breaks perpendicular to the manufacturing marks where possible. Petrographic descriptions and identifications were made using a polarising microscope on thin sections prepared to a thickness of 30 microns. The terms used and the general format of the macroscopic descriptions follow those outlined by Nordström and Bourriau (1993, 162–70). The format of the petrographic descriptions below is a slight modification of the system proposed by Whitbread (1995). The grain sizes were estimated using the graticule in the eyepiece of the microscope and the frequencies were estimated using the visual comparator charts in Matthew *et al.* (1991). The frequency labels used follow Kemp (1985, 17) and are as follows: Predominant: > 70%; Dominant: 50–70%; Frequent: 30–50%; Common: 15–30%; Few: 5–15%; Very Few: 2–5%; Rare: 0.5–2%; Very Rare: < 0.5%.

Macroscopic Description

The following description is based on the examination of approximately 30 sherds of B23 fabric from various find contexts throughout Dakhleh. B23 is a dense-bodied, medium-textured fabric. Exterior and interior surface colours include light brown, orange/pink, orange/brown and grey in various combinations. The groundmass generally has a central blue/grey core and orange/brown margins. Colours at the core can also include light brown and at the margins orange/pink and light brown. The firing pattern may display two bands rather than a distinct core, in which case the same colours are present as noted above, but with blue/grey occurring with any one of the other colours. A variant with orange/pink and grey/yellow bands also exists. The width of the central core varies immensely, ranging in size from approximately 50% to 90% of the area. A variant of this fabric exists that appears to have been fired in almost entirely reducing conditions, producing a light grey groundmass throughout.

Macroscopically visible inclusions include few to frequent, fine to medium limestone, few to common, fine to medium quartz/sand and few, fine to medium clay pellets. Some of the limestone has spalled during firing leaving the characteristic reaction rims around the voids and occasionally pitting on the surfaces. The colour of the clay pellets includes red/brown, orange/brown and light brown, while the quartz/sand in the fabric is clear and black.

Table 1: Suggested New Kingdom oasis amphorae fabric concordance based on published comparisons

	Dakhleh	Memphis/Saqqara	Amarna	Qantir
Group 1	B23	P44		V.01
		P45	IV.2	V.02
		P25		
Group 2	B23	P23	IV.3	V.02
		P90		
		P91	V.10	
		P92		
		P93		

Petrographic Description

The following description and comments should be considered preliminary as they are based on three samples only. Further analytical work is anticipated on the new material from site 30/435-P9-3 and on several other sherds from Dakhleh.

Dakhleh Samples Analysed

Sample Number	Site Number	Vessel Type
94-66	32/390-J3-1	Amphora neck with folded rim; **Fig. 3** m, **Plate 69**, right.
94-68	31/420-B10-1	Body sherd from an amphora; **Plate 69**, centre.
94-69	31/435-B4-1	Body sherd probably from amphora; **Plate 69**, left.

Microstructure

The voids comprise rare meso channels, rare meso to macro vesicles and rare meso to macro vughs. All voids are < 2.0 mm in length and mostly c. 0.1 mm to 0.15 mm. Generally the more elongated voids have a preferred orientation parallel to the vessel walls.

Groundmass

In thin section, the groundmass seems to be homogeneous, however, there is a colour differentiation between the margins and the core of the section. The colour in the margins varies from orange/brown (PPL x40) to orange (XP x40), that of the core is brown (PPL x40) and brown to brown/grey (XP x40). The groundmass is optically inactive.

Inclusions

$c{:}f{:}v_{10\mu}$ c. 25:70:5 to 30:68:2. Overall the inclusions seem to be moderately sorted with a modal size of c. 0.1 mm, a maximum size of c. 1.25 mm, and are rounded to very angular in shape.

Coarse Fraction, 0.1 mm.

Frequent to Dominant: Monocrystalline quartz, rounded to angular, generally c. 0.1–0.15 mm, max. c. 0.5 mm.
Frequent: Limestone (micrite), rounded to angular, generally c. 0.2–0.3 mm, max. c. 1.25 mm.
Few: Clay pellets and silty clay pellets, rounded to sub-angular, generally c. 0.2–0.25 mm, max. c. 0.9 mm.
Rare to Very Rare: Polycrystalline quartz, rounded to sub-rounded, mode c. 0.1 mm, max. c. 0.2 mm.

Fine Fraction, < 0.1mm.

Dominant: Monocrystalline quartz, rounded to angular.
Frequent to Common: Limestone, rounded to angular. Clay pellets, rounded to sub-angular.
Very Few: Opaques (iron oxide), rounded to sub-rounded.
Very Rare: Muscovite, laths.

Comments

This fabric is characterised by the frequent limestone, dominant monocrystalline quartz and few clay pellet inclusions in a groundmass that is orange to orange-brown in the margins with a brown to grey/brown core. Hypercoating of limestone or calcite is visible around the edges of a large number of voids indicating that they could have been produced as a result of limestone decomposition or spalling during firing. The inclusions in this fabric would indicate that it was produced using clay from a purely sedimentary environment. This is consistent with an origin in Dakhleh and/or Kharga Oasis.

A combination of the limestone spalling and optical inactivity of the groundmass seems to indicate that a firing temperature of at least 900°C is possible for this fabric. However, to be more certain it would be desirable to examine the internal vitrification of the clay matrix of this fabric using a SEM.

Discussion

As was mentioned above by Hope, all of the material from the excavations and surveys in Dakhleh has been placed within one fabric group. **Table 1** shows that the material from Memphis/Saqqara, Amarna and Qantir falls into two basic groups. It is possible that the Dakhleh B23 fabric could be sub-divided further on the basis of the proportion of limestone temper and other factors. It is, however, uncertain whether this would be of any real benefit given the nature of the differences within the fabric and whether this would assist in creating two distinct oasis fabric groups that parallel those found in the Nile Valley.

Thin section analysis of several sherds of the B23 fabric from Dakhleh has shown that the clay from which it is made is from an environment consisting of sedimentary deposits. The dominance of monocrystalline quartz in a paste that appears to have originated from a mudstone clay is characteristic of many other Dakhleh fabrics (Eccleston 1998). The presence of frequent micritic limestone inclusions in a mudstone clay is also consistent with some of the clay beds in Dakhleh described by Kleindienst et al. (1999, 5). It is possible that some of the variants noted in the Nile Valley might be a reflection of the production of comparable vessel types in similar fabrics in Dakhleh and Kharga, and possibly other oases in the Western Desert during the same period. The geology of Dakhleh and Kharga is virtually the same (Hermina 1990, 259–92); therefore any regional differences would not immediately be obvious macroscopically or petrographically.

Nicholson's (Nicholson and Rose 1985, 172) petrographic descriptions of Amarna fabrics IV.2 and IV.3 agree generally with the description of the three thin sections from Dakhleh. The only minor difference seems to be the presence of very rare microcline present in one example of IV.3. Whilst no microcline was noted in any of the Dakhleh samples, this alone does not preclude Dakhleh as being a source for Amarna fabric IV.3. Geologically, it is possible for microcline to occur in a sedimentary environment such as Dakhleh (Tucker 1991, 43) and it has been noted in other definite Dakhleh fabrics (Eccleston 1998, 50).

The primary Nile Valley amphora fabric during the New Kingdom, Marl D, was also compared to these fabrics in thin section. The texture and inclusions in the fabric are different enough from those of B23 to show that they are not variants of the same fabric. In addition to quartz, limestone and clay pellets that are common to both fabrics, Marl D also contains, in varying quantities, plagioclase and K-feldspar, amphibole, pyroxene and biotite mica.[36]

Bourriau (below) has suggested that there were workshops throughout the oases, implying that Bahariya might have been a possible provenance for at least one of the oasis fabrics she has identified. Evidence for wine manufacture in Bahariya has been mentioned by Hope above, who suggests that amphorae would have been manufactured in association with viniculture. On a recent visit to several sites in that oasis it was possible to make a cursory examination of some of the surface ceramics. Amongst this material was one fabric that Hope thought was very similar to the Amarna IV.2 fabric. Although this does not imply that it was produced in Bahariya and the diagnostics were not of the New Kingdom, it is interesting to note that the briefest examination of surface ceramics in Bahariya yielded a fabric that resembles one found in the Nile Valley and Dakhleh, but one that is not at all common in the corpus of ceramics from Dakhleh. The geological formations at Bahariya include variegated shales, limestone and sandstone (Said 1962, 81), which is consistent with the general mineralogy of these oasis amphora sherds as identified from thin section analysis. Bahariya, however, also contains several igneous dolerite intrusions (Said 1962, 81), which does not correlate with the mineralogy of the sherds discussed here. Due to the limited number of places in Bahariya where this rock type occurs, it may be possible that it was not part of the clay beds exploited by the potters during the New Kingdom. Until ceramics known to have been produced in Bahariya are examined by thin section analysis, however, it will not be possible to comment on whether or not small dolerite inclusions are a feature of ceramics from that region.

Bourriau (below) has also identified the presence of kaolin as a possible feature characteristic of ceramics produced in the oases. The presence of kaolin in ceramics made in Dakhleh was noted by Segnit (Edwards *et al.* 1987, 6–7) when examining five mid-Holocene samples by X-ray diffraction. He further noted that clays from the pottery workshop at Amheida contained kaolinite. Several clays from Dakhleh analysed by Professor R Heiman of McMaster University in 1980 also contained kaolinite and one contained dolomite. Given that the geology of Kharga is very similar to that of Dakhleh, it is suggested that clays containing kaolin would exist there. Kaolin deposits are also known to occur in Egypt in the region around Aswan, in the Eastern Desert and west central Sinai (Said 1962, 265, 267). Sampling and analysis of clay beds in Bahariya and Farafra would have to be undertaken before it is possible to rule out these locations as a source for the kaolin clays used for making some of the vessels recently analysed by Doherty for Bourriau (see below).

McGovern (1997) has published results of the Neutron Activation Analysis (NAA) of various ostraca from Malkata. Three of these ostraca, Inscription 19.1 (PMG331), Inscription 49.1 (PMG258) and Inscription 73.1 (PMG333), mention the oases in their texts, however, only PMG331

and PMG258 are identified as being from the oases on the basis of their chemical composition (McGovern 1997, 80). As he does not seem to have made a close examination of the fabric of the samples that were analysed, photographs of the sections of the three ostraca and a chip from 19.1 were obtained by Hope for macroscopic evaluation. McGovern (1997, 95) describes two of these sherds as being 'of a whitish ware', similar to modern *kulleh* ware from Qena. This description does not readily allow one to correlate the fabric of these ostraca to known fabrics from Dakhleh and the proposed oasis material from Nile Valley find contexts. Preliminary examination of the small chip from 19.1 and the accompanying photograph indicates that it is possibly one of the coarser oasis fabrics similar to Amarna IV.2. Until it is possible to examine the piece itself, a definite identification will not be possible.

Two other sets of NAA data also seem to show that ceramics thought to have been produced in Dakhleh and/or Kharga are generally chemically distinct from Nile Valley and Canaanite ceramics. The set used by Eccleston (1997) is made up of 156 sherds of mid-Holocene to fifth century AD date that were sampled and analysed during the early stages of the survey of Dakhleh in the 1980s. In general, it was shown that ceramics thought to have been produced locally were sufficiently different chemically from non-Dakhleh material to be separated with the aid of multivariate statistical analysis of 30 elements (Eccleston 1997; this volume). Only four New Kingdom B23 sherds were included in this sample set. At the time the samples were taken, these pieces were not known to be from the New Kingdom. Two of these pieces were chemically similar and grouped together, but away from other Dakhleh and Nile Valley sherds (Eccleston 1997, 33 and Appendix H); of the other two, one grouped with Dakhleh material and one stood on its own. The fact that three of these do not seem to be chemically similar to other Dakhleh ceramics could be explained by the fact that a different clay source or mix of clays was exploited during the New Kingdom than in other periods.

A large body of material from Nile Valley find contexts, analysed recently by al-Dayal (1995, 99–100), included examples of the fabrics Amarna IV.2 and IV.3 and Memphis P25, P45 and P90. He concluded that none of these fabrics were chemically comparable with any of the known Nile Valley silt and marl fabrics or Canaanite Jar fabrics that were also included in the analysis.

These three independent studies have all gone some way toward showing that ceramics produced in the oases seem to be distinctive enough chemically to be differentiated from Nile Valley ceramics with the aid of computer statistical packages.[37] There are, however, many methodological pitfalls in assigning a provenance to ceramics on the basis of chemical analysis alone. This is highlighted by the fact that the two B23 samples from Dakhleh used in my 1997 study did not group with the remainder of the Dakhleh material or with the comparative material from the Nile Valley.

Conclusions

The ability to provenance 'oasis' ceramics of the New Kingdom with confidence would assist the general study of contact between the oases and the Nile Valley during the New Kingdom and help quantify the possible extent and nature of royal control in the area, which has been suspected for many years (Giddy 1987, 96–7). Due to the paucity of sherds of New Kingdom date from any oasis other than Dakhleh it is impossible at this stage to identify positively any fabric traits that are particularly distinctive of any one of the oases. The finer limestone-tempered variants are by far the most commonly-occurring general fabric type used for amphorae in Dakhleh, as opposed to the coarser fabrics such as Amarna IV.2 and its correlates found in the Nile Valley. It would be unwise, however, to suggest that a coarse fabric could not have been produced in Dakhleh or that a fine fabric such as B23 could not also have been manufactured in Kharga, or in Bahariya, or Farafra for that matter.

Further work in Dakhleh on locating clay beds exploited by potters in antiquity is planned for forthcoming field seasons. It is anticipated that subsequent analysis of these clays and comparison with the results of typological, thin section and chemical analyses of ceramics from Dakhleh and Nile Valley find contexts will clarify some of the overlaps in these fabrics and the problems associated with assigning a definite provenance to them.[38] The problem with Amarna IV.2 and IV.3 fabric not containing kaolin may have to be addressed in more detail after further analyses and sampling have been undertaken. It is not certain that kaolin occurs in all clays throughout Dakhleh and the identification of clay beds containing kaolin may allow conclusions to be drawn concerning the region of the oasis in which certain fabrics were produced. This would assist in the task of discovering where the workshops that produced these vessels were located.

'Oasis Ware' Vessels from Amarna

Pamela Rose

From the beginning of the current excavations at Amarna, two rare but distinctive wares have been noted both in stratified deposits and, more commonly, amongst the sherds scattered in abundance over the surface of the city. The wares appear closely related, and differ in fabric, form and technology from contemporary 'Egyptian' vessels. Because of this, they were included in the imported fabric series from the site as fabrics IV.2 and IV.3, although their point of origin was then unknown. Recently, a third ware, even scarcer than the others but used for similar forms, has been distinguished (fabric V.10). Research, described above, suggests that fabric IV.3 may come from Dakhleh Oasis; IV.2 is so similar in form that it certainly also originates in one of the western oases, although where precisely is as yet unknown. The third fabric has fewer features in common with IV.2 and IV.3, but vessel form, and jar labels discussed below, show that it too is a product of the region. The wares are, then, technically 'Egyptian', but their striking differences from the ceramic traditions and products of the Nile Valley (including the Delta) mean that their separate origin must be acknowledged. In what follows, therefore, the term 'Nile Valley' is used to denote the commonly recognised ceramic assemblage of the late Eighteenth Dynasty. Likewise, because the specific origin(s) of the oasis wares are not yet certain, the term 'oasis' is used in an all-embracing manner, and may well include Kharga, and even perhaps Bahariya and Farafra.

Fabrics IV.2 and IV.3

These two fabrics constitute the vast majority of oasis ware found at Amarna, and each exhibits a striking degree of homogeneity in its attributes.

Fabric IV.2, which is the more common of the fabrics, is light orange at the exterior, and often shades to a pale grey towards the inner surface in thick-walled parts of the vessel. In thinner-walled areas, there can be a similar pale grey core, or there may be none. On examination with a 10x hand lens conspicuous inclusions are: common fine sand; some small to very large irregular opaque cream-coloured lumps, probably limestone, which sometime show signs of decomposition and leave hollow whitish-edged rims; and some small and medium opaque red rounded particles (Nicholson and Rose 1985, 139, 148). No vegetable matter has been noted. The fabric also occurs in a finer version that contains far fewer prominent large inclusions. Visually, fabric IV.2 appears similar to Memphis fabric P45 and the finer variant to Memphis fabric P44. Thin-section and chemical analysis, however, show up significant differences between the Memphis and Amarna material (see Bourriau's comments below). Aston (1998, 73) equates Amarna fabric IV.2 with his fabric V.02 at Qantir.

Fabric IV.3 is hard and dense, and most commonly of a reddish-orange colour, often with a brownish core towards the inner surface in thick-walled areas (Nicholson and Rose 1985, 139–40, 148). Conspicuous inclusions are common fine sand and abundant small, and some medium to large, white opaque particles of limestone that show signs of decomposition. The uncoated surfaces often appear considerably pitted where the particles have exploded during firing. There are also sparse small dark red opaque inclusions. No vegetable matter has been noted and the fabric is visually similar to Memphis fabric P23.

Whilst at Amarna the two fabrics are visually easy to distinguish, there are certain similarities in the inclusions and colouring that suggest they may be related, and perhaps come from similar locations. On both fabrics, the exterior surfaces are usually slipped. The most commonly-observed coating is a matte grey, and there are also many examples with matte red slips and others without a coloured coating. There are no certain examples of vessels with cream slips.

By far the commonest vessel form in these fabrics is the amphora. The tall, narrow-bodied jars have moulded bases, a lower interior body, which shows long vertical grooves made by the potter's fingers in the course of joining the separately manufactured elements, and a wheel-thrown upper body.

The neck is short and has an externally thickened rim, of which the diameter varies between 8 and 12 cm. Two vertical handles run between the shoulder, or just below it, and the upper body. Whilst individual 'diagnostic' elements of the vessels suggest that the amphorae are fairly standardised in form, reconstruction of vessel bodies shows that there is conspicuous variation in height, and a concomitant change in diameter so that shorter vessels have slightly wider bodies. The only complete example from Amarna, type XLIII/1015 (Peet and Woolley 1923, pl. LI), here reproduced as **Fig. 11** a, shows a vessel from the shorter end of the range, as do those in **Fig. 11** bc, and probably that in **Fig. 11** d, all of which come from recent excavations in the Central City. The taller amphorae are known from two examples from recent excavations in the Main City (**Fig. 12** ab). Tall forms occur in both fabrics; examples of the shorter vessels are only known in fabric IV.2, but this may be merely a factor of preservation.

A third form, known only from one small fragment, appears to be part of a miniature handled vessel (**Fig. 12** c). This is a surface find from the so-called palace rubbish heaps in the Central City. The fabric is IV.2, and although the surface is mainly lost, a small area of pinkish coating survives, perhaps a self-slip. The sherd preserves a small area of the lower shoulder and the lower handle stump of a vessel of c. 10–11 cm external diameter.

The most commonly encountered forms other than amphorae are small shallow dishes, which are almost certainly lids (**Fig. 12** de). Their identification as such initially rested on the fact that they were the only other oasis form found regularly at Amarna, and it was therefore logical to associate them with the amphorae. A recent find of a conical mud sealing preserving such a vessel in place within the neck of an oasis amphora (**Fig. 13** a) now confirms this. The lids have a diameter of between 8 and 10 cm, and are usually poorly finished with an uneven string-cut base. As with the miniature amphora noted above, lids of fabric IV.2 are sometimes made from a finer preparation of the clay than that used for the larger amphorae, but the inclusions appear identical. Lids of both fabrics are grey-slipped or uncoated.

A less common form encountered at Amarna is the gourd-shaped vessel. Only one example of the body of such a vessel has been found (**Fig. 13** b; Rose 1995, 138, 141), but necks have come from both excavated contexts and from surface collections (**Fig. 13** c). Examples occur in both fabrics, and are unslipped or grey slipped. The method of manufacture of the vessel bodies is unusual; rather than throwing the body in two halves and then luting them together, as was done for Egyptian pilgrim bottles, the body appears to have been thrown in one piece as a jar, and the orifice closed with a clay plug. The body was turned through 90 degrees, pierced, and the separately-manufactured neck and handles then attached.

Finally, a small rim sherd was found incorporated into the wall of the amphora shown in **Fig. 11** c. Its diameter is not ascertainable, but the sherd clearly comes from a red-slipped open form with a slightly upturned rim (**Fig. 13** d). The fabric is a fine IV.2. The form and finish are both well in keeping with types of red-slipped bowls of Nile silt fab-rics, which are extremely common at Amarna, and suggest that in some cases at least Nile Valley pottery norms were followed in the oases.

Fabric V.10

Fabric V.10 has only recently been identified and is as yet represented by very few sherds. It has not been subject to any scientific analysis. The fabric is strikingly different in appearance to those described above, but the only known form for which it is used, the amphora, is in most of its characteristics similar to the better-known oasis vessels. In colour, the fabric is dark brown, with a lighter greyish core in thicker-walled areas, and shading to a lighter red in thinner parts towards the exterior of the vessel. Inclusions visible under a 10x hand lens are: very common fine to coarse sand; common tiny cream-coloured to pinkish hollow particles and some fine white opaque particles, both probably limestone; some opaque fine and medium dark grey to black particles; sparse opaque red lumps; and also a few elongated whitish-edged voids, which may be the remains of vegetable matter. A jar label from earlier excavations at Amarna (BM 59379), mentioning the Southern Oasis, appears to be on a sherd of fabric V.10, but here the shoulder has fired bright orange with a thin grey core toward the inner surface. The orange areas appear similar to a fine IV.3, albeit with smaller and fewer whitish inclusions and more additional tempering material than usually seen in that fabric. This raises the possibility that the two fabrics are related in origin. Visually fabric V.10 can be equated with Memphis fabric P91. A distinguishing feature of the vessels made from this fabric is the use of a matte cream slip to cover all exterior surfaces including the underside of the base; no other slip colours have been noted.

Because of the paucity of examples, there is little evidence from which to examine vessel form. The few bases (**Fig. 13** e) indicate a manufacturing technology different from that described above; the bases themselves are mould-made, but are joined directly to the wheel-made body without the conspicuous vertical finger-scored area seen in vessels of fabrics IV.2 and IV.3. Externally, however, the base form and wall thickness are identical to other oasis amphorae. No rims or necks of the fabric have yet been recognised, and the only other 'diagnostic' fragment is a surface find preserving an area of the shoulder, handle scars and a potmark in the form of a wavy line running vertically between the handles (**Fig. 13** f). There is a vestigial cord impression just below the potmark, and the use of cord to support the vessel during manufacture is another technological feature not otherwise noted on amphorae of fabrics IV.2 and IV.3. What is most unusual about this fragment is, however, the positioning of the handles: rather than the setting seen on the other oasis amphorae, whereby the ends of the handle are aligned vertically on the shoulder and upper body, the scars show that the handle ends were aligned horizontally.

It is likely that these sherds come from a vessel form closely similar to type XVI.4 from the earlier excavations at Amarna (Frankfort and Pendlebury 1933, pl. LIII), here reproduced as **Fig. 13** g. This vessel is described in the corpus as of 'buff pottery, polished drab slip'. Such terms are usually applied to Nile Valley vessels of marl clay, but archive records show that the published descriptions are not always reliable. The vessel's form, the heavy base and the proportions of the body find their closest parallels in oasis amphorae. The principal discrepancy lies in the way the handle appears to be attached in the drawing, where the bulge on the inside suggests that the end of the handle may have been inserted through a hole in the vessel wall. The Amarna shoulder fragment has the handles attached to the exterior surface. However, there is some evidence for oasis vessels with handles inserted through the vessel wall (Bourriau and Eriksson 1997, fig. 7 no. 10; for the fabric see Bourriau's comments below). A vessel from the Deutschen Orient-Gesellschaft excavations at Amarna (Ägyptisches Museum, Berlin, no. 29223) is a further example of the horizontally-handled type, although the method of handle attachment could not be ascertained. What is of interest is the slight exterior modelling of the base, a trait that becomes more common in the later New Kingdom (for example, at Qantir, see **Fig. 5** b–c). The lower interior is vertically gouged. The fabric is not sufficiently visible to identify as a particular type; the surface is coated with a matte cream slip.

Similar handles feature on what have been identified as vessels of oasis origin in the Ramesside period from Qantir (Aston 1998, 539, no. 2208, fabric V.02). A jar label from the 1936 excavations at Amarna (Pendlebury 1951, pl. LXXXVI, no. 51), which specifies the contents as wine from the vineyards of s3-wḥ3t, came from a jar that was noted in archive records as of type XVII.7 or XVII.8 (Archive document 11.5 no. 75). The uncertainty as to the precise type suggests that the sherd preserved only the horizontally-placed handle(s). Whilst it is possible that the vessel was of Nile Valley origin, as are the cited types, it is more plausible that it came from the region of the oases, and was of fabric V.10. No other forms in the fabric have yet been identified.

What evidence we have suggests that vessels of fabric V.10 may show more mainstream Nile Valley traits than those of fabrics IV.2 or IV.3. These can be seen in the use of a cream slip and the direct attachment of the moulded base to the wheel-made lower body. However, jar labels, such as a fragmentary label on a sherd of this fabric (32019), which mentions the 'Southern? Oasis' (M A Leahy, pers. comm.), and BM59379 confirm its origin, as does the vessel form. Whilst the significance of this is as yet unknown, it may eventually have implications for the organisation of the pottery industries of the oases.

Comments

A feature that amphorae of all three fabrics outlined above have in common is the use of a similar potmark (a mark incised into the wet clay before the vessel was fired). This is a wavy line that can occur close to the base of the vessel and/or on the shoulder (cf. **Fig. 11** d; **Fig. 12** b, with potmarks in both places; **Fig. 13** f). The potmark is known also from an oasis ware vessel from Thebes, perhaps of the earlier Eighteenth Dynasty (Rose 1996, pl. 68 no. 124; **Fig. 10** b), and continued into the Ramesside period, albeit having turned through 90 degrees (Aston 1998, 537 no. 2203). The only other potmark noted at Amarna is a 'sm3'-sign

lightly marked in the wet clay on the lower body of the vessel shown in **Fig. 11** c.

Amphorae are, par excellence, vessels for the transportation of commodities rather than vessels with an intrinsic value of their own. Unlike amphorae made in the Nile Valley, on which jar labels detailing the vessel contents are not uncommon, there is very little inscriptional evidence that can definitely be associated with vessels of the fabrics described above from which to identify their contents. From the current excavations, only one fragment (32062), a shoulder sherd of a vessel of fabric IV.2, mentions the transported commodity and partially preserves the word for wine (M A Leahy, pers. comm.). Jar labels found in earlier excavations at the site that mention an oasis origin (some of which are listed in Giddy 1987, Table I) also indicate that wine was the commodity transported, but it is rarely possible to confirm that the vessels in question are of oasis origin. A single sherd from the North City had a coating of *Pistacia* sp. resin on the interior, but this remains unique, and there is no other evidence to suggest that resin was a commodity brought from the oases (Serpico 1996, 222–3, sample TA222). The vessel in question may have been reused as a container for this substance.

For transportation, the vessel mouths were closed with the lids, already mentioned, and a mud seal was applied covering the neck and shoulder. Only one such sealing has come from the current excavations (**Fig. 13** a), but shoulder sherds sometimes show a line of mud where the seal originally rested. That shown in **Fig. 13** a still retains the neck of an amphora of fabric IV.2 and its lid. It is of cylindrical shape (Hope 1978, 27), and is made of a light-coloured mud tempered with large pieces of chaff; it is probably local to the vessels' place of origin. The sides and top are stamped four times with an oval impression beginning 'Menkheprure ...'

A remarkable feature of the oasis trade is the apparent difficulty of transportation when the weight (and indeed size) of the vessels is taken into consideration: the vessel shown in **Fig. 12** b weighs just under 12 kg as preserved. Given the modes of transport available, bringing such vessels in quantity into the Nile Valley must have been a slow, laborious and difficult process. Their cumbersome nature may be the reason for the complete lack of oasis wares on the 'water trail', a supply route littered with sherds of amphorae that connected the Workmen's Village with a well on the edge of the Main City, Q48.4 (Rose 1987, 124–26). The amphorae used on the route were exclusively of Nile Valley and Canaanite origin.

On the basis of jar labels mentioning an oasis origin for the contents, Giddy (1987, 79) suggested that the wine transported in the amphorae constituted a luxury product 'destined for use by the king and/or his court exclusively'. Whilst it is not possible here to give an extensive discussion of the distribution of oasis wares at Amarna, some preliminary and general points can be made. The first is the scarcity of oasis wares over most of the site. In all areas examined by the current mission, oasis vessels are far outnumbered by both amphorae of Nile Valley origin, and also by imported Canaanite jars. Whether this indeed reflects the exclusivity of oasis products, or, and perhaps a more likely explanation, the limited production capacity of the oases, is unknown.

Distribution is summarised in **Table 2**, which separates areas for which information is available by type of occupation and source of information. For excavated areas, it shows the percentage of diagnostic oasis ware sherds against the entire diagnostic sherd total, and the percentage of oasis diagnostics against the total diagnostic amphora count (grouping local and imported types). For areas examined in the surface survey, it shows the percentage of oasis ware sherds against the total sherd count, and the percentage of oasis ware sherds against the total amphora count. Because different things are being quantified, the figures from the excavated and surface survey areas are not strictly comparable, but can together be taken as an indication of quantity.

In terms of areas of the site, the principal contrast is between the Workmen's Village and the rest of the city (see **Fig. 14**). Only a handful of sherds of oasis vessels was found in excavations at the Village and its immediate environs. Only in Site XI, a complex separated from the village proper, is there a greater concentration, suggesting the presence of more than one such vessel in the complex. This may reflect on the status or administrative role of the occupants of the area, and certainly serves to differentiate them from the occupants of the Village proper. Very low figures also characterise the industrial area of Q48.4 and the site of the well from which the Village's water supply was drawn.

In areas of domestic occupation within the Main City, by contrast, oasis wares are usually present, albeit in small quantities. The exceptionally high figure of oasis wares against amphorae from house P46.33 may be misleading in that there were only 68 amphora sherds in total from there. However, surface surveys along two transects across the city, covering areas essentially of domestic occupation probably similar to that in which P46.33 stands, show they were present in over half the areas of the first transect, and in three-quarters of those surveyed in the second (Rose 1989, 102–14). The figures show that oasis wares formed a not uncommon feature of the assemblage. Surface survey in the North Suburb showed a similar picture. Oasis wares were present in half the areas surveyed, with a concentration of sherds on the southeastern edge of the area, particularly in and around house V37.1. The vessel illustrated in **Fig. 13** g came from V35.6, also in the North Suburb. Oasis wares are present in similar quantities in the North City. These come from areas of both small-scale housing and the larger complex, U24.1.

In the Central City, in the area of the Clerks' Houses and the adjacent rubbish dumps, the percentage of oasis wares is higher than that noted above. Why this should be so is unclear. Kemp and Garfi (1993, 62) suggest that since the buildings lack normal domestic fittings, they form a relatively low status 'battery of scribal workplaces'. Whether the presence of oasis wares indicates some degree of domestic occupation, or whether the vessels represent one of the benefits of a close connection with the administration, is unknown. Elsewhere in the Central City, oasis wares are found principally in two areas. The first lies in what is apparently an open area toward the eastern edge of the city (Rose

1987, 121–2, area 13). Here, there are traces of a much destroyed mud-brick building, as yet unexcavated, and a dense sherd scatter, which contains the highest proportions of oasis wares yet encountered anywhere at Amarna. The scatter, which also contains many oasis ware lids, includes other unusual and distinctive pottery types (principally large marl clay biconical jars with post-firing painting). The type of occupation here is unknown, although the presence of lids may suggest a storage area. The second area lies within O43.1 and is currently under excavation. It consists of what appears to be an official storage area, the enclosing wall of which includes bricks stamped with a *wedjat* eye, perhaps here a writing of *wḏ*, storehouse (B Kemp, pers. comm.; see also Kemp and Garfi 1993, 65). Although very little of the pottery from it is as yet recorded in detail, the recent work has produced sherds from many oasis amphorae as well as the seal already mentioned. It seems from this that oasis wine formed part of the supplies stored in the complex. A further surface concentration has been noted in the area of the magazines east of the King's House (P42.2; M Serpico, pers. comm.), but this has yet to be studied in detail.

The other formal building that has been extensively excavated is the complex of Kom el-Nana, and here oasis wares are very rare indeed. The few sherds found come from just two areas of the site, the bakery complex and the south house. Neither suggests the presence of any significant quantity. Oasis ware amphora sherds have also been identified from amongst late Roman deposits from one small area close to the northern edge of Kom el-Nana. These are unquantified, but they appear in greater numbers here than elsewhere. The sherds are found alongside other Eighteenth Dynasty imported amphora fragments, and suggest that there was a storage facility in this area. The other amphorae include imported vessels that seem to have associations with religious usage (Serpico 1996, 225–7), but there is little other evidence to suggest that the same could be said of the oasis wares. It should be noted, however, that sherds of oasis ware were observed in the dumps of pottery immediately south of the Great Aten Temple (Rose 1987, 119–21, area 12). A surface survey at Kom el-Nana in an area extending from the rear of the bakery block to outside the northern enclosure wall of the building showed a higher proportion of oasis wares. The origin of the deposit is not clear, but the higher quantity of oasis wares suggests that they may be exterior rubbish heaps, the source of which is an area not yet identified, but may be the hypothetical storage area already noted.

In summary, oasis wares, although scarce, form part of the ceramic assemblage over the greater part of the city. Their associations appear to be on the one hand domestic; fragments occur throughout the length and breadth of Amarna, with the conspicuous absence of the Workmen's Village and its supply base. This may have implications for the status of the population housed there. The presence of oasis vessels even in areas of small-scale housing in the Main City presents a striking contrast. Outside the domestic sphere, the wares occur in quantity in magazine areas that are of an official and elite nature. Since we know almost nothing of the practices by which vessels and their contents reached their final resting places, it is impossible to say whether the trade was one monopolised by royalty, so that vessels came into official stores and were thence distributed as the king's largesse, or whether they could be obtained through private trading agreements by sufficiently well-connected or wealthy individuals amongst Amarna's residents.

Table 2: Distribution of oasis wares at Amarna

AREA	EXCAVATED AREAS		SURFACE SURVEY	
	% total diagnostics	*% amphorae*	*% total diagnostics*	*% amphorae*
Domestic areas				
Workmen's Village	0.06	nc		
Workmen's Village: Site X1	0.30	5.00		
Main City: P46.33	0.43	10.30		
Main City: Transect 1			0.16	1.08
Main City: Transect 2			0.30	2.26
North Suburb			0.23	1.96
North City	0.45	7.40	0.55	3.00
Other				
Q48.4	0.14	nc	0.04	0.13
Kom el-Nana: all areas	0.03	1.32		
Kom el-Nana: Bakery	0.02	0.56		
Kom el-Nana: South house	0.06	8.20		
Kom el-Nana: Outside bakery			0.68	5.00
Central City: Clerks' Houses			0.60	5.20
Central City: Area 13			13.70	16.50
Central City: Area 12			0.20	8.00

Fabrics of the Oasis Amphorae of the New Kingdom from Memphis, Kom Rabi'a

Janine Bourriau

The area of domestic housing excavated at Memphis, Kom Rabi'a, by David Jeffreys and Lisa Giddy for the Egypt Exploration Society uncovered a continuous series of settlement remains from the mid-Thirteenth Dynasty to the Third Intermediate Period (Bourriau and Eriksson 1997, 101–2). Pottery was abundant; 85,000 diagnostic sherds were recovered during the first season, and a sampling strategy was eventually devised to cope with this abundance (Bourriau 1992, 263–8). All sherds (body sherds and diagnostics) of non Nile Valley vessels were recorded and 358 sherds of oasis vessels, almost all of them amphorae, were found. This may most easily be compared to the 838 sherds of 'Canaanite' transport amphorae retrieved. Of the total of imported amphorae, oasis products amounted to 30% as opposed to 70% for Canaanite Jars. To put the oasis element into perspective against the pottery as a whole, we can say that the oasis vessels account for 0.018% of all rims recorded. The chronological distribution shows a steady increase from the beginning of the Eighteenth Dynasty until the Ramesside period, with sherds most numerous in Level III, corresponding roughly to the late Eighteenth–early Nineteenth Dynasties.

None of the sherds were inscribed, which is hardly surprising given this damp site and the necessity of washing all pottery before it could be identified and sorted. Diagnostics were also scarce for the less common fabrics. As a result, matching the Memphis fabrics to examples from other sites where preservation is better is an important part of our post-excavation work and I am grateful to Colin Hope for the opportunity of contributing to this article. Laurence Smith, Margaret Serpico, Pamela Rose and I have worked on a concordance between Memphis and Amarna for this group of fabrics as well as for the Egyptian New Kingdom fabrics (Bourriau and Nicholson 1992; Bourriau, Smith and Nicholson, 2000). The thin section analysis by Laurence Smith, which has just been completed, will be referred to but full publication will appear elsewhere. The illustrations of the diagnostics will appear in the publication of the New Kingdom pottery, currently being written.

In comparing Memphis and Amarna fabrics, we have three sets of data: visual descriptions based on the appearance of a fresh sherd break seen with a 10x hand lens and confirmed by microscopic examination at 25x; results of thin section analysis, identifying and quantifying the inclusions in the clay; and chemical analysis (NAA) of samples of fabric P25, P45, P90 (Memphis) and IV.2 and IV.3 (Amarna). Samples of P25, P45, IV.2 and IV.3 were also submitted to Chris Doherty at the Research Laboratory for

Table 3: Visual concordance of oasis fabrics by Bourriau and Rose
based upon sherds examined under microscope

Memphis	Amarna	Karnak North	Theban Tombs
P23	IV.3		99, courtyard
P25			
P44	IV.2, fine		
P45	IV.2		99, courtyard
P90			99, burial
P91	Similar to V.10		
P92		1/12/88-4;15/12/86-8	
P93			

Archaeology and the History of Art who used FTIR (Fourier Transform Infrared Spectroscopy) to check for the presence of kaolin. The results may be briefly summarised: the FTIR analysis suggested that the clay sources for P25 and P45 probably contained kaolin, whereas the sources for IV.2 and IV.3 were probably marl clays. The NAA analysis grouped most of the 'oasis' samples together, well separated from the Canaanite Jar samples. All the P45 and P25 samples (with kaolinite) were in this separate group. Some samples of the other fabrics, IV.2, IV.3, and P90, dominated by limestone, joined two large messy subgroups that also contained Canaanite Jar samples. Within the 'oasis' group there were seven subgroups, four of which were composed entirely of IV.2 and IV.3 samples and one entirely of P45 and P25 samples. The remaining two contained samples of both fabric groups, in each case IV.2 and P45 (which have the greatest visual similarity) grouped together. For further comparisons with examples from Dakhleh, Karnak North and Thebes, we have compared sherd breaks under the microscope. It might be possible at a later date to do further analysis on this latter material. For a definition of the terms used in the fabric descriptions, see Bourriau and Nicholson 1992.

Oasis Fabrics at Memphis, Kom Rabi'a

Fabric P23 is characterised by small quantities of fine and medium sand and abundant angular limestone particles, fine, medium, coarse and very coarse. There are coarse particles of unmixed clay and small quantities of fine and medium black rock and soft red particles. The material is dense, sorting is poor and the colour of the break is a uniform reddish yellow (5YR 6/6). This is a relatively rare fabric at Memphis, but it is present throughout the New Kingdom levels and most common in the late Eighteenth to early Nineteenth Dynasty. Visually this fabric appears close to Amarna IV.3 but thin sections suggest that the two fabrics, although internally homogeneous, do not match sufficiently well to indicate that they came from the same clay source. The fabric also visually matches an example from Theban Tomb 99, Courtyard 40–4 recorded by Pamela Rose.

Fabric P25 is characterised by small quantities of fine, medium and coarse sand; occasional impressions from fine plant remains; abundant coarse, medium and fine limestone particles, showing signs of decomposition; scattered fine, medium and coarse, soft red-brown particles; occasional coarse particles of unmixed clay; and rare fine black rock

particles. Sorting is only fair, porosity dense and the material medium hard. The vessel wall is usually very thick, up to 11 mm, and the break exhibits distinctive zones, from outer to inner – cream, pink and grey. In appearance the fabric seems to be related to P45 and P44. Sherds are rare at Memphis before Level II, the Nineteenth Dynasty, which explains why it has not been found at Amarna.

Fabric P44 is characterised by rare scattered particles of fine to coarse sand; fine to coarse limestone, abundant only in the very fine size fraction; rare soft red-brown particles; medium to fine scattered grey and red-brown clay particles; and fine to coarse scattered black rock particles. The sorting is fair and porosity dense; all the limestone shows signs of decomposition and there are elongated pores. The surface often has a grey slip and the break always shows zones, a pink outer zone and a wide grey core. This fabric does not appear in the earliest New Kingdom level at Memphis but shows up first in Level III, mid to late Eighteenth to early Nineteenth Dynasty. It is used for amphorae of the types illustrated from Dakhleh Oasis by Marchand and Tallet (1999, fig. 14).

Fabric P45 is characterised above all by very coarse particles of limestone within which fine particles of quartz can be seen. Otherwise, it contains occasional fine impressions of plant remains; fine and medium scattered limestone particles; fine and medium red-brown particles; fine scattered black rock particles; and coarse and very coarse particles of unmixed clay. Sorting is poor, porosity dense and some limestone shows signs of decomposition. The vessel wall can be up to 12 mm thick and the break always shows colour zones, usually pink/yellow and grey. The fabric is evenly spread over the New Kingdom levels at Kom Rabi'a. Visually some examples (but not all) match Amarna IV.2, but again the thin section analysis does not support the concordance very strongly. FTIR has shown that P45 and IV.2 almost certainly came from different clay sources, but bulk sampling by NAA has grouped some samples together. This is perhaps explained by the coarse limestone inclusions that dominate both fabrics.

P90 is dominated by highly decomposed abundant particles of limestone in all sizes from very fine to very coarse. In contrast there are only rare fine to coarse particles of sand. There are scattered coarse and medium red-brown particles and shiny black rock particles. Trails of red-brown unmixed clay and round particles of grey clay are distinctive. Sorting is poor, porosity dense. Vessel walls are very thick, up to

10 mm and the material medium hard. The colour zoning in the break is characteristic: a grey-brown to grey core with red (2.5 YR 5/6) outer zones. This is the most common oasis fabric at Memphis and occurs in all New Kingdom levels, but most plentifully in Level III, late Eighteenth to early Nineteenth Dynasty. It is clear from the diagnostics that some of the vessels were enormous and this may account for the more numerous sherds. The fabric does not occur at Amarna but it does occur at Thebes, from the burial group in Tomb 99 recorded by Pamela Rose (see **Fig. 9**).

P91 is a very rare fabric at Memphis and was identified by comparison with Amarna V.10. The only diagnostic is a handle from RAT 281 13124. The fabric is characterised by scattered fine to coarse sand and limestone. The limestone extends from the very fine to the very coarse range. There are scattered soft medium to fine red-brown particles; fine black rock particles; and frequent dark grey and light brown fine to coarse clay particles. The sorting is poor, porosity medium but the material is very hard. The sherd break is not zoned but a uniform light brown (7.5 YR 6/4).

P92 is another very rare fabric at Memphis, and the top of the handle of an example is published in Bourriau and Eriksson (1997, 115, 10). The article was written long before the recent work was completed and it is necessary to correct the fabric attribution. The amphora is not P23 fabric, nor is it a Canaanite Jar. Visually the fabric matches that of examples of Karnak North Form 1155 (15/12/86-8 and 1/12/88-4; **Fig. 7** a, **Plate 75**). It occurs only in the early Eighteenth Dynasty level at Memphis, which would explain why it does not occur at Amarna. The fabric is characterised by scattered coarse and fine sand particles; and abundant fine to medium and rare coarse limestone particles. There are coarse soft red-brown particles and scattered fine to medium black rock particles. The appearance is dominated

by the decomposed limestone particles. The porosity is dense and the material is medium hard. The break is a uniform light brown (7.5 YR 6/4) colour.

P93 is a rare fabric characterised by abundant fine sand and fine to coarse limestone. The coarse particles contain very fine particles of sand. In addition there are fine red-brown rock particles. The sorting is poor and the porosity medium; the material is crumbly and the break is an even reddish brown (5 YR 5/4) without zones. It occurs in levels up to and including Level III at Memphis, late Eighteenth to early Nineteenth Dynasty. Only one unattached handle and a base survive as diagnostics and are not well enough preserved to determine whether they are 'oasis' types. As a result the identification of the fabric is not quite certain but it appears visually to relate to P23 and P90. It does not occur at Amarna.

Conclusion

It is evident that using our collective experience of the shapes and technology of oasis vessels together with the distinctive general appearance of the fabrics (defined by inclusions, colour and texture), it is not difficult to identify sherds as of oasis origin. Classifying them further can be much more difficult, since establishing the boundaries between one fabric and another is not easy. This situation contrasts sharply with the fabrics of the imported Canaanite Jars, which are internally more homogeneous and easier to match between one site and another. The picture that is indicated, ready to be adjusted as new evidence emerges, is of a fragmented amphorae industry in which a relatively small output was produced by many workshops spread over the oases of the Western Desert. Each would have had its own 'recipes' for the paste, its own clay sources and variation in production methods, and so produced the variability that we see.

Notes

1. I would like to thank all of those mentioned in the notes below for their willingness to share information with me on discoveries of oases amphorae, for providing drawings of the same and for permission to publish such material. I am indebted to Bruce Parr who prepared the line drawings that illustrate my section of this article and to Olaf E Kaper for his comments upon an earlier draft.

2. This material has been reviewed in extenso by Giddy (1987) and summarised recently in relation to the Southern Oasis by Marchand and Tallet (1999, 308–14).

3. I shall use this term for the standard, two-handled transport and storage jar of the New Kingdom (Hope 1989a). Whilst this form is ultimately derived from the Canaanite Jar, I feel that it is extremely misleading to use that name for the Egyptian-made derivatives, and that this practice (e.g., by Leonard 1995) should be abandoned.

4. Marchand and Tallet (1999, 311–2) list 29 such items of which 21 come from these two sites; the number is incomplete and to it should be added the hieratic docket Ashmolean Museum 1925.574b and the pieces referred to by Rose. I am grateful to Dr Helen Whitehouse for permission to study the Ashmolean Museum piece and for providing me with slides.

5. This term was used in administrative contexts to indicate the oases of Dakhleh and Kharga (Kaper 1992).

6. E.g., P. Anastasi IV 14,7; P. Chester Beatty IV Vs. 9, 10; P. Harris I 7, 10; The Onomasticon of Amenemope G7, 6–8. All discussed in Giddy 1987, 83–9.

7. These might include *dkrw*-fruit (Tallet 1996, 379–81) and the specialised product termed *sdh*, perhaps a sweet, heated wine rather than pomegranate-wine as previously thought, some of which seems also to have been made in the oasis (Tallet 1995). In all of the Theban tombs that include oasis tribute-bearers, they are shown bringing jars/amphorae, which may be assumed to contain wine; the only other product they invariably present is basketry.

8. For studies of wine manufacture in New Kingdom Egypt see Lerstrup 1992; Lesko 1977 and 1996; Murray 2000; Poo 1995; Tallet 1998a and b.

9. It is pertinent to note here that Dakhleh Oasis has yielded evidence for the cultivation of vines from the Old Kingdom to late Roman period. Amongst the botanical samples from the late Old Kingdom site of Ein el-Gazareen (see Mills this volume) there is a 1% component of grape/vine. Seeds and leaves have also been found in a variety of contexts at Ismant el-Kharab (second to fourth centuries AD); the vine features regularly in its wall-paintings and Shesemu, god of the wine press, is represented on the walls of the mammisi. One Greek text from the site refers to a vineyard, see Bagnall 1999. The earliest reference from the Nile Valley to the wine of *wḥ3t* is from the Thirteenth Dynasty in P. Bulaq 18,

which refers to four jars of wine being amongst provisions consumed by the court (Giddy 1987, 62–3).

10. I must express my gratitude to the authors of this study for making a text of their manuscript available to me before its publication.

11. I can cite other possible examples of oasis amphorae. In the British Museum, EA 4947 is a long-bodied vessel with narrow base (see Parkinson 1999, 95 no. 19); its morphology and manufacturing technique resemble those of oasis-made vessels. It is unprovenanced. I am grateful to Dr R Parkinson for enabling me to examine this vessel and also New Kingdom ostraca in the British Museum collection. In Cairo, a pictorial ostracon with a representation of a house plan is certainly from the oasis: JE 51865, displayed in Room 24 case 15. An amphora from the mortuary temple of Amenhotep II at Thebes (UC 15937; Petrie 1897, 5, 21 and pl. V) resembles an oasis vessel.

12. For discussions of the results of the survey of Dakhleh and a summary of pottery manufacture in the area by this writer, see now Churcher and Mills (eds) 1999. It should be noted that the conclusion presented in that volume as it relates to the New Kingdom (Hope 1999, 226) needs to be amended in light of the present study.

13. For discussion of ceramics from these sites see Hope and Eccleston this volume.

14. In discussing this docket, Tallet (1999, 171–2) used the decoration on the sherd and its fabric type, both typical of Dakhleh manufactures, to confirm the identity of *Iw-mrw* with *Jmrt*. This is, of course, not accurate; the fabric and decoration of the piece only prove that it was made in Dakhleh, not that the two toponyms refer to the same locality.

15. It also occurs on examples from Memphis; information courtesy of Janine Bourriau.

16. The original ascription of some of the tombs to the Roman period has subsequently been proved incorrect. On the basis of the ceramic data (Hope 1999, 229; Hope *et al.* 2000) and several radiocarbon dates derived from human skeletal material, the cemetery does not appear to have been used after the Ptolemaic period.

17. This temple may have been dedicated to Thoth and be the origin of the inscribed blocks presently located in el-Qasr to the north (see Kaper 1992, 128–30); in addition, a head of Serapis and part of a stela depicting Seth have been found at the site.

18. Tallet (1999, 169–71; Marchand and Tallet 1999, 312–3) has cast doubt upon Kaper's location of this toponym while concluding that it did refer to a region in the west of the oasis.

19. I would like to extend my thanks to Sylvie Marchand for bringing this find to my attention and showing me drawings of the pottery found at the site before their publication.

20. I am most grateful to Susanna Thomas for bringing this vessel to my attention, and for providing me with a drawing and a sample of the fabric. I am also grateful to Dr Steven Snape for permission to mention it in this study.

21. I am grateful to Dr David Aston for additional information concerning these pieces and to Verlag Philipp von Zabern for permission to reproduce the drawings of the oasis amphorae from Qantir.

22. I am most grateful to Dr D Aston for bringing these pieces to my attention and for providing information.

23. I am grateful to the Committee of the Egypt Exploration Society for permission to reproduce a drawing of this vessel.

24. These were kindly provided by Susan Allen of the Egyptian Department, Metropolitan Museum of Art, New York.

25. I am grateful to Deborah and John Darnell for showing me a sample of the fabric of this vessel.

26. The classification and designation of the two types have been changed since the original recording of the material to that given here as a result of discussion between the writer and Helen Jacquet-Gordon. All comments on the find contexts of the vessels from Karnak North have been provided by Helen Jacquet-Gordon. I am grateful to Helen and Jean Jacquet for permission to reproduce illustrations and photographs of material from their excavations.

27. This vessel was originally classified as Form 430 and is referred to as such in the publication (Jacquet 1983, 86).

28. The identification was made by Helen Jacquet-Gordon on the basis of her observations of Old Kingdom and modern pottery in Dakhleh Oasis; I have not been able to examine the vessel.

29. I am grateful to Dr D Aston for providing a drawing of this vessel and for permission to reproduce it here.

30. I am grateful to the Griffith Institute, Oxford for permission to reproduce a drawing of this vessel.

31. The description of this material and the drawing illustrated here were kindly provided by Pamela Rose. I am grateful to Dr Nigel Strudwick for permission to include this unpublished material.

32. I am indebted to Dr N Strudwick for permission to reproduce drawings of these vessels.

33. The occurrence of oasis wine at Buhen should also be noted, see Smith 1976, 183 and Table III.

34. In addition to the evidence from the reliefs in the tomb of Amenhotep Huy there, grapes and wine from the Northern Oasis are mentioned on two dockets from Amarna (Fairman 1933, 106, pl. LVIII.37; 1951, 166).

35. This may account for the thickness of the walls of many oasis amphorae.

36. This conclusion is based on my own visual comparison of a number of thin sections and the descriptions of Marl D published in Nicholson and Rose 1985, 140–70 and Bourriau and Nicholson 1992, 37–71.

37. One problem with this hypothesis is that two studies have shown that Marl A1 seems to be chemically similar to ceramics produced in Dakhleh. This is discussed further by Eccleston earlier in this volume.

38. It is anticipated that L Smith and M Eccleston will prepare a more detailed discussion of the petrographic analysis of samples from Dakhleh, Memphis and Amarna for publication. This study will concentrate further on a more technical discussion of the petrographic similarity of the known Dakhleh pieces to the samples from Nile Valley find contexts and the problems associated with attempting to differentiate petrographically between clays originating in Dakhleh and Kharga.

Bibliography

Al-Dayel O A F, 1995. *Data from Characterisation of Ancient Egyptian Ceramics by NAA.* Unpublished PhD dissertation, University of Manchester.

Aston D A, 1991. Section 5: Pottery. In M. J. Raaven *et al.,The Tomb of Irudef. A Memphite Official in the Reign of Ramesses II.* Leiden and London: 47–54.

Aston D A, 1992. Two Decorative Styles of the Twentieth Dynasty. *Cahiers de la céramique égyptienne* 3: 71–80.

Aston D A, 1996. *Egyptian Pottery of the Late New Kingdom and Third Intermediate Period.* Studien zur Archäologie und Geschichte Altägyptens 13. Heidelberg.

Aston D A, 1998. *Die Keramik des Grabungsplatzes QI. Teil 1: Corpus of Fabrics, Wares and Shapes.* Die Grabundendes Pelizaeus-Museums Hildesheim in Qantir-Pi-Ramesse I. Mainz am Rhein.

Aston D A, 1999. *Elephantine XIX. Pottery from the Late New Kingdom to the Early Ptolemaic Period.* Archäologische Veröffentlichungen, Deutsches Archäologisches Institut Abteilung Kairo 95. Mainz am Rhein.

Aston D A, Aston B and Brock E C, 1998. Pottery from the Valley of the Kings – Tombs of Merenptah, Ramesses III, Ramesses IV, Ramesses VI and Ramesses VII. *Ägypten und Levante* VIII: 137–214.

Aston D A and Pusch E B, 1999. The Pottery from the Royal Horse Stud and its Stratigraphy. *Ägypten und Levante* IX: 39–55.

Bagnall R S, 1999. The Date of *P. Kell* I G. 62 and the meaning of χωριον, *Chronique d'Egypte* 74/148: 329–33.

Bourriau J D, 1992. The Memphis Pottery Project. *The Cambridge Archaeological Journal* 2: 263–68.

Bourriau J D and Nicholson P T, 1992. Marl Clay Pottery Fabrics of the New Kingdom from Memphis, Saqqara and Amarna. *Journal of Egyptian Archaeology* 78: 29–91.

Bourriau J D and Eriksson K O, 1997. A Late Minoan sherd from an early 18th Dynasty context at Kom Rabi'a, Memphis. In J Phillips, *et al.* (eds), *Ancient Egypt, the Aegean, and the Near East: studies in honor of Martha Rhoads Bell.* San Antonio: 95–120.

Bourriau J D, Smith L M V and Nicholson P T, 2000. *New Kingdom Pottery Fabrics: Nile clay and mixed Nile/Marl clay fabrics from Memphis and Amarna.* London.

Churcher C S and Mills A J (eds), 1999. *Reports from the Survey of the Dakhleh Oasis, Western Desert of Egypt, 1977–1987.* Dakhleh Oasis Project Monograph 2. Oxbow Monograph 99, Oxford.

Colin F, Laisney D and Marchand S, 2000. Qaret el-Toub: un Fort Romain et une Necropole Pharaonique. *Bulletin de L'Institut français d'archéologie orientale* 100: 145–92.

Edwards W I, Hope C A and Segnit E R, 1987. *Ceramics from the Dakhleh Oasis: Preliminary Studies.* Burwood.

Eccleston M A J, 1997. *Provenance Study of Ceramics from the Dakhleh Oasis, Egypt.* Unpublished BA(Honours) dissertation. Department of Classics and Archaeology, Monash University, Melbourne.

Eccleston M A J, 1998. *Petrographic Study of Locally Produced Ceramics from the Dakhleh Oasis, Egypt.* Unpublished MSc dissertation. Department of Archaeology and Prehistory, University of Sheffield, Sheffield.

El-Saghir M.1992.The Great Processional Way of Thebes (The Avenue of the Sphinxes at Luxor). In *Sesto Congresso Internazionale di Egittologia Atti. Volume I.* Turin: 181–7.

Fairman H W, 1933. The Inscriptions. In H Frankfort and J D S Pendlebury, *City of Akhenaten Part II.* Egypt Exploration Society Memoir 40. London: 103–9.

Fairman H W, 1951. The Inscriptions. In J D S Pendlebury, *City of Akhenaten Part III.* Egypt Exploration Society Memoir 44. London: 143–223.

Frey R, 1986. Dakhleh Oasis Project: Interim report on Excavations at the 'Ein Tirghi Cemetery. *Journal of the Society for the Study of Egyptian Antiquities* 16: 92–102.

Frankfort H, and Pendlebury J D S, 1933. *The City of Akhenaten Part II.* Egypt Exploration Society Memoir 40. London.

Gardiner A H, 1933. The Dakhleh Stela. *Journal of Egyptian Archaeology* 19: 19–30.

Giddy L L, 1987. *Egyptian Oases.* Warminster.

Gosline S L, 1990. *Bahariya Oasis Expedition. Season Report for 1988. Part 1: Survey of Qaret Hilwah.* San Antonio.

Hayes W C, 1959. *The Scepter of Egypt. Part II.* New York.

Hermina M, 1990. The Surroundings of Kharga, Dakhla and Farafra Oases. In R Said (ed.), *The Geology of Egypt.* Rotterdam: 259–92.

Hölscher U, 1939. *The Excavation of Medinet Habu. Volume II: The Temples of the 18th Dynasty.* Chicago.

Holthoer R, 1993. The Pottery. In J Baines (ed.), *Stone Vessels, Pottery and Sealings from the Tomb of Tut'ankhamun.* Oxford: 37–85.

Hope C A, 1977. *Jar Sealings and Amphorae of the 18th Dynasty: a technological study. Excavations at Malkata and the Birket Habu 1971–1974.* Warminster.

Hope C A, 1979. Dakhleh Oasis Project: Report on the Study of the Pottery and Kilns. *Journal of the Society for the Study of Egyptian Antiquities* 9: 187–201.

Hope C A, 1983. Dakhleh Oasis Project: Preliminary Report on the Study of the Pottery – Fifth Season, 1982. *Journal of Society for the Study of Egyptian Antiquities* 13: 142–57.

Hope C A, 1989a. Amphorae of the New Kingdom. In C A Hope, *Pottery of the Egyptian New Kingdom: Three Studies.* Burwood: 87–110.

Hope C A, 1989b. Pottery of the Ramesside Period. In C A Hope, *Pottery of the Egyptian New Kingdom. Three Studies.* Burwood: 47–60.

Hope C A, 1989c. The XVIIIth Dynasty Pottery from Malkata. In C A Hope, *Pottery of the Egyptian New Kingdom: Three Studies.* Burwood: 3–20.

Hope C A, 1991. Blue-Painted and Polychrome decorated Pottery from Amarna: A preliminary Corpus. *Cahiers de la céramique égyptienne* 2: 17–92.

Hope C A, 1993. The Jar Sealings. In J Baines (ed.), *Stone Vessels, Pottery and Sealings from the Tomb of Tut'ankhamun.* Oxford: 87–138.

Hope C A, 1999. Pottery Manufacture in the Dakhleh Oasis. In C S Churcher and A J Mills 1999. Oxford: 215–43.

Hope C A, 2001. Observations on the Dating of the Occupation at Ismant el-Kharab. In M Marlow (ed.), *The Oasis Papers I: Proceedings of the First International Symposium of the Dakhleh Oasis Project.* Oxford: 43–59.

Hope C A, Eccleston M A J, Kaper O E, Marchand S, and Darnell D, 2000. Kegs and Flasks from the Dakhleh Oasis. *Cahiers de la céramique égyptienne* 6: 189–234.

Hummel R, and Schubert S B, 1994. Kom el-Ahmar: Ceramic Analysis. In D B Redford (ed.), *The Akhenaten Temple Project. Volume 3: The Excavation of Kom el-Ahmar and Environs.* Toronto: 30–82.

Jacquet J, 1983. *Karnak Nord V: Le Trésor de Thoutmosis Ier. Étude Architecturale.* Cairo.

Janssen J J, 1968. The Smaller Dakhla Stela. *Journal of Egyptian Archaeology* 54: 165–72.

Kaper O E, 1992. Toponyms of Dakhleh Oasis. *Bulletin de L'Institut français d'archéologie orientale* 92: 117–32.

Kaper O E, 1997. *Temple and Gods in Roman Dakhleh. Studies in the Indigenous cults of an Egyptian oasis.* PhD thesis submitted to the Rijksuniversiteit Groningen.

Kemp B J and Garfi S, 1993. *A survey of the ancient city of el-'Amarna.* London.

Kemp B J and O'Connor D, 1974. An Ancient Nile Harbour: University Museum Excavations at the 'Birket Habu'. *The International Journal of Nautical Archaeology and Underwater Exploration* 3: 101–36.

Kemp R A, 1985. Soil Micromorphology and the Quaternary. *Quaternary Research Association Technical Guide No. 2.* Cambridge.

Kleindienst M R, Churcher C S, McDonald M M A and Schwarcz H P, 1999. Geomorphological Setting and Quaternary Geology of the Dakhleh Oasis Region: Interim Report. In C S Churcher and A J Mills 1999. Oxford: 1–54.

Leahy M A, 1978. *The Inscriptions. Excavations at Malkata and the Birket Habu 1971–1974.* Warminster.

Leonard A, 1995. 'Canaanite Jars' and the Late Bronze Age Aegeo-Levantine Wine Trade. In P E McGovern, S J Flemming and S H Katz (eds), *The Origins and Ancient History of Wine.* Amsterdam.

Lerstrup A, 1992. The Making of Wine in Egypt. *Göttinger Miszellen* 129: 61–82.

Lesko L H, 1977. *King Tut's Wine Cellar.* Berkeley.

Lesko L H, 1996. Egyptian Wine Production during the New Kingdom. In P E McGovern, S J Flemming and S H Katz (eds), *The Origins and Ancient History of Wine.* Amsterdam: 215–30.

Marchand S and Tallet P, 1999. Ayn Asil et l'oasis de Dakhla au Nouvel Empire. *Bulletin de L'Institut français d'archéologie orientale* 99: 307–52.

Matthew A J, Woods A J, and Oliver C, 1991. Spots Before the Eyes: New Comparison Charts for Visual Percentage Estimation in Archaeological Material. In A Middleton and I Freestone (eds), *Recent Developments in Ceramic Petrology.* British Museum Occasional Paper No. 81. London: 211–63.

McDonald M M A, 1998. Early African Pastoralism: View from Dakhleh Oasis (South Central Egypt). *Journal of Anthropological Archaeology* 17: 124–42.

McGovern P E, 1997. Wine of Egypt's Golden Age: an archaeochemical perspective. *Journal of Egyptian Archaeology* 83: 69–108.

Mills A J, 1979. Dakhleh Oasis Project: Report on the First Season of Survey, October–December *Journal of the Society for the Study of Egyptian Antiquities* 9: 163–85.

Mills A J, 1980. Dakhleh Oasis Project – Report on the Second Season of Survey, September–December 1979. *Journal of the Society for the Study of Egyptian Antiquities* 10: 251–82.

Mills A J, 1981. Dakhleh Oasis Project: Report on the Third Season of Survey, September–December, 1980. *Journal of the Society for the Study of Egyptian Antiquities* 11: 175–92.

Mills A J, 1982. Dakhleh Oasis Project: Report on the Fourth Season of Survey. October 1981–January 1982. *Journal of the Society for the Study of Egyptian Antiquities* 12: 93–101.

Mills A J, 1983. Dakhleh Oasis Project: Report on the Fifth Season of Survey: October, 98–January, 1983. *Journal of the Society for the Study of Egyptian Antiquities* 13: 121–41.

Mills A J, 1999. Pharaonic Egyptians in the Dakhleh Oasis. In C

S Churcher and A J Mills 1999, Oxford: 171–8.

Murray M A, 2000. Viticulture and Wine Production. In P T Nicholson and I Shaw (eds), *Ancient Egyptian Materials and Technology.* Cambridge: 577–608.

Nicholson P T and Rose P J, 1985. Pottery fabrics and ware groups at el-Amarna. In B J Kemp (ed.) *Amarna Reports II.* London: 133–74.

Nordström H-Å, and Bourriau J, 1993. Ceramic Technology: Clays and Fabrics. In Do Arnold and J Bourriau (eds), *An Introduction to Ancient Egyptian Pottery.* Mainz am Rhein: 147–90.

Osing J, Moursi M, Arnold Do, Neugebauer O, Parker P A, Pingree D and Nur el-Din M A, 1982. *Denkmäler der Oase Dachla aus dem Nachlass von Ahmed Fakhry.* Archäologische Veröffentlichungen, Deutsches Archäologisches Institut Abteilung Kairo 28. Mainz am Rhein.

Parkinson R, 1999. *Cracking Codes. The Rosetta Stone and Decipherment.* London.

Peet T E and Woolley L, 1923. *The City of Akhenaten* I. Egypt Exploration Society Memoir 38. London.

Pendlebury J D S, 1951. *The City of Ahenaten* III. Egypt Exploration Society Memoir 44. London.

Petrie W M F, 1894. *Tell el-Amarna.* London.

Petrie W M F, 1897. *Six Temples at Thebes.* London.

Poo M-C, 1995. *Wine and Wine Offering in the Religion of Ancient Egypt.* London and New York.

Rose P, 1987. The pottery survey. In B J Kemp (ed.), *Amarna Reports IV.* London: 115–29.

Rose P, 1989. Report on the 1987 pottery survey. In B J Kemp (ed.), *Amarna Reports V.* London: 102–14.

Rose P, 1995. The pottery. In B J Kemp (ed.), *Amarna Reports VI.* London: 137–45.

Rose P, 1996. The pottery. In N Strudwick and H Strudwick, *The Tombs of Amenhotep, Khnummose, and Amenmose at Thebes (Nos. 294, 253, and 254).* Oxford: 166–81.

Said R, 1962. The Geology of Egypt. New York.

Serpico M T, 1996. *Mediterranean resins in New Kingdom Egypt: a multidisciplinary approach to trade and usage.* Ph.D dissertation, University College, University of London.

Smith H S, 1976. *Buhen II: The Inscriptions.* London

Tallet P, 1995. Le shedeh: étude d'un procédé de vinification en Égypte ancienne. *Bulletin de L'Institut français d'archéologie orientale* 95: 459–92.

Tallet P, 1996. Une jarre de l'an 31 et une jarre de l'an 10 dans la cave de Toutânkhamon. *Bulletin de L'Institut français d'archéologie orientale* 96: 369–83.

Tallet P, 1998a. Quelques aspects de l'économie du vin en Égypte ancienne au Nouvel Empire. In N Grimal and B Menu (eds), *Le commerce en Égypte ancienne.* Cairo: 241–67.

Tallet P, 1998b. Les 'étiquettes' de jarres à vin du Nouvel Empire. In C J Eyre (ed.), *Proceedings of the Seventh International Congress of Egyptologists.* Leuven: 1125–33.

Tallet P, 1999. A Particularity of the Toponomy of Dakhla Oasis: *S3-wḫ3t* and *Jw-mrw. Göttinger Miszellen* 173: 169–74

Tucker M E, 1991. *Sedimentary Petrology: An Introduction to the Origin of Sedimentary Rocks.* 2nd Edition. Oxford.

van Siclen C, 1981. *Wall Scenes from the Tomb of Amenhotep (Huy), Governor of Bahria Oasis.* San Antonio.

Whitbread I K, 1995. *Greek Transport Amphorae: A Petrographical and Archaeological Study.* Fitch Laboratory Occasional Paper, No. 4. Athens.

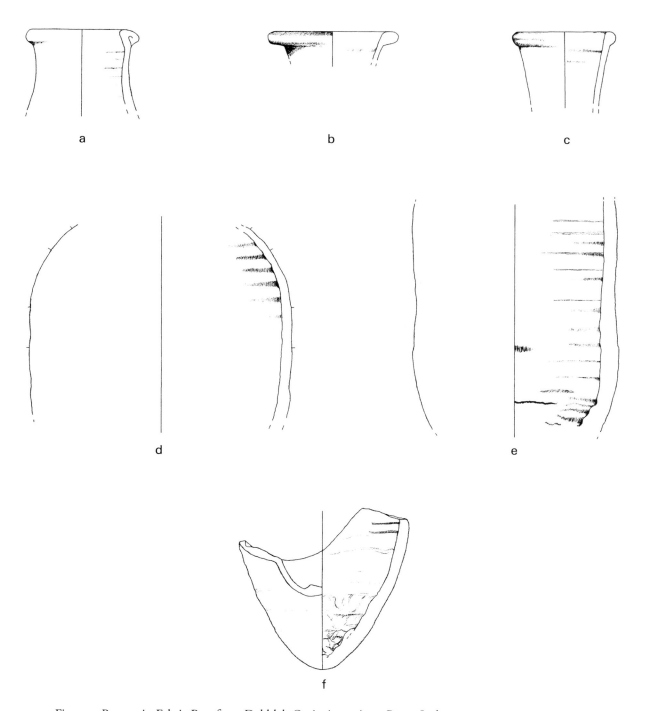

Fig. 2   Pottery in Fabric B23 from Dakhleh Oasis site 30/435-P9-3. Scale 1:4.

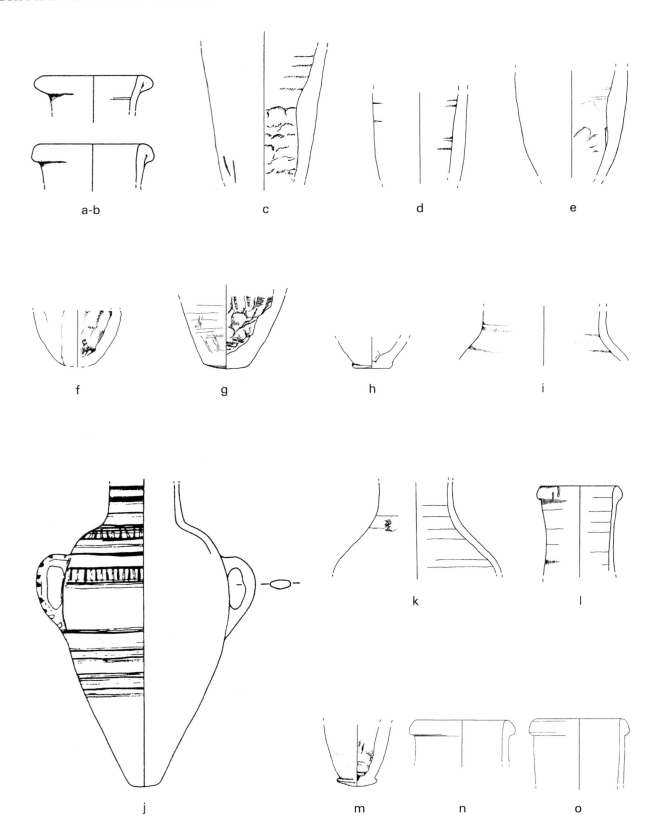

Fig. 3   Pottery in Fabric B23 from Dakhleh Oasis: *a-i*: East of site 31/435-I1-1; *j-l*: site 31/435-D5-2; *m*: site 31/420-D6-1; *n-o*: Necks from site 32/390-J3-1. Scale 1:4.

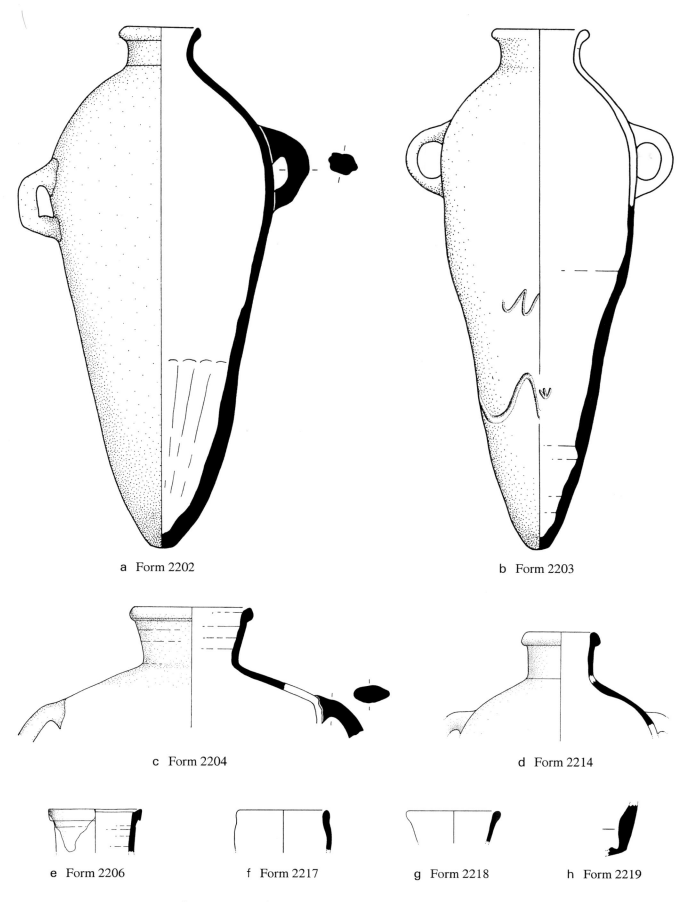

a Form 2202

b Form 2203

c Form 2204

d Form 2214

e Form 2206

f Form 2217

g Form 2218

h Form 2219

Fig. 4   Oasis ware from Qantir. Scale 1:4.

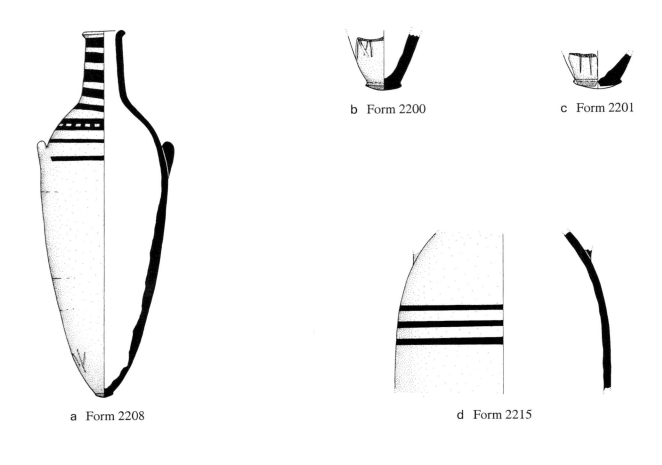

a Form 2208

b Form 2200

c Form 2201

d Form 2215

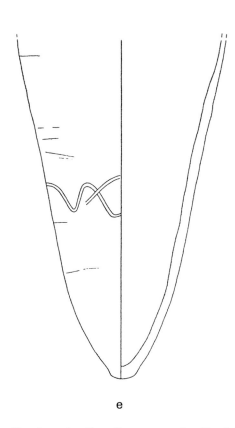

e

Fig. 5   Oasis ware *a–d*: from Qantir, and *e*: from Saqqara, tomb of Irudef. Scale 1:4.

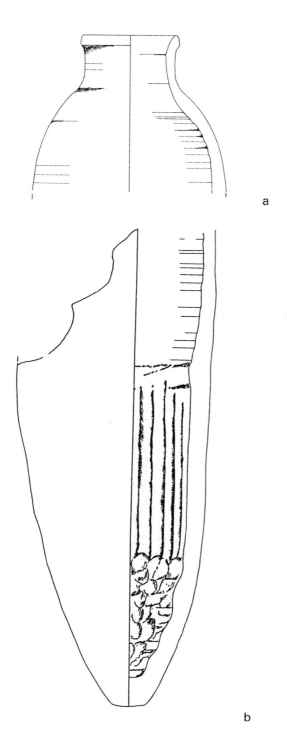

a

b

Fig. 6   Amphorae from Malkata: *a*: M73/E191/1488; and *b*: M73/Eac20(w)/630. Scale 1:4.

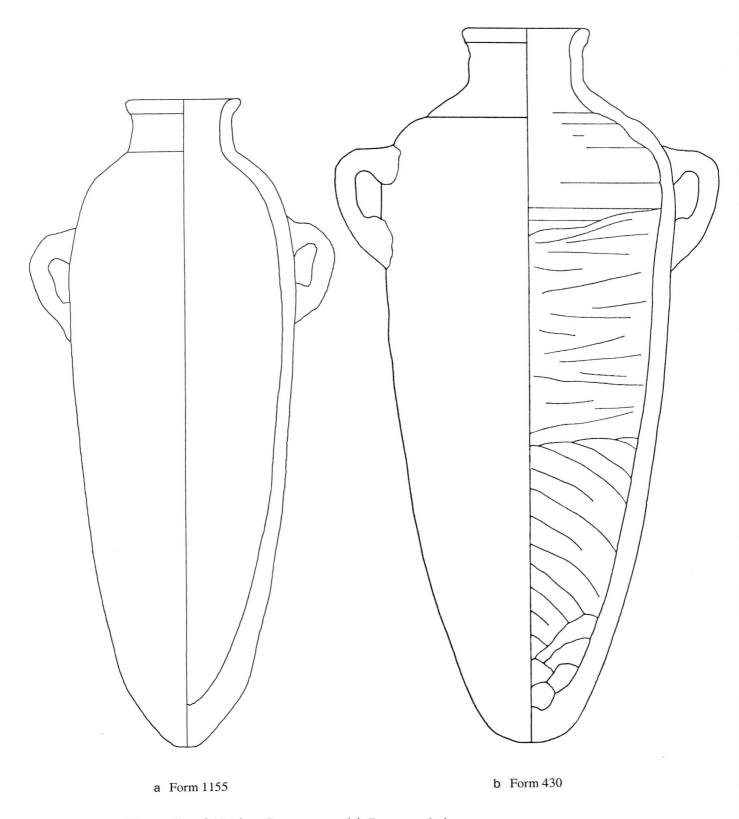

a Form 1155   b Form 430

Fig. 7   Karnak North: *a*: Form 1155; and *b*: Form 430. Scale 1:4.

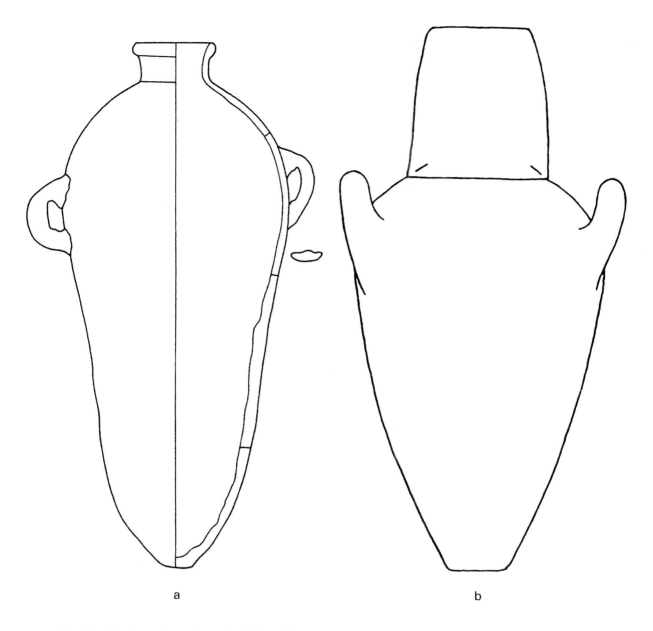

a   b

Fig. 8   Oasis amphorae from the Valley of the Kings: *a*: KV2; and *b*: KV62. Scale 1:4.

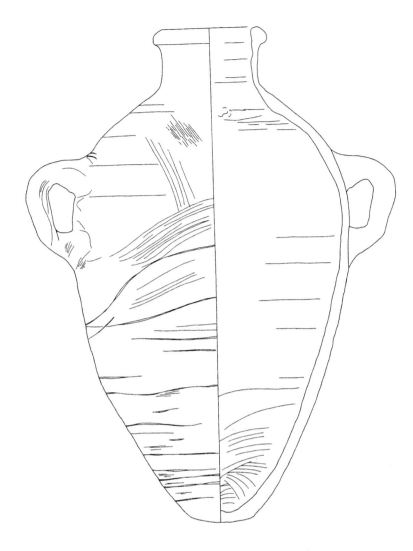

Fig. 9   Amphora from Theban Tomb 99. Scale 1:4.

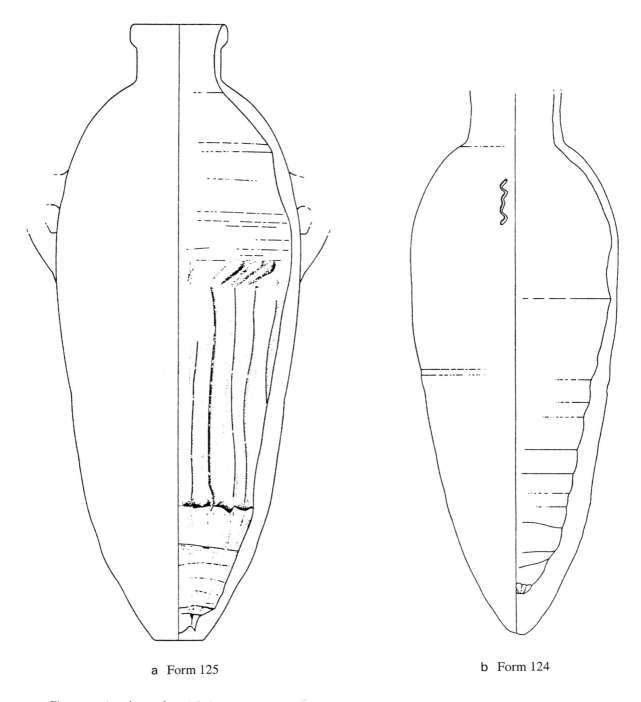

a Form 125   b Form 124

Fig. 10   Amphorae from Theban Tomb 253: *a*: Form 125; and *b*: Form 124. Scale 1:4.

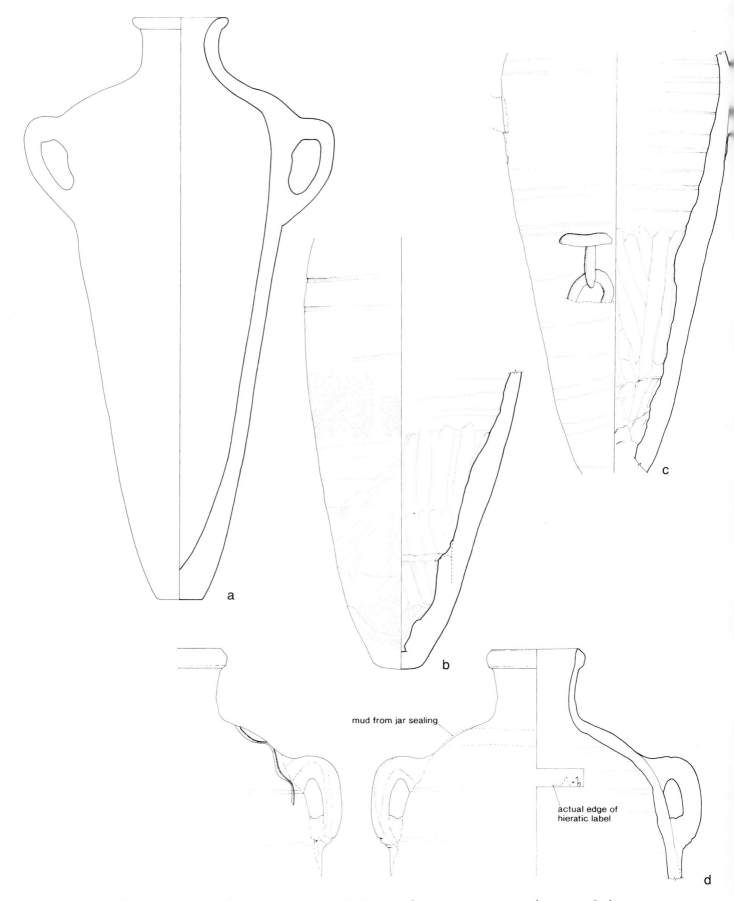

mud from jar sealing

actual edge of
hieratic label

Fig. 11   Oasis ware from Amarna, *a*: type XLIII/1015; *b*: 103058; *c*: 103071; *d*: 103056. Scale 1:4

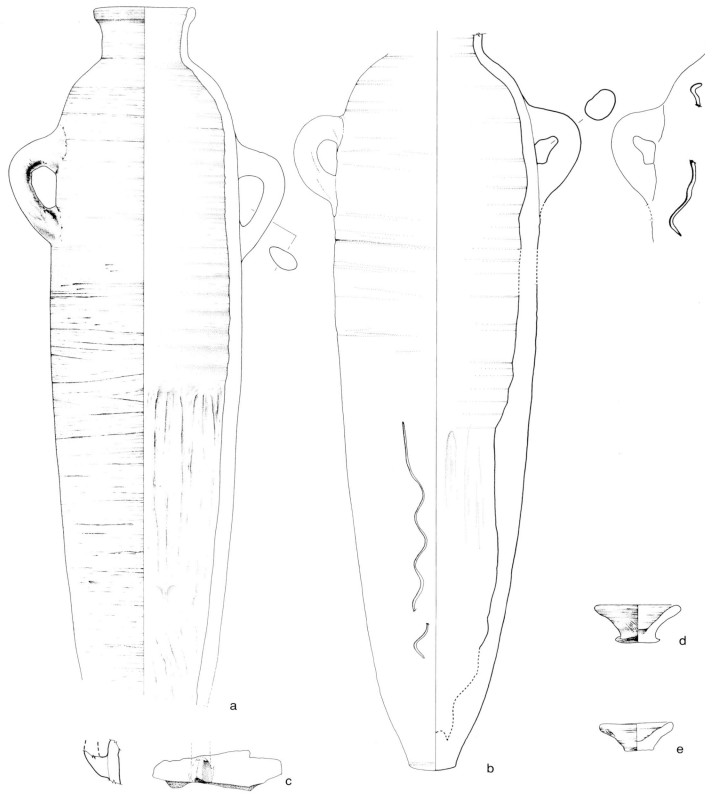

Fig. 12   Oasis ware from Amarna: *a*: Vessel 19; *b*: Vessel 28; *c*: Surface 130; *d*: Vessel 135; *e*: 98216.
Scale 1:4.

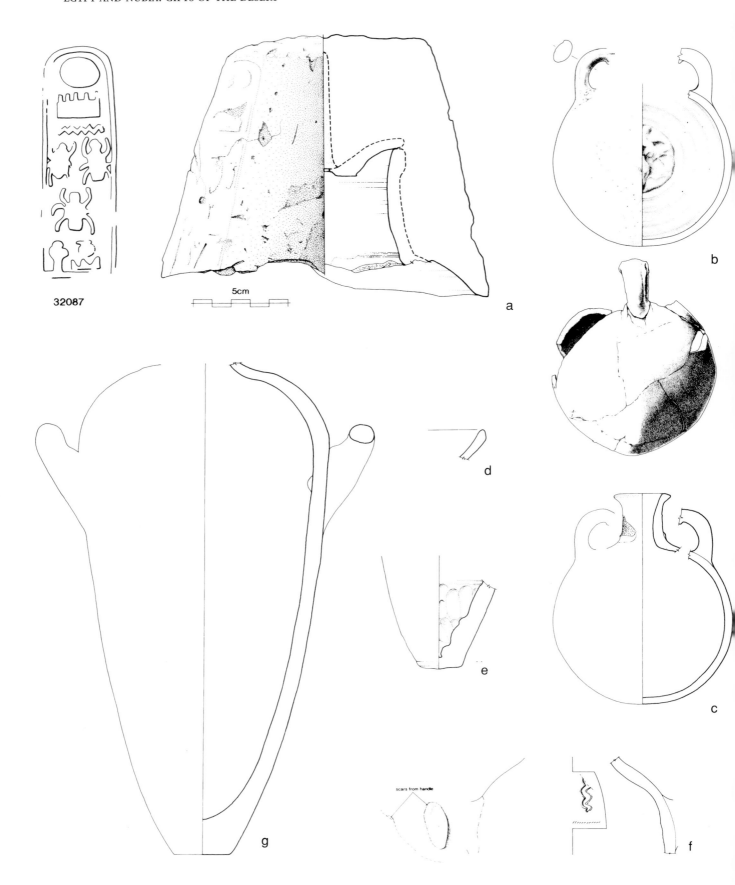

32087

5cm

Fig. 13 Oasis ware from Amarna: *a*: Find no, 32087; *b*: Vessel 39; *c*: Composite of Vessel 39 and Surface 118; *d*: surface 161; *e*: 103078; *f*: Surface 116; *g*: XVI/4. Scale 1:4.

North City

(north part)

North Suburb

(south part)

Central City

unexc.

P46.33

Transect 1

Workmen's Village
Site X1

Q48.4

Transect 2

Main City

unexc.

///// DOG excavations

⌐⌐⌐ EES excavations

Kom
el-Nana

Fig. 14   Areas containing oasis ware sherds from excavation and surface survey.

Opening the Narrow Doors of the Desert: Discoveries of the Theban Desert Road Survey

John Coleman Darnell

with the assistance of Deborah Darnell

For nine seasons the Theban Desert Road Survey has been exploring the pharaonic routes of the Theban Western Desert (for initial descriptions of these discoveries see Darnell and Darnell 1993–8). The survey began by seeking to ascertain if it would be possible to identify the desert routes of the Thebaïd that were in use during the pharaonic period. The Theban Desert Road Survey has indeed been able to do this and much more. The results of this continuing work have been the identification of numerous ancient routes and a wealth of associated archaeological and epigraphic sites, including hundreds of rock inscriptions, and the remains of caravansaries, encampments, fortifications, and sanctuaries. The abundance of ceramic material (see D Darnell this volume) has made it possible to classify the routes by the main periods of use and the nature of the traffic on them.

Unexpectedly, much of the evidence from these desert sites and features dates to periods of conflict and fragmentation/unification in the Nile Valley (Protodynastic, First and Second Intermediate Periods). The archaeological and epigraphic remains compliment one another in a remarkable manner, and produce an unexpectedly complex picture of pharaonic activity in the Western Desert. Far from being considered a frightening marginal zone, the Western Desert teemed with Egyptian activity. Ancient armies marched across it to turn the flanks of their adversaries, exploiting geophysical peculiarities of the Qena Bend of the Nile (**Figs 1 and 2**) and almost incidentally making of Thebes a great military power. Priests and pilgrims linked distant shrines in their travels along the desert roads, horse-mounted couriers and patrols raced between caravansaries, and humble travellers left their names.

The following is an overview of the discoveries of the first nine seasons of the continuing expedition. Unfortunately considerations of space do not allow for a complete presentation; what follows is therefore a selective representation of the highlights of the work to date.[1]

The Farshût Road

Gebel Antef

Prominent along the west bank of Luxor are the peaks of the gebel that serve as a boundary between the Nile Valley and the expanses of the Libyan Desert. Slightly to the north of the Valley of the Kings lies Gebel Antef (**Plate 78**), where in 1992 the Theban Desert Road Survey discovered the remains of the only major monument uniquely attributable to the Seventeenth Dynasty. Surviving fragments of inscribed door-jambs show a temple to have been constructed by a king Antef, son of (*ir.n*) a king Sobekemsaf (**Plate 79**), and dedicated to the Abydene Osiris. By virtue of the road on which it is located, connecting Thebes with Abydos, the temple was considered to be an extension of the Abydene cemetery. This association with Abydos explains the votive objects also discovered at the temple site, which include a Thirteenth Dynasty naos-stela and the statue of a Seventeenth Dynasty military official bearing the rare title 'King's Son of the Victorious Ruler'.

Random sampling of pottery at several locations in the vicinity of the chapel showed that the overwhelming majority of the ceramic material is Middle Kingdom through early New Kingdom in date. Thorough surface survey of the area of cairns and dry-stone huts on the west end of the Gebel Antef promontory revealed considerable amounts of Pan Grave pottery and Seventeenth Dynasty Egyptian storage jars. These results strongly imply that the area was a provisioning site for Medjay patrols, perhaps similar to the supply depot for a group of Medjay depicted in the tomb of Mahu at Amarna (Davies 1906, pl. 26). The Medjay were operating in the Theban area during the Second Intermediate Period, and appear to have had cattle herds in the area of Gebelein during the Thirteenth Dynasty (Vernus 1986:141–4).[2] Also during the Thirteenth Dynasty, the Theban court was granting supplies of Egyptian provisions to visiting Medjay (Scharff 1922, 60–1; Quirke 1990, 19–22; Spalinger 1986, 222).

Stelae of the Twenty-First Dynasty

At the site of the Antef temple at the Theban terminus of the Farshût Road, and several kilometres behind Gebel Roma (see below), we have found the remains of sandstone stelae of Twenty-First Dynasty date (**Plate 80**). The lunettes are surmounted by winged sun disks, below which appears a form of Amun, accompanied by Mut and Khonsu, before whom stands a figure of the ruler.

Records in the office of the Egypt Exploration Society in London reveal that an Egyptian workman with the Mond and Myers Armant Expedition discovered a stela of Panedjem son of Paiankh near the Wadi el-Hôl during the 1930s. Though it was never published and its present whereabouts are unknown, the stela exists in a photograph, a photographic enlargement partially inked by Margaret Drower and a partial handcopy. The texts of all three stelae are fragmentary, but they do appear to be parallel. The text copied by Ms Drower from the best preserved of the stelae (**Fig. 3**) reads:

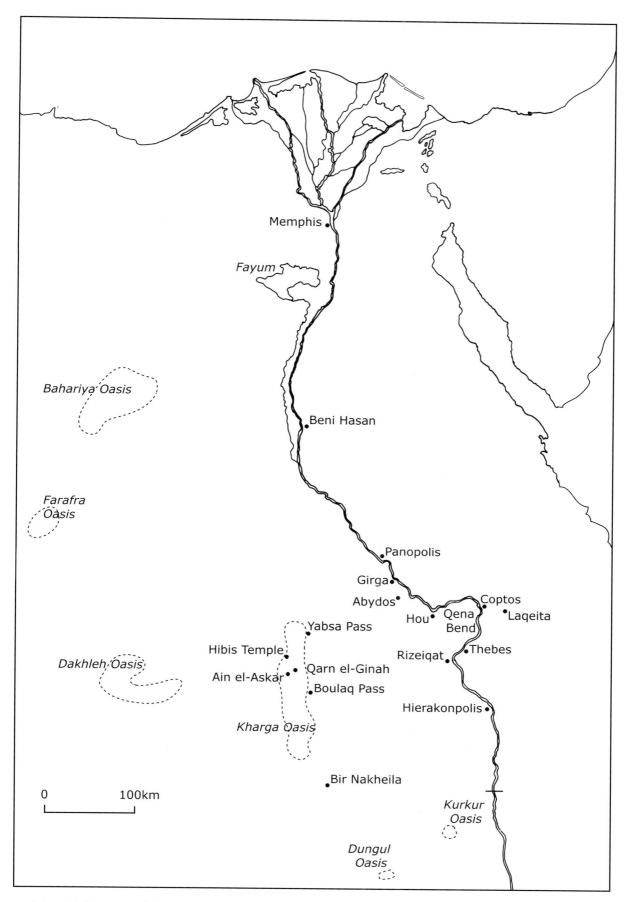

Fig. 1   Map with locations of places mentioned in the text (map prepared courtesy of Claire Thorne).

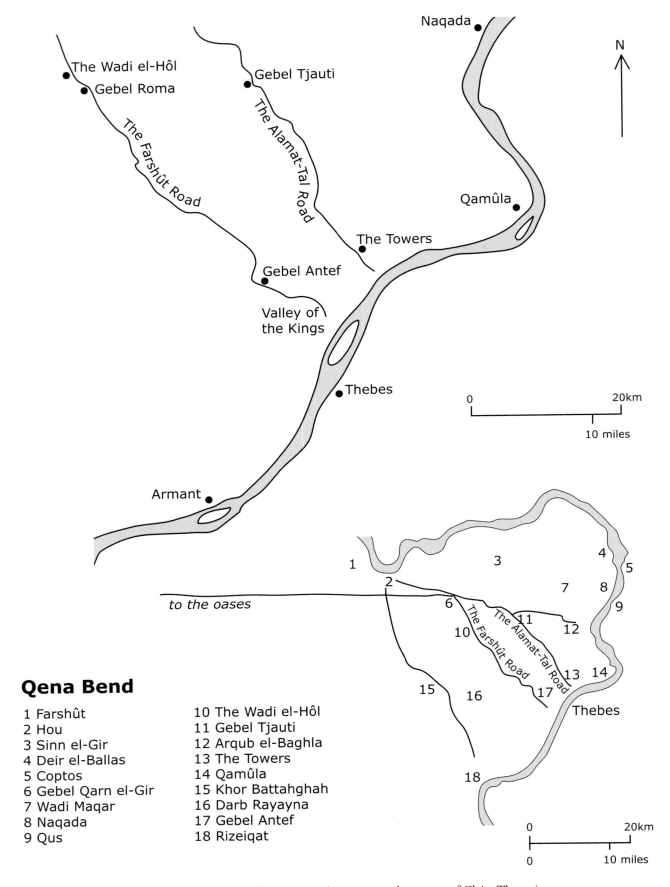

Qena Bend

1 Farshût
2 Hou
3 Sinn el-Gir
4 Deir el-Ballas
5 Coptos
6 Gebel Qarn el-Gir
7 Wadi Maqar
8 Naqada
9 Qus
10 The Wadi el-Hôl
11 Gebel Tjauti
12 Arqub el-Baghla
13 The Towers
14 Qamûla
15 Khor Battahghah
16 Darb Rayayna
17 Gebel Antef
18 Rizeiqat

Fig. 2   Map of the Qena Bend region and the desert routes (map prepared courtesy of Claire Thorne).

[1] … [*imy-r*] *ḥm.w*[*-nṯr*] *n ip.t-s.wt di ꜥnḫ ḏ.t ḥrw* [*pn*…]

[2] … [*ḥm nṯr tpy n imn-Rꜥ n*]*sw.t-nṯr.w nb-Tꜣ.wy Pꜣ-nḏm* [*sꜣ ḥm-nṯr tpy n imn-Rꜥ Pꜣy-ꜥnḫ* …]

[3] … [*n*]*sw.t Mn-ḫpr-Rꜥ iw ṯs*=[*t*]*w* […]

[4] … *ꜣw m wꜣ.t ḥr.t ssm.wt in ḥm-nṯr tpy n imn-Rꜥ* [*nsw.t nṯrw* …]

[5] … *imn-rꜥ ḫnty-ip.t-s*[*.w*]*t* …

[6] … *sꜣ Pꜣy-ꜥnḫ m-ḫt gm sw*(?)…[…]

[7] … *qnw ḥry.w-nṯr mitt iry rmṯ*(?) … *wꜣ.t* …

---

[1] … [overseer of] [pro]phets of Karnak, given life forever…

[2] …[high priest of Amun-Re k]ing of the gods, lord of the Two Lands Panedjem, [son of the high priest of Amun-Re Paiankh …]

[3] … [k]ing Menkheperre.[3] One ascended[4] …

[4] … widened in the High Road of Horses by the high priest of Amun-Re [king of the gods …]

[5] … Amun … foremost of Karnak …

[6] … son of Paiankh, after finding it …

[7] … stonemasons likewise, people(?) … the road …

The surviving text on the Gebel Antef stela also mentions: x+2 … *tꜣ*=*f t*(*ꜣ*) *mi.t* …, '… he showing the way …,' possibly a reference to Amun or some other deity as one who shows the way (*Wb* V 347, 20).[5] This recalls the concluding lines of the 'Stela of the Exiles', in which Menkheperre addresses Amun (l. 21): 'set my feet on your path, and lead me upon your way'. Referring to more than a physical path, this alludes to the deity setting one on the proper path of piety.[6] All of these images fit well within the overriding topos of the deity as good shepherd (Müller 1961, 126–44).

Considering Menkheperre's interest in the oases and desert routes, one may suggest that the Farshût Road stelae belong to the pontificate of Menkheperre. He has forts on routes to Bahariya and Kharga Oases, as well as near the Qus end of the Wadi Hammamat road (Kitchen 1986, 249 [map 1], 269–70).

The stelae agree in referring to the 'road of horses' (for early road names similarly formed, see Fischer 1991, 59–64). This name suggests horses moving along the roads, probably for military or communication purposes rather than trade (cf. rider in Martin 1989, 43–4 [scene 22], pls. 32–4).[7] A similar road name, describing a road as used by a certain animal, occurs in three inscriptions as *tꜣ mi.t n iḥ.w*, 'the way of cattle', attested to in three inscriptions of year 19 of Taharqa from Bab Kalabsha (see Hintze 1960, 330–3).

This portion of the Gebel Antef stela recalls Diodorus Siculus (Bk. I, ch. 45.7). Diodorus records that the Egyptians once had one hundred horse-relay stations positioned between Memphis and Western Thebes. Such horse patrols and postal relays may continue the earlier Medjay patrols, and the cavalry and dispatch riders may themselves descend from a tradition of mounted Nubian scouts.[8] The Chester Beatty papyri from Panopolis give evidence of letters travelling the roughly 120 miles (192 km) between Hermopolis and Panopolis within a single day, a feat only possible with horse relays (see Skeat 1964, xx). One may suggest that these horses, travelling around AD 300, could only attain such speed by travelling along a desert highway, avoiding the dykes, canals, crops, and habitations of the cultivation. The statement of Diodorus Siculus and the evidence from the Armant and Gebel Antef stelae suggest that horse roads in the Egyptian deserts may be of pharaonic origin.

The letter Berlin 10463 was written by Sennefer, mayor of Thebes, to the farmer Baki of Hou. In the letter, Sennefer warns of a royal visit to Hou by river within three days, and instructs Baki to perform several tasks before the king arrives. As Caminos (1963, 32 and 36) has pointed out, the letter must have been intended to reach Baki early enough to allow him time to fulfil the directives. As Caminos recognised, Sennefer's letter to Baki probably travelled along the Farshût Road. The Twenty-First Dynasty stelae from the Farshût Road suggest that mounted couriers may have transported Sennefer's letter across the Qena Bend.

The stelae may also be associated with efforts to control the potentially lawless, exile-filled oases, efforts that culminate in the fortresses constructed and pardons granted under Menkheperre. The stelae are also further evidence for the importance of Abydos for Thebans during the Third Intermediate Period, as the routes on which they stood also lead to Abydos.

The Wadi el-Hôl

Near the middle of the Farshût Road, in the cliffs behind el-Halfaya, the Theban Desert Road Survey has recorded the wealth of inscriptions in the Wadi el-Hôl (**Plate 81**) This site, partially discovered but only sampled photographically by Terence Grey and Hans Winkler in the 1930s, is being vandalised. A number of inscriptions had been completely destroyed by the time we began work at the site, and during our third season we surprised vandals in the act of desecration. Vandalism and wanton destruction of the inscriptions unfortunately continues.

The Theban Desert Road Survey has completed photographic documentation of the main concentrations of graffiti,[9] and has copied and collated all of the recoverable inscriptions and depictions. Although there are a number of prehistoric depictions, the majority of the carvings are hieratic, and some hieroglyphic, inscriptions, mostly dating to the Middle Kingdom, especially the late Middle Kingdom. One of the earlier pharaonic inscriptions in the Wadi el-Hôl is nothing less than the signature of King Mentuhotep III when he was a prince.

The pharaonic inscriptions in the Wadi el-Hôl are quite varied. Several stand out due to their great significance. Next to the graffito left by a man travelling from Abydos to Deir el-Bahari late in the reign of Amenemhat III is a letter carved on the face of the gebel (**Fig. 4**). The letter is addressed to 'this (particular) *wꜥb*-priest', apparently the priest Kheperka, next to whose large signature the letter was carved. The letter's author addresses the priest in the praise of a number of deities. The combination of deities that appears in this late Middle Kingdom letter finds its closest parallel in Sinuhe's letter to Senwosret I in the Story of Sinuhe. In fact, the deity Sopdu-Neferbauenra-Semseru is otherwise attested only in Sinuhe's letter. At least two readings in the Wadi el-Hôl inscription support variants from the Ashmolean Ostracon version of the Story of Sinuhe.

One of the most important rock inscriptions at the Wadi

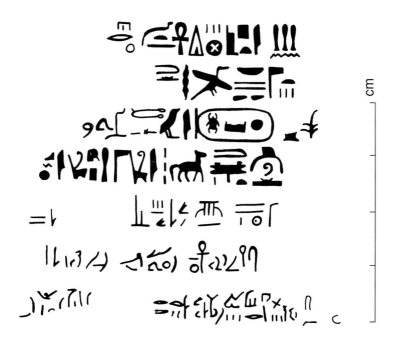

cm

Fig. 3   Text of a Farshût Road stela.

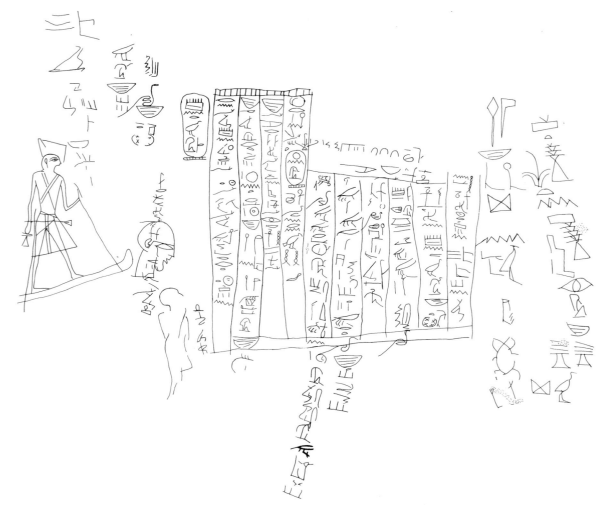

Fig. 4   Letter to Kheperka in the Wadi el-Hôl.

Fig. 5 Man on horse back from the Wadi el-Hôl.

Fig. 6 Inscription of Bebi in the Wadi el-Hôl.

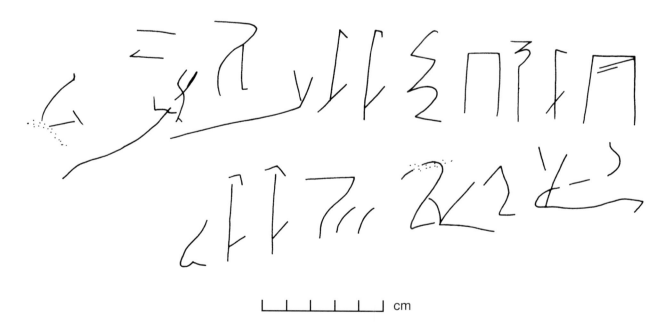

Fig. 7 Inscription of the stablemaster from the Wadi el-Hôl.

el-Hôl site is a five line literary text in hieratic carved below the letter described above (Darnell 1997, 85–100). Patterned after the opening to Sinuhe's encomium on the pharaoh Senwosret I in the Story of Sinuhe, the text begins:

(*i*) *rmṯ nb.t ʿ3.w šr.w m[šʿ] mi-ḳd=f m=tn s m niw.t n rḫ ḳd(?) [=f(?)…]*

Oh people great and small, and the army in its entirety—behold, a man is in the City (Thebes), [whose li]ke(?) has not been known!

The text relates how the 'foreigners fall to his pronouncements', and concludes by describing the ruler's bravery and intelligence. Then, in a stark description of the 'good shepherd' motif common to royalist texts from ancient Egypt, the text states that:

<*s*>*ḏr=f ḥḳr r ḥḏ.t t3 m33=f p.t mi sḏ.t rš=f pw km s3w.(t)*

he goes to sleep hungry, and at dawn he sees the sky like a flame—his joy is the successful completion of the watch.

Palaeography and content suggest that this literary text is a paean to a Theban ruler of the Second Intermediate Period, keeping watch in the desert and driving back the foreign hordes.

Nearby is a depiction of a statue of the king (**Fig. 4** left), shown on a sledge (cf. el-Saghir 1992, 21–7, esp. 24, Abb. 50), with the annotation: 'As for anyone who shall read these writings/view these images, he shall reach home safely'. Perhaps such a portable statue once visited or resided in the Wadi el-Hôl. The depiction provides a concrete illustration of the statement of Ibiau on the late Middle Kingdom stela Cairo 20086 that he 'followed the statue of the king into the foreign/desert countries'.

Another group of texts at the Wadi el-Hôl are the 'Spending the Day' inscriptions, which relate how people came to the Wadi el-Hôl to 'spend the day on holiday' (Darnell 2002). The vocabulary of the inscriptions suggests the worship of the goddess Hathor.[10] A depiction of Hathor in her bovid form accompanies one of the texts. These inscriptions allude to the veneration of Hathor in the Wadi el-Hôl, and a Ptolemaic stela from Hou actually describes a desert procession in honour of the goddess, travelling along a desert road that most likely led into the Wadi el-Hôl (Collombert 1995, 63–70).

The inscriptions also provide genealogical information about families of the late Middle Kingdom. They demonstrate that many people with rather humble titles, including many apparently low ranking soldiers, had attained at least a certain level of literacy. This fits in well with what we know of the high efficiency of the late Middle Kingdom bureaucracy, which must have required literacy of a fairly large proportion of the population.

In the Wadi el-Hôl is a pharaonic depiction of a man riding a horse (**Fig. 5**). The site also yields the signature of a stable master (**Fig. 7**), the: *ḥry-iḥ t3y=f in.t ʿš3w*, Chief of the Stable 'Its-Fetchings-Are-Frequent'.[11] These bits of information strongly support the conclusion that the main Farshût Road was in antiquity a major postal 'pony express' route (see below, Gebel Roma).

One of the most unexpected discoveries at the Wadi el-Hôl was the presence of two short early alphabetic inscriptions (**Plate 83**). Palaeographically, these texts are more archaic than previously discovered 'Proto-Sinaitic' inscriptions and reveal a derivation from Egyptian lapidary hieratic script at some point during the early Middle Kingdom. A hieratic inscription in the Wadi el-Hôl names one Bebi, *imy-r mšʿ n ʿ3m.w Bbi*, 'General of the (Semitic language speaking) Asiatics' (**Fig. 6**), and suggests a late Middle Kingdom date for the carving of the early alphabetic inscriptions. Bebi writes the seated man and woman over plural strokes as the determinatives of *ʿ3m.w*, 'Asiatics', suggesting that he is in charge of a group of men and women, probably soldiers or workmen and their families. The Wadi el-Hôl early alphabetic inscriptions can thus be explained as the adaptation of lapidary hieratic forms to carve the names of Asiatic members of Bebi's retinue.

In the inscription Bebi is accompanied by a number of messengers, one of them an *wpwty-nswt*, 'royal messenger', and others *sin.w*, 'express couriers'.[12] Apparently, Bebi (whose title is attested in a letter from Kahun) and his male and female Asiatic troops were providing support for the runners who used the Farshût Road before the introduction of horse-mounted couriers during the Seventeenth Dynasty. This epigraphic evidence augments the archaeological material from Gebel Roma discussed below.

Gebel Roma

The Theban Desert Road Survey has also mapped the road to the north that ascends the gebel over the Wadi el-Hôl graffiti areas. This led to the discovery not only of a concentration of huts with Middle Kingdom ceramics (to the northwest), but also, more spectacularly, of the largest area of caravan debris that we have thus far located in the Theban Western Desert. The site is a mountain of pottery, animal dung, straw and other archaeological material, covering nearly 3,000 square metres of the gebel. Although disturbed, enough remains to allow one to sketch the stratigraphy of the remains, the bulk of which date to the Middle Kingdom, Second Intermediate Period and early New Kingdom. There are also areas where animal dung was collected in the form of patties, apparently for use as fuel, as is well attested in documents from Deir el-Medina. Near the stratified caravan deposits are several tent bases. Scratched in hieroglyphs on a rough boulder forming part of one of these wind-breaks was an inscription (**Plate 82**):

ir.n ḥm-nṯr sn.nw n imn Rmʿ

Made by the second prophet of Amun, Roma

This is the name of Roma, called Roy, carved when he was second prophet of Amun. The text is a visitor's note left by an important clergyman of the Ramesside period, and direct evidence of Roma's travels. Apparently Roma once rested in this very rough stone shelter, and for this reason we have called the site Gebel Roma.

In his inscription at Karnak, Roma says that after becoming Second Priest of Amun, he took charge of the treasury and the granary of Amun; he further states that Ramesses II rewarded him with the high priesthood because of the prosperity of the treasury and granary. When Roma left his name above the Wadi el-Hôl he was Second Priest of Amun, administering the financial affairs of the temple of Karnak. The Chronicle of Osorkon at Karnak informs us that the temple of Amun possessed fields in the district of Hou (Caminos 1958, 126–7, 132–3), one of the termini of the ancient track from Thebes passing through the Wadi el-Hôl. In the Wadi el-Hôl we also have the graffito of a grain accounting scribe of Amun named May, apparently a man known from the reign of Thutmose III, and one may reasonably suggest that May was on his way to or from inspecting the grain of the domains of Amun at Hou. Much later the priest Nesmin was in charge of matters in Thebes and Hou (Haikal 1970, 13–6). From the Gebel Roma graffito, the priest Roma appears in fact to have been as diligent and personally involved with the affairs of Amun as he stresses in his autobiographical inscriptions.

Gebel Qarn el-Gir

This site contains another mass of material like that atop Gebel Roma. At Qarn el-Gir, there is further physical evidence of the transportation of grains for the temple of Amun at Karnak discussed above. Throughout the deposit, grain predominates in the botanical remains. There is a dearth of small objects like those found at the Gebel Roma debris mound.

In the light of the inscriptions from the Wadi el-Hôl and Gebel Roma, one may suggest an interpretation of the remains at Gebel Roma and Gebel Qarn el-Gir. The grain accounting scribe in the Wadi el-Hôl and the presence of Roma at Gebel Roma suggest the shipment of grain from the fields of Amun at Hou for the *ḥtp-nṯr* of Amun at Karnak. The presence of the chief of the scales of Amun in the Wadi el-Hôl also suggests the possibility that some weighing of grain may have taken place at some point or points along the road. Additionally, a grain accounting ostracon from Gebel Roma supports the image of accountants tracking grain shipments here, and perhaps in the Wadi el-Hôl. Some form of customs centre may have existed at Qarn el-Gir, the junction of the Theban route and the oasis roads, and at Gebel Roma/the Wadi el-Hôl, the back door of Thebes.

North of the caravan stop, at the very tip of the gebel, is another concentration of rock inscriptions, both Predynastic and pharaonic. The latter were of early Middle Kingdom date and included several names and titles as well as two longer compositions in vertical columns of text.

The debris mounds in the Wadi el-Hôl, atop Gebel Roma, and at Gebel Qarn el-Gir are features that set the Farshût Road apart from the other pharaonic tracks of the Theban Western Desert. On the basis of the stela of Menkheperre, which we discovered on Gebel Antef at the start of our desert explorations, we know that the Farshût Road was then known as the 'Road of Horses'. The graffito of a man on horseback in the Wadi el-Hôl (**Fig. 5**), and the signature of a late Nineteenth Dynasty stable overseer from the same location (**Fig. 7**), together with Twenty-First Dynasty stelae from the Farshût Road (**Fig. 3**), provide evidence for the use of the Farshût Road as a pony express postal route. This use would explain the large debris mounds that begin to accumulate during the Seventeenth Dynasty in the Wadi el-Hôl and at Gebel Qarn el-Gir, and would explain the enormous expansion of the Gebel Roma site at that time. However, the Gebel Roma deposit began during the Middle Kingdom, albeit modestly, with some increase in activity during the late Middle Kingdom. Messengers of various sorts frequented the road already by the time of the late Middle Kingdom (see below). The presence of debris mounds and the definite presence of special couriers distinguish the main Farshût Road. The earliest of the mounds, Gebel Roma, began to grow at the time of the presence of the late Middle Kingdom letter carriers, and expanded when mounted couriers began to travel the road. Other mounds then grew at points where mounts were changed.

The Alamat Tal Road

The northern of the two major pharaonic routes leading west out of the Thebaïd is the Alamat Tal Road, named for a toponym on Georg Schweinfurth's map of Western Thebes. This route joins the main Farshût Road at the Gebel Qarn el-Gir caravansary. The route was in use from Predynastic times through about 1000 BC, at which time–except for visits by random Coptic travellers–it fell out of use.

The Towers

The Theban terminus of the Alamat Tal Road was guarded by two towers. The structures were built of mud-brick (each brick approximately 8 × 15 × 32 cm in size) laid in headers. Each course of headers was stepped back along the outer edge of the wall to create a tapering mud-brick base. The structures were roughly circular, with the lower courses surrounded by stones. Such construction recalls certain features of the Second Cataract fortresses in Nubia (Borchardt 1923, 21, 32). The interiors reveal bricks occasionally intermingled with large stones; a form of construction suggestive of the rubble-filled brick chambers in the buildings at Deir el-Ballas (Lacovara 1997), and the much later and larger, though similar, Palace of Apries at Memphis (Kemp 1977).[13] These structures are round towers of a sort known early in Egypt (Badawy 1977, col. 194 and n. 4),[14] and surviving through the New Kingdom. The Alamat Tal towers, with diameters of *c.* 11 m, may have been larger than the besieged outposts depicted at Beni Hasan (Newberry 1893a, pl.14).

The inner masses of the two towers were laid at times in slightly overlapping courses of headers.[15] The internal headers rest on the bare gebel surface, but towards the outside the bricks lie atop a layer of mud plaster.[16] The sides of the square cores received added brick work in the form of a conical slice to give it its final form of a round base with sides sloping in to the top.[17] The exterior of the brick structures then received a coating of mud plaster and over this coating of the glacis are two layers of large desert boulders.[18]

The bricks frequently contain a considerable amount of late Middle Kingdom and Second Intermediate Period/early New Kingdom pottery fragments; there is every reason to believe that this pottery should date from about the time of the making of the bricks (D Darnell and J C Darnell 1996, 42, n. 16). The ancient gebel surface beneath the outer bricks of the southern tower yielded sherds of many periods, the latest being pieces of large Seventeenth Dynasty storage jars further supporting a Seventeenth Dynasty date for the surviving tower bases.

The mud plaster coating the brick structures and underlying the stone glacis is extremely hard, stronger and more difficult to cut through than the mud-bricks themselves. This coating contained a large proportion of limestone and flint, some of the latter of considerable size. These admixtures suggest a local source for the mud plaster. This source appears in fact to be an area of mud and broken mud-bricks to the northeast of the north tower, where the ancient builders reduced broken bricks to silt, and mixed this with eroded limestone from the gebel surface, with the inevitable stone inclusions. The inclusion of limestone powder with the alluvial mud made a strong mortar suitable for the outer layer of bricks.[19]

If these towers were constructed in a manner similar to the models cited above, they were entered by ladders giving access to second floors.[20] The tops probably had overhanging battlements of wood, perhaps with protective crenellations above, and murder holes (or machicolations) through the overhang. A stone glacis provided a modicum of protection from sappers. The superstructures have disappeared, and the erosion of wind and water, much in evidence on the surviving bricks, would account for much of this loss. The mining away of the bricks for reuse could easily account for the rest, possibly at an early date.[21]

Representations of such towers appear in the tomb of Mahu at Amarna, shown filled with the supplies and arms of the desert city's patrols (Davies 1906, pls 21 and 24). The closest parallel for the physical remains of these towers appears to be at Abkenissa, near Amara West in Nubia. A fortified structure there, with associated Middle Nubian and New Kingdom Egyptian remains, is located atop a hill, approximating in appearance and relative size the glacis of the Alamat Tal towers; on the hill is located 'une enceinte presque carré, aux angles arrondis, de 10m sur 9m'. (Vila 1977, 58–60). The enclosure is made of stone, the inside apparently formed of local soil. In the southwest quadrant of the enclosure is a triangular platform of stones, perhaps the base for a ladder to the top of a now lost superstructure.

The πύργοι-towers of the Hellenistic and Roman periods, standard features in farm-house complexes (Nowicka 1969, 100, fig. 69; 129–39), are the direct descendants of earlier fortification towers. At the time of the Napoleonic expedition into Egypt, such towers were still in use. In the *Description de l'Égypte* (État moderne vol. 1, 1822, pl. 74, no. 6) two 'tourelles contre les arabes' are shown. The towers are round, the height approximately 1.5 times the diameter of the base. Like the Old Kingdom towers they have external ladders entering the towers near the top and are surmounted by a battlement. Also, the two round towers in the *Description de l'Égypte* occur in pairs like the Alamat Tal towers. A pair of towers would be adequate to discourage small robber bands, and the presence of two would require an attacking

force to be large enough to attack both towers simultaneously.[22] The Alamat Tal towers may have been intended both as supply depots for Theban desert patrols and as sanctuaries for those escaping the bands of roving brigands (see Gardiner 1946, pl.6, ll.37–8). Descendants of the towers appear in a photograph of a poor tower-like house of mud, with storage in the bottom, a door in the middle giving access to a winter room, and an open top with a low wall for summer use (Lozach and Hug 1930, pl. 10, fig. 1).

In front of the northern tower is an area of loose bricks, whole and broken, thrown into place with no visible arrangement. The solid brick mass forms a wedge to the east of the northern tower, sloping up to the south. A number of rings of stones of two standard circumferences surround the wedge of brick. Depressions in the mud within these stone circles show significant cracks, the result of repeated wetting and drying. Storage jar sherds from within some of these rings, and the vast number of storage jar sherds from the area, reveal that the area east of the north tower had been a large *zir* (water jar) emplacement (**Fig. 8**), similar to such an area at Amarna (Hulin *et al.* 1984, 60–80). The stone rings supported pottery vessels of two basic sizes. As at Amarna, the mud-brick base, made up of rejected, broken and leftover bricks formed a surface that would absorb the water trickling from the jars, aiding in the evaporation cooling process. The ramp-like slope up from the north appears to have allowed for water-pot-laden donkeys to climb, and the contents of their burdens to be poured down into the large and small jars lining the ramp.

Gebel Tjauti

Where the Alamat Tal road ascends the plateau towards the northwest, there is a major concentration of rock inscriptions (**Plate 84**). We have called this area Gebel Tjauti after the Coptite nomarch whose road construction stela is one of the major inscriptions at the site (Darnell and Darnell 1997, 241–58; Darnell 1997, 101–8). Tjauti, the last Heracleopolitan nomarch of the Coptite nome, who governed from Qamûla, says in his rock inscription (**Fig. 9, Plate 85**):

i[r].n(=i) nn n-mrwt ḏ3.t ḫ[3s.t] tn ḥtm.t.n ḥk3 n k.t sp3.t [iw?] ᶜḥ3 [.n](=i) ḥnᶜ sp3.t[=f] ipзy(?) [...]p...

I have made this for crossing this gebel, which the ruler of another nome had sealed off. I fought with [his] nome. I flew(?) [...] ...

Tjauti has left us perhaps the only known pharaonic road construction text. He has also provided us with important information regarding the wars of unification at the end of the First Intermediate Period. Not only do we now know that Tjauti improved the road, but the inscription actually states that the road was made as a response to Theban aggression. The euphemistically termed 'ruler of another nome' is most likely the Theban nomarch Antef I, who also assumed the same title as Tjauti, 'Overseer of the Narrow Door of the Desert of Upper Egypt'. Tjauti, knowing that the Thebans could march directly on Abydos via the desert tracks, outflanking the Fifth, Sixth, and Seventh Upper Egyptian nomes, appears desperately to have sought to maintain a

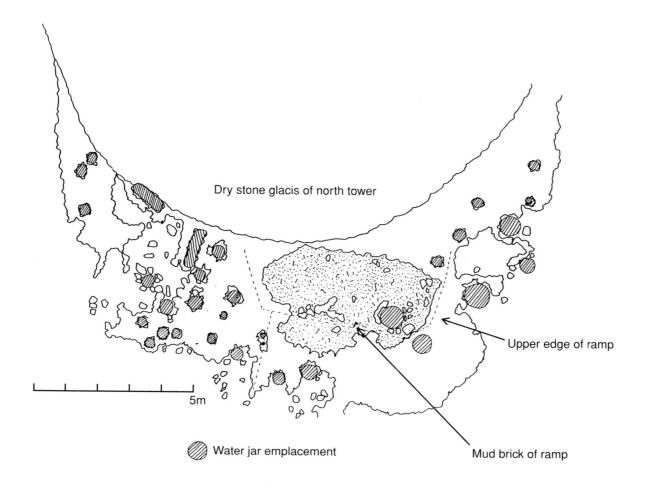

Fig. 8 Plan of *zir*-emplacements in front of the north tower on the Alamat Tal Road.

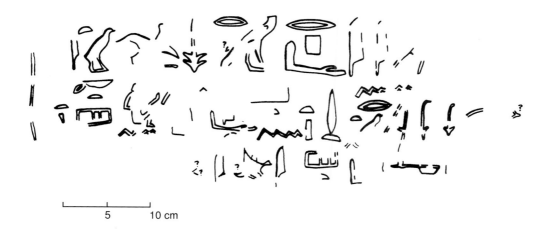

Fig. 9 The Tjauti road construction inscription.

10 cm

Fig. 10   Scorpion tableau from Gebel Tjauti.

direct desert link with the north. We know that Antef II, after an abortive attack on Thinis in the Eighth Upper Egyptian nome, attacked farther down the Nile, capturing the Tenth Upper Egyptian nome before returning to mop up resistance in the Thinite nome. The Gebel Tjauti inscription shows that this strategic use of the 'indirect approach' was no accident, but was part of Theban military policy during the Eleventh Dynasty.

The inscription of Tjauti also implies that the Coptite nome retained control of the desert routes, the 'narrow door of the desert of Upper Egypt', until the time of the early Eleventh Dynasty at Thebes. As was the case during the Old Kingdom, the Coptites administered the Upper Egyptian deserts, including apparently the routes leading out from Thebes.

One of the earliest and most imposing inscriptions at Gebel Tjauti is a tableau carved by a Naqada IId/IIIa ruler, labelled Horus Scorpion, possibly the owner of tomb U-j at Abydos. The scene (**Fig. 10**, **Plate 86**) possibly records the Abydene conquest of Naqada at the dawn of pharaonic history. The tableau incorporates both images and early

hieroglyphic groups, juxtaposing a stork with a serpent, symbolic of order over chaos, with a depiction of an armed man leading a bound captive on a rope. The figure of the ruler is perhaps identified by a falcon above his head, possibly the earliest attestation of the use of the Horus title without the serekh as a reference to the ruler. The Gebel Tjauti Protodynastic tableau is one of the earliest historical documents from ancient Egypt, a record of a military expedition at least as informative as the later Narmer palette. The tableau is a document of the unification of Upper Egypt, predating the palette of Narmer by at least a century (Friedman and Hendrickx 2002).

The serekhs and early kings' names at two other Alamat Tal Road sites show a close connection with names and serekhs known from the early tombs at Abydos. They support the implications of early cylinder seal art regarding an established iconography for Egyptian art at a very early date. This in turn encourages one to hope that we shall be able increasingly to understand and even read many Pre- and Protodynastic Egyptian representations and combinations of images. Correspondingly, the uniformity of late Predynastic utilitarian vessels, which we have been finding on the northernmost and southernmost routes under study, suggests that the politically independent areas of the Qena Bend were already economically integrated or at least interdependent prior to the First Dynasty.

The Gebel Tjauti tableau of Horus Scorpion appears to record the use of the Alamat Tal Road by an Abydene army to outflank the area of Naqada during the time of the initial unification of Egypt. This fits well with what the late First Intermediate Period graffiti from Gebel Tjauti tell us about the use of the same road by the Thebans to secure access to the area of Abydos. A red ink inscription of late Middle Kingdom/Second Intermediate Period date refers to the king travelling along the Alamat Tal Road on his way to Thebes. All of these inscriptions show important royal and military activity on the road over at least 1500 years, a remarkable continuity of use.

In addition to furthering our knowledge of Egyptian military history, the desert tracks and graffiti sites also enhance our understanding of religious practices. On a branch of the Alamat Tal/Gebel Tjauti Road with a marked late Predynastic-Early Dynastic ceramic presence, including Nubian A-Group pottery, we have discovered a concentration of well-built huts surrounded by sherds of Protodynastic vessels, and a Predynastic Egyptian campsite. At the latter site there are also a number of figural depictions, including two large crocodiles, paralleling several crocodiles at Gebel Tjauti, and two falcons on serekhs. The presence of drawings of crocodiles and fish at many of our graffiti sites suggests clear allusion to the Nile, and specifically–through the associations of the *tilapia* fish and the Sobek crocodile–to the inundation (cf. Kuentz 1929, 162–9). Stars at a number of these sites, and the actual record of the observation of the heliacal rising of Sothis in an inscription at Gebel Tjauti, suggest astronomical observations of the rising of the star Sothis, herald of the inundation, at a number of desert sites. These fit well with inscriptions from the Wadi el-Hôl and elsewhere referring to the worship of the goddess Hathor. These seemingly disparate inscriptions point to a widespread worship of the returning goddess of the eye of the sun, Hathor-Bastet as the star Sothis, returning atop the head of her father Re and signalling both the coming of the flood waters and the rejuvenation of the world (see J C Darnell 1997, 35–48).

Patrol Paths and Wadis immediately South of the Caravan Tracks

As part of our efforts to understand the use of the Alamat Tal Road and its hinterland, we examined a number of features immediately to the south of the caravan tracks. Associated with the towers is a system of criss-crossing swept paths on the middle desert south of the towers, apparently sentries' patrol paths of a sort known from the plateau behind the Valley of the Kings (Petrie 1909, 2), and from the high desert behind Amarna (Davies 1905, 5–6, pl. 1). These tracks controlled southern access to the caravan tracks and to the wadis on the north side of the Theban gebel promontory.

One of the patrol tracks leads up a slope about fifty

metres to a truly striking view of an unnamed wadi. At this site, which we named the 'Place of Horses', there are numerous depictions of Nubian soldiers (**Fig. 11**), grooms (**Fig. 12**), and plumed horses (**Fig. 13**). One even depicts a man on horseback – a rare pictorial example paralleled by a similar depiction in the Wadi el-Hôl. Additionally, writings of Amenhotep I and Thutmose III appear at this site. From the graffiti, it can be surmised that the 'Place of Horses' may have been a lookout post for a group of mounted Medjay patrolmen (for whom see Zivie 1985).

Northern Branches of the Alamat Tal Road

In a northern branch of the Wadi Maqar are two concentrations of rock inscriptions along the track connecting the region of Naqada with the Arqub el-Baghla ascent and the high desert plateau portion of the Alamat Tal Road. The main concentration of inscriptions consists of primarily Early Dynastic and Coptic graffiti near a large Protodynastic tableau incorporating images of boats with cabins and many crocodiles, some hoisted above the vessels on long poles. Over one boat is the image of a bull, a semi-hieroglyphic label occurring in a similar position in a petroglyph at Hierakonpolis (Berger 1982); in another vessel rides a large, Protodynastic Horus falcon. Along with a nearby depiction of a crocodile, across whose body are drawn a series of increasingly larger maces, this tableau appears to assert the power of a Horus king over the forces of chaos. Like the Horus Scorpion tableau from Gebel Tjauti, the Wadi Maqar North tableau appears to be annotated with several early hieroglyphic groups. At the Wadi Maqar North, Arqub el-Baghla, and Gebel Tjauti sites, large Protodynastic tableaux, executed at roughly the same time, express the triumph of order over chaos, and show the extension of the rule of the Horus king out along the routes into the Western Desert.

Not far away, near a high pinnacle of stone in the middle desert, is a concentration of New Kingdom graffiti. These include a number of semi-hieroglyphic images of Seth, Osiris, and Isis and Nephthys. The most elaborate image is a smiting scene, with the pharaoh in the Blue Crown brandishing his mace over the head of a long-haired and bearded foreigner.

Route Connecting the Farshût Road and the Alamat Tal Road

The Rock Inscription Site 'Dominion Behind Thebes'

At the southern terminus of an ancient track connecting the Farshût Road with the Alamat Tal Road, near the ascent to the main Farshût Road, we discovered an enormous concentration of rock inscriptions, stretching for a kilometre across the face of the gebel. Two inscriptions at the site have preserved that rarity, an ancient desert toponym (**Plate 87**): *Wȝs ḫȝ Wȝs.t*, 'Dominion[23] around/behind Thebes'.[24] This was the name of an outpost near the junction of the north-south route with the main Farshût Road, controlling access to the gebel behind Thebes at the final narrowing of the plateau before the high desert fans out towards el-Tarif and the Qurn. Gebel Roma and the Wadi el-Hôl probably made up

Fig. 11   Nubian soldiers from the 'Place of Horses'.

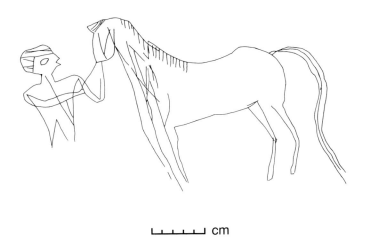

Fig. 12   Horse and groom from the 'Place of Horses'.

Fig. 13   Plumed horse and Hathor in a shrine on a sledge from the 'Place of Horses'.

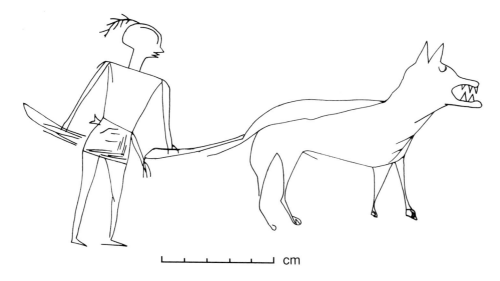

Fig. 14   Nubian with dog at 'Dominion behind Thebes'.

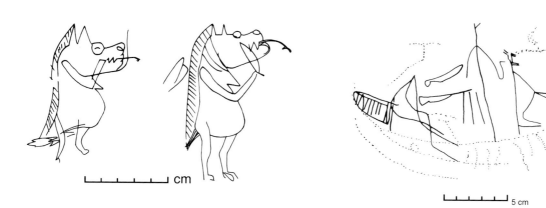

Fig. 15   Hippopotamus goddesses from 'Dominion behind Thebes'.

Fig. 16   The shrine depiction at 'Dominion behind Thebes'.

the Thebaïd's *r3-ʿ3 wr*, 'Great Desert Pass', but there were surely several smaller strong points, of which the 'Dominion Behind Thebes' track's ascent is one (for *r3-ʿ3 wr*, see Fischer 1960, fig. 1,1.1). According to Wahankh Antef I, Abydos and its strongholds are behind him (Clère and Vandier 1948, text 16)–thus behind Thebes–and they are at the northern Nile Valley terminus of the roads from the Thebaïd linked together by the 'Dominion Behind Thebes' track.

At 'Dominion Behind Thebes' we found the rock cut stela of an early Middle Kingdom Theban *imy-r i'3.w*, 'overseer of Nubian auxiliaries'. There is also an elaborate depiction of an Eleventh Dynasty/early Middle Kingdom Nubian and his growling patrol dog (**Fig. 14**). The man wears the uniform of Nubian soldiers of the First Intermediate Period: a feather in the hair, and a short kilt with sporran in front, the tie for which appears at the back (see Fischer 1961; Williams 1986, pls 34 and 38). The Nubian carries a bundle of arrows in the left hand; with the right hand he holds a bow and the leash of his dog (cf. Newberry 1893b, pl. 5).

At several sites behind Thebes, from near Gebel Tjauti in the north to *W3s ḫ3 W3s.t* in the south, there are Middle Kingdom depictions of hippopotamus goddesses, Rerit or Tawaret. Several appear at 'Dominion Behind Thebes' and two of these are particularly lively depictions (**Fig. 15**). These protective deities, at times wielding knives or torches, appear to represent the fiery power of the sun (see Gutbub 1961, 31–72; Verner 1969, 52–9). Their positions along the routes north and west of Thebes represent a hemispheric line of goddesses 'around behind' Thebes–a magical force field protecting the back door to Thebes, and the religious counterparts to the towers and patrols of the Alamat Tal Road and the Nubian soldiers.

'Dominion Behind Thebes' is home to an impressive array of Predynastic and Protodynastic graffiti, including many depictions of boats. There is also a tableau of strange hunters (**Fig. 17**), the most elaborately executed depiction thus far discovered of a type Winkler (1938, 26–8; 1939, 18) called the 'Eastern Invaders'. Two of the hunters wear depictions of facing hippopotami on their chests (**Plate 88**). The closest later parallels for these helmetted, feather-adorned, tail-wearing figures are the hunters on the Lion

Fig. 17   Hunters at 'Dominion behind Thebes'.

Hunt palette (Spencer 1980, 79, pl. 63), whom Helck (1987, 8) has identified as later representatives of Naqada II period leaders of _Ṯḥnw_, desert hunters sharing a common ancestry with the Nile dwelling Naqada II folk. Other cap-wearing figures appear on the Brooklyn palette fragment, on the Narmer palette, and the Scorpion mace head (Needler 1984, 332 and 334, fig. 266a). Leather caps are not infrequent in A-Group graves (Junker 1919, 38–9). For a close fitting cap adorned with feathers one may cite the actual cloth cap, extending down to the nape of the neck and over the cheeks to the jawbones, to which feathers have been attached with a resinous substance, from A-Group grave no. 601 near Abka (Bates and Dunham 1927, 8, no. 13, pl. 4, fig. 3 and pl. 57, fig 4).

These feather-wearing hunters share not only costumes with their Eastern Desert counterparts; both feather-wearing groups appear on the roads heading east and west out of the region of Naqada. An etched leather pouch in a burial containing Tasian pottery in the Wadi el-Hôl (see D Darnell this volume, **Fig. 4a**) provides stylistic evidence suggesting that the hunters may have been members of the 'Tasian' culture. All of this points to the 'Eastern Invaders' and their Western Desert manifestations here being representations of the desert folks who patrolled the caravan routes over which Naqada held sway. Their prowess and success in controlling traffic east and west out of Naqada may have prompted the Scorpion of the Gebel Tjauti tableau to launch the attack on Naqada commemorated in his desert victory inscription.

Of Archaic date is the representation of an Upper Egyptian shrine (**Fig. 16**), the forecourt occupied by a sacrificial

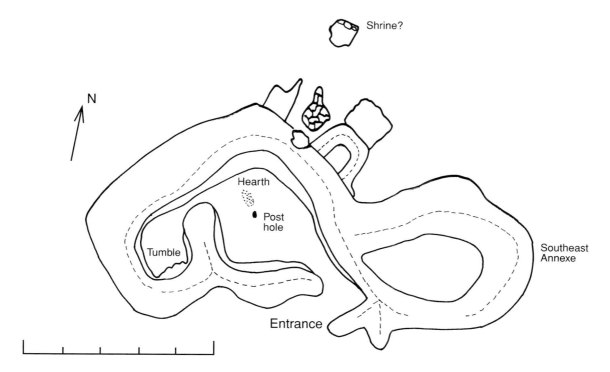

Fig. 18   Plan and elevations of the West Feature at Tundaba.

animal hanging from a forked pole, to the left of which is the representation of a flint knife above the sign for *nm.t*, 'slaughtering place'.[25] The ceremonial complex at Hierakonpolis locality HK29A appears to have consisted of a gateway, a mud-paved slaughtering place of roughly oval shape surrounded by a sinusoidal wall, a tall pole of some sort at the southern apex of the paved floor, and a *pr-wr* shrine (Friedman 1996). These elements appear to be present in our depiction, and the parallels are too striking to be coincidental.

The Routes between the Nile and Kharga Oasis

Tundaba

The site called Tundaba is in the middle portion of the desert between the northern Thebaïd and the northern part of Kharga Oasis, along the shortest route connecting the two areas. This site had been mentioned only briefly by two or three authors around the turn of the century (most fulsome being Beadnell 1909, 29). Several features of uncertain date had been noted, but no one ever contemplated the presence of pharaonic material. Only after our findings on the Theban desert routes could the possibility of the existence of early material near this site be recognised.

The main features at Tundaba are three dry-stone structures. The two larger features consist of a floor excavated several centimetres into the top of the natural outcroppings, with dry-stone walls approximately a half metre high built up around the sides of the cuttings. A shallow posthole in the West Feature (**Fig. 18**) suggests that the structures were at least partially roofed by tents, the wind break walls and

tent roofs corresponding to Roman military camp architecture in the east (Richmond 1962, 146).[26] The dry-stone structures at Tundaba are the first of pharaonic date found on the high plateau of the Western Desert. The combination of ceramic types in fabrics of both Nile Valley and oasis origin suggests that Tundaba marks the point of the utmost extent of Theban control of the desert to the west, as well as the easternmost extent of oasis administrative influence. For more on the ceramics at Tundaba see D Darnell this volume.

Within the East Feature we discovered a number of fragmentary mud seals, several preserving the impressions of stamps. The largest seal (**Fig. 20**) preserves part of a short inscription consisting of a man holding a round-topped shield, followed by the words *kз* and *dfзw*, 'food and provisions'. This appears to be a stamp indicating that the contents of the vessel it once capped were intended as military rations. Another stamp shows the god Bes and heads of a hippopotamus goddess (Taweret or Rerit) (**Fig. 19**). Several fragmentary seals show 'walking *wsr*-signs' (**Fig. 21**), a motif consistent with the Second Intermediate Period date of some of the pottery. The walking *wsr*-signs, aside from occurrences in late Old Kingdom hieratic and in certain Ramesside titularies, are common in the names of Hyksos rulers (Fischer 1977, 17 n. 156; 1996, 188) and one may suggest that the seals with the walking *wsr*-signs came from vessels shipped through Hyksos territories (see below for the possible implications of this).

To the north of the three structures is a roughly circular, sand-filled feature. Pottery lying atop debris from its initial construction include Second Intermediate Period/New Kingdom and later sherds, suggesting a pharaonic date for the feature. Modern references to this feature are few and

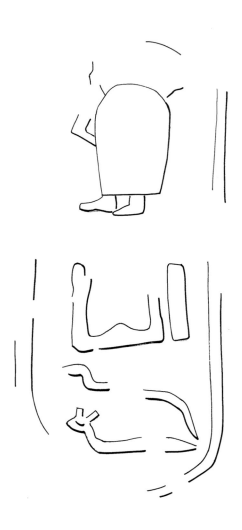

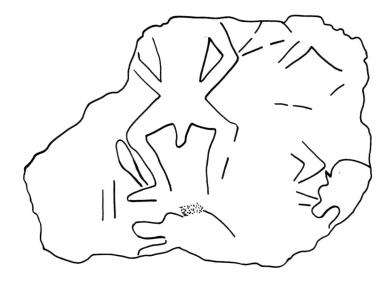

Fig. 19   Tawaret and Bes seal from Tundaba.

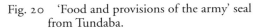

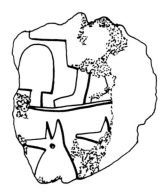

Fig. 20   'Food and provisions of the army' seal
from Tundaba.

Fig. 21   Walking *wsr*-sign seal from Tundaba.

brief, citing only the existence in this area of a 'deep shaft' of uncertain depth and date.

Clearance has revealed a remarkable pharaonic well of over 15 m in depth (**Fig. 22**). The amount of labour that went into its construction suggests that the pharaonic presence at Tundaba was neither transient nor ephemeral. Most likely the well or cistern at Tundaba was intended to provide a collection point and holding tank of sorts for the run-off rain water entering into the Tundaba depression from numerous surrounding wadis. The well appears in fact to be constructed at the edge of the lowest point within the depression and we encountered wet clay already at a depth of approximately 8 metres.

The well or cistern was excavated into a hard deposit of fossil alluvium, the soil remnants of a wetter Western Desert, aeons old. Beneath this alluvium the shaft passes through limestone rubble and boulders mixed with soil, then a layer of solid limestone, before passing again into a layer of mixed stone and clay. The upper edge of the well was partially built and levelled through the use of bricks made from the local silt. As flooring for the mouth of the well, the ancient build-

ers added atop the brick layers a harder layer of mixed clay, pebbles, and limestone powder, similar to the hardening shell of the mud-brick towers on the Alamat Tal Road. This feature of the well's construction fits the evidence for a Seventeenth to early Eighteenth Dynasty date for the structures nearby, and suggests that they functioned alongside it.

The upper area of the well, approximately 7 m in diameter, was accessed by one small and another longer set of stairs cut into the hardened soil, spiralling down the interior of the well for about 4 m (**Fig. 22**). Beneath the bottom step, footholds and handholds, some cut into the sides of the well, others protruding as stone ledges, provided access through a roughly square (1.5 m to the side), 9 m deep portion of the well to a ledge on the north and east sides, some 13 m beneath the mouth. The ledge gives access to a lower and more irregular shaft that leads toward the south and west. Parallel rope marks on the sides of the upper walls suggest that workmen standing on opposite sides of the well pulled together to haul up large containers of water from the bottom of the shaft.

The closest parallel to the Tundaba well is the *grand puit*,

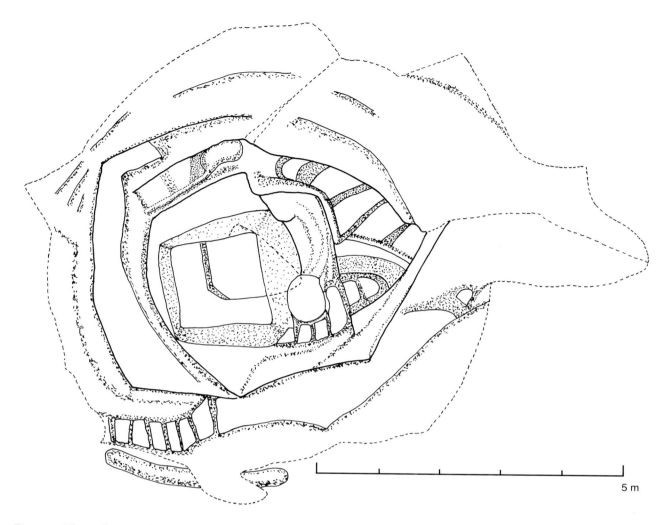

Fig. 22   The well at Tundaba.

a cistern at Deir el-Medina serving the New Kingdom community. The pottery in the area is overwhelmingly pharaonic, and many sherds were found atop the debris embankments left from the excavation of the well. Either those sherds were dropped on the embankment after the construction, or they were dumped there at some later date after a periodic clearance. In either case, their presence atop a debris pile shows that the Tundaba well is a Second Intermediate Period/New Kingdom construction.

These disparate bits of evidence indicate the presence of a Seventeenth Dynasty Theban outpost at Tundaba. Furthermore, the information gathered at Tundaba in conjunction with material of similar date found in Kharga Oasis itself and remains along Western Desert routes all indicate a greater importance of Kharga Oasis in pharaonic times than has previously been recognised.

The tracks from Tundaba appear to enter Kharga through the Yabsa and Boulaq Passes. The recent discovery by the Supreme Council of Antiquities of pharaonic cemeteries at Ain el-Askar at the base of Qarn el-Ginah, and near Hibis Temple, suggest a continuous use of these passes (Bahgat Ahmed and Magdi Hussein, pers. comm). For more details, see D Darnell this volume.

Bir Nakheila

Bir Nakheila, the northernmost of the small Nubian oases, was linked with Dungul Oasis, possibly Kurkur Oasis, and points south. It is important in relation to the overall network of pharaonic caravan routes that the Theban Desert Road Survey has been studying and documenting. Scholarly visits to Bir Nakheila were made by geographers in the early part of the last century and by Egyptologist Ahmed Fakhry nearly thirty years ago. The latter noted rock inscriptions, only two of which were posthumously published; no mention was made of ceramic or other archaeological remains at the site (Fakhry 1974, 216–7; Osing et al. 1982, 39–40, pl. 9, nos 47–8).

The major area of epigraphic interest at Bir Nakheila is atop a spur of the plateau that overlooks an area of palm trees. At this point we relocated the rock drawings and inscriptions described by Fakhry. These proved to be more extensive than his initial reconnaissance had suggested; there are hundreds of depictions on the exposed limestone at the top of the escarpment, stretching roughly from west to east, with a second, smaller concentration farther east. Most of the depictions are pecked, and certain of the motifs allow

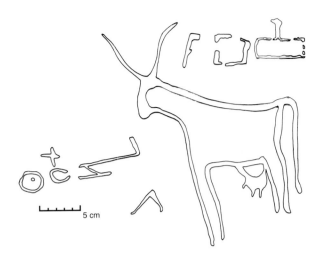

5 cm

Fig. 23   Hieratic inscription at Bir Nakheila.

one to suggest a date for the art. Depictions of hunters holding giraffes by ropes around their necks are part of a Predynastic Egyptian tradition that stretches from late Naqada I/early Naqada II down through the Narmer palette. Numerous examples of this motif in a more 'Nilotic' style occur at the site 'Dominion Behind Thebes', dating to the early to mid-Naqada II period.

Semi-hieratic late Old Kingdom/early Middle Kingdom inscriptions at Bir Nakheila list three men , and mention the 'good day of going back' (*ḥrw nfr ꜥn*) (**Fig. 23**). Unless it is a reference to the return of the goddess Hathor, this is probably a reference to a group Egyptians about to make the journey from Bir Nakheila back to the Nile, perhaps passing through Kurkur Oasis. The walking legs determining the word *ꜥn* have been reversed in order to face the distant Nile.

The Darb Rayayna and the Southern Roads

Between Thebes and the great Khor Battaghah a number of routes cross the Qena Bend. Inscriptions are less abundant along these southern routes, none of which appear to have been as important or heavily travelled during pharaonic antiquity as either the Farshût Road or the Alamat Tal Road.

One site deserving more than a brief mention in this overview is a dry-stone structure on the Darb Rayayna, on a hill near the juncture of that road with the Darb Rizeiqat. The structure is a truncated pyramidal shape, approximately 8.5 m on a side at the base, with a long narrow ramp leading up to the top on the east side. The structure is surrounded by several concentrations of pottery, the remains of large pithoi of late Naqada II date. In appearance it seems to foreshadow the earliest version of Userkaf's Abu Gurob solar altar (Ricke 1965, 4–5) and the later Amarna desert altars.

Coptic Remains

Space will not allow more than a brief mention of the numerous Coptic inscriptions, anchorite dwellings, and hermitages along a number of the desert roads. Many of the inscriptions are simple names and requests for prayer for one who considers himself a wretch. More interesting texts abound, however, including inscriptions in cryptography, announcements of the dates of the Lentin fast and Easter, and indications of the location of a number of toponyms previously unplaced on the map of Christian Egypt. This material belongs to an Egypt far different from that with which this publication is concerned, and a summary of the Coptic remains on the roads of the Theban Western Desert belongs elsewhere.

Conclusions

The physical makeup of the Qena Bend (**Fig. 2**) makes the region of ancient Thebes the southern goal of the routes across the desert filling that bend. Most of the high desert plateau is restricted to the southeastern half of the bend; this plateau is cut by many wadis, most of them running toward the northwest or southeast. The high-walled Khor Battaghah/Wadi Abu Madawi, beginning behind Rizeiqat and ending near Farshût, effectively severs the gebel filling the Qena Bend from the rest of the Western Desert plateau (see Schweinfurth 1901, 3–4). Gebels Qarn el-Gir and Sinn el-Gir, two arms of the escarpment extending toward the northwest in the middle of the Qena Bend, and the wadi system of the area together ensure that routes crossing the Qena Bend desert cannot travel directly east or west. The roads across the Qena Bend must in fact pass between Gebels Qarn el-Gir and Sinn el-Gir, avoiding the Khor Battaghah; the viable routes must therefore originate and terminate at or near ancient Thebes.[27] Thebes is thus the one area in the southern Qena Bend from which one may access the shortest route from the Nile to the oases of the Western Desert (Brugsch 1878, 4–10, pl. 1; Moritz 1900, 430; Paoletti 1900 476–8).[28] It is thereby also in the best position to control traffic between Nubia and the Thebaïd (see Posener 1952, 163–6). A track from Thebes also leads to Laqeita in the Eastern Desert (Cora 1891, facing 538), allowing access to the Wadi Hammamat Road as well (cf. Floyer 1891, 637–8).

In contrast to other centres in Upper Egypt, only the region of Thebes could exercise equally effective control of the Western and Eastern Deserts.

This brief and geographically organized gazetteer of sites and remains has, of necessity, omitted many more sites than it contains. This wealth of interesting, but seemingly disparate bits of information is, however, more integrated than it may first appear.

The region of the Qena Bend, although somewhat less than agriculturally rich in comparison to much of Middle and Lower Egypt, is exceptionally well positioned to control the routes leading into the Eastern and Western Deserts. The shortest route between the Upper Egyptian Nile and both the Red Sea and Kharga Oasis converge on the Bend, creating a desert travelling economy possibly based on long distance trade. The Qena Bend is a region that has long interacted with the deserts through which the Nile flows. In the remains of all periods on the desert routes of the Western Thebaïd we can see the mechanics and results of the interactions of the Nilotes and the desert dwellers. At 'Dominion behind Thebes' and in the Wadi el-Hôl as well as at several other sites, we may glimpse some of these desert dwellers.

The early feather-wearing desert folk were perhaps the associates of the Predynastic rulers of Naqada, who patrolled the roads on which the economy of Naqada was almost certainly based. With the Scorpion Tableau at Gebel Tjauti we may see the conquest of this region by the incipient Dynasty 0, possibly at the hands of one Horus Scorpion. One may now suggest that Naqada's desert traffic, sitting astride the north-south routes linking Hierakonpolis and Abydos, was in the end her undoing. In Naqada's desert commerce, her desert allies, and perhaps her attempts to control traffic in the area between Hierakonpolis and Abydos, we may have both the reason for Scorpion's aggressions, and the origin of the ancient enmity between Horus, old god of Hierakonpolis and patron of the nascent pharaohs of Abydos, and Seth, strange god of deserts and confusion.

With the collapse of the Old Kingdom and the rise of the pugnacious nomarchs of the Head of the South, we see a similar use of the desert roads of the west. Just as Naqada, old power of the Qena Bend, controlled the desert roads and ultimately fell because of it, so geography and the political events of the First Intermediate Period determined the future glory of Thebes. When the Theban nomarch Antef wrested control of the Western Desert from the Coptite Tjauti, ally of the Heracleopolitans, the fall of the Fifth, Sixth, Seventh and Eighth nomes of Upper Egypt was inevitable, and the future triumph of Mentuhotep II virtually assured.

During the Middle Kingdom, police and military patrols travelled the roads of the western Thebaïd, leaving both rock inscriptions and the physical remains of their bivouacs and mess kits. We have considerable evidence for the existence of perambulating border patrols, a network of roads and small outposts, ultimately linking major bases on the Egyptian Nile with the forward bases of this network at the Second Cataract.

With the collapse of the Thirteenth Dynasty and the loss of the north to the Hyksos, the remaining powers fell back on Thebes. The vestigial late Middle Kingdom state based at Thebes logically turned to consolidating its control of the deserts. Along with asserting its control over the Wadi Hammamat, it established a base in the Wadi el-Hôl. From here she could protect the desert door to the rear of Thebes, and maintain a link with forward bases at Abydos. The Alamat Tal towers demonstrate the strengthening of routes already routinely patrolled and more lightly fortified during the Middle Kingdom. Thebes also established a major outpost midway between the Nile and Kharga. Our discoveries at the latter site provide physical proof of the Theban control of the Western Desert long known from Kamose's capture of the unsuccessful Hyksos messenger to Kerma.

Not only did Theban control stretch across potential routes of communication between the Hyksos and Kerma, it also touched on the major north-south trade routes of northeastern Africa. Both Kerma and the Hyksos realm may be characterised as trade empires. Both needed trade in order to survive; because of Thebes' control of the deserts, and particularly the Western Desert, both appear also to have needed Thebes. Through reliance on Theban control of trade in the Upper Egyptian deserts, both Kerma and the Hyksos may have unwittingly financed their own destruction.

During the New Kingdom, as we know from the Wadi el-Hôl and the 'Place of Horses', mounted patrols and messengers travelled the routes of the Theban Western Desert. The enormous debris mounds of the New Kingdom caravansaries such as those at Gebel Roma and Gebel Qarn el-Gir provide physical evidence complementing the epigraphic information in the Wadi el-Hôl for the transport of grain shipments along the Farshût Road. Following the internal strife that marked the end of the Ramesside period, the high priest-king Menkheperre reasserted Upper Egypt's control of the desert hinterlands, erecting a series of stelae on the Farshût Road and providing us with the ancient name of that route, the 'Road of Horses'.

A number of sites on various roads show a religious significance. The Farshût Road connects among other things the cities of Thebes and Abydos. Remains at Gebel Antef, including small shrines apparently dedicated to Abydene Osiris, suggest that Gebel Antef was viewed as an extension of the Abydene holy land. Inscriptions and depictions in the Wadi el-Hôl and at Gebel Tjauti (to name but the most significant) attest to the worship of the goddess Hathor on the roads of the Western Desert.

There is not sufficient space to discuss the material of later date we have discovered in the Theban Western Desert, but this is not to minimize the interest of what comes after the end of the New Kingdom. Major trade continues well into the Coptic period, and there is a proliferation of new routes. Other roads essentially abandoned after the Predynastic period in favour of the concentration of activity on a few major roads—a feature of the Middle Kingdom and New Kingdom—see a renewed traffic during the Graeco-Roman and Coptic periods. At some point, however, the desert shrines fell out of use, and the chants of monks and the murmured prayers of lone anchorites replaced the hymns sung to Hathor. This belongs to a world far removed from earlier days when the wadis of the Western Desert echoed with clashing weapons of young states.

The Theban Desert Road Survey has discovered ample evidence that Thebes well understood and exploited the benefits of her location. The Protodynastic tableau of a Horus Scorpion, the First Intermediate Period inscription of Tjauti, the evidence for Seventeenth Dynasty activity and the abundance of ceramic remains of southern and western origin – all these reveal that the ancient Egyptians, and particularly the dwellers along the Qena Bend, well understood the importance of the Western Desert and moved freely and often within that now so inhospitable but beautiful terrain.

Notes

1. The permanent staff of the expedition consists of John Darnell, director, and Deborah Darnell, co-director. Numerous people have assisted in the work over the years, and many continue to do so. They have been acknowledged in works already published, as well as those in press and in progress.

2. Possible C-Group cattle herds are attested at Meir during the Middle Kingdom. Compare Blackman (1914, pls 9 and 10) and Blackman (1915, pls 3, 6, and 11) with the remarks of Williams (1983, 98–9 [and n. 6], 116–7, and pls. 104–5). For Nubians at Gebelein see Hodjash and Berlev 1982, 86–9 (no. 40).

3. Either the great Eighteenth Dynasty ruler Thutmose III or the high priest of the Twenty-First Dynasty. Although Menkheperre, son of Panedjem, did not consistently employ a cartouche (Kitchen 1986, 51–2, 262), his use of kingly titles and attributes is sporadic, evincing increasing claim to royal status (see Jansen-Winkeln 1992, 35–6), and his name does occur in a cartouche on occasion: El-Hibeh (Gauthier 1914, 268, nos 18 and 19); Gebelein (Gauthier 1914, 267, no. 15; Weigall 1910, 298); and Karnak (Roeder 1924, 390, no. 15725). The Kôm es-Sheikh Mubarek fortress bricks appear to preserve Menkheperre's name in ovals only (see Spencer 1979, pl. 34, *contra* Gauthier 1914, 268, no. 17). According to Wainwright (1927, 76–7), the Shurafa bricks bear the name of Menkheperre in ovals but not true cartouches. See also the brick with the title and name of Menkheperre in cartouches in Sliwa 1992, 23–6. The *Königsring* does not need the closing horizontal tie in order to be a true cartouche (cf. Kaplony 1980, col. 612; Ricke 1939, 34–5).

4. One may raise a number of things, including troops – *ts dšmw*, (*Wb* V 523, 17; Smith 1987, 88–9 [note to col. V, l. 18]). The verb *tsi* can also describe a trip into a foreign land (*Wb* V 406, 21–2), a journey which required climbing up out of the Nile Valley onto the gebel of the surrounding desert. A desert journey is *tsi hsi*, 'going up and going down' (*Kuban Stela*, l. 11; see also Gardiner 1911, 31, ll. 6–7), and referring to climbing the gebel at the outset of the trip and descending to the desired place, see Schott 1961, 142 (§B.6) n. 9. Such a meaning for *tsi* would suit the high plateau location of the stela.

5. Compare 'Amun-of-the-Way' (*Wenamun* 2, 55), and 'Amun Lord of the Ways' at Wadi es-Seboua (Habachi 1960, 52; see also De Meulenaere 1977, 245–51; Jasnow 1984, 91–3). Sakhmet also appears as *nb.t ws.t*, 'lady of the road' (Gauthier 1920, 187, no. 21), and there is an Atum of the road (Spiegelberg 1906, pl. 107 = P. Cairo 31168 A recto col. 2, l. x+7).

6. For *mi.t* as 'teaching', see Ritner 1986, 244 and n. 5.

7. The mule is hardier than a horse in carrying loads all day, see Dixon and Southern 1992, 234–8.

8. For mounted Nubian troops and cavalry in Egypt, see Zivie 1985, 379–88; Morkot, 1995, 237–8; Schulman 1957, 266 and n. 23; Gubel 1991, 281, 285 (no. 367). The love poem P. Chester Beatty I, Group B, no. 38, mentions 'horses at rest stations' (*ssm.wt n=f hr htp.t*) awaiting a royal messenger, see Fox 1985, 399, l. 9).

9. This photographic documentation was made possible by grants from the American and Swiss branches of the Michela Schiff-Giorgini Foundation.

10. For the Hathoric overtones of 'holiday', see Husson 1977, 222 n. 14; Kessler 1988, 171–96.

11. Compare the name of the census house in Zaba 1974, 151, no. 135.

12. On the *sin.w* see Posener 1987, 41–2. On his stela from Naqada, the messenger *Fgw* states *ink kn mm kn.w sin mm sin(.w)*, 'I was the bravest of the brave, the swiftest of the swift' (Spiegelberg and Pörtner 1902, no. 14). Fegu may have used the Alamat Tal Road.

13. For a text describing brick architecture with spaces for debris filling, see Fischer-Elfert 1986, 121–32. On rubble-fill see also Simpson 1963, 53 and 73–4.

14. Badawy (1977, 48), suggests that such 'independent towers' guarded 'the boundaries and desert roads'.

15. Compare the brick construction in Saleh 1981, 54 and pl. 48A. For stone blocks so arranged see Reisner 1917, 220.

16. For the use of a mud plaster base and headers, note that Spencer (1979, 128–9) describes these features as typical of 'solid brick construction in mastabas and pyramids'. J Jacquet (pers. comm.) suggests that the mud foundation would be necessary on the rubble hills in order to guard against bricks breaking over stones.

17. For bricks laid in order to give a rounded shape to a portion of a structure, compare Williams 1993, 168, fig. 103.

18. A parallel for the construction of the Alamat Tal towers is the east tower of the north gate of the fortress of Semna, but compare also Kumma; Reisner, Dunham, and Janssen 1960, 6 and pl. 5 C; 114. Compare also Emery, Smith and Millard 1979, 37, fig. 22, section A–A. Certain walls at Buhen are built atop a solid stonework base with glacis.

19. A similar mud mixing area was located along the slipway near the fortress of Mirgissa, see Vercoutter 1970, 214–6.

20. Compare The Prophecy of Neferti §33 (Helck 1992) mentioning a *hnr.t* fort and the scaling of an access ladder.

21. Compare the statement in the harper's song in the tomb of Djehutyemheb (TT194) that 'not a brick' of the house of the deceased is left (Wente 1962, 123–4, note f; pl. 16) and Sarenput I regarding the sanctuary of Heqaib on Elephantine (Franke 1994, 154–155, ll. x+5–x+6, and x+8).

22. Compare passage VIIf in the Prophecy of Neferti (Helck 1992, 30): a *hnr.t*-fortification with another to the side (*ky r gs*).

23. An abutted composite, on which see Fischer 1977, 5–19.

24. The feather of *Wss.t* is vestigial, compare James 1962, XI B 4; abbreviated without feather in Simpson 1965, 45 (no. 11).

25. This sign appears as early as the reign of Qa'a, see Kahl 1994, 903. One of the lines could represent blood, the other two forming the slaughtering block, compare Verner 1986, 185–6.

26. The tents may have been of cloth (cf. Helck 1970, 97, XVIe, 98–9) or of leather, see Forbes 1957, 31.

27. Most ancient routes crossing the desert filling the Qena Bend originate between Rizeiqat/Armant in the south and Naqada in the north; the most heavily used pharaonic tracks leave the valley between Malkata in the south and Qamûla in the north.

28. A journey from Luxor to Kharga is shorter than a trip from

Rizeiqat/Armant to Baris (southern Kharga); the road remains near the Nile as it crosses the Qena Bend, and it has a much shorter por-

tion of its length atop the exposed desert.

Bibliography

Badawy A, 1954. *A History of Egyptian Architecture Vol. I. From the Earliest Times to the End of the Old Kingdom.* Cairo.

Badawy A, 1977. Festungsanlage. In W Helck and W Westendorf (eds), *Lexikon der Ägyptologie* 2. Wiesbaden: 194–203.

Bates O and Dunham D, 1927. Excavations at Gammai. In E A Hooton and N I Bates (eds), *Harvard African Studies* 8, *Varia Africana* 4. Harvard: 1–121.

Beadnell H J Ll, 1909. *An Egyptian Oasis.* London.

Berger M, 1982. The Petroglyphs at Locality 61. In M A Hoffman (ed.), *The Predynastic of Hierakonpolis.* Cairo and Illinois: 61–5.

Blackman A M, 1914. *The Rock Tombs of Meir* 1. Archaeological Survey of Egypt 22. London.

Blackman A M, 1915. *The Rock Tombs of Meir* 2. Archaeological Survey of Egypt 23. London.

Borchardt L, 1923. *Altägyptische Festungen an der zweiten Nilschwelle.* Veröffentlichungen der Ernst von Sieglin-Expedition in Ägypten 3. Leipzig.

Brugsch H, 1878. *Reise nach der grossen Oase El Khargeh in der libyschen Wüste.* Leipzig.

Caminos R A, 1958. *The Chronicle of Prince Osorkon.* Analecta Orientalia 37. Rome.

Caminos R A, 1963. Papyrus Berlin 10463. *Journal of Egyptian Archaeology* 49: 29–37.

Clére J and Vandier J, 1948. *Textes de la première période intermédiaire et de la XIéme dynastie.* Bibliotheca Aegyptiaca 10. Brussels.

Collombert P, 1995. Hout-Sekhem et le septième nome de Haute-Égypte I: la divine Oudjarenes. *Revue d'Egyptologie* 46: 55–79.

Cora G, 1891. La Route de Kéneh à Bérénice levée en 1873 par le Colonel R E Colston. *Bulletin de Société khédiviale de Géographie.* 3rd. ser., no. 7: 533–38.

Darnell D and Darnell J C, 1996. The Luxor-Farshût Desert Road Survey. *Bulletin de liaison du Groupe international d'étude de la céramique* 19: 36–50.

Darnell J C, 1997. A New Middle Egyptian Literary Text from the Wadi el-Hôl. *Journal of the American Research Center in Egypt* 34: 85–100.

Darnell J C, 1997. The Message of King Wahankh Antef II to Khety, Ruler of Heracleopolis. *Zeitschrift für Ägyptische Sprache und Altertumskunde* 124: 101–8

Darnell J C, 1997. The Apotropaic Goddess in the Eye. *Studien zur Altägyptischen Kultur* 24: 25–48.

Darnell J C 2002. *Theban Desert Road Survey in the Egyptian Western Desert* I: *Gebel Tjauti Rock Inscriptions 1–45 and Wadi el-Hôl Rock Inscriptions 1–45.* Oriental Institute Publication 119. Chicago.

Darnell J C and Darnell D, 1993. The Luxor-Farshût Desert Road Survey. *The Oriental Institute Annual Report (1992–93).* Chicago: 48–55.

Darnell J C and Darnell D, 1994. The Luxor-Farshût Desert Road Survey. *The Oriental Institute Annual Report (1993–94).* Chicago: 40–8.

Darnell J C and Darnell D, 1995. The Luxor-Farshût Desert Road Survey. *The Oriental Institute Annual Report (1994–95).* Chicago: 44–54.

Darnell J C and Darnell D, 1996. The Luxor-Farshût Desert Road Survey. *The Oriental Institute Annual Report (1995–96).* Chicago: 58–66.

Darnell J C and Darnell D, 1997. The Luxor-Farshût Desert Road Survey. *The Oriental Institute Annual Report (1996–97).* Chicago: 66–76.

Darnell J C and Darnell D, 1997 New Inscriptions of the Late First Intermediate Period from the Theban Western Desert, and the Beginnings of the Northern Expansion of the Eleventh Dynasty. *Journal of Near Eastern Studies* 56/4: 241–58.

Darnell J C and Darnell D, 1998. The Luxor-Farshût Desert Road Survey. *The Oriental Institute Annual Report (1997–1998).* Chicago: 77–92.

Description de l'Égypte, 1822. *État moderne* vol. 1. 2nd ed. Paris.

Davies N deG, 1905. *The Rock Tombs of El Amarna* 2. Archaeological Survey of Egypt 14. London.

Davies N deG, 1906. *The Rock Tombs of El-Amarna* 4. Archaeological Survey of Egypt 16. London.

Dixon K R and Southern P, 1992. *The Roman Cavalry from the First to the Third Century AD.* London.

Emery W B, Smith H S and Millard A, 1979. *The Fortress of Buhen Archaeological Report.* Egyptian Exploration Fund Memoir 49. London.

Fakhry A, 1974. The Search for Texts in the Western Desert. In *Textes et Languages de l'Egypte pharaonique. Hommage a Jean-François Champollion a l'occasion du cent-ciquantieme anniversaire du dechiffrement des hieroglyphes (1822–1972).* Bibliothèque d'Étude 64/2. Cairo: 207–22.

Fischer H G, 1960. The Inscription of *In-it.f,* Born of *Tfi. Journal of Near Eastern Studies* 19: 258–68.

Fischer H G, 1961. The Nubian Mercenaries of Gebelein during the First Intermediate Period. *Kush* 9: 44–80.

Fischer H G, 1977. The Evolution of Composite Hieroglyphs in Ancient Egypt. *Metropolitan Museum Journal* 12: 5–19.

Fischer H G, 1991. Sur les routes de l'Ancien Empire. *Cahier de Recherches de l'Institut de Papyrologie et d'Égyptologie de Lille* 13: 59–64.

Fischer H G, 1996. *Egyptian Studies* 3, *Varia Nova.* New York.

Fischer-Elfert H-W, 1986. *Der satirische Streitschrift des Papyrus Anastasi I.* Ägyptologische Abhandlungen. 44. Wiesbaden.

Floyer E A, 1891. Note sur les Sidoniens et les Erembes d'Homère. *Bulletin de la Société khédiviale de Géographie* 3rd ser., no. 7: 629–43.

Forbes R J, 1957. *Studies in Ancient Technology* 5. Leiden.

Fox M V, 1985. *The Song of Songs and the Ancient Egyptian Love Songs.* Madison.

Franke D, 1994. *Das Heiligtum des Heqaib auf Elephantine.* Studien zur Archäologie und Geschichte Altägyptens 9. Heidelberg.

Friedman R, 1996. The Ceremonial Centre at Hierakonpolis Locality HK29A. In J Spencer (ed.), *Aspects of Early Egypt.* London: 16–35.

Friedman R and Hendrickx S 2002. Protodynastic Tableau (Gr. No. 1). In J C Darnell 2002: 10–18.

Gardiner A H, 1946. Davies's Copy of the Great Speos Artemidos Inscription. *Journal of Egyptian Archaeology* 32: 43–56.

Gardiner A H, 1911. *Egyptian Hieratic Texts, Series I: Literary Texts of the New Kingdom, Part I: The Papyrus Anastasi I and the Papyrus Koller, Together with the Parallel Texts.* Leipzig.

Gauthier H, 1920. Les Statues thébaines de la déesse Sakhmet. *Annales du Service des Antiquités de l'Égypte* 19: 177–207.

Gauthier H, 1914. *Livre des rois* 3. Memoires de l'Institut français d'archéologie orientale 19. Cairo.

Gubel E, 1991. No. 367. Deux Nubiens a Cheval. In *Van Nijl tot Schelde/Du Nil a l'Escaut*. Exhibition Catalogue. Brussels: 285.

Gutbub A, 1961. Un Emprunt aux textes des pyramids dans l'hymne à Hathor, dame de l'ivresse. In *Melanges Maspero I: orient ancien*. 4th fascicle. Memoires de l'Institut français d'archéologie orientale, Cairo: 31–72.

Habachi L, 1960. Five Stelae from the Temple of Amenophis III at Es-Sebua' now in the Aswan Museum. *Kush* 8: 45–52.

Haikal F M H, 1970. *Two Hieratic Funerary Papyri of Nesmin*. Bibliotheca Aegyptiaca 14, Brussels.

Helck W, 1970. *Die Lehre des Dwȝ-Ḫty*. Kleine Ägyptische Texte 3/2. Wiesbaden.

Helck W, 1987. *Untersuchungen zur Thinitenzeit*. Ägyptologische Abhandlungen 45. Wiesbaden.

Helck W, 1992. *Die Prophezeiung des Nfr.tj*. Kleine Ägyptische Texte 2. Wiesbaden.

Hintze F, 1960. Eine neue Inschrift vom 19. Jahre König Taharqas. *Mitteilungen des Instituts für Orientforschung* 7: 330–3.

Hodjash S and Berlev O, 1982. *The Egyptian Reliefs and Stelae in the Pushkin Museum of Fine Arts, Moscow*. St. Petersburg.

Hulin L *et al.* 1984. Report on the 1983 Excavations Commodity Delivery Area (Zir-Area). In B Kemp (ed.), *Amarna Reports* 1: 60–80.

Husson C, 1977. *L'offrande du miroir dans les temples égyptiens de l'époque gréco-romaine*. Lyon.

James T G H, 1962. *The Hekanakhte Papers and other Early Middle Kingdom Documents*. The Metropolitan Museum of Art Egyptian Expedition. New York.

Jansen-Winkeln K, 1992. Das Ende des Neuen Reiches. *Zeitschrift für Ägyptische Sprache und Altertumskunde* 119: 22–37.

Jasnow R, 1984. Demotic Graffiti from Western Thebes. In H J Thissen and K T Zauzich (eds), *Grammata Demotika: Festschrift für Erich Lüddeckens*. Würzburg: 87–105.

Junker H, 1919. *Bericht über die Grabungen der Akademie der Wissenschaften in Wien auf den Friedhöfen von El-Kubanieh-Süd, Winter 1910–1911*. Akademie der Wissenschaften in Wien, philosophisch-historische Klasse Denkschriften 62.3. Vienna.

Kahl J, 1994. *Das System der ägyptischen Hieroglyphenschrift in der 0.–3. Dynastie*. Gottinger Orientforschungen IV/29. Wiesbaden.

Kaplony P, 1980. Königsring. In W Helck and W Westendorf (eds), *Lexikon der Ägyptologie* 3. Wiesbaden: 610–26.

Kemp B J, 1977. The Palace of Apries at Memphis. *Mitteilungen des Deutschen Archäologischen Instituts Abteilung Kairo* 33: 101–8.

Kessler D, 1988. Der satirisch-erotische Papyrus Turin 55001 und das Verbringen des schönen Tages. *Studien zur Altägyptischen Kultur* 15: 171–96.

Kitchen K A, 1986. *The Third Intermediate Period in Egypt (1100–650 BC)*. 2nd rev. ed. Warminster.

Kuentz C, 1929. Sur un passage de la stèle du Naukratis: la lecture du signe ⌷. *Bulletin de l'institut français d'archéologie orientale* 28: 103–6.

Lacovara P, 1990. *Deir el Ballas. Preliminary Report on the Deir el-Ballas Expedition, 1980–1986*. American Research Center in Egypt Reports 12. Winona Lake.

Lacovara P, 1997. *The New Kingdom Royal City*. London.

Lozach J and Hug G, 1930. *L'Habitat rural en Égypte*. Cairo.

Martin G T, 1989. *The Memphite Tomb of Horemheb Commander-in-Chief of Tut'ankhamun 1 The Reliefs, Inscriptions, and Commentary*. Egypt Exploration Society Excavation Memoir 55. London.

de Meulenaere H, 1977. Derechef Arensnouphis. *Chronique d'Égypte* 52(104): 245–51.

Moritz B, 1900. Excursion aux oasis du désert libyque. *Bulletin de la Société khédiviale de Géographie*, 5th ser. no. 8: 429–75.

Morkot R, 1995. The Foundations of the Kushite State: a Response to the László Török. *Cahier de Recherches de l'Institut de Papyrologie et d'Égyptologie de Lille* 17: 229–42.

Müller D, 1961. Der gute Hirte, ein Beitrag zur Geschichte ägyptischer Bildrede. *Zeitschrift für Ägyptische Sprache und Altertumskunde* 86: 126–44.

Needler W, 1984. *Predynastic and Archaic Egypt in the Brooklyn Museum*. Wilbour Monographs 9. Brooklyn.

Newberry P E, 1893a. *Beni Hasan I*. Archaeological Survey of Egypt 1. London.

Newberry P E, 1893b. *Beni Hasan 2*. Archaeological Survey of Egypt 2. London.

Nowicka M, 1969. *La maison privée dans l'Égypte ptolémaïque*. Bibliotheca Antiqua 9. Warsaw.

Osing J, Moursi M, Arnold Do, Neugebauer O, Parker P A, Pingree D and Nur el-Din M A, 1982. *Denkmäler der Oase Dachla aus dem Nachlass von Ahmed Fakhry*. Archäologische Veröffentlichungen, Deutsches Archäologisches Institut Abteilung Kairo 28. Mainz am Rhein.

Paoletti H, 1900. Route de Ghirgheh à Khargheh. *Bulletin de la Société Khédiviale de Géographie*, 5th ser. no. 8: 476–78.

Petrie W M F, 1907. *Gizeh and Rifeh*. British School of Archaeology in Egypt 13. London.

Petrie W M F, 1909. *Qurneh*. British School of Archaeology in Egypt 16. London.

Posener G, 1952. A propos des graffiti d'Abisko. *Archiv Orientální* 20: 163–6.

Posener G, 1987. *Cinq figurines d'envoûtement*. Bibliothèque d'Étude 101. Cairo.

Quirke S, 1990. *The Administration of Egypt in the Late Middle Kingdom, the Hieratic Documents*. New Malden.

Reisner G A, 1917. The Barkal Temples in 1916. *Journal of Egyptian Archaeology* 4: 213–27.

Reisner GA, Dunham D and Janssen J M A, 1960. *Semna Kumma*. Second Cataract Forts 1. Boston.

Richmond I A, 1962. The Roman Siege Works of Masada, Israel. *Journal of Roman Studies* 52: 142–55.

Ricke H, 1939. *Der Totentempel Thutmoses III*. Beiträge zur ägyptischen Bauforschung und Altertumskunde 3. Cairo.

Ricke H, 1965. *Das Sonnenheiligtum des Konigs Userkaf. Volume I, Der Bau*. Beiträge zur ägyptischen Bauforschung und Altertumskunde 7. Cairo.

Ritner R, 1986. Review of M. Lichtheim, *Ancient Egyptian Literature: a Book of Readings* vol. 3. *Journal of Near Eastern Studies* 45: 243–4.

Roeder G, 1924. *Aegyptische Inschriften aus den staatlichen Museen zu Berlin. Vol. 2, Inschriften des Neuen Reichs*. Leipzig.

el-Saghir M, 1992. *Das Statuenversteck im Luxortempel*. Deutschen Archäologischen Instituts Abteilung Kairo Sonderschrift 26. Mainz.

Saleh A A, 1981. *Excavations a Heliopolis* 2. Cairo.

Scharff A, 1922. Ein Rechnungsbuch des königlichen Hofes aus der 13. Dynastie (Pap. Boulaq nr. 18). *Zeitschrift für Ägyptische Sprache und Altertumskunde* 57: 51–68 and 1**–24**.

Schott S, 1961. *Kanais, der Tempel Sethos. I im Wadi Mia*. Göttingen.

Schulman A R, 1957. Egyptian Representations of Horsemen and Riding in the New Kingdom. *Journal of Near Eastern Studies* 16: 263–71.

Schweinfurth G, 1901. Am westlichen Rande des Nilthals zwischen Farschût und Kom Ombo. In Dr A Petermanns, *Mitteilungen aus Justus Perthes' geographischer Anstalt* 47: 1–10.

Simpson W K, 1963. *Papyrus Reisner I*. Boston.

Simpson W K, 1965. *Papyrus Reisner II*. Boston.

Skeat T C, 1964. *Papyri from Panopolis*. Chester Beatty Monographs 10. Dublin.

Sliwa J, 1992. An Unpublished Stamped Brick of Menkheperre, High Priest of Amun. *Studies in Ancient Art and Civilization* 2: 23–6.

Smith M, 1987. *The Mortuary Texts of Papyrus BM 10507*. Catalogue of the Demotic Papyri in the British Museum 3. London.

Spalinger A, 1986. Foods in P. Boulaq 18. *Studien zur Altägyptischen Kultur* 13: 207–47.

Spencer A J, 1979. *Brick Architecture in Ancient Egypt*. Warminster.

Spencer A J, 1980. *Catalogue of Egyptian Antiquities in the British Museum V. Early Dynastic Objects*. London.

Spiegelberg W, 1906. *Die demotischen Papyrus*. Vol. 2. Catalogue général des antiquités égyptiennes du Musée du Caire, Die demotischen Denkmäler 2. Strassburg.

Spiegelberg W and Pörtner B, 1902. *Ägyptische Grab- und Denksteine aus süddeutschen Sammlungen 1: Die Stelen in Karlsruhe, Mülhausen, Strassburg, Stuttgart*. Strassburg.

Vercoutter J. *et al.* 1970. *Mirgissa I*. Paris.

Verner M, 1969. Statue of Tweret (Cairo Museum no. 39145) Dedicated by Pabesi and Several Remarks on the Role of the Hippopotamus Goddess. *Zeitschrift für Ägyptische Sprache und Altertumskunde* 96: 52–9.

Verner M, 1986. A Slaughterhouse from the Old Kingdom. *Mitteilungen des Deutschen Archäologischen Instituts Abteilung Kairo* 42: 181–9.

Vernus P, 1986. Études de philologie et de linguistique (V). *Revue d'Égyptologie* 37: 139–47.

Vila A, 1977. *La prospection archéologique de la Vallée du Nil au sud de cataracte de Dal (Nubie soudanaise)*. Fasc. 7, *Le district d'Amara Ouest*. Paris.

Wainwright G A, 1927. El Hibeh and Esh Shurafa and their Connections with Herakleopolis and Cusae. *Annales du Service des Antiquités de l'Égypte* 27: 76–104.

Weigall A, 1910. *A Guide to the Antiquities of Upper Egypt, from Abydos to the Sudan Frontier*. London.

Wente E F, 1962. Egyptian 'Make Merry' Songs Reconsidered. *Journal of Near Eastern Studies* 21: 118–28.

Williams B M, 1983. *C-Group, Pan Grave, and Kerma Remains at Adindan Cemeteries T, K, U, and J*. Oriental Institute Nubian Expedition 5. Chicago.

Williams B B, 1986. *Excavations Between Abu Simbel and the Sudan Frontier, part 1: The A-Group Royal Cemetery at Qustul: Cemetery L*. Oriental Institute Nubian Expedition 3. Chicago.

Williams B B, 1993. *Excavations at Serra East, Parts 1–5. A-Group, C-Group, Pan Grave, New Kingdom and X-Group Remains from Cemeteries A-G and Rock Shelters*. Oriental Institute Nubian Expedition 10. Chicago.

Winkler H A, 1938. *Rock-Drawings of Southern Upper Egypt I* Archaeological Survey of Egypt 26. London.

Winkler H A, 1939. *Rock-Drawings of Southern Upper Egypt II*. Archaeological Survey of Egypt 27. London.

Zaba Z, 1974. *The Rock Inscriptions of Lower Nubia (Czechoslovak Concession)*. Prague.

Zivie A-P, 1985. Cavaliers et cavalerie au Nouvel Empire: a` propos d'un vieux probleme. In *Mélanges Gamal Eddin Mokhtar* 2. Bibliothèque d'Étude 97/2, Cairo: 379–88.

Gravel of the Desert and Broken Pots in the Road: Ceramic Evidence from the Routes between the Nile and Kharga Oasis

Deborah Darnell

The observation from the Metternich Stela quoted in the title (Sander-Hansen 1956, 52, §118–19) suggests that, already in ancient times, caravan routes were distinguished by a considerable number of potsherds littering the desert surface. Investigations by the Theban Desert Road Survey of the region west of the Nile between the Qena Bend and Kharga Oasis have uncovered a wealth of evidence for an energetic human presence in this area, beginning with the very earliest, formative period of Egyptian culture (see also J Darnell this volume). In addition to numerous sites with hundreds of rock inscriptions and depictions, we have encountered substantial archaeological remains, including hut clusters and campsites, tombs and monumental edifices, and above all, pottery, both scattered on the desert surface and in stratified deposits. This paper is intended as an introduction to the ceramic evidence that sheds light on connections between the Nile Valley and the Western Desert, especially Kharga Oasis and its environs, during the Predynastic period and the Second Intermediate Period to mid-New Kingdom. Selected examples from a number of sites are presented for each of these two periods. Material from the most recent field season is included, despite the fact that its analysis in still in the preliminary stages, because of its particular relevance to the theme of this colloquium. Further assessment of this new evidence will augment what years of fieldwork have already demonstrated: that desert routes are an important and formerly untapped source of information about the origins and development of the ancient Egyptian civilization, as well as the enterprising character of both Nile Valley and desert dwellers in traversing the barren expanses of the Eastern Sahara.

I. The Earliest Links: Badarian and Naqada Period Nile Valley Dwellers and Libo-Nubian Groups

Never an impenetrable barrier, the great desert bordering the ancient Egyptians' Nile Valley home often served as a conduit through which flowed people, products and ideas. Many elements of what was to become pharaonic Egyptian civilization have their origin in the cultures of the Western Desert. Yet the identities of these early desert peoples remain obscure, and links with known cultural groups continue to be reconsidered. The identification of the relationships of various early Sudanese, Nubian and 'Libo-Nubian' (i.e., belonging to the region to the west and south of the Upper Egyptian Nile Valley) groups is still an ongoing process. As a result of the continuing study of the system of desert routes by the Theban Desert Road Survey and the Yale Toshka

Desert Survey, a firm connection has now been established between certain Libo-Nubian ceramic traditions, the cultures that produced them and various phases of the Egyptian Predynastic period. The association of Nile Valley imports with locally manufactured pottery at sites in the Western Desert provides a valuable chronological anchor for the desert Neolithic; the occurrence along the routes between Kharga and the Qena Bend of vessels of fabrics originating in the oases and Western Desert demonstrates the means by which these early desert populations entered the Nile Valley. Some of the most exciting evidence has emerged from our most recent work at sites with assemblages comprising an abundance of both Libo-Nubian and Egyptian (Badarian through Naqada III) types in clear association.

I.1 Gebel Rayayna and the Oasis Road

In the past, as today, the extremely broad Wadi Rizeiqat served as a corridor for human movement between the Nile at the southern portion of the Qena Bend and the southern part of Kharga Oasis, and thereby also the southwestern desert of Egypt (see J Darnell this volume, **Figs 1–2**). A number of sets of caravan tracks attest to use over a long period of time. Although the pottery observed on the surveyed portions of the tracks themselves was almost exclusively late Roman/Coptic, we found substantial early remains in the middle desert and in and around a number of branch wadis. In particular, pooling areas at the heads of wadis, as might be expected, appear to have drawn travellers and desert-dwellers. In the Predynastic period, when the climate was wetter, these wadi heads might have been semi-permanent water sources, the high rock faces providing some degree of shade for any runoff rainwater that might collect there (cf. Newbold 1924, 56, 75–6: 'rockwell' with associated rock depictions).

Over a century ago, Legrain travelled this route and discovered a number of flint sites (de Morgan 1897, 45–50; Hayes 1965, 102–3); subsequently a good deal of research has been undertaken to evaluate the relationship between early material from Kharga Oasis and the Armant area, first postulated by Caton-Thompson (1952) and pursued by other prehistorians, but it has been almost exclusively devoted to the lithic assemblages. Furthermore, material from the areas between the Nile Valley and Kharga Oasis has never before been sought or considered. The evidence encountered by the Theban Desert Road Survey in this desert region allows us to suggest possible routes of entry for peoples from and via the Western Desert, along which continued interaction with Nile Valley populations took place.

On the basis of data recovered thus far, one may postulate an influx of people from the Western Desert, likely belonging to or bearing elements of cultures far to the south as well as west, into the Nile Valley at the southern portion of the Qena Bend. From this region, the desert routes crossing the bend gave access to other nodes of Predynastic occupation including the Naqada area and, via the Wadi el-Hôl and the Khor Battaghah, the Hou/Halfaya region, Abydos, and points further north, as well as routes continuing south past Gebelein, Adaima, and Hierakonpolis. Oliver Myers was one of the first scholars to examine critically the influences on and interactions with the Nile Valley by the cultural groups of the Western Desert; his ideas about what he termed the 'Saharan' culture and how it might have entered the Nile Valley have been borne out by new finds much further from the cultivation than those on which he based his insightful predictions (Mond and Myers 1937, 1, 267–78). Some of the most notable are detailed below.

1.1.1 The Cave of the Wooden Pegs

This previously unknown site is located at the lower head of a short east/west wadi off of the Wadi Rizeiqat. The opening is broad and the interior now fairly well lit, but judging by the quantities of bat guano incorporated in the interior debris mound, the opening may have been more restricted in the past. Large boulders and slabs of limestone that now stand at the eastern edge of the apron before the cave entrance may have fallen from the rock overhang that now shades the forepart of the cave. The apron itself is covered with water-borne gravel. Straw trapped beneath some of the boulders proves that human activity on the apron (probably an area for animals) preceded the presence of the boulders. To either side of the opening are remains of dry-stone constructions, including a U-shaped hut and a tumbled dry-stone wall. These may be the remains of shelters, once possibly roofed with perishable material, as suggested by the presence of portions of wooden pegs in natural holes in the upper areas of the rock faces behind the hut and near the wall. Alternatively, the pegs may have been used to suspend vessels or food items above the ground—if so, this feature is perhaps a link with cultures of the Western Desert, both ancient and recent. At Gebel Uweinat Oliver Myers noted depictions of suspended pots and the remains of poles 'in the cracks of the walls of (a) cave, near the roof' (Myers nd.b, 9).

As one approaches the cave, two easily visible boats signal the presence of Predynastic rock depictions; other images include additional boats, quadrupeds, and birds. In the cave, on the apron and on the slope below it are abundant quantities of Predynastic pottery; there is also a considerable quantity of Predynastic flint working. The interior of the cave is of extraordinary significance. Sustained and vigorous Predynastic activity produced a mounded accumulation of copious amounts of ash and burned material, other organic matter, water-borne debris and pottery. Though there had been some disturbance by modern digging, much of this deposit, which includes several packed living floors, was undisturbed. Predynastic habitation sites are of great significance wherever their location; the presence of this occupation area, along a desert road and far from the Nile or

any other permanent source of water, together with its combination of Nile Valley and Libo-Nubian ceramic remains, give this site a unique importance.[1]

Excavation and planning of the interior of the cave produced exciting results. The smattering of Coptic pottery on the surface belied the fact that the bulk of the material in the deposit was of Predynastic date. Site formation processes were taken into consideration in interpreting the stratigraphy, as wind- and water-action, trampling and pitting were all in evidence. Though turbation and modern disturbance accounted for some earlier material on the surface and in the upper levels of the loose, silty debris, there was no intrusive material below an upper packed floor in which both Coptic and Predynastic sherds were embedded. To account for the presence of pottery of two epochs so widely separated in time on this surface, one may postulate that no significant use of the cave was made after the Predynastic. In fact, the only evidence of visits to the site between Predynastic and late Roman times are two sherds of a Marl D amphora from the spill and one spiral-painted Twenty-First Dynasty vessel from a disturbed area on the interior left side of the cave. During this interim period, wind-blown and water-borne silt would have covered the old living surface. But this lightweight silt was not hard packed until later, more intensive Coptic occupation, so it allowed some late sherds to migrate below to the last Predynastic surface and its build-up of debris.

This and lower living surfaces seem to have been hardened both through burning and possibly by intentional tamping-down. The matrix of this upper packed layer contained ash, charcoal and organic matter including bone, as well as some flint (implements and chips). Earlier levels contained these same elements to varying degrees—it was the difference in the matrix that distinguished one stratum from another. The upper packed floor was atop an ashy layer, below which lay light sand with burned elements throughout; this in turn was atop a lower hard-packed floor. Prior to this earlier living surface, periods of disuse may have been more pronounced, as indicated by the presence of large and small rocks mixed in with the debris and hearth material accumulation. Some small rocks were probably water-borne; a number of flat slabs, often burned on one side, were clearly pieces of the ceiling that had cracked and fallen off due to expansion after being heated by the fires in the cave. Significant quantities of bat guano were encountered at various points, probably signalling periods without occupation. The lowest level with cultural material was almost pure ashy silt; beneath this was clean sand atop the bedrock.

Among the ancient activities carried out in the cave, food preparation may have been paramount. Some of the abundant quantities of animal bones showed butchering marks and many were charred; a number of the flint tools recovered, such as knives and scrapers, were no doubt those used in slaughtering, cleaning and preparing for cooking the hunters' take. Areas of burning were often not clearly demarcated, however, there were a number of hearths with built-stone fire baffles. The lack of significant evidence for direct smoke blackening in the interior of the cave, but the clear evidence for intense heat and the falling of large slabs of rock

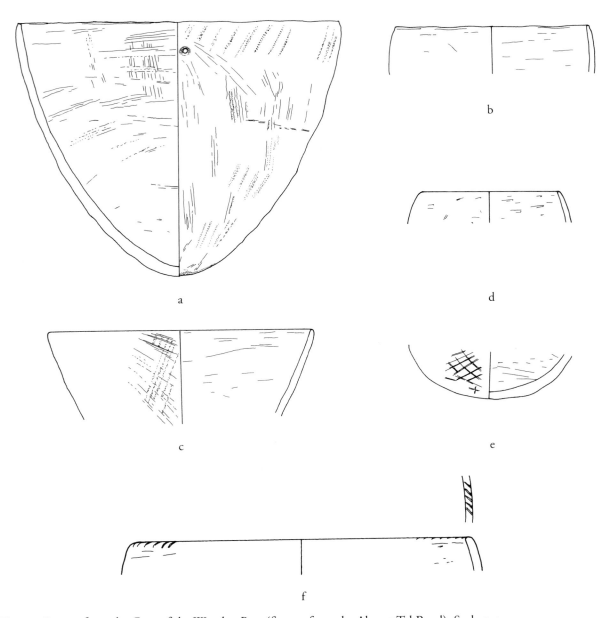

Fig. 1   Pottery from the Cave of the Wooden Pegs (fig. 1 a from the Alamat Tal Road). Scale 1:4.

from the roof, along with the enormous quantities of ash, suggest large but contained fires, probably primarily charcoal fed.

The array of ceramic types is of great importance for the study of the relationships and synchronisation of Nile Valley and Libo-Nubian cultures, including the Abkan and the early A-Group. One of the most common forms at the oasis road sites, also occurring in isolated drops along other routes of the Qena Bend, is the Badarian form RB 27T (and related Rough Brown forms 27M, 31H, 36E, and 37H). It appears with similar surface treatment in oasis as well as Nile Valley fabrics alongside more diagnostic Badarian types as identified by form and ware, including Black-topped Brown, ripple-burnished and Black-topped Red, all of very fine silt with no or few inclusions. At the Cave of the Wooden Pegs, it also occurs in closed contexts with middle Predynastic sherds, suggesting a long-lived persistence in the desert rep-

ertoire. The illustrated example (**Fig. 1a** and **Plate 89**) is from the Alamat Tal Road, not far from Gebel Tjauti. The vessel walls retain traces of coil-building; the rim is irregular, a simple lip at some points, but finished overall as a flattened, burnished edge, slightly in-turning–a subtle but unmistakable diagnostic feature of a number of Badarian bowl types. The exterior of the vessel is irregularly ripple-burnished with broad undulations diagonal to the rim crossed by vertical and curving (pebble?) burnishing streaks. The upper portion of the interior has narrow vertical rippling crossed by horizontal and curving burnishing strokes. The fabric is Nile silt with sparse to moderate, medium-sized straw (burned-out in firing), abundant fine to medium sand, including some larger sub-rounded quartz particles, very abundant mica, and sparse carbonate particles.

At the Cave of the Wooden Pegs, this form occurs in both Nile silt and Western Desert/oasis fabrics. The shale-tempered fabric used for this and other forms found at sites in the Gebel Rayayna region of the oasis road also occurs at the Western Desert sites of Bir Nakheila, Kurkur, Yabsa, and Qarn el-Ginah (see J Darnell this volume, **Figs 1–2**) and may be related to Dakhleh Oasis 'Coarse Shale Fabric' (see Hope this volume, section I.1, and Eccleston in this volume).[2] Significantly, this shale-tempered fabric may also be related to a fabric found at a Nubian cave with Abkan remains described by Williams (1989, 3–12). Although Williams identifies this as a silt variant, and attributes the unusual colours to difference in firing (Williams 1989, 6, Table 1, Form Group II, pl. 12b), the appearance as well as the description of the fabric suggests it is similar to our shale-tempered oasis variant.

Most of the Egyptian pottery at the Cave of the Wooden Pegs can be dated to the late Naqada I through Naqada II periods, although Naqada III vessel types are also represented among the substantial variety of Nile Valley sherds. In addition to Black-topped Red ware, Decorated ware, Marl A1 jars and red-burnished bowls and various forms of Rough ware, are some distinctive fabrics we have encountered elsewhere in the southern Theban desert. These include a low-fired, cocoa-coloured silt that also occurs near the Predynastic solar altar on the Darb Rayayna (see J Darnell this volume), and a dark red-slipped sandy marl variant, or 'imitation plum red', corresponding with Friedman's fabric/temper class 8 (Friedman 1994, plate 4.6.3 for colour photograph of fracture). First identified by Friedman in assemblages of the Naqada region, it occurs on the desert routes of that area, but with even greater frequency on the southern Qena Bend roads.

In association and contemporary with this datable corpus is a great deal of pottery originating with Libo-Nubian cultures of the Western Desert and Nubia, including the shale-tempered fabric mentioned above, as well as other variants of oasis ware that may have been manufactured from locally available clay sources by groups moving across the desert. The best parallels for these vessels are the oasis/Libo-Nubian types at Kurkur, Bir Nakheila and Yabsa (see below). Still other sherds bear a great resemblance to Nilotic Nubian ceramics. The date for much of the Egyptian pottery in the cave corresponds well with that given by Nordström (1972, 28) for the early A-Group (Naqada Ic–IId). The northernmost limit of the A-Group was formerly thought to be Kubbaniya (Nordström 1972, 17), but there is significant evidence of both early and classic A-Group presence on the desert routes of the Qena Bend. Recently, attention has been focused on the far-reaching relationships between A-Group ceramics and those found at many Nilotic and desert sites (Rampersad 2000); certainly this is the direction to be taken if we are to achieve a full understanding of the fascinating interactions of a variety of distinct but related culture groups at that critical time. In fact, the Terminal Abkan and early A-Group corpora provide the closest parallels for some of the non-Egyptian material from the cave. The desert-dwellers, the Abkan and the A-Group seem to belong to one cultural tradition, most likely originating in what is now the Sahara Desert.

Some of the Nile silt vessels at the Cave of the Wooden

Pegs may be imports of Nubian origin, while others may have been locally manufactured. The vessels illustrated in **Fig. 1 b c** and **d** are all from a single locus, each of a very different type of silt. **Fig. 1 b** is paralleled in the Badarian Rough Brown corpus, but is of fine Nile silt, with burnishing on the interior and exterior. The more open form of **Fig. 1 c**, also burnished inside and out, resembles some A-Group bowls (e.g., Nordström 1972, pl. 36, form type AIa2; Williams 1989, 27e though smaller) and is of a coarse limestone-tempered silt fabric. The chaffy silt fabric of **Fig. 1 d** differs from Rough ware, and may possibly be related to the 'brown polished ware' of an A-Group vessel of similar form with large, burned-out straw voids visible on the surface (Nordström 1972, 175, pl. 163,1, 332/17:5, type AIIIa22, described as red-polished). A vessel of what appears to be a Nubian, possibly dung-tempered, fabric with polished black interior bears on the lower portion of the exterior an irregular cross-hatched incised decoration (**Fig. 1 e**), a trait found in the early A-Group.

A few types are known otherwise from sites far to the south and west, such as a vessel with notched decoration on the rim (**Fig. 1 f**), the fabric of which is unusual and possibly of Western Desert origin. Parallels for incised ticks or notches as a rim-top decorative feature are widespread in Sudanese and the Western Desert neolithic material (cf. Rampersad 2000, 129–30, pattern 25), ranging from Abka (Nordström 1972, 213, pl. 121, 25–31) and Kadruka (Reinold et al. 2000, 47)[3] to Abu Ballas, the Gilf Kebir, Selima Sandsheet, and the Laqiya area (Kuper 1995, 131–2, figs 4–5; Schon 1994, 141 and 171, pl. 17, fig. 11). The Theban Desert Road survey has also found similar rim sherds at Yabsa (**Fig. 5**) and between Gebel Tjauti and 'Dominion Behind Thebes'. In the Nile Valley, this type of rim decoration occurs at Khattara, where it may be the result of oasis influence (Friedman 1994, section 8.4.2.5).

At the Cave of the Wooden Pegs and its hinterland, short ceramic cylinders, tapering to one end and open at both ends (vividly called 'lampshade' stands by G W Murray), and large disks with central holes are present in abundance. We have encountered this 'lampshade' cylinder and disk combination in association with Predynastic and Protodynastic pottery at a number of other sites, especially along the oasis road and at Kurkur, Yabsa and Bir Nakheila. It has been found thus far exclusively at desert sites, primarily in the Western Desert of Egypt and Sudan, but also in the Eastern Desert (Murray 1939, 38–9, pls VIII and IX, dated to the First to Second Dynasty; Murray and Myers 1933, 129–32, pl. XX.1; see also Hope this volume). Caton-Thompson (1952, 43) compiled a list of occurrences, but offered no suggestion as to their function, which remains unknown. Riemer and Kuper's (2000) comprehensive study is a substantial contribution toward understanding these objects, yet, as they point out, no conclusive evidence of how they were used has been forthcoming.

The 'lampshade' cylinders on the desert routes are made either of silt (sometimes dung-tempered)(**Fig. 2 a**, of coarse silt) or Marl A1. Some disks are of silt (**Fig. 2 c**, very low-fired straw and sand-tempered, cf. Riemer and Kuper 2000, fig. 3/1–2), while others are clearly cut down from Marl A1

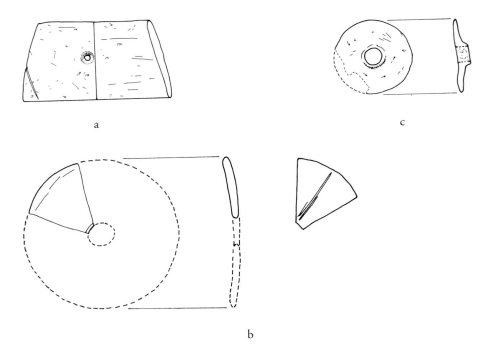

a

c

b

Fig. 2   Ceramic cylinders and disks from the Cave of the Wooden Pegs. Scale 1:4.

jars (**Fig. 2** b, with post-firing potmark) and red-burnished bowls. The presence of an incised potmark, often of a bird or an element suggestive of a bird track, is not infrequent on both disks and cylinders (cf. Caton-Thompson 1952, pl. 123.3; Riemer and Kuper 2000, fig. 3/7–9), and may signal a connection with the trapping of small birds. Ethnographic parallels (personal observation) confirm that such tiny desert fowl are, surprisingly, thought of as a delicacy and perhaps were caught and consumed in the past as well. The presence of these stands and disks inside the cave in association with food preparation may at last shed some light on the mystery of the function of this curious combination that occurs only in desert environments.

I.1.2 The Wadi of the Dance of the Four Winds and the Cave of the Hands

This wadi, beyond the extent of most detailed maps, contains spectacular evidence of ancient occupation. Examination of the rock faces revealed a number of locations with Predynastic drawings, including some very imposing and important depictions. On a tall flat face are two very large boats, a sacred barge and smaller towboat– part of a recurrent tableau related to the royal jubilee. Other nearby distinctive depictions include a large figure holding a mace, with a possible shrine behind him, and a female figure in the backbend pose of a dancing-girl. She is wearing a long ankle-length dress, has her hands over her head and one leg lifted; her hair hangs down and she holds a flower in one hand. This pose appears in a number of representations of an acrobatic religious dance evoking the actions of the four winds, thus the name we have given to the wadi.

One of the smallest and most endearing of the drawings is a tiny basenji, a little stick dog with a well-made curly tail (distinctive to the breed). This type of dog commonly occurs in early rock depictions as part of hunting scenes, usually running and/or biting the rump of a gazelle or other quadrupeds. Among the Predynastic scenes we copied at the site of Apa Tyrannos, there are four basenjis in a group with a man holding a curved throw-stick (Winkler 1938, pl. XVI.2, site 34). The example under discussion is distinctive because of its standing posture and its occurrence as a single, isolated element. It is likely to be a depiction of a dog with which the artist was acquainted, and is a further link with peoples and cultures of the Western Desert. The basenji type appears in early rock art of the Sahara, in Predynastic Egyptian rock depictions and in glyptic and formal compositions from the Early Dynastic through the Middle Kingdom, after which time the basenji virtually disappears from the iconographic repertoire. The descendents of this type of dog were found in the last century in modern Congo.

A short fork of this same wadi contains an amazing number of rock depictions, all Predynastic, including many unusual, even unique, elements. Animals, both pecked and incised, some very nicely executed, include horned quadrupeds, giraffes, elephants, hyenas and a possible wild boar. In the upper portion of a cleft, the images are on a gigantic scale. Among them are two boats with an elaborate standard over them, an extremely long-necked giraffe (a forerunner of later solar giraffes and the serpopards of the Narmer Palette). There is also a giant figure with a distinctive long garment, belonging to an iconographic tradition unlike any we have encountered in the Theban desert; this same type of figure is also depicted walking behind and holding the tail of an elephant.

A number of stick figures with large hands are present, paralleled at the Wadi el-Hôl (environs of the Tasian Burial Cave, see below), as well as in the Eastern Desert (wearing two antennae-like feathers, standing in a boat; Winkler

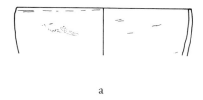
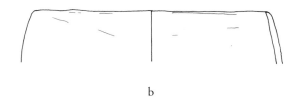

a   b

Fig. 3   Pottery from the 'Predynastic Feature'. Scale 1:4.

1938, site 26), and along the Darb el-Ghubari, between Kharga and Dakhleh (Winkler 1939, site 60). There are also repeated small elements resembling lotus-like flowers or papyrus umbels, but which may actually represent animal tracks,[4] and odd U-shaped forms with parallel lines that are also known from distant Saharan sites as well as Abka (Myers 1958, pls 38–9; Hellström 1970). These enigmatic symbols may represent paths going to the wadi head(s), or possibly some form of trap. There is also a depiction of a standard-like element projecting sideways out of a pole. Though unusual in the iconography of early Egyptian rock art, the peculiar standard is paralleled in the boulder graffiti in the vicinity of the 'Predynastic Feature' (see below).

Not far from this rich rock art site is a cave-like area with a slanted rock 'floor' and a curved 'ceiling'. Overhead and on flat rock surfaces within this space is a great deal of incision, some depictive but primarily scratches and patterns of lines. There are also elaborate 'woven' scratched designs, similar to a number of depictions at 'Dominion Behind Thebes' (see J Darnell this volume) and the etched design on the tooled leather pouch we discovered in the Tasian Burial Cave in the Wadi el-Hôl (see **Fig. 4** a).

Most astonishing is the presence of a number of negative human handprints outlined in spattered or daubed red paint (**Plates 90-91**), as well as several red handprints and other red-painted decorations. This type of rock art has never been found so close to the Nile Valley, and indeed is otherwise known in Egypt only from a cave near Farafra Oasis (Barich 1999; but also pecked hands at Abka, Myers 1958, pl. 33; Myers 1960, 177). It does occur much further west in the great Sahara Desert.[5] Incised depictions carved over some of the handprints prove that they must be dated no later than (and in fact probably considerably predate) the Naqada II period. The handprint motif in the Cave of the Hands is one of the most remarkable and strongest pieces of evidence for connections between early Egyptians and the Sahara/inner Africa.

Excavation at the site should provide further details about the people who left the handprints and the activities carried on at the site. Hearths and other evidence of occupation are present, and the surface pottery is exclusively of early date, including possible Tasian or Abkan/early A-Group as well as early oasis ware. A relationship with the Cave of the Wooden Pegs is likely, as the network of nearby caravan tracks suggests that people were likely to be moving back and forth along the base of the gebel near potential water sources. One of the questions yet to be answered is whether the creators of these sites were travellers from the oasis and Western Desert,

pausing to rest in the wadis and shelter areas, or permanent nomadic desert dwellers.

I.1.3 The 'Predynastic Feature'

On gravel terraces north of the oasis road are extensive remains of early Predynastic occupation, the most imposing element of which is a large dry-stone hut. Roughly circular in form, this structure has quite substantial walls and is of particular significance. Thieves had made a small digging along the interior of the northern side, revealing hearth remains below the surface. Tossed out of the thieves' trench were fragments of a quartzite 'mortar', similar to examples we have found at the more remote Western Desert sites of Bir Nakheila, Tundaba, Yabsa and Kurkur Oasis, charred from use as a brazier. A significant number of early Predynastic sherds in and around the feature attest to the probable date of its construction. A footpath leading north in the direction of a wadi, on the other side of which are a number of additional features, passes two additional stone constructions on the same gravel terrace. With the exception of two isolated late Roman pot drops, all surface pottery was exclusively early Libo-Nubian and Badarian. Badarian types include ripple-burnished sherds, red- and brown-polished (including Black-topped) vessels, and a 'keel' of a classic Badarian bowl, all of the distinctively fine Badarian version of Nile silt A. There are also Rough Brown and Smooth Brown wares, as well as a number of open vessels in variant silt fabrics: **Fig. 3** a is of silt with sparse fine calcareous inclusions, sparse medium sand, and very sparse fine straw; **Fig. 3** b is of silt with abundant coarse limestone/carbonate particles, as well as very fine straw, possibly dung temper.

The structure remained essentially unused after the middle Predynastic period. Rainwater washing down from the gebel heights brought silty debris into and around the hut, creating a series of hard crusts that encapsulated the remains within the structure. After careful surface collection, we made an initial test excavation that produced exclusively early sherds, worked flint, bird bones, a charred date pit, as well as ostrich eggshell pieces. As at the midden at the Seventeenth Dynasty military outpost at Tundaba (section II.1 below), the shell pieces are fire-blackened. There is no doubt that the ostrich eggshell is contemporary with the pottery. The ostrich eggs clearly were cooked and consumed by the desert dwellers here, as they were in the Middle Kingdom in the Alamat Tal and during the Second Intermediate Period at the outpost (cf. Newbold 1924, 49, 59).

We began a plan of the structure, and opened up horizontally in a limited area on a packed living floor that had several small postholes. We hope next season to expose fully and complete the planning of this surface throughout the whole structure where it is still preserved.

A wadi leading from the structure towards the gebel contains several boulders with pecked decorations, many elements of which also occur among the rock depictions near the Cave of the Hands. This rock art, pecked onto the vertical and horizontal surfaces of hard boulders, resembles in both manner of execution, placement and iconography the rock depictions we are studying at Bir Nakheila, south/southeast of Kharga Oasis. There are giraffes with serpentine ropes around their necks, representing the giraffe as solar carrier controlled by the ropes that represent human intervention in the divine realm (see also Huyge this volume). These images appear in multitudes at 'Dominion Behind Thebes'. There is also a depiction of a human figure with raised arms meeting above the head in the so-called bird-like dance of early Egyptian iconography. A number of meandering elements are well-paralleled at Bir Nakheila and also at Abka Site IX (Myers 1958, pl. 33), where they have beendated by excavated context to between 4000 and 5000 BC (Myers 1960, 177).[6] Together with the ceramic material nearby, as well as the ceramic and epigraphic material from Bir Nakheila, these rock depictions provide further evidence for the interaction of desert and Nile Valley cultures at the dawn of the Egyptian Predynastic.

I.2 The Burial Caves in the Wadi el-Hôl

I.2.1 Burial and Storage Caves

Overlooking the tracks of the Farshût Road as they pass into a branch of the Wadi el-Hôl, an opening in the rock face leads to a complex of three small natural caves. In the pharaonic period, a portion of the southernmost cave was used for the storage of provisions, as evinced by the presence of fragments of Middle Kingdom and New Kingdom pots, and many well-preserved mud jar stoppers and sealings. The use of this cave as a sort of natural 'refrigerator' can be attributed to the existence of a second, narrower opening towards the southeast, which allows a cool breeze to blow through the interior space even when the noonday heat is great in the wadi outside. This ventilation had an important impact on the preservation of much earlier remains; long before the presence of pharaonic Egyptians travelling through and stationed at the Wadi el-Hôl, a number of individuals of the Tasian culture were buried in the cave. Their bodies and organic grave goods were quickly desiccated by the dry desert air circulating within the gebel sepulchre. Notwithstanding the inevitable desecrations by later tomb robbers, the Tasians of the Wadi el-Hôl are the best-preserved representatives to date of that still-enigmatic cultural group.

Post-pharaonic visits to the site are represented by a scattering of Roman sherds in the vicinity, and also outside and below the southern cave, at the bottom of a spoil heap underlying the burial remains thrown out of the cave by the grave robbers. Excavation and sifting of this debris heap showed the various strata, through which the despoilers had dug, preserved in an inverted order. On the basis of this, one can suggest that the burials, though perhaps robbed, were

basically intact at least into the Roman period. The horrible crushing of the bodies and grave goods, and their dispersal throughout the caves, is most likely a result of modern desecration of the interments.

The first and only previously recorded visit to the caves was by Terence Gray while he was working with Hans Winkler at the Wadi el-Hôl in 1937.[7] His brief observations on site were limited by lack of time and illumination. The burials had already been disturbed; he noted fragmentary human remains and 'quantities of leather'; though he found no intact vessels, he saw 'numerous remains of large broken red pots' outside the caves, and what he described as black pottery with white decoration. When two such sherds were shown to Myers he astutely recognized that they came from Tasian vessels (Myers nd.a, 11). Myers' plans to 'do a three days' dig' at the caves were never fulfilled. Based on Gray's descriptions of the sorry state of the remains, we expected that when we relocated the site, our task would consist of clearing and sifting only disturbed material. Much to our surprise and delight, however, four burials remained *in situ* in the southernmost chamber, protected to some extent by a heavy covering of wadi deposit gravel, apparently brought in at the time of interment to cover the bodies and grave goods. Each burial suffered a degree of disturbance from above, yet major portions of the bodies as well as a number of associated grave goods remained as they had been placed to rest thousands of years ago.

Preliminary analysis of the human remains recovered from both the *in situ* burials and the material disturbed by the robbers indicates that a minimum of nine individuals were buried in the cave, of both sexes, with ages at death ranging from fetal to old adult (50+ years of age). The grave goods and many features of the burials are comparable to those found in Tasian, as well as Badarian, burials excavated by Brunton in Middle Egypt (Brunton 1937); selected parallels are cited in the discussion below. The process of assigning objects to original burials is complex and ongoing, but we can with reasonable certainty present the following features of the four *in situ* individuals (discussed further below):

H1: Juvenile, 8–12 years of age. Vegetal matter was found beneath the body. A leather bag containing strung steatite beads and grain was found in the area of the head, which was missing. Associated with the burial were Tasian sherds and a tooled leather pouch (**Fig. 4** a) that may, however, belong to adjacent disturbed burial.

H2: Middle-aged male, 35–50 years of age. The body had been wrapped in leather, tied with twisted leather cord and then laid upon thick hide. Vegetal matter was found underlying. A leather cap and a possible mask was still attached to the skull. Other finds include an ivory/bone hairpin (**Fig. 4** d), cloth, associated Tasian sherds, and a quartzite palette with malachite stains (**Fig. 4** e).

H3: Old adult female, 50+ years of age. The body had been wrapped in leather. A leather bag containing food matter was found under and behind the head. A schist palette, beneath which was a leather vessel, was recovered in the area of the hands.

H4: Old adult male, 50+ years of age. The body had been

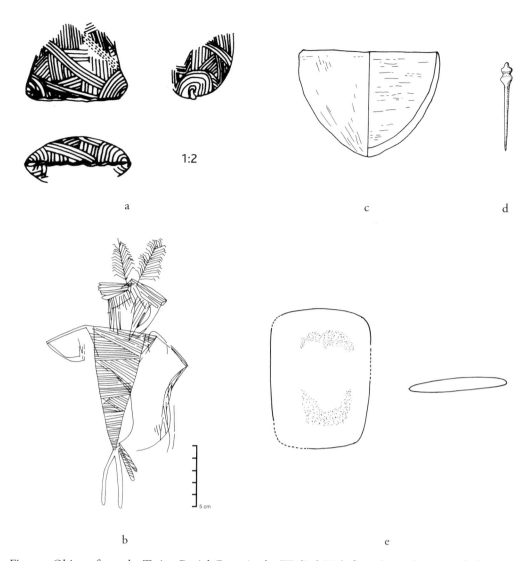

1:2

a

c

d

b

5 cm

e

Fig. 4   Objects from the Tasian Burial Caves in the Wadi el-Hôl; fig. 4 b is a drawing of a hunter
from 'Dominion Behind Thebes'. Scale 1:4 unless otherwise noted.

wrapped in leather. A leather bag with fibre threads, under which was a bone kohl tube, was recovered from behind the head and back. A limestone palette was also found.

The preservation of the bodies was fairly good, and we were able to recover many elements of soft tissue and some of the skin remaining in place on the bones. A large amount of hair from the body in H2 was preserved; it was fairly fine brown, somewhat wavy and seems to have been dressed with a fatty substance. Portions of the hair from the body in H4 survived as well, and is of a light golden colour. It is possible that this is tinted or discoloured grey hair, or he may have been a natural blonde or redhead as yellow and ginger hair colour is known among Badarian individuals (Brunton 1937, 34–6). Perhaps most remarkably and unexpectedly, from the skull of H3 came the dried remains of the right eye, including muscles and a portion of the optic nerve. The body of H4 yielded a considerable quantity of coprolites, found *in situ* in and just outside the intestinal cavity. Such portions of the bodies, not known from the water-damaged burials excavated by Brunton during his original identifica-

tion of the Tasian culture, should eventually tell us much about the appearance, diet, and pathology of these desert Tasians. Two of the skulls were essentially intact (H2 and H3), increasing the existing number of complete crania of people belonging to the Tasian culture by fifty percent. Due to the conditions of the burials, Brunton was able to recover only four complete skulls from the original 44 Tasian burials he excavated in Middle Egypt.

In contrast with Badarian burials, wherein the dead usually faced to the west (Brunton 1929, 465), there was no consistency to the orientation of the bodies, a feature Brunton noted during his excavations of Tasian burials in Middle Egypt. The bodies were all flexed. The bodies in H1 and H4 lay on their right sides; H3 was on her left side. The body in H2 lay on his back, a pose rare but not unattested in the early Predynastic (cf. Brunton and Caton-Thompson 1928, pl. IX 13, burial 5701), and he appears to have had the most singular burial of the four we uncovered.

All of the bodies were in shallow depressions in a thin layer of water-borne silt deposit, at least some of them atop vegetal matter, which may represent the remains of matting (cf. Brunton and Caton-Thompson 1928, 2), although no woven elements were recovered. Apparently gravel and larger rocks, including some boulders, were then brought into the cave from the wadi bed and placed atop the burials; some of the gravel and rocks were embedded between the limbs, individual bones, and filling the eye sockets, as the material settled after the soft tissues decayed. At least three of the bodies had originally been wrapped in leather, some of it quite thick and multiply folded.[8]

The bit of ancient cloth associated with H2 was found in the pelvis area, and may indicate the original presence of cloth wrappings under the leather, as attested in Badarian burials (Brunton and Caton-Thompson 1928, 19). Although the fabric appears to be linen, analysis may prove otherwise, as flax was ruled out as the 'vegetable fibre' used in Badarian fabrics (Brunton and Caton-Thompson 1928, 67; cf. Brunton 1937, 30 for Tasian cloth).

With the notable exception of H2, most of the leather over the faces and the upper bodies had vanished completely. This, along with the total absence of jewellery around the necks, and the greater and lesser degrees of damage to the hands of the bodies, suggest the activities of grave robbers, who appear to have searched the neck and hand areas seeking valuable objects. As mentioned above, the evidence from the robbers' spoil heap outside the left chamber suggests that the Tasian burials remained largely undisturbed through the early Roman period. However, as the robbers' activities on the Tasian bodies imply that the robbers understood the probable locations of valuables, we suggest that the Tasian burials may initially have been robbed by 'professional' thieves of the Tasian period, who took with them whatever they may have found in the area of the hands and neck.

Nevertheless, H2, apparently the body of a man of particular importance, preserved a large fold of thick leather over the face and head. When this was removed, the skull was seen to be covered by parallel strips of a soft, dark leather, apparently the remains of a leather cap, parts of which extended under the right eye and below the right cheekbone. A possible parallel for this cap is illustrated in **Fig. 4** b, the rock drawing of a hunter from the tableau at 'Dominion Behind Thebes' discussed further by J Darnell in this volume. The cultural identity of the figures depicted in that tableau may be related to, or even identical with, that of the Tasians buried at the Wadi el-Hôl. This possibility is further strengthened by the most remarkable object from the burial caves, an elaborately etched stiff leather pouch (**Fig. 4** a and **Plate 92**) that may have belonged to H1. The stunning tooled decoration, consisting of overlapping bands of parallel lines, executed so as to give the appearance of being interwoven, is as far as we know unique among early leather remains; however, it is well paralleled in certain motifs in rock art, particularly at 'Dominion Behind Thebes' (**Fig. 4** b). This distinctive pattern appears not only on the costumes of these Naqada II hunters, but in an enigmatic depiction of something very similar in shape to the actual leather pouch. Whether the depiction is of such an object, or whether both petroglyph and object represent some form of significance, is as yet unknown.

A minimum of nine Tasian and Badarian vessels were present in the cave. Much of the pottery is impossible to assign to a particular burial with any degree of certainty, although it appears from the find spots of the various fragments that at least several of the vessels originally belonged to H2. We have a number of vessels at various stages of restoration and have been able thus far to reconstruct the rim to base profile of one cup (**Fig. 4** c). The fabric of this cup corresponds with one of the variants commonly occurring in the Gebel Rayayna material, a medium-fine silt with moderate fine calcareous particles, moderate coarse sand and sparse fine straw. Elements of its simple form are paralleled in the Badarian Rough Brown corpus as well as in A-Group material, including a vessel from a grave which also contained a palette of light-grey quartzite (Nordström 1972, pl. 163, 2; cf. Williams 1989, 137, Table 26), and its exterior bears the distinctively Tasian vertical burnishing strokes (Brunton 1934, 94, 96). The interior bottom retains traces of its original contents, apparently a type of cereal mush (cf. Brunton and Caton-Thompson, 25, 41 for 'porridge' found in pots in Badarian graves; Brunton 1937, 6 for Tasian pots with organic contents).

Among the other fragments of early vessels associated with the burials were sherds of very fine Badarian silt with almost no inclusions, reddish-brown burnished exterior and brown burnished interior, and portions of a globular black-topped pot of a coarse silt with moderate organic but abundant mineral inclusions. This vessel in not of Badarian Black-topped Brown ware, but rather exhibits surface treatment consistent with the Tasian biconical bowl type. The most diagnostic of the Tasian forms is well-represented by at least four flared-rim beakers bearing incised patterns infilled with white pigment (Brunton 1937, 27–9). Three silt fabric variants are present, but do not correspond directly with the different firing colours and surface treatments. True black polished surfaces occur in both extremely fine Badarian silt with almost no inclusions as well as in a coarser fabric with moderate medium straw temper. Dark chocolate brown, moderately burnished surfaces are present in both the extremely fine silt as well as in a fabric including sparse fine straw, and also sparse very fine sand and calcareous particles. Decoration includes horizontal lines below the rim and incised triangles (**Plate 93**). Although Tasian beakers are known predominantly from settlement as opposed to burial contexts,[9] the related Sudanese Neolithic calciform beakers occur mainly at cemetery and not settlement sites (e.g., Welsby 1995, 105; 1997, 27; Reinold et al. 2000, 61). Perhaps the presence of at least four beakers with the burials is indicative of a retention of an older tradition originating in the far south.

Various sorts of leather bags were found in definite association with at least three burials, two of which contained grain, apparently emmer wheat (cf. Brunton and Caton-Thompson 1928, 41; and Brunton 1937, 40, 58 for a leather bag with grain found either at the head or foot of Badarian body no. 2224; cf. Wetterstrom 1993, 216), and also, in the case of H1, a string of steatite beads, which thus escaped the prehistoric robbers' attentions. A hairpin with stylized feminine figure atop it was found in the vicinity of

H2 (**Fig. 4** d). H3 had a rough slate palette in front of the hands, and in H4 a limestone palette lay between the back of the head and the leather bag behind the body. Two of the fragments of the finely shaped palette shown in **Plate 94** and **Fig. 4** e were displaced through robbers' activity, but were later found to join pieces apparently still *in situ* near H2, to whom it likely belongs. The palette, which appears to be made of quartzite, still retains the green stain of the malachite once ground upon it. The Tasians, unlike the contemporary Predynastic Egyptian cultures, made use of stones other than greywacke for palettes (Brunton 1937, 29–30). A portion of a large shell from the burials probably originally contained a quantity of malachite for the deceased. A number of white feathers, an ostrich feather and bits of ostrich eggshell, and several pieces of resin also appear to have belonged to the burials (cf. Brunton 1937, 29; section 77).

The location of these Tasian burials—at a point far from the cultivation in the middle of the Qena Bend, on a route leading to and from the Western Desert—supports the notion that the home of the Tasian culture was outside the Nile Valley. The use of quartzite and limestone, as opposed to greywacke, for two of our Tasian palettes suggests a Nubian connection for the Tasians (Brunton 1937, 30; Junker 1919, 85), or at least for the Tasians buried in the caves on the Farshût Road. Another feature consistent with Libo-Nubian traditions is the presence of at least one dog burial in the southernmost cave—compare, for example, the canine burials associated with the later Pan Grave people of Hou, a tradition that can be traced back to the A-Group and central Sudanese cultures.[10] When all the evidence is considered, a south Western Desert origin for the cultural complex to which the Tasians belonged seems increasing probable (see also Friedman and Hobbs this volume). The developments in the desert, as we know in many places, such as Nabta Playa, predate the introduction of a number of domesticates and techniques into the Nile Valley. We may now with some confidence see the Tasians as important links between the Nile and the more developed but increasingly arid West during the early Predynastic.

I.2.2 Environs of the Tasian Burials

Evidence of an early Libo-Nubian presence is scattered throughout the Wadi el-Hôl, and included Libo-Nubian sherds along the caravan tracks in an area 1–1.5 km from the major birfurcation of the wadi where the Tasian Burial Caves are situated. On the eastern side of the wadi, across from the Tasian caves, was an occupational area marked by another concentration of Tasian/Libo-Nubian pottery, including punctate-decorated sherds, a Tasian beaker rim sherd, and a classic Badarian form RB 27T in the same limestone-tempered silt fabric in which this form occurs at the 'Predynastic Feature' and at the Cave of the Wooden Pegs. A connection with the nearby Naqada I rock depictions at the head of a small branch of the wadi (Winkler 1938, site 31) is possible; in fact, the petroglyphs we recorded at that site, including depictions of elephants with internal chevron decorations, a style known from Amratian/ Naqada I White Cross-line pottery and decorated palettes, also contain some elements

paralleled in the cleft next to the Cave of the Hands in the Rayayna desert. Integrating the epigraphic and ceramic information from all these sites will shed light on the earliest Predynastic periods, particularly the relationship of Nile Valley and Libo-Nubian cultures at that formative time, and on the chronological position of the Tasians.

I.3 Western Desert Sites

I.3.1 Yabsa Pass

Although portions of this pass extending into the northeastern Kharga depression were examined by Caton-Thompson (1952) and subsequently by other prehistorians (Simmons and Mandel 1985), the association of an abundance of Libo-Nubian ceramic material with Predynastic Nile Valley imports went unnoticed until our discovery and study of a number of high plateau sites in the vicinity of Yabsa. The source of the clay for much of the Libo-Nubian pottery appears to have been local, that is, oasis-derived. For example, **Fig. 5**, a ticked-rim cup discussed above, is made of an oasis version of silt with fine sand temper. However, certain sherds are paralleled in both form and fabric (limestone-tempered Nile silt) by vessels from the Cave of the Wooden Pegs and the 'Predynastic Feature' in the Rayayna desert. In association and contemporary with this pottery is a great amount of worked flint, resembling some elements of the corpus from an extensive site we discovered in the middle of the Farshût–Kharga route. Comparative studies of the ceramic and stone tool corpora will certainly shed more light on the identity and movements of Western Desert peoples.

Fig. 5   Pottery from Yabsa Pass. Scale 1:4.

Mat-impressed sherds were noted at Yabsa by Caton-Thompson (1952, 42–3, pl. 123, 1–2), who, quoting Arkell's observation of similarities with Meroitic as well as modern Sudanese vessels, tentatively assigned a relatively late date to them. The trait of basketry- or mat-impressions on pottery is a long-lived feature, widespread across North Africa in the southern Sahara. Some pottery from Iron Age sites in what is now Burkina Faso, Mali and Niger, as well as contemporary vessels from these regions, bears a remarkable resemblance to the Sudanese basket-impressed examples. However, it is likely that this trait had very early origins in the Saharan cultures. Tangri (1991, 141) maintains that such sherds at Dakhleh are 'broadly contemporary with Badarian, Nagadian and later Predynastic sites in the Nile Valley' (see also Hope in this volume) and indeed, we have found similar sherds at a number of sites in the Theban desert, as well as at Yabsa, in association with Predynastic Egyptian pottery (**Plate 95**). We have recovered mat-impressed vessels that also bear C-Group decorative elements along a route heavily used in both the Predynastic period and the early Middle Kingdom. Objective laboratory dating of specimens of basket-impressed sherds from a number of sites may offer the best chance for distinguishing early from late examples of this type of vessel.

Nile Valley imports are also present, as well as sherds of local oasis clay from pots imitating Nile Valley forms (cf. Hope 1999, 219). The pottery includes late Predynastic to Early Dynastic Nile Valley wares (e.g., Marl A1 jars, red-slipped bowls with radial burnishing, and Rough ware vessels including jars and pithoi). This evidence provides a clear demonstration of Predynastic and Protodynastic traffic between Kharga Oasis and the Nile; the abundance of material further shows this traffic to have been intensive. Similarly, the significant amounts of late Predynastic to Early Dynastic pottery we discovered in the Wadi Karnak (south of Farshût and Gara) during initial surveys of the ancient routes leading from Gebel Qarn el-Gir and the region of Hou westwards toward the oases attests to travel between the northern Qena Bend and northeastern Kharga.

I.3.2 Bir Nakheila and Kurkur Oases

In response to the imminent threat to archaeological sites posed by the grand scale of the Toshka Canal/New Valley Development Project and the swift pace of its progress, we asked permission to initiate the Yale Toshka Desert Survey in order to search for and document evidence of Predynastic and pharaonic activity in the wide area of Egypt's Western Desert that will be affected. We conducted an archaeological survey of the small and northernmost Nubian oasis Bir Nakheila, and have surveyed several key areas in and around Kurkur Oasis, c. 150 km nearly due east of Bir Nakheila, at the intersection of a number of important caravan routes traversing the Nubian desert. The evidence we encountered augments and enhances that at the more remote Theban Desert Road Survey sites, particularly Yabsa, and also helps explain and date ceramic evidence found elsewhere in the Western Desert. This material provides links between the earliest ceramic traditions of the Western Desert and those of the Nile Valley, both in Upper Egypt and in Nubia, and will hopefully enhance our understanding of the North African origin of Egyptian civilization.

Despite its small size and isolated locale, Bir Nakheila holds much promise for future work. Our investigations at this tiny oasis focused on the important rock depictions and inscriptions, for which see J Darnell in this volume, and on an occupational area close to and south of the palm trees at the base of the low gebel, with a considerable spread of ceramic material. The greatest concentration of these remains was around the largest clumps of palms now existing at the site, suggesting that the main focus of water-bearing strata at Bir Nakheila has always been in the same area. The presence of multiple-layered hearths suggests that a trial excavation in the area of apparent heaviest occupation may be warranted in order to determine if levels undisturbed by more recent activity exist. We hope to undertake an initial trial excavation on our next visit to the site.

Although a number of sherds and other material of Roman and later date were present, the majority of the archaeological remains were potsherds of Libo-Nubian tradition, contemporary with Egyptian Predynastic through

Fig. 6   Pottery from Bir Nakheila. Scale 1:4.

Middle Kingdom periods. The early Libo-Nubian pottery at the site is discussed below with the related material from Kurkur. A Bir Nakheila vessel type not found at Kurkur is illustrated in **Fig. 6**; more than one such example was recovered. The incised rim-top decoration and heavily ridged exterior of the vessel walls, together with the very black, apparently Nubian silt fabric, recall A-Group as well as early central Sudanese traits. Comparable bowls occur at Kadada (Geus 1984, 367), but the closest parallels are in the C-Group corpus (Gratien 2000, 122 and fig. 17D, esp. Wadi es-Sebua rim sherd). Geus (1984, 368–9, 371) states that the Kadada culture is contemporary with the classic A-Group and has 'a number of affinities with the A-Group and C-Group culture of Lower Nubia'; he also notes the similarity of the pottery decoration to that of Tasian beakers. To be added to the increasingly complex web of cultural interrelationships is the fact that the ceramic material at Bir Nakheila includes other probable C-Group pottery, the presence of which in this area, as well as at Kurkur and Dunqul, supports previous hypotheses concerning the south Western Desert origins of the C-Group culture. Space prohibits discussion here of the C-Group material, except to note that at Bir Nakheila there is also a considerable number of mat-impressed sherds of the so-called 'Saharan' style, which, when considered along with the vessel from the Rayayna desert route incorporating both C-Group features and mat-impression (mentioned above in section I.3.1), further supports a relationship between them. Further work on the ceramic material at Bir Nakheila may help clarify the temporal and cultural relationships between early and later Nubian, Sudanese and Western Desert traditions.

Although the wadi-oasis of Kurkur (**Plate 96**) has been visited many times by various groups of people with different research interests, the Yale Toshka Desert Survey's December 1999 campaign was the first investigation devoted to assessing the presence and extent of evidence for activity in the oasis during the Predynastic and pharaonic periods. Though previous expeditions reported almost nothing of that date, happily our suspicions were correct and there is in fact an appreciable amount of material.

The last and most comprehensive scientific survey of Kurkur was also sponsored by Yale University, taking place in 1963 during the Nubian Salvage Campaign, but was manned entirely by geologists and prehistorians (Butzer and Hansen 1968). A wealth of important information was recovered from this geologically unique locale. Palaeolithic material was sought and found, but archaeological material of the Predynastic and later periods was only rarely recognised and never published. The brief visits by archaeologists to Kurkur in the 1960's concentrated on high plateau loca-

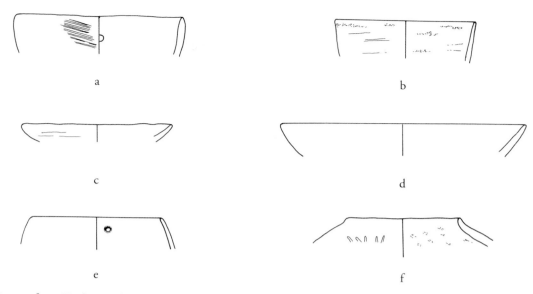

Fig. 7   Pottery from Kurkur and Bir Nakheila. Scale 1:4.

tions around the rim of the oasis wadis; this concentration on upper areas resulted in an over-representation of Palaeolithic material in relation to overall occupation of the area. Reports of sites of roughly Neolithic (Predynastic/Protodynastic) date were conspicuously absent.

During two short but intensive campaigns we achieved our initial survey goals: to determine which of the possible routes in and out of the oasis were used during various periods and to identify evidence of ancient occupation in the oasis proper. Our first survey covered three main areas of Kurkur: the main wadi, with its central well area; the northwest wadi; and the north wadi. In the main wadi, we were able to identify the sole location in which (Nubian) pottery dated to the pharaonic period was reported to have been found by the previous missions at Kurkur, but in addition, we discovered that there is in fact much more pharaonic material than was acknowledged by those prior surveys (see below, section II.4).

We also discovered an important late Predynastic-Early Dynastic occupation area in association with the caravan tracks running through the northwest wadi. The Naqada II-III ceramics include Rough ware from the Nile Valley, complete with a pre-firing potmark of the same type as is found on pithoi and roll-rim jars from Hierakonpolis and the Darb Rayayna, and red-polished Marl A1 bowl sherds. As at Bir Nakheila, the enigmatic tapered cylindrical 'lampshade' cylinders (discussed above, section I.1.1) were present, made of both Marl A1 (thus manufactured in the Nile Valley) and of local desert clay. At Bir Nakheila stands were made of Marl A1, but a silt disk was present. These datable forms and fabrics provide a chronological anchor for the locally manufactured pottery that is present in great abundance. The majority of the sherds scattered on the desert surface at this site were of various compositions of local oasis fabric. A number of them bore drilled mending holes.

Ostrich eggshell was also present. Lithics show that both flint and quartz were worked, the latter a distinctly Nubian

practice. Parallels for the Kurkur northwest wadi site pottery, as well as that from Bir Nakheila, occur at the Yabsa Pass. At all three sites, the presence of datable Nile Valley pottery in context with the more enigmatic local, oasis types, as well as sherds of local oasis clay from pots imitating Nile Valley forms, emphasises the increasingly clear connection between the earliest Egyptian sites in the Nile Valley and the rich cultural tradition of the Sahara.

The early ceramic assemblages from Bir Nakheila, Kurkur, and the Yabsa Pass share many features including form (mostly open), technique of manufacture (hand-made, vessel walls of uneven thickness, surfaces often compacted but unevenly finished) and fabric. The two basic fabric categories for sherds of Libo-Nubian tradition are Nile silt and various types of oasis clay. Many of the sherds from the desert surface, particularly from along the caravan tracks, have been trampled into fragments too small to be drawn. However, we have been able to determine stance and rough diameter for a number of vessels, a selection of which is depicted in **Fig.** 7 (examples from Kurkur, but representing types also present at Bir Nakheila). In general, inclusions are abundant (usually limestone and shale), and surface colours are variable and uneven (indicating open firing as opposed to the use of a kiln, though exposure and 'desert varnish' must also be taken into consideration). **Fig.** 7 a, d-f are of silt, but are different variants. Vessels illustrated in **Fig.** 7 a and d have abundant large inclusions (which probably allowed them to fire to a greater hardness at a lower temperature); **Fig.** 7 e is of a much finer silt, though limestone inclusions are still detectable. **Fig.** 7 f is of dung-tempered Nubian silt; the form and decoration have near parallels at Hierakonpolis (HK29A; Friedman 1994, 855, pl. 9.1.2), Armant (Mond and Myers 1937, pl. 54, 6) and on the Naqb Umm el-Salma in the Theban Western Desert. The vessel in **Fig.** 7 b is of a coarse desert ware that is probably a local Kurkur fabric. **Fig.** 7 c may also be of a Kurkur variant of oasis ware. An apparent Kurkur fabric occurs among the

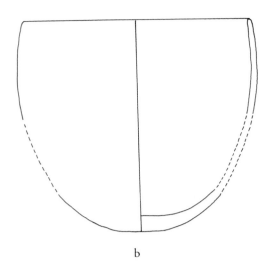

a   b

Fig. 8   Pottery from Qarn el-Ginah. Scale 1:4.

potsherds collected at the desert outpost HK64 at Hierakon-polis (Friedman *et al.* 1999). The sherd in question has tickings on the rim, a Nubian and Western Desert motif that usually occurs on vessels made of Nile silt or oasis ware. This is further evidence for the use of the desert 'corridor' by ancient travellers moving from Kurkur north to Hierakonpolis and beyond.

1.3.3 Qarn el-Ginah

Important evidence of early Nile Valley contact with the oases is present at Qarn el-Ginah. At the Yabsa Pass in the northeast we discovered plentiful evidence for Nile Valley wares coming into Kharga Oasis during the late Predynastic. At Qarn el-Ginah, well within the actual oasis depression of Kharga, we can report more evidence of Nile Valley Badarian pottery in the oases of the Western Desert (see Hope and Eccleston this volume). Contrary to what many still believe, the Nile Valley and the oases can be shown to have been in direct contact with an exchange of goods, to judge from the mixture of Nile Valley and oasis fabrics in the Yabsa Pass material. The Badarian material from Qarn el-Ginah suggests that this contact may be as old as the oldest Upper Egyptian culture of the Predynastic period. In addition to the black-topped rim of fine Badarian silt shown in **Fig. 8** a (associated sherds suggest the rim was from a Black-topped Red vessel), we recovered a diagnostic Badarian 'keel' as well as (brownish) red- and black-polished body sherds.

Of apparently roughly equal date is pottery of a Libo-Nubian tradition from Qarn el-Ginah (**Fig. 8** b),[11] in association with which we found quantities of ostrich eggshell, hearth remains, and much worked flint. Some of the forms and fabrics here match those from the Nile Valley end of the oasis road. Of great interest is a sherd of the same shale-tempered oasis ware that we identified in the early Predynastic levels at the Cave of the Wooden Pegs. The Qarn el-Ginah ceramic material corresponds well with that at the other end of the desert route leading to the Nile at Rayayna, and suggests that Libo-Nubian groups were moving between Kharga Oasis and the Nile Valley during the formative

Badarian and early Predynastic periods. Such links with known and datable Nile Valley cultures are extremely important; they may shed light on the relationships of other early oasis and Western Desert cultural material labelled 'Neolithic' but otherwise chronologically afloat. By comparing material throughout the entire system of desert routes connecting southern Upper Egypt and Kharga, we have found at last the crucial temporal anchors for this important body of material.

1.4 Conclusions

As was noted when the Badarian culture was first identified (Brunton and Caton-Thompson 1928, 39–40), it has a strong relationship to Naqada I (Amratian) culture, which has generally been presumed to be either an outgrowth of it, or a regionally distinct development influenced by it. The nature of the connection between the Badarian and the Amratian/Naqada I has not yet been resolved.[12] The existence of a separate Tasian culture and its temporal range continues to be much debated. First thought to precede the Badarian, it was subsequently dismissed, the distinctive Tasian objects considered to be part of the Badarian repertoire (cf. Midant-Reynes 2000, 165–6). The possibility that the Tasians belonged to a nomadic group interacting with Nile Valley dwellers, analogous to the relationship of later Nubian peoples with dynastic Egyptians, was proposed by M Murray (1956, 86, n. 1), perhaps influenced by Firth's suggestion of such a characterization for the Badarian itself (Firth 1929, 243; Brunton 1929, 459). Friedman's (1994, 15–16, 20; 1999, 9) insightful use of data not previously considered to support the concept that the Tasians were a nomadic people contemporary with the Badarian and Amratian, rather than a chronologically distinct culture, has been further advanced by recent work in the Eastern Desert (see Friedman and Hobbs this volume).

Rather than representing a northern influence filtering down to the area of Badarian occupation (Kaiser 1985; Midant-Reynes 2000, 186), it is instead likely that the Tasians entered the Nile Valley from the south Western

Desert via the region of the Qena Bend. It is not unreasonable to suggest that the material culture that was to develop into the Badarian also came out of the Western Desert.[13] It was probably not the Nile dwelling Badarians who were responsible for the appearance of Badarian pottery and objects in remote areas, but rather the Libo-Nubian groups, of which the Tasian may be one manifestation, who brought certain distinctly 'southwestern' features to the Nile Valley and in turn carried elements of Egyptian material culture across the desert expanses. The links of Naqada I–II cultures with the desert are numerous (see J Darnell this volume) – perhaps the Badarian and the overlapping Naqada I cultures represent developments of the same cultural groups coming out of the desert. By Naqada III-Early Dynastic times, the Egyptian influence is evident far afield and is more likely to have been the result of economic and possibly political expansion by the emerging pharaonic state.

Based on the ceramic and other evidence from the sites discussed above, one can posit that the early Libo-Nubian group(s) occupying the region between greater Kharga Oasis and the Nile are related to the Abkan and A-Group cultures (Nordström 1972, 28; Schon 1994, 150–1; Rampersad 2000, 140). Wendorf and Schild (2001) have noted the resemblance of Western Desert 'Late Neolithic' pottery to both Badarian and Abkan ceramics. The cultural tradition identified up until now as 'Tasian' may have evolved from the same cultural complex as this Libo-Nubian group. It is quite possible that many of the distinctive features of both the Badarian and Naqada I cultures originated far to the south and entered the Upper Egyptian Nile Valley from the Western Desert via these Libo-Nubians, whose culture continued to develop on its own path (cf. Hays 1984, 217–8). The common ancestor of the Badarian and the Naqada I cultures, as well as the Abkan, A-Group and other Nilotic Nubian and Sudanese groups, is to be sought in the expanses of what is now a vast desert.

II. The Pharaonic Evidence

A growing body of ceramic material discovered by the Theban Desert Road Survey at Western Desert sites where previously no pharaonic presence had been known points to a close association of Kharga Oasis with the Thebaïd beginning in the Middle Kingdom and developing considerably during the Seventeenth Dynasty and into the New Kingdom. The implications are far-reaching, particularly for reassessing the extent of Theban economic, political and cultural influence during the Second Intermediate Period. Conventional concepts regarding commercial interaction between Upper Egypt, Nubia, the Hyksos-controlled north and the eastern Mediterranean during that time must be altered in light of this new evidence. The importance of Kharga Oasis in the pharaonic period is much greater than was ever before recognized.

II.1 Seventeenth Dynasty Military Outpost

The Seventeenth Dynasty outpost is located in the middle of a depression on the high plateau, midway between the northern portion of the Qena Bend and Kharga Oasis, at Tundaba. It is centred on three outcroppings of fossil soil atop each of which a dry-stone structure was built: the multiple-roomed East and West Features, and the single-roomed South Feature, which is rich in midden remains and appears to have been the site of food preparation. For more on the site in general, including the pharaonic well, see J Darnell in this volume.

The ceramic evidence recovered during the excavation of these features is of unique importance. Each of the three features contained and was surrounded by pottery that originated in both the oases and the Nile Valley. The proportion of oasis-manufactured vessels in relation to Nile Valley vessels was about 50 percent in the East Feature, and even higher in the West and South Features on the west side of the site, suggesting that this remote desert outpost was provisioned not only from the Nile Valley, but also from Kharga Oasis itself. This had led us at the time of discovery to postulate the existence of an as yet unknown pharaonic habitation and ceramic production site during the Seventeenth to early Eighteenth Dynasty in Kharga, a notion that has been confirmed by the recent discovery by the Kharga Antiquities Inspectorate of tombs of that date not far from the Hibis Temple, as well as by our own discovery of pharaonic occupation at Gebel Ghueita (see below section II.3).

The pottery recovered from the interior as well as the immediate exterior of the two-room East Feature is of exclusively Seventeenth to very early Eighteenth Dynasty date, and provides the primary evidence for the date of construction and initial occupation of the outpost. Pottery of the same date also occurs inside two rooms of the West Feature, at the South Feature, in surface scatters in the general area, along the caravan tracks, at the well, at dry-stone huts both west of the well and at a remote site far to the southwest, as well as at the hinterland site discussed in the following section.

Most of the Nile Valley pottery at the outpost is likely to have originated in the Theban area and is represented by silt fabrics Nile B1 and B2 in the form of Seventeenth Dynasty short-necked restricted jars with parallel incised lines below the rim (**Fig. 9** a), red-polished Seventeenth Dynasty to early Eighteenth Dynasty ring-base bowls (**Fig. 9** b), beer jars, large and small wine jar/drop pots (**Fig. 9** d), a small jar with folded rim and a deep carinated bowl with folded rim, also characteristic of the Seventeenth and early Eighteenth Dynasties (**Fig. 9** c; probably a ring base type, cf. Bourriau 1997, 169, fig. 6.8, associated with Kerma cooking pottery, dated to Amenhotep I). Nile Valley Marls A2 was used for a carinated jar with brown painted decoration, a shallow carinated bowl with everted rim, both of which are characteristic of the Seventeenth to early Eighteenth Dynasty, and a biconical jar with mould-made bottom.

The major oasis wares thus far analysed include an oasis version of Nile silt, straw-tempered and identical to Nile Valley silt in consistency and surface treatment, but the colour indicates the use of shale-containing oasis soils in lieu of riverine silt deposits. The oasis 'marl' equivalents are in greater variety. The basic categories identified thus far are the pink/blue-grey New Kingdom 'amphora fabric' first identi-

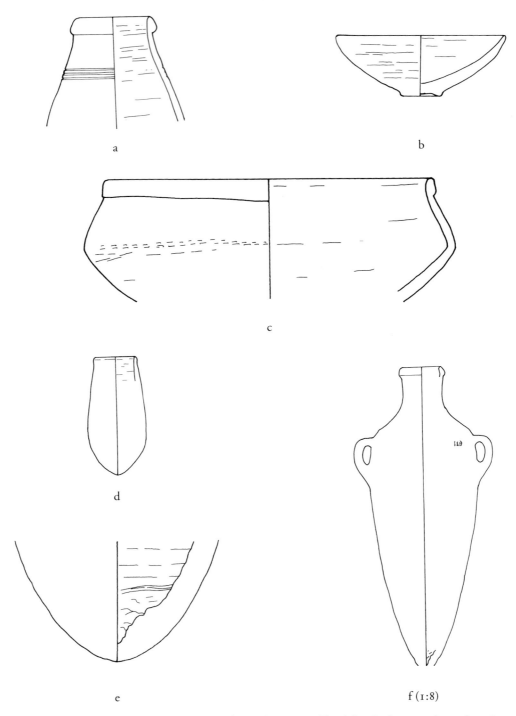

a

b

c

d

e

f (1:8)

Fig. 9   Pottery from the Seventeenth Dynasty Military Outpost at Tundaba. Scale 1:4 unless otherwise noted.

fied in the form of very thick-walled, large, dense amphorae with compacted surfaces, but used also for thinner-walled, smaller vessels (**Fig. 9** e). Chemical analysis may provide insight into variations in inclusions and firing temperatures to suit the functional requirements of various vessel types. This fabric also occurs with a red slip in forms that in the Nile Valley are made of silt. A dark grey fabric may be a more highly fired version of this same paste and occurs primarily in medium-large amphorae and ovoid jars. A lightweight, sandy green marly fabric with a buff slip, seemingly over-

fired, apparently corresponds to Nile Valley Marl E, which was identified at the site of Deir el-Ballas as a local Seventeenth to early Eighteenth Dynasty innovation. The presence of this fabric in significant quantities at the outpost, and the fabric's resemblance to known oasis wares, would suggest rather that it is another oasis fabric.

The vessels from the Hibis tombs mentioned above (to be published by the author) are also of both Nile Valley and oasis fabrics and show evidence of the influence of Theban ceramic traditions. Furthermore, some of the unusual forms in oasis ware from these tombs occur at Seventeenth to early Eighteenth Dynasty sites along the routes of the Theban Desert, in both Nile Valley and oasis fabrics. These new finds provide insight into the links between the Thebaïd and Kharga that have previously been denied in the literature (D Darnell nd).

Stamped impressions on some of the many fragments of mud jar-seals from the East Feature (see J Darnell in this volume) include a possible Hyksos name, suggesting these seals may have capped jars originating in Hyksos-controlled territories. Yet foreign products did not necessarily have to pass through the region under Hyksos control to reach the Seventeenth Dynasty Thebans. Even before the Thebans captured Avaris and re-established sovereignty over all of the Nile Valley, they were far from isolated economically and maintained access to commodities from the north not only via the Hyksos middlemen, but also by exploiting the unsurpassed Theban control of the desert routes. Certain of the Seventeenth Dynasty Theban ceramic innovations are influenced by (northern as well as southern) Syro-Palestinian forms and styles to an extent that suggest more than transient contact. Adoption of some of those same forms and stylistic elements, often in a quite unusual manner, is evident in the contemporary pottery manufactured in Kharga Oasis, indicating that the influence was there as well. Contrary to commonly held assumptions, the Western Desert acted not as barrier, but as corridor, not only to Nubia and points south and west, but also to the northern coast, and thereby to the eastern Mediterranean world. This continued to hold true well into the New Kingdom.

Imported early Canaanite amphorae, as well as imitations and adaptations of this form in oasis fabric are present at the outpost and also on the Farshût Road in the Qena Bend.[14] Later Eighteenth Dynasty Marl D (Nile Delta) amphorae (e.g., **Fig. 9** f, virtually intact and labelled with a hieratic date 'regnal year 9, first month...' in ink on the shoulder; from the exterior of the West Feature), as well as numerous contemporary imported Canaanite amphorae from a hinterland site (see the following section II.2) show that northern imports continued to reach this remote desert outpost throughout the New Kingdom.

Thus, soldiers stationed at the site may have partaken of wine from the Delta and Palestine (cf. the mud seal referring to 'food and provisions of the army', J Darnell in this volume); alternatively, the vessels may have been reused as containers for shipment of other commodities such as grain, oil, and resin (Cline and Cline 1991, 53, fig. 11). These vessels may have been brought south via the Nile to Thebes and thence to this outpost at Tundaba, but more likely, they represent shipments heading to the Nile Valley via Tundaba and the Western Desert routes from distant northern sites, including ports on the Mediterranean coast. Evidence from later in the New Kingdom for the use of ports far to the west of the Delta supports this notion; significant quantities of imported vessels have recently been unearthed at the early Ramesside coastal fortress of Zawiyet Umm el-Rakham, including Canaanite amphorae, Syro-Palestinian or Aegean jugs and Aegean stirrup vessels (Snape 2000).

II.2 Outpost Hinterland Survey

In the spring 2001 season, we discovered a new area of pharaonic activity, site PCG, to the northwest of the main area of construction at the Tundaba outpost. The quantities of ceramics, primarily of oasis fabrics, were considerable and represent an important contribution to our growing corpus of pharaonic pottery most likely manufactured in Kharga Oasis. The area now appears to be a relatively flat sheet of blown sand overlying pebble-covered ancient silt deposits. Clearance, however, revealed that the area was once—perhaps quite recently—a place of plants and trees.

Though the pharaonic pottery was scattered over an area of about 1400 square metres, the heaviest concentration occurred in a c. 100m2 area surrounding the sub-surface remains of a number of trees, most of which had been burned. Botanical analyses of the wood will be necessary for an identification of the species, but it is likely that the trees, which thrive today near this new site, are the last surviving examples of a small high plateau forest. A local man who had travelled the caravan route in the first half of this century described to us the former presence of a number of trees of various types. The fact that the pharaonic pottery was so heavily focused on the area of burned tree roots, leads one to speculate that pharaonic travellers on the route from Kharga Oasis to the region of the Qena Bend of the Nile might have found repose in the shadow of a number of trees, in an area which was once better watered than it is today (for ancient tree roots attesting to climatic change in the low desert west of Armant, see Mond and Myers 1937, 7 and pl. 8). The ancient silts, trees and a nearby well suggest that the area was once a rain-fed semi-oasis on the high plateau, at precisely the mid-point of the shortest route connecting the Nile Valley with Kharga Oasis.

We attempted a total collection of pharaonic and earlier pottery in this area; we inventoried post-pharaonic types, and collected a representative range of diagnostics as well as fabric samples. The ceramic types in this apparent camping area suggest that, as might be expected, transport vessels were the most common sort of pottery carried along the desert road. An overwhelmingly high percentage of the forms represented in the pharaonic material were amphorae, especially of the 'Canaanite Jar' type (cf. Bourriau 1990). **Fig 10** illustrates some of the rims and bases in the two most common amphora wares: **Fig. 10** ab, d and f are of a grey-brown fabric; **Fig. 10** c and e of a fine, hard, dense rosy fabric. Initial macroscopic analysis suggests that the grey-brown amphorae may be of two varieties, an imported Canaanite fabric and the local oasis imitation of the same. Among the inclusions in the examples shown in **Fig. 10** a, b and d is grey shale, a diagnostic feature for a clay source in the oases, whereas that illustrated in **Fig. 10** f lacks shale and has very abundant fine-medium white calcerous inclusions and macroscopically resembles a common Palestinian ware (cf. Group 3 of Smith *et al.* 2000, fig. 11). The fact that Canaanite forms were copied in oases clay is itself of great interest, pointing to a familiarity with vessels imported from the Levant at a time when Kharga was previously thought to be a remote 'backwater' cut off from regular contact with the

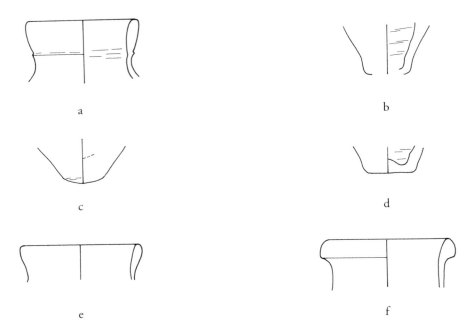

Fig. 10   Pottery from the Outpost hinterland. Scale 1:4.

Nile Valley, much less the wider Mediterranean world. Further analysis of the fabric of **Fig. 10** c and e will determine whether it is also of foreign origin, which seems probable.

Farther to the west, we surveyed the rim of the depression, identifying two distinct sets of caravan tracks. Cairns marked the routes; one cairn sits atop a high point, beneath which is a crevice in the rock. This natural space has been transformed into a 'room' by the construction of a dry-stone screen wall over a metre high, most likely erected to provide not only shelter, but also concealment for watchmen posted here to guard the road. The space was used in Roman times, but was probably created much earlier, as we found pharaonic pottery atop the hill. These and other pharaonic ceramics recovered during this survey are of great importance, as they predate the main occupation at Tundaba; the vessels are of Middle Kingdom date. The pottery therefore confirms the use of the Qena Bend–Kharga route prior to the Second Intermediate Period; the association with a 'look-out' post suggests that this desert road was already being policed by the Middle Kingdom at the latest. The site may be considered another component of the network of way-stations and fortresses strategically placed to monitor movement through the desert. The clusters of dry-stone huts established in the First Intermediate Period to Middle Kingdom along the routes of the Theban desert and similar installations in association with certain Egyptian fortresses in Nubia, as well as the fortresses themselves, are further manifestations of this system (D Darnell forthcoming). The network undoubtedly extended to the northern portions of the Western Desert as well. Archaeological evidence for this has yet to be investigated, but may include the temple site of Amenemhat I at Qaret el-Dahr in the Wadi Natrun (Fakhry 1940), where the author observed Middle Kingdom pottery of apparent northern oasis fabric in association with contemporary pottery, including Marl C storage jars.[15]

II.3 Qarn el-Ginah and Gebel Ghueita

An integral part of our study of the desert roads connecting the Theban region with Kharga Oasis is the study of the ancient remains at the termini of these routes. Thus the presence of the fortress temple of Ghueita, which appears to guard the entrance into the central Kharga depression from the east and northeast, is of extreme interest and relevance to the study of desert connections. The possibility of prior (pre-Persian) occupation on the site of Ghueita Temple was first suggested by the observation of surface pottery that was clearly both pharaonic and oasis-made. A pharaonic presence in the vicinity of Ghueita and Qarn el-Ginah had already been demonstrated by the recent discovery by the Kharga Antiquities' Inspectorate of Middle Kingdom tombs at nearby Ain el-Askar. Surveys have shown that connections with the Nile Valley in fact go back much earlier in time.

II.3.1 Survey of Qarn el-Ginah

Our work thus far at Qarn el-Ginah has concentrated on the southern and southeastern regions of the main southwestern pinnacles of the Qarn el-Ginah gebel. Caton-Thompson (1952, 41, fig. 5) reported Libo-Nubian sherds of pharaonic date in the area of the southern slopes of Qarn el-Ginah (apparently of a Pan Grave tradition based on her illustration), and we can now report evidence for considerable pharaonic Egyptian presence in the general area. There is New Kingdom oasis ware from more than one locus at Qarn el-Ginah, including a mould-made amphora bottom, another amphora of Canaanite form and a wealth of pharaonic pottery at Gebel Ghueita (see below). At Qarn el-Ginah we also discovered a rock depiction of a standing man facing right, with three feathers(?) in his hair, holding a fork-topped staff and wearing a kilt; a probable representation of one of the Nubian auxiliaries of the pharaonic patrols in the area. The ample evidence for Nubian patrolmen at many

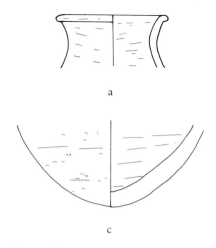

a

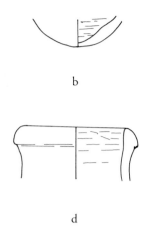

b

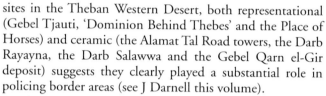

c

d

Fig. 11   Pottery from Gebel Ghueita. Scale 1:4.

sites in the Theban Western Desert, both representational (Gebel Tjauti, 'Dominion Behind Thebes' and the Place of Horses) and ceramic (the Alamat Tal Road towers, the Darb Rayayna, the Darb Salawwa and the Gebel Qarn el-Gir deposit) suggests they clearly played a substantial role in policing border areas (see J Darnell this volume).

The Pan Grave sherds mentioned above suggest that some of the pharaonic pottery at Qarn el-Ginah and Gebel Ghueita, if not in fact the majority of the material, may be related to the pharaonic patrols in the area and the people they guarded and policed, i.e., the caravans entering Kharga Oasis along the central eastern escarpment and travelling north and south along the Darb el-Arba'in.

II.3.2 Gebel Ghueita and Ghueita Temple

An initial survey of the environs of Ghueita Temple and the slopes of Gebel Ghueita yielded an astonishing amount of pharaonic ceramic material of Middle Kingdom through New Kingdom date. Many forms were present, the majority of oasis fabrics. This assemblage is the most conclusive evidence to date of a permanent pharaonic settlement in Kharga Oasis from the Middle Kingdom onward. **Fig. 11** illustrates just a small sample of this exciting new corpus. The Middle Kingdom rim to neck (**Fig. 11** a) and jar bottom (**Fig. 11** b) are of a coarse oasis version of silt, with abundant straw-, limestone- and shale-temper and yellowish grey-brown surfaces. The same sorts of inclusions are present in the 'oasis silt' variant of which the Second Intermediate Period to early New Kingdom ovoid jar bottom (**Fig. 11** c) is made, but the surface colour of that vessel is a medium pink. **Fig. 11** d is the rim of a New Kingdom oasis ware amphora, one of the most frequently occurring forms and fabrics in the sample at Gebel Ghueita. Seventeenth to early Eighteenth Dynasty forms seemed to outnumber other pharaonic types, as we might have predicted based on the evidence we have recovered elsewhere, pointing to an explosion of activity on the Western Desert routes at that time. One very special sherd of a smooth-surfaced grey oasis fabric may be the 'polished grey ware' that Helen Jacquet-Gordon (pers. comm.) identified as a unique Second Intermediate

Period type at Karnak North, the origin of which has remained a mystery.

Considering the relatively small surface area in which such a mass of pottery appears, one may suggest an extensive pharaonic presence on Gebel Ghueita. This leads to the inevitable suggestion that the fortress temple of Ghueita may in fact sit atop the remains of a pharaonic predecessor. A series of test trenches within and outside the present temple precinct may help to determine more precisely the history of the site.[16] The fortress temples of Kharga Oasis are not well understood, and a possible pre-Persian period pedigree for Ghueita could go far toward explaining the origins and functions of the fortress temples.

II.4 Kurkur Oasis

As mentioned above (section I.3.2), surveys in the main wadi led to the discovery of a significant pharaonic presence at Kurkur. At least 16 separate loci with material of pharaonic date were identified. Examples of ceramics from these loci include: the lower portion of a New Kingdom jar of Marl D, a Delta fabric; the rim of a Marl B New Kingdom amphora; an Eighteenth Dynasty silt flask rim; and simple and flanged rim sherds of the same date. There is also Nubian pottery of Middle Kingdom to New Kingdom date, including C-Group and Kerma sherds. At least some of the strategically-placed dry-stone huts built on the heights overlooking the Kurkur wadis are of pharaonic date. The spatial distribution of the pharaonic period material leads us to believe that more remains to be discovered in what must have been the focus of habitation following prehistoric times: the well area in the main wadi. Future fieldwork is planned to search for further evidence of a pharaonic presence.

The existence of important concentrations of pharaonic pottery in Kurkur will assist in the proper understanding of the inscriptions of the Nubian soldier Tjehemau at Abisko, now submerged beneath the waters of Lake Nasser. Those inscriptions, along with the Deir el-Ballas inscription of Montuhotep II, suggest that one of Montuhotep's first accomplishments was to secure Theban control over Lower

Nubia (Wawat) by means of the capture of an unnamed oasis. This oasis is likely to have been Kurkur. We know that Montuhotep II recruited Tjehemau and presumably other Nubian soldiers in the area of Aniba. Tjehemau refers to the use of a desert route to Thebes, and one may suggest that Montuhotep utilized the Darb el-Bitan (beginning at the southern portion of the Qena Bend) and the Darb Gallaba to travel southward via Kurkur Oasis to the region of Aniba, thereby securing direct control of Wawat through a land route bypassing the First Cataract.

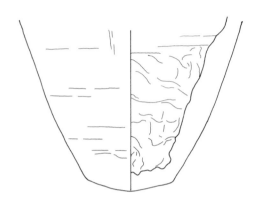

Fig. 12   Oasis amphora from the Theban Desert Roads.

II.5 Conclusions

The study of pharaonic period oasis pottery is still in its infancy, as evidence for ceramic production in the oases of the Western Desert, particularly during the New Kingdom, has only very recently come to light. Thus the material recovered by the Theban Desert Road Survey is extremely important for establishing a fabric type series. This information will be of use for research not only in the oases, but in the Nile Valley as well, where it is likely that many oasis imports await identification (see Hope *et al.* in this volume).

Following the example of the publication of the Old Kingdom centre at Balat in Dakhleh (Soukiassian 1990), a comprehensive, integrative study must be undertaken regarding later pharaonic pottery manufactured in the oases. The limited but ever-growing body of material available for comparison with the Theban Desert Road Survey's new corpus includes New Kingdom ceramics from occupation areas in Dakhleh uncovered recently by the French Institute expedition (Marchand and Tallet 1999; for the Thirteenth Dynasty settlement, see Baud 1997), the Dakhleh Oasis Project evidence published from initial surveys (Edwards, et al. 1987; Hope 1999, and Hope *et al.* in this volume), and probable 'oasis ware' vessels from multiple Nile Valley contexts.

Of the latter, Karnak North in particular has a wide array of vessels imported from the oases (H Jacquet-Gordon, pers. comm.); these are likely to have entered the Theban area via the Farshût Road. Several pot drops of New Kingdom oasis amphorae, probably originally containing wine (cf. Giddy 1980, 123; Bavay *et al.* 2000, 84–5, fig. 6), occur at the Theban end of both the Farshut and Alamat Tal Roads, including an extremely thick-walled amphora from along the descent from Gebel Antef. The exterior colour of the vessel is a dull rosy-flesh tone, while the section ranges from blue-grey to pink. Shale is the predominant inclusion. The method of manufacture is shown by the deep vertical pulling marks on the lower portion of the interior, which was apparently formed separately and then attached to the wheel-turned upper portion. Undulations in the thickness of the vessel walls occur at the joining points of the top to the bottom, and at the attachment of the handles. The vessel, published by Rose (in Strudwick 1996, 176, pl. 68, no. 125), is a close parallel for the Theban desert example. This form and its finishing features occur exclusively in an oasis fabric, and the amphora type is probably of Kharga origin. It is known from Eighteenth Dynasty contexts at Karnak North, Malkata, Qurna and Amarna (see Hope *et al.* in this volume).

Conventional early amphorae types in oasis fabric are more common in the Theban Desert, e.g., **Fig. 12** from the hinterland of the Alamat Tal Road; paralleled by examples from Gebel Roma and the Theban descent of the Farshût Road. The vessel has a mould-made bottom and is distinguished from its Nile Valley formal parallels by the colour and composition of its fabric. In section, a blue-grey core (5Y 6/1–2.5Y 6/1) with indistinct zoning is surrounded by colours ranging from pink (2.5YR 7/4) to butterscotch (10YR 7/4) to salmon (7.5YR 6–7/6). The percentage of inclusions relative to the matrix is high, including abundant medium to coarse calcareous particles, as well as darker elements that are probably shale. Re-examination of the fabrics of amphorae from Nile Valley loci which, like this example, may outwardly appear to be of Egyptian or Canaanite manufacture, would be a worthwhile undertaking at this time.

As more previously unrecognized pharaonic oasis material is identified at Nile Valley sites, an increasingly vigorous and regular contact between the desert and Egypt proper is emerging. Moreover, new discoveries in the Southern Oases and along the routes which link them to the Nile indicate that distant Western Desert locales were integrated into the Egyptian administrative system to a greater extent than was ever imagined. Future research can only increase our appreciation of the ancient Egyptians' knowledge and mastery of the great desert out of which their own extraordinary civilization is likely to have arisen.

Acknowledgements

This paper draws on season reports of the Theban Desert Road Survey and Toshka Desert Survey by J and D Darnell; for a description of the project, its origins and work to date see J Darnell in this volume; illustrations are by J Darnell; photographs by D Darnell. The author wishes to thank Vivian Davies and Renée Friedman for the invitation to participate in the colloquium, as well as Helen Jacquet-Gordon, Colin Hope and Sylvie Marchand for generously sharing information on pottery manufactured in the oases. The project is currently funded by Yale University and a grant from the National Endowment for the Humanities.

Notes

1. For the most similar published parallel to this cave with petro-glyphs and occupational remains, see Bietak and Engelmayer 1963 and the comments thereon in Nordström 1972, 21.

2. This fabric has been assigned to the early Holocene Masara cultural unit, but also occurs near and at later Bashendi B and Sheikh Muftah sites. Hope (1999, 216 [by D. Tangri] and 237–8) suggests the coarse and irregular character of the ware may 'be indicative of manufacture by people not permanently resident in the oasis and who were either unaware of, or who did not have the time to exploit, more suitable clay deposits'. The latter explanation would fit the desert road context well.

3. From site KDK 1; SNM 26877; although there is a subtle outward flare as opposed to the inward turn of the Cave of the Wooden Pegs example, the rim decoration and finishing marks interior/exterior in the rim areas of the two vessels are very similar.

4. Similar elements occur in association with 'stick figure' crocodiles viewed from above, whose feet they very much resemble. These are found in the Eastern Desert at Winkler (1938) sites 14 and 17; he suggested they represent the footprints of the animals.

5. Sozzani and Negro 1989, 100–101, figs 1, 2, negative handprints, but executed in white, as opposed to red, pigment in the Grotta delle Mani, Wadi Berigh, Tassili N'Ajjer; and Mori 2000, 247, fig. 169, with negative handprints outlined with white pigment, and possibly one positive handprint in red pigment at Tadrart Acacus. As in our Cave of the Hands, the negative prints are of the left hand.

6. The Abka images occur below Level 5, which has a corrected C14 date of 4650 BC (Hellström 1970, 29).

7. Comments written up by Gray under the heading 'Caves in the Wadi al Hôl' are included among the notes of Myers in the archives of the Egypt Exploration Society, London.

8. Brunton and Caton-Thompson (1928, 19) note that leather skins, sometimes sewn into a garment of sorts, 'were the common material for clothing for the dead', but were more frequently found with Badarian males than females. Leather in many folds occurred in Tasian burials of adults, both male and female, as well as children: e.g., Brunton 1937, 5, Tasian graves 438, 439, and 464; 27 ff for sewn and knotted leather.

9. Cf. Friedman 1994, 348, 357; Friedman 1999, 3–6 and 9; and note a single sherd, apparently from a Nile Valley Tasian beaker–though whether it is of fine Badarian silt is unclear–found in possible association with Bashendi B cultural material in Dakhleh Oasis, Hope 1999, 239 and Hope section I.3.1 in this volume, **Fig. 10** c.

10. Specifically Kadada–see the discussion by Rampersad 2000, 136–7. Also see Brunton and Caton-Thompson 1928, 42 for Badarian burials of dogs and other animals wrapped in matting and sometimes linen, noting a comparison with Nubian traditions. The Predynastic multiple dog burial (pl. LXIX) at Hemamieh seems to represent a different phenomenon.

11. See Brunton and Caton-Thompson 1928, pl. 18, RB 31R for the form, but the fabric is an oasis version of silt, with coarse straw, sand and shale temper.

12. Hays (1984) maintains that the Badarian and Amratian are contemporary; Holmes (1996, 189) suggests a local persistence or evolution of the Badarian into Amratian times. On the widespread influence of the Badarian on the Upper Egyptian Predynastic, see Friedman 1994, 351–60 and in Holmes and Friedman 1994, 137.

13. Cf. the often-discussed similarities among Neolithic pottery of Sudan and the Western Desert; Hays (1984, 218) suggests that ripple-burnishing techniques started in the Sudan and then moved down the Nile to Egypt; also, see Midant-Reynes 2000, 164, citing Holmes 1989; Holmes 1996 for the 'African' origins of Badarian and Naqada I; and especially Hope in this volume, concluding paragraphs.

14. For example, Upper Egyptian and Kharga Oasis copies of the transitional MB IIA-B type of Canaanite amphora with a pronounced rounded ridge on the exterior of the neck and a slight ridge at the base of the neck, for which see McGovern and Harbottle 1997, 142–45 (fig. 5.1), and elements thereof appear in Seventeenth Dynasty contexts.

15. The identification is based on personal observation of sherds of the same distinctive fabric at sites along the desert edges of the Fayum and its resemblance in certain aspects to oasis wares from Kharga and Dakhleh.

16. We are grateful for the collaboration kindly suggested by Mr Bahgat Ahmed, General Director for the Kharga Inspectorate, in studying the evidence recovered during past SCA excavations in the temple precinct.

Bibliography

Banks K M, 1980. Ceramics of the Western Desert. In F Wendorf and R Schild (eds), *Prehistory of the Eastern Sahara*. New York: 299–315.

Barich B, 1999. The archaeology of Farafra Oasis. *Egyptian Archaeology* 15: 37–9.

Baud M, 1997. Balat/'Ayn-Asil, oasis de Dakhla: La ville de la Deuxième Période intermédiaire. *Bulletin de l'Institut français d'archéologie orientale* 97: 19–34.

Bavay L, Marchand S and Tallet P, 2000. Les jarres inscrites du Nouvel Empire provenant de Deir el-Medina. *Cahiers de la céramique égyptienne* 6: 77–89.

Bietak M and Engelmayer R, 1963. *Eine frühdynastische Abri-Siedlung mit Felsbildern aus Sayala-Nubien*. Österreichische Akademie der Wissenschaften, Philosoph.-Hist. Klasse, Denkschriften 82. Vienna.

Bourriau J, 1990. Canaanite Jars from New Kingdom Deposits at Memphis, Kom Rabi'a. *Eretz-Israel* 21: 18*–26*.

Bourriau J, 1997. Beyond Avaris: The Second Intermediate Period in Egypt Outside the Eastern Delta. In E Oren (ed), *The Hyksos: New Historical and Archaeological Perspectives*. University Museum Monograph 96; University Museum Symposium Series 8. Philadelphia: 159–82.

Brunton G, 1929. The Beginnings of Egyptian Civilization. *Antiquity* 3: 456–67.

Brunton G, 1934. Some Tasian Pottery in the Cairo Museum. *Annales du Service des Antiquités de l'Égypte* 34: 94–6.

Brunton G, 1937. *Mostagedda and the Tasian Culture*. British Museum Expedition to Middle Egypt. London.

Brunton G and Caton-Thompson G, 1928. *The Badarian Civilisation and Predynastic Remains near Badari*. British School of Archaeology in Egypt and Egyptian Research Account 46. London.

Butzer K W and Hansen C L, 1968. *Desert and River in Nubia: Geomorphology and Prehistoric Environments at the Aswan Reservoir*. Madison, Milwaukee, and London.

Caneva I, 1987. Pottery Decoration in Prehistoric Sahara and Upper Nile: A New Perspective. In B E Barich (ed.), *Archaeology and Environment in the Libyan Sahara.* British Archaeological Reports International Series, 368. Oxford: 231–54.

Caton-Thompson G, 1952. *Kharga Oasis in Prehistory.* London.

Cline E H and Cline M J, 1991. Of Shoes and Ships and Sealing Wax: International Trade and the Late Bronze Age Aegean. *Expedition* 33/3: 46–54.

Darnell D, nd. *The Theban Origins of New Kingdom Ceramic Features in the Nile Valley and Kharga Oasis.* PhD thesis in preparation

Darnell D, forthcoming. Securing His Majesty's Borders: Middle Kingdom Features on the Routes of the Theban Western Desert.

Darnell D and Darnell J C, 1994. The Luxor-Farshût Desert Road Survey. *Bulletin de liaison du groupe international d'étude de la céramique égyptienne* 18: 45–9.

Darnell D and Darnell J C, 1996. The Luxor-Farshût Desert Road Survey. *Bulletin de liaison du groupe international d'étude de la céramique égyptienne* 19: 36–50.

Darnell J C and Darnell D, 1997. New Inscriptions of the Late First Intermediate Period from the Theban Western Desert and the Beginnings of the Northern Expansion of the Eleventh Dynasty. *Journal of Near Eastern Studies* 56/4: 241–58.

Edwards W I, Hope C A and Segnit E R, 1987. *Ceramics from the Dakhleh Oasis: Preliminary Studies.* Victoria College Archaeology Research Unit Occasional Paper 1, Burwood, Australia (with recent corrections by verbal communication of C A Hope).

Fakhry A, 1940. Wâdi-El-Natrûn. *Annales du Service des Antiquités de l'Égypte* 40: 845–8.

Firth C M, 1929. Review of 'The Badarian Civilization'. *Antiquity* 3: 242–5.

Friedman R, 1994. *Predynastic Settlement Ceramics of Upper Egypt: A Comparative Study of the Ceramics of Hemamieh, Nagada, and Hierakonpolis.* University of California at Berkeley, PhD Dissertation. University Microfilms, Michigan.

Friedman R, 1999. Badarian Grave Group 569. In W V Davies (ed.), *Studies in Egyptian Antiquities: A Tribute to T.G.H. James.* British Museum Occasional Paper 123. London: 1–11.

Friedman R. et al., 1999. Preliminary Report on Field Work at Hierakonpolis: 1996–1998. *Journal of the American Research Center in Egypt* 36: 1–35.

Geus F, 1984. Excavations at El Kadada and the Neolithic of the Central Sudan. In L Krzyzaniak and M Kobusiewicz (eds), *Origin and Early Development of Food-Producing Cultures in North-Eastern Africa.* Poznan: 361–72.

Giddy L L, 1980. Some Exports form the Oases of the Libyan Desert into the Nile Valley–Tomb 131 at Thebes. *Livre du Centenaire 1880–1980.* Memoire de l'Institut francais d'archéologie orientale 104. Cairo: 119–25

Gratien B, 2000. Les pots de cuisson nubiens et les bols décorés de la premie`re moitié du IIe millénaire avant J.-C.: Problèmes d'identification. *Cahiers de la céramique égyptienne* 6: 113–48.

Hays T R, 1984. Predynastic development in Upper Egypt. In L Krzyzaniak and M Kobusiewicz (eds), *Origin and Early Development of Food-Producing Cultures in North-Eastern Africa.* Poznan: 211–9

Hayes W C, 1965. *Most Ancient Egypt.* Chicago.

Hellström P, 1970. *The Rock Drawings.* The Scandinavian Joint Expedition to Sudanese Nubia 1. Stockholm.

Holmes D L, 1989. *The Predynastic Lithic Industries of Upper Egypt: A Comparative Study of the Lithic Traditions of Badari, Nagada and Hierakonpolis.* Cambridge Monographs in African Archaeology 33. British Archaeological Reports International Series 469. Oxford.

Holmes D L 1996. Recent investigations in the Badarian region (Middle Egypt). In L Krzyzaniak, K Kroeper and M Kobusiewicz (eds), *Interregional Contacts in the Later Prehistory of Northeastern Africa.* Poznan: 181–92.

Holmes D L and Friedman R F, 1994. Survey and Test Excavations in the Badari Region, Egypt. *Proceedings of the Prehistoric Society* 60: 105–42.

Hope C A, 1999. Pottery Manufacture in the Dakhleh Oasis (with a contribution by Daniel M. Tangri). In C S Churcher and A J Mills (eds), *Reports from the Survey of the Dakhleh Oasis, Western Desert of Egypt, 1977–1987* Dakhleh Oasis Project Monograph 2. Oxford: 215–43.

Junker H, 1919. *Bericht über die Grabungen der Akademie der Wissenschaften in Wien auf den Friedhöfen von El-Kubanieh-Süd, Winter 1910–1911.* Akademie der Wissenschaften in Wien, philosophisch-historische Klasse Denkschriften, 62.3, Vienna.

Kaiser W, 1985. Zur Südausdehnung der vorgeschichtlichen Deltakulturen und zur frühen Entwicklung Oberägyptens. *Mitteilungen des Deutschen Archäologischen Instituts Abteilung Kairo* 41: 61–87.

Kuper R, 1995. Prehistoric Research in the Southern Libyan Desert: A brief account and some conclusions of the B.O.S. project. *Cahier de Recherches de l'Institut de Papyrologie et d'Égyptologie de Lille* 17/1 Actes de la VIIIe conférence internationale des études nubiennes, Lille. 11–17 Septembre 1994: 123–40.

Marchand S and Tallet P, 1999. Ayn Asil et l'oasis de Dakhla au Nouvel Empire. *Bulletin de l'Institut francais d'archéologie orientale* 99: 307–52.

McGovern P and Harbottle G, 1997. 'Hyksos' Trade connections between Tell el-Dab'a (Avaris) and the Levant: A Neutron Activation Study of the Canaanite Jar. In E D Oren (ed.), *The Hyksos: New Historical and Archaeological Perspectives.* Philadelphia: 141–57.

Midant-Reynes B, 2000. *The Prehistory of Egypt: From the First Egyptians to the First Pharaohs.* Oxford.

Mond R and Myers O H, 1937. *Cemeteries of Armant I.* Egypt Exploration Society Excavation Memoirs 42. London.

de Morgan J, 1897. *Recherches sur les origines de l'Égypte–Ethnographie préhistorique et tombeau royal de Négadah.* Paris.

Mori F, 2000. *La grandi civiltà el Sahara Antico.* Nuova Cultura 7. Turin.

Murray G W, 1939. An Archaic Hut in Wadi Umm Sidrah. *Journal of Egyptian Archaeology* 25: 38–9, pls. VIII and IX.

Murray G W and Myers O H, 1933. Some Pre-dynastic Rock-drawings. *Journal of Egyptian Archaeology* 19: 129–32, pl. XX.

Murray M A, 1956. Burial Customs and Beliefs in the Hereafter in Predynastic Egypt. *Journal of Egyptian Archaeology* 42: 86–96.

Myers O H, nd.a unpublished. *Armant 1936–7 season report.* Manuscript in archives of the Egypt Exploration Society, London.

Myers O H, nd.b unpublished. *Armant 1937–8 season report.* Manuscript in archives of the Egypt Exploration Society, London.

Myers O H, 1958. Abka Re-excavated. *Kush* 6: 131–41.

Myers O H, 1960. Abka Again. *Kush* 8: 174–81.

Newbold D, 1924. A Desert Odyssey of a Thousand Miles. *Sudan Notes and Records* 7: 43–92.

Nordström H-Å, 1972. *Neolithic and A-Group Sites.* Scandanavian Joint Expedition 3:1. Stockholm.

Rampersad S R, 2000. Relationships of the Nubian A-Group. *Journal of the American Research Center in Egypt* 37: 127–42.

Reinold J *et al.*, 2000. *Archéologie au Soudan, les civilisations de Nubie*. Paris.

Riemer H and Kuper R, 2000. <<Clayton rings>>: enigmatic ancient pottery in the Eastern Sahara. *Sahara* 12: 91–100.

Sander-Hansen C E, 1956. *Die Texte der Metternichstele*. Analecta Aegyptiaca 7. Copenhagen.

Schild R and Wendorf F, 2001. The Combined Prehistoric Mission Field School, 2000 field season report. *American Research Center in Egypt website*: www.arce.org/research2.html.

Schon W, 1994. The Late Neolithic of Wadi El Akhdar (Gilf Kebir) and the Eastern Sahara. *Archéologie du Nil Moyen* 6: 131–75.

Simmons A H and Mandel R D, 1985. *Human Occupation of a Marginal Environment: An Archaeological Survey near Kharga Oasis, Egypt*. The University of Kansas Museum of Anthropology Project Report Series 57. Kansas.

Smith L M V *et al.*, 2000. The Provenance of LBA Transport Amphorae Found in Egypt. *Internet Archaeology* 9: http://intarch.ac.uk/journal/issue 9.

Snape S, 2000. Imported Pottery at Zawiyet Umm el-Rakham: Preliminary Report. *Bulletin de liaison du Groupe international d'étude de la céramique égyptienne* 21: 17–22.

Soukiassian G, Wuttmann M and Pantalacci L, 1990. *Balat III. Les ateliers de potiers d'Ayn Asîl*. Fouilles de l'Institut francais d'archéologie orientale 34. Cairo.

Sozzani M and Negro G, 1989. Due interessanti incisioni del Tadrart algerino. *Sahara* 2: 100–5.

Strudwick N, 1996. *The Tombs of Amenhotep, Khnummose, and Amenmose at Thebes (Nos. 294, 253, and 254)*. Oxford.

Tangri D, 1991. Neolithic basket-impressed pottery from Dakhleh Oasis, Egypt: New evidence for regionalism in the Eastern Sahara. *Sahara* 4: 141–3.

Welsby D, 1996. 1.75 Beaker. In T Phillips (ed.), *Africa The Art of a Continent*. London: 105.

Welsby D, 1997. Early Pottery in the Middle Nile Valley. In I Freestone and D Gaimster (eds), *Pottery in the Making: World Ceramic Traditions*. London: 26–31.

Wetterstrom W, 1993. Foraging and farming in Egypt: the transition from hunting and gathering to horticulture in the Nile Valley. In T Shaw, P Sinclair, B Andah and A Okpoko (eds), *The Archaeology of Africa: Food, Metals and Towns*. London and New York: 165–226.

Williams B B, 1986. *Excavations Between Abu Simbel and the Sudan Frontier, part 1: The A-Group Royal Cemetery at Qustul: Cemetery L*. Oriental Institute Nubia Expedition 3. Chicago.

Williams B B, 1989. *Excavations Between Abu Simbel and the Sudan Frontier, parts 2, 3, and 4: Neolithic, A-Group, and Post-A-Group Remains from Cemeteries W, V, S, Q, T, and a Cave East of Cemetery K*. Oriental Institute Nubia Expedition 4. Chicago.

Winkler H A, 1938. *Rock-Drawings of Southern Upper Egypt I* Archaeological Survey of Egypt 26. London.

Winkler H A, 1939. *Rock-Drawings of Southern Upper Egypt II*. Archaeological Survey of Egypt 27. London.

A 'Tasian' Tomb in Egypt's Eastern Desert

Renée Friedman and Joseph J Hobbs

Introduction

The investigation of a burial site in the central Eastern Desert of Egypt has yielded important dated information about the Neolithic inhabitants of the Eastern Desert. Despite the abundance of rock drawings that attest to their presence, the actual remains and datable material culture of these early desert inhabitants have been notable for their absence. Although possibly plundered in antiquity, and certainly violated twice in recent times, the large tomb, hollowed out of soft sandstone, still contained a diverse set of artefacts that give some indication of the original wealth and cultural milieu of its multiple occupants. The ceramic assemblage, dominated by distinctive flared-rim beakers, which are often decorated with incised and/or punctate designs, finds its closest parallel with the Tasian, the most poorly-understood of the early Predynastic cultures within the Egyptian Nile Valley. Conventional radiocarbon and AMS dating of the remains produced strikingly early calibrated dates of between 4940 and 4455 BC (5850 ± 50 bp and 5760 ± 70 bp uncalibrated), supporting the original early date proposed for the Tasian. However, analysis of the ceramics suggests that they are locally made, and the recent discovery of similar material deep in the Western Desert indicates that the makers are apparently far-ranging desert dwellers. The presence of related pottery at various locations in the Egyptian Nile Valley may be the most distinctive evidence for the early interaction of the desert and the sown.

Context and Objectives

In 1983 Joseph Hobbs was accompanied by a Bedouin guide to a plundered grave site in the Wadi Atulla, in the central portion of Egypt's Eastern Desert, north of the Wadi Hammamat (**Fig. 1**). The crude excavation had apparently yielded nothing of perceived value to the diggers, and they left what had been taken out–mainly human bones, pottery, beads, palettes, flint knives and sea shells–by the pit. These were photographed (**Plate 102**), and the pottery was later identified as having its closest parallels with a series of incised beakers now in the Egyptian Museum, Cairo. These vessels were published by G Brunton (1934), and he attributed them to the Tasian culture he had discovered in the Badari region of Middle Egypt (1929; 1937, 25–33). Brunton believed the Tasian culture to precede the Badarian, making it the earliest ceramic-bearing Predynastic culture then known in Upper Egypt. However, from the start, the existence and chronological placement of the Tasian has been a subject of controversy (e.g., Baumgartel 1955, 20–1;

Holmes 1989, 177–8; Kaiser 1985; Midant-Reynes 2000, 165–6, 186; Hendrickx and Vermeersch 2000, 40).

The Neolithic and early Predynastic cultures of Upper Egypt are still poorly understood. There are many unanswered questions about the origins and influences that contributed to the Predynastic cultures of Upper Egypt. No connection with the Epi-Palaeolithic fishing and gathering communities has yet been established, and a gap of approximately 2000 years (7000–5400 BC) still exists in the record of habitation along the Egyptian Nile Valley. Yet this time period corresponds to the increasingly complex and diverse societies being discovered within the Western Desert, which are discussed in several contributions to this volume (e.g., Kuper; Wendorf and Schild; D Darnell). Thus the west has figured large in discussion of Predynastic origins and influences, despite the lack of uncontroversial evidence to support this connection.

The Tasian-related material in the Eastern Desert and now at a site near Nabta Playa in the Western Desert (Schild and Wendorf 2001) suggests that this culture may be the most distinctive 'missing link' in the picture of interaction between desert dwellers and the Nile Valley cultures, which led ultimately to the development of Egyptian civilization.

This burial in the Eastern Desert is also a significant new addition to our understanding of that desert during the Neolithic and early Predynastic. Despite an abundance of rock drawings attributed to this early period and the recovery of a wide variety of Eastern Desert products in Predynastic graves, material, and especially ceramic, evidence of the desert's inhabitants has for a long time been limited to an inadequately published Badarian/Naqada I settlement and burial in the Wadi Hammamat discovered by Debono (1950; 1951) and a possibly 'Tasian' burial near Ras Samadi reported by Murray and Derry (1923) and reassessed by Resch (1963). Fortunately this state of affairs is beginning to change with recent and on-going investigations at Wadi Sodmein (Vermeersch *et al.* 1994; 1996), the Wadi Allaqi (Sadr *et al.* 1994, 1995), the Wadi Gash (Alfano 1994) and the Wadi Hammamat (Wright and Herbert 1993). As this work continues and sees full publication, our understanding of the lifestyle and role played by these seemingly elusive desert inhabitants of the Eastern Desert will be dramatically enriched.

The major objective of the research was to learn more about this desert culture through field study of this rarunusual site. Going into the project, the research team knew that the tomb had been plundered. However, because of the paucity of information about the Eastern Desert and the Tasian culture, it was deemed worthwhile to salvage what we could.

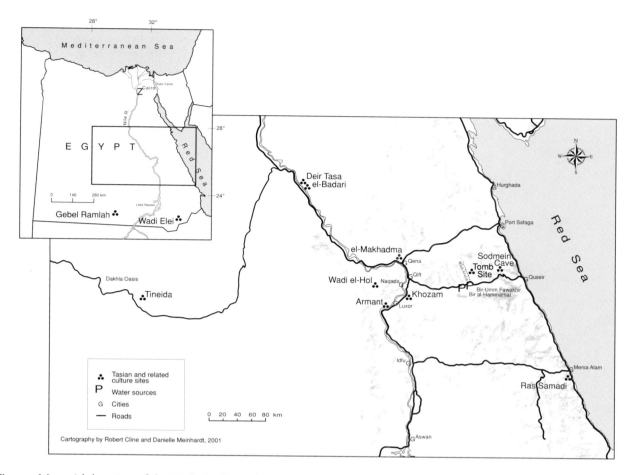

Fig. 1   Map with location of the Wadi Atulla tomb and other Tasian-related sites.

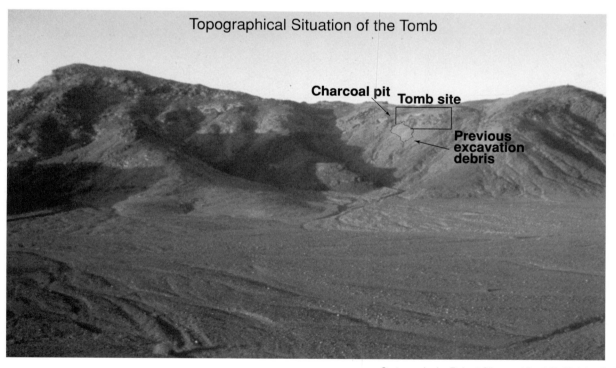

Cartography by Robert Cline and Danielle Meinhardt, 2001

Fig. 2   Topographical situation of the tomb in the Wadi Atulla.

179

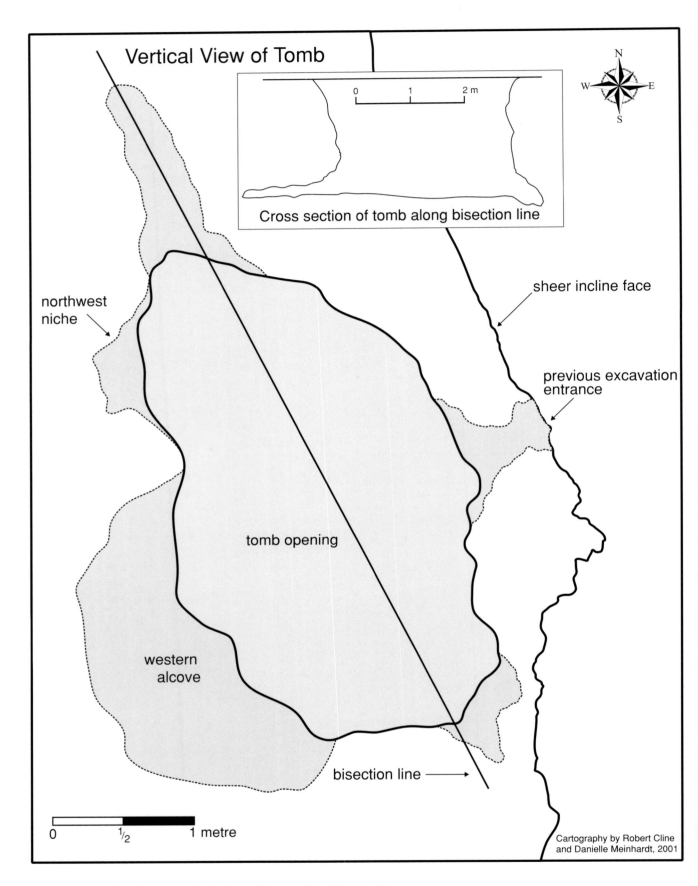

Vertical View of Tomb

0   1   2 m

Cross section of tomb along bisection line

northwest
niche

sheer incline face

previous excavation
entrance

tomb opening

western
alcove

bisection line

0   ½   1 metre

Cartography by Robert Cline
and Danielle Meinhardt, 2001

Fig. 3   Vertical and cross-sectional views of the tomb in Wadi Atulla.

Findings

The grave is located on the eastern edge of a sloping ridge overlooking a confluence of two wadis. It is within a narrow geological band identified as the Atud Sedimentary Formation and had been hollowed out of a relatively soft and friable intrusion of light coloured sandstone set within a parent material of darker siltstone (**Fig. 2** and **Plate 97**). This sandstone is very friable and easily broken along longitudinal fractures, and as a result the tomb cutting has relatively sheer, although somewhat sloping, walls. The opening is oblong in shape, measuring roughly 4 m long (N-S) by 3 m wide (E-W) with a maximum depth of approximately 4 m (**Fig. 3** and **Plate 98**). At floor level the main area is only about 1.6 m wide. At surface level, the ground slopes down from west to east following the natural slope of the ridge to a sheer face drop just beyond the east wall of the tomb. Several niches were dug into the walls of the tomb, the most prominent being a large alcove cut into the west wall and smaller niches on the north (**Plates 99–100**).

One extremely unusual and useful aspect of the field work was that we were able to speak with two of the four men who had plundered the tomb in 1981 and again in 1992 (the other two had died). This enabled us to learn how the tomb had been discovered and roughly what its surface features and contents looked like before and during these disturbances, thereby helping to fill in some of the missing pieces of the archaeological puzzle. It also offered us the opportunity to educate these men and other potential future grave-robbers about the importance of leaving sites undisturbed. We told them (as they had already learned) that the likelihood of their finding treasures was slim, and that their rewards would be greater by working for expeditions that would excavate their finds properly. We also informed them how to get the word to the appropriate authorities when they found new sites.

Prior to the recent activity, the tomb appears to have already been plundered in ancient, perhaps Predynastic times, but has remained undisturbed since that time. The first modern discovery of the tomb was in 1981, and the tomb diggers attributed their find to a supernatural prophecy. The surviving one of the two brothers who first breached the tomb told us they were drawn to the site by an account related by an elderly 'Ababda seer living at Qena, in the Nile Valley. This 'Ababdi reportedly had a book describing, among many other treasure tales, a rich site in the Eastern Desert containing forty graves. The text read that if one stood at the pharaonic inscription near Bir Kubbaniya in Wadi Atulla and looked in the direction of the sunrise, one would see the place where the graves lie. The text added that there were both inscriptions and treasures of great value in these graves. With this information the two brothers proceeded to the pharaonic inscription (removed by thieves some time after 1993) and looked eastward. A single upright stone at the edge of the ridge closest to their location caught their eyes. They climbed up, began to look around, and soon spotted, lower on the ridge, a prominent cluster of perhaps twenty boulders protruding from the ground. These were darker than other rocks in the area, and the men concluded

that they had been brought by people from the wadi bed below. Over the next two hours they extracted these partially-buried heavy stones and dug several shallow pits below where a few of them had lain. They found only some small bone fragments and decided this site did not warrant further excavation.

The next day they returned to the site, and began looking under another cluster of dark, obviously introduced boulders some ten metres to the east of where they had already dug (**Plate 101**; **Fig. 2**). Their shallow excavation yielded only charcoal fragments (which they identified as *Acacia raddiana*), and they abandoned this site. Exploring the hillside north of here, they came across about ten oblong, half-metre long rocks set vertically in the ground. They pulled back two of these, causing sediment to spill into a hole below. They now believed had found a tomb (they had), and began digging in the loose sediment. The surviving brother expressed repeatedly and emphatically that as soon as they began digging (at an estimated depth of 4 cm) they were finding human bones in badly-weathered, disassociated fragments. This point leads to the conclusion, related above, that the tomb was probably disturbed in ancient times.

At the end of the day, having dug about two metres though sediment strewn with human bone fragments, the brothers reached some artefacts at the rear of the tomb's prominent western alcove (**Plate 99**). These were the beakers and cups, lying mostly empty on their sides, along with two flint knifes and some of the assorted artefacts illustrated in **Plate 102**. Judged to be worthless by the diggers, these were left on the site.

In 1992 a distant relative of the brothers reflected further on the 'Ababda revelation of forty graves with treasure, and decided to give the site a closer look. He continued to dig below the level of the 1981 excavation and, finding that there was an enormous amount of loose, bone-strewn sediment, called for assistance from two more men. The three dug furiously in the belief that there would be several bodies and accompanying treasures in branches leading off from the central pit. However, after a day and a half, they had found only small quantities of bone and pottery fragments. They did find a promising shaft leading northwestward from the base of their excavation and followed it about a metre, again finding no artefacts but only badly-preserved human bone. Surmising that there was no treasure after all, they elected to dig no further here or below into the loose sediments at the bottom of the tomb.

As a result of these multiple disturbances, few artefacts remained in the tomb itself. Nevertheless, careful clearance has revealed some apparently undisturbed sediments and allowed us to reconstruct some of the activities that took place within the tomb. The largest alcove, dug into the higher west wall of the tomb, is approximately 1.5 m above the sloping bedrock floor (**Fig. 3** and **Plates 98–99**). Here, a semi-circular opening within the west wall, measuring approximately 1.3 m (N-S) along the base, and 1.6 m high, leads to an alcove with a sharply sloping ceiling that extends 1.4 m toward the west. The floor of the alcove was cut down behind the remnant of the main west wall of the tomb for another 40 cm to a roughly oval shape, about 130 × 80 cm in dimensions, its long axis oriented north-south, appropriate for a crouched adult burial. Within this area, the irregular bedrock was levelled with a layer of ashy, grey granular soil, on top of which was a compacted reddish-brown sediment about 3–5 cm thick that may be the remains of organic material, possibly matting, basketry or wickerwork (cf. Brunton 1937, 27). Unfortunately no identifiable organic material could be observed in the depression within the alcove, although some bleached bones, charcoal and potsherds were recovered from this area. Additional niches, about 50 × 60 cm in dimension, appear to have been hollowed out on the west and south sides of this alcove. It is in one of these that the beakers were found in 1981.

Infant bones and unidentifiable bone fragments were also embedded in compacted and undisturbed silts in the low ceiling and back walls of the niches. How they came to be there is not entirely clear. Water action would appear to be responsible, although at what point in time is unknown.

Another large niche hollowed out at the northwest corner of the tomb is at a lower level (**Fig. 3**, **Plate 100**). Approximately 130 cm deep and 90 cm wide with a sloping ceiling, it also contained the compacted reddish-brown soil atop ashy grey sediments as found in the western alcove. Again these sediments lay upon the irregular bedrock in an oval configuration, approximately 130 × 80 cm in dimensions, with the longer side oriented north-south.

Further to the north, a niche originally cleared in 1991 retained no clear indication of human interment. The compact silty sediments were followed for an additional metre and half, but only animal bones were found, suggesting that this might have been an animal burrow at some point. Notable, however, was the recovery of a large bone that may be *Bos* sp., although this identification has not been confirmed. Another possible niche on the south cut into and below floor level was examined, but only silt and the remnants of rodent burrows were found. Thus at least two areas, the western alcove and the northwest niche, were clearly used for human burial, but whether the main area of the tomb was used for this purpose remains unknown.

Soft silt and loose stone debris was cleared to bedrock in the main part of the tomb; no undisturbed sediments were found. The tomb bottomed out on a smooth, possibly water-scoured, floor of soft serpentine and the parent siltstone. The floor sloped sharply from west to east, funnelling into an opening at the base of the east wall (**Fig. 3**). This opening was cleared by the Bedouin during their diggings to facilitate the removal of dirt, and although it was no doubt enlarged by them, it may have been a natural opening created by the build-up and subsequent draining of water.

The extensive disturbance of the tomb makes it difficult to determine what induced its users to select such a seemingly unlikely place (**Fig 2**). Certainly of all the places on the top of this ridge, some 40 m above the surroundings wadis, this vein of friable sandstone would be the easiest to dig; the extensive fissures would make it quite easy simply to pull away. However, the great depth to which it has been dug seems excessive and is more suggestive of mining operations.

Talc and serpentine are prevalent throughout the area, and the talc is still actively mined on a small scale in the immediate vicinity. The tomb may thus be the opportunistic use of an abandoned mining operation. Yet, its users must have been aware that its down-slope location would make it prone to at least episodic flooding, and it is therefore possible that its water collection properties were in fact part of its attraction. The burial niches, which are clearly secondary man-made cuttings, have been placed well above the main floor.[1] Evidence from Sodmein Cave indicates that the climate in this part of the Eastern Desert at this time and earlier was not substantially different from what it is today (Vermeersch *et al.* 1994). Burial near or in conjunction with a water source, however intermittently it acted as a reservoir, may have been the intention, providing water for life in the hereafter, similar in conception to the siting of cemeteries on the banks of wadis common in Predynastic Egypt.

Regarding the original above-ground appearance of the tomb, we must rely on the Bedouin reports. The ten oblong, half-metre long rocks set vertically in the ground above the tomb cutting suggest that the tomb was marked in some way.[2] The large dark boulders on the top of the ridge may also have been related to the tomb superstructure. Limited investigation of an area once covered by these stones to the southwest of the tomb opening revealed a roughly circular deposit of soft ash-filled material set above and within hard yellow rocky sediments (**Fig. 2**; **Plate 101**). At its base, approximately 40 cm below the current surface, was a concentration of charcoal sitting upon rubified rock. A conventional C14 date from this charcoal produced a date of 5760 ± 70 bp, or 4765–4455 cal BC (Beta 143776), closely corresponding to the AMS date derived from pottery from the tomb itself (see below). Aside from unidentified bones scrapes, no other cultural material was recovered from this area.

A lack of parallels (well dated or otherwise) hampers a full understanding of this disturbed site. Nevertheless, the tumulus burials at Wadi Elei, east of the Wadi Allaqi (see **Fig. 1**), may be of use. Here a relatively undisturbed grave (D5.1) has been found with a superstructure composed of a ring of boulders approximately 7 m in diameter, filled with sand. Within the circle were upright stelae, or slabs of stone, marking the offering area. This offering pit was dug some 50 cm into the bedrock and filled with ash and charcoal, as well as pots, beads and animal offerings. A radiocarbon date from the charcoal in this pit produced a similarly early date: 5650 ± 70 bp. Therefore it may be possible to envision a similar configuration of boulders surrounding the hearth emplacement and the tomb cutting at Wadi Atulla. However, at Wadi Elei the actual burial was placed in a shallow cutting off to one side (single interment), which contained among other things a gold wire bracelet. This discovery in conjunction with an offering pit dug deeply into the bedrock has led the excavators to suggest that gold mining, even if in elementary form, was already practiced at this time (Sadr 1997; Sadr *et al.* 1994). This is a suggestion with possible relevance for explaining the presence of the tomb and its builders in Wadi Atulla, a wadi with rich and extensively mined gold resources.

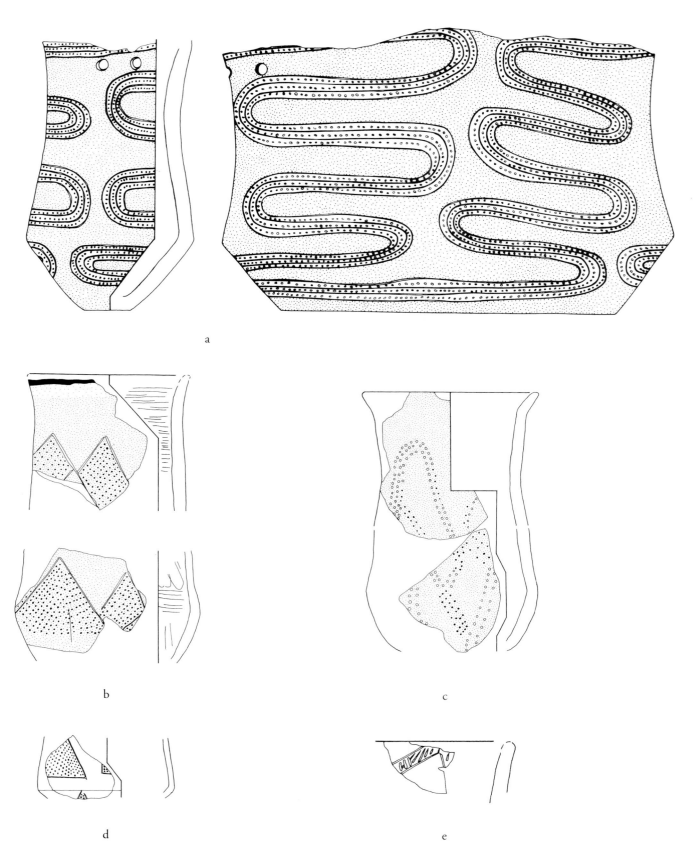

Fig. 4   Decorated beakers from the tomb at Wadi Atulla. Scale 1:2.

Human Remains

The majority of artefacts and human bone was recovered by sifting through the debris dumped mainly to the west of the tomb opening, but material was found in a wide arc around the tomb. Human bone, badly weathered and fragmentary in the extreme, has not yet been fully analysed. However, preliminary examination has revealed the left and right petrus portions of the temporal bones of at least 14 individuals. It was impossible to determine gender from these remains.

Teeth recovered from the debris were examined by Dr Joel Irish (University of Alaska, Fairbanks). Despite their poor condition, a number of crowns and roots could be identified from a minimum number of six individuals with the following age distributions: 18 months ± 6 months; 4 years ± 1 year; 14–15 years; 19–21 years; an older adult; and an old adult (based on extensive dental wear; chronological age is unknown). Teeth belonging to two additional individuals may also be present: one molar crown may belong to a second infant of approximately 18 months of age, the coloration and preservation being distinct from the other infant; and, based on molar crown scraps that do not seem to match the others, an adolescent or young adult may also be present. There are a few traits among the teeth suggestive of sub-Saharan affiliation (LM1 cusp 7, LP1 Tome's root, 6 cusped LM1, 3-rooted LM2, LM2 Y-pattern); however, these traits can occur in North Africans, and there are other simple traits present that are common among North Africans. While it is possible that a mixture of both groups is present, the sample is too small and poorly preserved to make any definitive statement.

A limited number of teeth had small cavities, and several had slight calculus deposition. This pattern indicates that these people may have been eating some high-carbohydrate, processed food, but not at the level seen in fully agricultural societies. Instead, the teeth suggest an intensive gatherer type of economy with some level of food processing of high carbohydrate plants. The small sample size affects this interpretation and it must be considered preliminary. Nevertheless it does not contradict what one would expect from the admitted limited information on Eastern Desert habitation at this time (cf. Vermeersch *et al.* 1994; 1996).

The level of disturbance is such that it is impossible to reconstruct the history of interments in this tomb with any certainty. The number of individuals present suggests that the tomb was opened on several occasions for the deposition of subsequent burials, rather than a group interment of such a large number of people all at one time. Parallels for this practice have been observed at comparable sites with related material culture. At a natural cave in the Wadi el-Hôl located in the desert behind Thebes, burials attributed to the Tasian on the basis of ceramic finds including incised beakers, were discovered by JC and D Darnell (see D Darnell this volume). Although disturbed, a minimum of nine individuals were apparently buried in this cave, four of whom were found *in situ* in discrete shallow graves, some with remnants of organic material, possibly matting, beneath them. At Gebel Ramlah, 25 km north of Nabta Playa, a Late Neo-lithic burial area (site E-01-2) containing incised beakers has recently been investigated (see below). Of the nine graves examined, six had been reopened for the addition of later burials, with up to four bodies being interred consecutively in the same pit. That care was taken to restore order to anything displaced when the grave was opened suggests that there was a familial relationship with the deceased (Schild and Wendorf 2001). It is indeed highly likely that the Wadi Atulla site and the Wadi el-Hôl cave represent a family sepulchres in which related members were buried together whenever possible.[3]

Ceramics

Investigations in and around the tomb revealed over fifty fragments of hand-made pottery. Many of the fragments could be joined and a minimum of fifteen individual vessels (all fragmentary) were recorded. These vessels are in addition to those observed in 1983, during the first reconnaissance at the site (**Plate 102**), of which no remnants were found during the recent investigation. It was disappointing to find that so much of the original material had disappeared. In addition to the removal of the intact vessels, it would appear that sherds were also taken, resulting in an irregular ceramic assemblage that is composed almost entirely of rims (**Plate 103**), the decorated body sherds having been collected, possibly as tourist trinkets. Nevertheless, at least part of the tomb's unique assemblage can be reconstructed from the remaining sherds and archival photographs.

The most interesting feature of the pottery from this site is the number of beakers with a bulbous or sharply carinated base. These beakers may be undecorated except for a red slip and a blackened rim, or they may be elaborately ornamented with a combination of incised and impressed decoration.

Of the ten complete or nearly complete beakers observed in 1983 and photographed at that time, only one was drawn (see **Fig. 4** a; **Plate 102** centre). Examples recovered from the debris around the tomb were reconstructed from the remaining fragments and drawn to the best of our abilities (**Figs 4-5**). These vessels occur in several varieties, but all are hand-made out of one of two basic fabrics. One fabric is composed of a sandy clay mixed with greater or lesser amounts of dung temper. The voids from the burn-out of this organic matter are visible in the break and on the surfaces, especially where worn. The other fabric is a moderately sandy and very micaceous clay. Flecks of mica are visible in the break and twinkle on the surfaces. Both of these clay types are probably local to the desert region and do not appear to be Nilotic in origin. Most are low fired; those with dung temper have thick black carbon cores.

Four examples of decorated beakers were recovered from the debris and have been reconstructed from non-mending fragments; the full nature of the decoration is unknown. The vessel illustrated in **Fig. 4** b (**Plate 103** upper row, centre) was decorated with at least one band of incised diamonds running around the upper body. The area within each diamond was impressed with small pin-prick-like dots set in relatively orderly diagonal lines, but a stamp or multiple

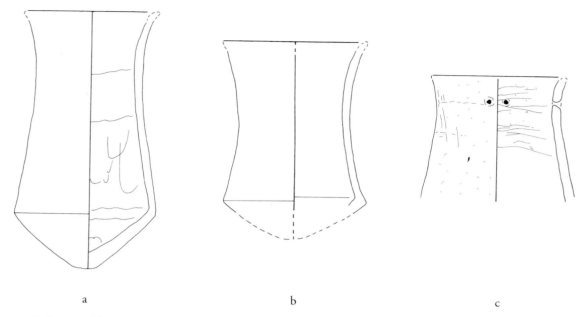

a   b   c

Fig. 5   Undecorated beakers. Scale 1:2.

pronged implement was not used. Below, around the bulbous base, another band of irregular diamonds or triangles was incised and similarly filled with dots. The surface of the vessel was coated with a micaeous red slip or wash (see below) and lightly polished, but much of the slip has worn away, so it is unclear whether or not the impressed decoration was placed on unslipped, or reserved, zones. The rim appears to have been black-topped and the interior is blackened. There is no evidence of white pigment in the incisions or impressions. The fabric is the moderately sandy micaeous silt.

The vessel illustrated in **Fig. 4** c is made of the same fabric (**Plate 103** upper right). It was red slipped and lightly polished over its entire exterior surface before it was impressed with multiple rows of small dots, similar to those described above, and larger hollow circles, probably made with a bird bone or hollow stick, arranged in a sinuous pattern. It is hard to determine how this rather free-form ornamentation may originally have appeared. This vessel was not black-topped and the red slip is present on the interior lip.

The beaker shown in **Fig. 4** d, of which only the carination area of the base was recovered, is composed of a very thin dung- tempered fabric. If the exterior surface was ever slipped, this has now completely washed off leaving no trace on the tan-coloured surface. The decoration is composed of individual triangles outlined with a light incised line and filled with tiny, but very deep and closely spaced, impressed dots. These dots almost pierce through the vessel's wall. The interior surface is blackened and the break has a thick black carbon core.

Another decorative motif is preserved only on a small rim fragment (**Fig. 4** e). All that remains is an angular band (part of a chevron?) that has been defined by incised lines and then filled internally with a series of irregular incised dashes.

The fine dense fabric may have been red slipped, but it was not black-topped.

Other types of decoration are visible on the vessels recorded in 1983. **Fig. 4** a, a beaker with a sharp carination at the base and an intentionally shaved-down rim, is decorated with a well-arranged composition of a continuous band made up of four incised lines filled with impressed dots that snakes around the body. A red slip was applied to only the undecorated areas; the decorative band is in reserve. The interior is blackened, but there is no evidence of a black top, though nothing of the original rim remains.

The decoration on the other vessels can be described from the evidence of the 1983 photograph alone (**Plate 102**). The vessel second from the right is decorated in a similar manner to that illustrated in **Fig. 4** a, except here the two interlocking reserve-slip bands have created a large diamond design around the beaker's body. The blackening of the rim is clear in the photograph. The beaker on the far right was apparently decorated with large incised triangles pendant from the neck that have been filled in with impressions from a serrated rocker stamp. A horizontal band around the neck and zig-zag band around the lower part of the vessel are filled in the same manner. On the far right, the body of another beaker, although incised with zig-zag bands, is covered completely with well spaced punctations that must also have been made with a stamp. The other beakers appear to be undecorated, and three additional examples of undecorated beakers were recovered from the debris around the tomb (**Fig. 5**).

In all cases it would appear that effort was taken to make the decoration of the beakers both pleasing and individualistic. These vessels were obviously important to their owners. The extensive wear on the rims among the collected fragments suggests that the beakers were also well-used. The rim of the vessel in **Fig. 4** a was so badly chipped or broken that its owner shaved it down and continued to use the pot. Each

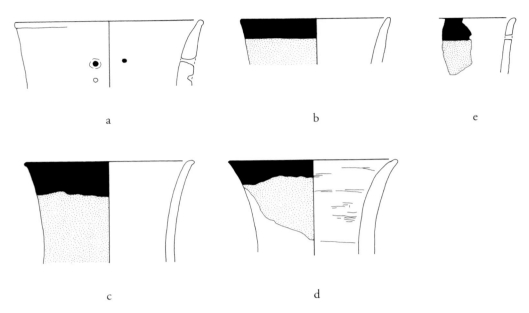

Fig. 6   Black-topped pottery from the tomb at Wadi Atulla. Scale 1:2.

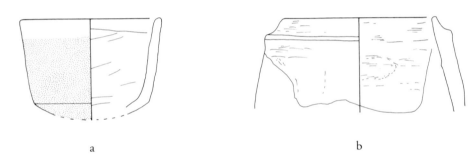

Fig. 7   Red slipped/washed pottery. Scale 1:2.

of these beakers also has a pair of holes bored into the neck while the clay was still wet. These holes may have facilitated the attachment of a lid or enabled the suspension of the pot from a cord for transport or storage. It should be noted that the configuration of the base makes it impossible for these vessels to stand on a flat surface, but they will stand well in a shallow hole or in sandy soil.

All of the undecorated beakers may originally have been coated with red ochre and burnished or polished to a moderate lustre (**Fig. 5**). This red ochre appears to have been applied as a wash, rather than a slip, as it has not been mixed with clay. It has not adhered well to the vessel walls and is water soluble. As a result the red is now preserved only as patches on the vessel surfaces.

All three of the undecorated beakers had sharp carinations to the base. **Fig. 5** a (**Plate 103** upper left) is made from the sandy fabric without organic temper, the others are of a dung-tempered clay and were low fired. An AMS date derived from the carbon core of the vessel illustrated in **Fig. 5** c provided a date of 5850 ± 50 bp (Beta 143775). A single hole drilled into the vessel wall from the exterior, unlike the characteristic paired holes at the neck of other beakers,

appears to be for mending and securing the now missing rim. In all three cases, the rims had been blackened and the interior surface is also black, suggesting that the pots were fired rim down in the bonfire. While it is unclear whether the blackened rims on these and some of the decorated beakers were intentional produced as a decorative effect or were simply a by-product of the firing process, other sherds recovered from the debris leave no doubt that intentional black-topping was practiced.

Several rims of black-topped, red polished flaring walled cups were recovered. They have orifice diameters of between 8 and 10 cm (**Fig. 6**). While these pieces could be the upper parts of beakers, the burnished black interior surface of many suggests that they belong to small cups instead. The type of base they might have had is unknown, as no base fragments were found. This shape is rare among known Tasian/Badarian ceramics (see Friedman 1994, fig. 7.20, type 22.1d). Nevertheless it may be possible to suggest MS4 (Brunton and Caton-Thompson 1928, pl. 16) or MS 28 and 29 (Brunton 1937, pl. 18) as potential parallels: roughly cylindrical vessels with thick flat bases and everted or thickened rims. However the early Naqada I B18 series of cups

Fig. 8   Bead types from the tomb at Wadi Atulla. Scale 1:1.

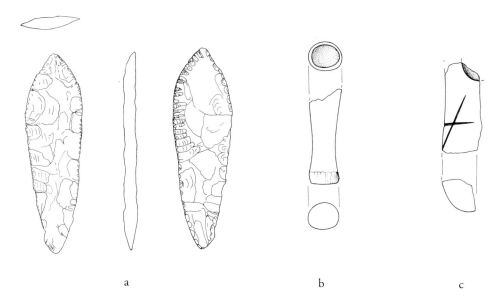

a   b   c

Fig. 9   Flint knife, bone handle and soapstone object. Fig. 9 a, b scale 1:2, c scale 1:1.

(Petrie 1921, pl. 2; cf. Brunton and Caton-Thompson 1928, pl. xiv, BR5p) may be closer. Rims are direct, tapering on the interior, but a few have exterior thickening, which in one case has been accentuated by underscoring (**Fig. 6** a). The fabric ranges from thick and very sandy (rounded quartz up to 3 mm) to extremely thin (3 mm wall thickness) with fine dung/organic-temper. Burnishing strokes on the exterior run diagonally down from the left, horizontally or vertically. The lustre produced is moderate but not metallic. These vessels were also highly prized, as two have holes drilled probably for the mending of cracks and breaks.

Another small cup (**Fig. 7** a, **Plate 104** lower) has a simple rim and a sharp keel before a slightly rounded base. The pottery is moderately sandy micaceous clay, well fired, and coated with a micaceous red slip that has been lightly polished. While it is possible that this slip has worn away at the rim, it does appear that it was intentionally omitted here, leaving a reserve band. The interior is uncoated, but lightly compacted and well smoothed. The base shape is attested in the Badarian repetoire (see Friedman 1994, fig. 7.20, types 22.1b1 and 22-keel), but exact parallels for the shape are lacking.[4]

The final vessel recovered from the debris is without parallel (**Fig. 7** b; **Plate 104** upper). It is a slightly restricted vessel with a pinched flange, or exterior ledge, possibly meant to support a lid. It is composed of the same micaceous clay as the cup above and coated with a mottled red slip that has been lightly polished. Two mending pieces, making up almost half the diameter, ensure that the stance is correct.

The 1983 photograph (**Plate 102**) shows a shallow bowl in the foreground, but further information on this vessel is lacking. One body sherd collected from the debris, with a red slipped and polished exterior and a suggestion of a blackened rim, may derive from a closed, globular vessel, but this cannot be confirmed.

Objects

The unique assemblage of pottery is augmented by a number of other finds. Although none have a distinctive cultural affinity, they do show that the tomb owners were well acquainted with the resources of the Eastern Desert. Even in its sadly plundered state, the assemblage from this tomb suggests a people who roamed widely and were far from isolated.

Items of personal adornment included numerous pieces of malachite and lumps of red ochre (**Plate 103** lower right). A roughly-shaped oval palette of hard grey stone may have been used to grind these pigments, but no trace of them appeared on either of its surfaces (**Plate 103** lower left). Fragments of a thick-walled bivalve shell were also recovered. Heavily weathered, it resembles the Nile oyster (*Aspatharia*) shells known from Tasian and later burials (Brunton 1937, 31); however this identification has not been confirmed.

Many beads were also collected from around the tomb, most made of the soft serpentine or soapstone prevalent in the immediate vicinity. The beads occurred in three basic

187

sizes (**Fig. 8**; **Plate 103** lower right). The largest bead (1.4 cm in diameter, maximum thickness 0.5 cm) may originally have been covered with a green glaze. Other beads of a brownish serpentine (?) were irregularly shaped, approximately 0.8 cm in diameter and 0.2 cm thick. The majority of the beads collected were small, ranging from 0.4 to 0.25 cm in diameter, with a thickness of 0.05–0.1 cm and made of grey soapstone. Five beads of a harder, slightly translucent white stone (0.3 cm in diameter, 0.1 cm thick) were carefully made, with even round drill holes and polished edges. Shells from the Red Sea were also filed down and pierced for stringing. *Conus* and *Nerita* shells can be identified among them (**Plate 103** lower centre).

No bead or bead blanks were observed among the fifteen relatively large fragments of undecorated ostrich eggshell (**Plate 103** lower center), suggesting that the whole or partial egg was used, possibly as a container. None of the fragments showed evidence of burning or cooking. The practice of placing an egg, either plain or decorated, in the graves of children is well documented in A-Group Nubia (cf. Nordström 1972, 122–3); but fragments have also been recovered from Tasian and Badarian burials in the Nile Valley (Brunton 1937, 30; Brunton and Caton-Thompson 1928, 3, 28).

Fragments of a slab of mica (**Plate 103** middle right) were perhaps part of a mirror. Similar slabs have been found in contemporary Neolithic burials at Kadruka (Reinold 2001, pl. xii) and more recently at Gebel Ramlah, near Nabta Playa (F Wendorf, pers. comm.).

The lithics were all made from the same fine grained beige flint (**Plate 105**). The finest piece recovered during the recent investigation is a bifacially worked knife, retouched on both sides (**Fig. 9** a). It is similar to, but smaller than, that photographed in 1983 (**Plate 102** centre). The other lithics include unifacial scrapers and an *ad hoc* piece with unifacial retouch.

Other finds include what appears to be a handle, possibly for a flint tool, made from the terminal part of the long bone of an unidentified mammal (**Fig. 9** b; **Plate 103** middle left). A fragment of worked soapstone, possibly part of a figurine, was also recovered. So very little of this remains, it is difficult to determine what it might have been (**Fig. 9** c; **Plate 103** lower, third from left). Only one carefully smoothed and rounded side is preserved, upon which are two intentional and deeply incised crossing lines. A smoothed concave edge at one end suggests a bifurcation and that the original piece may have been at least twice as wide. This may be the trunk or a limb of a slender human or animal figurine (cf. Nordström 1972, pl. 56.1), but it is impossible to say more.

The photograph from the 1983 visit to the site (**Plate 102**) shows further grave goods, including a large sea shell and two drop-shaped pendants of hard stone drilled for stringing. More intriguing is the object of smoothed green stone in the centre of the photograph. This may be a small palette or possibly a ground stone axe, or 'celt', considered by Brunton (1937) to be one of the distinguishing features of his Tasian culture.

The handful of parallels presented for these objects is by no means exhaustive, but demonstrates that parallels, although wide-ranging, can be found in contemporary cemeteries and even individual graves that contain the most distinctive element of the Wadi Atulla assemblage, the incised beakers.

Discussion

The closest parallels for the Wadi Atulla beakers are those purchased in Luxor by Capart in 1933–4 and subsequently acquired for the Cairo Museum and published by Brunton (1934). The collection included: four beakers very similar to those from Wadi Atulla, two of which are strikingly so (Brunton 1934, nos 4 and 5; Cairo JE 62932–3); a black incised, wide-flaring 'tulip-shaped' beaker of the type excavated at Deir Tasa in Middle Egypt by Brunton; a deep bowl with coarse vertical rippling; and a rectangular palette of grey 'schist' with convex sides. When Capart purchased the collection he was told that the entire group had come from a single grave at Khozam. While dealer's reports are notoriously suspect, and the likelihood that all came from the same grave remote, this reported find spot is of great interest, being on the east bank about 10 km south of the mouth of the Wadi Hammamat (see **Fig. 1**). Predynastic burials are known from Khozam (Hendrickx 1992), but one cannot help but wonder if some of the material actually originates from deeper into the Eastern Desert. Another collection of beakers observed by Hobbs in the Eastern Desert strongly suggests this may be the case (**Plate 106**). Additional parallels for the Wadi Atulla beakers can be found amongst purchased pieces now in Munich (Scharff 1928, 269–70, fig. 6; Meisterwerke 1978, 85, no. 49) and in the Petrie Museum (UC 17871, a black-topped unincised example purchased by Petrie in Luxor).[5] Where it has been possible to examine the purchased vessels personally, all exhibit fabric similar to the Wadi Attula examples, either sandy or dung-tempered, and where preserved, all have the distinctive two holes just below the lip punched out from the interior.

Because of the general similarity in shape to the tulip-shaped Tasian beakers, these purchased beakers have been attributed to the Tasian culture as defined by Brunton in Middle Egypt, but obviously without any evidence for this cultural attribution or date. In light of the discoveries at Wadi Atulla and now Gebel Ramlah near Nabta Playa and a fuller understanding of the cultural context, this attribution needs to be re-explored.

At Gebel Ramlah, a small Late Neolithic burial area, containing thirty individuals in nine grave clusters, was examined in 2001 by Michael Kobusiewicz, Jacek Kabacinski and Joel Irish (Schild and Wendorf 2001). Within the richer burials were beakers with complex incised and stamped decoration closely paralleled by those at Wadi Atulla. Made of a sandy clay, these beakers have also been fired in an oxidizing atmosphere resulting in a red or brown/mottled surface colour. They have flaring lips, and the same distinctive two holes at the neck (F Wendorf pers. comm.). These beakers are the closest contexted parallels for the Wadi Atulla material. Undisturbed, the numerous objects buried in some of the graves provide further parallels for the Atulla material and include: sheets of mica; bone and stone tools including knives of beige flint; Red Sea shells; and rectangular and oval hard stone palettes. In addition, the graves contained ivory bracelets, beads and lip plugs of carnelian and turquoise, amongst other things. These grave goods indicated far-reaching contacts with the Eastern Desert and the Red Sea, while mortars and pestles of hard stone, pottery with rocker stamp decoration, crescent-shaped lithics and the mica slabs point to connections with the far south (Schild and Wendorf 2001, 17), most notably with contemporary Kadruka, where highly decorated flared-rim beakers were also placed in the elite graves (Reinold 2001).

It is hoped that investigation of the associated settlement at Gebel Ramlah, located some 60 m to the east of the cemetery, will provide further information to link these people with the complex megalithic structures and calendar circle in the Nabta Playa region (Wendorf and Schild this volume). Nevertheless, together with the discoveries at Wadi Atulla, the Gebel Ramlah graves attest to a wide-ranging desert culture that found neither the deserts nor the river an impediment to movement.

But what is the relationship of this desert Neolithic with the Tasian culture as known from Nile Valley discoveries? A number of shared traits certainly indicates a relationship between the desert and the valley and strongly suggests that the Tasian is distinct culturally, if not temporally, from the Badarian, as Brunton first maintained (Brunton 1937, 25–33; Friedman 1999). Some of these shared attributes include rectangular stone palettes, celts, burials with niches at side for vessels, but most notably, the beakers.

More than anything else, it is the highly distinctive shape and decoration of the Tasian beakers, especially when compared to the open and generally unincised forms predominant in the Egyptian Nile Valley, that indicate a connection with the beakers found in the deserts. However, the desert beakers differ from the excavated Middle Egyptian Tasian examples in clay fabric–the Middle Egyptian Tasian pottery is always made of fine, dense Nile clay; colour –Tasian pottery has a black surface with designs filled with white paste; design motifs –Tasian pottery is decorated mainly with pendant triangles and vandykes; and shape– Tasian vessels have wide flaring lips decorated on the interior (see Brunton 1937, 28–9). Furthermore, with only one exception (Badari grave 569; Friedman 1999), the Tasian beakers found in Middle Egypt have been recovered only from settlement debris, while those of the desert are found almost exclusively in graves.

Examples of the Middle Egyptian type of beaker have also been found at Armant (Mond and Myers 1937, 6; Ginter *et al.* 1986, 62) and possibly Mahgar/Makhadma, where incised sherds probably derived from beakers, but made of coarser fabrics, were excavated (Hendrickx and Midant-Reynes 1988; Hendrickx *et al.* 2001, 70, 84–5, pl. 56). Where not simply isolated finds, these beakers are always associated with Badarian to very early Naqada I ceramics, suggesting that differences between the desert and the valley manifestations may be chronological as well as regional. The earliest radiocarbon date for the Badarian culture is 5580 ± 80 bp from excavations in the Badari region, site 3400, which also produced two Tasian beaker sherds (Holmes 1993, 23–4; 1994; Hendrickx 1999, 63).

The recent discoveries of Middle Egyptian type Tasian beakers in the burial caves at Wadi el-Hôl (D Darnell this volume, **Plate 93**) and possibly also at Dakhleh (Hope this volume, **Fig. 10** c) suggest that the owners of this type of beaker were also desert based,[6] and that the cultural complex we call Tasian should be considered a desert, rather than an Egyptian Nile Valley, phenomenon. Although the exact date of these new finds is unknown, it may be possible to suggest that the beakers are the first hard evidence for the interaction posited to have taken place between the inhabitants of the desert and those of the valley and oases as the desert climate deteriorated over time. This was an interaction that was no doubt complex and variable, but we may propose that it also involved the exchange of these highly ornate vessels, which the Nile dwelling Badarians may have prized, but clearly did not consider them appropriate in their graves.

In 1985 Kaiser argued that the Tasian culture should be viewed as the direct ancestor of the main line of cultural, and especially ceramic, development in Upper Egypt that begins with the Naqada I period. He saw the Tasian as coming from the north, a view no longer tenable based on the new finds in Wadi Atulla, Gebel Ramlah and the growing number of beakers being found in the Sudan from the Dongola Reach and further south (e.g., Chlodnicki 1997; Reinold 2001; Welsby 2001). These southern examples further suggest a connection via the desert corridors given the stark lack of beakers within Nubia itself.[7]

The influence of desert cultures on Upper Egyptian developments is probably hard to overestimate. As work in the deserts continues, evidence for this particular gift of the desert will surely grow.

Acknowledgments

The authors wish to thank the National Geographic Society Committee for Research and Exploration for supporting this project. We are grateful to Egypt's Supreme Council for Antiquities and the American Research Center in Egypt for in-country assistance. Deborah Darnell and Robert Cline assisted in the field; Gillian Pyke and Will Schenck inked the object drawings. We are also grateful to Carol Wicks and Dietrich Klemm for assistance in identifying the rock types, and to Joel Irish and Tammy Greene for examining the skeletal material. We are indebted to Pierre Vermeersch and stan Hendrickx for information on Wadi Sodmein and especially to Romuald Schild and Fred Wendorf for sharing information on their exciting new finds at Gebel Ramlah.

Notes

1. Man-made extensions to natural caves have been noted in the Neolithic cave behind Cemetery K, south of Abu Simbel. Here a loculus almost 2.5 m deep was carved into the back wall of the natural cave by cutting a shallow shelf backward at ceiling height and then carving out parallel grooves that were then broken up with stone hammers until the desired level was reached. The rock in the Wadi Atulla did not require a great deal of effort to carve, but similar methods may be detected. The cave behind Cemetery K has been dated to the Abkan, a culture considered contemporary with the Tasian and one that has many ceramic elements in common (see Williams 1989, 3–12, 136–7 and D Darnell this volume), including beakers (M Gatto, pers. comm.).

2. Stelae or oblong slabs set vertically along the edge of the grave pit have also been found in the Dongola Reach at Kadruka cemetery KDK21. Although known from A-Group, C-Group and even Kerma culture graves, the stelae at Kadruka are amongst the earliest known in the Sudan and have been dated by C14 to between 4790 and 4720 cal BC. Incised tulip shaped beakers also been found in this cemetery (Reinold 2001, 9).

3. Further to the south, at Kadruka and other Neolithic cemeteries in the Dongola Reach, burials grounds clearly arranged along family lines have been found, in which the opening of the grave pit for a later burial is relatively common, but not the rule. Little care was taken with the earlier remains, but at cemetery KDK18, the bones from earlier burials were collected and bundled to one side when the grave was reopened (Reinold 2001).

4. Closer shape parallels can currently be found at Merimde in the published data from the earliest level, with which the Wadi Atulla finds may be contemporary (Eiwanger 1984, pls 10, 21, 34, 35). Pottery with the incised herringbone design distinctive of the Merimde *Urschicht* has also been found at Wadi Sodmein (Vermeersch *et al.* 1996, 416).

5. Two beakers purchased by Gayer Anderson reportedly from Edfu appear to be closer in fabric and decoration to the beakers known from Deir Tasa (Bourriau 1981, 24; Lugn 1931).

6. Fragments of an incised beaker possibly of the desert type were also collected from the Yabsa Pass near Kharga Oasis as an isolated find by Caton-Thompson (1952, 42, pl. 123.2 second left and right; see also D Darnell this volume).

7. Only one incised beaker is published from Nubia. It was excavated by Firth (1927, 147, pl. 25a3, upper right) in Cemetery 118, located in the Eastern Desert near the Wadi Allaqi, burial 188, which was apparently a C-Group grave. Earlier graves were also present in the cemetery and Firth noted that not only had the C-Group people reused the area, but they had also reused some of the earlier pottery. Thus it seems more likely to assume the reuse of this vessel than posit a long duration for this distinctive shape (*contra* Welsby 2001).

Bibliography

Alfano C, 1994. Rock Pictures of the Eastern Desert of Egypt (1989 Campaign). In C Bonnet (ed), *Etudes Nubiennes. Conference de Geneve. Actes du VIIe Congres international d'études nubiennes II.* Gevena: 117–124.

Baumgartel E. 1955. *The Cultures of Prehistoric Egypt.* Vol. 1. Oxford.

Bourriau J D, 1981. *Umm el Ga'ab. Pottery from the Nile Valley before the Arab Conquest.* Cambridge.

Brunton G, 1929. The Beginnings of Egyptian Civilization. *Antiquity* 3: 456–67.

Brunton G, 1934. Some Tasian Pottery in the Cairo Museum. *Annales du Service des Antiquités de l'Égypte* 34: 94–6.

Brunton G, 1937. *Mostagedda and the Tasian Culture.* British Museum Expeditions to Middle Egypt, 1928–9. London.

Brunton G, and Caton-Thompson. G, 1928. *The Badarian Civilization and the Predynastic Remains near Badari.* British School of Archaeology in Egypt and Egyptian Research Account 46. London.

Caton-Thompson G, 1952. *Kharga Oasis in Prehistory.* London.

Chlodnicki M, 1997. New types of the Neolithic pottery in Kadero (Sudan). *Cahier de Recherches de l'Institut de Papyrologie et d'Égyptologie de Lille* 17/2: 29–35.

Debono F, 1950. Desert Oriental Mission archeologique royal 1949. *Chronique d'Égypte* 50: 237–40.

Debono F, 1951. Expédition Archéologique Royale au Désert Oriental (Keft-Kosseir). *Annales du Service des Antiquités de l'Égypte* 51: 59–91.

Eiwanger J, 1984. *Merimde-Benisalame I. Die funde der Urschicht.* Archäologische Veröffentlichungen, Deutsches Archäologisches Institut Abteilung Kairo 47. Mainz am Rhein.

Firth, C.M. 1927. *The Archaeological Survey of Nubia, Report for 1910–1911.* Cairo.

Friedman R F, 1994. *Predynastic Settlement Ceramics of Upper Egypt: A Comparative Study of the Ceramics of Hemamieh, Nagada and Hierakonpolis.* PhD Thesis. University of California, Berkeley. University Microfilms International, Michigan.

Friedman R, 1999. Badarian Grave Group 569. In W V Davies (ed.), *Studies in Egyptian Antiquities: A Tribute to T.G.H. James.* British Museum Occasional Paper 123. London: 1–11.

Ginter B, Kozlowski J and Pawlikowski M, 1986. Investigations into Site MA 6/83 and MA 21/83 in the Region of Qurna–Armant in Upper Egypt. *Mitteilungen des Deutschen Archäologischen Instituts Abteilung Kairo* 43: 45–66.

Hendrickx S, 1992. Predynastic Cemeteries at Khozam. In R Friedman and B Adams (eds), *The Followers of Horus.* Oxford: 199–202.

Hendrickx S, 1999. La chronologie de la prehistoire tardive et des debuts de l'histoire de l'Egypte. *Archeo-Nil* 9: 13–81.

Hendrickx S. and Midant-Reynes B, 1988. Preliminary Report on the Predynastic Living Site Maghara 2 (Upper Egypt). *Orientalia Lovaniensia Periodica* 19: 5–16.

Hendrickx S, Midant-Reynes B and Van Neer W, 2001. *Mahgar Dendera 2 (Haute Egypt). Un site d'occupation Badarien.* Egyptian Prehsitoric Monographs 3. Leuven 2001.

Hendrickx S and Vermeersch P, 2000. Prehistory: From the Palaeolithic to the Badarian Culture. In I Shaw (ed), *The Oxford History of Ancient Egypt.* Oxford: 17–43.

Holmes D L, 1989. *The Predynastic Lithic Industries of Upper Egypt: A comparative study of the lithic Traditions of Badari, Nagada and Hierakonpolis.* British Archaeological Reports International Series 469. Oxford.

Holmes D L, 1993. Archaeological Investigations in the Badari Region, Egypt: A Report on the 1992 Season. *Nyame Akuma* 39: 19–25.

Holmes D L, 1994. Egypt, Badarian Region Site 3400. In R E M Hedges, R A Housley, C Bronk Ramsey and G J van Klinken, Radiocarbon Dates from the Oxford AMS System: Archeometry Datelist 18, *Archaeometry* 36 (2): 367–8.

Kaiser W, 1985. Zur Südausdehnung der vorgeschichtlichen Deltakulturen und zur frühen Entwicklung Oberägyptens. *Mitteilungen des Deutsche Archäologischen Instituts Abteilung Kairo* 41: 61–87.

Lugn P, 1931. A 'Beaker' pot in the Stockholm Egyptian Museum. *Journal of Egyptian Archaeology* 17: 22.

Midant-Reynes B, 2000. *The Prehistory of Egypt. From the First Egyptians to the First Pharaohs*. Oxford.

Meisterwerke, 1978. *Meisterworke Altagyptischer Keramik*. Exhibition catalogue. Montabaur.

Mond R and Myers O H, 1937. *Cemeteries of Armant I*. Egypt Exploration Society Excavation Memoirs 42. London.

Murray G and Derry D, 1923. A Pre-Dynastic Burial on the Red Sea Coast of Egypt. *Man* 23: 129–3.

Nordström H-Å, 1972. Neolithic and A-Group Sites Scandanavian Joint Expedition 3:1. Stockholm.

Petrie W M F, 1921. *Corpus of Prehistoric Pottery and Palettes*. Egypt Research Acount 32. London.

Reinold, J. 1987. Les Fouilles Pre- et Proto-historiques de la section Francaise de la Direction des Antiquites du Soudan: Les Campagnes 1984–85 et 1985–86. *Archeologie du Nil Moyen* 2: 17–67.

Reinold J, 2001. Kadruka and the Neolithic in the Northern Dongola Reach. *Sudan & Nubia* 5: 2–10

Resch F E, 1964. Eine vorgeschichtliche Grabstätte auf dem Ras Samadai. *Mitteilungen des Anthropologische Gesellschaft in Wien* 93–94: 119–21.

Sadr K, 1997. The Wadi Elei finds: Nubian desert gold mining in the 5th and 4th millennia BC? *Cahier de Recherches de l'Institut de Papyrologie et d'Égyptologie de Lille* 17/2: 67–76.

Sadr K, Castiglioni A and Castiglioni A, 1995. Nubian Desert Archaeology: A Preliminary View. *Archeologie du Nil Moyen* 7: 203–29.

Sadr K, Castiglioni A, Castiglioni A and Negro G, 1994. Archaeology in the Nubian Desert. *Sahara* 6: 69–75.

Scharff A, 1928. Some Prehistoric Vases in the British Museum and Remarks on Egyptian Prehistory. *Journal of Egyptian Archaeology* 14: 261–276.

Schild R and Wendorf F, 2001. The Combined Prehistoric Expedition Results of the 2001 Season. *American Research Center in Egypt Bulletin* 180: 16–7.

Vermeersch PM, Van Peer P, Moeyersons J and Van Neer W, 1994. Sodmein Dave site (Red Sea Mountains, Egypt). *Sahara* 6: 31–40.

Vermeersch PM, Van Peer P, Moeyersons J and Van Neer W, 1996. Neolithic Occupation of the Sodmein Area, Red Sea Mountains, Egypt. In G Pwiti and R Soper (eds), *Aspects of African Archaeology*. Papers 10th Congress Pan African Association for Prehistory and Related Studies. Harare: 411–20.

Welsby D, 1997. Early Pottery in the Middle Nile Valley. In I Freestone and D Gaimster (eds), *Pottery in the Making: World Ceramic Traditions*. London: 26–31.

Welsby D, 2001. *Life on the Desert Edge. Seven thousand years of settlement in the Northern Dongola Reach, Sudan*. Sudan Archaeological Research Society Publication 7. London.

Williams B B, 1989. *Excavations Between Abu Simbel and the Sudan Frontier, parts 2, 3, and 4: Neolithic, A-Group, and Post-A-Group Remains from Cemeteries W, V, S, Q, T, and a Cave East of Cemetery K*. Oriental Institute Nubia Expedition 4. Chicago.

Wright H T and Herbert S. 1993. *Archaeological Survey in the Eastern Desert of Egypt*. Report of the University of Michigan/University of Asiut Project to the Egyptian Antiquities Organization. <http://rome.classics.lsa.umich.edu/projects/coptos/desert.html>

Cosmology, Ideology and Personal Religious Practice in Ancient Egyptian Rock Art

Dirk Huyge

Rock art in Upper Egypt and Lower Nubia (Northern Sudan) has been the subject of a vast body of literature, both ancient and modern (over 420 references in Hendrickx 1995). As is the case for many rock art areas in the world, studies in this field have focused primarily on the recording of images, thematic and stylistic classification, and, to a much lesser degree, chronological seriation and cultural-historical attribution (Davis 1990, 274–9). Aspects of interpretation, that is, the meaning and motivation of the art, have for the most part been left unaddressed.

In this contribution I would like to explore, to a certain extent, a strategy for rock art interpretation that has recently been proposed on the basis of the study of petroglyph localities at the Upper Egyptian site of Elkab (Huyge 1995; 1999). Before presenting a general overview of the Elkab rock art, however, it may be useful to discuss briefly the history and methodology of ancient Egyptian rock art hermeneutics.

The Historical-Methodological Perspective

On the basis of its principal subject matter, i.e., boats, anthropomorphic figures and animals (especially elephants, giraffes and other large 'Ethiopian' fauna), much of the Upper Egyptian and Lower Nubian rock art has been dated to the late prehistoric (Predynastic) or Early Dynastic period (Davis 1984; Cervicek 1986; 1992–3). This general attribution is corroborated by the various physical characteristics and organisational features of the drawings, including rock patina development and patterns of superimposition. It is therefore logical that assumptions put forward in the field of interpretation are often closely linked to the cultural (especially iconographic) and archaeozoological evidence of the Badarian and Naqada I–III periods (c. 4400–3150 BC) and to that of the first two dynasties (c. 3150–2650 BC). Setting aside (too) simplistic explanations, for instance that the rock drawings would be the outcome of casual pastime or merely exercises of artists' apprentices, four main motivations have been put forward to account for the ancient Egyptian rock art tradition: 1) magic; 2) totemism; 3) religion; and 4) ideology. Let us examine each of these critically.

Magic

The magical hypothesis as an explanation of ancient Egyptian rock art (its animal figures in particular) was first formulated by the Egyptologist J Capart (1904, 207–10). Capart's approach relied heavily on hunting magic hypotheses (especially the ethnographically inspired ideas of S Reinach) that had been introduced to explain the abundance of animal representations in the Upper Palaeolithic

cave art of Western Europe. Of crucial importance is the distinction that can be made between 'desirable' and 'undesirable' animals: animals fit for human consumption versus unsavoury and savage beasts. The apparent artistic predilection for 'desirable' animals in the rock art was considered indicative of an opportunistic mental attitude. The conclusion was that rock art was neither more nor less a ritual act of imitative and/or sympathetic imagery magic, implemented to multiply the number of game available, guarantee the success of the hunt and ensure a daily subsistence.

For reasons that have been fully discussed elsewhere (e.g., Bahn and Vertut 1988, 150–8), hunting magic is no longer regarded as a valid comprehensive explanation for Upper Palaeolithic art. Equally it cannot be retained as a primary motivation for ancient Egyptian rock art. Already in the oldest phases of the Egyptian Neolithic (Fayum A and Merimde) and Predynastic (Badarian) the economic subsistence pattern was largely characterised by animal husbandry and agriculture. As far as may be inferred from the osteological information available (Boessneck 1988, 13–31), hunting played a minor economic role. Clearly the stock available (cattle, goats, sheep and pigs) supplied their breeders and herders with amply sufficient animal protein and various other utilitarian products. At the same time, the almost complete absence of depictions of classic household animals in the older rock art horizons (see below) makes it highly unlikely that other types of imitative and/or sympathetic imagery magic (at least via the medium of the rock art) were implemented to improve the quality or quantity of livestock produce.

Totemism

The totemistic interpretation of rock art, considered complementary to the magical hypothesis by Capart (1904, 209–10, 213–4), relied on the anthropological principle that so-called primitive societies often display an intimate relationship between certain animal species (more rarely plant species or inanimate objects) and human groups (most often lineage groups). This phenomenon, social and religious in nature at the same time, is especially externalised by rites executed with the intention to proliferate the totem species. As a rule, the intimate connection with the totem is moreover expressed by certain taboos, for instance with regard to the killing and consuming of the totem species. In the case of ancient Egyptian society, the totemistic interpretation was founded on the fact that the religious order is characterised already in its early phases by a cult in which theriomorphism (the representation of deities in animal shape) is a fundamental constituent (see Ries 1975, 295–9).

The development of such a cult was considered to be the logical outcome of the totemistic principles adhered to by the tribal groups of the Predynastic (and possibly earlier). As such, animal representations in rock art would represent totem species that are guardian spirits essential to the survival and well-being of their totemic owners.

The totemistic origin of ancient Egyptian religion is currently being questioned by many scholars (*int. al.*, Quirke 1995, 73) for a number of reasons, among them, because characteristic side-effects of totemism like exogamy are not documented with regard to ancient Egyptian society. Predynastic iconography in general and rock art in particular moreover display a large variety of animal (and other) motifs, without any apparent chronological-geographical preferences. A further fundamental counter-argument is the fact that the Predynastic and Early Dynastic rock art repertoire contains for the most part animals (elephants, giraffes, asses, ibexes and antelopes) that did not hold a divine status in the early Pharaonic periods. In the light of the assumed cultural and religious continuance between Predynastic and later dynastic times (see below) it is therefore unlikely that these animals would ever have had a function as a venerated ethnic emblem or totem.

Religion

Magic and religion are often hard to distinguish. In a general sense magic is a matter of supernatural, impersonal forces that bring about human targets or aspirations (insofar as clearly defined magical acts are correctly performed), whereas religion involves self-willed, personified powers to which human beings are subordinate (but that can be propitiated by means of certain rituals). The existence of religious ideas and pious practices in the latter sense cannot be demonstrated directly with regard to the Predynastic period. Indeed, with the exception of funeral rituals implemented to guarantee life in the hereafter, religiousness is difficult to detect in the archaeological record. In view of the ubiquitous devotional practices in the early pharaonic periods (Early Dynastic and Old Kingdom), however, it can be conjectured with confidence that (at least) substantial seeds of religiousness must have been present in the Predynastic. Depictions in Predynastic art of possible ritual structures and several manifest prototypes of classical ancient Egyptian deities (or their primeval emblems) can be called in confirmation (for an enumeration and discussion of the archaeological evidence suggesting the existence of developed concepts of the divine in the Predynastic period, see Hornung 1971, 91–101; Silverman 1991, 10–4; Traunecker 1993, 31–3).

According to the religious interpretation, rock art is in essence a devotional outlet; human figures pose in cultic attitudes, perform liturgical actions (such as prayers and sacrifices), or represent anthropomorphic deities. Boats are meant to be sacred or funeral barques, and animals relate to offering rituals or represent a zoomorphic pantheon. In this context the execution of a rock drawing is not merely an illustration of religion, but a devotional act in itself. Illustrative examples of this interpretative approach are, par excellence, the numerous treatises by P Cervicek (e.g., 1986;

1992–3). Even though this approach, often carried to extremes, is subject to serious criticism, the religious interpretation of rock art is attractive (to the point of being self-evident) because of the apparent permeation of ancient Egyptian society with religion. I shall elaborate on this later.

Ideology

The concept of ideology, being in a lexicographic sense the whole range of political, social, and religious thought that underlies human behaviour and action, has been introduced in Predynastic iconographical research by B Williams and T J Logan (1987). Reconsidering in detail a large number of Predynastic and Early Dynastic elite artefacts, such as wall paintings, painted linen, ivory knife handles, slate palettes, and indurated 'clay' incense burners, Williams and Logan have convincingly argued that the decoration on these very different types of objects does not consist of an amalgam of unrelated motifs, but, on the contrary, represents sequences (or cycles) of standard themes. The basic idea behind their approach is that these various scenes constitute the visual synopsis of a number of highly important politico-religious duties that had to be performed periodically by the ruling headman. At the centre of this series of ceremonial assignments, which is defined by Williams and Logan as the 'Greater Pharaonic Cycle', is the Heb-Sed ritual or 'Royal Jubilee', a symbolic renewal of the coronation ceremony intended to enable the ruler to acquire new vigour. Politico-liturgical tasks within the Heb Sed ritual are, amongst others, 'The Victory', 'The Sacrifice', 'The Hunt' and 'The (Barque) Procession'. By no means do all of the documents involved show the whole of the cycle; individual themes and excerpts ('lesser cycles') can be represented separately, even in a highly abbreviated or cryptic form. According to the specific requirements of the ceremonial occasion, they can moreover be combined in various ways.

It is questionable to what extent rock art can be related to these politically and religiously inspired iconographical sequences. With the exception of a renowned terminal Predynastic (Naqada III) rock carving at Gebel Sheikh Suleiman in Lower Nubia (Murnane 1987) and some elaborate panels recently discovered in the Theban desert (J Darnell this volume, **Fig. 17**, **Plate 86**; Friedman and Hendrickx 2002), compositions that can with any degree of certainty be identified as fragments of the 'Greater Pharaonic Cycle' seem to be lacking in the Upper Egyptian and Lower Nubian rock art repertoires. Numerous individual motifs occur that can have relevance to the above-mentioned cycle, however, for the most part they appear without any evident syntactical coherence. According to Williams and Logan these motifs (such as specific types of barques and serekhs) are perhaps abbreviated tags used as a substitute to evoke major parts of the cycle. This viewpoint, however plausible, can hardly be used as a comprehensive explanation for the whole of ancient Egyptian rock art. If, indeed, this graphic tradition was a common means of expression and not an officially instigated and controlled medium, it is logical to assume that it was only to a limited extent part of iconographical constructs that were mainly

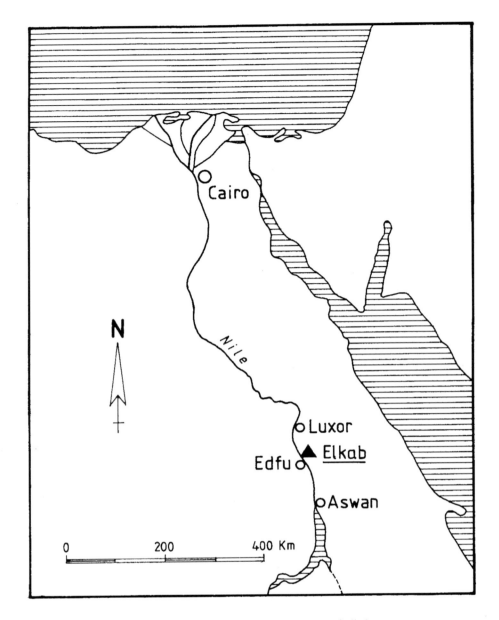

Fig. 1   Map of the Egyptian Nile Valley showing the location of Elkab.

conceived by and for the intellectual elite (i.e., the ruler and his entourage).

On the basis of the discussion above, it appears that religion and, albeit to a lesser degree, ideology offer more satisfactory, and certainly less circuitous, approaches to rock art interpretation than magic and totemism, both of which are grounded on indirect ethnographical comparisons. On a more general level, it may be suggested that any interpretative approach to rock art should ideally be conceived as a historical exegesis. This implies that the search procedure for meaning and motivation should basically be founded on contemporaneous source materials. With regard to the prehistoric and early historic periods such information is often only sparsely available or even non-existent. Non-synchronous sources then have to be sought. To a considerable extent this is the case for the Upper Egyptian rock art pro-

duction. Moreover, unlike, for example, South Africa where living or oral traditions may elucidate the contents, meaning and motivation of the historical rock art, modern sources are not available in the Islamized Nile Valley and its neighbouring deserts. Fortunately, from the Predynastic through the pharaonic period, ancient Egyptian civilisation seems to display a single line of progress and a considerable degree of conceptual conservatism. In fact, what occurred in Egypt between c. 3200 and 3050 BC (the time of state formation) was not an abrupt change of iconography, but rather a profound formalisation, standardisation and officialisation. Image-making passed from a less disciplined 'Preformal' artistic stage (a term introduced by B Kemp 1991, 66) to a 'Formal' canonical phase. This change is indeed 'huge', but basically it is a change on the exterior. The content of the iconography (the themes) and the underlying beliefs (the meaning and motivation) remain very much the same and

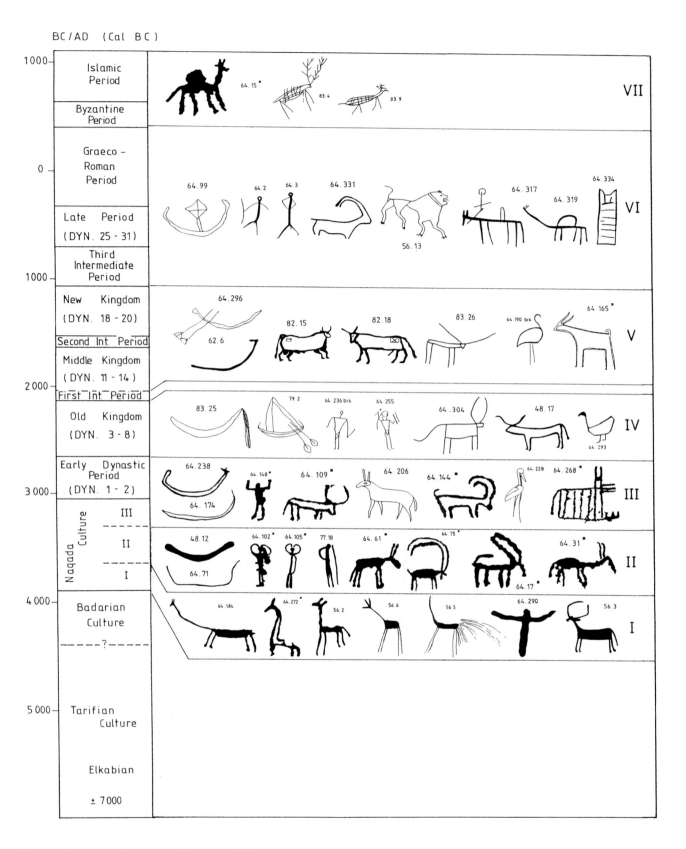

Fig. 2 Chronological seriation (Horizons I–VII) of the Elkab rock art.

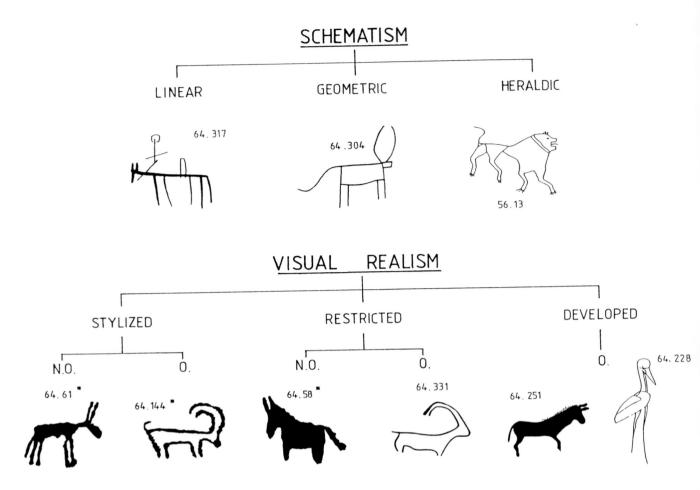

Fig. 3   Prevailing types of style in the Elkab rock art. O = outline drawings; NO = designs consisting of an area not surrounded by an outline.

The Rock Art of the Elkab Area

will continue to be so for several millennia. With that in mind, a diachronic approach to rock art, in which phenomena are not considered individually, but as integral parts of the historical chain of development, can therefore be considered scientifically admissible (cf. Westendorf 1966c, 201–2; Silverman 1991, 9).

The Upper Egyptian town site of Elkab, ancient Nekheb, especially noticeable in the landscape because of its massive Late Period mud-brick enclosure walls, is situated on the east bank of the Nile, about 80 km south of Luxor (**Fig. 1**). The site, investigated by Belgian archaeologists since 1937, had been continuously occupied in antiquity from the Palaeolithic onwards (for a topographical index of archaeological features, see Hendrickx and Huyge 1989). The presence of prehistoric rock drawings in the environs of Elkab had been recorded in the early part of the last century (Green 1903), and an extensive rock art survey was undertaken between 1979 and 1983 by the Committee for Belgian Excavations in Egypt (Huyge 1984a; 1984b). This project led to the discovery of eleven petroglyph localities, together containing well over 500 incised and hammered

figures. The majority of these localities are situated at the mouth of Wadi Hilal, a dry stream channel that ultimately joins the Nile. By far the most impressive is the 'Rock of the Vultures' (locality 64), an 80 m long and 30 m high steep-sided inselberg of Nubian sandstone, exhibiting 350 rock drawings and hundreds of Old Kingdom hieroglyphic inscriptions.

Following the recording and cataloguing of the Elkab rock art in the field, a chronological and cultural seriation was undertaken (Huyge 1995, 264–399). The technical details of the seriation procedure, too copious to be expounded here, will be dealt with in a forthcoming study. In brief, over 350 rock drawings or almost 70% of the total assemblage could be attributed to seven distinct chronological horizons (I to VII) on the basis of internal criteria, such as superimposition and rock patina formation, and external reference sources, such as iconographical and archaeozoological documents. The oldest horizon that could be identified in the Elkab rock art (Horizon I) can with good confidence be attributed to the Naqada I period (c. 3900–3650 BC); the youngest (Horizon VII) spans the Christian and Arabic eras. All important phases of ancient Egyptian history from the middle Predynastic onwards appear to be represented in the Elkab rock art. Its apogee, represented by

Table 1: Overall thematical composition of the Elkab rock art according to chronological horizons

Category/Horizon	Horizon I		Horizon II		Horizon III		Horizon IV		Horizon V		Horizon VI		Horizon VII		Total
	N	%	N	%	N	%	N	%	N	%	N	%	N	%	
Boats	–	–	19	15.8	12	17.4	14	25.5	11	20.3	2	7.4	–	–	58
Anthropomorphic figures	2	8.3	13	10.8	17	24.6	7	12.7	1	1.9	9	33.4	1	20.0	50
Cattle	–	–	–	–	10	14.5	23	41.8	27	50.0	–	–	–	–	60
Asses	–	–	45	37.5	8	11.6	2	3.7	–	–	–	–	–	–	55
Ibexes	–	–	23	19.2	5	7.2	–	–	1	1.9	1	3.7	–	–	30
Antelope and gazelle	3	12.5	12	10.0	3	4.3	4	7.2	7	13.0	1	3.7	–	–	30
Giraffes	19	79.2	–	–	2	2.9	–	–	–	–	–	–	–	–	21
Dogs	–	–	8	6.7	2	2.9	1	1.8	–	–	2	7.4	–	–	13
Camels	–	–	–	–	–	–	–	–	–	–	10	37.0	1	20.0	11
Birds	–	–	–	–	4	5.8	2	3.7	3	5.5	–	–	–	–	9
Goats	–	–	–	–	–	–	–	–	3	5.5	–	–	–	–	3
Elephants	–	–	–	–	1	1.5	–	–	–	–	–	–	–	–	1
Scorpions	–	–	–	–	3	4.3	1	1.8	–	–	–	–	–	–	4
Crocodiles	–	–	–	–	1	1.5	–	–	–	–	–	–	–	–	1
Deer	–	–	–	–	–	–	–	–	–	–	–	–	3	60.0	3
Plants	–	–	–	–	–	–	–	–	1	1.9	–	–	–	–	1
Architectural constructions	–	–	–	–	1	1.5	1	1.8	–	–	2	7.4	–	–	4
Total	24	100.0	120	100.0	69	100.0	55	100.0	54	100.0	27	100.0	5	100.0	354

53% of the seriated rock drawings, occurred in Horizons II and III; the corresponding time span encompasses the Naqada II period up to the Early Dynastic (c. 3650–2650 BC). **Table 1** gives the overall thematic composition of the rock art at Elkab, arranged according to chronological horizons.

For the sake of convenience, the seven rock art horizons distinguished above have been reassembled in four chronological phases: 1) Horizons I and II: the Middle and Late Predynastic; 2) Horizon III: the Terminal Predynastic and Early Dynastic; 3) Horizons IV and V: the Old to New Kingdom; and 4) Horizons VI and VII: the late Pharaonic to Post-antique period. Before venturing onto the domain of interpretation, I shall now briefly and with considerable simplification present the thematic, technical, stylistic and syntactic particulars of each of these phases. Representative examples of Elkab drawings are given in **Fig. 2**; **Fig. 3** illustrates the prevailing types of style (designations after Lefèbvre 1967).

Phase 1. Horizons I and II: the Middle and Late Predynastic

This phase encompasses the Naqada I and II periods (c. 3900–3300 BC). From a purely thematic point of view Horizon I is clearly distinct from Horizon II (see **Table 1**). The former is almost exclusively characterised by the presence of giraffe-drawings, whereas the iconographic spectrum of the latter is much wider. Diagnostic for Horizon II are primarily sickle-shaped boats (often with slightly 'clubbed' ends) and right-angled vessels of Types I and VII respectively in P Cervicek's (1974, 98–138) boat typology (see **Plates 107–108**). Other distinctive components of Horizon II are of an anthropomorphic nature: figures with raised arms are especially typical. Amongst the animal drawings of this horizon are numerous wild asses, ibexes, and several kinds of antelope and gazelle. Cattle, however, are conspicuously absent. In both horizons the vast majority of the drawings are executed in a stylised visual realistic manner (see **Fig. 3**). Hammered designs, with and without outline, are by far the most common; incised drawings are almost

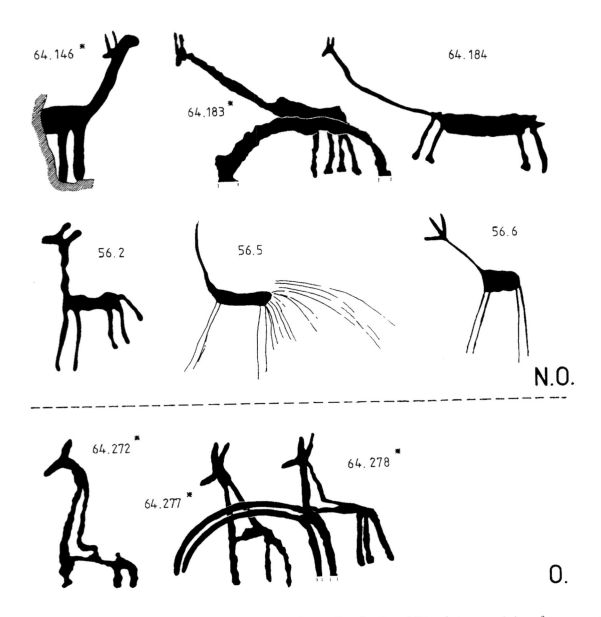

Fig. 4   Representative selection of Elkab giraffe drawings. O = outline drawings; NO = designs consisting of an area not surrounded by an outline.

completely lacking. A further distinctive feature of Horizon II is the occurrence of several stereotypical spatial compositions consisting of a Type VII boat surrounded by animal figures, principally asses (**Plate 111**).

Phase 2. Horizon III: the Terminal Predynastic and Early Dynastic

This phase, comprising the Naqada III period and the first two dynasties (*c.* 3300–2650 BC), is characterised by an extremely wide range of motifs. Boats are again well represented and vary in morphology. The sickle-shaped specimens belong to Cervicek's Types III and XV on the basis of the hull shape (see **Plate 109**), and the right-angled ones can be attributed to Type II. Human figures are also of diverse nature. Especially characteristic are representations with square-shaped trunk and so-called false steatopygia. As

regards animal figures, depictions of asses and ibexes are clearly less common than in the previous phase. Cattle, mostly of a long-horned breed with U-shaped horns, make their first appearance in rock art and immediately constitute the best-represented animal category. Worth mentioning is also the unique representation of a primitive temple: the *perwer* ('great house'), or traditional shrine of Upper Egypt. From a stylistic point of view, restricted and developed visual realistic drawings now clearly outnumber stylised ones. As in Horizons I and II, hammered designs, with or without outline, are still the most common; incised outline drawings account for about 40% of the total assemblage. The spatial compositions of the previous phase no longer occur, the main type of structural association now being small scenes or compositions with a narrative content, implying an interaction between the individual figures (e.g., hunting scenes).

Phase 3. Horizons IV and V: the Old to New Kingdom

This phase, encompassing the period from about the Third to the Twentieth Dynasty (*c.* 2650–1070 BC), is likewise characterised by a broad variety of motifs. Boats are exclusively sickle-shaped and now mainly belong to Cerviček's Types XVI (Middle Kingdom craft) and XXII–XXIII (Old and New Kingdom vessels) (see **Plate 110**). Human figures are relatively rare; they are mostly of small dimension and highly schematised, displaying a triangular trunk and matchstick-like limbs. The zoological repertoire consists, for the greater part, of cattle; different breeds can be identified. Most common are long-horned bovids with lyrate (Old Kingdom) and V-shaped (mainly Middle Kingdom) horns. The few indisputable examples of short-horned cattle, among which are some highly remarkable branded bulls (Huyge 1998a), can with good confidence be attributed to the New Kingdom. With regard to style, the majority of drawings are again stylised visual realistic. A substantial component of the assemblage, however, is geometrically schematic (about 30%). In contrast to the previous phases, the greater part of drawings in Horizons IV and V are incised. Outlined designs, even among the hammered drawings, clearly prevail. Apart from some juxtapositions and confrontations of boats and bovids, structural associations between figures appear to be absent.

Phase 4. Horizons VI and VII: the late Pharaonic to Post-antique period

The iconographic repertoire of Horizons VI and VII, corresponding to the period from about the Twenty-First Dynasty to the Islamic period (*c.* 1070 BC–after AD 641), is very restricted. Boat-drawings are exceptional; the sole example that can with any degree of certainty be attributed to this phase belongs to Cerviček's Type XXIX. Human figures and dromedaries are dominant. The former are even more rudimentarily executed than in the previous phase; most are matchstick figures with linear trunk and limbs. Dromedaries, exceptionally mounted, are drawn in very much the same way. Cattle are absent. Peculiar to this phase are also the representations of a Roman 'horned altars' and a number of palaeo-Christian (?) deer-drawings. From a stylistic point of view, the great majority of drawings are linear schematic. A small number are executed in a distinctive heraldic schematic style, reminiscent of the Eastern Desert nomads' (Blemmye) iconography (see Winkler 1938, 15–7). The near-totality of drawings in this phase are incised, either linear or outlined. As in Horizons IV and V, structural associations are only occasionally recorded.

Elkab provides a fairly representative sample of Egyptian rock art motifs and the above chronological and cultural seriation of the Elkab petroglyphs is in overall agreement with several other seriations of rock art in Upper Egypt and Lower Nubia (cf. in particular Almagro Basch and Almagro Gorbea 1968; Hellström 1970; Cerviček 1974; 1986; 1992–3). However, the intensively patinated, curvilinear and geometric designs that apparently constitute the oldest rock art horizon in this area, and are possibly of Late Palae-olithic or Early Predynastic age, are completely lack in the Elkab assemblage (see Davis 1984; Huyge 1998b; 1998d; 1998e; Huyge *et al.* 2001).

Meaning and Motivation of the Elkab Rock Art

In the following discussion the different Elkab rock art phases will be subjected to a synchronic and diachronic interpretative approach. This is neither the place nor the occasion to deal with all the aspects that can add to the argumentation. Only the main lines of reasoning will be advanced here.

Horizons I and II: the Middle and Late Predynastic

As stated above, giraffes (see **Fig. 4**) far outnumber other iconographic themes in the oldest rock art horizon at Elkab. Any attempt at interpreting the art of Horizon I will therefore have to concentrate on the significance, either utilitarian or symbolic, of this key motif. Unfortunately, few details are available regarding the importance of the giraffe to the Egyptians of the Predynastic and Early Dynastic periods. On archaeozoological grounds, it is clear that hunting this long-necked mammal was not a major economic preoccupation. What hypothesis can then be forwarded to account for its graphic popularity? Some information, both iconographic and lexicographic, is available suggesting that the giraffe may have had an emblematic role and a religious connotation in Graeco-Roman and palaeo-Christian times (Debono 1979, 425–7). A conceivable antecedent of this may be the suggested function of the animal as an heliophorous being (sun-bearer or *Hebekraft der Sonne*) in the Terminal Predynastic period and the early Old Kingdom. According to this hypothesis, advanced by W Westendorf (1966a, 539; 1966b, 37, 84–5) and based essentially on the recurrent appearance of this animal on Terminal Predynastic ceremonial palettes, the giraffe had a role as intermediate between the earthly and heavenly spheres. Its particular responsibility was to act as a bearer or vehicle of the sun-god. By performing this duty on a daily basis, the giraffe made it possible for this cosmic deity to bring his voyage along the heavenly vault to a favourable conclusion. The reason why the giraffe was considered in such relationship to the sun is probably self-evident (though not formulated as such by Westendorf). Because of its height (up to 6 m) it is closer to this celestial body than any other living creature and such a notion is certainly consistent with the ancient Egyptian 'outlook on nature' (see Wilson 1977, 40).

Although Westendorf's hypothesis regarding the solar character of the giraffe, among several other motifs, has been subject to criticism (e.g., Cialowicz 1991), it seems to be corroborated by the rock art evidence (which Westendorf only incidentally took into account). Of probable significance for the interpretation is the fact that the giraffes at Elkab are drawn facing almost exclusively (80%) to the (viewer's) left. This lateralisation, which contrasts sharply with that of other animal representations (only 30%, 28%, and 14% are lateralised to the left in the case of cattle, asses, and ibexes respectively), may be thought to indicate the local sense of the apparent rotation of the sun (see **Fig. 5**). As far

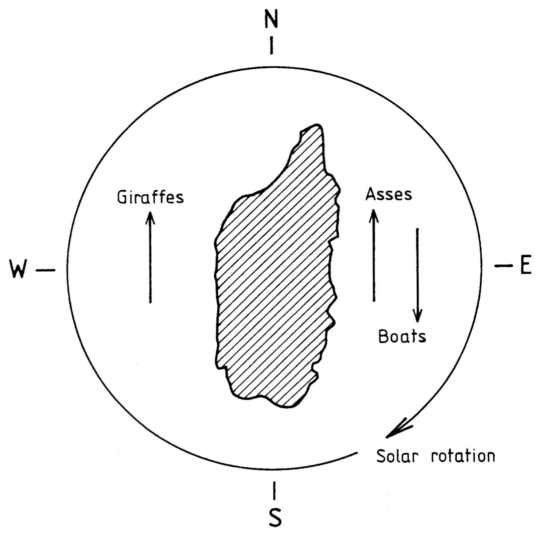

Fig. 5 Cosmological symbolism in the Elkab rock art. The shaded area portrays the 'Rock of the Vultures' (locality 64).

as the other internal aspects are concerned, it is also remarkable that the greater part of the Elkab giraffe-drawings are oriented westward (over 60%). Because the orientation of the rock drawings in general is predominantly eastward (over 70%), this westward orientation is no doubt significant. The West, being the heavenly direction where the sun sets, is considered as the location of the hereafter in the traditional religious symbolism of the ancient Egyptians (and this is already evident in Predynastic times from the standard burial orientation with face to the west). In the daily orbit performed by the sun-god, the transitional phase from day to night is especially perilous; adversaries of the sun, demons and malignant deities inhabit this twilight zone and must be kept at bay. By representing heliophorous powers facing west (the giraffe as *Hebekraft der Sonne*), the rock art creators may have been attempting to influence this hazardous event favourably. The fact that the sun-god or his subordinate representatives predominantly face west in classical dynastic representations of the solar cycle may strengthen this argument (Westendorf 1966b, 83).

The principal themes in Horizon II, boats of Type I and

VII (**Plates 107–108**), human figures with raised arms, and asses and ibexes create a more complex scene. Among these subjects, boats of Type I, human figures with raised arms, and ibexes are common motifs on funerary ceramics ('Decorated ware') of the Late Predynastic (Naqada II) period. Boats of Type VII and asses, on the other hand, are rarely if ever represented on this type of pottery. It is obviously not accidental that precisely these last two mentioned themes constitute the main ingredients of the stereotypical spatial compositions that characterise Horizon II (see **Plate 111**).

Rare iconographic parallels, particularly on ceramics from the Early Dynastic temple precinct at Abydos (see Petrie 1903, pl. XII, 266), suggest that the Type VII boats are sacred vessels and therefore not primarily funerary in nature. Certain details, such as the pendant banner-like ornamentation of the stern or prow (possibly a prototype of the later solar 'mat', see Thomas 1959), suggest that they may actually be solar barques. Their conceivable solar character is moreover corroborated by the internal characteristics of the drawings: not only are these boats almost exclusively oriented eastward (the heavenly direction where the sun rises), they are also mainly lateralised to the left. On this basis it can be suggested that these boats are propitiously related to the sun (their preferential lateralisation is consistent with the apparent sense of rotation of the sun). By analogy with the giraffes, they may therefore be considered symbolic bearers of the sun.

One of the underlying reasons why the vitally important task of *Hebekraft der Sonne* might have devolved *vom Sonnentier zum Sonnenboot* (Westendorf 1979) may be that the river had now become the principal artery of traffic and transport (Westendorf's suggestion). Another perhaps more fundamental cause might be that the giraffe had become uncommon in the landscape (experienced as a sign of weakness) to such a degree that it could no longer symbolically function in good confidence. In this intricate symbolism the numerous co-acting asses seem to play an antagonistic part. As opposed to the boat-drawings (and the giraffes!), they are for the most part lateralised to the right (72%), which presumably suggests their negative relation to the sun (they run counter to its apparent sense of rotation). The most obvious conclusion, completely consistent with the negative status of donkeys in ancient Egyptian religious symbolism (see Brunner-Traut 1977; Houlihan 1996, 32–3), is that the asses in the rock art are waylayers of the sun or *Sonnenfeinde*. Several passages in the Pyramid Texts, the Coffin Texts, and the Book of the Dead, in which asses are staged as malicious creatures, epitomes of evil, and even explicitly as animals that hamper the safe crossing of the solar barque, may support this hypothesis (see Blok 1929, 110; Borghouts 1971, 144–5). It could also be argued that the ass-drawings represent sacrificial animals which, in a not necessarily unrelated role, were ritually destroyed as part of the solar cult (for pertinent archaeozoological evidence, see Boessneck, von den Driesch and Eissa 1992).

As stated above, boats of Type I, human figures with raised arms, and ibexes are recurrent motifs on Late Predynastic funerary ceramics and this suggests a function with respect to the symbolic care of the dead. In my opinion, boats, human figures, and ibexes alike can most adequately be explained in terms of regeneration symbolism. This seems particularly likely for the boats of Type I. On the basis of strong morphological resemblance (e.g., the occurrence of upturned 'clubbed' ends), these vehicles are closely related to the basic design of the divine barque (Henu-barque) of the Memphite mortuary god Sokar (Huyge forthcoming). The latter funerary boat, one of the earliest-known and most characteristic of its type, is also provided with solar connotations. Sokar, being a god who 'resides in death and possesses in potency rejuvenating life' (Bleeker 1967, 66), is equated in certain passages with the rising sun (Brovarski 1984, 1061). It is therefore reasonable to assume that Sokar's Henu-barque and, by extrapolation, the Type I boats can be equated with the ascending sun-ship. A funerary vessel, which at the same time supports the rising sun-disk, must evidently be considered as a symbol of regeneration. The human figures with raised arms that often accompany these boats, and are also seen in the rock art (e.g., Winkler 1938, pl. XXXV), can be explained in similar terms; their distinctive arm-pose may moreover be interpreted as a sun-bearing posture (cf. Westendorf 1980). Likewise, the status of the ibex (and its often hypertrophically executed horns in particular) as a symbol of renewal and rejuvenation is generally acknowledged (see Hornung and Staehelin 1976, 139–40).

Summarising, it may be suggested that two symbolic constituents characterise the rock art of Horizon II: a solar and a funerary component. These constituents are perfectly complementary. The solar component (Type VII boats versus asses), guaranteeing the smooth working of the solar cycle, is closely linked to the funerary aspect (Type I boats, human figures with raised arms, and ibexes) through the concept of renewal and rejuvenation, which is perhaps the cardinal tenet of ancient Egyptian religious thought (Bleeker 1967, 21–2). Ultimately, all these images appear intricately interwoven; they indiscriminately symbolise and engineer the diurnal rise of the sun, and by extension, the regeneration of the deceased.

Horizon III: the Terminal Predynastic and Early Dynastic

The solar and funerary motivations prevailing in Horizons I and II can also be detected in Horizon III. In this horizon, however, the complex spatial compositions with boats and asses characterising Horizon II have given way to small narrative scenes in which human figures and different kinds of animals play the leading part. The interaction displayed is predominantly either hunting or ritual killing. The scene represented in **Plate 112** for instance, in which a human figure with square-shaped trunk confronts a crocodile, may be interpreted in terms of cosmological symbolism ('order triumphant'). As was the case for asses and several other kinds of animals, the troublesome crocodile was traditionally considered as a *Götterfeind* (Hornung 1977) and fearsome foe of the sun.

What particularly distinguishes Horizon III from the earlier (and later) horizons are the numerous and varied images that can be explained in terms of royal ideology. This is pre-eminently the case for a number of boat-drawings that belong to Types II and XV (see **Plate 109**). These vessels, having close counterparts on Terminal Predynastic and Early Dynastic elite artefacts (e.g., the famous Narmer Palette and the Gebel el-Arak knife handle), can in all probability be considered as ships of state or royal procession barges, which symbolically express the dominion of the ruler. Some of these depictions may even have been executed in commemoration of the actual periodic passage of a royal ship and the human figures on board may represent the skilful royal helmsmen (as in **Plate 109**). The concept of regal power and triumph is probably also embodied in a number of individual animal representations, including wild ('raging') bulls, vultures and scorpions, all of which are recognised bestial allegories of kingship.

Also characteristic of Horizon III is an important number of domestic cattle drawings. These animals most likely had a special status in the rock art. In contrast to other kinds of animals, such as the above-discussed asses and ibexes, it is difficult to relate them to religious symbolism, either cosmological or funerary. The complete absence of diagnostic paraphernalia, such as a solar disc between the horns, also

Fig. 6   Solar symbolism on a White Cross-line platter of the Naqada I period (after Westendorf 1966b, fig. 27).

seems to preclude their identification as divinities. In my opinion, these bovid images probably represent sacrificial beasts with a specific function in the local temple cult (cf. Ghoneim 1977, 196–216). It may not be coincidental that their appearance in rock art concurs with the oldest surviving traces of religious architecture in the Elkab area.

Horizons IV and V: the Old to New Kingdom

Clear-cut ideological and solar motifs are unusual in the rock art of Horizons IV and V. In all probability, the main motivations are funerary concerns and sacrificial practices. Figured prominently among the drawings of these horizons are the sickle-shaped boats of Types XVI and XXII–XXIII (see **Plate 110**), which in most cases can be related to funerary symbolism. Representatives of these vessel types may allude to funerary journeys, either the actual or mythical crossing of the Nile to the place of interment on the west bank (Wilson 1944, 205–10) or the 'mystical' nautical pilgrimage of the soul to a major sacred locus like Abydos (Yoyotte 1960, 30–40). The predominant westward orientation of these boats, contrasting sharply with the orientation of the earlier vessel images, is a firm argument favouring this interpretation.

Largely outnumbering all other animal species in Horizons IV and V, the domestic bovids most probably represent sacrificial animals (as in Horizon III). Some remarkable New Kingdom examples, unmistakably fattened and provided with brands on their hindquarters, have close counterparts in formal religious iconography (see Huyge 1998a).

Horizons VI and VII: the late Pharaonic to Post-antique period

With the exception of a limited number of symbols and allegorical images, most rock art of the late Pharaonic to Post-antique period does not seem to have a profound religious background (see Huyge 1998c). This is particularly evident for the main subject, the camel, which plays no part in ancient Egyptian religion or mythology. There is no indica-

tion whatsoever that it was offered or otherwise exploited in the cult. The use of the camel is entirely confined to the profane domain. If drawings of this animal have any underlying significance in rock art, it is more likely that they served as symbols of prestige, pride, prosperity, opulence and power. Likewise, the human figures of this phase are devoid of any religious aura. Often armed and engaged in warlike undertakings, they convey a bellicose ethos and a primary preoccupation with violent acquisition and the safeguarding of moveable property.

An additional argument that may be brought forward to confirm the rather trivial motivations of the rock art of this period is related to the particular location and orientation of the drawings. In the Elkab area, no less than 70 percent of the figures that have been attributed to Horizons VI and VII have been executed either on horizontal rock surfaces or on vertical rock faces facing west. In earlier phases of the rock art (with the exception of Horizon I) such drawings are rare, the majority having been executed on vertical rock faces facing east. Although it remains to be confirmed that these external features of the later Elkab rock art are traceable on a larger geographical scale, they possibly point to the fact that flat surfaces and faces providing shade were preferred, not because of the high-minded principles that underlie the earlier art, but for the sake of convenience only.

Summary and Discussion

The Middle and Late Predynastic: Cosmology

The common characteristic of Horizons I and II is that the majority of rock art representations can be related to cosmological (solar) symbolism. Giraffes in Horizon I and spatial compositions with asses and Type VII boats in Horizon II are the central features. As far as their meaning and function are concerned, giraffes and boats are interchangeable; both apparently perform the vitally important task of sun-bearer.

Some animal species (particularly the asses in Horizon II) may represent the adversaries of the sun. Of crucial importance in this cosmological symbolism is the orientation and lateralisation of the drawings. The eastward or westward orientation indicates the particular phase of the solar cycle (sunrise/day or sunset/night respectively) during which the images in question were intended to intervene. The lateralisation to the left (consistent with the apparent sense of rotation of the sun) are sympathetically solar; those to the right (counter to this apparent sense of rotation) have an explicit anti-solar character. The assumption that solar concepts already held a prominent place in the early Predynastic rock art horizons need not be a matter of surprise. The rejoicing on the occasion of daybreak (birth or renewal of life) and the dread of the night (expiration and death) were indubitably deeply embedded in the ancient Egyptian body of thought since time immemorial (see Wilson 1977, 35). The immutable rhythm of sunrise and sunset probably always has been correlative with the human dilemma of life and death. As a matter of fact, an incontestable pictorial representation of the main heavenly directions or major phases of the solar cycle, indicated by two radiant sun-disks, can already be pointed out on a White Cross-line platter of the Naqada I period (see **Fig. 6**).

It would probably be erroneous to consider the rock art of this early period as a mystical or philosophical treatise intended for liturgical or didactic application. The fragmentary nature of the cosmological symbolism (only some highly relevant excerpts of the solar cycle have been retained) appears to preclude such an interpretation. Evidently, the societal (and probably also private) motivation for the solar imagery should be sought on another level. In my opinion, the creation of rock art was a well-considered attempt to influence favourably certain critical phases of the solar cycle by means of the magical discharge of the petroglyphic image itself (which has been carefully levelled at a specific target by means of its orientation and lateralisation). The central features in all of this are the diurnal phenomena of sunrise and sunset, considered at the same time an instance and a guarantee for continued existence after death (hence the emphasis on representing heliophorous beings and powers). A second crucial aspect is the elimination of solar enemies (symbolised by desert game as representations of evil and chaos). The representation of these noxious creatures in the rock art may then have the function of a sympathetic substitute-offering or even an extermination in effigy of the sun-threatening powers (at the same time it cannot be excluded that it refers to the commemoration and/or the symbolical reinforcement of an actual deed of sacrifice). The societal (but also private) opportunism behind this intricate symbolism seems obvious: if the rock drawings guarantee the smooth working of the solar cycle, then the necessary conditions are fulfilled for each mortal (and consequently also the creator of a particular rock drawing) to be reborn. Just as the sun god renews himself on a daily basis, so each human being will achieve regeneration (cf. Quirke 1995, 23). Rebirth, in other words, is a natural spin-off from good cosmological order.

Obvious funerary meanings and motivations, of little or no account in Horizon I, play an important role in Horizon II. The symbolism sustained by the Type I boats, human figures with raised arms, and ibexes is evidently grafted firmly onto the fundamental ancient Egyptian concept of regeneration. The probable derivation of the Henu-barque of the mortuary god Sokar (equated with the ascending sun-ship) from the Type I boats can be a major argument for this thesis. Cosmology hides just around the corner: the daily rise of the sun (or the ascending solar barque) is by symbolic extension also the rebirth of the deceased. The sun's fate is therefore closely connected to that of all mortals; sunrise and regeneration are basically one and the same. The solar component in Horizon II (implying the idea of rebirth) can only be separated artificially from the funerary aspect (making the concept of rebirth explicit): both meanings and their underlying motivations are intimately interwoven.

The Terminal Predynastic and Early Dynastic: Ideology

The same motivations characterising Horizons I and II, cosmological (solar) symbolism and funerary concerns (merging in the concept of rebirth), can also be pointed out in Horizon III. What distinguishes Horizon III from the earlier horizons is the prominent ideological component. Indeed, a whole series of rock drawings (boats, anthropomorphic figures, and animals alike) can directly or indirectly be associated with royal ideology. All these images ultimately serve the same purpose: they externalise and proclaim symbolically the dominion, triumph and power of the ruler. In all probability the societal motivation underlying these figures is popular royalism and the growing recognition of the ruler as the upholder of the universe. Because of their unequal quality of manufacturing and the simplicity of their structural associations, these drawings are certainly not part of formal iconographic constructs that have been conceived and traced out by 'professional' ideologists and artisans. At the same time, however, it is manifest that every one of these representations has directly been inspired by the standardised, elitist imagery of the Terminal Predynastic and Early Dynastic periods. The ideological component in the rock art might therefore be labelled 'semi-official'; it is in all probability the product of an 'educated' local elite, perhaps priests and other dignitaries.

The reason this ideological component turns up in Horizon III can be found in the radical socio-political and religious reforms of the Terminal Predynastic and Early Dynastic periods. The official political unification of Egypt in late Naqada III times (Naqada IIIb or Dynasty 0), accomplished on a cultural-technological level already at the Naqada II stage (see Pérez Largacha 1993, 87–94; Wilkinson 1996, 5–7), resulted in a far-reaching centralisation of power and a concentration of the governmental apparatus at the royal court. The concretisation and personification of the state machinery also implied an hierarchical restructuring of religion and a royal annexation of the pre-existing devotional symbolism. As a consequence, certain fundamental religious practices, such as the concern for the cosmological order (a central feature in Horizons I and II), became less and less a public affair and increasingly a royal prerogative. In the light of these developments, it is perfectly understandable that ideologically motivated drawings entered the rock art repertoire. Corresponding to a profoundly modified mental attitude in society, these images are basically graphical manifestations of loyalty to the ruler and glorification of his worldly and divine power.

Of a completely different nature in Horizon III are the drawings of domestic cattle. Probably directly related to the attested existence of early cult infrastructure, these animals most likely represent sacrificial beasts that were offered up in the context of institutional or private religious rites. Their meaning and motivation will be further discussed below.

The Old to New Kingdom: private religious practice

Most conspicuous with regard to the rock art of Horizons IV and V is the rarity of cosmological (solar) symbolism. A plausible explanation for this can be found in the growing significance of the cult of the anthropomorphic chthonic fertility and mortuary god, Osiris. Indeed, toward the end of the Old Kingdom, the funerary cult of Osiris had significantly gained popular appeal. The emphasis on funerary concerns in the rock art of Horizons IV and V, pre-eminently expressed by means of nautical symbolism, has to be considered in the light of these developments. Some of the various boat-drawings in these horizons apparently relate to the actual funerary ritual, the transport of the deceased over water, and the journey to the final resting-place. Others, of a more 'mystical' nature, probably illustrate the posthumous pilgrimage of the soul to a major locus of worship. Eventually both types of drawings testify to an individual inclination in rock art motivation; they may be considered as graphical manifestations of personal devotion.

It remains debatable whether or not the sacrificial cattle drawings in Horizons IV and V should be interpreted in similar terms. If these drawings symbolically reinforce or commemorate actual cattle immolation, then the offering depicted was beyond doubt performed by the local propertied classes (e.g., the local priesthood). If, on the other hand, the offering depicted is nothing but a succedaneum (or a complement in effigy to the offer of a low-status animal), then it is likely that the creators of the drawings belonged to a lower class group. The question whether these cattle drawings refer to institutional sacrifice in the context of the local temple cult or individually motivated offering (or possibly both) must therefore be left unresolved.

The late Pharaonic to Post-antique period: Secularisation

In contrast to what has previously been the case, the rock art of Horizons VI and VII is essentially profane. Horsemanship and belligerence appear to have been the major sources of inspiration (for an in-depth discussion, see Huyge 1998c). Some of the rather trivial drawings of this period may be the outcome of casual pastime; others may purposely illustrate the pursuit of material prosperity or the tribal pride and prestige of their performers. Indeed, these late images associated with pomp, power and warfare display a mental attitude fundamentally different from that of the rock art seen in earlier periods. Such a mental shift in petroglyphic art, however, is not typical of the Egyptian situation alone. As a matter of fact, a far-reaching secularisation in the first millennium BC can be observed for almost the whole of North African rock art (see Muzzolini 1992, 42–3).

Conclusions

The rock art of Elkab is not a meaningless amalgam of obscure representations. The interpretative analysis presented above suggests that this graphical tradition was governed by subtle rules. Both content (themes) and formal peculiarities (orientation and lateralisation) appear intricately interwoven in a complex pictography. This language of imagery is clearly symbolic rather than narrative. As is the case for most of the official artistic manifestations in ancient Egypt (including the funerary-religious literature), it is only completely comprehensible to 'initiates'. Its hidden meanings and motivations can indeed be of diverse nature. They are mostly decipherable in the light of the general evolution of society and the historical succession of mystico-religious patterns of thought. In some horizons (especially I to III) the rock art may at the same time be a cosmography and a functional part of the cosmological machinery; it serves not only to illustrate the divine order of the universe and nature (the concept of ma'at), but effectively contributes to its maintenance. 'Perpetual return' or the endless process of death and birth, entirely correlative with the immutable rhythm of sunrise and sunset, is concretised and magically engineered by a multiplicity of metaphorical devices. The emergence of an important ideological component in Horizon III and the manifest emphasis on private funerary motivations and personal religious practice in Horizons IV and V are the direct reflection of fundamental political and socio-religious changes: the centralisation of government, the definitive legitimisation of the worldly and divine power of the ruler in the Terminal Predynastic and Early Dynastic periods and the increasing democratisation and regionalisation of cultic-funerary concepts from the later part of the Old Kingdom onward.

Admittedly, the statistical foundation underlying some of these interpretative constructs and claims carries insufficient authority (especially with regard to the oldest horizon; see **Table 1**). Quantitative data for other rock art assemblages in Upper Egypt, however, are rarely available, and it is questionable whether the Lower Nubian documentation would be useful, as the art of this area may, at least in part, correspond to a different type of symbolism. The intimate relationship between the rock drawings and the ancient *Weltanschauung* of which the Elkab petroglyphs seem to bear evidence can therefore be generalised only hypothetically for the whole of the ancient Egyptian rock art tradition. The broad thematic affinities, however, between the different assemblages, lead me to believe that such a generalisation may be warranted. Regional and local dissimilarities may be considered as vernacular variants of a communal language. They may be adequately explained in the light of the local historico-cultural context (e.g., the practical organisation of the indigenous temple cult). They may also be the consequence of the existence of socially or functionally distinct population groups in a certain region. In this sense the rock art of quarry workers and herdsmen will in all probability be thematically distinct, while at the same time possessing similar meanings and motivations, and subordinate to the same syntactical rules. Further research, paying full attention to intrinsic and external features alike, will be required to demonstrate whether ancient Egyptian rock art actually operated within a communal language with a standardised grammar and a universal semantic system. Clearly, this paper is only a beginning.

Acknowledgements

This article is partly based on a Ph.D dissertation that was supervised by Professor Pierre M Vermeersch and the late Professor Jan Quaegebeur (both Catholic University Leuven). Several friends and colleagues have commented on earlier drafts. They are (in alphabetical order): Ms Shawn Bubel (Catholic University Leuven), Dr Renée Friedman (British Museum), Dr Stan Hendrickx (Catholic University Leuven), Mr Charles Frank Herman (Catholic University Leuven) and Dr Luc Limme (Royal Museums of Art and History, Brussels). I am grateful to them for amicable advice and constructive criticism. Of course, I alone am responsible for any errors of interpretation and debatable standpoints taken.

Bibliography

Almagro Basch M and Almagro Gorbea M, 1968. *Estudios de arte rupestre nubio I. Yacimientos situados en la orilla oriental del Nilo, entre Nag Kolorodna y Kars Ibrim (Nubia egipcia)*. Memorias de la Misión Arqueológica X. Madrid.

Bahn P G and Vertut J, 1988. *Images of the Ice Age*. Leicester.

Bleeker C J, 1967. *Egyptian Festivals. Enactments of Religious Renewal*. Studies in the History of Religions 13. Leiden.

Blok H P, 1929. Eine magische Stele aus der Spätzeit. *Acta Orientalia* 7: 97–113.

Boessneck J, 1988. *Die Tierwelt des Alten Ägypten*. München.

Boessneck J, von den Driesch A and Eissa A, 1992. Eine Eselsbestattung der 1. Dynastie in Abusir. *Mitteilungen des Deutschen Archäologischen Instituts Abteilung Kairo* 48: 1–10.

Borghouts J F, 1971. The Magical Texts of Papyrus Leiden I 348. *Oudheidkundige Mededelingen uit het Rijksmuseum van Oudheiden te Leiden* 51: 1–248.

Brovarski E, 1984. Sokar. In W Helck and W Westendorf (eds), *Lexikon der Ägyptologie* V. Wiesbaden: 1055–74.

Brunner-Traut E, 1977. Esel. In W Helck and W Westendorf (eds), *Lexikon der Ägyptologie* II. Wiesbaden: 27–30.

Capart J, 1904. *Les débuts de l'art en Egypte*. Brussels.

Cervicek P, 1974. *Felsbilder des Nord-Etbai, Oberägyptens und Unternubiens*. Ergebnisse der Frobenius-Expeditionen 16. Wiesbaden.

Cervicek P, 1986. *Rock Pictures of Upper Egypt and Nubia*. Istituto Universitario Orientale–Napoli. Supplemento 46 fasc. 1. Roma.

Cervicek P, 1992–3. Chorology and Chronology of Upper Egyptian and Nubian Rock Art up to 1400 B.C. *Sahara* 5: 41–8.

Cialowicz K M, 1991. *Les palettes égyptiennes aux motifs zoomorphes et sans décoration*. Studies in Ancient Art and Civilization 3. Kraków.

Darnell J C and Darnell D, 1997. The Theban Desert Road Survey. *Newsletter American Research Center in Egypt* 172, 1: 10–5.

Davis W, 1984. The Earliest Art in the Nile Valley. In L Krzyzaniak and M Kobusiewicz (eds), *Origin and Early Development of Food-Producing Cultures in North-Eastern Africa*. Poznan: 81–94.

Davis W, 1990. The Study of Rock Art in Africa. In P Robertshaw (ed.), *A History of African Archaeology*. London: 271–95.

Debono F, 1979. A propos de la curieuse représentation d'une girafe dans l'ouvrage de Belon du Mans. In J Vercoutter (ed.), *Hommages à la mémoire de Serge Sauneron 1927–1976. II. Egypte post-pharaonique*. Bibliothèque d'Étude 82. Cairo: 417–58.

Friedman R and Hendrickx S 2002. Protodynastic Tableau (Gr. No. 1). In J C Darnell, *Theban Desert Road Survey in the Egyptian Western Desert I: Gebel Tjauti Rock Inscriptions 1–45 and Wadi el-Hôl Rock Inscriptions 1–45*. Oriental Institute Publication 119. Chicago: 10–18.

Ghoneim W, 1977. *Die ökonomische Bedeutung des Rindes im Alten Ägypten*. Habelts Dissertationsdrucke. Reihe Ägyptologie 3. Bonn.

Green F W, 1903. Prehistoric Drawings at El-Kab. *Proceedings of the Society for Biblical Archaeology* 25: 371–2.

Hellström P, 1970. *The Rock Drawings*. The Scandinavian Joint Expedition to Sudanese Nubia 1. Stockholm.

Hendrickx S, 1995. *Analytical Bibliography of the Prehistory and the Early Dynastic Period of Egypt and Northern Sudan*. Egyptian Prehistory Monographs 1. Leuven.

Hendrickx S and Huyge D, 1989. *Elkab IV. Topographie. Fascicule 2. Inventaire des sites archéologiques*. Brussels.

Hornung E, 1971. *Der Eine und die Vielen. Ägyptische Gottesvorstellungen*. Darmstadt.

Hornung E, 1977. Götterfeind. In W Helck and W Westendorf (eds), *Lexikon der Ägyptologie* II. Wiesbaden: 684–5.

Hornung E and Staehelin E, 1976. *Skarabäen und andere Siegelamulette aus Basler Sammlungen*. Ägyptische Denkmäler in der Schweiz 1. Mainz.

Houlihan P F, 1996. *The Animal World of the Pharaohs*. Cairo.

Huyge D, 1984a. Horus Qa-a in the Elkab Area, Upper Egypt. *Orientalia Lovaniensia Periodica* 15: 5–9.

Huyge D, 1984b. Rock Drawings at the Mouth of Wadi Hellal, Elkab (Upper Egypt). In L Krzyzaniak and M Kobusiewicz (eds), *Origin and Early Development of Food-producing Cultures in North-Eastern Africa*. Poznan: 231–4.

Huyge D, 1995. *De rotstekeningen van Elkab (Boven-Egypte): registratie, seriatie en interpretatie*. Unpublished Ph.D dissertation. Leuven.

Huyge D, 1998a. 'Battered Bulls': Rock Art Destruction in Egypt. *African Archaeological Review* 15: 3–11.

Huyge D, 1998b. Possible Representations of Palaeolithic Fish-Traps in Upper Egyptian Rock Art. *Rock Art Research* 15: 3–11.

Huyge D, 1998c. Art on the Decline? Egyptian Rock Drawings from the Late and Graeco-Roman Periods. In W Clarysse, A Schoors and H Willems (eds), *Egyptian Religion. The Last Thousand Years. Studies Dedicated to the Memory of Jan Quaegebeur*. Orientalia Lovaniensia Analecta 85, Leuven: 1377–92.

Huyge D, 1998d. Egypt's Oldest 'Art'? The Petroglyphs of El-Hosh. *Egyptian Archaeology. Bulletin of the Egypt Exploration Society* 13: 34–6.

Huyge D, 1998e. Hilltops, Silts and Petroglyphs: The Fish-Hunters of el-Hosh (Upper Egypt). *Bulletin des Musées royaux d'Art et d'Histoire* 69: 97–113.

Huyge D, 1999. Bearers of the Sun. *Discovering Archaeology* 1: 48–58.

Huyge D, forthcoming. *Recycling the Predynastic. Anachronisms in Historical Egyptian Cult.* MS.

Huyge D, Watchman A, De Dapper M and Marchi E, 2001. Dating Egypt's Oldest 'Art': AMS [14]C Age Determinations of Rock Varnishes Covering Petroglyphs at El-Hosh (Upper Egypt). *Antiquity* 75: 68-72.

Kemp B J, 1989. *Ancient Egypt. Anatomy of a Civilization.* London and New York.

Lefèbvre L, 1967. Les styles de l'art rupestre pré et protohistorique en Afrique du Nord (essai de typologie). In *Actes du VIème Congrès Panafricain de Préhistoire.* Chambéry: 226–30.

Murnane W J, 1987. The Gebel Sheikh Suleiman Monument: Epigraphic Remarks. In B Williams and T J Logan, The Metropolitan Museum Knife Handle and Aspects of Pharaonic Imagery before Narmer. *Journal of Near Eastern Studies* 46: 245–85: Appendix C: 282–5.

Muzzolini A, 1992. Le profane et le sacré dans l'art rupestre saharien. *Bulletin de la Société française d'Egyptologie* 124: 24–70.

Pérez Largacha A, 1993. *El nacimiento del Estado en Egipto.* Aegyptiaca Complutensia 2. Alcalá de Henares.

Petrie W M F, 1903. *Abydos. Part II.* Memoirs of the Egypt Exploration Fund 24. London.

Quirke S, 1995. *Ancient Egyptian Religion.* New York.

Ries J, 1975. La religion de la préhistoire égyptienne: les étapes de la recherche. In E Anati (ed.), *Actes du Symposium International sur les Religions de la Préhistoire, Valcamonica 1972.* Capo di Ponte: 293–312.

Silverman D P, 1991. Divinity and Deities in Ancient Egypt. In B E Shafer (ed.), *Religion in Ancient Egypt. Gods, Myths, and Personal Practice.* London: 7–87.

Thomas E, 1959. Terrestrial Marsh and Solar Mat. *Journal of Egyptian Archaeology* 45: 38–51.

Traunecker C, 1993. *Les dieux de l'Egypte.* Que sais-je? 1194. Paris.

Westendorf W, 1966a. Bemerkungen zu den Namen der Könige Djer-Athothis und Neferka. *Orientalistische Literaturzeitung* 61: 533–41.

Westendorf W, 1966b. *Altägyptische Darstellungen des Sonnenlaufes auf der abschüssigen Himmelsbahn.* Münchner Ägyptologische Studien 10. Berlin.

Westendorf W, 1966c. Ursprung und Wesen der Maat, der altägyptischen Göttin des Rechts, der Gerechtigkeit und der Weltordnung. In S Lauffer (ed.), *Festgabe für Dr. Walter Will.* Köln, Berlin, Bonn and München: 201–25.

Westendorf W, 1979. Vom Sonnentier zum Sonnenboot. In M Görg and E Pusch (eds), *Festschrift Elmar Edel.* Ägypten und Altes Testament 1. Bamberg: 432–45.

Westendorf W, 1980. Der Wortstamm *k3(j)*: 'heben, tragen' > 'hervorbringen, erzeugen'. *Bulletin de la Société d'Egyptologie Genève* 4: 99–102.

Wilkinson T A H, 1996. *State Formation in Egypt. Chronology and Society.* British Archaeological Reports International Series 651. Oxford.

Williams B and Logan T J, 1987. The Metropolitan Museum Knife Handle and Aspects of Pharaonic Imagery before Narmer. *Journal of Near Eastern Studies* 46: 245–85.

Wilson J A, 1944. Funeral Services of the Egyptian Old Kingdom. *Journal of Near Eastern Studies* 3: 201–18.

Wilson J A, 1977. Egypt: The Nature of the Universe. In H Frankfort, J A Wilson, T Jacobson and W A Irwin, *The Intellectual Adventure of Ancient Man. An Essay on Speculative Thought in the Ancient Near East.* Chicago and London: 31–61.

Winkler H A, 1938. *Rock-Drawings of Southern Upper Egypt I* Archaeological Survey of Egypt 26. London.

Yoyotte J, 1960. Les pèlerinages dans l'Egypte ancienne. In *Les pèlerinages.* Sources orientales 3. Paris: 17–74.

The Deserts and the Fifteenth and Sixteenth Upper Egyptian Nomes during the Middle Kingdom

Sydney H Aufrère

From the earliest times, the Eastern Desert has been criss-crossed by hunters, caravans and mining expeditions (Butzer 1982). To date, there is little evidence of settlement aside from a few camps and rock shelters, and there appear to have been no substantially built-up areas until the Graeco-Roman period. However, throughout the pharaonic period, this desert was at times the place of an economy parallel to that of the Nile Valley. The abundance of inscriptions left along the access routes confirms that the Eastern Desert was widely explored and that many individuals were able to stay there for extensive periods (see also Harrell; Klemm, Klemm and Murr; and Shaw in this volume).

Notwithstanding the apparent lack of records, a question comes to mind: who, during the Twelfth Dynasty, was in charge of the borders, frontiers and limits of the desert area on behalf of the pharaonic administration? To answer this question we must consider the tombs both at Beni Hasan, whose owners carried out important duties in the Oryx Nome (Newberry 1893=*BH I*; 1894=*BH II*; Shedid 1994), and those at El Bersheh (Newberry 1894b).

In the early Twelfth Dynasty, having been involved in the reconquest of the Delta and Nubia as well as the reorganisation of administrative structures during the reigns of Amenemhat I and his son Senwosret I, the nomarchs of the Sixteenth Upper Egyptian (Oryx) nome held very high ranks, which they recorded in their biographical inscriptions. Their tombs at Beni Hasan, where the nomarchs date their administration to the regnal years of the sovereigns, are particularly instructive for both the representations and the titles they contain. Before dealing with the question at hand, we must bear in mind that administrative titles were variable and the type of power held by their owners changed frequently (Simpson 1965, 63–8). We need therefore to determine whether the titles under discussion correspond to actual responsibilities.

From the Eleventh Dynasty onward, the princes of the Oryx nome knew how to maintain a close relationship with the royal court, and this allowed them to play an enviable role in Twelfth Dynasty Egypt. In this they followed the example of the great families of the Jackal and Hare nomes, who took part in the government of the country as well as in the royal achievements of the Twelfth Dynasty (see Montet 1961, 146–56).

Among the high officials of the Oryx nome, Khnum-hotep II, owner of Beni Hasan tomb number 3 and a contemporary of Senwosret II, the fourth ruler of the Twelfth Dynasty, held the title 'Administrator of the Eastern Deserts' (*jmj-rз sm.jwt jзb.tjw*). In his titulary, this title always appears immediately after those of *jrj-pʿt*-prince and *ḥзtj-ʿ*-prince (*BH I*, 39, 41, pls XXIV, B and A, southern archi-

trave; XXV, 1–2; XXXII; XXXIII; XXXV, 2nd reg. on the left). Its position within the sequence of titles allows us to observe to which level in the titulary's hierarchy it belongs, because it is not, *a priori*, an honorific title as the previous two, but a real administrative title whose meaning we will try to define.

If we dissect the title we can observe that *jmj-rз* is a common title for an individual playing the role of steward, administrator or supervisor. *Smjt* is traditionally considered to mean the fringes of the desert, either flat or hilly, located to either side of the Nile Valley. If by means of a paronomasis the word connotes the 'necropolis', its meaning gets closer to that of *ḥзst*, 'desert', in the wide sense of the word. By the association of one idea with another, a space composed of hollows and humps signifies 'foreign country', because Egypt, strictly speaking, is the flat earth, *tз*. In the context of the title, *smjt* represents the desert, considered as a hunting and economic working area, which was the property of Egypt and its nomes. Thus, the *sm.tjw jзb.tjw* correspond to the vast stretches of the east as well as the Arabic mountain range. *Jmj-rз sm.tjw jзb.tjw*, Administrator of the Eastern Deserts, is therefore not a meaningless title in the titulary of Khnumhotep (Kamrin 1993). In spite of the apparent simplicity and unequivocal character of this title, we must trace the history of its function within the nome itself.

One learns from the long biographical inscription left by Khnumhotep II in his tomb that his maternal grandfather (Khnumhotep I) was established by Amenemhat I as *jrj-pʿt* prince, *ḥзtj-ʿ* prince, Administrator of the Eastern Deserts in the town of Menat-Khufu' (*BH II*, 59, cols 30–31; cf. pl. XXXV). The expression 'in the town of Menat-Khufu' is quite relevant and we shall come back to this subject below (see also Montet 1961, 160). For the moment, it appears that Khnumhotep II is trying to connect this title with the founder of his dynasty, as the small tomb of Khnumhotep I (no. 14) does not mention it (*BH I*, 81–5). However, this is not the case in Nakhty's tomb (no. 21). Nakhty is a *ḥзtj-ʿ*-prince and Administrator of the Eastern Deserts, who, like Khnumhotep I (presumably his father), holds the title of 'Great Chief of the Oryx Nome' (*ḥrj-tp ʿз n Mз-ḥd*) (*BH II*, 26, pl. XXIIA). This latter title disappears after the administration of Ameny-Amenemhat, whose tomb is the most impressive after that of Khnumhotep II.

Among a number of rulers who wielded power in the Oryx Nome, only four held the title 'Administrator of the Eastern Deserts': possibly Khnumhotep I, according to the inscription of Khnumhotep II; Nakhty I; Netjernakht, the owner of the tomb number 23 (*BH II*, 27); and Khnum-hotep II. This title in particular causes problems for our understanding of the succession of dignitaries and the hand-

Table 1: List of the nomarchs holding the titles 'Great Chief of the Oryx Nome' and 'Administrator of the Eastern Deserts'

Baqet I Tomb No. 29		Great Chief of the Oryx Nome	*BH II*, 32–6
Baqet II Tomb No. 33		Great Chief of the Oryx Nome	*BH II*, 37–40
Romushenty Tomb No. 27		Great Chief of the Oryx Nome	*BH II*, 30–1
Baqet III Tomb No. 15		Great Chief of the whole Oryx Nome	*BH II*, 43–50
Khety Tomb No. 17		Great Chief of the whole Oryx Nome	*BH II*, 51–62
Khnumhotep I Tomb No. 14	(Administrator of the Eastern Deserts)	Great Chief of the Oryx Nome	*BH I*, 81–5
Nakhty Tomb No. 21	Administrator of the Eastern Deserts	Great Chief of the Oryx Nome	*BH II*, 26
Ameny-Amenemhat Tomb No. 2		Great Chief of the Oryx Nome	*BH I*, 11–38
Netjernakht Tomb No. 23	Administrator of the Eastern Deserts		*BH II*, 27–9, pls XXIII–XXV
Khnumhotep II Tomb No. 3	Administrator of the Eastern Deserts		*BH I*, 41–72

ing down of responsibility in the Oryx nome. It forces us to examine chronological issues. Thus, the tomb in which Netjernakht is buried apparently owes its existence to Khnumhotep II, who left his own portrait on its wall as he acts as donor. His originally standing figure is surmounted by an inscription of seven columns that reads:

'(Here is) the *ḥзtj-ꜥ*-prince, Chief of the prophets, the Administrator of the Eastern Deserts, Neheri's son Khnumhotep II, born of Baqet, justified, lady of Imakh: He made (this) for his father whom he loves, the *ḥзtj-ꜥ*-prince, the Chief of the prophets, [Netjerna-kht] born of Aryhotep, justified' (*Hnm-htp sз Nḥrj jr n Bзqt jr=f n jt=f mrj=f ḥзtj-ꜥ jmj-rз ḥmw-ntr [...] jr n ꜥrjt-ḥtp, mзꜥt-ḥrw*) (BH II, pl. xxxiv).

The expression 'for his father whom he loves' is not evidence of a familial link, but simply means that Neheri's son Khnumhotep II[1] succeeded Netjernakht (*BH II*, 27). We notice that among his titles, Netjernakht is only an 'Administrator of the Eastern Deserts' but not a 'Great Chief of the Oryx Nome'. Thus it is not possible to be certain that he lived before Ameny-Amenemhat, the last to hold the latter title, particularly since only two persons – Nakhty I and Khnumhotep I – ever held both of the titles 'Administrator of the Eastern Deserts' and 'Great Chief of the Oryx Nome'.

How do we then explain the fact that Ameny-Amenemhat, who held office between the years 18 and 43 of Senwosret I, had the title 'Great Chief of the Oryx Nome', but not that of 'Administrator of the Eastern Deserts'? It seems difficult to plead an omission when dealing with a tomb whose decoration was so perfectly executed, particu-

larly since his two predecessors introduced the tradition and titles of the Eastern Desert administration. Ameny-Amenemhat therefore reveals a discontinuity in the use of the title 'Administrator of the Eastern Deserts', unless we consider that the two titles 'Great Chief of the Oryx Nome' and 'Administrator of the Eastern Deserts', previously held by a single individual, were now separated and held by two different officials. If this is the case, Ameny-Amenemhat would have inherited the function of nomarch as 'Great Chief of the Oryx Nome', while Netjernakht, who shared with him a series of honorific titles, would have taken up a career as 'Administrator of the Eastern Deserts'. In this respect Netjernakht would appear to have been a true heir of the Khnumhotep I dynasty, as the desire of Khnumhotep II to pay homage to him suggests. Yet, we must not forget that Khnumhotep II chose to build his own hypogeum next to the one belonging to Ameny-Amenemhat.

We must also bear in mind that after Nakhty I neither Ameny-Amenemhat – although he had a son, called Khnumhotep[2] – nor Netjernakht had descendants able to succeed them.[3] By referring to Netjernakht as 'his father whom he loves', his successor Khnumhotep II appears to take over the filial duty for an official with no children of his own at the time of his death. It is Khnumhotep II who leads Netjernakht's funeral and decorates his funerary chapel.

Table 1 summarises the sequence of the dignitaries of the Oryx nome during both the Eleventh and Twelfth Dynasty and allows us to consider the sequence of events.

Among the 'Administrators of the Eastern Deserts', Khnumhotep II holds centre stage because of the unusual

Table 2: List of the finished and unfinished tombs of the nomarchs of the Sixteenth Upper Egyptian (Oryx) nome

No. 1	unfinished		No. 21	Nakhty I	*BH II*, 26
No. 2	Ameny-Amenemhat	*BH I*, 9–38, pls II–XXIIIA	No. 22	unfinished	*BH II*, 27
No. 3	Khnumhotep II	*BH I*, 39–72, pls XXIV–XXVIII	No. 23	Netjernakht	*BH II*, 27–9
No. 4	Khnumhotep IV	*BH I*, pls XXXIX–XL	No. 24	unfinished	
No. 5	unfinished		No. 25	unfinished	
No. 6	unfinished		No. 26	unfinished	
No. 7	unfinished		No. 27	Remushenty	*BH II*, 30–1
No. 8	unfinished		No. 28	unfinished	*BH II*, 32
No. 9	apparently unfinished		No. 29	Baqet I	*BH II*, 32–6
No. 10	unfinished		No. 30	unfinished	*BH II*, 36
No. 11	unfinished		No. 31	unfinished	*BH II*, 36
No. 12	unfinished		No. 32	nearly finished	*BH II*, 36–7
No. 13	royal scribe Khnumhotep	*BH I*, 73–7, pl. XLVI	No. 33	Baqet II	*BH II*, 37–40
No. 14	Khnumhotep I	*BH I*, 79–85, pls XLII–XLVII	No. 34	unfinished	*BH II*, 40
No. 15	Baqet III	*BH II*, 41–50, pls II–VIIIA	No. 35	unfinished	*BH II*, 40
No. 16			No. 36	unfinished	*BH II*, 40
No. 17	Khety	*BH II*, 51–62, pls IX–XIX	No. 37	unfinished	*BH II*, 40
No. 18	unfinished	*BH II*, pls XX–XXI	No. 38	unfinished	*BH II*, 40
No. 19	unfinished		No. 39	unfinished	
No. 20	unfinished				

importance of his tomb, decorated in the local traditional style. According to his biographical inscription, he was invested with his official duties in year 29 of Amenemhat II. As the son of a prince, he had certainly been brought up in the palace. He was probably a companion, or even a childhood friend, of Senwosret II, since royal heirs were raised with the children of the peers of the realm.

Khnumhotep II did not formally hold the title 'Great Chief of the Oryx Nome', as this prestigious princely title had been abandoned during the Twelfth Dynasty. Nevertheless, one cannot fail to notice Khnumhotep's high position. Thus, according to the titles held by dignitaries of the Oryx nome, their activity seems to have been progressively transferred, from Nakhty I onwards, toward the administration of the desert; a process we should try to explain.

During this period the Egyptian élite were in charge of one or more economic departments. The administrative situation seems to have been frequently modified to suit the various parties who shared in administrative power and were in competition to become vizier, an office whose holder was always selected from the high provincial dignitaries (Valloggia 1974, 123–34). We know that the nomarchs of Assiut, like Hapydjefai, succeeded in putting Nubia under their military and commercial control during the reigns of Amen-

emhat I and Senwosret I, while during the reign of Senwosret II the organisation of expeditions to the Wadi Hammamat was the responsibility of the vizier Antefoker. We can observe during the second half of the Twelfth Dynasty the effects of an economic policy that focused on the East. The three pharaohs Amenemhat II, Senwosret II and Senwosret II successively conducted a policy of economic expansion toward both Nubia and Asia. For this one can refer to the recently published Memphite historical inscription of Amenemhat II (Altenmüller and Moussa 1991; Malek and Quirke 1992, 13–8, pls 2–3) as well as the Sobek-khu stela, dated to the reign of Senwosret III, in the collection of the Manchester Museum (Baines 1987).

Coming back to Beni Hasan, it would be risky to consider an official tomb such as that of Khnumhotep II as a precise reflection of reality or of the whole Egyptian economic sphere. A tomb is, as far as we know, a version, or an image, of the administration of the official meant for his funerary use, and Khnumhotep's tomb is no exception. As in the tomb of Hapydjefai, whose administrative activities both in Egypt and abroad are recorded, the decoration of the tomb principally reflects the workings of an estate economy rather than that of a centralised administration. Indeed, local events are not to be excluded, as shown by the transport of the huge statue of Djehutyhotep as depicted on one of the walls in his tomb at el-Bersheh (Vandier 1943, 185–90).

If we accept the idea that the exploitation of the Eastern Desert represented one of the most important duties of the Oryx Nome administrators, we must see if such an interpretation can be proven, particularly by examining the evidence in Khnumhotep II's tomb, as it is the most detailed (*BH II*, 61). Indeed, it is interesting to learn that Khnumhotep was attended by other local officials whose duties were related to desert exploitation. The most important among them are the two superintendents of the desert-land (*jmj-r3 smjt*) Nakht (*BH I*, pl. xxxv) and Nakht's son, Nakht (*BH I*, pl. xxx), who probably succeeded his father in the same post, unless they worked together. We can also observe other people linked to the activity in the desert, including three 'herdsmen' (*ssw*), whose names are Khnumhotep, Pepy and Khnumnakht, a 'donkey-herder' (*ssw ʿ3w*) named Khnumnakht and an unnamed 'gazelle-herder' (*ssw ʿwt*) (*BH I*, pl. xxx).

Among the officials shown surrounding Ameny-Amenemhat in his tomb, the dimensions of which are quite similar to that of Khnumhotep II, there are no equivalent desert-based officials; we find only the names of four herdsmen who probably took care of the cattle in the pasture-land on the desert's fringe during winter and spring (*BH I*, 18). As Ameny-Amenemhet did not hold the title 'Administrator of the Eastern Deserts', the omission of such officials is perhaps not surprising. Moreover, in Khnumhotep's tomb, there is a 'superintendent of desert policemen' (*jmj-r3 nww*), whose name is Khety (*BH I*, pl. xxx). This title does not exist in Ameny-Amenemhat's tomb. These policemen, who crisscrossed the desert fringe, used dogs in order to control Bedouin people in the vicinity of the valley.

The scenes in these two tombs cannot be taken as evidence of the social relationship of the named officials nor the full significance of their economic duties; the owner's status and the desire to insist on his prominent role overwhelms other concerns. Thus it is advisable to reserve judgement on this question. Nevertheless, the presence of two officials holding the title 'superintendent of the desert-land' in Khnumhotep's tomb seems to confirm the specific character of the title 'Administrator of the Eastern Deserts' in Khnumhotep's titulary.

The religious duties of Khnumhotep II, although linked to aspects of the desert deities, do not allow us to confirm the nature of some of his civil duties, but nor do they invalidate them. Because he was in charge of the local cults, it is true that Khnumhotep plays an important role in the priesthood of Pakhet, the divine lioness of the nome who was worshipped in the wadi where the Speos Artemidos had been carved out in the reign of Hatshepsut (Bickel and Chappaz 1988, 9–24).

On the whole, Khnumhotep II's priestly duties[4] express the close link that every nome kept with desert forces inherent in the economy of their geographical area (Aufrère 1998; 2001). Pakhet, 'Lady of the Valley' (*nbt srt*), acts as the Distant One, a role belonging to almost all the lioness-goddesses worshipped along the edges of the Eastern and Western Deserts (DeWitt 1951, 285ff) starting with Smi-

this in the cult of Elkab. The legend of the Eye of Rê' specified that Elkab was one of the routes through which Hathor-Tefnut entered the valley on New Year's day when coming back from Punt (De Cenival 1988, 65). It was under the aegis of the lioness deities, equated with the Eye of Horus, that travellers and caravan traders placed themselves. In general, all desert exploitation, principally in the Eastern rather than in the Western Desert, was under their protection. Other Hathoric deities, of whom traces can be found here and there in the Eastern Desert and Sinai, corresponded to Min and Sopdu, Lords of the East. Local cults show that the Oryx nome's dignitaries were oriented toward the desert and particularly toward hunting therein, but neither more nor less, according to the decoration of their tombs, than those of every other Egyptian nome.[5] We have to admit that, as far as the religious titles of the Sixteenth nome are concerned (Montet 1961, 157–63), they indicate, from an economic point of view, only virtual activity. However, whatever this activity may have been, the titles reveal the existence of traditional links with the deep desert.

It must be admitted that such a general title as 'Administrator of the Eastern Deserts' is suggestive only of the activity within the desert areas, without the nome itself being implicated as a departure or arrival point of the expeditions into them. Khnumhotep I is, however, named as 'Administrator of the Eastern Deserts *in* Menat-Khufu', and this suggests a link between this town and the desert. Consequently we may consider Menat-Khufu to be a city linked with the Eastern Desert, although its location in the Oryx nome is very far from being decided (Gauthier 1926, 36–7).

First of all, we should determine whether the Oryx nome is suitable for communications with the east. If one looks at the wadi in which the Speos Artemidos was cut, one must acknowledge that despite the religious association, provided by the texts of the so-called speos that deal with the return of Pakhet from Punt,[6] this wadi is neither a penetrating route nor a commercial road into the desert (Bickel and Chappaz 1988). The location of the speos is related to the spiritual link between the population of the valley and the lioness-goddess' cult. Let us say, to simplify, that it is located on a virtual path leading toward the Eastern Desert.

In the north, the long track that joins the Gebel el-Qalala el-Qibliya follows the Wadi el-Tarfa to meet the Nile Valley below Sheikh Hasan, north to el-Sisiriya (Berg 1973, sheets X–XI). It is a direct route to the Sinai and has a few wells, which were occasionally a focus of short-term settlement (e.g., Bir-Murêr, see Berg 1973, sheet X). The Egyptians of the Sixteenth nome could also cross the rocky plateau and enter the valley at the latitude of Sheikh Mubarek, northeast of Minieh, which earlier scholars considered to be the location of Menat-Khufu. To the south, the Wadi el-Tarfa joins the Wadi Qena system by means of adjacent tributaries. In short, there were enough routes of penetration to allow us to imagine that the Sixteenth nome was widely opened toward the east.

On the other hand, the southern part of the Sixteenth nome is where the *via Hadriana* formerly ended. This track left the Red Sea shore in the neighbourhood of Gebel el-Zeit and made an arc across the rocky plateau to join the valley just above Deir el-Bersheh. Desert tracks usually follow traditional roads that have been used for generations, and the Bedouin still use the Sikka el-'Agam, their name for the remnants of the *via Hadriana*.[7] However, this link with the Eastern Desert through the southern part of the Sixteenth nome is only a possibility for which we do not really have evidence from this period; it should be examined in the field.

The problem of the traffic eastward allows us to consider once more the problem of the famous scene whose inscription says that it concerns the arrival of a tribe of 37 Asiatic Bedouin (*ʿꜣmw*) led by a patriarch named Abishai (*BH I*, pls xxviii, xxx, xxxi).[8] Much has been written about this scene from Khnumhotep II's tomb in Egyptological and Biblical circles partly because it is a unique document. The papyrus sheet presented to Khnumhotep II by the scribe Neferhotep is dated to year 6 of Senwosret II, a *terminus ante quem* of this nomarch's activity (*BH I*, pl. xxxviii, 2). The event must have been quite striking to find inclusion among the dramatic scenes of the nomarch's administration, and in this way, it follows the example of the transport of Djehutyhotep's statue in his tomb at Deir el-Bersheh (Newberry 1894b, pls xii, xv).

As suggested by Donald Redford (1967), we are dealing here with a real event that is historic and dated, even if the designer of the tomb chose to attach the arrival of the Asiatics to scenes within the desert; an area where the real and the fantasy worlds could potentially mix together, as conveyed by the various mythical animals such as griffins and unicorns in the hunting scenes (Keimer 1944, 135–47). Yet, although we have a date – year 6 of Senwosret II – and the number of Asiatics (37), we do not know where the meeting took place. Scenes of a desert environment are depicted on the same tomb wall, but nothing *a priori* suggests that this event took place in the Oryx nome. Janice Kamrin has regarded the arrival of the Bedouin and the scenes dedicated to desert activities together with the entire northern wall as part of a universal microcosm (Kamrin 1993, 126–160, especially 157–60; 1999, 82–104).

On the other hand, we could explain the presence of these Asiatics as part of an official visit by tribute-payers.[9] It may seem strange that the Asiatics decided to come to Egypt, relatively distant from their natural cultural area, Southern Palestine, using northeastern desert tracks. The attraction was no doubt very strong, particularly during times of scarcity. Traveling with donkeys in the desert-land did not represent an impossible challenge. The evidence of regular desert crossings between Maadi and Southern Palestine by means of donkeys is attested from the earliest times (Shaw and Nicholson 1996, 166).[10]

As we know that the principal trade product of these Asiatics was galena, whose value was prized by every Egyptian, we must look, as many others have done, to the galena deposits of Gebel el-Zeit, which seem to have been the main source of this product during the Middle and New Kingdoms (Castel and Soukiassian 1989; 1985, 285–93; Castel, Gout, and Soukiassian 1985, 15–28; Mey, Castel and Goyon 1980, 299–318). Access to these deposits would have necessitated a long detour to the southeast, if these Asiatics were coming from Palestine, and this would lead us to

the conclusion that these people were used to living in the desert, a fact that is not contradicted by the activities at Gebel el-Zeit, as revealed by the excavations themselves. If Khnumhotep, as the one in charge of the Eastern Desert, was responsible for providing the courtiers with luxury goods, then this meeting between Egyptians and Asiatics may have been an official rather than an serendipitous event, probably taking place at a traditional trading post used by the Asiatic nomads. In this regard we can recall the Walls of the Prince in the Wadi Tumilat where fortresses were built that probably functioned in a very similar way to those at the Second Caratact in the reign of Senwosret III.

We must leave this problem unresolved to observe the link between Menat-Khufu, capital of the Sixteenth nome, and the Red Sea in the inscription of Se'ankh, dating to the reign of Nebtawyra Mentuhotep, at the end of the Eleventh Dynasty (Couyat and Montet 1912, 12, cf. 32–3 no. 1; Vandersleyen 1989, 156–8). This inscription, carved into the rock in the Wadi Hammamat, relates that this aged official was entrusted by his lord with a mission of organising an expedition into the desert in order to found a settlement to be inhabited by young people. The mention of Menat-Khufu as the northern limit of the explored range is surely not a mere coincidence. Indeed, because of the material into which it was carved and the conditions under which it was written, the text is brief and concise; each word is important. In spite of Claude Vandersleyen's hypothesis (1989),[11] let us postulate that Se'ankh refers in his speech to two urban areas corresponding to the departure and arrival points of his expedition, namely one to the northwest in the Nile Valley at Menat-Khufu, and the other to the southeast at Tja'au.

Even if the author of this record is naturally inclined to pomposity, one cannot doubt that the formulations and the words have real meaning. Quarry records are known for their practical if not pragmatic character. Even though he is reduced to brevity and concision, why would Se'ankh mention Menat-Khufu if it did not represent an important place for the understanding of his speech? This indicates that Menat-Khufu already occupied a strategic position with regard to the Eastern Desert during the Eleventh Dynasty, following the example of Coptos whose specific link to the exploitation of Wadi Hammamat is well known.

If we agree that Menat-Khufu was a place where one could enter the desert, the reality of Khnumhotep's duties in the Eastern Desert may find further confirmation on one of the two stelae found at Wadi Gawasis, 60 km north of Qoseir.[12] The first one dates to year 28 of Amenemhat II, which is a year before Khnumhotep took up his duties, and the second to the first year of Senwosret II, when Khnumhotep II is still 'Administrator of the Eastern Deserts'. These stelae have been the subject of a detailed study by Alessandra Nibbi (1976). They can be related to substantial archeological evidence discovered by Abd el Monem el-Sayed (1977, 138–78, esp. pl. 8) at Wadi Gawasis and Mersa Gawasis. All the elements of the archeological record in this area are nearly contemporary and in any case entirely homogeneous, which suggests that both stelae originate from the place where they were discovered or, failing that, from somewhere not far distant.

The man who erected the Stela of the Year One of Senwosret is named Khnumhotep, a high official since he holds the title 'god's sealer' (*sdꜣwtj ntr*), a title usually borne by those in charge of expeditions into the Eastern Desert and the Sinai during the Middle Kingdom (e.g., Goyon 1957, nos 28, 30, 31; Couyat and Montet 1912, 46, no. 35). Detlef Franke (1991), having gathered together the elements of an interesting file on Khnumhotep III, established the identity of this man as Khnumhotep II, who introduces himself as: 'The sole one of the (Lower Egyptian) King, who was made in the palace (and) educated of Horus'.

If these two Khnumhoteps are indeed one and the same person,[13] the biographical approaches of the stela and the Beni Hasan tomb are quite different. The first is a royal record; the second is a personal document. The stela has no reason to surprise us. This record from the first year of Senwosret II suggests that the reign was inaugurated with an expedition to a foreign country, in this case 'God's land' (*Tꜣ-ntr*), which was meant to make a strong impression on contemporary memories (see also Shaw this volume). To accomplish this, Senwosret II sends a childhood friend experienced in relations with the east and its populations. Moreover, the expedition takes place under the banner of Sopdu, '*Lord of Tꜣ-šmt*' and 'Lord of the East', a deity ordinarily worshipped in the eastern Delta and particularly in Wadi Tumilat, which was one of the routes taken by Egyptian expeditions to Southern Palestine and Sinai.[14]

Is the role of this Khnumhotep with regard to the desert theoretical? Surely not! We know from a note of Gustave Jéquier published in the report of the Dahshur excavations conducted by Jacques de Morgan (1895, 20, fig. 24, 19, fig. 23), and confirmed by Detlef Franke's (1991, 61–3) study, that the Khnumhotep who lived at the court of Senwosret III was probably Khnumhotep III.[15] The *membra disjecta* of his biographical record give us many details of his life. We know he received the 'gold of the reward in front of the officials' (de Morgan 1895, 95, fig. 23). Another fragment of his biographical record alludes to his military exploits. Thus, as a 'chief of the army' (*jmj-rꜣ mšꜥ*), he 'criss-crossed the Asiatics country, being on the battle field' (*ḥḥ ḥr Tꜣ-ꜥꜣmw wnn ḥr pgꜣ*) and 'he defended the borders of Kem-wer...' (*nḫt.n=f [t]ꜣw Km-wr*), that is to say the area of the Bitter Lakes, a place of traditional contacts between Egypt and Asia. These traces of Khnumhotep's biography recall Senwosret III's campaigns in Asia and bring us closer to the Wadi Tumilat than to the Oryx nome (de Morgan 1895, 21, second fragment, second row from the right; central inscription, upper row; fig 26, upper part, third fragment from right).

In his own tomb Khnumhotep II eulogizes his son, Khnumhotep III (*BH I*, 61 lines 150–160), whose tomb is not at Beni Hasan, while that of his brother Khnumhotep IV was cut into the cliff (*BH I*, 17). For the moment, let us bear in mind the last title of Khnumhotep III explaining his principal activity. He is [hieroglyphs] (*jnn ꜣḥwt nb šps (m) rꜣ ꜥꜣ ḫꜣswt*) 'the one who brings precious goods (coming from) the doors of the foreign countries'.[16] Khnumhotep, the defender of the borders, also appears to be a customs officer who collects taxes on the goods coming from the foreign Asiatic countries,[17] and one who controls the access of the Asiatics to the area of the Bitter Lakes and the Wadi Tumilat. He also controlled the secondary access routes to Egypt supposedly used by these populations, notably the different wadis that led the nomads into the Nile Valley in the Oryx nome, starting with the Wadi el-Tarfa.

Thus, far from falling into disfavour after the reign of Senwosret III as Detlef Franke has concluded, Khnumhotep's family at Beni Hasan prospers and continues to exert a certain influence during the reign of Senwosret III and probably later. From a general point of view the texts show that we can compare the duties of the nomarchs of the Oryx nome and those of the Fifteenth Upper Egyptian (Hare) nome.

Among the dignitaries of the Hare nome, Djehutyhotep displays once in his tomb at el-Bersheh the title [hieroglyphs] 'door of every foreign country' (*ꜥꜣ n ḫꜣst nbt*) (Newberry 1894b, 6, no. 7; 16). This indicates that he too carried out administrative duties in relation to foreign lands, especially as he resided in Megiddo (Posener 1957, 160). Also of note is the title held by Djehutynakht's son Ahanakht, 'Administrator of the Western Deserts' (*jmj-rꜣ smjwt jmn.tjwt*) (Griffith and Newberry 1895, pl. xi, lintel line 3), the Western Desert equivalent to the title *jmj-rꜣ smjwt jꜣb.tjwt* of Sixteenth nome's princes. If this title is unique among the Hare nome's nomarchs, we can at least suspect a real link, although perhaps only temporary, with the west.

If after a long tradition the dignitaries of the Oryx nome have specialised in communications with the Eastern Desert, those in the Hare nome seem to have turned toward the economic activity of the Western Desert. Hermopolis and Cusae were located at the departure points of the desert routes leading to Farafra and Bahariya Oases. Despite the quarrying at Hatnub by the inhabitants of the Fifteenth nome, a relationship with the deep desert and probably the mines located to the north of Wadi Qena together with the main galena deposits of Gebel el-Zeit were considered a privilege of the Sixteenth (Oryx) nome during the Twelfth Dynasty. Theoretically or religiously speaking, each nome was linked to an aspect of the traditional desert economy, and most of these links can still be observed in the late religious texts.

Acknowledgements

I am indebted to Jaromir Malek and to Renée Friedman for helping me to improve the English version of this manuscript.

Notes

1. On the father of Khnumhotep II, see Redford 1967, 158.

2. This son (*BH I*, 14) bears the titles *ḥrj-ḥb ḥrj-tp, sḏꜣwtj bjtj, smr wꜥtj, nswt-rḫ mꜣꜥ m smꜥ, jmj-rꜣ msꜥ*.

3. Unless one imagines that many incomplete tombs represent the attempts of those who did not rule long enough to finish their projects. See **Table 2**.

4. Khnumhotep holds the complementary responsibilities of 'stolist of Horus' (*smꜣtj Ḥr*) and 'stolist of Pakhet' (*smꜣtj Pꜣḫt*) (*BH I*, 42, pl. xxiv, b), commemorating the close link between Horus and this local form of Hathor. The Horus whose name frequently appears as 'Horus who strikes the Rekhyt' (*Ḥr ḥw rḫjt*) is probably that of Hebenu. Khnumhotep II is given the religious titles 'Chief of the offices in the temple of Pakhet' and 'Chief of the procession taking back the goddess in the temple of Pakhet' (*BH I*, 42, pl. xxxiii). The mother of Khnumhotep II, Baqet, was a 'prophetess of Pakhet' (*BH I*, 43). Amongst her daughters is one 'prophetess of [Pakhet], lady of the Valley' (*BH I*, pl. xxxvi).

5. It is necessary to say that Khnum, in the nome of Shashotep (Eleventh Upper Egyptian nome), was supposed to be the modeller of animals; cf. Sauneron 1983, 61–4.

6. She is also considered as the lady of the ebony-tree of Punt; cf. Kœmoth 1994, 89–90.

7. At the end of the nineteenth century, a portion of the Via Hadriana was still in use as a route to the monastery of Saint Paul; cf. the map compiled by the Intelligence Branch War Office in 1883, principally from the survey made by the Egyptian General Staff and Mr. John Fowler C.E. Scale 1/200.000 (Griffith Institute, nr. 321 War).

8. For the interpretation of this scene see: Kessler 1987, 147–66; Goedicke 1984, 203–10; Staubli 1991, 30–4 and also Posener 1957, 145–63. More recently Kamrin (1993, 142–8; 1999, 93–6) has summarised the different views on this subject. Concerning Semitic people in Egypt, note the recent study devoted to this subject by Hoffmeier 1997, 52–78.

9. It may be considered a tribute scene inasmuch as it was part of Khnumhotep's responsibility to deal with peoples living in the desert. The artist, faithful to Egyptian tradition, has represented the most significant episode of the arrival and has emphasised more of the spirit than the letter of the event. He has taken care to depict the main features of the patriarch leading the small troop and the members of this tribe. This was undoubtedly based on a sketch painted from life and kept in the archives of the palace, although one could perhaps suppose that the artist was gifted with the ability to remember all the distinctive accessories and the small details of the weaponry and saddles.

10. A well-developed understanding of desert resources during seasons with sufficient rainfall and the inherited knowledge of natural cisterns and springs allowed these groups as well the Egyptians themselves to cross significant distances. At the end of the last century, the Darb el-Tarabîn was used to go between Helwân and Shalluf. It was then lengthened by the Darb el-Hadj; cf. Carte Lith.d of the Intelligence Dept, War Office. June 1882 (Griffith Institute, nr. 321 War).

11. This an answer to Bradbury 1988, 127–56.

12. One was discovered by Gardiner Wilkinson and the other by Burton. These two stelae are now kept in the Gulbenkian Museum of Oriental Art, Durham (Northumberland 1934–1935).

13. We must keep in mind the son of Ameny-Amenemhat named Khnumhotep (*BH I*, 14), who held a number of important titles, if only for a limited time.

14. Sopdu watched over the mythical defense of the Eastern Desert as Ha protected the Western Desert; cf. Aufrère 1995, 35–40. On the role of Sopdu with regard to relations with the east, see Yoyotte 1989, 17–63.

15. Khnumhotep III was the owner of mastaba number 2 in the vicinity of the pyramid of Senwosret III at Dahshur (see de Morgan 1895, 16, fig. 18; 18–23 and particularly 19, figs 20–21). Khnumhotep III is not only a noble and prince (*rꜣ-pꜥt, ḥꜣtj-ꜥ*), but also 'steward of the pyramid-town (*jmj-rꜣ njwt*), judge (*sꜣb*), and vizier (*ṯꜣtj*)', as well as 'treasurer of the king of Lower Egypt, sole friend, and great steward (*sḏꜣwtj bjtj, smr wꜥtj, jmj-rꜣ pr wr*)'. This great figure, as Franke (1991) has shown, is associated with the Oryx nome. One of the inscriptions of his tomb quotes the name of 'Khnum, lord of Her-our' (de Morgan 1895, 20, fig. 24b), a deity worshipped in the Sixteenth nome. In addition, he is 'Guardian of Nekhen' (*jrj Nḫn*), a title the dignitaries of the Sixteenth nome (de Morgan 1895, 21, fig. 25) shared with other in this period, starting with Djehutyhotep of El Bersheh (Newberry, 1894b, 6).

16. My point of view differs notably from that of Franke (1991, 57), who reads it as: 'one who brings useful things to their owner (i.e., the king), Door-post of the foreign countries'. The phrase in question, about which Franke gives neither detail nor transliteration, includes the written form ⌫. This he has translated as if it were composed of two elements (*n nb*), while it is probably a writing for *nb*, especially during the Middle Kingdom (cf. *Wb II*, 234). In addition, there are many reasons to consider it to be the expression *ꜣḫwt nb(w)t špswt* 'all precious goods' as in the expression *ꜥꜣwt nbwt špswt*. Moreover, the following words allude to a locality, not to a title. Franke seems to disregard *rꜣ* in the title *rꜣ-ꜥꜣ ḫꜣswt*. Hennu, the stewart from the time of Nebtawyra, in his inscriptions in the Wadi Hammamat, dating from years 2 and 8 of this king, is 'the steward of the Southern Door' (*rꜣ ꜥꜣ Rsj*) (Couyat and Montet 1912, nos 113, 6; 114, 8). This title is also used by another official from Elephantine (Couyat and Montet 1912, no. 35; *Wb II*, 390, 15–6). On the title 'steward of the narrow Southern Door' see Fischer 1968, 12, n. 54; cf. Montet 1936, 87, 105, 108. This door opened up in the vicinity of Qamula (cf. Fischer 1968, 12 ; 1964, 5, 47; see also J Darnell this volume).

17. Undoubtedly there were costly products coming from Asia that were especially appreciated by the members of the court. With some imagination, we can suppose he was among those responsible for the procurement of the precious minerals used to create the funerary jewels discovered at Illahun and at Dahshur in the tombs belonging to the princesses. We can also postulate he was a purveyor of perfumes and costly cosmetics like galena and malachite from the Eastern Desert; this would explain the scene of the Asiatics in the tomb of Khnumhotep II, presumed to be his father.

Bibliography

Abdel Monem A H E, 1977. Discovery of the 12th Dynasty Port at Wâdî Gawâsîs on the Red Sea Shore. Preliminary Report on the Excavations of the Faculty of Arts, University of Alexandria, in the Eastern Desert of Egypt–March 1976. *Revue d'Egyptologie* 29: 138–78.

Altenmüller H and Moussa A M, 1991. Die Inschrift Amenemhet II. aus dem Ptah-Tempel von Memphis. Vorbericht. *Studien zur Altägyptischen Kultur* 18: 1–48.

Aufrère S H, 1995. Dieux du désert égyptien. Ha et la défense mythique des déserts de l'ouest. *L'Archéologue, Archéologie nouvelle* 11: 35–40.

Aufrère S, 1998. Un prolongement méditerranéen du mythe de la Lointaine à l'époque tardive. In N Grimal and B Menu (eds), *Le commerce en Égypte ancienne*. Bibliothèque d'Étude 121, Cairo: 19–39.

Aufrère S, 2001. Convergences religieuses, commerce méditerranéen et piste des oasis du Nord à la Basse Époque. Un aspect des incidences commerciales du mythe de la Lointaine (= Autour de l'Univers minéral XIII). In S Aufrère (ed.), *Actes du colloque ''L'Égypte et la Méditerranée. Voies de communication et vecteurs culturels'*. Montpellier: 11-33.

Baines J, 1987. The Stela of Khusobek: Private and Military Narrative and Values. In J Osing and G Dreyer (eds), *Form und Mass. Festschrift für Gerhard Fecht*. Wiesbaden: 43–61.

Berg W, 1973 *Historische Karte des alten Ägypten*. Sankt Augustin.

Bickel S and Chappaz J-L, 1988. Missions épigraphiques du Fonds de l'égyptologie de Genève au Spéos Artémidos. *Bulletin de la Société française d'Egyptologie* 12: 9–24.

Bradbury L, 1988. Reflections on Traveling to 'God's Land' and Punt in the Middle Kingdom. *Journal of the American Research Center in Egypt* 25: 127–56.

Butzer K W, 1982. Ostwüste. In W Helck and W Westendorf (eds), *Lexikon der Ägyptologie* IV. Wiesbaden: 637–8.

Castel G, Gout J-F and Soukiassian G, 1985. Gebel Zeit: Pharaonische Bergwerke an den Ufern des Roten Meeres. *Antike Welt, Zeitschrift für Archäologie und Kulturgeschichte* 16 (3): 15–28.

Castel G and Soukiassian G, 1985. Dépôt de stèles dans le sanctuaire du Nouvel Empire au Gebel Zeit. *Bulletin de l'Institut francais d'archéologie orientale* 85: 285–93.

Castel G and Soukiassian G, 1989. *Gebel el-Zeit I. Les mines de galènes*. Fouilles de l'Institut francais d'archéologie orientale 35. Cairo.

Couyat J and Montet P, 1912. *Les inscriptions hiéroglyphiques et hiératique du ouâdi Hammâmât*. Memoires de l'Institut francais d'archéologie orientale 34. Cairo.

de Cenival F, 1988. *Le mythe de l'œil du soleil*. Sommerhausen.

de Morgan J, 1895. *Fouilles à Dahchour mars–juin 1894*. Vienna.

deWitt C, 1951. *Le rôle et le sens du lion dans l'Égypte ancienne*. Leyden.

Franke D, 1991. The Career of Khnumhotep III of Beni Hasan and the so-called 'Decline of the Nomarch'. In S Quirke (ed.), *Middle Kingdom Studies*. Reigate: 51–68.

Fischer H G, 1964. *Inscriptions of the Coptite nome. Dynasties VI–XI*. Analecta Orientalia 40. Rome.

Fischer H G, 1968. *Dendera in the third millenium B.C.* New York.

Gauthier H. 1926. *Dictionnaire des noms géographiques contenu dans les textes hiéroglyphiques. Vol. 3*. Cairo.

Goyon G, 1957. *Nouvelles inscriptions rupestres du Wadi Hammamat*. Paris.

Griffith F Ll and Newberry P, 1895. *El-Bercheh. Part II*. Archaeological Survey of Egypt. London,

Hoffmeier J K, 1997. *Israel in Egypt. The evidence for the Authenticity of the Exodus tradition*. New York, Oxford.

Kamrin J, 1993. *Monument and Microcosm: The 12th Dynasty Tomb Chapel of Khnumhotep II at Beni Hasan*. University Microfilms International. Michigan.

Kamrin J, 1999. *The Cosmos of Khnumhotep II at Beni Hasan*. London and New York.

Keimer L, 1944. L'horreur des Égyptiens pour les démons du désert. *Bulletin de l'Institut égyptien* 26: 135–47.

Kessler D, 1987. Die Asiatenkarawane von Beni Hassan. *Studien zur Altägyptischen Kultur* 14: 147–66.

Kœmoth P, 1994. *Osiris et les arbes. Contribution à l'étude des arbles sacrée de l'Égypte ancienne*. Aegyptiaca Leodiensia 3. Liége.

Malek J and Quirke S, 1992. Memphis, 1991: Epigraphy. *Journal of Egyptian Archaeology* 78: 13–8.

Mey P, Castel G and Goyon J-C, 1980. Installations rupestres du Moyen et du Nouvel Empire au Gebel Zeit (près de Râs Dîb) sur la Mer Rouge. *Mitteilungen des Deutschen Archäologischen Instituts Abteilung Kairo* 36: 299–318.

Montet P, 1936. Les Tombeaux dits de Kasr el Sayad. *Kêmi* 6: 81–129.

Montet P, 1961. *Géographie de l'Égypte ancienne*. Paris.

Newberry P E, 1893. *Beni Hasan. Part I*. Archaeological Survey of Egypt 1. London [= *BH* I].

Newberry P E, 1894. *Beni Hasan. Part II*. Archaeological Survey of Egypt 2. London [= *BH* II].

Newberry P E, 1894b. *El-Bercheh Part I (The Tomb of Tehutihetep)*. Archaeological Survey of Egypt. London.

Nibbi A, 1976. Remarks on the two stelae from the Wadi Gasus. *Journal of Egyptian Archaeology* 62: 45–56.

Posener G, 1957. Les Asiatiques en Égypte sous les XIIe et XIIIe dynasties (à propos d'un livre récent, Hayes, *A Papyrus of the Late Middle Kingdom*). Syria 34: 145–63.

Redford D B, 1967. The Father of Khnumhotep II of Beni Hasan. *Journal of Egyptian Archaeology* 53: 158–9.

Sauneron S, 1983. *Villes et légendes d'Égypte*. 2nd edition, Bibliothèque d'Étude 90. Cairo.

Shaw I and Nicholson P, 1995. *British Museum Dictionary of Ancient Egypt*. London .

Shedid A G, 1994, *Die Felsengräber von Beni Hassan in Mittelägypten*. Zaberns Bildbände zur Archäologie 16. Mainz am Rhein.

Simpson W K, 1965. The Stela of Amun-wosre, Governor of Upper Egypt in the Reign of Ammenemes I or II. *Journal of Egyptian Archaeology* 51: 63–8.

Staubli T, 1991. *Das Image der Nomaden im alten Israel un in der Ikonographie seiner sesshaften Nachbarn*. Orbis Biblicus et Orientalis 107.

Valloggia M, 1974. Les viziers des XIe et XIIe dynasties. *Bulletin de l'Institut francais d'archéologie orientale* 74: 123–34.

Vandersleyen C, 1989. Les inscriptions 114 et 1 du Ouadi Hammamat (11e dynastie). *Chronique d'Égypte* LXIV/127–28: 148–58.

Vandier J, 1943. Note sur le transport du colosse d'El-Bersheh. *Chronique d'Égypte* XVIII/36: 185–90.

Yoyotte J, 1989. Le roi Mer-djefa-Re et le dieu Sopdou. Un monument de la XIVe dynastie. *Bulletin de la Société française d'Egyptologie* 114: 17–63.

Ancient Gold Mining in the Eastern Desert of Egypt and the Nubian Desert of Sudan

Dietrich D Klemm, Rosemarie Klemm and Andreas Murr

Nub was the ancient Egyptian word for gold and consequently the land called Nubia was regarded as the legendary land of gold. The exact borders of Nubia are questionable and might have varied significantly during different historical periods. In any case, modern Nubia, as ethnographically defined, starts south of Aswan and is restricted to the cultivated areas inhabited by non-Bedouin tribes along the Nile to about as far as Atbara in the Sudan.

The main gold producing sites of Nubia in the past were confined to the region of the Wadi Allaqi and that south of it. This area is currently within the territory of the Bisharin nomads and includes the entire Eastern Desert, east of the Nile River to the Red Sea, and southward to about the 19th parallel latitude.

In spite of the etymological relationship of *nub* and Nubia, during the main period of ancient Egyptian gold mining in the New Kingdom, from the reign of Thutmose III (1479–1425 BC) to Amenhotep IV (1351–1334 BC), this region was not known by an alliteration with *nub*, but was called Wawat (the region around Wadi Allaqi) and Kush (the undifferentiated remainder of the area).

Geologically the Nubian Desert might be regarded as the southern continuation of the Eastern (or Arabian) Desert of Egypt, where an intensively folded Precambrian basement is overthrust by napes of late Precambrian island arc terrains that are partly composed of mafic to ultramafic units, representing former basalts and serpentinitic remains of the upper mantle. This complex unit, during the time span of 700–550 million years before present (bp), was penetrated by huge granitoitic intrusions that heated up their host rocks and caused local thermal anomalies. As a result of those thermal anomalies, the interspace waters in the rock units moved as 'hydrothermal' convection cells of hot water solutions from the heat centres toward cooler surface regions, using any type of aquifers as pathways. Because of the higher solubility, due to elevated temperature and pressure, the hydrothermal systems dissolved all of the mineral species available from the percolated rocks along the aquifers and, if present, also gold in low concentrations. If the aquifers had open spaces, like veins or shear zones, a drop in temperature and pressure caused the hydrothermal fluids to precipitate their dissolved mineral contents within these open spaces. The main constituent of such fluids was silica and consequently quartz is by far the dominant mineral in the shear zones or veins. Other minerals like calcite, baryte, hematite and chlorite are present only in small amounts (less than 5 vol %), and metal sulphides like pyrite, arsenopyrite, chalcopyrite and galena occur in amounts even less than 1%. If the fluids also transported gold in the form of dissolved gold sulphide complexes, gold might become co-precipitated with the metal sulphides in concentrations of a few grams per ton of quartz ore.

After a long period of erosion during the Cretaceous (about 90 million years bp), the basement sequences were covered by sand, which became the Nubian Sandstone. This in turn was eroded after the relatively recent continental upraising of the flanks of the Red Sea rift system. During this phase of erosion, the Precambrian basement together with the gold containing quartz-veins and shear zones were exposed to the surface, and consequently to exploitation. But this 'gift of the desert' is distributed over an extremely large area and searching for it is like searching for a needle in a huge haystack.

In modern times such mineral prospection is assisted by complex computer-aided analyses of satellite spectral imagery and highly sophisticated geochemical, petrographical and geophysical investigations, together with detailed geological fieldwork. Nothing like this was available to the ancient prospectors, who did their job in the vast regions of the Nubian Desert almost exclusively during the relatively short period of only 140 years between the reigns of Thutmose III and Amenhotep IV (about 1480–1330 BC). During this time almost all of the important gold mining sites in the Eastern Desert of Egypt and in the Nubian Desert were discovered and exploited.

In the 1960s and 1970s expert teams from the Egyptian Geological Research Authority (EGSMA), the Geological Research Authority of the Sudan (GRAS) and the Soviet Techno Export group carried out extensive gold prospection programmes in Egypt and in Nubian Sudan. Even with the latest equipment, wherever they discovered any economically significant gold anomaly, they also found the remains of ancient mining activity in the form of stone mills, traces of settlements and mine-shafts, indicating that ancient prospectors had already discovered the place long before.

Unfortunately these teams had no archaeological experts with them to examine the many ancient mines and tools, and thus this interesting aspect was left unexplored. We have tried to fill this gap and, thanks to a generous grant from the German Volkswagen Foundation, we have been able to visit, in co-operation with EGSMA, most of the *c.* 90 previously known gold production sites and have succeeded in raising this figure to over 150 (**Figs 1–3, 6–7, 9**). During this survey only the surface inventory, the remains of open cast and underground operations, and the remnants of the ancient settlements were investigated in a preliminary fashion, as we had neither the licence nor the time for detailed excavations. Some of our results have already been published (R Klemm and D Klemm 1994; D Klemm and R Klemm 1997). In northeastern Sudan, along the Nile and in the Nubian Desert, we carried out comparable investigations in co-operation with GRAS, again generously supported by the Volkswagen Foundation. This work resulted in the examination of roughly another 100 ancient gold mining sites (**Figs 4–5, 8**).

In the Eastern Desert of Egypt traces of gold production sites can be dated back to the time of the 'Earliest Hunters' according to H A Winkler (1938), who associated this nomadic population with the Predynastic Amratian culture of the mid-fourth millennium BC. During this time small nuggets of gold were simply picked up from the wadi beds. As one would hardly expect an accumulation of gold nuggets in the more recent wadis, which lacked actively flowing river systems by which to flush the nuggets out, the occurrence of visible nuggets is restricted to the few wadis of Pleistocene age. Such a Pleistocene system is preserved in the area around Umm Eleiga, in the southern part of the central Eastern Desert of Egypt, where petroglyph sites with drawings of the 'Earliest Hunters' have in fact been found (R Klemm 1995) (**Plate 113**).

The first traces of true gold mining sites within the Eastern Desert (**Fig. 1**) date to the later Predynastic and Early Dynastic period. They take the form of open cast and underground mining trenches, where the gold containing quartz ore was crushed down to a fine powder fraction by calabash-shaped two-hand stone hammers of 6–10 kg in weight (**Plate 114**). This mining method produced conspicuously smooth surfaces both on the walls and the terminus of the underground operations. If the wall rocks, due to tectonically dependant shearing, had a shistosity-type exfoliation, disk-shaped stone hammers of 20–30 cm in diameter were also used as mining tools to remove the barren host rock from the gold containing quartz ore.

No archaeological evidence could be recognised for the further treatment of the powder-fine, crushed quartz ore or for the recovery of the freed gold particles within it. But, taking into account the hydro-metallurgical concentration processes used during later periods of gold production, comparable methods can be assumed for this epoch.

During both the Old and Middle Kingdoms only sporadic gold mining activities within the Eastern Desert of Egypt could be detected (**Fig. 2**), making it doubtful whether even the relatively meagre finds of gold artefacts of these periods could have originated from only the Eastern Desert mining sites. According to expedition reports from the Old Kingdom, in addition to skins, ivory, exotic stones and so forth, the import of gold from Nubia is explicitly mentioned (Gundlach 1977). The first military campaign in year 18 of Senwosret I, at the beginning of the Middle Kingdom, was most probably organised to obtain access to the Nubian gold, as the nomarch Ameni reports in his tomb at Beni Hasan on three expeditions to Nubia from whence he returned with gold and gold ore for his king (Newberry 1893).

During the Old Kingdom a remarkable change in mining tools and mine exploitation took place that lasted until the end of the Middle Kingdom. One-hand hammers created with comfortable ergonomically-formed upper handles (**Plate 115**) replaced the calabash-shaped two-hand hammers. These hammers were 20–30 cm long and 5–8 cm in diameter. It is worth noting that the ergonomic handles fit

hand sizes 17–19 cm long and 10–11 cm wide. This is a size that does not correspond to the smaller than average hand sizes documented for the inhabitants of the Nile Valley during that time. Thus, it may be suggested that gold production operations within the Eastern Desert were carried out mainly by non-Egyptian ethnic groups, and only the trade of gold was organised by Egyptian representatives, whose presence is indicated by the numerous rock inscriptions that they left all over the Eastern Desert. A more detailed study of the ethnic groups involved in the production of gold requires careful excavations of the scattered tombs still extant in the vicinity of Old Kingdom and Middle Kingdom gold mining sites.

A stone axe tool with a medial groove (about 0.5–1 cm deep and 1–1.5 cm wide) to allow hafting to a forked stick (**Plate 116**) is another common artefact at Old and Middle Kingdom gold mining sites. Thanks to these new mining implements a more effective exploitation of the gold-containing quartz veins was possible.

In spite of the fact that almost all ancient gold mines of these times have more or less collapsed and that any estimations of the depth is inexact without archaeological excavation, a maximum depth in open trenches of about 25 m seems realistic.

During the Middle Kingdom stone mortars (**Plate 117**) were also introduced, which allowed the lump of quartz ore first to be crushed down to about pea size and then ground to powder fraction. Again, no archaeological evidence for further treatment to recover the gold has been found. However, the above-mentioned Ameni noted in his Beni Hasan tomb, 'I forced their [Nubian] chiefs to wash the gold' (Newberry 1893), and this remark strongly suggests that hydro-metallogenic concentration processes were well established by this period.

A revolutionary change in gold production in the Eastern Desert becomes obvious with the establishment of the New Kingdom. This probably took place during the reign of Thutmose I (1504–1492 BC), who expanded Egyptian economic and military influence to the heart of Kerma, and according to rock inscriptions even as far as Kurgus, south of the Fourth Cataract (Davies 2001)(**Figs 3–4**).

The most striking innovation of this period is the introduction of an oval millstone (**Plate 118**), fitted with a hand sized rubbing stone, with which a much faster and more efficient grinding of the gold-containing quartz ore to a powder-fine fraction was possible. A comparative mill type had already been in use for the milling of flour within the Nile Valley since at least Old Kingdom times, and its introduction into the gold production process in the Eastern Desert might be regarded as an indication that from hence forward gold production was entirely in Egyptian hands. The unprotected location of the many New Kingdom gold miners' settlements (**Plate 119**), in places still relatively well-preserved, indicates clearly that during this time no serious danger to the Egyptian miners and to their supply infrastructure was present in the Eastern Desert of Egypt (see also Shaw this volume).

Another important tool for gold ore processing was the ore crusher: a small stone anvil and rounded stone pestle

(Plate 120), with which the gold-containing quartz ore lumps were crushed down to an about pea size fraction for further grinding with the above-described oval stone mills.

At quite a few New Kingdom gold production sites one can observe inclined gold washing tables constructed of stone fragments, consolidated with crude clay/sand mortar and covered by a layer of the same material (Plate 121). The length of these washing tables varies between 2.5 and 4 m; they are 40–60 cm wide and 80–100 cm high, with an inclination angle of 15–20°. At the downslope end washing water was recovered in a box, about 60 cm wide and deep, created from stone slabs and sealed again with the mortar described above. Here the detritus of the barren quartz tailings were precipitated to be dumped later at nearby tailing heaps, still partly preserved in many cases today. A gutter, also constructed of stone slabs and mortar-sealed, conducted the water back into a basin, 80 × 60 cm in size, from whence most probably a primitive 'shadouf' lifted the water for reuse in further gold washing operations.

How the surface of the inclined table was prepared to facilitate the separation of the fine-grained gold particles freed by the grinding process from the more or less barren quartz sand tailings remains a mystery. Until now no direct archaeological evidence exists for this important step in ancient gold recovery. Due to the lack of any archaeological indication in this respect, it might be assumed that a covering for these inclined tables was made of organic materials. If this is the case, there are two general possibilities: 1) a wooden grid; or 2) a simple sheep skin. Both have been used in the past for the separation of gold flitters from barren quartz sand fractions. The most likely option is the sheep skin, as sheep were available at the mining sites for food purposes. In addition, both the lanolin-grease and the wet fibres of the skin's hair capture the sharp-edged gold flitters, whereas the barren quartz particles flow off in the water suspension. The legend of the Golden Fleece could thus be of Egyptian origin and far older than the voyage of the Argonauts. Finally, burning the skins with the trapped gold particles yielded the raw gold product.

Mining techniques were improved significantly in New Kingdom times mainly by the introduction of bronze chisels, which allowed the gold-containing quartz in a multi-phased quartz vein to be much more selectively separated from the barren parts of the host rock. Thus, the miners could selectively follow the most promising ore shoots, and this often resulted locally in a somewhat chaotic course of underground operations. Fortunately, in most of them the miners left supporting pillars of various sizes at appropriate points both for their own safety and for ours. Obviously during New Kingdom times no sophisticated ventilation of the underground operations was possible, thus the maximum depth of the mines never exceeded about 30 m, this being the limit of the oxygen supply by normal air exchange for men and burning oil lamps.

The most surprising fact of the New Kingdom gold story is the singular success in field prospection. Almost all productive gold mining sites, with the exception of those already known from the Old and Middle Kingdom, were discovered during this period; a period that lasted in Nubia

only until the reign of Amenhotep IV (about 1330 BC) and in the Eastern Desert of Egypt at most until the end of the Ramesside period (about 1150 BC). The New Kingdom prospectors must have had detailed knowledge of the complicated multi-staged geological and petrographical conditions favouring the formation of a gold quartz vein system. Further, they were well aware of the tectonic dependence of the direction followed by the productive quartz veins, as only those and never any of the other variously oriented veins were touched. Only with such a highly sophisticated knowledge was it possible to separate the chaff from the wheat in the vast areas of the Nubian and Eastern Deserts in such a relatively short period of time. It is, in fact, most probable that all this successful prospecting is limited solely to the time of Eighteenth Dynasty, as the main Ramesside mining sites like el-Sid, Bir Umm el-Fawakhir and Barramiya (Seti I) as well as Wadi Allaqi with Umm Grayat (Ramses II) were already known earlier.

Other forms of gold production no doubt also augmented the gold stores of the New Kingdom. According to the report of Ameni, this Middle Kingdom nomarch forced the chiefs of the Nubians to wash gold. As alluvial river gold is today still panned (washed) in parts of Nubia, especially in the area around Shamkhiya, some 30 km west of Abu Hamed, the idea should not be ruled out that this or a similar technique was already known during pharaonic times. Dedication lists at New Kingdom Egyptian temples, like Medinet Habu, where 'gold of the water' is registered (Hölscher 1957) suggest gold extraction from alluvial (wadi and river sediments) sources. Nevertheless, no convincing archaeological evidence exists that panning or equivalent techniques were practised in ancient times. The only possible gold washing plant, which Vercoutter (1959) reported in the vicinity of Faras (now under the water of Lake Nasser), is unlikely to be for this purpose, and he himself questioned whether it could instead be an installation for wine production.

In many wadis, extended fringe settlements of New Kingdom date with the typical oval shaped stone mills and crusher stones have been observed together with the occasional remains of tailing dumps, indicating sites of intensive gold production. However, instead of open cast or underground mining operations, the wadi bed at these sites is covered with small heaps up to 50 cm high of barren quartz and gravel rock fragments (Plate 122). Of course, in most cases, due to water erosion, these heaps can be recognised only as relics on those flanks of the wadis protected from erosion. They are the remains of dumps from intensive activity during which the wadi beds were dug up to obtain rock samples that promised some gold content. Certainly these wadi works were established only in areas with outcroppings of primary gold-containing quartz veins, which were too small for individual mining operations or had already been eroded, leading to an accumulation of productive material within the wadi itself. For this type of work no special skill was required; only workers familiar with handling a field-hoe and who could be trained to separate the barren from the productive quartz ore.

In an open cast or underground mine only one worker

can do his job at the face, obtaining a maximum of a basket of ore per shift with the available stone or bronze tools. On the other hand, workers grubbing up the wadi bed could fill far more baskets depending on the number of ore lumps present in the wadi sediments. Thus, a huge work force could be employed in this manner, doing the job in pre-selected areas with high efficiency for a relative short time of perhaps one or two seasons. Comparable recent alluvial workings were studied by the authors during a 1999 field campaign into Wadi Singeir of the Bayuda Desert (Sudan), where many tributary wadis had been dug up in only one season without the aid of machinery. The subsequent grinding and milling is now performed by primitive gasoline-driven mills, but the gold separation itself is done by hand panning, which is actually a much less effective method compared to the inclined washing tables used by the ancients.

Well-organised housing areas were constructed at the various gold working sites in New Kingdom times. These were composed mainly of two roomed houses, in many cases with a front terrace, constructed of dry packed stone walls, about 30 cm wide and up to 1.5 m high. The lack of any enclosure wall to provide protection indicates that during this period the Eastern Desert of Egypt was a rather peaceful area under the sole control of pharaonic Egypt (**Plate 123**).

In Nubia, from Wadi Allaqi onward, this situation was different. At Umm Grayat the New Kingdom settlement is protected by a large enclosure wall, and at other sites, like Duweishat and Abu Sari, the New Kingdom settlements are hidden in side wadis. Gold production further to the south, in places like Sai Island, Shamkhiya, Tanta and Mograt Island, seems to have operated only at strongly fortified sites. However this is an assumption based on the fact that almost all of these southern sites can today only be identified indirectly from the typical New Kingdom stone mills and crusher stones incorporated into the walls of far later medieval fortifications of the Christian kingdom of Makuria. It is very likely that these later fortifications are actually reused and rebuilt defensive installations of New Kingdom times. This assumption is supported by a site called Ras el-Gazira, at the western edge of Mograt Island, where a relatively untouched New Kingdom gold production site is protected by an impressive stone fortification with a field of rock palisades extending toward the open eastern plain of the island. Here, as at the other sites, only scanty ceramic remains are detectable on the surface and detailed archaeological excavation is urgently required.

Fig. 4 shows the distribution of the many New Kingdom gold production sites currently known in northeastern Sudan, both along the Nile and in the remote regions of the Nubian Desert. This figure together with **Fig. 3**, showing the synchronous sites in the Eastern Desert of Egypt, gives an idea of the vast extent of gold production activities carried out during New Kingdom times. Again, it should be emphasised that in Nubia these activities were restricted to the period between about Thutmose III and Amenhotep IV. From the time of Amenhotep IV and his weak Egyptian government on through the Ramesside period no archaeological evidence for pharaonic gold mining within the Nubian Desert south of Wadi Allaqi could be detected by us.

In the Egyptian Eastern Desert primary gold production collapsed totally at the end of the Ramesside period and seems to having been suspended throughout the entire Late Period until early Ptolemaic times. On the other hand, in Nubia quite a few New Kingdom sites were reworked using the older tools, especially the stone mills. At such sites one can observe that the typical, rather flat, New Kingdom oval trough-shaped stone mills have a distinctly deeper secondary concavity (**Plate 124**), indicating re-use of the milling equipment in a manner somewhat different from that of the New Kingdom workers. The best guess for the date of the secondary use of these sites would be during the most powerful episodes of the Kushite Kingdom. Unfortunately, only local Nubian ceramics, hard to assign to a distinct period, have so far been found at these sites. Here again, only detailed excavations will result in a better dating. It must be emphasised once again, we had neither the licence, nor the intention to conduct any excavations during our surveys. Our main purpose was only to inspect the surface inventory.

The relatively few sites where we could identify this reworked mill stone variety might not have been the only gold source available during the Kushite Kingdom (**Fig. 5**). According to Ameni's report, since at least Middle Kingdom times, gold panning took place in Nubia, despite our ignorance of the production methods due to the lack of relevant archaeological evidence.

In the Egyptian Eastern Desert a new gold production boom started with Ptolemaic rule. The Greek conquerors brought with them from Macedonia and above all from Laurion in Attika long experience in mining techniques, and improved significantly on the already evolved New Kingdom methods. The most striking innovation is the introduction of a new concave stone mill type with a length of 60–80 cm and width of around 30 cm (**Plate 125**). Along the long side of the concave milling surface of many of these millstones are flat grooves, 2 mm wide. A nearly semicircular-shaped hard stone of 4–6 kg in weight was used as a rubbing stone and fit into the milling plain with two ergonomically modelled handles. This type of stone mill seems to have originated from the island of Crete, where we have found them at Gurnia and Festos, but not in the Laurion district of Attika.

In many cases, flat hollows of 5–8 cm in diameter on the top side of the rubber stones indicate that they also were used as crusher stones. In addition to this crusher type, heavy stone plates of about 70 × 50 cm in size were used, especially close to entrance of underground mines.

Mining techniques also improved significantly during the Ptolemaic period with the introduction of iron chisels and the construction of dome-shaped roofs for underground workings. At flat inclined gold quartz veins in particular, the new roof construction allowed a considerable reduction in the size of support pillars, increasing the amount of extractable ore.

From Laurion, the Ptolemaic miners imported a circular heavy mineral concentrator about 8–12 m in diameter. It had a groove, approximately 5 cm wide and 2–3 cm deep, running around its periphery, into which small hollows were carved out at about every 10 cm (**Plate 126**). With a controlled water flow, a mixture of barren quartz powder and fine heavy ore grains could be separated step by step in this device, yielding a pre-concentrate for a more effective final separation using the inclined washing tables, already known from the New Kingdom. This heavy mineral concentrator also allowed efficient separation from the gold and barren quartz of the different sulfide minerals, such as pyrite, arsenopyrite and galena, which could not have easily been collected in New Kingdom times. This type of heavy mineral concentrator has been well documented at the Laurion mining district in Attika, Greece by C Conophagos (1980), who called it a 'laverie hélicoidale'. We also studied a well-preserved example at the Demoliaki site in the same district (**Plate 127**).

Ptolemaic gold mining sites are exclusively located on former New Kingdom sites. Fortunately the Ptolemaic settlements are always some distance away from those constructed in the New Kingdom, thus preserving them to the present. The reuse of mining sites indicates that during this period no serious new gold prospection took place. Previously worked gold production sites were reopened and their exploitation taken to deeper levels. Ptolemaic sites are entirely restricted to the central parts of the Eastern Desert of Egypt (**Fig. 6**), and apart from the well-guarded desert roads with the many fortified hydreumata established during Ptolemaic times, no gold mining sites south of latitude 24°40' could be detected during our surveys. No doubt, during the entire Ptolemaic period, the Eastern Desert of Egypt was only sufficiently under governmental control to allow gold production within the limited area roughly between the Qena–Safaga road and some 40 km south of the road between Edfu and Marsa 'Alam. This fact is somewhat surprising as the genuine Ptolemaic foundation of Berenike south of latitude 24° gives the impression of control further to the south. However, gold mining in the Wadi Allaqi district, as insistently reported by Agatharchides and referred to in Diodorus (Book III, 12), never actually took place. This mistaken assumption stems most probably from a misinterpretation by scholars of Diodorus' reference to the 'border to Ethiopia' as meaning the Wadi Allaqi. This is clearly misleading and the 'border' must be positioned much further to the north. Also the spectacular 'discovery' of a site identified as Berenike Panchrysios as published by A & A Castiglioni (1991) in the upper Wadi Allaqi must be questioned due to a serious lack of archaeological evidence. It would seem that as a result of more intensive fieldwork these authors have recently distanced themselves from their former hypothesis, (Sadr *et al.* 1994; Castiglioni, Castiglioni and Vercoutter 1995).

The reasons for the restriction of Ptolemaic gold mining activities to the central Eastern Desert of Egypt are not recorded in historical documents, but we know from later Roman information that during their rule large parts of the Eastern Desert and Nubia became uncontrollable due to the aggressive attitudes of the local nomadic tribes (Updegraff 1978), which the Romans called Blemmyes. The present-days Bisharin tribes, still dangerously armed with sharp swords and daggers, are regarded as their descendants.

Consequently in Nubia no Ptolemaic gold production took place, but of course the roughly contemporary Meroitic Kingdom also sought gold. We have not yet found any clearly Meroitic gold production sites in Sudan. Only at Mograt Island, within the ruins of the medieval Christian forts of Karmel and Sehan, have we found, in addition to pieces of New Kingdom stone mills, fragments of a concave stone mill type originally about 80–100 cm long and 40–50 cm wide that closely resembles the above described Ptolemaic mills (**Plate 128**). However, the rubber stones, which here in Nubia were only simple double fist sized stones, lack the comfortable handles used at the Ptolemaic sites. Any possible Meroitic ceramics within the surface inventory of the sites are totally overwhelmed by the younger Christian pottery and better dating arguments will require detailed excavations. As no underground mines could be recognised in this region, one has to assume that the mills were used for working hand picked gold quartz lumps collected in the alluvial wadi sediments. Thus, hints for Meroitic gold production in Nubia are more than scanty. Perhaps the majority of Nubian gold production, from the first Old Kingdom reports until the present-day in Shamkhiya and the Bayuda, concentrated on the washing of alluvial sediments at the banks of the Nile and within the fossil alluvium of the wadi beds close by. If this washing was performed with wooden pans or other organic materials, hardly any remains could be expected in surface inventories. In other words, Meroitic gold production continues to be enigmatic (**Fig. 5**).

In Egypt after the Roman conquest another significant change in gold production techniques was introduced: a cylindrical rotation mill (quern) with a diameter between 30 and 50 cm and an upper hand-driven rotating stone fitting in it. This upper stone contained a central hole to hold a wooden axel and also a peripheral hole for a wooden stick as handle (**Plate 129**). The Romans inherited this mill type from the Celts (Cauuet 1991), who used it at their mining sites spreading from the Carpathians to Scotland (Childe 1943).

This new mill type led to an approximately five-fold increase in milling efficiency and consequently should have led to a comparable increase of gold production in Egypt. However, due to the violent attacks of the nomadic Blemmyes and their equally sudden disappearance in the unknown vastness of the desert, the Romans were unable to reopen and protect the many scattered gold mining sites in the Eastern Desert. Only a few sites were exploited (**Fig. 7**). These were located along the well-guarded roads of Quft–Quseir, with the Bir Umm el-Fawakhir and el-Sid mines, the desert road via Lykabettos to Berenike and possibly the Edfu–Marsa 'Alam road. For the Romans the 'gifts of the desert' existed mainly in the prominent quarry sites like Mons Claudianus, Mons Porphyrites or Semna (Klemm and Klemm 1993), to which they constructed special roads (Sidebotham 1991), highly protected by day-march distant forts, preferably located around water wells.

For the Byzantine period only very little archaeological evidence concerning gold mining exists. Even at Bir Umm el-Fawakhir, which was inhabited during Byzantine times, despite the assumption of Meyer and Heidorn (1998), no unquestionable evidence of gold ore dressing could be found by us during an extended survey there.

219

The Bedouin tribes, dominating the entire Eastern Desert of Egypt and the Nubian Desert, traditionally were not interested in mining and remain so today (Fadl Hassan 1967), refusing to dig in the ground even for agricultural purposes in water-sufficient wadi beds. Thus, the still partially rich gold mining sites fell into obscurity for about nine centuries, until the Arab adventurer El-Omari, during the reign of Ibn Tulun around AD 960, started a most impressive gold rush. Equipped with an army type workforce, he penetrated from Upper Egypt via Wadi Allaqi into Nubia as far as Omar Kabash in the Wadi Gabgaba. The fifteenth century historian Makrizi reported that he engaged 60,000 camels to supply the many gold producing sites (Fadl Hasan 1967), and we have found in quite a few places, such as Deraheib, Uar, Bir Kiaui, Omar Kabash and Terfawi, the well-organised settlements that he founded as supply stores for the many scattered gold working sites (Plate 130).

After this short-lived gold rush, which most probably collapsed immediately after El-Omari's early murder, a more peaceful westward penetration from the Arabian peninsula led to a revitalisation of gold production, especially in the Nubian Desert (Fig. 9), and due to its obvious success, consequently also in the Eastern Desert of Egypt (Fig. 8).

The Arab gold miners reused, where profitable, the ancient sites that had been discovered during New Kingdom times. They also concentrated to a high degree on wadi workings, and not only did they gather promising quartz lumps from the wadi beds and the colluvial flanks of the mountain slopes, but also introduced the technique of sieving the wadi sands that contained finely distributed gold flitters and then panning it, as is still done today in the Bayuda gold rush regions.

For dressing the gold-containing quartz ore, the Arabs inherited the stone rotation mills (querns) introduced by the Romans, and for concentration, the slightly modified inclined washing tables in use since New Kingdom times. But the systematic use of always re-hardened forged steel chisels, for which the existence of blacksmith's slag at many Arab sites provides evidence, made underground mining much more effective, resulting in increased exploitation.

The Arab penetration of the Nubian Desert in search of gold never reached the Nile provinces, but ended in the desert at a line approximately marked today by the railway between Wadi Halfa and Abu Hamed. This was also the approximate eastern limit of influence of the Christian Kingdoms of Nobadia and Makuria (Fig. 8).

It is unknown why at around AD 1350 Arab gold working became paralysed. It may be that the productive wadi grounds were now worked out and the few underground mines had reached the lowest-most levels of ventilation, precluding further deepening. Around the same time the above-mentioned Christian kingdoms collapsed and their populations converted to Islam. Whether this religious-political step has any connection to the cessation of gold production in the Nubian Desert must be left to further investigations. However, it is worth considering that the conversion to Islam provided for the Arabs, who had until this time been earning their livings in the gold mines of the Nubian Desert, the possibility of moving into and settling on the fertile ground of the Nile Valley by systematic intermarriage with the local Nubian population. This certainly would have offered them far better living conditions than the hard and troublesome work full of privations in the gold mines of the desert (Fig. 10).

Acknowledgements

We wish to express our thanks to EGSMA, and especially to Dr Abu Bakr Hawari. We also wish to express our gratitude to GRAS and especially to its General Director, Dr Mohammed Omer Kheir, and the two GRAS geologists, Mohamed el-Hag Hassan and Mustafa Kasim, who bravely and helpfully accompanied us during our most difficult desert trips in northeastern Sudan. Further, we are most grateful for the manifold assistance to our German students: Axel Kraus, Gernot Langwieder, Ruppert Utz, Markus Lang, Christian Tichatschke and Florian Schmid, who suffered with us on different field trips in Egypt and the Sudan the many privations but also the great enjoyment of the remote desert regions. Last but not least, the generous financial support of the German Volkswagen Foundation for these many projects is gratefully acknowledged.

Bibliography

Castiglioni A and Castiglioni A, 1991. A la recherche de Bérenice Pancrisia dans le Désert Oriental Nubien. *Bulletin de la Société française d'Égyptologie* 121: 5–24.

Castiglioni A, Castiglioni A and Vercoutter J, 1995. *Das Goldland der Pharaonen*. Mainz.

Cauuet B, 1991. L'exploitation de l'or en Limousin des Gaulois aux Gallo-Romains. *Ann. Midi* 103, Nr.194: 149–81.

Childe V G, 1943. Rotary querns on the Continent and the Mediterranean basin. *Antiquity* 17: 19–26.

Conophagos C E, 1980. *Le Laurium antique et la technique Greque de la production de l'argent*. Athens.

Davies W V, 2001. Kurgus 2000: The Egyptian Inscriptions. *Sudan & Nubia* 5: 46–58.

Fadl Hasan Y, 1967. *The Arabs and the Sudan*. Edinburgh.

Gundlach R, 1977. Expedition(en). In W Helck and W Westendorf (eds), *Lexikon der Ägyptologie* II. Wiesbaden: 55–9.

Hölscher U, 1957. *Medinet Habu vol. 5: The Temple proper, Part I.* University of Chicago Oriental Institute Publication 83. Chicago.

Klemm D and Klemm R, 1997. Antiker Goldbergbau in der ägyptisch-sudanesischen Ostwüste. *Nürnberger Blätter zur Archäologie* 13: 149–66.

Klemm R, 1995. Umm Eleiga. Ein prädynastischer Goldfundplatz in der Ostwüste Ägyptens. In D Kessler and R Schulz (eds), *Gedenkschrift für Winfried Barta*. Münchener Ägyptologische Untersuchungen 4: 247–60.

Klemm R and Klemm D D, 1993. *Steine und Steinbrüche im Alten Ägypten*. Berlin.

Klemm R and Klemm D D, 1994. Chronologischer Abriss der antiken Goldgewinnung in der Ostwüste Ägyptens. *Mitteilungen des Deutschen Archäologischen Instituts Abteilung Kairo* 50: 189–222.

Meyer C and Heidorn L, 1998. Three Seasons at Bir Umm Fawa-khir in the Central Eastern Desert. In O E Kaper (ed.), *Life on the Fringe*. Leiden: 197–209.

Newberry P E, 1893. *Beni Hasan I*. Archaeological Survey of Egypt 1. London.

Sadr K, Castiglioni A, Castiglioni A and Negro G, 1994. Archaeology in the Nubian Desert. *Sahara* 6: 69–75.

Sidebotham S E, 1991. Römische Strassen in der ägyptischen Wüste. *Antike Welt* 22/3: 177–89.

Updegraff R T, 1978. *A Study of the Blemmyes*. Ann Arbor.

Vercoutter J, 1959. The Gold of Kush. *Kush* 7: 120–53.

Winkler H A, 1938. *Rock-Drawings of Southern Upper Egypt I* Archaeological Survey of Egypt 26. London.

Winkler H A, 1939. *Rock-Drawings of Southern Upper Egypt II*. Archaeological Survey of Egypt 27. London.

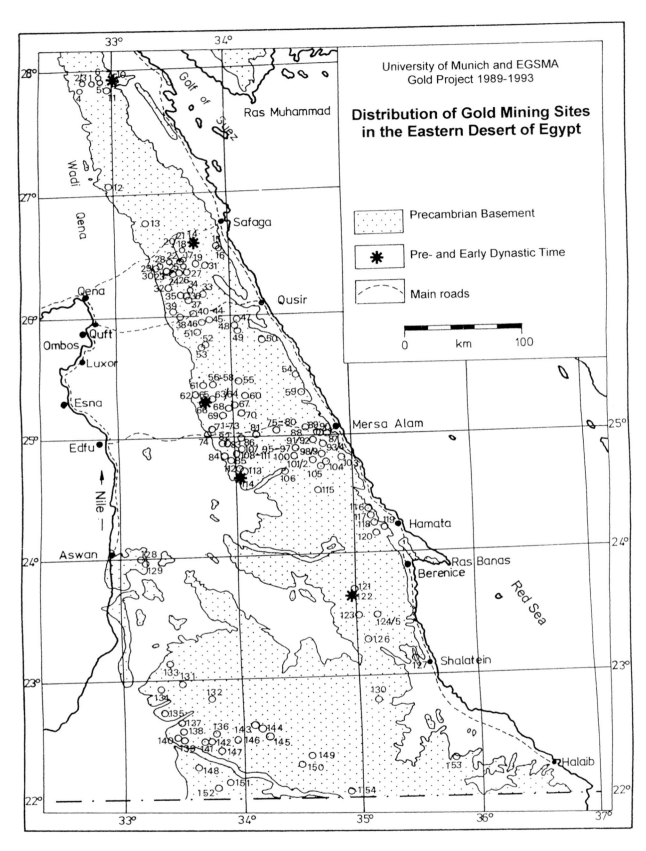

Fig. 1   Distribution of currently known gold mining sites of the Pre- and Early Dynastic periods within the Eastern Desert of Egypt. In the Nubian Desert of Sudan no gold mining during this period could be located. The open circles represent gold production sites that were worked in later periods.

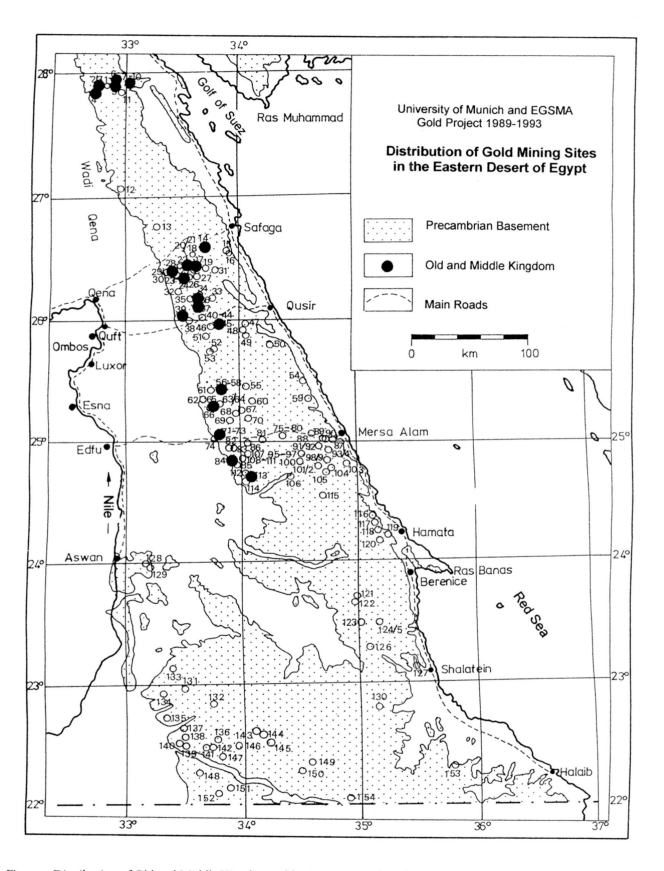

Fig. 2   Distribution of Old and Middle Kingdom gold mining sites within the Eastern Desert of Egypt. Note the restricted range of the sites in the northern and central Eastern Desert only.

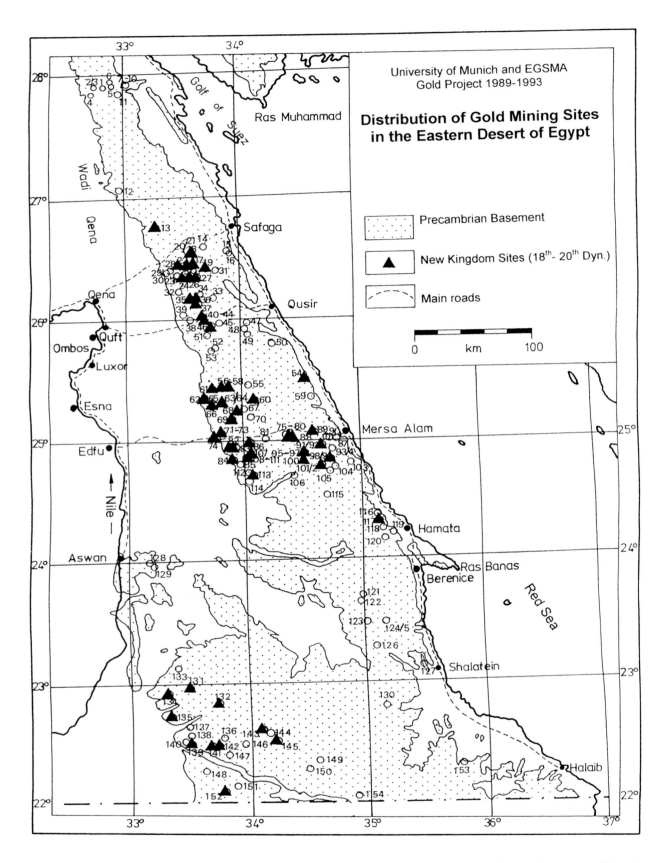

Fig. 3   Distribution of the New Kingdom gold production sites within the Eastern Desert of Egypt. Note that gold production in the northern Eastern Desert was abandoned during this period, but expanded significantly to the south, deep into the Nubian Desert.

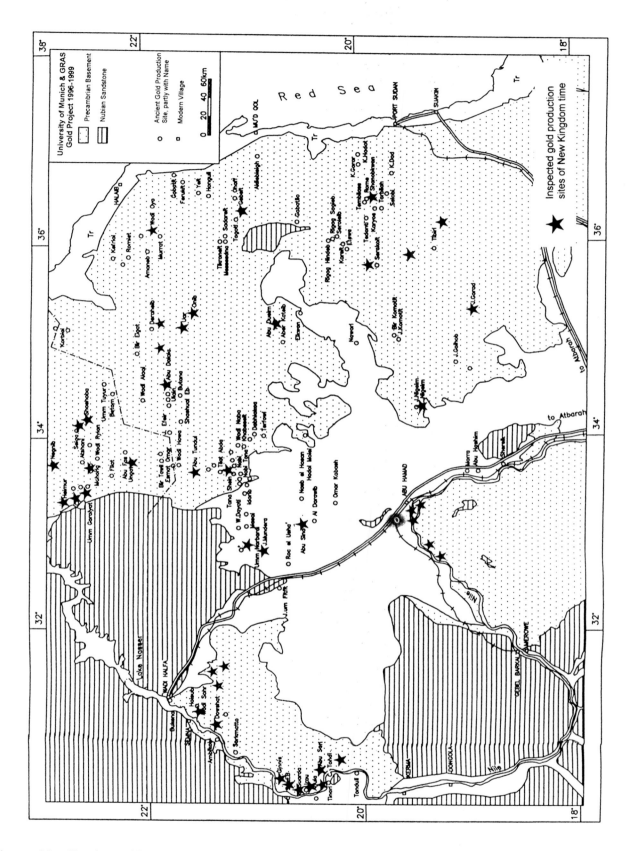

Fig. 4   New Kingdom gold production sites in the Nubian Desert. Note the extensive penetration of Egyptian activities deep into the Nubian Desert.

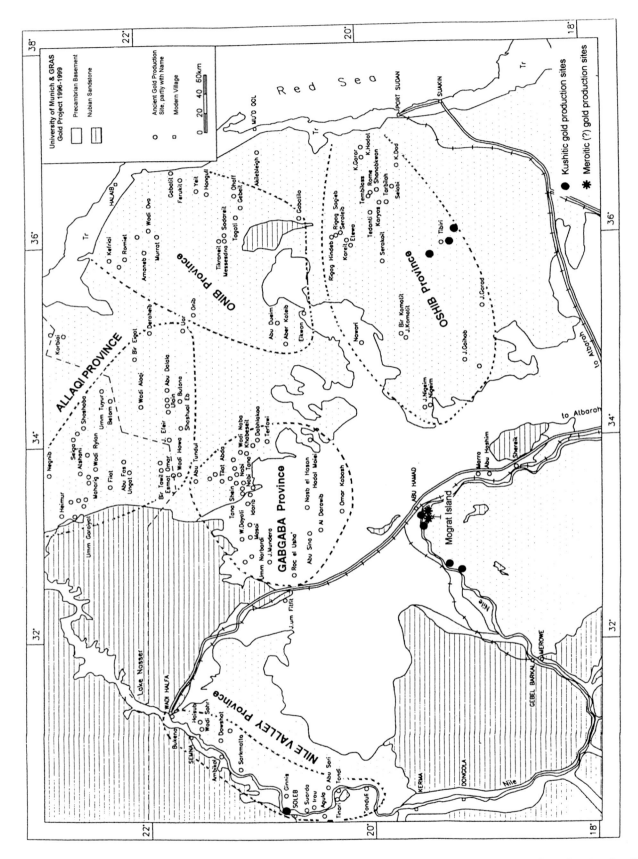

Fig. 5   Distribution of the currently known remains of Kushitic and Meroitic gold production sites. These few sites hardly represent the total number of gold sources in these periods, and further field work is required before a more complete picture can be formed.

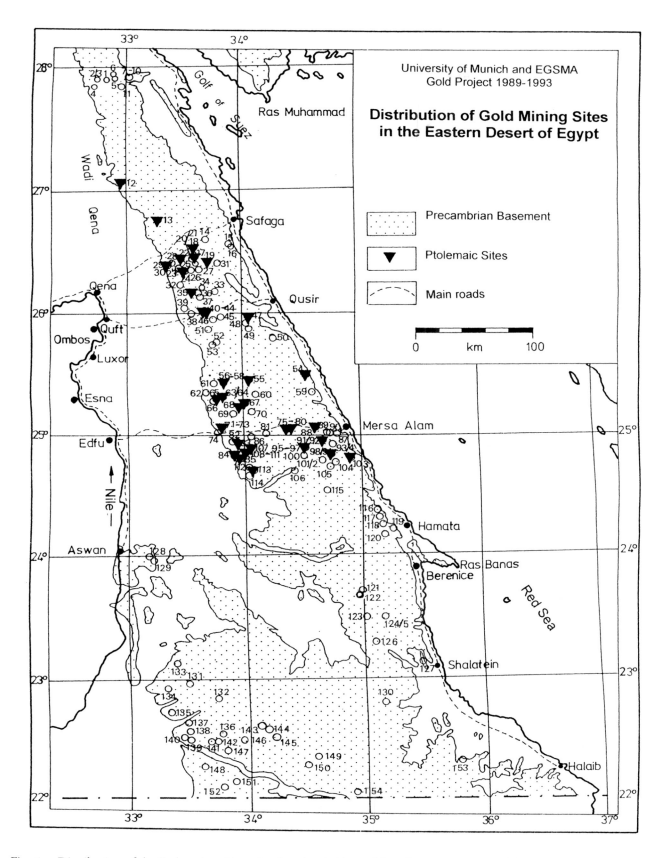

Fig. 6   Distribution of the Ptolemaic gold production sites in Egypt. Note the concentration of these activities only within the central Eastern Desert.

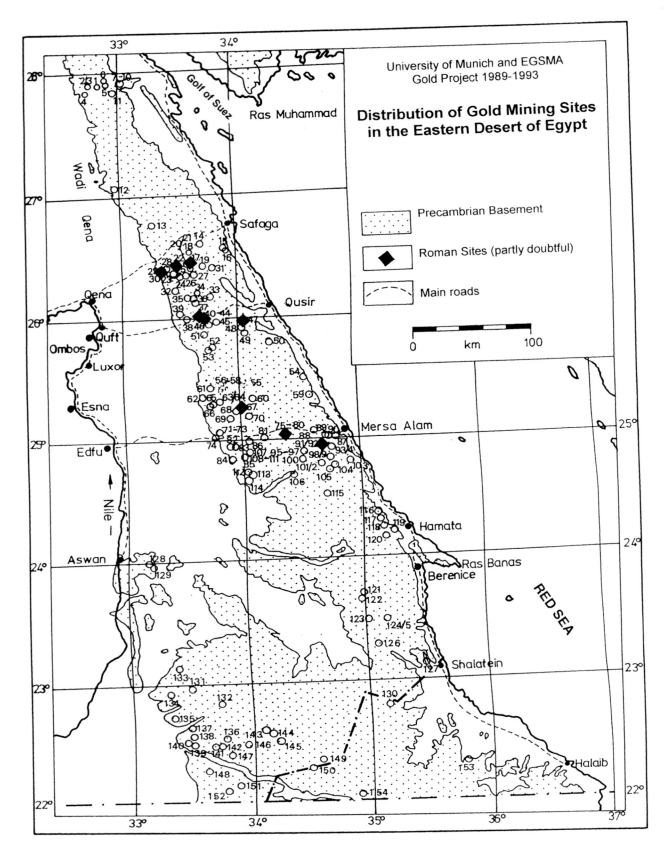

Fig. 7   Distribution of the very few (partly doubtful) Roman gold mining sites along protected desert roads in the central part of the Eastern Desert of Egypt.

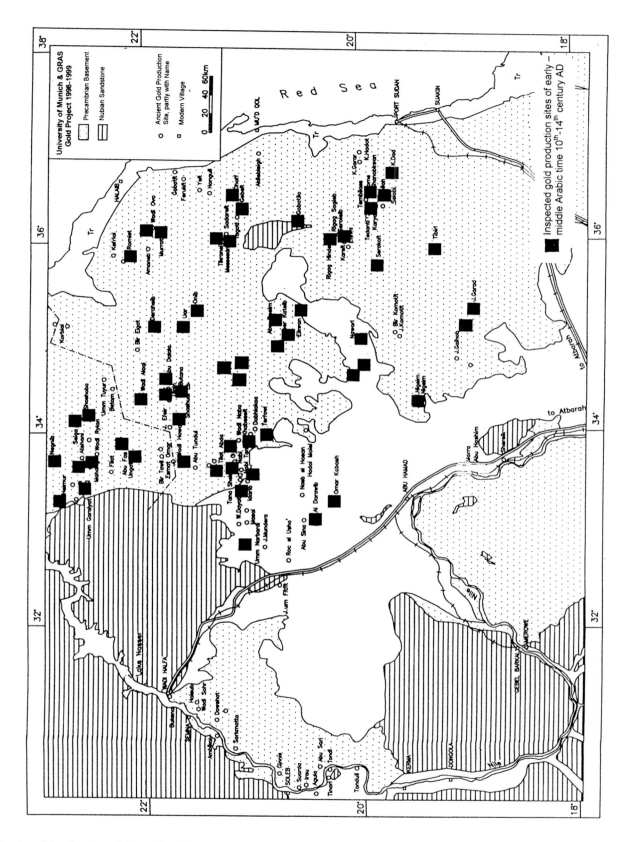

Fig. 8   Distribution of the Arab gold production sites in the Nubian Desert. Note the western limit of this activity, which extended only to the ancient borders of the Christian kingdoms of Nobadia and Makuria in the Nile Valley.

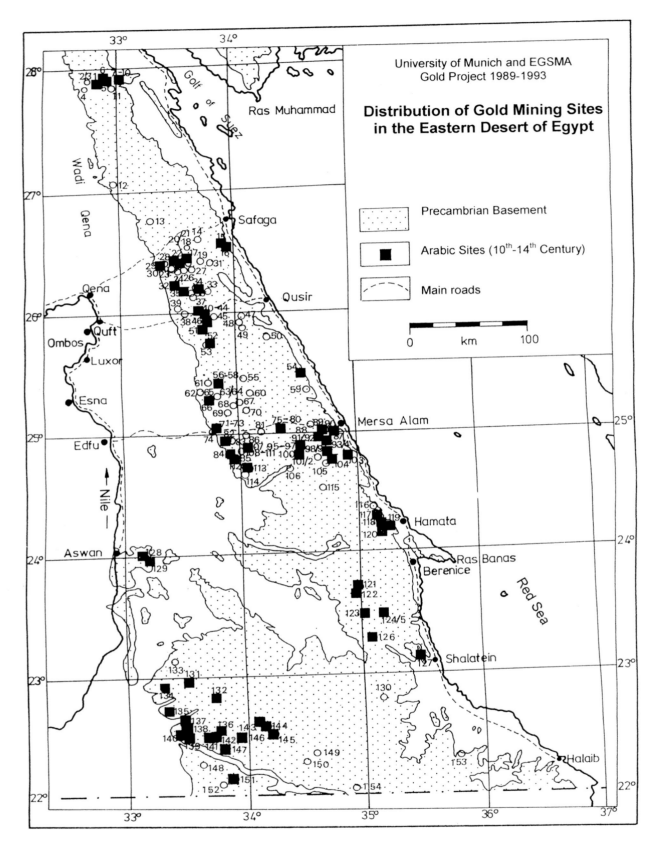

Fig. 9   Distribution of the Arab gold production sites in the Eastern Desert of Egypt. Note the wide dispersion of the sites, indicating governmental control over the entire Eastern Desert.

Time	Historical Period	Relative Rate of Gold-production	Eastern Desert of Egypt	Nubian Desert and River Nile Valley
3000 BC	Predynastic	?	Sporadic gold findings in wadi beds. First systematic gold mining with large two hand stone hammers.	No archaeological evidence for gold mining.
2500 BC	Old Kingdom		Sporadic gold mining with ergonomically shaped one-hand stone hammers limited to north and central Eastern Desert.	Sporadic gold mining in close proximity to river Nile (Duweishat) with grooved stone axes
2000 BC	First.Intermed Period / Middle Kingdom		Sporadic gold mining with ergonomically shaped one-hand stone hammers and mortar milling limited to north and central Eastern Desert.	No archaeological evidence for gold mining by Kerma Culture. Gold washing along the Nile (?) (Ameni report at Beni Hassan) but no archaeological evidence for it
1500 BC	Hyksos Period			
	New Kingdom		Systematic gold prospection, intensive mining in underground and wadi workings (oval rubber stone mills, inclined washing tables, bronze chisels, well organised housing areas).	Intensive gold prospection and mining in underground but mainly wadi workings in the Nubian Desert and along the Nile Valley (oval rubber stone mills, inclined washing tables and bronze chisels).
1000 BC	Late Period		No archaeological evidence for gold mining.	
	Kushite Kingdom		Intensive gold mining reusing New Kingdom underground and wadi workings (two-lugged rubber stones on concave stone mills, circular heavy mineral concentrators, inclined washing tables).	Reorganisation of some New Kingdom gold production sites and reuse of New Kingdom tools, especially of oval rubber stone mills.
500 BC				
0	Ptolemaic Period			Isolated findings of Meroitic (?) stone mills at Mograt Island.
	Roman Period		Scarce gold mining close to protected desert roads (quern mills, inclined washing tables).	
500 AD	Byzantine Period			During Christian Kingdoms in Nubia no archaeological evidence for gold mining.
641 AD	Arab Conquest of Egypt			
	A.Ibn Tulun			
1000 AD				
1200 AD	Salah ed Din		Intensive gold mining reusing old underground operations, but also new wadi workings (quern mills, inclined washing tables, (?) panning). Gradual abandonment of gold mining.	El-Omari's expedition starts intensive gold rush, reuse of New Kingdom mines and wadi workings around well-organised settlements (quern mills, inclined washing tables). Intensive gold mining mainly of wadi workings by Arabs penetrating from Arabian Peninsula into Nubia (quern mills, inclined washing tables, (?) panning).
1350 AD	Collapse of Christian Kingdoms in Nubia			Gradual abandonment of gold mining.

Fig. 10   Summary of gold production activities in the Eastern Desert of Egypt and the Nubian Desert from Predynastic time (about 4000 BC) until the collapse of the Christian Kingdoms in Nubia (about AD 1350).

231

Pharaonic Stone Quarries in the Egyptian Deserts

James A Harrell

Introduction

The ancient Egyptians used many varieties of stone for their temples, pyramids, statuary, reliefs, sarcophagi, vessels, jewelry, tools and other applications (Aston *et al.* 2000). The Nile Valley and adjacent desert fringes provided the bulk of the stones (limestone, sandstone, travertine, granite and granodiorite), but among the most esteemed were those coming from deep inside the Western and Eastern Deserts. The long distances and harsh environments endured in the quest for desert stones were no deterrent to the Egyptians, who in Pharaonic times operated seven known quarries (**Fig.** 1). These are the subject of the present paper. The quarry localities, along with their stone types and ages, include: Gebel Manzal el-Seyl (tuff and tuffaceous limestone – Early Dynastic period); Umm el-Sawan (alabaster gypsum – Early Dynastic and Old Kingdom); Widan el-Faras (basalt – Old Kingdom); Gebel el-Asr (anorthosite gneiss – Late Predynastic through Old Kingdom, and Twelfth Dynasty); Wadi Hammamat (greywacke sandstone and siltstone, and conglomerate – Early Dynastic through Roman periods); Gebel Rokham (marble – Eighteenth Dynasty); and Rod el-Gamra (dolerite porphyry–Thirtieth Dynasty). Discussion of ancient gemstone and gold mining in the desert are provided in this volume by Shaw, and Klemm, Klemm and Murr, respectively.

Gebel Manzal el-Seyl

Bowls, cylinders, dishes and other vessels made from stone were common burial offerings from the late Predynastic through the Old Kingdom (Petrie 1937; Lucas 1962, 406–28; El Khouli 1978; Aston 1994). In terms of numbers produced and stone varieties used, these vessels reached their greatest development during the First through Third Dynasties. Only three quarries with evidence of vessel production are known; those at Gebel Manzal el-Seyl, Umm el-Sawan and Gebel el-Asr. Stones from other known quarries were also used for vessels but no evidence of this industry has yet been found in the quarries themselves. The sources for several other stone varieties used for vessels have not been located and perhaps for some no quarries even exist. In the latter case, it is possible that the stones were merely collected as already loose boulders lying on the desert surface.

The Gebel Manzal el-Seyl quarry is the largest one devoted to stone vessel production. It is located in the north-central part of the Eastern Desert (**Fig.** 1 no. 1) and was discovered in 1994 by V M Brown, M S Masoud and the present author, who also provide the only description of it (Harrell *et al.* 2000). The quarry consists of about 200 excavations scattered across the 3 km-long ridge of Gebel Manzal el-Seyl (**Plate 131**). These workings are mostly 5 to 10 m across but range up to 50 m in maximum dimension.

The quarry supplied two related stones that were widely employed for vessels: a dark green, commonly banded, calcareous tuff and a slightly bluish, medium green, tuffaceous limestone. Earlier writers routinely misidentified these stones as volcanic ash, schist, slate or greywacke. Tuff is an igneous rock composed largely of volcanic ash (a sediment consisting of fine pieces of glass, rock and mineral fragments blown out of an erupting volcano), and limestone is a sedimentary rock consisting mainly of the mineral calcite. At Gebel Manzal el-Seyl the two stone varieties are gradational with each other, and thus the tuff is calcareous (contains abundant calcite) and the limestone is tuffaceous (contains some volcanic ash).

No pottery, ruins or other datable remains have been found in or near the quarry, but there is no doubt as to its age being of the First through Third Dynasties, as established from the dating of tuff and limestone vessels (Aston 1994, 26–7). The quarry is probably operationally related to an Early Dynastic mining settlement in Wadi Abu Had, 20 km to the northeast (site WAH-29 of Bomann 1994, 29–30; 1995, 14–6).

Littering the quarry are several hundred vessel blanks made from tuff and limestone (**Plate 132**). Some are found in the excavations, but most are concentrated in 15 areas that served as the quarry workshops. The vessel blanks are not hollowed out but have been roughly shaped into the forms of cylinders, bowls and dishes. The final carving and polishing was apparently done in Nile Valley workshops. In a practice repeated at every other desert quarry, as well as at many of those in the Nile Valley, objects were roughed out not only to reduce their bulk and so facilitate transport, but also to assure that only good quality material, with no hidden flaws, made the trip to the workshops. Eleven vessel blanks in two of the quarry excavations at Gebel Manzal el-Seyl are inscribed with a sign resembling the hieroglyphic character *mḏ* (∩), the numeral 10. These are analogous to the potter's marks seen on many ceramic vessels, but unlike for ceramics, this sign cannot represent contents or volumetric capacity. It also cannot signify the quarry itself as the same sign appears on many ceramic vessels made in the Nile Valley (van den Brink 1992, figs 9 and 12). The sign may have been used instead as an accounting device to mark every tenth blank produced (see also Kaper and Willems this volume) or, less likely, it is the toponym for the administrative region or center in the Nile Valley that operated the quarry and to which the vessel blanks were taken.

The vessel blanks were quarried with primitive stone

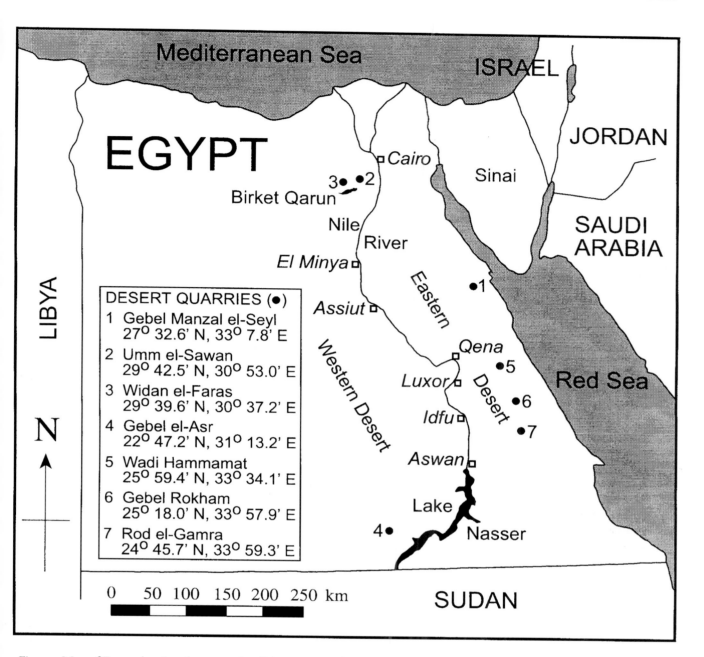

Fig. 1   Map of Egypt showing the quarry localities mentioned in the text.

tools known as mauls or pounders (Arnold 1991, 258–63) that were made from dolerite, a locally available stone. Both the large two-handed and smaller one-handed forms of these roughly shaped tools now litter the quarry grounds. Blocks of tuff and limestone were extracted by using the heavier two-handed mauls to hammer along natural fractures in the bedrock where, after repeated pounding, the stone would break away. The extracted blocks were then shaped into the forms of vessels using the one-handed mauls. Most of the latter were simply held within the hand, but some had encircling notches for taking a wooden handle.

The vessel blanks, weighing up to 25 kg apiece, were carried about 200 km across the desert to the Nile Valley. Of all the known desert quarries, none was more distant from the Nile than Gebel Manzal el-Seyl. Given the relatively small

size of the vessel blanks, it is likely that they were carried on the backs of donkeys. The caravan route would have passed through the mountains to the west by following either Wadi Mellaha or its tributary, Wadi Mellaha Umm Barmil. These wadis connect with Wadi Sobir, which then leads to Wadi Qena, a broad, easily traversed valley that continues to the Nile River at Qena. Alternatively, the donkey caravans may have crossed Wadi Qena on their way to Wadi Assiut, which reaches the river at Assiut.

Umm el-Sawan

Another desert quarry for stone vessels is at Umm el-Sawan (Fig. 1, no. 2) in the Fayum Depression, and it was in operation at about the same time as the one at Gebel Manzal el-

Seyl. The site was discovered in 1928 by G Caton-Thompson and E W Gardner who also published the only report on it (Caton-Thompson and Gardner 1934 v. 1, 103–23; v. 2, pls 58–73). The description that follows is based largely on their account with some supplemental field observations provided by the present author.

The Umm el-Sawan quarry supplied a variety of rock gypsum known as alabaster, which is a stone consisting predominantly of the mineral gypsum with a massive, fine-grained crystalline texture. Alabaster is a petrological term that is commonly but incorrectly applied to travertine (the so-called 'Egyptian alabaster'), which consists of calcite and is a variety of limestone (Harrell 1990). The travertine quarried anciently in Middle Egypt was called *alabastrites* by the Classical Greeks and Romans, and the modern version of this name, alabaster, has continued to be misapplied by archaeologists and others, despite the fact that it was redefined centuries ago by geologists as a variety of rock gypsum (Harrell 1995, 33). In the present paper, the term 'alabaster' is used to refer only to a gypsiferous rock.

At Umm el-Sawan the alabaster is generally white with common parallel streaks and veins of dark grey or brown clay. Gypsum can be scratched with a fingernail, and so the stone is very soft and easy to carve. This also means, however, that it is not durable. The softness together with the unsightly clay impurities suggests that alabaster vessels may have been a low-quality, low-cost alternative to ones made from the harder and more attractive stones like Gebel Manzal el-Seyl's tuff and tuffaceous limestone, or Gebel el-Asr's anorthosite gneiss.

The alabaster occurs in a dense network of sub-vertical, cross-cutting veins that are up to 25 cm thick (**Plate 133**). The veins, which somewhat resemble walls and owe their exposure to wind erosion, occur in an area of about 1 km long by up to 300 m wide. These are cut in turn by thin (2–3 cm) sub-horizontal sheets of transparent, colourless selenite, which is another variety of rock gypsum. The selenite sheets are too thin and brittle to be quarried for vessels, but Caton-Thompson and Gardner (1934 v. 1, 108–9) suggested that they were worked as a source of gypsum for wall plaster and mortar, the ingredients for which are produced by burning the pulverized rock. There is, however, no evidence that the selenite was actually quarried at Umm el-Sawan. There are also no obvious quarry excavations among the alabaster veins. Instead, these merely appear to be broken up by something other than natural erosional processes. Interspersed among them are piles of extracted alabaster blocks.

Along the east side of the alabaster outcrop there are three workshops where thousands of alabaster vessel blanks were found along with great piles of gypsum powder and chips. The vessels are roughly shaped into cylindrical, discoidal and oblate-spheroidal forms (**Plate 134**) that were intended for cylinders, dishes and bowls, respectively (Caton-Thompson and Gardner 1934 v. 1, 105–7). None of the vessel blanks are hollowed out, but a few show some incipient internal carving. The size of the blanks is limited by the maximum thickness of the alabaster veins (25 cm) and, thus, they are generally much smaller than the blanks at Gebel

Manzal el-Seyl. Rarely do the blanks found in the workshops exceed a few kilograms in weight.

All the quarrying and carving was done with unhafted, hand-held stone tools (Caton-Thompson and Gardner 1934 v. 1, 104–5 and 113). Three types were employed: hand picks and crescent drills of chert (made from chert nodules weathering out of the limestone bedrock to the southeast) and mauls of dolerite (from the Eastern Desert) and anorthosite gneiss (from the southern Western Desert). The mauls, which come in both the two- and one-handed sizes, are found among the alabaster veins and, to a lesser extent, within the nearby quarrymen's camp. Although alabaster is a soft stone, the thick veins are not easily broken into blocks. It was for this that the mauls were needed. Hand picks were found both among the alabaster veins and at the workshops. From the grooves and pits found on the surfaces of the vessel blanks, it is clear that these were carved with the hand picks. The crescent drills were found only in the workshops, and from the couple of thousand recovered it would seem that a great many vessel blanks were hollowed out by drilling prior to their removal from Umm el-Sawan. Curiously, however, only a few of the several thousand blanks found show any evidence of drilling. Either the so-called crescent drills were used for something else or, less likely, all drilled blanks, including the broken ones, were taken from the quarry.

About half a kilometre southeast of the alabaster workings is the quarrymen's camp (Caton-Thompson and Gardner 1934 v. 1, 120–2). It consists of over 200 stone rings that are ovoid to circular in plan and 1.5–6 m across (**Plate 135**). These are made from undressed, dry-laid pieces of stone taken from the underlying ferruginous sandstone and conglomerate bedrock. The stone came from the interiors of the rings which, as a consequence, have floors excavated below the original surface by as much as 0.5 m. The piles of stone forming the rings are up to another 0.5 m high, and this combined with the sunken floors made shelters about 1 m deep on the inside. No post holes or other constructions were found. The stone rings are clearly not the walls of roofed huts, but rather mere windbreaks open to the sky.

There is some disagreement on the age of the Umm el-Sawan quarry. Based on pottery sherds, Caton-Thompson and Gardner (1934 v. 1, 110–3) suggest that the site was most active during the Third and Fourth Dynasties but may range in age from the First through Fifth Dynasty. Aston (1994, 47–53), on the other hand, found that alabaster vessels were used as burial offerings from the late Predynastic period to the early Old Kingdom with the principal use during the First through Third Dynasty.

Twenty kilometres southwest of Umm el-Sawan is another workshop for alabaster vessels that also dates from the same general period (Caton-Thompson and Gardner 1934 v. 1, 133–4). It is located on the slope just below the late Twelfth or early Thirteenth Dynasty temple of Qasr el-Sagha and contains vessel blanks, chert hand picks and crescent drills, and mauls of dolerite and anorthosite gneiss. A large outcrop of alabaster veins, like that at Umm el-Sawan, occurs 4 km northeast of the temple and just above Deir

Abu Lifa, a collection of rock-cut cells used by Christian ascetics during the late first millennium AD. Although there is no obvious evidence of quarrying here, it is the closest source of suitable alabaster deposits and so probably supplied the stone for the Qasr el-Sagha workshop.

The alabaster vessel blanks would have been carried overland, by donkey, to the Nile Valley where the final carving was done. The distance is just 40 km, a long day's walk. Caton-Thompson and Gardner (1934 v. 1, 109) suggest that the Dahshur Road discovered by Petrie (1888, 33–6) was the route the quarrymen followed. This track, which starts near the Dahshur pyramids, heads toward the Fayum but disappears well short of it, apparently due to its removal by erosion. It has a fairly uniform width of about 26 m and was constructed by sweeping the larger pieces of gravel to the sides. The age is uncertain but it could well be contemporaneous with the quarry. It seems, however, rather too grand a road to have served Umm el-Sawan alone or even both it and the nearby Widan el-Faras basalt quarry. It might well have been used by the quarrymen, but it seems more likely that it was built for general communication with the Fayum.

The presence of mauls of anorthosite gneiss at Umm el-Sawan and Qasr el-Sagha is particularly interesting. The only known outcrops in Egypt of this stone are at the contempory Gebel el-Asr quarry 750 km to the south. On present evidence, it appears that mauls made from the gneiss have not been found outside this quarry and the northern Fayum, suggesting that there is some connection between the two localities. Perhaps the men who worked at Gebel el-Asr also quarried in the Fayum and simply brought their stone tools with them when they left the southern site. Alternatively, the gneiss mauls may have been tools favoured by Old Kingdom stonemasons and so were imported by the Fayum quarrymen. In either case, it is quite clear that the gneiss, like dolerite, was a favoured material for mauls and this is because it was highly durable.

Widan el-Faras

From the Third through Sixth Dynasty, basalt was used for interior pavements, and occasionally for walls and causeways, in the pyramid temples of kings Djoser, Userkaf and Pepi I at Saqqara, Sahura and Nyuserra at Abusir, and Khufu at Giza. The black, fine-grained basalt symbolized the dark, fertile Nile alluvium (Hoffmeier 1993) on which Egyptian civilisation depended for its existence. It was from this alluvium, deposited by the annual Nile floods, that ancient Egypt took its name of *kmt* or *kemet*, 'the black land'.

Basalt has also been reportedly used for some Old Kingdom sarcophagi and pyramidia but most, if not all of these, are carved from two other dark stones; granodiorite from Aswan and greywacke from Wadi Hammamat. Basalt was used, however, for vessels from the late Predynastic period through the Fourth Dynasty and rarely thereafter until the end of the Old Kingdom (Aston 1994, 18–21). The stone for the vessels could have come from any of the numerous basalt outcrops in the desert just outside the Nile Valley in the Giza–Saqqara region, with Abu Rawash being the closest source. No ancient quarries have been found among these outcrops, but a large basalt quarry does exist further west at the northern edge of the Fayum Depression on Gebel el-Qatrani, near the two prominent buttes of Widan el-Faras (**Fig. 1**, no. 3). This site is just 26 km southwest of Umm el-Sawan, and is now known to be the source of basalt used for the Old Kingdom pyramid temples (Harrell and Bown 1995).

The presence of a quarry near Widan el-Faras had long been suspected because of the existence of an ancient road leading to it from the south with pieces of discarded basalt strewn along its length (Beadnell 1905, pl. 18; Caton-Thompson 1927, 338–9; Caton-Thompson and Gardner 1934 v. 1, 136–8; Klemm and Klemm 1993, 414–6). The actual quarry was discovered only recently, the western part in 1987 and the eastern part in 1993, by T M Bown, S E and G A Cornero, and the present author. The quarry, road and other associated features have been described by Harrell and Bown (1995).

The western and eastern parts of the quarry are separated by 0.5 km and both have an excavated bench on top and along the edge of the Gebel el-Qatrani escarpment (**Plate 136**). These benches have a combined length along the escarpment of about 900 m, and are typically 3–5 m deep (below the original surface) by 5–10 m wide. Numerous dolerite mauls were found, but none made from anorthosite gneiss. The quarry is large and so mauls of the latter rock type could easily have been overlooked if present. All the mauls seen were one-handed tools, both the helved (notched) and unhelved forms, but larger ones may yet be found.

The two-handed mauls used to dislodge blocks at Gebel Manzal el-Seyl and Umm el-Sawan cannot be used for this purpose at Widan el-Faras because of the great size of the basalt blocks extracted. Based on the dimensions of pieces of basalt used in the pyramid temples, these blocks must have been commonly on the order of 0.5–1 m thick by 1–2 m across. The only way to remove blocks of this size is to excavate around their edges. The trenches and other distinctive markings made by stone mauls in the Aswan granite-granodiorite quarry (Clarke and Engelbach 1930, 26–30; Arnold 1991, 36–40) are not seen at Widan el-Faras, but perhaps none should be expected. The basalt is naturally broken up by cross-cutting fractures with spacings comparable to the sizes of the basalt blocks in pyramid temples. Quarrying may, thus, have involved using mauls to break up the basalt along the fractures and copper gads (like the one found in the Gebel el-Asr quarry; see below) hammered into the fractures to further split the stone. Once a block was isolated, wooden levers and ropes were probably used to move it. The extracted blocks would have received some shaping and trimming with stone mauls, but must have been taken from the quarry in fairly rough form. The final shaping was certainly done at the temple work sites where pavements and walls of close-fitting blocks were constructed, often by sawing (Moores 1991).

The quarrymen's camp lies at the foot of the escarpment below the quarry (Harrell and Bown 1995, 77–8). It consists of at least 160 ovoid to circular, dry-laid stone rings ranging from 2 to 7 m across. They are similar to the shelters found at Umm el-Sawan, and so are either windbreaks or perhaps tent weights. There is no bedrock below the floors to excavate for stone, and so the rings were made from pieces of basalt taken from the nearby talus slopes below the quarry. A second, smaller and less well-preserved collection of shelters lies 400 m to the south.

Unlike Umm el-Sawan, no archaeological excavations have been conducted at Widen el-Faras and so there is much more yet to be discovered about the quarry and its operations. Fully visible on the surface, however, is the site's most significant feature: a sophisticated network of paved roads (**Plates 137–138**; Harrell and Bown 1995, 78–83). From both pottery found on-site and known uses of basalt in pyramid temples, it is clear that the quarry was in operation from the Third through Sixth Dynasty. This makes the quarry road the oldest known paved road in the world. The next oldest was built by the Minoans on the island of Crete and dates, at the earliest, to the Egyptian Eleventh Dynasty (Forbes 1934, 51–4; Lay 1992, 43–5). The road's main trunk runs along the foot of the Gebel el-Qatrani escarpment, below the quarry, and is joined in several places by short branches coming from different parts of the quarry. The pavement has a uniform width of 2.0–2.1 m or about 4 Egyptian cubits (1 royal cubit = 52.4 cm). It is made from a single course of dry-laid, unshaped pieces of whatever stone was close at hand: basalt and sandstone near the quarry, and sandstone, limestone and silicified wood elsewhere. The road passes down the middle of the quarrymen's camp and then turns south toward the centre of the Fayum Depression. The total length of the road, including all its branches and several short sections now removed by erosion, is nearly 12 km, the last ten of which follow a nearly straight and mostly downward course from Widan el-Faras to its final destination on the shore of an ancient and now vanished lake.

The paved road was clearly built to facilitate the removal of large blocks of basalt from the quarry. These would have been placed on wooden sledges pulled by teams of men. The two largest dressed blocks known to the author are a paving slab in the Khufu pyramid temple measuring 2.10 by 1.85 by 0.80 m and weighing about 9000 kg (assuming an average density of 2.9 gm/cc for basalt), and a wall slab in the Nyuserra pyramid temple measuring 2.60 by 1.05 by 0.95 m and weighing about 7500 kg. The original pieces from which these blocks were cut would have been larger. Most blocks were much smaller, but still would have weighed on the order of a few thousand kilograms. Sledges carrying such heavy loads cannot be pulled across a soft, sandy surface like that over which the road passes. Where the road pavement is well-preserved one does not see any abrasions or other wear left by the passage of the sledges (**Plate 137**), and this suggests that they were pulled over closely spaced, stationary wooden beams (not rollers, which do not work well on an uneven surface) that were laid crosswise on the road. The beams behind would be picked up and set down ahead of the advancing sledge. Similar systems are well known from many ancient and modern examples. For instance, at the Twelfth Dynasty pyramids of Senwosret I at Lisht and Senwosret II at Lahun there are ancient construction ramps with embedded wooden crossbeams over which

sledges were pulled (Arnold 1991, 86–90), and in the 1900s, in Italy's Carrara marble quarry, sledges were lowered down slopes over wooden crossbeams that were advanced with the sledge (Pieri 1964, 154). It is obviously much easier to pull a sledge over smooth wooden beams than over a rough stone pavement, and this fact would not have escaped the ancient quarrymen. But why have a paved road at all, and why not simply place the beams directly on the sandy desert surface? While this might work for the sledges, the men doing the pulling could not obtain the necessary traction in the loose sand. The road may, thus, have been built more for the men pulling the sledges than for the sledges themselves.

Widan el-Faras is 66 km from the Nile Valley by the shortest overland route. Supplies and quarrymen may well have moved along the Dahshur Road, but the basalt blocks would not have been taken along this track when there was water transport just 10 km from the quarry. The quarry road ends at an artificial, rectangular structure that is 311 m long by 19 m wide, and is nearly covered with pieces of basalt. It slopes from +21–22 m above mean sea level at its north end to +18 m at its south end where it reaches its greatest height of 3 m above the more steeply inclined desert surface. Birket Qarun, a salt lake occupying the lowest part of the Fayum Depression and now 8 km south of this structure, has a surface elevation of −45 m below mean sea level. During the Old Kingdom it was a much larger and higher body of water (ancient Lake Moeris) with an elevation of +19–21 m (Harrell and Bown 1995, 83–7). The structure at the end of the quarry road is, thus, a quay that once jutted out into the waters of Lake Moeris. This lake was at the same level as, and in free communication with, the Nile River during its annual summer flood. The connection between the two bodies of water was then, as now, through the gap in the hills between Hawara and Lahun. Barges came to the quay to pick up loads of basalt and then sailed across the lake, through the Hawara/Lahun gap, and down the Nile River to the royal centres where the stone was used.

Gebel el-Asr

The Gebel el-Asr quarry is located 65 km northwest of Abu Simbel and the Nile River (**Fig. 1**, no. 4). The actual site does not have a geographic place name and so it is commonly referred to by that of the nearest prominent landmark, a high hill known as Gebel el-Asr that is 10 km to the east. The site is also sometimes called by two other names: Chephren's Quarry, after the four well-known statues of this Fourth Dynasty king (Khafre) made from the quarry stone; and the Tushka Quarry, after a village on the Nile River near the terminus of an ancient road coming from the quarry. The northern and southern parts of the quarry were discovered in 1933 and 1938, respectively, by R Engelbach and G W Murray following an initial discovery of stelae in the area by a military patrol in 1932. Brief descriptions of the quarry have been published by Engelbach (1933; 1938), Murray (1939; 1967, 139–48), Harrell and Brown (1994), Shaw and Bloxam (1999) and Shaw (2000), but despite these investigations, the site is still largely unexplored. Excavations currently in progress by E G Bloxam and I M E Shaw will provide much needed new information (see Shaw this volume).

The Gebel el-Asr quarry supplied two gradational varieties of metamorphic rock: anorthosite gneiss, which is light grey with dark green to black speckles, streaks and thin bands; and gabbro gneiss, which is darker with alternating, contorted layers of light grey and dark green to black (Harrell and Brown 1994, 52–3). These stones have commonly been misidentified by archaeologists as diorite or, more recently, diorite gneiss. The light grey portions of the stones consist of either the labradorite or bytownite variety of plagioclase feldspar. It is the percentage of plagioclase that determines how these stones are classified: anorthosite gneiss if over 90 percent, otherwise gabbro gneiss. The plagioclase is iridescent and, in the bright desert sunlight, cause the stones to have a striking blue glow that is easily seen from hundreds of metres away. The glow is not visible, however, under the much weaker indoor lighting of museums. This unusual visual effect, which is known from the same rock types elsewhere in the world, has been commented on by many visitors to the quarry (Engelbach 1933, 66; 1938, 389; Murray 1939, 107; Harrell and Brown 1994, 54–5). It is probably the reason why the quarry was opened in the first place, as the site would otherwise seem too distant, the environment too harsh, and the stones too unremarkable to justify the great efforts required for their extraction and transportation. Because objects made from the gneisses glowed in the sunlight, they must have seemed to onlookers imbued with a magical or supernatural quality. Although the many vessels made from these stones were placed inside tombs, the gneiss statues may originally have been set outside in the sun.

Anorthosite gneiss was used for vessels during the late Predynastic period through the Sixth Dynasty, with production peaking in the Second and Third Dynasties (Aston 1994, 62–4). The stone was also employed for other objects, such as two stelae of the Second Dynasty king Peribsen, but especially, along with the gabbro gneiss, for royal statuary during the Fourth through Sixth Dynasty and again in the Twelfth Dynasty. The few known objects of gneiss postdating the Middle Kingdom were probably recarved from earlier statues or blocks (Aston *et al.* 2000, 23).

The two stone varieties come from well-separated parts of the quarry. The speckled and streaked variety of anorthosite gneiss was obtained from northern outcrops near Quartz Ridge (Harrell and Brown 1994, 50–1). This topographic feature is a long, narrow spine of metamorphic rock that is tens of metres wide and up to 10 m high. The ridge gets its name from a large, ancient cairn on its summit made from pieces of white quartz (**Plate 139**). Nearby were found stelae of kings Radjedef (Fourth Dynasty), Djedkara Izezi and Nyuserra Izi (Fifth Dynasty), and Amenemhat II (Twelfth Dynasty) (Engelbach 1933, 66 and 1938, 369–70; Shaw and Bloxam 1999, 17). The latter stela identified the quarry stone by its ancient name, *mntt*, or *mentet* (Engelbach 1933, 66, 70; Simpson 1963, 50–3), a name well attested from other textual sources (Harris 1961, 87–8). No obvious quarry workings exist near Quartz Ridge. Instead, on its

west side, there is a low, mostly sand-covered outcrop of anorthosite gneiss that parallels the ridge for a few kilometres both north and south of the quartz cairn. This outcrop is perhaps a couple of kilometres wide and is littered with loose pieces of stone naturally eroded from the underlying bedrock. It appears that the ancient quarrymen simply harvested the already loose boulders. Because the anorthosite gneiss here was used almost exclusively for small vessels, it would seem that there was no need to excavate the bedrock so long as boulders of sufficient size and quality were still available. If excavations ever did exist, they are now hidden under a blanket of sand.

About 4 km southwest of the cairn on Quartz Ridge is the main part of the Gebel el-Asr quarry and it is from here that the gabbro gneiss and the banded variety of anorthosite gneiss were obtained. The workings consist of numerous shallow depressions, now filled with sand, scattered over 1–2 km^2 (**Plate 140**). There has been no detailed mapping done here, so the size and other characteristics of these excavations remain unknown. Previous investigators focused their attention instead on two sites at the western and eastern edges of the workings where antiquities were found.

On the east side is a low pile of quarried blocks of gneiss that is 20 m across. On top of this was a stela of king Khufu (Fourth Dynasty) and beside the pile was a stela of king Sahura (Fifth Dynasty) (Rowe 1938, 393–96). Both stelae give what may be the name of the quarry or surrounding district, *ḥmt or hemet*. The workings around these stelae have been referred to as the Khufu Quarry by early writers. On the west side of the southern workings a copper gad was found that dates to the Fourth Dynasty (Rowe 1938, 391–3). Such a tool would have been hammered into fractures to split rocks during quarrying. Despite the fact that it has no cutting edge and so is not a true chisel, the workings where it was found were referred to by its discoverers as the Chisel Quarry.

Rare stone mauls of anorthosite gneiss are found in the Gebel el-Asr quarry, as are mauls of what may be imported dolerite and quartzite. The quarrying that took place in the southern excavations would have followed the method used at Widan el-Faras: blocks of gneiss were isolated by using stone mauls and, to exploit the natural fractures, copper gads. Apart from the extracted blocks of gneiss, which are piled and scattered everywhere, no worked pieces of this stone have so far been observed in the quarry. Murray (1939, 107), however, reports finding on the quarry road, about 6 km east of the Khufu stela, five pieces of gneiss weighing about 18 kg apiece. These had been roughly shaped into the form of bowls but had not been hollowed out, and are clearly vessel blanks like those found at Gebel Manzal el-Seyl and Umm el-Sawan. Vessel blanks of anorthosite gneiss have also been recently observed on Quartz Ridge (E G Bloxam, pers. comm. 1999).

The habitations of the quarrymen are found scattered throughout the site but most are concentrated on Quartz Ridge which, by virtue of this, would seem to have served as the administrative centre (Murray 1939, 108; Shaw and Bloxam 1999, 17; Shaw 2000, 29). These structures of dry-laid stone are quite different from those found at Umm el-

Sawan and Widan el-Faras. Some are rectangular in plan (**Plate 141**) and may have been true walled and roofed huts, whereas the others are low crescent-shaped structures that are probably windbreaks. The non-banded anorthosite gneiss was the first stone used from the Gebel el-Asr quarry and this together with the concentration of ruins at Quartz Ridge suggests that the northern workings are the oldest and, like the vessels made from the stone, date from the late Predynastic period onward. It was not until the early Old Kingdom that the two gneisses in the southern workings were quarried for statues.

Starting near the east side of the southern workings, an ancient track heads for the Nile River at Tushka (Engelbach 1938, 388; Murray 1939, 110). Unlike the Widan el-Faras and Dahshur roads, this track has no prepared surface, but instead is marked by a series of intervisible stone cairns, discarded pieces of gneiss and pottery, and the well-worn tracks of the donkey caravans. The greater distance involved and a paucity of nearby stone for long stretches precluded construction of a paved road like that in the Fayum. The straight-line distance between the quarry and Tushka is 75 km, but the track, with its meanderings through Wadi Tushka, would have been about 80 km long. However, if the gneiss were shipped down-river during the annual summer flood, the floodwaters would have extended up Wadi Tushka (west of Tushka village) for several kilometres, in much the same way that Lake Nasser does today, thereby shortening the distance. Only Twelfth Dynasty pottery has been found along the road (Engelbach 1938, 388) and so this may be the date of the cairns, but it is almost certainly the case that the same track was also used in earlier periods. A southeasterly route to Abu Simbel is a little shorter, but the track along Wadi Tushka is the only one that provides a steady downslope all the way to the river.

A Twelfth Dynasty stela found near Tushka specifically mentions quarrying *mentet*-stone (Simpson 1963, 50–3). It was left by one Horemhat during the reign of Amenemhat II and says the quarrying expedition included, among other personnel, 50 stonecutters, 200 quarrymen, 1006 workmen and 1000 donkeys (Simpson 1963, 50–3). Presumably, the quarrymen extracted the blocks of gneiss, the stonecutters carved them into roughed-out statues, and either the workmen or donkeys pulled the sledges with their loads of stone.

Two structures that appear to be loading ramps are found on the east side of the southern workings. These are constructed from pieces of unworked, dry-laid gneiss. One is near the Khufu stela, but the largest and best preserved is about 2 km east of this stela and at the beginning of the quarry road to the Nile (Engelbach 1938, 372; Murray 1939, 108). The latter ramp is 8.2 m long, 4.7 m wide and rises to 1.2 m above the original ground level (Engelbach 1938, 372; Shaw and Bloxam 1999, 18; Shaw 2000, 29–30). The other ramp is 5.5 m wide and rises to 1 m above the original desert surface. Extending several metres from the eastern elevated ends of both ramps are two straight, parallel trenches cut into the underlying hard-packed desert soil (Engelbach 1938, 372; Murray 1939, 108; Shaw and Bloxam 1999, 18; Shaw 2000, 30). Each is about 30–35 cm deep immediately adjacent to the ramps and 70–100 cm

wide along their length, and each pair is separated by a ridge about 70 cm in width. The great regularity of the trenches indicates that they were purposefully cut rather than inadvertently worn into the desert surface. They progressively shallow away from the ramps, disappearing when their bottoms merge with the original surface. These ramps have been a puzzle not only to their discoverers, but also to all subsequent investigators. It would seem that they were used to load gneiss blocks onto sledges, but, if so, why are their ends so high and why were the trenches cut?

The largest wooden sledge to survive from ancient Egypt is 4.2 m long and about 1 m wide with two runners (each 12 cm high by 20 cm wide) connected by at least four crossties (Arnold 1991, 276; Partridge 1996, 131–2). It is now in the Cairo Museum (CG 4928), but was found at the Dahshur pyramid of Senwosret III (Twelfth Dynasty) where it was apparently used to transport six funerary boats from the river to the pyramid. At 1.7 m high, one of the four Khafra statues in the Cairo Museum (CG 14) is the largest known object made from gneiss. The original block from which it was cut would have weighed around 3000 kg. Transporting it from the quarry to the Nile would have required a sledge about as large as the one from Dahshur. It is impractical to pull sledges over soft sandy ground because the runners will quickly dig themselves into the sand that then piles up in front of the cross-ties, thereby hindering, if not altogether stopping, forward progress. However, this problem can be avoided if the runners are high enough to keep the cross-ties well above the sand (at least a few tens of centimetres). Perhaps the ramps were built to load such a high sledge, but why then the cut trenches? Their width suggests that the sledge runners were several tens of centimetres wide, a feature that would also facilitate travel over soft ground. Perhaps the ramps were built before the dimensions of the sledges were known and so the trenches were cut later to lower a sledge when it was backed up against the ramp face, allowing its upper surface to be flush with the top of the ramp. Shaw and Bloxam (1999, 19–20) suggest that rather than using a conventional sledge, which could not be so high, a river raft mounted on runners was used to haul the stone to the Nile.

Wadi Hammamat

The shortest route across the Eastern Desert, between the Nile River and Red Sea, passes through the valley of Wadi Hammamat. This was, consequently, a much used track throughout antiquity as is well attested by the over 500 rock-cut inscriptions on the wadi walls (Couyat and Montet 1912; Goyon 1957; Simpson 1959; Bernand 1972; Gundlach 1986). Many of these were left by traders and others passing through the desert, but the rest are associated with a stone quarry (**Fig. 1**, no. 5; **Plate 142**), which is 75 km east of Qift (ancient Koptos) on the Nile River. Wadi Hammamat along with Aswan have the longest records of activity among the quarries in Egypt: they span the late Predynastic through Roman periods.

The quarry was apparently first rediscovered around 1800 by scholars attached to the Napoleonic Expedition to

Egypt with the first published notice of it being that of de Rozière's (1813, 88–90), a member of this expedition. The quarry has subsequently been mentioned by many writers who, with rare exception, were concerned only with the inscriptions. The quarry itself has only been described by Hume (1934, 258–66), Harrell and Brown (1992a; 1992b), Klemm and Klemm (1993, 355–76) and Brown and Harrell (1995), but none of these authors have provided a detailed account of the quarry workings.

The principal stone extracted was a dark grey or greenish grey to mainly dark greyish green, slightly metamorphosed sedimentary rock that varies texturally from a sandstone to a finer-grained siltstone. These rocks were originally rich in clay minerals (now replaced by epidote and chlorite mica, the source of the green coloration) and so can be said to have a greywacke texture. To simplify the petrological nomenclature, both the sandstone and siltstone can be referred to simply as either greywacke or metagreywacke, with the latter name reflecting the effects of metamorphism that produced the epidote and chlorite. In the past, the greywacke has been incorrectly identified as schist and slate, and also occasionally as basalt. The ancient Egyptian name for the greywacke is *bekhen* (*bḫn*) (Lucas and Rowe 1938; Harris 1961, 78–82), a name that evolved over the ages, first by transliteration into the Greco-Roman *basanites* and then by a medieval transcription error into the modern basalt (Harrell 1995, 30–3).

After the Aswan granite and granodiorite, the Wadi Hammamat greywacke was the most widely used hardstone in ancient Egypt. For example, it was employed for vessels and commemorative palettes (including the famous Narmer Palette) of the late Predynastic and Early Dynastic periods, royal and private statuary from the Early Dynastic period onward, and sarcophagi from the Old Kingdom onward. Its ability to take a good polish, its uniform fine-grained texture, and especially its green colour account for greywacke's great appeal over the millennia. For the ancient Egyptians, green had many positive connotations (such as fruitfulness, pleasant appearance and joyfulness) because of its association with growing, life-sustaining vegetation (Harris 1961, 224–5).

Another very different-looking stone was also taken from the Wadi Hammamat quarry. It is a conglomerate (or metaconglomerate), which is just a coarser-grained version of the greywacke sandstone. The conglomerate contains abundant gravel clasts (rounded pebbles and cobbles) of many rock types with a wide variety of compositions and colours. Overall, the conglomerate has a greenish appearance (due to abundant epidote and chlorite), but the multicoloured gravel clasts caused the Romans to call it *hexacontalithos* ('sixty stones in one'). More recently, the rock has been referred to as *breccia verde antica* or *d'Egitto*, a name given to it by Italian stonecutters. The term breccia is inappropriate, however, because the rock lacks the angular gravel clasts typical of a true breccia. The conglomerate was quarried mainly by the Romans, but was also worked to a minor extent during the Twentieth, Twenty-Fifth and Thirtieth Dynasties, when it was used for three known sarcophagi and one stela (Aston *et al.* 2000, 58).

The Wadi Hammamat quarry extends for about 1 km

along the valley, with the Roman workings occurring on both sides and the earlier ones restricted to the north side. The sandstone comes from throughout the quarry, the siltstone was taken just from the central part around a tributary wadi that enters from the north, and the conglomerate was obtained only from the west side. Apart from the many quarry excavations and rock-cut inscriptions, the only other features to be seen are all Roman: a shrine built on the wadi floor; a slipway descending the south valley wall; signaling towers (*skopeloi*) on the hilltops; and, near the shrine, what have been variously interpreted as bathtubs, naoi and sarcophagi carved from the greywacke. The excavations span three and a half millennia and consequently exhibit the full range of ancient quarrying technologies from stone mauls to, in later periods, iron wedges pounded into pre-cut holes. Unlike the other hardstone quarries previously discussed, at Wadi Hammamat one finds traces on the quarry walls of the use of stone mauls (for example, see Klemm and Klemm 1993, fig. 414). Here the stone was bruised away by pounding in a series of adjacent rectangular compartments. The same kind of quarrying traces are also seen at Aswan (Clarke and Engelbach 1930, 26–30; Arnold 1991, 36–40).

Many of the rock-cut inscriptions provide interesting details of the quarrying activity. Two of them commemorate the largest known quarrying expeditions in ancient Egypt: that of king Senwosret I (Twelfth Dynasty) with 17,000 men (inscription no. 61 of Goyon 1957, 81–5; Simpson 1959, 28–32); and that of king Ramesses IV (Twentieth Dynasty) with 8,368 men (**Plate 143**) (inscription no. 12 of Couyat and Montet 1912, 34–9; Christophe 1948). The Senwosret I stela states that blocks of stone for 60 sphinxes and 150 statues were hauled by teams of 2000, 1500, 1000 and 500 men (Simpson 1959, 30).

A by-product of the Ramesses IV expedition is a well-known papyrus that is one of the world's oldest surviving maps and the only one with topographical information so far discovered in Egypt (Gardiner 1914; Murray 1942; Goyon 1949; Shore 1987, 121–4; Klemm and Klemm 1988; Harrell and Brown 1992a; 1992b). The papyrus was found at Deir el-Medina and is now in Turin's Egyptian Museum. It was prepared for Ramesses IV's expedition and was probably drawn by the Scribe of the Tomb Amennakhte, son of Ipuy (Harrell and Brown 1992a, 100–3). The map, which is remarkably modern in its depiction of topography, shows a 15 km stretch of Wadi Hammamat and illustrates this valley's confluence with Wadis Atulla and el-Sid, the surrounding hills, the greywacke-conglomerate quarry, and the gold mine and associated settlement at Bir Umm el-Fawakhir. It also includes numerous annotations identifying the features shown on the map, such as the destination of the wadi tracks, the distance between the quarry and gold mine, the locations of gold deposits in the hills, a statement of the expeditions' purpose (to quarry *bekhen*-stone for a statue of the king), and the sizes of the stone blocks quarried written around representations of the blocks themselves. One of these blocks, for example, is labeled with dimensions of 'breadth of 2 cubits, 2 palms; thickness of 2 cubits … fingers' (or approximately 1.2 m and 1.3 m, respectively), and another text refers to a 'stone that is pulled by men …[that is] 3 cubits wide' (or about 1.6 m; Harrell and Brown 1992a, table 1). Only one statue of Ramesses IV with similar dimensions is known and its badly fragmented remains stand today beside the Eighth Pylon at Karnak temple in Luxor. The papyrus is also of great interest to geologists who consider it a geologic map (the oldest one known) because it shows the areal distribution of different rock types (represented by differently colored hills) and the lithologically diverse wadi gravels (represented by multicolored dots). It also provides information on quarrying, mining and the locations of gold deposits (Harrell and Brown 1992b).

The problems of distance and terrain are essentially the same for the quarrymen hauling stone from the Gebel el-Asr and Wadi Hammamat quarries, and similar methods may have been employed. However, wheeled carts were in use by the time of Ramesses IV's reign. The stela describing his 8,368-man expedition (**Plate 143**) mentions food supplies being brought in on 'ten wagons, there being six yokes of oxen to [each] wagon' (Christophe 1948, 26–7; Arnold 1991, 281). Rather than sending the supply wagons back to the Nile Valley empty, perhaps they were loaded with quarried stone. The fact that each wagon was pulled by 12 oxen suggests that they carried heavy loads, but could they have borne the largest *bekhen*-stone blocks, which may have weighed up to a few thousand kilograms? No trace of the quarry road from Wadi Hammamat to the Nile River has been found, but it probably followed the most direct route across the desert plateau; the same one used by the Romans and now marked by a series of their ruins, *skopeloi*, cairns and inscriptions between Qift on the Nile and Wadi Hammamat (Bernand 1972, 1–58; Zitterkopf and Sidebotham 1989).

Gebel Rokham

Although white marble was the sculptural stone of choice for the classical Greeks and Romans, it was rarely used in pharaonic Egypt. This is not surprising given that deposits of marble are found only as thin veins in the distant mountains of the Eastern Desert. One of these veins, however, was quarried anciently at Gebel Rokham, near the confluence of Wadis Miya and Abu Qaria, 110 km east of the Nile River (**Fig. 1**, no. 6). The site was discovered in 1899 by C J Alford and his brief description is the only one extant: 'enormous heaps of chippings show that the marble had at one time been extensively worked, but, with the exception of one fragment of a broken vase, we could find no worked pieces' (Alford 1901, 14–5). In recent decades the ancient excavations were destroyed by modern quarrying. The only remaining traces of earlier activity are New Kingdom, Late Period and Roman pottery sherds found in the ancient tailings on the north side of the new quarry and, on the south side, in a pile of marble chips marking the site of an ancient workshop (**Plate 144**; Brown and Harrell 1995, 231). The marble would have been transported to the Nile Valley by taking Wadi Miya to Wadi Abbad, a route that passes the site of the Nineteenth Dynasty rock-cut temple at Bir el-Kanais and reaches the Nile River at Edfu.

Among white marbles from throughout the Mediterra-

nean region, the one from Gebel Rokham is compositionally unique. It consists mainly of calcite, like most marbles, but is unusual for containing abundant brucite (Lilyquist 1989, 40; Klemm and Klemm 1993, 427–9; Brown and Harrell 1995, 231). It is additionally distinctive for having crosscutting veins (up to 5 mm wide) of pure white, finergrained, brucite-free calcite. Only a handful of objects are known to have been made from this stone and all date to the Eighteenth Dynasty. The best known examples are two statues of king Thutmose III. One of these and part of another are in the Cairo Museum (JE 43507A and JE 90237, respectively), and the rest of the second one is in New York's Metropolitan Museum of Art (07.230.3). The other white marble objects date to the reigns of Thutmose III and his successors, Amenhotep II, Akhenaten and Tutankhamum.

Rod el-Gamra

The youngest of the pharaonic desert quarries is also the most recently discovered. It was found in 1998 by V M Brown, M S Masoud and the author, and a preliminary description of it has been given by Harrell and Brown (1999). The quarry is located midway between the Red Sea and Nile River (110 km from both; **Fig. 1**. no. 7), and occurs in the broad valley of Rod el-Gamra, near the prominent ridge of Gebel Urf Hammam.

The quarry stone is a dolerite (or, equivalently, diabase) porphyry with large greenish grey crystals (up to 15 cm across) set in a fine-grained greenish black matrix (**Plate 145**). The single quarry excavation measures 5 by 15 m in area and is at least 2 m deep (**Plate 146**). The actual depth is greater at the bottom, but is now covered by sand. There are two other smaller areas at the site where the uppermost 1–2 m of weathered dolerite porphyry has been stripped away to expose fresh rock. These are places where the stone was being evaluated for future quarrying.

Lying in the debris field immediately adjacent to the quarry are five unfinished naoi (shrines) carved from the dolerite porphyry (**Plate 147**). These have the shape of a rectangular box with a pointed top or pyramidion, giving them the appearance of stubby obelisks. They are undecorated and uninscribed, and come in only two sizes. The two large naoi measure, on average, 1.48 m high by 0.80 m wide by 0.77 m deep, and the three smaller ones average 1.02 m high by 0.45 m wide by 0.47 m deep. It is probably no coincidence that the heights of the large and small naoi are approximately 3 and 2 Egyptian cubits, respectively. Scattered around these naoi are fragments of several others that were originally cut to one of the two standard sizes.

Stone naoi were used from the Middle Kingdom through the Roman period, and typically were placed in temple sanctuaries where they held a statue of the god to which the temple was dedicated. No naoi of dolerite porphyry are known outside Rod el-Gamra, but the author is aware of twelve naoi with the same unusual shape. All date to the Late Period and this suggests that the quarry may be of the same age. Three are dedicated to King Apries of the Twenty-Sixth Dynasty and the other nine are dedicated to kings Nectanebo I and II of the Thirtieth Dynasty. Pottery found at

Rod el-Gamra further confirms a general Late Period date, but several small statues carved from the dolerite porphyry and now in museums all date to the Thirtieth Dynasty (for example: De Putter and Karlshausen 1992, 124; Bothmer 1960, 112–3). The quarry, thus, almost certainly dates to the Thirtieth Dynasty as well. If true, this may suggest why the five whole naoi were never taken to the Nile Valley: before this was possible, the quarry was abandoned when the Thirtieth Dynasty collapsed with the Persian invasion of Egypt.

Adjacent to the quarry workings are the well-preserved remains of five huts. These are rectangular structures with walls of dry-laid, stacked stone that still stand, in many cases, to their original maximum height of 1.2 m. They might be windbreaks, but it is more likely that they originally had upper walls and roofs made from perishable materials: some sort of wooden framework with a reed mat, palm frond or animal hide covering. The hut interiors are quite small, ranging between 5.6 and 9 m², and if used for sleeping could have accommodated about a dozen men. This might also be the size of the workforce, but it seems too small by at least half. The larger naoi weigh about 2000 kg apiece and if there were only a dozen men available to move them around the quarry, each man would have had to handle about 170 kg, which is too great a weight. Perhaps the huts were used only for storing provisions and tools, and a larger number of men lived out in the open.

The most archaeologically significant aspect of the Rod el-Gamra quarry is the use of iron tools. From the markings left on the surfaces of the naoi, it is evident that both pointed and flat-edged chisels were utilized in carving the stone. Dolerite porphyry is a very hard material (similar to the dolerite mauls) and such a stone cannot be worked with soft copper or bronze tools; only iron will suffice. The most compelling evidence for the use of iron tools at Rod el-Gamra are the wedge-shaped holes seen on many pieces of stone (**Plate 145**). Throughout the ancient world these are a clear indication that iron wedges were used to split the rock. The quarrying process proceeded as follows: a series of wedge-shaped holes were cut along a straight line using iron tools, and wedge-shaped pieces of iron were then set into the holes and hammered until the rock broke along the line of holes. Many early writers have argued that such holes were cut for wooden wedges which, when wetted, expanded and split the stone. It has now been amply demonstrated that wedge holes of the size and spacing seen at Rod el-Gamra could only have been intended for iron wedges (Waelkens et al. 1988, 103–6; 1990, 62–5). Yet another indication of iron use at Rod el-Gamra is a 4 m-diameter deposit of black, glassy, vesicular slag that appears to be the result of iron-working. There must have been a blacksmith at the quarry whose task it was to repair, sharpen and perhaps even cast the iron tools, and slag would be a by-product of his forge.

The first evidence for the use of iron wedges is found in Greek quarries dating to the early sixth century BC (Waelkens et al. 1990, 62–3), but the technology may have originated a century earlier. Prior to the discovery of the Rod el-Gamra quarry, the oldest known wedge holes in Egypt were in the Aswan granite-granodiorite quarry and were

thought to date to the second century BC at the earliest (Röder 1965, 522). A textual source refers to the use of iron tools at Aswan in the early third century BC, but it is not clear that this also included iron wedges (Röder 1965, 523–4). The Rod el-Gamra quarry, which was active in the mid-fourth century BC, thus provides the earliest evidence in Egypt for the iron-wedge technology. Iron wedges were undoubtedly also employed at the same time in other hard-stone quarries, but the tool marks have so far gone unrecognised. It is, in fact, likely that the technology was being used in Egypt by the end of the Twenty-Sixth Dynasty (late sixth century BC), a dynasty that is well known for its close ties to ancient Greece. It was during this period that Greeks founded a commercial settlement at Naukratis in the western Delta (and smelted iron there), and Greek mercenaries served in the Egyptian army. Naukratis was located just 16 km from Sais, the capital of the Twenty-Sixth Dynasty.

Stone from the Rod el-Gamra quarry was probably transported on wheeled carts. The route taken to the Nile Valley would have followed either Wadi Muweilha (on the north side of Rod el-Gamra) or, less likely, Wadi Sibrit (on the south side) west to Wadi Shait, which leads to the Kom Ombo area, a total distance of a little over 110 km.

Concluding Remarks

There are several known quarries for travertine (calcitic 'Egyptian alabaster') along the western fringe of the Eastern Desert (Aston et al. 2000, 59–60), but they have not been described in the present paper, as it is only concerned with those quarries found deep within the desert. The seven pharaonic quarries described above cannot be the only ones that exist in the desert interior. There are numerous other varieties of stone used anciently in Egypt that have no known sources, but which almost certainly came from the mountains of the Eastern Desert. For example, pegmatitic diorite, red-and-white andesite (or dacite) porphyry, and black-and-white andesite (or dolerite) porphyry were commonly used for vessels and occasionally for small animal figurines from the late Predynastic period into the Old Kingdom (Aston 1994, 13–5 and 21–3; Aston et al. 2000, 30–1, 48–50). It is probable that these stones were quarried, like others during the same period, as opposed to being simply harvested as already loose boulders. The andesite-dacite porphyry (also known as the Imperial Porphyry) and pegmatitic diorite were later quarried by the Romans at Gebel Dokhan (Mons Porphyrites) and Wadi Umm Shegilat, respectively (Brown and Harrell 1995, 222–30). It is possible that these localities are also the pharaonic sources, and that all traces of earlier workings were destroyed by Roman activity. This is especially the case for Wadi Umm Shegilat, which has the only known outcrop in Egypt of the distinctive pegmatitic diorite.

Serpentinite is another important stone and was used throughout the pharaonic period, initially just for vessels and then later for kohl and unguent jars, scarabs, shabtis, and occasionally small statues (Aston et al. 2000, 56–7). Both black and green varieties were employed and so there may be more than one quarry. A Roman quarry for the green variety was discovered near Wadi Umm Esh (Brown and Harrell 1995, 225–30), and this could be the earlier source as well, but this particular rock type is widely distributed across the Eastern Desert and so could have come from another locality.

In visiting the desert quarries, one is struck by how utterly remote most of them are. They are found on mountain tops and in small wadis that are seemingly far removed from the well-traveled ancient tracks. Given this, one might well wonder how the stone sources were discovered in the first place? It is evident not only from the quarries, but also especially from the mines for metals, that the deserts were thoroughly explored in antiquity. For example, there are today 86 known gold deposits in the Eastern Desert and 85 percent of these were worked anciently (EGSMA 1979), including all of the richest ones (see also Klemm, Klemm and Murr this volume).

Ancient Egypt must have had its own versions of the storied gold prospectors of the nineteenth century American West. These were people who knew how to read the often subtle clues that point to valuable rock and mineral occur-rences. They did not have to climb every mountain and walk every wadi to know what was present. They understood that the full spectrum of an area's geologic resources can be seen in the gravel of the wadi that drains the area. Most prospecting, therefore, can be done by simply examining the gravel in the lower reaches of the main wadis because through them pass the eroded fragments of every variety of stone in the drainage basin. When something interesting is found, it can then be tracked to its source by following the trail of telltale signs up the wadi. One can imagine as well that ancient Egyptian prospectors also made use of the desert nomads who, in the course of grazing their herds, probably did visit virtually every wadi. Modern-day Bedouin pride themselves on remembering the things seen during their wanderings (see Hobbs this volume), and the ancient nomads were probably no different. One has only to ask the right questions to get useful answers from these people. This is, in fact, how the present author 'discovered' the Gebel Manzal el-Seyl and Rod el-Gamra quarries. More modern-day prospecting for ancient sites remains to be done and one can fairly anticipate that much new information will be forth-coming on the desert quarries.

Bibliography

Alford C J, 1901. Gold mining in Egypt. *Transactions of the Institute of Mining and Metallurgy* 10: 2–28.

Arnold D, 1991. *Building in Egypt – Pharaonic Stone Masonry.* New York.

Aston B G, 1994. *Ancient Egyptian Stone Vessels: Material and Forms.* Studien zur Archäologie und Geschichte Altägyptens 5. Heidelberg.

Aston B G, Harrell J A and Shaw I, 2000. Stones. In P T Nicholson and I Shaw (eds), *Ancient Egyptian Materials and Technology.* Cambridge: 5–77.

Beadnell H J L, 1905. *The Topography and Geology of the Fayum Province of Egypt.* Cairo.

Bernand A, 1972. *De Koptos à Kosseir.* Leiden.

Bomann A, 1994. Discoveries in the Eastern Desert. *Egyptian Archaeology* 4: 29–30.

Bomann A, 1995. Wadi Abu Had – Wadi Dib, Eastern Desert. *Journal of Egyptian Archaeology* 81: 14–7.

Bothmer B V, 1960. *Egyptian Sculpture of the Late Period, 700 B.C. to A.D. 100.* Brooklyn.

Brown V M and Harrell J A, 1995. Topographical and petrological survey of ancient Roman quarries in the Eastern Desert of Egypt. In Y Maniatis, N Herz and Y Bassiakis (eds), *The Study of Marble and Other Stones Used in Antiquity – ASMOSIA III, Athens.* Transactions of the 3rd International Symposium of the Association for the Study of Marble and Other Stones in Antiquity. London: 221–34.

Caton-Thompson G, 1927. Explorations in the northern Fayum. *Antiquity* 1: 326–40.

Caton-Thompson G and Gardner E W, 1934. *The Desert Fayum* (2 Vols.). Royal Anthropological Institute of Great Britain and Ireland. London.

Clarke S and Engelbach R, 1930. *Ancient Egyptian Masonry.* Oxford.

Couyat J and Montet P, 1912. *Les inscriptions hiéroglyphiques et hiératiques du Ouâdi Hammâmât.* Mémoires de l'Institut français d'archéologie orientale 34. Paris.

Christophe L, 1948. La stèle de l'an III de Ramsés IV au Ouâdi Hammâmât (No. 12). *Bulletin de l'Institut français d'archéologie orientale* 48: 1–38.

De Putter T and Karlshausen C, 1992. *Les Pierres Utilisées dans la Sculpture et l'Architecture de l'Égypte Pharaonique – Guide Pratique Illustré.* Brussels.

De Rozière M, 1813. Description minéralogique de la Vallée de Qoceyr. In *Description de l'Égypte, Histoire Naturelle* (Vol. 2). Paris: 86–98.

EGSMA (Egyptian Geological Survey and Mining Authority), 1979. *The Mineral Map of Egypt – Explanatory Notes and Lists.* Egyptian Geological Survey and Mining Authority, Cairo.

El Khouli A A-R H, 1978. *Egyptian Stone Vessels: Predynastic Period to Dynasty III* (2 vols.). Mainz am Rheim.

Engelbach R, 1933. The quarries of the western Nubian Desert – a preliminary report. *Annales du Service des Antiquités de l'Égypte* 33: 65–74.

Engelbach R, 1938. The quarries of the western Nubian Desert and the ancient road to Tushka. *Annales du Service des Antiquités de l'Égypte* 38: 369–90.

Forbes R J, 1934. *Notes on the History of Ancient Roads and Their Construction.* Amsterdam.

Gardiner A H, 1914. The map of the gold mines in a Ramesside papyrus at Turin. *Cairo Scientific Journal* 8: 41–6.

Goyon G, 1949. Le papyrus de Turin – dit 'des mines d'or et le Wadi Hammamat'. *Annales du Service des Antiquités de l'Égypte* 49: 337–92.

Goyon G, 1957. *Nouvelles Inscriptions Rupestres du Wadi Hammamat.* Paris.

Gundlach R, 1986. Wadi Hammamat. In W Helck and W Westendorf (eds), *Lexikon der Ägyptologie* 6/7. Wiesbaden: 1099–113.

Harrell J A, 1990. Misuse of the term 'alabaster' in Egyptology. *Göttinger Miszellen* 119: 37–42.

Harrell J A, 1995. Ancient Egyptian origins of some common rock names. *Journal of Geological Education* 43: 30–4.

Harrell J A and Bown T M, 1995. An Old Kingdom basalt quarry at Widan el-Faras and the quarry road to Lake Moeris in the Faiyum, Egypt. *Journal of the American Research Center in Egypt* 32: 71–91.

Harrell J A and Brown V M, 1992a. The oldest surviving topographical map from ancient Egypt (Turin Papyri 1879, 1899 and 1969). *Journal of the American Research Center in Egypt* 29: 81–105.

Harrell J A and Brown V M, 1992b. The world's oldest surviving geological map – the 1150 BC Turin papyrus from Egypt. *Journal of Geology* 100: 3–18.

Harrell J A and Brown V M, 1994. Chephren's Quarry in the Nubian Desert of Egypt. *Nubica* 3/1: 43–57.

Harrell J A and Brown V M, 1999. A late-period quarry for naoi in the Eastern Desert. *Egyptian Archaeology* 14: 18–20.

Harrell J A, Brown V M and Masoud M S, 2000. An Early Dynastic Quarry for Stone Vessels at Gebel Manzal el-Seyl, Eastern Desert. *Journal of Egyptian Archaeology* 86: 33–42.

Harris J R, 1961. *Lexicographical Studies in Ancient Egyptian Minerals.* Deutsche Academie der Wissenschaften zu Berlin, Institut für Orientforschung 54. Berlin.

Hoffmeier J K, 1993. The use of basalt in floors of Old Kingdom pyramid temples. *Journal of the American Research Center in Egypt* 30: 117–23.

Hume W F, 1934. *Geology of Egypt* (Vol. 2, Pt. 1). Cairo.

Klemm R and Klemm D D, 1988. Pharaonischer goldbergbau im Wadi Sid und der Turiner minenpapyrus. *Akten des Vierten Internationalen Ägyptologen Kongresses München 1985.* Hamburg: 73–87.

Klemm R and Klemm D D, 1993. *Steine und Steinbrüche im Alten Ägypten.* Berlin.

Lay M G, 1992. *Ways of the World – A History of the World's Roads and of the Vehicles That Used Them.* New Brunswick.

Lilyquist C, 1989. The marble statue of Tuthmosis III from Deir el Bahari. *Göttinger Miszellen* 109: 39–40.

Lucas A (revised by J. R. Harris), 1962. *Ancient Egyptian Materials and Industries.* London.

Lucas A and Rowe A, 1938. The ancient Egyptian Bekhen-stone. *Annales du Service des Antiquités de l'Égypte* 38: 127–56.

Moores R G, 1991. Evidence for use of a stone-cutting drag saw by the Fourth Dynasty Egyptians. *Journal of the American Research Center in Egypt* 28: 139–48.

Murray G W, 1939. The road to Chephren's Quarries. *Geographical Journal* 94: 97–114.

Murray G W, 1942. The gold-mine of the Turin-papyrus. *Bulletin de l'Institut l'Égypte* 24: 81–6.

Murray G W, 1967. *Dare Me to the Desert.* London.

Partridge R, 1996. *Transport in Ancient Egypt.* London.

Petrie W M F, 1888. *A Season in Egypt, 1887.* London.

Petrie W M F, 1937. *The Funeral Furniture of Egypt with Stone and Metal Vases.* British School of Archaeology in Egypt 59. London.

Pieri M, 1964. *I Marmi d'Italia – Graniti e Pietre Ornamentali.* Milan.

Röder J, 1965. Zur steinbruchgeschichte des rosengranits von Assuan. *Archäologischer Anzeiger, Jahrbuch des Deutschen Archäologischen Instituts:* 467–552.

Rowe A, 1938. Provisional notes on the Old Kingdom inscriptions from the diorite quarries. *Annales du Service des Antiquités de l'Égypte* 38: 391–6.

Shaw I, 2000. Khafra's quarries in the Sahara. *Egyptian Archaeology* 16: 28–30

Shaw I and Bloxam E, 1999. Survey and excavation at the ancient pharaonic gneiss quarrying site of Gebel el-Asr, Lower Nubia. *Sudan & Nubia* 3: 13–20.

Shore A F, 1987. Egyptian cartography. In J B Harley and D Woodward (eds), *The History of Cartography.* Vol. 1. Chicago: 117–29.

Simpson W K, 1959. Historical and lexical notes on the new series of Hammamat inscriptions. *Journal of Near Eastern Studies* 18: 20–37.

Simpson W K, 1963. *Heka-nefer and the Dynastic material from Toshka and Arminna.* Pennsylvania-Yale Expedition to Egypt 1. New Haven.

van den Brink E C M, 1992. Corpus and numerical evaluation of the 'Thinite' potmarks. In R Friedman and B Adams (eds), *The Followers of Horus: Studies Dedicated to Michael Allen Hoffman 1944–1990.* Egyptian Studies Association Publication 2. Oxford: 265–96.

Waelkens M, De Paepe P and Moens L, 1988. Patterns of extraction and production in the white marble quarries of the Mediterranean: history, present problems and prospects. In J C Fant (ed.), *Ancient marble quarrying and trade.* British Archaeological Reports International Series 453. Oxford: 81–116.

Waelkens M, De Paepe P and Moens L, 1990. The quarrying techniques of the Greek world. In *Marble – Art Historical and Scientific Perspectives on Ancient Sculpture.* Malibu: 47–72.

Zitterkopf R E and Sidebotham S E, 1989. Stations and towers on the Quseir-Nile road. *Journal of Egyptian Archaeology* 75: 155–89.

Life on the Edge: Gemstones, Politics and Stress in the Deserts of Egypt and Nubia

Ian Shaw

Introduction

This paper is concerned with several mining and quarrying sites in the Egyptian and Nubian deserts. It deals primarily with the links between politics, economics and gemstone mining during two periods: the Middle Kingdom and the Roman/Byzantine period. We cannot be sure whether the Egyptian king – or, in later periods, the Roman emperor in his role as pharaoh – monopolised the large-scale mining of metals and gemstones, but the practicalities of such expeditions suggest that this kind of control over mineral resources might have been a reality, if only because few others would have been capable of it.

It seems likely that mining and quarrying expeditions, like military campaigns, were exploited to reinforce centralised political control. On a symbolic level, they could demonstrate the king's control over the most far-flung regions, and on a socio-political level they enabled the king to obtain the precious materials that would allow him to reward his high officials appropriately (see Shaw 1998). Many funerary texts on stelae and in private tombs clearly indicate that officials relied upon the king for gifts of funerary equipment made from exotic materials, such as lintels, jambs, sarcophagi and jewellery (see also Aufrère this volume).

The conventional view is that mining and quarrying would tend to proliferate in times of political stability and prosperity and diminish during periods of weakness or political fragmentation (see, for instance, Grimal 1992, 170, concerning the procurement of stone in the reign of the Twelfth Dynasty ruler Amenemhat III). Precisely because of the significance of mining expeditions as political or economic virility symbols, however, it is argued in this paper that quarrying and mining teams might, paradoxically, have been sent in greater numbers by those regimes that were attempting to fend off severe political or socio-economic pressures.

Early Gemstone Mining

The Egyptian mining and processing (carving and piercing) of gemstones clearly dates back to prehistoric times. Beit Arieh (1980), for instance, found evidence for turquoise mining near Serabit el-Khadim during the Chalcolithic period. Such prehistoric workings, however, were on a comparatively small scale compared with the huge state-sponsored expeditions that began in the Early Dynastic period. Many surviving spells and prophylactic texts indicate that particular stones were regarded as appropriate, indeed essential, materials for different kinds of amulet. A

wide variety of types of stone was exploited by the Egypians, such as malachite, garnet, haematite, mica, serpentinite, lapis lazuli, olivine, fluorspar, turquoise and microcline (amazon stone), as well as varieties of quartz (e.g., amethyst and rock crystal), and by the Roman period they were also using emeralds.

From the Old Kingdom (*c.* 2650–2180 BC) onward, a great deal of archaeological and textual information has survived concerning mining expeditions in pursuit of turquoise, malachite, amethyst and a variety of other gemstones. The inscriptions and graffiti associated with mining and processing sites of the Old and Middle Kingdoms provide information on the dates of the expeditions, as well as occasional lists of personnel, and even narrative accounts of specific expeditions.

The Middle Kingdom

Many gemstones occur widely over the desert surface and must simply have been collected from certain spots – in the case of carnelian and jasper, for instance, we have no large-scale workings at any particular site. The situation, however, is somewhat different for some of the varieties of quartz gemstones, such as amethyst. During the pharaonic and Greco-Roman periods the Egyptians exploited various sources of amethyst; in the Middle Kingdom they established mines at Wadi el-Hudi and Gebel el-Asr (see **Fig. 1**).

It is difficult to calculate the relationship between mining or quarrying expeditions and the pharaonic economy as a whole. We can, however, at least gain some idea of the fluctuations in frequency and intensity of mining by examining the inscriptions and graffiti carved in the vicinity of certain mines and quarries. In the Middle Kingdom, judging from surviving inscriptions alone, at least 39 expeditions were sent to the turquoise mines in Sinai, 15 to the Wadi el-Hudi amethyst mines, and 13 to the Wadi Hammamat siltstone/greywacke quarries (on which see Harrell this volume). It is interesting to observe that there is a strong similarity between the numbers of expeditions sent to these three destinations in each reign, particularly during the early and middle Twelfth Dynasty, i.e., from Amenemhat I to Senwosret III. Apart from an unusual surge of turquoise expeditions to Sinai in the reign of Amenemhat III, there is a surprising consistency both within and between reigns (see **Figs 2-3**).

The procurement of siltstone from Wadi Hammamat appears to have been the steadiest and most consistent of the three activities. For most of the Middle Kingdom there was no more than one expedition every five years sent to each of the three destinations. We can see that in most reigns during this period there was a fairly constant ratio between regnal

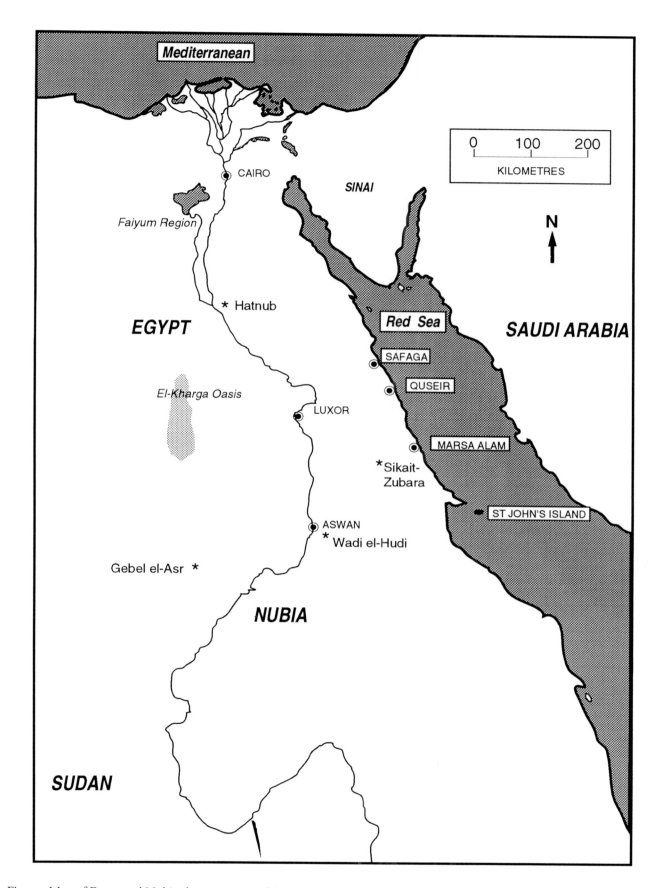

Fig. 1   Map of Egypt and Nubia showing some of the sites mentioned in the text.

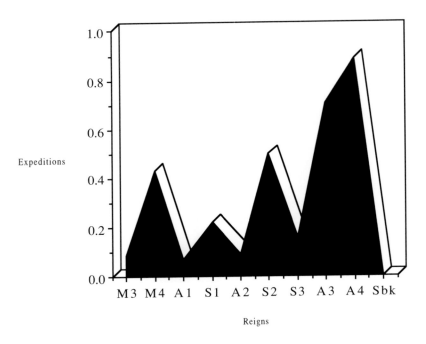

Fig. 2   Chart showing the number of quarrying and mining expeditions per reign of the Middle Kingdom.
Abbreviations: M=Mentuhotep, A=Amenemhat, S=Senwosret, Sbk=Sobekneferu.

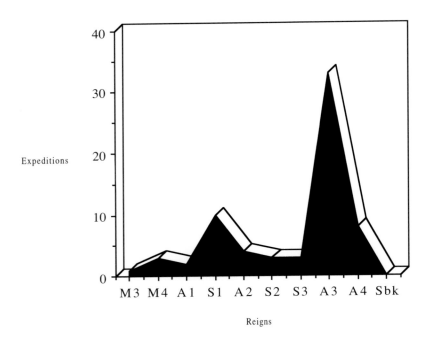

Fig. 3   Chart showing the number of quarrying and mining expeditions per regnal year during the Middle Kingdom.
Abbreviations: M=Mentuhotep, A=Amenemhat, S=Senwosret, Sbk=Sobekneferu.

length and number of expeditions (see **Fig. 3**). The only two real exceptions are Mentuhotep IV and Amenemhat IV, both of whom undertook an amount of mining that was much higher than we would expect for the lengths of their reigns. Is it a coincidence that both ruled at the end of a dynasty, at a time when there may have been greater political instability? In the case of the last Eleventh Dynasty ruler, Mentuhotep IV, the quarrying inscriptions are virtually the only written records that his reign took place at all. It is perhaps also significant that his vizier Amememhat, the man whom many Egyptologists identify as the one destined to become the first ruler of the Twelfth Dynasty, Amenemhat I, is encountered in a rock inscription describing a quarrying and trading expedition along the Wadi Hammamat. The control of such expeditions must have been one of the more effective routes to political power. The Eleventh and Twelfth Dynasty amethyst mines at Wadi el-Hudi are discussed below as a case-study for the links between mining, politics and society.

The Middle Kingdom amethyst mines at Wadi el-Hudi

Wadi el-Hudi is a wide and geologically varied region covering some 300 km² in the Eastern Desert, about 35 km southeast of Aswan (**Fig. 1**). The location of the site is interesting in that it lies essentially at the interface of the Egyptian mines in the Eastern Desert and the Nubian mines further to the south. The Wadi el-Hudi mines were therefore probably in some respects a stepping stone from the more familiar territory of the Eastern Desert down toward the more distant gold mining region of the Wadis Allaqi and Gabgaba.

The Wadi el-Hudi region is situated in the southern section of the Arabo-Nubian massif, which stretches from northeastern Sudan up through the Eastern Desert to the Gulf of Suez. The Arabo-Nubian massif consists of a series of deformed and metamorphosed sediments with numerous igneous intrusions. Like many other parts of the Eastern Desert, the Wadi el-Hudi region includes deposits of auriferous quartz. The region has been exploited for its minerals (including mica, barytes, gold and amethyst) since at least the early second millennium BC, and modern miners and quarriers are still extracting haematite and building stone from the immediate area.

The area is dominated by a large hill, the Gebel el-Hudi, which is located about halfway along the broad flat floor of the main wadi. The latter stretches for about 12 km from northwest to southeast, with a complex network of ridges and smaller wadis spreading out across the surrounding area to the west and the east. The traces of ancient mining and quarrying expeditions are scattered throughout this adjacent region of smaller valleys rather than on the floor of the main wadi itself (see **Fig. 4**).

Exploitation of the amethyst mines at Wadi el-Hudi appears to have peaked in the Middle Kingdom, a period to which many inscriptions and graffiti at the site date (Fakhry 1952; Sadek 1980–85; Shaw and Jameson 1993). Three distinct areas were in use during the Middle Kingdom: Site 5, which is a low hill adjoining an amethyst mine and surmounted by the remains of a rough stone fortified enclosure containing about 40 dry-stone workmen's shelters; Site 6,

which is another hill (about 200 m to the southeast of Site 5) with a large number of Middle Kingdom texts and images carved into the rocks at its summit; and Site 9, comprising a rectangular dry-stone fortified settlement (70 × 50 m), located a further 400 m to the south and associated with two amethyst mines (see **Plate 148**).

The rock-carved inscriptions and stelae at Wadi el-Hudi can be interpreted to provide a schematic chronological structure for the site, in which the Site 5 mine would have been opened first (probably in the late Eleventh Dynasty), while the two mines associated with the fortress at Site 9 might have been opened some time in the Twelfth Dynasty, possibly later than the reign of Senwosret I. If Sadek is correct in interpreting inscription WH148 as a record of the opening of *fresh* mines at Wadi el-Hudi (rather than the continuation of work at an existing mine), and WH21 as a reference to prospection for new lodes of amethyst, then it might even be possible to suggest that the two mines at Site 9 were opened in the reigns of Amenemhat II and Amenemhat IV respectively. This would place the date of the construction of the fortress well within the mid-Twelfth Dynasty, which would synchronise comfortably with its architectural style and associated ceramics.

The 1992 preliminary survey of the site (Shaw and Jameson 1993) enabled a few basic conclusions to be reached concerning the quantity and dating of the ceramics in the Middle Kingdom zone (Sites 5–9). The hilltop settlement at Site 5 contained large quantities of sherds, the vast majority of which appears to date to the Middle Kingdom. Although numerous sherds were also scattered within the walls of the fortress at Site 9, there were far fewer concentrations compared with the hilltop settlement. The pottery scattered inside the fortress included pharaonic sherds (probably of late Middle Kingdom date) as well as some sherds considered to date to the Roman period, suggesting that there may have been a later re-use of the fortress. The assemblage also included Pan Grave sherds, suggesting either that the nomadic Medjay were providing supplies or assistance to the Egyptian expedition, or that they were already being employed by the Egyptians as workmen or guards.

In terms of dating, the ceramic evidence from the Middle Kingdom mines at Wadi el-Hudi is broadly in line with that of the inscriptions. There already appears to be a small amount of data to suggest that the hilltop settlement was in use earlier than the fortress, but this suspicion will only be corroborated by a much more detailed analysis of the ceramics at both sites.

The Gebel el-Asr amethyst mines

Reginald Engelbach (1938) reported the existence of a set of amethyst mines possibly dating to the Old Kingdom at the northern end of Gebel el-Asr (the so-called 'Chephren Diorite Quarries', source of the gabbro/diorite gneiss from which the royal statues found in Khafra's Valley Temple were carved; see Harrell this volume). If Engelbach is correct in his dating, these would be earlier than the Middle Kingdom Wadi el-Hudi mines. In our 1999 and 2000 surveys (Shaw 2000; Shaw *et al.* 2001), we were able to identify not only Middle Kingdom pottery and one Roman amphora in the

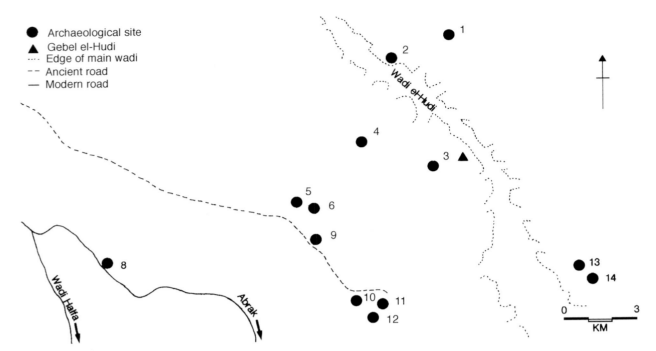

Fig. 4   Schematic map of Wadi el-Hudi showing the location of Middle Kingdom and Roman mining sites (1–14). Sites 1–4, 8, 10, 13 and 14 are late Roman or early medieval gold, barytes or mica mines or gold-miners' settlements. The following sites relate to amethyst mining: Site 5 (Eleventh Dynasty hilltop settlement and amethyst mine); Site 6 (peak with amethyst miners' rock-drawings and inscriptions); Site 9 (Twelfth Dynasty fortress and amethyst mine); Site 11 (late Roman amethyst miners' hilltop settlement); Site 12 (late Roman amethyst mine).

Stele Ridge part of the site, but also several Old Kingdom sherds (one deriving from a Fourth Dynasty footed bowl or stand, and others from red-polished marl jars and Meidum bowls, D Darnell, pers. comm. 2000), suggesting that this area of amethyst, carnelian and multi-coloured quartz mines may well have been exploited at an earlier date than the Wadi el-Hudi mines. Thus not only were the Stele Ridge mines clearly a source of amethyst in the late Middle Kingdom, but they also probably pre-date the mines at Wadi el-Hudi.

Middle Kingdom amethyst mining

Both texts and ceramics at Wadi el-Hudi suggest two successive major phases of amethyst exploitation, dating to the Eleventh and then to the Twelfth–Thirteenth Dynasties. The Eleventh Dynasty hilltop settlement at Wadi el-Hudi (Site 5) is clearly comparable with the Old Kingdom settlement at Wadi Maghara in Sinai: both are densely concentrated and crudely fortified versions of the more dispersed dry-stone quarriers' encampments at Hatnub and Umm el-Sawan (see Harrell this volume, **Plate 135**), and are thus adaptations of the conventional quarrying or mining settlement to more dangerous circumstances. On the other hand, the Twelfth Dynasty fortified settlement at Wadi el-Hudi (Site 9) – a small dry-stone version of the archetypal Nubian fortress – is more than a local adaptation. It is perhaps an expression of new Egyptian attitudes both to quarrying expeditions and to Nubia.

Lower Nubia had effectively become a colonised province of Egypt after the reign of Senwosret I (*c.* 1971–1926 BC). The area between the First and Fourth Cataracts was con-

trolled by Twelfth Dynasty fortresses and watchtowers, some as much depots as garrisons, concerned with military control over the Nubians and with trading and mining expeditions into the Middle Nile and surrounding deserts. The Twelfth Dynasty mining settlement at Wadi el-Hudi appears to have been affected by the new military style of organisation and bureaucracy that characterises most Egyptian activities during the period. Quarriers were housed like colonists in a quasi-permanent settlement and the whole business of amethyst mining took on a more military air.

At the same time, however, we can compare the Twelfth Dynasty fortified mining settlement at Wadi el-Hudi with the contemporary (or perhaps slightly later) mines at Gebel el-Asr, which were situated considerably further south into Nubia (see Harrell this volume, **Fig. 1**). At Gebel el-Asr there are few traces of settlement, let alone fortifications, and the major architectural features at the site are a series of large cairns with courtyards containing stelae and votive deposits. How do we explain this contrast between the two sites? Since the Gebel el-Asr mines are some 200 km deeper into Nubian territory than those at Wadi el-Hudi, we might theoretically expect a much more heavily fortified settlement. Three factors, however, may explain the discrepancy. One possibility is that the Gebel el-Asr mines might have been regarded as a temporary and far-flung outpost of one of the Middle Kingdom fortresses in the Nile Valley, therefore the expeditions might have been very brief forays undertaken by the inhabitants of one or more of the permanent Nubian fortresses (e.g., Kubban or Aniba). Another possibility is that the demographic situation in the Sahara might possibly have differed from that of the Eastern Desert; in other words, there may have been less perceived threat from local bedouin groups. Finally there is the possibility that the very remoteness of the site (80 km from the nearest Egyptian fortress and 240 km from Aswan) might have made it a target for very brief expeditions, whose aim would have been to obtain the maximum amount of stone in the minimum amount of time. This last factor seems also to have applied to the Old and Middle Kingdom gneiss quarrying expeditions at Gebel el-Asr, which, although fairly extensive, have left few traces of settlement (fortified or not) (see Harrell this volume, **Plate 141**).

The Middle Kingdom mines at Wadi el-Hudi and Gebel el-Asr suggest a fairly complex set of conditions, whereby the duration of mining 'seasons' and the locations of the mines themselves would have conditioned the Egyptians' strategies. The contrasting nature of two sites that might ostensibly be expected to have had many shared characteristics should be taken as a warning that Egyptian 'policy' in Lower Nubia was not necessarily uniform or inflexible, but might well have been adapted to changing circumstances, both geographically and chronologically.

Mining and Quarrying in the Roman and Byzantine Periods

The question of the links between politics and mineral procurement can also be pursued in much later periods, when the Eastern Desert in particular was still proving to be a reliable source of metals and gemstones. Indeed, during the periods of Roman and Byzantine domination of Egypt, the levels of mining and quarrying in the Eastern Desert seem to have reached something of a peak, with certain sites (e.g., Mons Claudianus, Mons Porphyrites and Bir Umm el-Fawakhir) being occupied for long periods rather than simply visited intermittently, as was usually the case in the pharaonic period. These activities took place amid flourishing trade along such official routes as the Via Hadriana (see Sidebotham and Zitterkopf 1998) and via such Red Sea ports as Myos Hormos and Berenike. Both the commerce and quarrying of the Roman and Byzantine periods necessitated a complex infrastructure of roads, way-stations and fortified wells.

Amethyst was used comparatively rarely in New Kingdom and Late Period jewellery, perhaps suggesting that it had become very difficult to obtain. By the late Ptolemaic period, however, it had once again become a popular gemstone. Pliny makes reference to Egyptian amethysts, and in AD 200, Clement of Alexandria writes that amethysts, emeralds, peridot and jasper were among 'the stones which silly women wear fastened to chains and set in necklaces'. The most typical types of amethyst beads in the late Ptolemaic and early Roman period were truncated biconical beads often of a very dark colour (in contrast to some of the paler pharaonic varieties), whereas those of the sixth and seventh centuries AD were characteristically pear-shaped.

On a map of known Roman roads and stations in the Eastern Desert, we can see that one Roman road passes

southeastward from Aswan down toward Wadi Allaqi. On its way it passes through Wadi el-Hudi, which had once again begun to be exploited for amethysts in the Roman period (the other amethyst mines at this date being in the Safaga region, near Gebel Abu Diyeiba). From a political point of view, Wadi el-Hudi lay within the territory of the Christian kingdom of the Nobatae, although for at least part of the period it may well have lain within the territory of the Blemmyes, the same nomadic group in the Eastern Desert that is said to have gained control of the Egyptian emerald mines in the late Roman and early Byzantine period (see below and Klemm, Klemm and Murr this volume).

The Roman amethyst and gold mines at Wadi el-Hudi

On the western side of the Wadi el-Hudi there are a number of areas of archaeological interest, clustering together amid a succession of high rocky ridges and valleys. These include the two Middle Kingdom mining settlements (Sites 5 and 9) mentioned above and, about 3 km to the south, another hilltop settlement and a possible amethyst mining area surrounded on three sides by a low perimeter-wall. This hilltop settlement (Site 11, see **Plate 149**) is similar in basic appearance to the Eleventh Dynasty hilltop settlement (Site 5), although it is somewhat smaller and all of the sherds examined proved to be of Roman date.

The walled mining area at the foot of the hill (Fakhry's site 12) is enclosed to the north, east and south but there is no wall on the western side, where the ground slopes steeply upward to a ridge. Five stone shelters were erected at regular intervals around the mine's circumference, and about twenty low stone windbreaks are scattered throughout the enclosure. The site contains only a small number of potsherds, primarily along the northern edge of the enclosure. The roughly D-shaped area enclosed by the wall appears to have been a working area around the mine rather than an actual settlement, since the houses of the workers were located further to the north, in the hilltop settlement Site 11. The spoil heaps from the mine are situated immediately outside the enclosure wall to the north and east.

The amethyst mine and associated settlement appear to date largely to the late Roman and Byzantine periods, although the pottery needs to be studied in much greater detail before it can be confidently ascribed to a particular century. The equipment is similar to that in use at Bir Umm el-Fawakhir in the sixth and seventh centuries AD, but the hilltop settlement has more in common with the nearby early Middle Kingdom amethyst mining settlement than with the Byzantine gold and emerald mining settlements at Umm el-Fawakhir and Wadi Gimal. This perhaps suggests that local workers were being used to some extent in Lower Nubian mines, and that these workers were creating settlements that drew on local traditions rather than those of Roman Egypt itself.

The Sikait-Zubara Roman and Byzantine emerald mines

It was during the Late Roman and Byzantine periods that the emeralds of the Eastern Desert began to be quarried on a fairly large scale in the area of the Eastern Desert between Myos Hormos and Berenike (principally the Sikait-Zubara region). The region of Mons Smaragdus (Gebel Zubara) was sufficiently important for it to be specifically mentioned in an inscription in Wadi Semna describing the mines controlled by the *archimetallarchos* (chief overseer of mines) in the Roman period.

The Egyptian emerald mines, which were perhaps first worked at least as early as the Ptolemaic period (*c.* 332 BC), are widely believed to have been one of only two sources of emeralds for Europe and Africa during the Graeco-Roman period (the other being the Habachtal mines in Austria). Although an uncut emerald has been tentatively identified in a necklace from the Predynastic site of el-Kubbaniya, immediately to the north of Aswan, such gem-quality beryls do not appear to have been used regularly in Egyptian jewellery until the Roman period (*c.* 30 BC–AD 395), when techniques for polishing the stones were probably introduced. The Egyptian mines continued to be exploited until at least the Middle Ages, when Arab writers document the appearance of larger, heavier stones from the Indian subcontinent. In the sixteenth century AD, the Spanish conquest of the New World resulted in the export of emeralds from Columbia and Brazil to Europe and Asia on a massive scale, thus finally eclipsing the trade in Egyptian emeralds. In more recent times, fine emeralds have also been mined in a number of other Old World countries, including Zimbabwe, Zambia and Pakistan.

In 24 BC Strabo described emerald mines in the southern part of the Egyptian Eastern Desert, but these had fallen out of use by the seventeenth century AD, and it was not until AD 1816 that they were rediscovered by the French goldsmith, Frédéric Cailliaud (1821), who was searching for mines on behalf of Muhammad Ali Pasha. Cailliaud is said to have found an emerald after descending through a winding passage for a distance of about one hundred metres, reaching a depth of thirty metres below the ground surface. The principal emerald mining sites in the region have not been scientifically studied since the expeditions of Donald MacAlister (1900) and E S Thomas (1909).

Judging from the surface ceramics, the emerald mining sites in the Eastern Desert cover an extremely wide chronological range, extending at the very least from the late Roman period at Wadi Gimal to the sixteenth century at Gebel Zubara. Since the rock temples at Gebel Sikait are usually assigned to the Ptolemaic period, the full period of exploitation at Sikait-Zubara must have spanned more than 1500 years.

At Wadi Sikait there are numerous stone structures of a type similar to those at the Wadi Nuqrus mines, but this time they are on both sides of the wadi. In addition, there is a huge three-storey stone watch-tower at the entrance to the wadi, providing a commanding view of the surrounding area (see **Plate 150**). Opposite the watch-tower are two rock-temples perhaps dating as early as the Ptolemaic period, which would suggest that the mines were already being worked as early as the first or second centuries BC, although no pottery in the vicinity has yet been found that can be dated this early.

The largest emerald mining sites are Nuqrus, Sikait, Zubara and Umm Kabu, but it is one of the smaller sites (Wadi Gimal A) that has provided an interesting piece of cultural evidence. Wadi Gimal A (probably to be dated to the fourth–fifth centuries AD on the basis of its pottery) is an emerald mining site on the southern side of the Wadi Gimal, approximately 15 km west of the Red Sea coast (see Shaw *et al.* 1999 for a summary of the remains).

The pottery at Wadi Gimal A supplies the first tangible archaeological evidence for the involvement in emerald mining of the Blemmyes, a nomadic tribe based in the Eastern Desert. The ceramics include four fragments of hand-made cups and bowls with well-burnished surfaces decorated with incised designs and different coloured slips; these are typical Blemmyes potsherds (similar to those recently discovered further to the south at the Egyptian port of Berenike). Although it would certainly be overstating the case to say that these sherds support documentary evidence that the emerald mining region had fallen into the hands of the Blemmyes during the late Roman and early Byzantine period, the pottery at least indicates that the Blemmyes were to some extent involved in the operations, either as workers or as the suppliers of goods and services.

Olympiodorus claims that in AD 423 he met the 'phylarchs' of the Blemmyes at Aswan and then accompanied them on a visit not only to their principal settlements, but also to their emerald mines. According to A Paul (1971, 56), 'The Blemmyes, while uninterested in gold, seem to have maintained control of the emerald mines and to have supplied Abyssinia for trade with India'. Parallels for the Blemmye pottery from Wadi Gimal can be found as far south as Qasr Ibrim, taking in Berenike on the coast and a number of other sites in northern Lower Nubia. The distribution therefore coincides quite well with Olympiodorus' description of the area occupied by the Blemmyes in the early fifth century AD.

Conclusions

At this point it is worth returning to the theme discussed initially in terms of Middle Kingdom mining: the idea of gemstone mining as a response to economic and social stress. There are some grounds for believing that rulers in the pharaonic period were obliged to send out mining and quarrying expeditions for quite pragmatic reasons, given that the produce of the mines was one of the most important ways in which the king could buy off his high officials and therefore prevent any threat to his own position (see also Aufrère this volume).

Bearing this in mind, it is interesting to note that the peak of emerald mining appears to have been in the late Roman and early Byzantine period. Carol Meyer (1995), in her recent description of the Umm el-Fawakhir gold mines in the Wadi Hammamat, makes the point that problems with the gold supply in the early Byzantine period may have forced the rulers of Egypt to seek out more gold in the Eastern Desert in order to solve their money supply.

If the emerald mining was also part of this process of renewing reserves at a time of economic stress, then we may well have identified an overall theme in Egyptian mining that runs all the way through history from the Early Dynastic to the Byzantine period. Rather than the peak periods of mining always being indications of prosperity and stability, they may sometimes be an indication that the government was in some kind of trouble and was perhaps more in need of precious materials than at times of greater peacefulness and tranquility. The title of this paper – *Life on the Edge* –

therefore refers not only to the experiences of the miners themselves, out on the peripheries of the civilised world, but also to the stress faced by successive Egyptian governments, which were perhaps occasionally sent careering over the edge – or at least out to the desert peripheries – in a great frenzy of mining.

Bibliography

Beit Arieh I, 1980. A Chalcolithic site near Serabit el-Khadim. *Tel Aviv* 7: 45–64.

Cailliaud F, 1821. *Voyage à l'oasis de Thebes et dans les déserts situés à l'orient et à l'occident de la Thébaide, fait pendant les années 1815–1818.* 2 vols. Paris.

Engelbach R, 1938. The Quarries of the Western Nubian Desert and the Ancient Road to Tushka. *Annales du Service des Antiquités de l'Égypte* 38: 369–90.

Fakhry A, 1952. *The Inscriptions of the Amethyst Quarries at Wadi El Hudi.* Cairo.

Grimal, N, 1992. *A History of Ancient Egypt.* Trans. I Shaw. Oxford.

MacAlister D A, 1900. The emerald mines of northern Etbai. *Geographical Journal* 16: 537–49.

Meyer C, 1995. A Byzantine gold-mining town in the eastern desert of Egypt: Bir Umm Fawakhir, 1992–3. *Journal of Roman Archaeology* 8: 192–226.

Murray G W, 1925. The Roman roads and stations in the Eastern Desert of Egypt. *Journal of Egyptian Archaeology* 11: 138–50.

Paul A, 1971. *A history of the Beja tribes of the Sudan.* 2nd ed. London.

Sadek A I, 1980–85. *The Amethyst Mining Inscriptions of Wadi el-Hudi.* 2 vols. Warminster.

Shaw I, 1998. Exploiting the desert frontier: the logistics and politics of ancient Egyptian mining expeditions. In A B Knapp, *et al.* (eds), *Social approaches to an industrial past: the archaeology and anthropology of mining.* London: 242–58.

Shaw I, 2000. Khafra's quarries in the Sahara: Old and Middle Kingdom activity at Gebel el-Asr. *Egyptian Archaeology: Bulletin of the Egypt Exploration Society* 16: 28–30.

Shaw I, 2000b. The evidence for amethyst mining in Nubia and Egypt. In L Krzyzaniak, K Kroeper and M Kobusiewicz (eds), *Recent Research into the Stone Age of Northeastern Africa.* Poznan: 219–27.

Shaw I and Bloxam E, 1999. Survey and excavation at the ancient pharaonic gneiss quarrying site of Gebel el-Asr, Lower Nubia. *Sudan & Nubia* 3: 13–20.

Shaw I, Bloxam E, Bunbury J, Lee R, Graham A and Darnell, D, 2001. Survey and excavation at the Gebel el-Asr gneiss and quartz quarries in Lower Nubia (1997-2000). *Antiquity* 75: 33-4.

Shaw I, Bunbury J and Jameson R, 1999. Emerald mining in Roman and Byzantine Egypt. *Journal of Roman Archaeology* 12: 203–15.

Shaw I and Jameson R, 1993. Amethyst mining in the Eastern Desert: a preliminary survey at Wadi el-Hudi. *Journal of Egyptian Archaeology* 79: 81–97.

Sidebotham S, and Zitterkopf R E, 1998. Survey of the Via Hadriana: the 1997 season. *Bulletin de l'Institut français d'archéologie orientale* 98: 353–66.

Thomas E S, 1909. The mineral industry of Egypt: emeralds. *Cairo Scientific Journal* 3/38: 267–72.

On the Antiquities of the Eastern Desert

Joseph J Hobbs

In his kind invitation to me to speak at the colloquium, Vivian Davies proposed that I address traditional usages of the desert as they might bear on ancient Egypt. This is a background theme of this essay, as there are many activities of pastoral nomads in today's Eastern Desert that are similar – even identical – to those pursued by their predecessors as long as 8000 years ago. More fundamentally though, I propose that precisely because the modern nomads have such an ancient and close relationship to the land, they are the archaeologist's most useful ally in the field. Here I describe some of the means by which the archaeologist and the Bedouin might develop a productive partnership.

The Setting

The Eastern Desert nomads interact with a wealth of antiquities. Dating from between about 6000 and 11,000 years ago are the abundant encampments, hunting blinds, rock shelters, rock paintings and stone tools of Epi-Palaeolithic and Neolithic peoples. Predynastic remains include burials and rock drawings. Dynastic Egypt is represented most strongly in the abundant inscriptions along the historic Wadi Hammamat desert crossing, and in the quarries from which the stone for some of the Early Dynastic palettes may have been hewn (see Harrell this volume). The Roman record is the strongest of all, with its staggering network of quarries, roads, and way stations (**Plate 151**). Nabatean traders left inscriptions along major transdesert routes. Christian monasticism began in the northern part of this area, and there are numerous remote cells, inscriptions and chapels testifying to the stamina and dedication of the early desert fathers.

The Ma'aza Bedouin inhabit roughly the northern half of the Eastern Desert, from the Qift–Qoseir road northward to the Wadi 'Araba. South of this line, the 'Ababda and then the Bishariin nomads prevail, while north of this line there is little Bedouin presence. The Ma'aza began migrating into this region from the Arabian Hijaz almost three centuries ago, and established supremacy through years of skirmishes with the 'Ababda and other groups that had prevailed here. Today, probably no more than 1000 people, primarily of the Khushmaan clan of the Ma'aza, describe this vast region of 146,000 square km (56,000 square miles) as home.

The Egyptian Ma'aza homeland is a diverse desert wilderness. Uplifted plateaux of Eocene limestone dominate the north and west. These are poorly watered and seldom-used labyrinths of deep hidden gorges and countless feeder tributaries. In the east and south are high mountains of Precambrian igneous and metamorphic origin, the so-called 'basement complex' country also found in southern Sinai

and western Arabia (**Plate 152**). The highest peak is that of Gebel ash Shaayib–'Old Man Mountain'–at 2187 m asl (7175 ft). Separating the limestone plateaux from this high country, which has the most abundant water sources, pastures and wildlife in Ma'aza territory, is the huge Wadi Qena. Much of its drainage basin is a broad, flat waterless gravel plain, with vegetation and animal life confined largely to the wadi's main trunk.

The Khushmaan Ma'aza practice their livelihood mainly in the basement complex country, with occasional forays into the Wadi Qena and the limestone plateaux when rain is unusually abundant and therefore pastures are rich. For more than 200 years here, following several thousand years in the Hijaz, theirs has been mainly a pastoral nomadic way of life. The average family has a herd of about fifty sheep and goats – usually about two-thirds goats – with two or three camels and donkeys, which serve as beasts of burden (**Plate 153**). They sell surplus animals in the sedentary communities of the Nile Valley and Red Sea littoral, where they buy their flour and other necessities. These livestock feed on a variety of drought-resistant perennial shrubs and trees, notably acacia, and on the annual or ephemeral vegetation, which appears only when and where rain has fallen. The Ma'aza use many of these plants in their own diets, medicine chests and material culture, and sell some–notably ben seeds and wormwood (*habb ghaaliya* and *shiih* in Egyptian Arabic)–to the traditional apothecaries ('*atariin*) of the Nile Valley. Dogs are invaluable allies in hunting ibex (*Capra ibex*), an important supplement to a diet generally focused on bread, rice and lentils. In the 1950s, hungry men and their dogs killed off the last Barbary sheep (*Ammotragus lervia*) in the area. Using so-called 'burrow traps', the Bedouin probably eliminated their public enemy number one, the leopard (*Panthera pardus*), more than one hundred years ago. Adding to this bleak picture of wildlife losses, in the past 20 years, wealthy armed hunters from the Gulf States have all but extinguished the once thriving gazelle (*Gazella dorcas*) population of Wadi Qena.

Also changing is the Bedouin way of life, which is increasingly focused on the wage economies of Hurghada, Ras Gharib and the Nile Valley. The typical pattern these days is for the male head of the household to earn cash from periodic or permanent jobs as mechanics, drivers, tour guides or oil installation guards, while women and children tend livestock year-round in the desert.

Reading the Ground

The Bedouin have developed a special set of skills to live in this wilderness. Many of these talents should be of great interest to archaeologists in the Eastern Desert. Most striking are their powers of observation. They watch the stars of the night sky to calculate the passage of time, from hours to seasons. By day they search the sky for clues of impending or actual rain. They study the contents of the horizon, searching for people, the various profiles of plant communities, the locations of their livestock and the movements of potential game.

Above all they read the ground. Their most precious resource, water, is there, both in standing quantities and in hidden stores revealed only by slight clues on the surface. There on the ground are the tracks of a meal. Was the ibex here a few minutes or hours ago? You must know the right answer before spending hours on a hunt. Which way was that car travelling – will it come back by this way? (How many of us can look at the sand and say which way the car was going?) Whose straying camel left those prints – yours? Is it safe to sit on the ground here? I was about to sit down on a spot when a Bedouin boy forcefully instructed me not to. When I asked him why, he used a stick to provoke a viper into revealing itself from beneath its sandy covering.

Such powers of observation, so useful for living today, also make the Bedouin keen observers of the ancient record of human life on this landscape. Here are a few examples. The basement complex country is very rocky, an apparent jumble of stones to the untrained eye. Many times while walking amidst rocks of all sizes and colours, I have seen a Bedouin companion pause and examine the single stone or few stones that stand out as different. These are almost always artefacts of human activity. In Wadi ash-Shifawiyya, well within the limestone plateau west of Wadi Qena, Muhammad Umbarak stooped down to pick up a flat rock – perhaps a grinding stone. Passing it for me to admire, he said 'it's from Wadi Jidhami'. He recognised the peculiar pattern in the igneous rock from a location 123 km (77 miles) distant. The Bedouin's discerning eyes often pick out the flint flakes left by Neolithic activities on the elevated gravel benches separating drainages throughout the Ma'aza area. Because these people took care to camp and to bury their dead well above the wadi floors, the Bedouin conclude there must have been much more abundant rain then than there is now.

They see many clues about ancient environments. Saalih 'Ali guided me over a barren gravel terrace above the watercourse of Umm Yasaar, where microliths lay in abundance. The terrace was thick with acacias when people used these tools, he said, but they gradually cut and burned them as fuel. He scraped away the surface gravel to expose a layer of charcoal dust, and pointed out the acacia's former area of coverage by patterns of relatively light and dark granite boulders. In the right lighting conditions, Bedouin often admire the lines revealing abundant hillside trails made when there were large populations of ibex, gazelle, Barbary sheep and perhaps other animals. To the Bedouin, these represent an ancient golden age of abundant water, lush pastures and teeming game. In contrast, they point out that when the Romans worked their quarries there was much less vegetation. Their evidence is the camel dung burned as fuel, indicating shortages of firewood (**Plate 154**).

Their observational skills lead these men to conclusions

about sequences of events and interactions between people. When I told Saalih 'Ali that individual hermits probably lived in rock huts around Wadi Naggaat, he responded that they must have worked together in a community – the stones in these structures are too large to have been manipulated by an individual. In the 1940s, Saalih's uncle told the English explorer Leo Tregenza that these people must have lived here long after the time of a distinct ibex hunting culture that the Bedouin recognise. Why? The anchor stones of the ibex-hunters palm wheel traps (**Plate 155**) appear in the walls of the hermits' hut. Who destroyed many of the frescoes on the walls of an early Coptic chapel in the limestone plateau, and when? A companion recalled walking by this place in 1962 – he calculated the date by the ages of family members – and seeing the bright red of iron oxides spilled near the mouth of the cave containing the chapel. The plastered frescoes of Christ and the angels were set upon the oxidised walls, so someone must have come along and gutted the frescoes before 1962. One man excitedly took me to a dog cemetery he had visited. I stared into a hole with a dog skeleton stretched out on a layer of ash. 'First,' the man explained, 'they dug the grave. Then they made a fire of acacia wood in the grave. They let the ashes burn down. No, they didn't carry they ashes here. Look, the rocks in the grave walls are singed by the flames. Then they buried the animal on the bed of ashes. Cremated? No, look – the bones are intact. The corpse was laid with its head on the west side, its nozzle pointing north'.

The Spirit of the Past

These, then, are some Bedouin observations of the material record of the past. In order to understand how they interact with that inheritance, it is also useful to consider how the Ma'aza perceive the peoples, cultures and chronologies of the past.

Diverse ancient cultures have left their marks on this land over a very long period. However, while the Bedouin clearly perceive that differences exist between the cultures represented by a flint-strewn gravel terrace and by a way station along the Via Porphyrites, they are not particularly interested in learning the archaeologist's version of history. They are not literate and have not been to school, and therefore have no method for creating a precise timeline for the past. They are content with the direct evidence on the ground that one event preceded another. We should, then, be forgiving about their rough categories and estimations.

The Ma'aza use three largely synonymous and interchangeable names to describe all past peoples of this desert: *Rumaani* (Roman), *Jahaliya* (meaning pre-Muslim) and *Kifri* (also meaning pre-Muslim or Infidel). *Fara'uuni* or Pharaonic is seldom used, and then only with difficulty. They know from television documentaries seen on shopping trips in Hurghada that there was a distinct pharaonic culture, typified by the pyramids and the tomb of Tutankhamen, but have difficulty placing it chronologically and equating it with Eastern Desert remains. Most Ma'aza believe the Romans identified with the quarrying sites preceded the pharaonic culture, but there is clearly uncertainty and curiosity, as they often ask me which really did come first. Many are surprised and disappointed by the answer. As for when the Romans of the quarries were here, one man estimated that the wagon tracks made by huge loads of porphyry have been on the ground for perhaps 200,000 years. Another man speculated that the Romans created the way station of Umm Sidr, and planted the still-surviving sidr (*Zizyphus spina-Christi*) trees around it, on the Via Porphyrites some 400,000 years ago. If these numbers seem preposterous, it is important to recognise that these men have no experience with numbers that high, and that they reckon time by human generations. The 15 or so generations they recall represent roots in antiquity.

They presume there has been an unbroken chain of human succession on the landscape. The Ma'aza believe, for example, that the Romans coined many of the local place names – including the Gebels Shaayib, Qattar, Umm Diisa, Abul Hassan, Abu Harba and Abu Dukhaan. Otherwise, they feel little affinity with or inheritance from these peoples. They are grateful for some of the legacies, and from time to time these have lifesaving and other useful worth. At Roman sites where fuelwood is absent, the men sometimes use charcoal excavated from blacksmiths' shops to heat water for tea (**Plate 157**). An ancient symbol incised into the rock face, which the Ma'aza call *dalu*, tells the Bedouin where they can dig for and find water – a very valuable gift from the past.

The Ma'aza perceive their predecessors, particularly the Romans of the quarries, as people of extraordinary energy and talent. They often describe them admirably as having been *afariit*, or otherworldly gifted spirits on earth. Incongruous natural features, such as stalactites and stalagmites in Galala Plateau caves, are frequently interpreted as having been made by the ancients. One man marvelled that the Romans ever found their quarry stone and precious metals, much less worked and exported them. 'They squeezed gold out of these mountains', another said. 'We've been here for so long, and so much later, but we are ignorant – we would not know how to begin'. They admire but do not envy the people who lived and worked here. Probably because of conversations with Leo Tregenza in the 1930s and 1940s, the Ma'aza know that much of the quarrying was done with convict labour. They refer to that era as the 'days of the whip', and pity the suffering of those who worked, died and were buried at places like Gebel Abu Dukhaan.

Losing Ground

Tales of desert treasures are always intriguing, and it is little wonder that they incite exploration. A Ma'aza man related this account: 'In Wadi al-Hayr, 'Awaad Suwaylim found what appeared to be copper statuettes of a man and a woman. The man had a tail tied to his leg and she was carrying a plate on her head. 'Awaad had these for ten years. An Egyptian came and bought them both for 100 pounds. He sold them in Cairo for 400 pounds, but the buyer later returned them and got his money back. The Egyptian took the figures back, took a young goat and slaughtered it on top of the images. Bathing them with blood, he discovered they were made of gold! He went to Cairo again and sold them for 12,000 pounds'.

There are many similar stories of lost or elusive treasures, including this account: 'Near the Qena–Safaga road, a woman found a complete piece of pottery, the size of a *hand-hal* (*Citrullus colocynthis*) gourd. She broke it open and found a black powder, resembling kohl, called *tibr*. They say it's more valuable than gold. But as soon as she broke it, this stuff blew away in the wind, and all was lost'. The most spectacular legend involves the lost treasure-filled tomb of a king named Maalik ad-Dinyaan. Men of previous ages have seen it; there are clues to its whereabouts, but its precise location has been unknown for a long time. It is somewhere on top of the plain viewed from Qasr el-Jinn, to the east of where the sun sets.

Quite often in these accounts there is an outsider, either an Egyptian or foreigner, who profits from the ignorance of the Ma'aza, usually by reselling what the Bedouin believe to be of little value. Oral testimonies of various foreigners who have come to dig by night in antiquities sites in the Eastern Desert, often stealing away with mysterious heavy bags, only fuel such legends of fabulous wealth just beyond the reach of these poor men. It is little wonder, then, that the Bedouin are well acquainted with the antiquities of the Eastern Desert. Yet a more profitable use can be made of this knowledge.

A Partnership?

Archaeologists might very effectively engage the local Ma'aza Bedouin in the identification, interpretation and conservation of antiquities in the Eastern Desert. The presumed benefits of such a partnership might parallel my experiences with the botanical knowledge of the Ma'aza. Although not botanists, the Ma'aza are unparalleled authorities in the realm of Eastern Desert botany. They named and helped me collect some 147 plant species, including scores of species that had not been collected previously in their tribal territory. These included several new records for trees in Egypt. No botanist had systematically sought Ma'aza ethnobotanical information, and so the occurrence of these trees went unknown to botany. In the same fashion, the Ma'aza are not archaeologists, but they know more than anyone about the locations of antiquities, and they have an indigenous ethnoarchaeology that is a treasure trove of information for professional archaeology.

Pursuing the theme of place names as undocumented sources, for example, the Ma'aza have several that they insist describe antiquities sites never visited by archaeologists. These include a drainage carrying large amounts of potsherds from an expansive settlement atop a limestone plateau. Another site reportedly has a rich collection of petroglyphs, with cattle a prominent theme. There is said to be a large terrace containing an abundance of mortars, fire pits and ostrich eggshells. And then there are the Bedouin oral descriptions of distant sites seen long ago, or described by deceased relatives, that the Bedouin themselves may one day find again. In one watershed we searched for two days for a settlement said to be made entirely of pottery. One member of our party had seen it many years ago, but in this limestone and gravel labyrinth failed to relocate it. There is a long list of such reports, describing sites that range from Neolithic to early Christian times. Several of these, particularly reports of graves and tombs, deal with what might be best described as sites only partially plundered, or not yet plundered (e.g., Friedman and Hobbs this volume).

Returning to the botany parallel, most of our new plant records came by following graybeards' oral descriptions of strange plants seen long ago near such-and-such a place. As unlikely as any one of these antiquity site reports might seem, they should be followed up, for there is a strong likelihood that they exist and can be located.

The second area of partnership is interpretation. Above are several examples of how well these native sons can read the ground, identify plant and animal remains and deduce sequences of events. In future anyone excavating in this region should have at least one Bedouin assistant on hand lending his trained eyes. Steve Sidebotham (University of Delaware) and Jim Harrell (University of Toledo) have benefited greatly by having Ma'aza companions on their surveys of Roman and other quarry sites, and associated routes and remains in the Eastern Desert (see Harrell this volume).

Finally there is conservation. The Ma'aza believe that destruction of antiquities in the Eastern Desert has accelerated in recent years. Incidents in the late 1990s include the thorough plundering of Umm Balad, a small Roman station on the southern flank of Gebel Abu Dukhaan (Mons Porphyrites). All inscriptions from the site were carried off, there was extensive digging for other portable objects and the walls of the settlement were knocked down. The Bedouin blame the destruction on 'fellahiin' looking for treasure. During this period numerous inscriptions, including Pharaonic, Roman and Neolithic, were hacked out of cliff faces and carried off in vehicles. The great gouges left in their wake may be seen in such places as Wadi Gasuus and Wadi Atulla. The Roman way station of Deir Semna in Wadi Semna was completely destroyed by a bulldozing crew working on the Qena–Safaga railway. One Ma'aza man praised Leo Tregenza and Steve Sidebotham for photographing, mapping and describing the monument, saying that is all that remains of it now.

The Ma'aza catalogue of such incidents is all too lengthy, but an opportunity exists to cut the mounting losses. The Ma'aza themselves are in the best position to monitor visits to antiquities sites, attempt to prevent looting, and report any destruction. The Bedouin simply need incentives and an effective framework within which to take such actions. The Bedouin Support Program of the St. Katherine Natural Protectorate project in Sinai offers a model for emulation. The programme, which receives about 10 percent of the total park budget (funded by the European Union and the Government of Egypt), is developing means by which Bedouin can assist in the park's natural resource conservation objectives, while providing limited health, education, economic development and employment opportunities for Bedouin within the protected area. These initiatives are linked because it is recognised that Bedouin will not necessarily protect plants and animals unless they perceive it is in their

interest to do so. In addition to benefits aimed at entire communities, like limited health services, there are activities that directly employ a handful of individuals but demand commitments by everyone. The most effective is a programme which has posted 20 so-called 'community guards', in effect rangers, to patrol specified districts within the vast park. They monitor and report on the status of wildlife and vegetation, assist backcountry tourists, and more generally spread the word about the park and its conservation objectives. Each community guard receives a salary of 250 Egyptian pounds per month. This programme has already had the noticeable effect of reducing hunting pressure on ibex. This is not necessarily because the people believe the protection of this animal is important in its own right. Rather, it relates more to kinship and territorial obligations. Traditional tribal law ('urfi) insists that one man cannot violate the livelihood of another. Since the employment of the community guard is explicitly linked to the preservation of wildlife within his zone, any poaching of ibex, for example, constitutes an attack on his livelihood.

The same tradition of 'urfi law prevails with the Ma'aza, and a programme similar to the community guard effort should prove effective. Six Bedouin men would probably suffice to monitor the condition of and impacts on antiquities within their respective districts of responsibility. Theirs would be salaried positions, but other economic incentives would promote conservation of antiquities among the wider Bedouin population. Safari-style tourism is booming in Ma'aza territory, with scores of foreigners setting out each day from Hurghada on guided jeep tours to enjoy spectacular desert scenery and Bedouin hospitality. Mons Claudianus and other antiquities sites are on some of these itineraries, and these attractions will likely become much more prominent as backcountry tourism grows. Tour operators need only to continue to employ the local Bedouin as guides and for other services on trips that highlight antiquities. The Bedouin are quite aware of the importance tourists attach to Egyptian antiquity, and so long as tourism benefits these local people, they are sure to do their best to preserve the archaeological resource.

Whether as tourist attractions, as world heritage, as links with former inhabitants of the landscape, or as objects of scientific study, the antiquities of the Eastern Desert must be protected. The Bedouin people of that desert are the best, indeed the only, people capable of providing that protection.

Acknowledgements

I thank Dr Vivian Davies for inviting me to participate in this colloquium, and Dr Renee Friedman for nurturing my interest in the antiquities of the Eastern Desert. I thank Roxie Walker and the Bioanthropology Foundation for their efforts to protect the region's ancient resources, which may lead to a Bedouin antiquities guardian programme. I am grateful for the companionship and encouragement of Leo Tregenza, who died at age 97 in Cornwall as our conference was underway in London. I thank Saalih 'Ali and many Ma'aza companions for sharing their knowledge with me, and for their unbounded kindness and hospitality.

1 (Left) Ralph Bagnold and his Expedition meeting with Italian officers at Sarra Wells on 16 October 1932 (from the left: Shaw, Sandford, Bagnold, Major Lorenzini, Craig, Paterson, Boustead, Prendergast, Harding-Newman).

2 (Below) The Libyan Desert Silica Glass expedition of December 1934 with P A Clayton, L J Spencer and O H Little (from the right) and their Egyptian companions.

3 Lazlo Almásy at his camp in the Great Sand Sea.

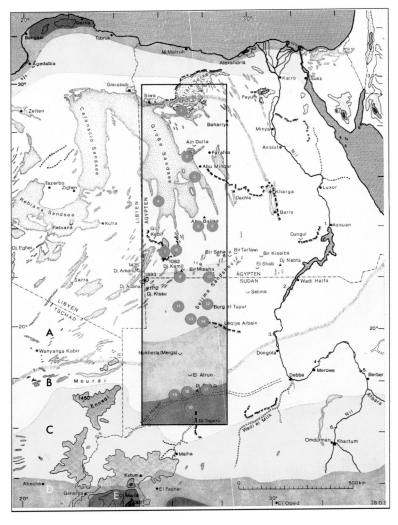

4 The BOS research areas in the eastern Sahara:
1 Qattara/Siwa
2–4 Great Sand Sea
5–6 Abu Ballas Area
7–8 Gilf Kebir
9–12 Selima Sandsheet
13–14 Laqiya Area
15–18 Wadi Howar
The colours within the transect show a reconstruction of the northward shift of the sahelian vegetation at *c.* 7000–6500 bp. While Egypt was mainly covered by contracted desert vegetation (pale yellow), environmental conditions in Sudan favoured acacia desert scrub (dark yellow), thorn savanna (light green) and deciduous savanna (dark green) (after Neumann 1989, 145).

5 The western cliff of the Gilf Kebir Plateau.

6 The BOS expedition crossing the Selima Sandsheet.

7 A comparative view of the distribution of prehistoric sites in northeast Africa at around 6000 BC (above) and at 4000 BC (below). The distribution supports the hypothesis of population movement towards the Nile as consequence of the southward retreat of sahelian vegetation.

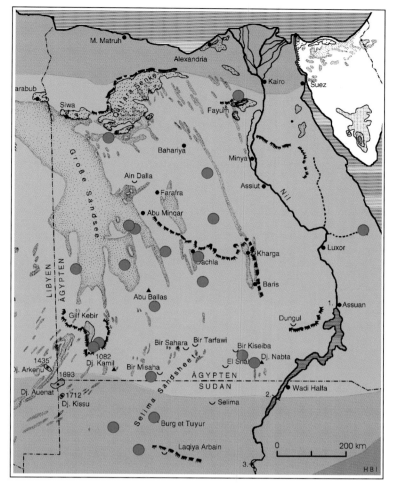

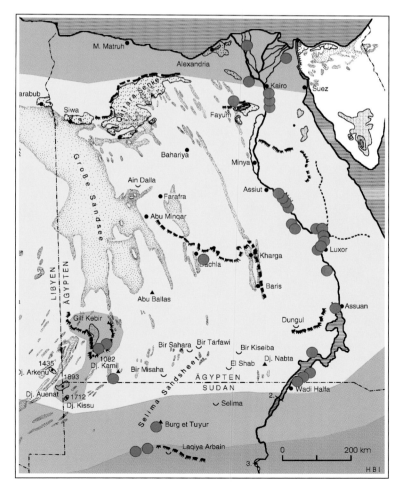

8 The playa barrier of Wadi Bakht in the Gilf Kebir viewed from the south. The falling dune in the centre overlies a fossil dune that dammed the wadi and caused the accumulation of still-water sediments visible on the lower left. A 10 m high section through these sediments provides a climatological sequence for the early Holocene from 8200 to 4800 bp. The camp is shown on the right for scale.

9 Rock paintings in the Cave of Swimmers in Wadi Sura (Gilf Kebir). A row of eight 'swimmers' begins in the upper left and continues to the bottom right. Rock exfoliation and tourist activities endanger the survival of the entire panel.

10 Almásy and his group in front of the Cave of Swimmers in Wadi Sura on 18 May 1942.

11 Excavation at the entrance of the upper basin of Wadi el-Akhdar (Gilf Kebir). Between these huge rocks sherds of Wavy Line pottery were discovered. In the background are the eroded playa deposits of the main habitation area.

12 Wavy Line sherds from Wadi el-Akhdar site 83/33.

13 At Regenfeld site 96/1 in the Great Sand Sea the stratigraphy of dune and playa deposits was examined by means of a mechanical excavator. The dates from this site provide clear evidence for early Holocene re-settlement of the northern Libyan Desert in the ninth millennium BC.

14 In some parts of the Abu Muharik Plateau the rough limestone surface is especially challenging for the ACACIA vehicles.

15 A column of the temple at Deir el-Hagar in Dakhleh Oasis bears the names of the members of the Rohlfs Expedition of 1873/74: G Rohlfs, G Zittel, W Jordan, P Ascherson, and Ph Remelé. On the right are their respective German servants.

16 The Rohlfs Expedition in front of their house in el-Qasr, Dakhleh Oasis in January 1874. Beside them are the 500 iron water containers brought from Germany.

17 The stalactite cave of Djara.

18 The pottery deposit at Abu Ballas as photographed during the Kemal el Din expedition of 1923.

19 The pottery deposit at Abu Ballas in 1985.

20 A hunting scene at Abu Ballas showing a man with the 'Libya' feather in his hair, holding a bow and a bundle of arrows.

21 A hunting scene painted on a bowl from Qubbet el-Hawa near Aswan.

22 The hieroglyphic inscription at 'Meri's Rock' west of Dakhleh. Transcription given by Burkard 1997 is shown above.

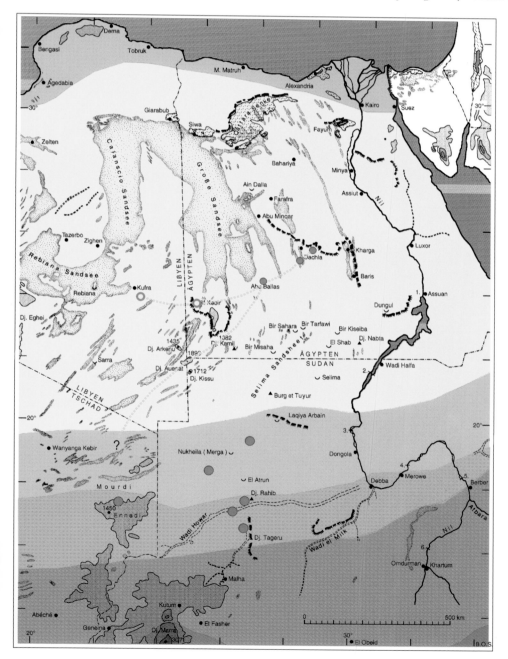

23 The hypothetical route from Dakhleh via Meri's rock to Abu Ballas and further through Wadi Abd el-Melik ('Zerzura') to Kufra, or through Gebel Uweinat into central Africa. The map also shows the proposed extent of sahelian vegetation at around 2000 BC and some desert sites dated to that period.

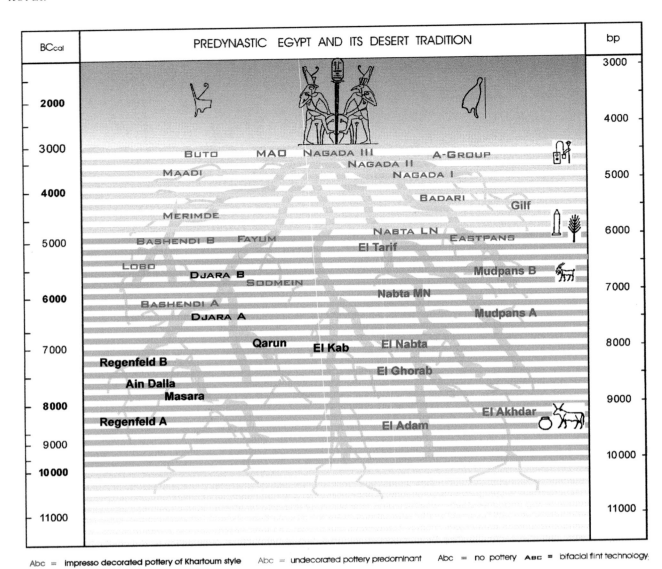

PREDYNASTIC EGYPT AND ITS DESERT TRADITION

Abc = **impresso decorated pottery of Khartoum style**   Abc = undecorated pottery predominant   Abc = no pottery   **Abc** = bifacial flint technology.

24 A hypothetical model of the roots of Egyptian civilisation with prehistoric groups and type sites from the time of the 'Green' Sahara between 10,000 and 6000 bp (*c.* 9500–5000 cal BC).

25 View across Nabta Playa, looking south along an alignment of megaliths. Megaliths 1 and 2 are in the foreground.

26 Megalith 2 was imbedded almost 1 m into silts of the Early Neolithic playa.

27 The 'calendar circle' after it had been partially destroyed.

28 The small rock-covered tumulus as first seen before excavation, partially buried by wadi sediments. Below the rocks was an oval, clay-lined chamber containing the burial of a complete young cow.

29 The young cow buried in the chamber below the small rock-covered tumulus.

30 View looking south over the area containing some of the thirty 'complex structures'. Each structure, like the one in the foreground, consists of an oval made of large roughly shaped rocks standing upright and a very large stone lying horizontal in the centre. Both the upright ovals and the central horizontal stones have their long axes oriented northwest–southeast.

31 Removing the sand from around Complex Structure A. Note the two large horizontal stones in the centre, under the standing archaeologist.

32 The modified table rock under Complex Structure A had carefully shaped sides. Below this rock is Nubian bedrock shale.

33 Another view of the modified table rock of quartzitic sandstone below Complex Structure A. Note the smoothed top and the projection at the northwest end at the top of the photograph. The north end of the 'sculpture' had been held in position by the slab on the right.

34 This large stone 'sculpture' was found placed upon the modified table rock in the fill of the pit directly beneath Complex Structure A. Like the overlying surface architecture the long axis of the stone was oriented northwest–southeast and had an unshaped head-like projection at the northwest end.

35 Using the tripod and equipment shown here the large stone 'sculpture' was moved to the surface.

36 The large stone 'sculpture' found under the surface of Complex Structure A. What it depicts is not clear, but some have suggested it resembles a cow.

37 The worked end of one of the large central horizontal stones from Complex Structure A. Note the repetitive flaking to shape the end and the smooth convex side of the stone by the tape.

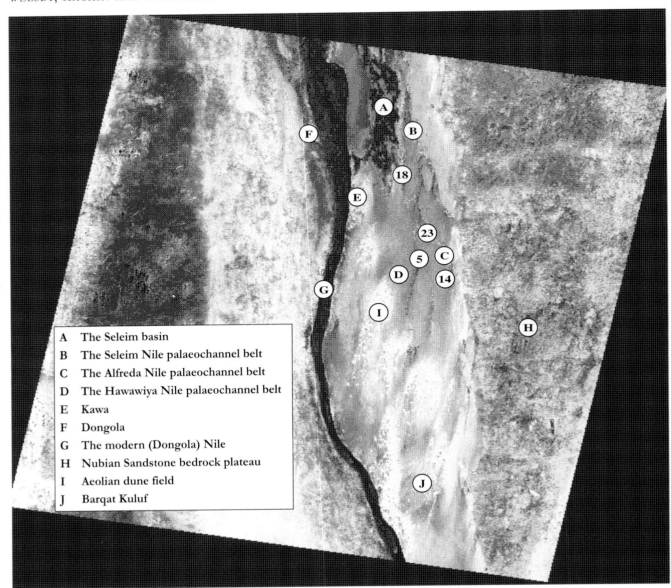

A	The Seleim basin
B	The Seleim Nile palaeochannel belt
C	The Alfreda Nile palaeochannel belt
D	The Hawawiya Nile palaeochannel belt
E	Kawa
F	Dongola
G	The modern (Dongola) Nile
H	Nubian Sandstone bedrock plateau
I	Aeolian dune field
J	Barqat Kuluf

38 A SPOT satellite image of the Northern Dongola Reach. Key sites, settlements, and major geomorphological features are shown (A to J). Note that aeolian dune fields cover a significant part of the valley floor to the east of the modern (Dongola) Nile but only one example has been labelled on this image (I). Within the palaeochannel belts, the location of the four ground water pump pits (Pits 5, 14, 18 and 23) whose stratigraphies are shown in Fig. 4 is also marked. This image covers an area of 60 x 60 km.

39 (Left) The Seleim Basin.

40 (Below) Neolithic occupation scatter at site L17.

41 Kerma settlements.

42 Mounds in the mound field at site H10 in the Northern Dongola Reach.

43 The well field at Gebel Fau.

44 A closer view of the well field at Gebel Fau.

45 Section of a sherd from Bashendi B Loc. 212. Fine quartz- and shale-tempered fabric (surface view in Plate 47, left).

46 Section of a sherd from Bashendi B Loc. 212. Fine quartz- and shale-tempered fabric (surface view in Plate 47, right).

47 Bashendi Cultural Unit ceramics in fine quartz- and shale-tempered fabric. Centre: Late Bashendi A Loc. 307. Right and left: Bashendi B Loc. 212 (cf. sections above).

49 (Above) Coarse Quartz Fabric: detail of a section of a sherd from Loc. 275 Cluster 1, Late Bashendi A Cultural Unit.

48 (Left) Sherds of the Late Bashendi A Cultural Unit. Top left: fine quartz- and shale-tempered fabric with compacted brown surfaces and lightly incised finger nail decoration, from near Loc. 174. Top right: coarse calcareous fabric, Loc. 307. Bottom left: black-topped, fine quartz- and shale-tempered fabric, Loc. 278. Bottom right: fine quartz- and shale-tempered fabric with brown surface, Loc. 174.

50 Decorated sherds from the Late Bashendi A Loc. 275 in coarse quartz fabric.

51 Decorated sherds from the Late Bashendi A Loc. 275 in coarse quartz fabric.

52 Bashendi B culture ceramics in fine quartz- and shale-tempered fabric from Loc. 74.

53 Decorated sherds from Bashendi B Loc. 74 in fine quartz- and shale-tempered fabric.

54 Vegetal-tempered sherd with woven-mat design from Bashendi B culture Loc. 212.

55 Early Sheikh Muftah Unit ceramics from Loc. 35.

56 Decorated sherds from the Early Sheikh Muftah culture Loc. 35.

57 Early Sheikh Muftah Unit ceramics from Loc. 135; sherd at bottom right is Badarian Black-topped Brown ware.

58 Rim and upper body sherds from a large jar with impressed, woven-mat design from the Early Sheikh Muftah culture Loc. 135.

59 Bowl in shale-tempered and rippled fabric from Loc. 222; Late Sheikh Muftah Cultural Unit.

60 Sherds in straw- and gypsum-tempered fabric from Sheikh Muftah culture Loc. 69 (top right) and Loc.100.

61 Sherd with impressed woven-mat design from Sheikh Muftah culture Loc. 48 in limestone-tempered fabric.

62 Black-fired, polished and impressed sherd in ash-tempered fabric from Loc. 5.

63 View from the south of site number 30/420-F3-1 (hilltop site no. 8) in the Dakhleh Oasis.

64 One of the huts on top of site number 30/420-F3-1 seen from the southeast. The hut is partly excavated into the surface of the hill and partly built of loose blocks.

65 Hut A upon Nephthys Hill seen from the south.

66 Hut B on Nephthys Hill seen from the northeast.

67 The portrait of a soldier from inside Hut A on Nephthys Hill.

68 Portable stone with a 'mute account' from Hut A.

Examples of Dakhleh Oasis fabric B23

69 Sites 31/435-B4-1 (left), 31/420-B10-1 (centre) and 32/390-J3-1 (S94.66, right); original magnification 1:1.

70 Site 31/435-D5-2 surface of tomb 48; original magnification 2:1.

71 Site 32/390-K1-1; original magnification 3:1.

72 Miscellaneous surface find; original magnification 3:1.

Oasis Fabrics from Karnak North

73 Form 1155–15/12/86-8; original magnification 2:1.

74 Form 1155–7/2/70-7; original magnification 1:1.

75 Form 1155–1/12/88-4; original magnification 1:1.

76 Oasis amphorae from Karnak North: Form 1155–15/12/86-8 (centre), 7/2/70-7 (front right); Form 430–15/12/75-2 (left) and 6/1/74-8 (right).

77 Interior of Karnak North amphora Form 430–15/12/75-2.

78 View of Gebel Antef.

79 Jamb of King Antef, son of King Sobekemsaf from Gebel Antef.

80 The remains of a stela from the Farshût Road.

81 View of the Wadi el-Hôl.

82 Inscription of Roma from Gebel Roma.

83 One of the early alphabetic Proto-Sinaitic inscriptions at Wadi el-Hôl.

84 A view of Gebel Tjauti.

85 The Tjauti road construction inscription.

86 The Scorpion tableau from Gebel Tjauti.

87 Inscription naming *W3s ḥ3 W3s.t*, 'Dominion behind Thebes'.

88 Hunter with hippopotami on his chest from 'Dominion behind Thebes'.

89 Badarian form RB27t
from Alamat Tal Road.

90 Paintings in the
Cave of the Hands.

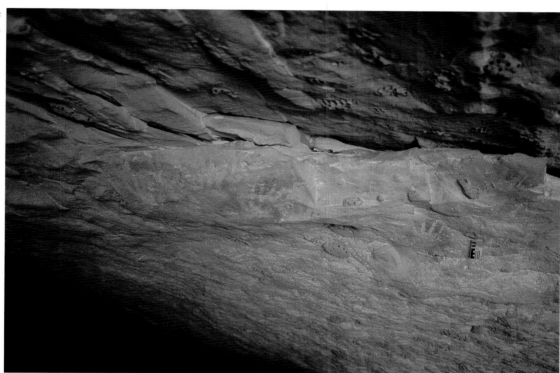

91 Detail of
painting in the
Cave of the Hands.

92 Leather pouch found in the Tasian Burial Cave.

94 Stone palette from the Tasian Burial Cave.

93 Fragment of a Tasian beaker from the Tasian Burial Cave.

95 (Above) Mat or basket impression on sherds from the Rayayna Desert.

96 (Left) Kurkur Oasis.

97 View of the tomb cutting in the Wadi Atulla.

98 View of the tomb cutting from above, looking south.

99 The western alcove prior to clearance.

100 The northwest niche (right) and the western alcove (left) of the tomb in Wadi Atulla.

101 Remnants of the stone tumulus over the charcoal pit are visible in the foreground. The tomb opening is on the right at the edge of the slope.

102 Artefacts removed from the tomb in 1981 and photographed in early 1983.

103 Artefacts recovered from the tomb and its surroundings during recent investigation.

104 Red slipped pottery from the Wadi Atulla tomb.

105 Lithic artefacts.

106 Beakers from an unknown site in the Eastern Desert, photographed in 1983.

107 Type I boat from Elkab rock art (type designations in Plates 107–11 after Cervicek 1974, 98–138).

108 Type VII boat from Elkab.

109 Type XV boat from Elkab.

110 Type XXII–XXIII boats from Elkab.

111 Spatial composition consisting of a Type VII boat surrounded by animal figures.

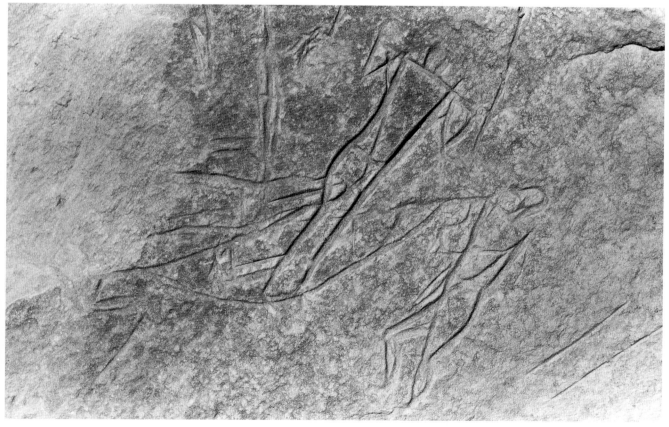

112 Human figure with square-shaped trunk (on the right) confronting a crocodile (partly destroyed, on the left).

113 Rounded stone (quartz-carbonate) with carved snake-type drawings of the 'Earliest Hunters' period. Vicinity of Umm Eleiga mine.

114 Collection of two-hand stone hammers (fine-grained granodiorite) used at Predynastic gold mining sites. Higalig mine, southern Eastern Desert, Egypt. Modern hammer at top: 30 cm.

115 Collection of one-hand stone hammers (fine-grained granodiorite and andesite) from the Old Kingdom waste dam at Abu Mureiwat, central Eastern Desert, Egypt. Scale is 10 cm.

116 Grooved stone (fine-grained granodiorite) axe from Abu Mureiwat mine, Eastern Desert, Egypt. Scale is 10 cm.

117 Stone mortar (andesite) from the Middle Kingdom site of Um Hugab mine, Eastern Desert, Egypt.

118 Oval millstone (grey granite) with two rubber stones (andesite) from the New Kingdom gold production site of Hairiri, tributary of Wadi Allaqi. Scale is 10 cm.

119 Remains of an unprotected settlement of the New Kingdom on both sides of the wadi within the Bokari mine district, Eastern Desert, Egypt.

120 Stone anvil (crusher stone) with pestle (both fine grained granite) for crushing quartz lumps to about pea size. Dungash mine, southern Eastern Desert, Egypt.

121 Inclined washing table for the separation of fine gold flitters and barren quartz powder. Note the water basins at the head and foot of the table and the stone-lined back flow channel. Arabic gold production site of Shashuateb in the Nubian Desert of Sudan.

122 Heaps of wadi gravel are the remains of wadi working to obtain gold in New Kingdom times at Sukkari, southern Eastern Desert.

123 Ruins of the rectangular houses of New Kingdom miners at Abu Sari, near the Nile, northern Sudan.

124 Part of a New Kingdom stone mill reused probably in Kushite times. The original concavity is recognisable by the lighter colour of the worked plane. Sehan/Mograt Island, west of Abu Hamed, Sudan.

125 Ptolemaic gold mill. Note the the depression on the rubber stone, which shows that it was also used to crush the ore lump to pea size. Hangaliya mine, south Eastern Desert, Egypt. Scale: 10 cm.

126 (Left) Remains of a Ptolemaic heavy mineral concentrator. Heavy minerals were concentrated in flat holes regularly deepened in the central channel, whereas the lighter barren quartz powder was washed off by water flow. Dagbagh Mine, central Eastern Desert, Egypt.

127 (Below) Remains of a heavy mineral concentrator from the site of Demoliaki in the Laurion District, Attika, Greece. Compare the similar design of the Ptolemaic concentrator from the Dagbagh mine in the Eastern Desert of Egypt above.

128 Remains of two broken concave-shaped gold ore mills of the Meroitic period. The milling plane is about 30 cm wide and resembles the more sophisticated design of the contemporaneous Ptolemaic mills. White scale: 25 cm. Sehan, Mograt Island, Sudan.

129 Cylindrical rotation stone mill. Originally a Celtic design, it was introduced by the Romans into Egypt, but was used at only a few sites for gold ore milling. It was more intensively used during the Arabic gold rush period. Arabic example from Attala Mine, central Eastern Desert. Width of inner milling hole is 48 cm.

130 A well-organised Arab settlement most probably set up during the short gold rush episode of El-Omari around AD 960. Uar in Wadi Hammisana, Nubian Desert, Sudan.

131 (Left) Quarry excavation (middle foreground) on Gebel Manzal el-Seyl.

132 (Below) Examples of vessel blanks in the Gebel Manzal el-Seyl quarry for a cylinder (above the pencil on the left), a bowl (above the pencil on the right) and a dish (below and in front of the pencil). Pencil is 14 cm long.

133 Alabaster veins in the Umm el-Sawan quarry.

134 Examples of vessel blanks at the Umm el-Sawan quarry with one cylindrical and several discoidal forms shown. Pencil is 14 cm long.

135 Stone ring in the quarrymen's camp at Umm el-Sawan.

136 Widan el-Faras quarry with its excavated bench along the top edge of the Gebel el-Qatrani escarpment (in the middle distance).

137 Close-up of the sandstone paving slabs on the Widan el-Faras quarry road. Pavement is 2.1 m wide.

138 Ancient paved road to the Widan el-Faras quarry (view looking south toward Birket Qarun).

139 Quartz Ridge at the Gebel el-Asr quarry with a quartz cairn in the foreground.

140 Quarry excavation with surrounding tailings piles in the southern workings of the Gebel el-Asr quarry.

141 Stone hut on Quartz Ridge in the Gebel el-Asr quarry.

142 Wadi Hammamat quarry with excavations on the far northern hillside (at center).

143 Author at the Ramesses IV stela in the Wadi Hammamat quarry.

Marble chips (foreground) in ancient workshop at the Gebel Rokham quarry.

145 Part of a wedge hole in dolerite porphyry at the Rod el-Gamra quarry. Pen is 15 cm long.

146 Rod el-Gamra quarry. Excavation area is 5 x 15 m.

147 Unfinished naos (one of two large ones) in the Rod el-Gamra quarry.

148 The Middle Kingdom fortress at Wadi el-Hudi.

149 The late Roman hilltop settlement at Wadi el-Hudi.

150 The late Roman watch-tower at Wadi Sikait.

151 A 200-ton column of granodiorite abandoned in the Roman quarry of Mons Claudianus.

152 Gebel Qattar (1963 m asl) in the heart of the basement complex country of the central Eastern Desert.

153 A man of the Khushmaan Ma'aza with his camel in the South Galala Plateau.

154 Ma'aza men studying ibex tracks imprinted in the drying wash of a Ptolemaic gold mining operation of about 2000 years ago.

155 An anchor stone (*dims habaala*) for an ancient palm wheel trap, with associated lithics.

156 A Ma'aza man examining remains from strata of the Roman way station of el Hayta, near lower Wadi Qena.

157 A Ma'aza man makes tea using charcoal from a Roman blacksmith's shop near the summit of Gebel Abu Dukhaan, where porphyry was quarried.